APOSTLES & PROPHETS

Their Roles in the Past, the Present, and the Last Days

RICK RENNER

APOSTLES & PROPHETS

Their Roles in the Past, the Present, and the Last Days

Unless otherwise indicated, all scriptural quotations are from the *King James Version* of the Bible.

Scripture quotations [marked *ESV*] are from *The ESV® Bible* (*The Holy Bible, English Standard Version®*), copyright © 2001 by Crossway, a publishing ministry of Good News Publishers. Used by permission. All rights reserved.

All Scriptures marked *NASB* are taken from the *New American Standard Bible*, New Testament, copyright © 1960, 1962, 1963 by The Lockman Foundation. All rights reserved.

Scripture quotations marked (*NIV*) are taken from the *Holy Bible, New International Version®*, NIV®. Copyright © 1973, 1978, 1984, 2011 by Biblica, Inc.™ Used by permission of Zondervan. All rights reserved worldwide. www.zondervan.com The "NIV" and "New International Version" are trademarks registered in the United States Patent and Trademark Office by Biblica, Inc.™

All Scriptures marked *NKJV* are taken from the *New King James Version* of the Bible © 1979, 1980, 1982 by Thomas Nelson, Inc. All rights reserved.

Scripture quotations marked *NLT* are taken from the *Holy Bible, New Living Translation*, copyright © 1996, 2004, 2015 by Tyndale House Foundation. Used by permission of Tyndale House Publishers, Inc., Carol Stream, Illinois 60188. All rights reserved.

Scripture quotations marked *RIV* are taken from *Renner Interpretive Version*, copyright © 2021 by Rick Renner.

Apostles & Prophets: Their Roles in the Past, the Present, and the Last Days

ISBN: 978-1-68031-897-5
eBook: 978-1-68031-898-2

Published by Harrison House
Shippensburg, PA 17257
www.harrisonhouse.com

2 3 4 5 6 7 / 29 28 27 26 25
2nd printing

Editorial Consultant: Rebecca L. Gilbert
Text Design: Lisa Simpson, www.SimpsonProductions.net

ENDORSEMENTS

Finally! For years we've seen the extreme behavior of self-defined apostles and prophets. Now, my friend Rick Renner unfolds Scripture as only he can, pointing us to hidden gems and giving us insight into these ministry callings. He does a masterful job unlocking the mystery!

As a student of revival and Church history myself, I so enjoyed the connection to the history as well as to the Scripture. *Apostles and Prophets — Their Roles in the Past, the Present, and the Last Days* is not a stuffy manual on how to be an apostle or prophet. You will, however, want to keep this book nearby the next time a question arises on the subject of apostles and prophets.

I am continually amazed at the calling on Rick Renner as demonstrated through the literary works he has penned! So grab your pen and notebook and buckle your seatbelt. You might be surprised at the truths Rick lays out in the following pages!

Gene Bailey
Author, revivalist, and host of Victory Channel's *FlashPoint*

In his newest book, Rick Renner expertly brings clarity in undeniable language concerning what the Scripture teaches about apostles and prophets. Not only does Rick understand this topic from a theological point of view, but many believe Rick is an apostle to Russian-speaking people worldwide; therefore, he has a unique understanding of this subject experientially.

With the misunderstanding by so many concerning these two ministry offices, the Church of the Lord Jesus' role is stymied somewhat. But, as Rick's book says, God intends for the Church to operate in the fullness of all that Christ has provided to cause it to be built, established, and influential in every part of the world.

I highly recommend this book because apostles and prophets are *needed.* Every tool that God has made available must be utilized to carry out His will.

Bishop Keith A. Butler
Pastor, Word of Faith International Christian Center
Southfield, Michigan

There are rare moments when a book comes along which speaks with such clarity, anointing, and urgency that it creates a new benchmark for Christian thinking. Rick Renner has given us this very thing with his instant classic *Apostles and Prophets — Their Roles in the Past, the Present, and the Last Days.* The writing is richly illustrated, deeply researched, and powerfully anointed. Each page drips with insights that will both inspire and challenge ministers and laymen alike to recapture a high view of the Church of Jesus Christ and those peculiar ministers upon which He has chosen to build it. Not only does Rick Renner clearly define the purpose and necessity of these gifts, he deftly calls out the error and excess that all too often have polluted the apostolic and prophetic ministries since the dawn of the Church. This work is a masterpiece of continualist theology that will be a standard reference for generations to come.

John Carter
Pastor, Abundant Life Church
Syracuse, New York

With the release of *Apostles and Prophets — Their Roles in the Past, the Present, and the Last Days,* Rick Renner has provided believers with what will be an enduring resource of incalculable value. I have no doubt that it will long be considered the definitive text on this important topic. Through expert scholarship and intensive research, Rick leaves no stone unturned in mining out the riches of Scripture relative to these two vital gifts that God has given to the Church. In addition, Rick covers a wide array of interconnected topics to create a highly contextualized understanding of the value that apostles and prophets bring when they function accurately and effectively. If you care about the Body of Christ achieving all that it was created for, you will want to study Rick's book and glean from its countless insights.

Tony Cooke
Bible teacher and author

Apostles and Prophets — Their Roles in the Past, the Present, and Last Days is knowledgeable, insightful, and timely. This book is filled with extensive study and revelation to educate the reader and bring much-needed balance to this important topic. It is a great honor to highly recommend this book!

Kenneth W. Hagin
Pastor, Rhema Bible Church
Broken Arrow, Oklahoma

I am confident that *Apostles and Prophets — Their Roles in the Past, the Present, and Last Days* is the most thorough, revelatory, scholarly, and magnificent work on the subject of apostles and prophets that has ever been published and may ever be in the future. The substance, glory, richness, and weight of each chapter will masterfully expose our modern-day pontification, networking, and conference hype surrounding apostles and prophets. In a sad Church age where grape juice is being advertised and sold as expensive wine, I thank God for Rick Renner, who has gifted this generation with this true treasure. May an entire generation of apostles and prophets, young and old, rise to inherit all that he has labored for in this groundbreaking work!

Jeremiah Johnson
Founder *The Altar Global* and best-selling author

I am so proud to be a tiny part of this great book *Apostles and Prophets — Their Roles in the Past, the Present, and the Last Days* that the Holy Spirit led Rick Renner to write, and its urgency cannot be overstated. We have had an explosion of social media along with an implosion of Bible teaching, and the result is a swamp of self-promotion and false doctrine. This wise, compassionate, scriptural, and academically solid tome is a must-read for any believer seeking truth and clarity.

Mario Murillo
Mario Murillo Ministries

Rick Renner is one of this generation's premier biblical researchers, writers, and biblical Greek scholars. I know of no one who has the knowledge, understanding, and wisdom to explore and explain this vast and rather controversial subject of apostles and prophets than Rick Renner. This dynamic book *Apostles and Prophets — Their Roles in the Past, the Present, and the Last Days,* is a must-read for anyone who loves the deep teaching of the Scripture.

Perry F. Stone Jr.
Founder of VOE, OCI, and ISOW

I've known Rick and Denise Renner for about four decades. I have not only benefited from their ministry personally, but I've seen the Lord use them to impact many lives all over the world. I've had them at our Charis Bible College, and the students are always blessed.

Rick is a *teacher's teacher*. He goes into a depth that very few are qualified to do, and he brings that same depth and research to this subject of apostles and prophets. This book is loaded with biblical references and examples to substantiate what he's saying, and I guarantee you will be enlightened and blessed by its content.

Andrew Wommack
Founder and President Charis Bible College
and Andrew Wommack Ministries

In Rick's latest book *Apostles and Prophets — Their Roles in the Past, the Present, and the Last Days*, he gives more than just a historical and scriptural background for these offices — he gives us the heart of God for His people. The gifts and callings of God are irrevocable and without repentance. So there could have never come a time God would withdraw these two ministry offices of *apostle* and *prophet*. They are not only "without repentance" for the one who has and operates in them, but they're also "without repentance" for the Church He gave them to. Apostles and prophets were necessary when the Church began, and they're even more necessary today. These two ministries are part of God's defense for the Church against Satan and the gates of hell, which uselessly try to prevail against it. Good job, Rick!

Bob Yandian
Bob Yandian Ministries

God has spoken through a general in the Church, just in time for it to rediscover its foundation!

When Rick Renner sent me a copy of *Apostles and Prophets — Their Roles in the Past, the Present, and the Last Days*, I devoured every page from cover to cover and must tell you, there is not another book like this one anywhere. At a time when many don't allow the Bible to get in the way of what they believe — in a culture where it seems Heaven is being visited every five minutes, angelic visitations are as regular as checking the mail, and nutty pseudo-revelations are abounding from people claiming to be apostles or prophets — this book cries out, *Enough!*

Armed with his Bible, extensive historical examples, and decades of tenured experience — Rick Renner has produced a scholarly masterpiece that will right-size the mania, purge the dysfunction, confront willful ignorance, and cause celebration among lovers of the Word of God. Should Jesus tarry, this book will be read by a generation long after us as a manual for building His Church.

To Rick Renner, your years of consistency and leadership have not only impacted this generation, but will continue making an impact for generations to come. *Thank you.*

I am profoundly honored to endorse this magnificent work!

Joseph Z
Z Ministries

CONTENTS

ACKNOWLEDGMENTS

I want to first of all acknowledge the ministers who directly or indirectly influenced my thinking about fivefold ministry when I was a younger man. Because I was reared in an atmosphere of cessationist beliefs, I'd never considered the possibility that apostles and prophets could still exist. But hearing the remarkable teachings of these unnamed men and seeing them operate so powerfully in their particular fivefold ministry gifts was a game-changer for me. Many of those who influenced me are now standing in their heavenly reward, but in life, they operated powerfully in different fivefold ministry gifts, and their teaching and examples tremendously influenced my earlier life.

Before each of my books is published, I always ask several people whom I consider to be trustworthy and spiritually mature to seriously read what I have written. I ask them to read deeply and to alert me to anything that may need to be more accurately articulated. For this book, I am especially grateful to Denise, who contemplated every word as she carefully read chapter by chapter; to Paul Renner, whose comments carry a lot of weight for me and whose life I respect immensely; to Joel Renner, who has a remarkable ability to analyze spiritual truths and an interesting way of articulating them; to Tony Cooke, a dear friend who took time out of his schedule to read major portions of this book that I felt needed examination by a keen doctrinal eye; and to my friend John Carter, who has insights in prophetic ministry, so I asked him to read the sections in this book about the prophet's ministry and to offer his comments.

I also want to acknowledge Becky Gilbert, the chief editor at Rick Renner Ministries. Becky is a gifted editor who has a deep commitment to Christ and who reads every word with spiritual eyes. I am also thankful to Becky's team of proofreaders that included Debbie Townsley, who also assisted the project with her capable research, Roni Bagby, Beth Parker, and Loretta Yandian.

LeRay Smith, our finance director at the ministry, also helped me with the monetary conversions and current-day values that I discussed in Chapter Two, for which I am grateful.

I additionally want to acknowledge my friend, Keith Trump, an American Bible Society scholar, who has been awarded the highest honors for his studies in Hebrew and Greek and who contributed his insights to this book regarding the Hebrew words for a *prophet*. I am also thankful to Maxim Myasnikov, my assistant in Moscow, who assisted me in my research of every Greek word that is used in this book.

I also acknowledge graphic artist Jenny Grisham for her work on the cover and for the way she so beautifully arranged all the illustrations contained in this book. The illustrations were created by Balage Balogh, and I want to express how impressed I am with his artistic renderings of biblical sites and historical figures — as well as my gratitude for being able to include many of his illustrations in this book. I wish also to acknowledge Lisa Simpson for her marvelous job of typesetting this book to make it enjoyable for readers — and I want to express my deepest gratitude to Don Nori and Brad Herman at Harrison House for working with me and for being such fabulous publishers.

Most of all, I am thankful to Jesus Christ, who called me and who is *the Perfect Apostle, the Perfect Prophet, the Perfect Evangelist, the Perfect Pastor*, and *the Perfect Teacher.* Through the Christ-given fivefold ministry gifts of apostle, prophet, evangelist, pastor, and teacher, He continues to express these various aspects of His ministry in His Church today.

In 1978, Jesus called me to write and promised that if I would *"write, write, write,"* He would bless what I wrote. As I look back over the many years I've been writing, my heart is filled with gratitude that in addition to *enabling* me to write, He indeed has blessed what I have written. *To Him be all the glory!*

INTRODUCTION

Years ago, much of what was being taught on the subject of spiritual warfare was not Bible-based, and I felt compelled by the Holy Spirit to write a book called, *Dressed To Kill* to do my part to bring balance to the important subject of spiritual warfare and armor. Since that time many years ago, God has mightily used *Dressed To Kill.* It has been distributed by millions of copies around the world, and it is even used as a textbook in many Bible schools. I am so thankful and humbled for how God has used that book.

But just as I felt a need to address spiritual warfare years ago, I now sense the Holy Spirit compelling me to address the subject of *apostles and prophets*, because so much of what is being taught today about this subject is not Bible-based. Some materials that have been written are exceptional, while others are built on personal opinion and personal experience. This subject is so important that I've felt the need to write a book that seriously examines what the Bible says on the subject of apostles and prophets in the past, in the present, and in the last-days Church.

My prayer is that those who read this book can take the information in it and apply it to what they are hearing, saying, writing, or teaching on this subject in various media. In no way do I intend to imply that I know everything on this huge subject, and perhaps there are even others who are more qualified to write this book. However, I am compelled by the Holy Spirit to do my part to help lay a spiritual, intellectual, biblical, and historical foundation underneath this very important topic.

Please let me help you navigate through this book.

I will begin by clearly stating that this book is *not* a manual about how to be an apostle or a prophet. Instead, it is a very serious examination of what the Bible tells us about the New Testament's vision for the Church and the specific roles that apostles and prophets play in the fulfillment of this God-given vision. In this book, I outline their roles in the past, in the present, and in the last-days Church. Other authors have written manual-type books, but my objective is to present materials from both the Bible and history to form a solid foundation upon which the reader may build as he or she continues the study of this subject. But starting with a good foundation is vital, and that is my role in writing this book.

In the first two chapters, I cover the New Testament apostolic vision of the Church — which is foundational to our understanding of the Church — and the role of all the Christ-given fivefold ministry gifts of *apostle*, *prophet*, *evangelist*, *pastor*, and *teacher*. Some readers will want to begin in Chapter Three where I define the ministry of the apostle and describe his or her Christ-given role. That information can certainly stand alone, but the beginning chapters are critical to understanding *why* the five-fold ministry gifts must function in their fullness.

But in those first two chapters, you will clearly see that God envisions the Church as a Body and as a Temple — His *House* — that is being built as a habitation for His Spirit. In Chapter One, you will also read about all the five-fold ministries, including the evangelist, pastor, and teacher as well, because they are Christ-given fivefold gifts with a God-assigned purpose. However, those specific gifts are not the focus of this book.

When I wrote *Dressed To Kill* in the early 1990s, the Body of Christ everywhere seemed to be seized with "spiritual-warfare mania." Now it seems the craze is *apostles and prophets*. If we believed all the videos on the Internet, advertisements in publications, and posts on social media, we could conclude that apostles and prophets exist in large numbers. But are there as many in existence as what is being publicized?

Some who claim to be an apostle or a prophet (or who are being called an apostle or a prophet incorrectly by others) do not even comprehend what the words "apostle" and "prophet" really mean. Hence, important biblical terms are being used too casually and often, albeit sincerely, very inappropriately. Please know that I do not feel a hint of criticism toward anyone who has incorrectly used these terms, but I believe that most people will be thankful for clarification about what these important words actually mean.

As you come to Chapter Three, you will learn the history of the word "apostle" so you can understand its roots and how its earliest meanings were carried into the New Testament Church's concept of the ministry of an apostle. In Chapters Four, Five, and Six, you will learn the number of people in the New Testament called apostles; what Paul said about the foundation-laying ministry of an apostle; and the actual signs of an apostle (there are distinctive *signs*). Finally, you will see important answers to other questions that people regularly ask about the ministry of an apostle.

In Chapter Seven, you will learn both the Hebrew and Greek meanings of the word "prophet," you will see how this word was used in antiquity by ancient writers, you will see a specific example of a surprising *false* prophet, you will learn what the apostle Peter taught about how true prophets do and do not operate, and you will read a balanced view of the warnings God issues to false prophets.

In Chapters Eight and Nine, you will find a long list of individuals whom ancient rabbis deemed to be prophets in the Old Testament, you will learn about various prophets who functioned in the intertestamental period and in New Testament times, and you will learn what the Bible says about the role of prophets in the last-days Church. Finally, in Chapter Ten, you will see what the apostle Paul said about the long-term effects of healthy Christ-given fivefold ministry in the Church.

In addition to what I have written in this book, I made the decision to additionally include illustrations by a fabulous biblical illustrator to help you "see" what has been discussed in its pages. Each illustration has been carefully selected and captioned to link you to the page where the ideas in the illustration are discussed. These illustrations are marvelous and will make this book a treasure you will cherish for years to come.

I thank you for being a faithful reader and for taking the time to carefully read the material contained in this book. My goal is to bring *teaching you can trust* to the Church, and because we are living in the last hours of the Church Age, it is imperative that we have correct apostolic vision for the church as it is laid out in the New Testament — and that we biblically understand the roles of apostles and prophets and how they are to function in these last days. This subject is too important to move forward from without having a rock-solid spiritual, intellectual, biblical, and historical foundation under it. My prayer is that this book will help provide that foundation to strengthen you as you take your journey onward.

— *Rick Renner*
Pastor, Bible teacher, author, and broadcaster
Moscow, Russia

CHAPTER 1

WHERE WE ARE HEADED AS THE CHURCH

That he might present it to himself a glorious church, not having spot, or wrinkle, or any such thing; but that it should be holy and without blemish.

— Ephesians 5:27

This book is about God's New Testament vision for the Church and what it is to become. We will particularly focus on two of the Christ-given fivefold gifts — the *apostle* and *prophet* (*see* Ephesians 4:11). In recent years, it has become woefully clear that inadequate and erroneous teaching has been provided about apostles and prophets, and it has created confusion in the Body of Christ. After spending time in prayer about this, I felt the Holy Spirit impressing me to address these subjects. This book is the outworking of my obedience to His promptings.

The roles of apostles and prophets have always been vital to the Church, *since its inception*, and they continue to be vital today. Therefore, it is imperative that we understand *what* and *who* apostles and prophets are.

In Colossians 1:25-29, Paul states his apostolic passion — to reveal the mystery of the Church — and his words echo the heartbeat of every person who is genuinely called into a Christ-given fivefold-ministry position.

> **Whereof I am made a minister, according to the dispensation of God which is given to me for you, to fulfil the word of God; even the mystery which hath been hid from ages and from generations, but now is made manifest to his saints: To whom God would make known what is the riches of the glory of this mystery among the Gentiles; which is Christ in you, the hope of glory:**
>
> **Whom we preach, warning every man, and teaching every man in all wisdom; that we may present every man perfect in Christ Jesus: Whereunto I also labour, striving according to his working, which worketh in me mightily.**

Paul was consumed with the mystery of God in the Church (vv. 26,27), and he embraced and stewarded it as his calling to reveal it to the saints. It is vital that we understand this apostolic vision of the Church — this "mystery" — as presented by Paul. So before we move to the subject of apostles and prophets, we must first establish *the New Testament apostolic vision of the Church*. Then we will be able to more clearly understand the roles apostles and prophets are to play in building the Church into what God intends for it to eventually become.

What Is the Apostolic Vision for the Church?

In various texts scattered all over the New Testament, Paul metaphorically compares the Church to *a vineyard, a temple*, and *a body*. Many people think most often of the metaphor of "the Body of Christ" in relation to the New Testament Church. Although the Church as the Body of Christ is certainly a very important metaphor, the Church as "vineyard" and "a temple" are also often-used illustrations in Paul's writings.

As you will see in the following chapter, Paul and Peter both primarily compare the Church to *a temple* that is to be filled with believers who each, individually, are members of a Church-wide holy priesthood. *Each* of these metaphors for the Church is unique and important in revealing the apostolic vision for the Church.

But in this chapter, we'll start with scripturally illustrating the Church as *a vineyard.*

The Church as a *Vineyard*

In First Corinthians 3:6-9, Paul compared the Church to *a vineyard* when he wrote, "I have planted, Apollos watered; but God gave the increase. So then neither is he that planteth any thing, neither he that watereth; but God that giveth the increase. Now he that planteth and he that watereth are one: and every man shall receive his own reward according to his own labour. For we are labourers together with God: ye are God's husbandry…."

In these verses, Paul described the Church as *a vineyard*, and he also depicted the various roles different people play in the growth and fruitfulness of the vineyard. For example, Paul described his role in Corinth as *a planter*. Of course, as a Christ-given apostle, he was indeed a planter — or a foundation-layer — as the work first got started. That's why in verse 6, He said, "I have *planted*...."

The word "planted" in this verse is translated from the Greek word *phuteuo*, which is a form of *phuton*, the Greek word for *a plant*, and it simply refers to *the act of planting a plant*. By using this word, Paul was metaphorically describing his work in Corinth. He was *a planter*. His task was to penetrate the darkness of the city with the Gospel — as a seed penetrates the dark soil from which it will eventually spring up — and to *plant* a church there.

There is no doubt that this city was some of the toughest spiritual ground Paul had ever encountered, as it was surely one of the most difficult places to minister in the ancient world. Like a neglected field overrun with pests and weeds, Corinth was a city infested with deeply rooted demonic powers. In order to plant the Gospel in people's hearts and firmly establish the Church in that tough environment, Paul had to press forward and till the ground with the very power of God. He knew his role was that of a planter, and his statement here is a clear reference to his founding of the Corinthian church. Paul was anointed to forge into new territory and challenge the powers of darkness in order *to plant*.

Paul was endowed with an anointing to find God-given opportunities, to push open those doors, and then to plant seeds for the Gospel that would grow into churches. And for one and a half years, Paul poured his life into this pioneering job in Corinth. When he finally left that city to pursue his apostolic calling in another city, the Corinthian church had not only been planted — it was deeply rooted and producing good fruit!

But how did this laborious and spiritually challenging work of planting occur? Paul and his apostolic team moved onto the site, removed the spiritual debris, pulled the weeds, chased away the pests, planted the seed, and established the new church plant in Corinth.

The Planting *and the* Watering of the Church as a Vineyard

Paul was also fully aware of where his responsibility ended and another's responsibility began. That is why he continued in First Corinthians 3:6, "I have planted, *Apollos watered....*"

The word "watered" is from the Greek word *potidzo*, which most often means *to water* or *to irrigate.* It is the very word that would have been used to depict a farmer watering his garden or vineyard to provide nourishment to his plants so they could grow. It can also be translated *to imbibe*, which in this context would convey the act of a field becoming *soaked* or *saturated* in water. By describing Apollos' role in Corinth with the Greek word *potidzo*, Paul actually gave Apollos a great compliment. It was as if Paul was saying, "Apollos didn't just *water* you; he *saturated* you...."

In other words, Paul acknowledged what a vitally important role Apollos played in the Corinthian church. Apollos had nurtured the new church plant, watering it regularly with the Word of God, which was absolutely critical to the vitality of the church. In other words, one was not better than the other — planting or watering — rather, each played a significant role as "planter" and "waterer" in the spiritual development of that church. Paul was a marvelous "planter" who was mightily anointed in his foundational role of starting the church, and Apollos was a marvelous "waterer" who was especially anointed *to come behind* Paul to water and nourish what Paul had planted.

Only God Can Give the Increase

Paul continued in First Corinthians 3:6 to say, "I have planted, Apollos watered; *but God gave the increase.*" This word "increase" is the Greek word *auxano*, which means *to cause to grow, to cause to increase*, or *to cause to become enlarged.* God ultimately gave the increase, so God was the One who was ultimately responsible. And the form of this word indicates *the continuous blessing* of God upon the work of Paul and Apollos. God was their Chief Partner in the process of bringing forth the Church at Corinth and sustaining it.

Various workers can till the ground, plant the seeds, pull the weeds, and lavishly water what has been planted, but only God can provide the blessing — the sunshine and the right environment or weather conditions — to make it all grow. We can nurture the soil, plant seeds, and water the work of our planting — and, of course, we do all of that by God's grace, gifts, provision, and power. But only *He* can ultimately cause growth. Therefore, even with all the help of faithful people who do their essential parts, God is the most important Partner in building the Church. So *all* the glory goes to Him!

The Church as a *Building* or *Temple*

In First Corinthians 3:9, Paul concluded the illustration of the Church as a vineyard and abruptly moved to a new metaphor to describe the Church. It was almost as if he said, "Hey, I know another illustration that is even better" — then added, "...Ye are God's *building.*"

To understand what kind of "building" Paul was alluding to in this verse, we must look at the conclusion of this passage in First Corinthians 3, where he wrote in verse 16, "Know ye not that ye are the *temple* of God, and that the Spirit of God dwelleth in you?"

The "building" Paul refers to is the Church, which he notably calls the "temple" of God. The word "temple" is a translation of the Greek word *naos*, a word that was used by Greeks in the ancient world to describe *a temple where a god dwelled.* For example:

- Pindar (c.518-438 BC), the lyric poet from Thebes in ancient Greece, used the word *naos* to describe *any habitation of a god.*[1]

- Herodotus (c.484-425 BC), an ancient Greek writer, geographer, and historian, used the word *naos* to depict *the innermost part of a temple where a god reputedly dwelled.*[2]

By using this same Greek word *naos* over and over throughout his epistles, Paul imparted the apostolic vision that God is building a body of believers into *a temple* for the habitation of the Holy Spirit in the earth. Paul importantly used the word *naos* to depict the Church as a temple where God today dwells by His Spirit. In fact, *naos* is a very commonly used metaphor that Paul employed in the New Testament to depict *who* and *what* the Church is.

This illustration comparing the Church to *a building* or *a temple* can also be found in Jesus' first depiction of the Church in Matthew 16:18 (*ESV*), where He said, "And I tell you, you are Peter, and on this rock *I will build* my church, and the gates of hell shall not prevail against it."

The words "I will build" are translated from a form of the Greek word *oikodomeo,* a word that is emphatically a construction term used to depict the building of a structure — in this case, the Church, which Jesus pictures as the new temple of God. This word *oikodomeo* is extremely important, and we will deal extensively with it in following chapters.

Paul, Peter, and John often metaphorically compared the Church to *a building* or *a temple* in their inspired writings. Among these notable examples are First Corinthians 3:9-17, Ephesians 2:19-22, and First Peter 2:5-9, which I encourage you to study, as well as other verses enumerated here that directly or indirectly refer to the Church as a building.

- 1 Corinthians 6:19; 14:12
- 2 Corinthians 6:16
- Colossians 2:7
- 1 Timothy 3:15
- Hebrews 3:6
- Revelation 3:12

We saw that in First Corinthians 3:9, Paul said, "...Ye are God's *building.*" We will extensively cover Paul's vision of the Church as a *building* or *temple* in Chapter Two and will return to it once again in Chapter Five, where we'll see Paul describing the ministry of Christ-given apostles to *assist* in building the new *"naos"* Temple of God in the earth today.

But for now, let's proceed to see another prominent metaphor Paul used in his epistles to portray the Church in the New Testament.

The Church as a *Body*

As I said, most people think the metaphor of the Church as "the Body of Christ" is the most commonly used illustration to depict the Church in the New Testament. Although the Church as the Body of Christ is certainly a very important metaphor, the fact is, the Church as *a temple* is also a critically important illustration in Paul's writings.

Nevertheless, Paul importantly called the Church the *Body* of Christ. In fact, it was a central part of his apostolic vision for the Church. For that reason, much of the balance of this chapter will focus on the Church as the Body of Christ.

There are many passages in the New Testament that compare the Church to *a body.* The following are just a few:

- Romans 12:5
- 1 Corinthians 12:12-27
- Ephesians 1:21-23; 4:12-16; 5:23,30
- Colossians 1:18,24; 2:19

But probably the most well-known of these is First Corinthians 12:27, where Paul wrote, "Now ye are the body of Christ, and members in particular." In this chapter, we will be looking primarily at Paul's words in Ephesians about the Church as *a body.* We'll begin with his use of this metaphor in Ephesians 1:18-23.

The eyes of your understanding being enlightened; that ye may know what is the hope of his calling, and what the riches of the glory of his inheritance in the saints,

And what is the exceeding greatness of his power to us-ward who believe, according to the working of his mighty power, which he wrought in Christ, when he raised him from the dead, and set him at his own right hand in the heavenly places, far above all principality, and power, and might, and dominion, and every name that is named, not only in this world, but also in that which is to come:

And hath put all things under his feet, and gave him to be the head over all things to the church, which is his body, the fulness of him that filleth all in all.

In these verses, Paul gloriously depicts Christ's highly exalted position over all principalities, powers, mights, and dominions — and that it is God's intention for Christ's presence to pervade and fill the Body of Christ, which is the Church.

In Ephesians 1:20-23, Paul wrote, "...When he [God] raised him from the dead, and [He] set him at his own right hand in the heavenly places, far above all principality, and power, and might, and dominion, and every name that is named, not only in this world, but also in that which is to come: And hath put all things under his feet, and gave him to be *the head over all things* to the church, *which is his body*, the fulness of him that filleth all in all."

How High Was Christ's Glorious Positioning?

In verse 21, Paul wrote of Christ's resurrection that exalted Him to a position at the Father's right hand, "Far above all principalities, and power, and might, and dominion, and every name that is named, not only in the world, but also in that which is to come." All the words in this verse are important, so we will look at them in-depth to see exactly *how* highly exalted Jesus is in the universe.

First, Paul said Jesus is exalted *"above all."* The word "above" is *huperano*, a Greek word that means *high above* or *far above* and refers to both *rank* and *dignity*. In the context of this verse, it means quite simply that no one in the universe has a higher rank, name, or position than Jesus Christ!

To affirm Jesus' highest position, Paul added the word "all," which is a translation of the Greek word *pas*, meaning *anything and everything*. By using these two words together — *huperano* and *pas* — Paul left no room for misunderstanding or doubt regarding his message that Jesus Christ holds the highest and most exalted position in the entire universe. Jesus is literally *"above all."*

Jesus Is Lord of All and Head of the Church, His Body

But Paul went on in verse 21 to describe the categories in which Christ is "above all." First, he stated that Christ is "above all *principality*." The word "principality," is from the Greek word *arche*, and it denotes *rulers of the highest level*. This encompassing term refers to *all* human rulers, including kings and politicians. However, it must be noted that the word *arche* is also used in Scripture to refer to *angelic beings*. This means Paul was declaring that Christ's exalted rank is far above all *human rulers* and all *angelic beings*. The natural and the spiritual realms are both under the dominion of Jesus Christ, and there is absolutely no one in any realm more highly exalted than Him.

Paul then named Christ's superiority "above all *power*." The word "power" is a form of the Greek word *exousias*. This word describes people who have received *delegated power* and therefore is often translated *authorities*. In the context of Ephesians 1:21, this word *exousias* likely refers to people who hold public office and wield authority entrusted to them by their superiors through an election or by governmental decree. Paul was teaching that although these individuals wield substantial power and influence in the affairs of the world, their authority pales in comparison to that of Jesus Christ.

At the time Paul penned these words in the First Century (c. 62 AD), this was a dangerous statement to make because Roman political powers were actively persecuting the Church and were attempting to suppress the message of the Gospel. But Paul wanted his readers to know that no matter what authority a politician might try to exert over the Church, Jesus has a rank that is higher than any human authority.

Next Paul wrote of Christ's superiority "above all *might*" (v. 21), from a form of the Greek word *dunamis*, denoting *explosive power*. But this word was also used to describe the full strength of a military force. By using this word, Paul declared that Jesus is exalted in His authority and power even above all the military forces in the world today.

Paul was declaring that Christ's exalted rank is far above all *human rulers* and all *angelic beings*. The natural and the spiritual realms are both under the dominion of Jesus Christ, and there is absolutely no one in any realm more highly exalted than Him.

As if this list isn't already complete enough, Paul added that Christ is supreme "above all *dominion*." The word "dominion" is from the Greek word *kuriotes*, which means *lordship*. It could refer to any world system — political, financial, or *any system* of *any type*. There are simply no principalities, powers, mights, or dominions more high-ranking than the Lord Jesus Christ!

Finally, Paul added "...And every name that is named, not only in this world, but also in that which is to come" (Ephesians 1:21). In one sweeping statement, Paul declared that Jesus is Lord over all. He is far superior to rulers (*arche*), elected leaders (*exousias*), military powers (*dunamis*), and constitutional authorities (*kuriotes*).

Jesus is quite literally Lord over all!

ALL THINGS WERE PLACED *IN SUBJECTION* UNDER CHRIST'S FEET

Remember, as a precursor to my teaching on the apostles' and prophets' roles in building the Church, we are talking about the various metaphors for the Church that are used in the Bible — Christ's *vineyard*, or *garden*; His *body*; and His *building*, or *temple*.

In this section, we're focusing on the Church as the Body of Christ, and we just established in Ephesians 1:21 that Jesus is the Head of the Church — the Head of His Body — and He is *"above all"* or, literally, Lord *over all.*

Then in Ephesians 1:22, Paul added, "And hath put all things under his feet...." When I read this verse, my mind always goes to the Egyptian Museum in Cairo, Egypt, where there is an exquisite display of the treasures of the Egyptian Pharaoh Tutankhamun (King Tut). Each time I've been there, I've found myself especially fascinated by one group of items in the collection — the walking canes that were once used by the pharaoh.

You may wonder what this has to do with God putting all things under Jesus' feet, but stay with me and you will understand my point.

As one might expect, those Egyptian canes were long and slender, decorated with gold, silver, ivory, precious stones, and rare woods. Each cane had a u-shaped hook at the base, which was engraved with images of conquered peoples from foreign lands lying prostrate on their stomachs with their backs arched upward and their hands at their sides, as if in complete captive subjugation to, or even in adoration of, the pharaoh. So every time the pharaoh walked with his cane in hand, with each heel-to-toe step, these figures rocked back and forth on the bottom of his cane — at his feet — symbolically bowing before him.

This imagery was not just artistry. It conveyed a strong message — namely, that all enemies were defeated and were directly *under the feet* of this mighty pharaoh.

When I first understood the meaning behind these carvings, it reminded me of the apostle Paul's words in Ephesians 1:22, where he wrote, "And hath put all things *under* his [Christ's] feet…." Paul's choice of words in this verse was very powerful, so let's take a moment to examine the original Greek language in this phrase in verse 22.

The word "under" in this verse is a translation of the Greek word *hupo*, and here it means *to subjugate* or *to dominate.* It could be used to describe forcibly subduing a conquered people and putting them in their place. But Paul's use of this word in Ephesians 1:22 was not figurative or symbolic at all. Through Jesus' death on the Cross, His subsequent resurrection, and His ultimate ascension on High, God literally put every foe that ever existed *under* Christ's feet.

Paul elaborated on this in Philippians 2:9-11, saying, "Wherefore God also hath highly exalted him, and given him a name which is above every name; that at the name of Jesus every knee should bow, of things in heaven, and things in earth, and things under the earth; and that every tongue should confess that Jesus Christ is Lord, to the glory of God the Father."

This means that *nothing* in the universe is more highly exalted than Jesus Christ. His throne rules above all — above all human authorities, including military authorities, and above spiritual authorities. There is simply no one who rules higher or more majestically than Jesus.

From His Head to His Feet, Christ's Body Is One

As wonderful as this already is, we must remember that the "feet" we are discussing are Christ's feet, which today are a part of the "Body of Christ." Hence, this also means that all the aforementioned powers are also *under* the feet of the Church. That's why Paul added in Ephesians 1:22, "And hath put all things under his feet, and gave him to be the *head* over all things to the church."

The word "head" is a translation of the Greek word *kephale*, which interestingly is a word that describes *a physical head* or *a capstone* that connects two sides of an arch in the center. It clearly means that Christ is the physical head of the Body of Christ and that everything in the Church comes together in Him and leans on Him for its existence.

But because the word *kephale* was used by a variety of famous ancient Greek writers as well, their use of the word gives us powerful additional insights into what it means for Christ to be the Head of the Church. For example:

- Plato used *kephale* to picture what is *main*, *basic*, or *core* and also used it to picture *investing a substantial sum of money* into a project. Thus, *kephale* became known as *the central point of investment.*[3]
- Aristotle (384-322 BC), the noted philosopher who taught Alexander the Great, (356-323 BC) used *kephale* identically to picture whatever is *main*, *basic*, or *core* and to portray *investing a substantial sum of money* into a project, and thus it was also used in Aristotle's writings as *the central point of investment.*[4]
- Plutarch used the word *kephale* to depict a person who was considered to be *the chief* or *the head* of something.[5]

When these various historical nuances are carried into Ephesians 1:22, where Paul described Christ as the "head" of the Church, it emphatically means Christ is the *chief* and *head* of the Church, so *central* that He is the *core* of it. Moreover, His exalted position means God made His greatest spiritual investment in Christ's exalted position, and as such, our focus, affection, and treasure should likewise be invested in His lordship over our lives and over the Church.

God made His greatest spiritual investment in Christ's exalted position, and as such, our focus, affection, and treasure should likewise be invested in His lordship over our lives and over the Church.

Paul then said Christ was made "...to be the head over all things to the *church*" (Ephesians 1:22).

Since this verse says Christ is the Head of the *Church*, it is imperative we understand the word "church" and what it meant to the ears that heard it when the word was first incorporated into the language of the New Testament.

As Westerners who have grown up with church buildings in our communities, we have certain images etched in our minds when we hear the word "church." However, the word "church" that was used in early New Testament times was not originally a biblical word. When early New Testament believers heard this word, they understood much more than most of us understand today.

It is so important to understand where the word "church" originates that I have included the following abridged excerpt from my book *A Light in Darkness*, where I wrote extensively about the origins of the word "church." I realize this is a long excerpt, but in this section from *A Light in Darkness*, I delve deeply into the historical origin of the word "church" and include many of the word's nuances so you'll understand what God longs for the *Church at large* to become in these last days. In short, God's plan is for His Church to emerge as a mighty force that rules and reigns!

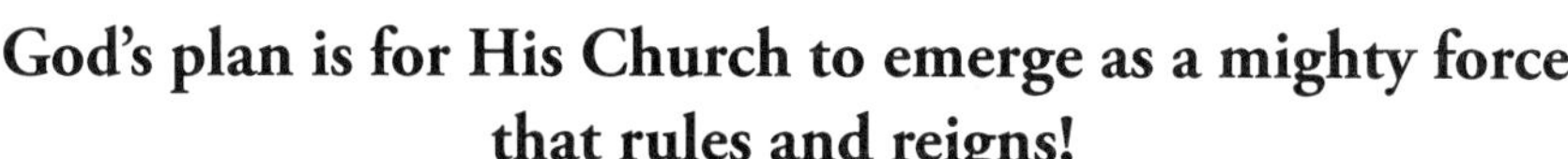

God's plan is for His Church to emerge as a mighty force that rules and reigns!

The excerpt reads as follows:

The Meaning of the Word 'Church' in Greek

The word "church" is a translation of the Greek word *ekklesia*, a compound of the words *ek* and *kaleo*. The meaning of the word *ek* can be slightly altered, depending on the context in which it is used. But it primarily means *out*. It can signify *an exit*, such as when a person *leaves* one room to relocate to another room. It can also convey the idea of *separation*, a point that is important in the context of the *Church*.

The second part of the compound word *ekklesia* is derived from the word *kaleo*. The basic meaning of *kaleo* is *to beckon*, *to call*, *to invite*, or *to summon*. When *ek* and *kaleo* are compounded, the new word *ekklesia* literally means *those who are called out*.

The Greek word *kaleo* is a very important component in the word *ekklesia*, and it is necessary to understand *kaleo* to grasp the great privilege and honor it is to be a member of God's *ekklesia*, His Church.

Studying the New Testament use of the word *kaleo* provides further insight into the meaning of the compound word *ekklesia* as it pertains to the local church and the Church collectively, worldwide. Although the word *kaleo* can simply mean *to call*, it is often used to convey the idea of *an invitation* that isn't made available to everyone else. Because everyone isn't invited, those who *are invited* should view the invitation as a privilege and a prestigious honor.

The New Testament has many examples of this word *kaleo*. Two notable examples are found in Matthew 22:2-10 and Luke 14:7-24. In Matthew 22, the word *kaleo* is used in Jesus' parable to describe a special *invitation* extended by a king who was asking people to attend a great marriage feast. Such royal events were closed to the public, and a person couldn't attend without being *called* or *invited*. Receiving an invitation to attend this type of special occasion was therefore considered a great honor.

Then in Luke 14:7-24, Jesus taught two parables in which various forms of the word *kaleo* are used 12 times to denote *invitations,* also given to people to attend a wedding and a great feast. Both parables in this passage of Scripture emphatically convey the idea of the great *honor* and *privilege* bestowed on a person who was *called* or *invited* to such an event.

Paul used the Greek word *kaleo* and its various forms 49 times in his epistles. For instance, he used the word *kaleo* to describe God's call to repent. This divine call comes to each person when God opens his or her spiritual ears to hear the Gospel's *invitation* to salvation. Without the Lord's participation, no sinner will ever enter the Kingdom of God, for entrance is *by invitation only*. When the Holy Spirit opens a person's spiritual ears to truly hear the Gospel message, that is precisely when God's *invitation* is extended to him or her. To be a recipient of this *invitation* is both an *honor* and a *privilege*.

Paul also used the word *kaleo* in First Corinthians 1:9 to state that God has *called* or *invited* us into fellowship with His Son. It says, "God is faithful, by whom ye were *called* unto the fellowship of his Son Jesus Christ our Lord." The word "called" would be more accurately translated *invited.* Like the king in Jesus' parable (Matthew 22:2-10), God has *invited* us to His banquet table, where we are honored to fellowship with Christ. Once again, this *invitation* is extended only to the called; therefore, it should be held in high esteem.

But in a much more personal way, Paul used the word *kaleo* and its various forms to describe his own *call* to be an apostle (*see* Romans 1:1; 1 Corinthians 1:1; 15:9). Paul also used the word *kaleo* in Galatians 1:15 to describe God's call on his life. He wrote, "But when it pleased God, who separated me from my mother's womb, and *called* me by his grace." The use of *kaleo* in this verse means it could be translated, "And *invited* me by his grace."

It is significant Paul would use this word to describe his call to be an apostle, because it lets us know Paul never lost sight of the fact that his position as an apostle wasn't a result of his own efforts. He recognized he had received a rare *invitation* to participate in a divine purpose not extended to many others (*see* 1 Corinthians 12:29). This call — this *kaleo* — was an honor and a privilege.

Hebrews 11:8 is another exceptional example of *kaleo*, describing the divine call that Abraham received. This divine invitation to Abraham was completely unique and it set him apart, for until that moment in history, no one had ever received such an invitation. Abraham's call was an honor and a privilege extended to no one else. Once again, the concepts of *honor* and *privilege* are integrally linked to the Greek word *kaleo* in this context.

So as noted, the word *ek* means *out*, and the word *kaleo* means *to call*. But whenever the words *ek* and *kaleo* are combined, they form the compound word *ekklesia*, and the meaning changes significantly. The compound word *ekklesia* describes *an entire assembly of individuals who are called out, called forth, and separated, and who therefore hold a position of honor and privilege.*

The Earliest Historical Use of the Word 'Church'

The Greek word *ekklesia* has a rich and meaningful history. One of the earliest appearances of this word was in ancient Athens, where the word *ekklesia* was used in a political context. This early meaning of *ekklesia* is significant because the application of its meaning was still in force when New Testament writers used this word to describe the Church of Jesus Christ. The writers of the New Testament clearly understood the meaning of the word *ekklesia* — a meaning that was far more profound than the one attributed today to its modern English counterpart, the word "Church."

Anyone with a knowledge of the Greek language in the First Century — and certainly this would include Paul — understood the historical, political, and judicial implications connected to this word. It was therefore no accident that New Testament writers used *ekklesia* to depict the Church and its role in God's plan. Yet because of this word's strong political implications, to use it in a separate context was a courageous act at that time. In other words, the use of this word could have resulted in charges of treason against the authors of these New Testament epistles and the church members to whom they wrote.

But in Classical Greece, the word *ekklesia*, which is translated "Church" in the New Testament, denoted a secular assembly of citizens who were *invited* to participate in a closed assembly in Athens. In this privileged assembly, a variety of functions were performed:

- Laws were created.
- Governmental decisions were debated.
- Policies affecting both internal and external affairs were formulated.
- Key judicial cases were decided.
- Customs and cultural norms were adapted and changed.
- Officials were appointed.
- State decisions were proclaimed.
- Chief magistrates of the land were elected.

Every Athenian citizen was invited to attend the meeting and participate in this ruling body regardless of his class or status in society. Then delegates were *called out* from their private lives and *summoned* to take their seats in this distinguished assembly. The Athenian *ekklesia* was considered the most prestigious group of people in the land, and it was a great privilege and honor to participate in this illustrious ruling body. Its decisions were far-reaching, affecting every aspect of public and private life.

The meetings of the Athenian *ekklesia* were conducted 30 to 40 times a year, and the site for these meetings was a small, artificial platform called the Pnyx in the southwestern district of ancient Athens, near the Acropolis. The *ekklesia* proceeded to deal with matters of law, public policy, and other business. Sessions frequently included speakers who made eloquent speeches, taught or debated law, argued for truth, or promoted specific agendas on behalf of the wider population. When meetings concluded, a closing prayer and a final sacrifice was offered to the gods.

This secular *ekklesia* was such an integral part of life that famous Greek orators and statesmen — such as Pericles, Aristides, Alcibiades, and Demosthenes — regularly delivered speeches at these meetings. Even Plato referred to events that occurred at Athenian *ekklesia* meetings in his writings. Political parties and factions were strictly forbidden in this respected assembly. The idea that such an illustrious group could degenerate into a group of contentious factions was an intolerable prospect. There was too much prestige attributed to the *ekklesia* for its meetings to deteriorate into ugly fights and divisions.

As frequently occurs when people become accustomed to privilege and honor, eventually citizens began to take for granted their right to participate in the *ekklesia* meetings, and over time attendance at the *ekklesia* dropped substantially. Many would attend meetings only when they were coerced to do so. It is important to also note that the Athenian *ekklesia* had different levels of leadership. It had a council that would operate when the *ekklesia* was not in session, which functioned as a kind of eldership. This council determined what would be brought before the people at the next general assembly *ekklesia* meeting. In many respects, the levels of leadership in the Athenian *ekklesia* were similar to the levels of leadership that later emerged in the early New Testament Church.

The fame of the Athenian *ekklesia* was so widespread that any educated writer during the First Century would have understood this word's historical roots and ramifications — including the apostles who penned the pages of the New Testament. The Holy Spirit inspired those writers to use the word *ekklesia* because it unmistakably means the Church is a body of individuals who have been called out, called forth, and separated for the purposes of God.

And just as the Athenian *ekklesia* ruled in matters of law, business, society, customs, culture, and judicial matters, God expects the Church to exert its spiritual influence in every arena of the society in which it exists. The mere use of the word *ekklesia* to depict the Church emphatically tells us it was never God's intention for the Church to be a small group of silent, unnoticed people who gathered to quietly discuss religious affairs. This power-packed Greek word tells us God's original intention was for the Church to exercise a voice of influence in private and public life.

So the concept of the Church, translated from *ekklesia,* is that of *a body of believers as called-out citizens of Heaven who are to apply God's laws in the affairs of the earth* — and *to be invited* to this distinguished Body is both an *honor* and a *privilege.*[6]

I alluded to this previously, but it was extremely courageous for New Testament writers to use the word *ekklesia* to describe the Church, for a pagan government could have perceived the Church to be declaring itself an alternate governing body. Rome had no tolerance for subversion, and everything about this word suggested, at the very least, a desire to influence society. The mere use of the word *ekklesia* could have been sufficient reason for a charge of treason to be brought against people who used it to describe the Church. Yet Paul and other New Testament writers bravely used this word because they knew God had ordained the Church to be *His ekklesia*, with His own vested authority, to rule and reign in the earth.

Although God's intention has not been achieved as yet, it is still in development. His plan has never altered or changed. His divine plan is that His called-out people exercise spiritual authority to dominate over the powers of darkness in every place where the Church has been established.

All Baptized By *One* Spirit Into *One* Body — the Work of the Holy Spirit To Build the Church

Before I write about the roles of apostles and prophets in building the Church, I am first biblically answering the question: *What is the Church?* We know the Church is referred to metaphorically in Scripture as a *vineyard*, a *building* or *temple*, and a *body*. Although most of the next chapter will address the Church as God's building, or Temple, we are looking now at the *Body* of Christ. We as individual members of that Body have been baptized into Him — and *collectively*, we are all members of this one Body, with Christ as the Head.

First Corinthians 12:13 tells us that when a believer is born again, he or she is "baptized by one Spirit into one body." This supernatural baptism takes place the moment one repents and calls Jesus the Lord of his or her life. In that split second, faster than you can blink your eyes and without your even being aware that it's happening, the Holy Spirit Himself *baptizes* or *immerses* you *into* Christ. Paul again referred to this initial baptism in Galatians 3:27 when he wrote, "For as many of you as have been baptized into Christ have put on Christ."

This is also the baptism Paul referred to in Ephesians 4:5 when he wrote, "One Lord, one faith, *one baptism*." It is a baptism into the Body of Christ that comes simultaneously with one's salvation. When a sinner repents and calls Jesus Lord, the Holy Spirit takes over from there and supernaturally baptizes and melds him or her into the Body of Christ. From that moment forward, that person is *in Christ*.

THE BODY OF CHRIST IS ONE

In First Corinthians 12:13, Paul wrote that regardless of our ethnicity, class, gender, or race, after we are baptized into the Body of Christ, these distinctions cease to exist in the Church in terms of partiality. Paul radically said, "For by one Spirit are we all baptized into one body, whether we be *Jews* or *Gentiles*, whether we be *bond* or *free*; and have been all made to drink into one Spirit." When Jesus looks at His Church, He doesn't see race, gender, or class distinctions — He simply sees one unified Body.

In that same verse, Paul additionally stated that each born-again believer is "...made to drink into one Spirit" (1 Corinthians 12:13). The word "drink" is a translation of the Greek word *potidzo*, which we saw previously, and it means *to water* or *to irrigate.* It is the word used to depict a farmer watering his garden or vineyard to provide nourishment to his plants so they can grow. The word *potidzo* can also be translated *to imbibe*, which conveys a picture of a field becoming *soaked* or *saturated.* Paul's use of this word means that, once baptized into the Body of Christ, each believer becomes a fully saturated recipient of the Spirit.

Paul radically said, "For by one Spirit are we all baptized into one body, whether we be *Jews* or *Gentiles*, whether we be *bond* or *free*; and have been all made to drink into one Spirit." When Jesus looks at His Church, He doesn't see race, gender, or class distinctions — He simply sees one unified Body.

God's intention is to water, irrigate, imbibe, soak, and saturate each one of us with the Spirit until we are full — regardless of our ethnicity, class, gender, or race — to bring us into spiritual growth and to demonstrate the glorious fullness of Christ in the Church.

More Revolutionary Talk — Where Societal Lines Cross

It is impossible to convey how *revolutionary* it was for Paul to write Galatians 3:28, which says that *in Christ* — and therefore in His Body — "there is neither Jew nor Greek, there is neither bond nor free, there is neither male nor female: for ye are all one in Christ Jesus."

In Colossians 3:11, Paul stated again that in Christ, "there is neither Greek nor Jew, circumcision nor uncircumcision, Barbarian, Scythian, bond nor free: but Christ is all, and in all."

When Paul wrote these verses, the Roman world was *strictly divided* by *ethnicity, class, gender,* and *race*. These distinctions were clear-cut and these societal lines were rarely crossed. To imagine these different categories of *ethnicity, class, gender,* and *race* sitting together, side by side, was unfathomable because these different classifications rarely mingled.

In the same way oil and water do not mix but, in fact, repel each other, all those various ethnicities, classes, genders, and races didn't mix well either — they *repelled* one another. To imagine these various groups united into a single body was completely revolutionary.

I want to help you understand just why this "declassifying of the classes" in Christ was such revolutionary thinking in the First Century. The unthinkable occurred when Paul wrote in Galatians 3:28 and Colossians 3:11 that in Christ there is neither *Greek, Jew, circumcision, uncircumcision, bond, free, male, female, barbarian,* nor *Scythian.*

Jew and Greek

Since the list in Colossians 3:11 begins with *Greeks*, that is where we will begin. The word "Greek" pictures anyone from the Greek-speaking world, but in the New Testament it is usually translated "Gentile." Most readers assume the word "Gentile" simply means non-Jewish, and although this is correct, it is more than that, as it pictures anyone who is *pagan*.

It is impossible to exaggerate how vastly different the pagans were from the Jews. While Jews grew up worshiping the One True God, pagans were notorious idol-worshipers from lands filled with drunkenness, debauchery, and multiple forms of unbridled sexual immorality.

The pagan world generally loathed Jews and regarded them as narrow-minded and bigoted because they only believed in the One True God compared to the pagans' open-mindedness to believe in a sundry of gods. They generally deemed Jews as a people with a disgusting language and a bloody religion. Although there were rare instances in which the Greek-speaking world valued Jews for their business acumen, they largely held Jews in contempt, and mingling with them would not have been a preference. The antagonism Greek-speaking pagans felt toward Jews was deeply rooted, and the division between Greeks and Jews could at times be severe.

Next, Paul mentioned *Jews*. Because of the Greeks' pagan beliefs and lifestyles, Jews similarly found Greek-speaking pagans to be disgusting. They especially felt disdain toward Romans who had forcefully occupied Jewish territories. The repugnance Jews felt toward pagan Gentiles — Greek *and* Roman — was so acute that Jews did all they could to keep distance between themselves and pagans, whom they judged to be sexually deviant, perverse idol-worshipers with no moral law. For these reasons and many more, Jews tended to look upon Gentiles as unclean, foul, polluted people.

In fact, a devout religious Jew would have found a pagan Gentile so reprehensible that he would not even permit someone in this category to cross the threshold of his house. Even if a Jew felt that a particular Gentile seemed better than others, to a devout religious Jew, pagans as a whole were nonetheless impure, contaminated people to be avoided if possible. The enmity Jews frequently held toward Greek-speaking pagans was deeply held. It is nearly impossible to exaggerate the division that existed between these two groups.

Circumcision and Uncircumcision

Paul then added *circumcision* and *uncircumcision* to his list. One might think this was simply another way of describing Jews and Gentiles, but the word "circumcision," as used in Colossians 3:11, could also depict *strict religious Jews* as compared to *non-religious Jews*, whom the strictly religious Jews considered to be *shameful* because those non-religious Jews often were uncircumcised.

So the word "uncircumcision" in this verse likely refers to those non-religious Jews whom religious Jews regarded as shameful. In this verse, it seems Paul was depicting a religious war that existed inside a single religious group. Deeply religious Jews who faithfully followed the rules of circumcision saw themselves as superior to the Jews who did not, and the deeply religious had little tolerance for the non-religious. Extreme hostility between religious Jews and non-religious Jews was so cold-blooded that these groups seldom got along in a civil manner.

Bond and Free

In Galatians 3:28, Paul then mentioned *bond* and *free.* The word "bond" is a translation of the Greek word *doulos*, which is *the most abject term for a slave* and pictures *one who is born into or sold into slavery*. The system of slavery was so entrenched in society that, as far back as the Classical period, Aristotle wrote that those born as slaves had inferior intellects and were biologically designed to be slaves; therefore, it was best for them to live contented lives in their natural subservient condition. While this mindset is outrageous today, and it is disgusting to us to think slavery is acceptable, Aristotle expressed what most believed at that time when he wrote, "From the hour of their birth, some are marked out for subjugation, others for rule."[7]

Those born to rule were the "free" that Paul referred to in Galatians 3:28. The word "free" in that verse is a translation of the word *eleutheros*, a Greek word that pictures one *born free* and who possesses rights and privileges only belonging to the free. The demarcation between "bond" and "free" was so stark that even if a slave was later granted freedom, he or she was still considered inferior to others.

A person's history of slavery was a blemish that permanently prohibited that individual from engaging in many aspects of society readily available to those who were born free. Although masters and slaves were in close contact domestically, the public social division between them was distinct and was rarely crossed in a social gathering. These societal prohibitions ensured that masters and slaves — the "free" and the "bond" — were rarely together in a public setting.

Male and Female

Paul implausibly (to our Western minds) added *male* and *female* to his list. The Greek phraseology is so strong in Galatians 3:28 that it emphatically means male-female distinction simply does not exist in Christ in terms of partiality. But a mere suggestion by Paul that there was no distinction between "male and female" was one of the most revolutionary statements ever written at that moment in history. It makes it altogether strange when modern critics charge Paul of being "anti-women," when, in truth, Paul — inspired by the Holy Spirit — wrote the most liberating words that had ever been written about women. And his actual practices in ministry provided women more freedom than had ever been granted in the ancient world up to that time.

In the First Century, there were simply societal restrictions that were applied to women, but not to men. Men could vote; women could *not* vote. Men could hold a political office; women could *not* hold any political office. This absence of women in key public positions explains why men are referred to by historical writers more than women. Men were allowed education; women were allowed *some* education, but generally less than what was provided to men.

Women's public lives were so restricted, they were not even permitted to shop in the public market. If a woman was seen in a public market, it was likely she was a prostitute, because decent women were not allowed to shop there. Men had many legal rights; women had fewer legal rights. Men freely attended public meetings and forums; women were usually prohibited from these meetings.

A lack of women's experience in public meetings was why Paul found it necessary to instruct women in his epistles about what to do when something was said in a service that needed explanation. That is not the focus of this book, but it's important to note, as many who have not deeply studied the subject of "male and female" in the Church have wrongly concluded that Paul was against women. Quite the contrary, he, for one, liberated them to sit side by side with men in public meetings.

Think about it. This unthinkable development only occurred *in Christ.* Women needed practical instruction about right and wrong behavior in a public setting so they would know how to conduct themselves in public meetings *where they had never been before.* Prior to Christ, such a thing would have never happened because the boundary lines between males and females in both the Jewish- and Greek-speaking worlds generally did not permit it. However, in Christ, those restrictive distinctions *were* and *are* obliterated.

But to imagine that men and women would sit side by side and participate together in public meetings was preposterous in that ancient culture. It only began to happen regularly *in Christ.*

Barbarian and Scythian

In Colossians 3:11, Paul also declared that in Christ, there was neither *barbarian* nor *Scythian*. The word "barbarian" is a translation of the word *barbaros*, a Greek word describing *anyone who didn't speak Greek or Latin* or *one who spoke it poorly*. Greek and Latin were the languages of the civilized world, so those who didn't speak these languages and speak them well were regarded as lacking in culture, as being uncivilized, and were therefore relegated to a lower class than others.

The word *barbaros* had such a negative connotation that Greek- and Latin-speakers also used it to picture those they deemed to be *ignorant* and *insensitive.* In a figurative sense, the word *barbaros* was used to picture any person or people group that was *brutal, cruel, warlike, uncultured, unsophisticated, ignorant*, and *insensitive.* Romans widely used *barbaros* to depict any person or people group they deemed *uncouth, rude*, or *uncivilized.*

Last, Paul listed *Scythians* in this astonishing list of people groups. Scythians were a nomadic type of people who originally lived in the steppes north and east of the Black Sea. They eventually moved westward where they became a menace to different empires, including Rome, who was terrified of Scythians because of their warmongering ways. Scythians had divided into a multitude of tribes over eons of time and had a long and diverse history. Among Scythians were the legendary *Amazons*, whom Herodotus, the famous

Greek historian, wrote were fearless female warriors whose strength matched that of men and they were notorious fighters.[8]

While common barbarians were deemed uncouth, even *they* deemed Scythians as *the lowest of all barbarians and the scum of the barbarian world.* You could say the general feeling toward Scythians of those who were "simply" barbarians was something like, "Well, we might be *barbarians*, but at least we're not *Scythians*!" So even barbarians considered Scythians to be the lowest rung on the ladder in the world of barbarians. And it would have been absurd to envision these various barbarian groups sitting together peacefully in a social setting.

When Paul listed all these groups — which were each on the farthest opposite spectrum and would never naturally find any commonality with each other — he astonishingly stated in Galatians 3:28 that they were now "all one in Christ Jesus." And in Colossians 3:11, Paul wrote that "Christ is all, and in all."

Against all odds and societal norms of that age, a single, united Body now existed that was comprised of all these various "conflicting" parts. After each part was baptized by one Spirit into the Body of Christ, they each became supernaturally, *mysteriously*, blended — joined, fused, intermingled, amalgamated, and divinely melded — into one, single body of believers!

Think of the magnificent, supernatural unifying work God performed by His Spirit at the moment of the new birth, in which — in one instant — classes and distinctions *vanished* inside this one, new Body, the Church.

Paul went on to say in Ephesians 1:23 that Christ is the Head of this remarkable "body." And since the word "body" is an important apostolic metaphor to describe the Church, we must pay close attention to that word in this text.

The word "body" was translated from the Greek word *soma*, a word that both figuratively and literally depicts a human body with all its various parts. It pictures a physical body with its head, neck, shoulders, arms, hands, torso — including chest, waist, and hips — legs, feet, and every inner organ required for a life: brain, heart, lungs, digestive system, and so on.

Paul used the word *soma* to declare that the Church is *figuratively* and *literally* the Body of Christ in the earth today. He *figuratively* likens the Church to a body, but also *literally* because the Church is, in fact, more than a metaphor. The Church is the actual living Body of Christ on the earth today.

The metaphor of the Church as a "body" is relatively easy for people to visualize — that is why it's probably the most popular view people have of the Church. They are able to visualize Christ as the Head who is seated "...far above all principality, power, might, and dominion" (Ephesians 1:21) — and His Body extending downward into the earth with His heart, His voice, His hands, and His feet, etc. doing the work of ministry as the Church. The Body of Christ is so connected to Christ as the Head that in Colossians 2:19, Paul said the Church becomes dysfunctional when it does not retain its relationship to Christ.

The 'Breath of Life' and the Newly Emerging Church

Every human body must have a *life-force* at its core in order to live, which is why James 2:26 says, "...The body without the spirit is *dead*...." The word "dead" is the word *nekros*, which pictures *a lifeless body* with no heartbeat, no breath in its lungs, and no pulse in its wrists. And just as any human body must have a life-force at its core to live, the Church also must have *a life-force* at its core for it to be the living and breathing Body of Christ in the earth. That divine Life-Force — the precious Holy Spirit — came into the Church after Jesus' resurrection from the dead when Christ appeared to the disciples in a closed room, where they were gathered after Jesus' crucifixion.

After showing them His hands and side and convincing them it was really Him, Jesus said, "...Peace be unto you: as my Father hath sent me, even so send I you" (John 20:21). Then He breathed on them and said, "...Receive ye the Holy Ghost" (v. 22). In that moment, the disciples were born again under the New Covenant, and the Holy Spirit literally came *into* them and, thus, *into* the Church — the newly emerging Church — filling all in all.

Notice John 20:22 tells us Jesus "breathed" on the disciples. The word "breathed" is the word *emphusao*, a Greek word that means *to breathe into.* In that moment, Jesus breathed His Spirit *into* their spirits. It is important to note that this Greek word *emphusao* in John 20:22 is the identical word used in Genesis 2:7 in the Septuagint version of the Greek Old Testament, where we read, "And the Lord God formed man of the dust of the ground, and *breathed into* his nostrils the breath of life; and man became a living soul."

Adam was unquestionably the most perfect man ever formed, a masterpiece of God's own hands. But until God "breathed into his nostrils the breath of life," he was simply a physical form with no beat in his heart, no pulse in his wrists, no breath in his lungs, and no movement in his limbs. But when God literally "breathed into his nostril the breath of life," Adam's heart began to beat, his lungs began expanding and contracting, the pulse in his wrist came alive, and his body began to move. In that moment when the "breath of life" was infused *into* him, Adam miraculously became a living soul.

Like that perfectly formed body of Adam, the disciples had been trained, prepared, and "formed" by Jesus, but the Holy Spirit had never come to live in them. But when Jesus "breathed on" them, which is the Greek word *emphusao*, He literally *breathed into* them in the same way God breathed into the nostrils of Adam, and the Holy Spirit came to live in them.

Simultaneously, Jesus had said, "*Receive* ye the Holy Ghost" (John 20:22). The word "receive" is the Greek word *labete*, meaning *to take right now.* In that exact moment, the Holy Spirit — God's divine breath of life — entered *into* the disciples and *into* the Church. Later, on the Day of Pentecost, they were baptized in the Holy Spirit. But the Holy Spirit, who is the Breath of God and Life-Force of the Church, entered *into* the hearts of the disciples and *into* the Church when Jesus breathed on them and told them to receive the Holy Spirit (John 20:22). It was at that exact moment that they were born again.

If the event recorded in John 20:22 had never occurred, the Church would be no more than a human, good-will organization like other organizations with no divine life-force at their core. But just as God breathed the breath of life into the nostrils of Adam and he became a living soul, Christ breathed the Holy Spirit — His divine breath of life — into the Church and caused it to become the living, breathing Body of Christ.

After Christ imparted the divine life of God into the Church's core, the Head and Body were supernaturally connected, and the Church was filled with the life of Christ Himself — "the fullness of Him who fills all in all" (*see* Ephesians 1:23). For this reason, the Church really is the living, breathing Body of Christ in the earth today.

Paul directly referred to this divine life-force in Ephesians 1:23 when he declared that Christ's Body is "...the *fulness* of him that filleth all in all." That word "fulness" ("fullness") is a translation of the word *pleroma,* a Greek word that means *to make full, to fill completely,* or even *to be filled to the point of satisfaction*. It is important to note that this word *pleroma* was used to describe any kind of container that was filled and packed to overflowing. Thus, we find God's intention is for the Church *to be filled to the point of overflowing* with Christ's presence. God intends for His divine life to *fill completely* the collective Christian Body.

A Stunning Revelation That the Body of Christ Must Grasp

According to John 3:34, when Jesus Himself walked the earth, the Father gave Him the Spirit without measure. But Paul stated in Colossians 1:18,19 that now, since Christ "…is the head of the body, the church…it pleased the Father that *in him* [and in all His Body] should all fulness dwell."

The words "in him" certainly refer to Jesus Himself, but the subject Paul is discussing in these verses is the Church, the Body of Christ. These verses remarkably mean that as God was pleased to give Jesus the Spirit without measure, now the Father is pleased for "all fullness" to "dwell" inside the Church, the Body of Christ — *Head to toe*.

The word "all" in the phrase "all fulness dwell" in Colossians 1:19 is a translation of the word *pan*, an all-encompassing Greek word. The word "fulness" is translated from the word *pleroma*, the same Greek word we saw in Ephesians 1:23 that depicts something that is *filled to the maximum*.

The word "dwell" in Colossians 1:19 is a form of *katoikeo*, a Greek word depicting *one who settles down into a home and feels so at home there that he has chosen to take up permanent residency*. These three words "all fulness dwell" unequivocally mean:

1. God's Spirit has settled into the Church (the Body of Christ).
2. He is pleased to permanently dwell there.
3. His plan is *to fill it to the maximum* with the life of Christ.

This stunning revelation is confirmed in Colossians 2:9 and 10, where Paul added, "For *in him* dwelleth all the fulness of the Godhead bodily. And ye are complete *in him*…."

The words "in him" in verse 9 emphatically declare that all the fullness of the Godhead dwells bodily in Jesus, but the following verse says, "And ye are complete *in him....*" In that verse, Paul was speaking plurally to the Church, so these words could be better translated, "And you (plural) have been given that same fullness." Thus, Paul declared that as the Father was pleased to give the Spirit to Jesus without measure, the Father is now pleased to give that same fullness to Christ's whole Body, the Church (*see* Colossians 1:19).

Individually, *every* believer carries the Spirit within, but when all the members of the Church are joined to become a larger body, all those various portions of Christ are divinely connected. United, we experience a fullness we cannot know apart from each other. God's long-term plan is for each member to be divinely joined to others and to function as the real, living Body of Christ in the earth with His heart, His pulse, and His hands and feet in order to touch others and carry the Gospel where it needs to go.

But to bring this plan out of the "mystical realm" into reality, something else that's divine must occur. This God-breathed plan requires the help of the Christ-given fivefold ministry gifts who are anointed to do their respective parts in *assembling* and *building* the Body of Christ so that this Body can house the fullness of the Spirit — the fullness of Christ Himself.

God's long-term plan is for each member to be divinely joined to others and to function as the real, living Body of Christ in the earth with His heart, His pulse, and His hands and feet in order to touch others and carry the Gospel where it needs to go.

Christ-Given Fivefold 'Body Builders'

Here is the good news. God has placed these Christ-given ministry gifts in the Church, and they are supernaturally anointed "Body-builders" who are equipped to do their part in assembling and building the Body of Christ to be what God longs for it to become. In Ephesians 4:11 and 12, Paul wrote, "And he [Christ] gave *some*, apostles; and *some*, prophets; and *some*, evangelists; and *some*, pastors and teachers; for the perfecting of the saints, for the work of the ministry, for the edifying of the body of Christ."

Notice Paul repeats the word "some" again and again in this verse. In each instance, the word "some" is a Greek word that should be taken as an *emphatic, categorical,* or *exclamatory* remark. It could be better translated: "And he gave *indeed*, apostles; and *indeed*, prophets; and *indeed*, evangelists; and *indeed,* pastors; and [it is understood to mean] *indeed* teachers...."

Or it could be translated, "And he gave *emphatically*, apostles; and *emphatically*, prophets; and *emphatically*, evangelists; and *emphatically*, pastors; and *emphatically*, teachers...."

It could also be translated, "And he gave *categorically*, apostles; and *categorically*, prophets; and *categorically*, evangelists; and *categorically,* pastors; and *categorically*, teachers...."

This tells us Christ has *indeed*, *emphatically*, and *categorically* given the Church the fivefold ministry gifts of *apostle*, *prophet*, *evangelist*, *pastor*, and *teacher.* Perhaps how each of these gifts operate can be debated, but the repetitious use of the word *indeed* means the present-day reality of these fivefold gifts should never be questioned — for Paul said Christ has *indeed, emphatically*, and *categorically* given each of these ministry gifts for the work of the ministry and for the edifying (building up) of the Body of Christ.

The reason they are called *fivefold gifts* is because there are *five* that fit into a unique category. While there are certainly many others with gifts in the Body of Christ, these five are in a separate category.

Again, this book focuses primarily on the Christ-given fivefold ministry gifts of *apostles* and *prophets*, but we will briefly look at the original meanings of all the words in Ephesians 4:11 — *apostle*, *prophet*, *evangelist*, *pastor*, and *teacher* to see how they were used historically and how believers in the Early Church heard and understood these words in the First Century.

The Meaning of the Word 'Apostle'

First, Ephesians 4:11 says, "And he [Christ] gave some, ***apostles***...."

As we have seen, the word "some" would be better translated *indeed*, *emphatically*, or *categorically*, so when Paul listed the gift of the apostle, he stated *emphatically* or *categorically* that this is a Christ-given gift that is *indeed* given to the Church.

The ministry of the apostle will be extensively covered in Chapters 3-6, but as an introduction, the word "apostle" is a translation of the Greek word *apostolos*, an old word that is compounded from the preposition *apo* and the word *stello*. The preposition *apo* means *away* and the word *stello* means *to send*. When these two words are compounded, it forms the word *apostolos* — which is translated "apostle" — and its most simplistic meaning depicts *one who is sent away*. (In later chapters, we will see more deeply the use of this Greek word in the New Testament and in the Old Testament Greek Septuagint.)

It is important to note the word *apostolos* predates the New Testament and was used in different ways by various writers in ancient Greece. Since the word *apostolos* is a notable Greek word, we must see how legendary Greeks used it and how that usage set the stage for how the word *apostolos* would be used in the New Testament.

- Herodotus used *apostolos* to describe *a high-powered ambassador who had been sent to represent a government or king.*[9]
- Euripides and the historian Thucydides (c. 460-400 BC) used *apostolos* to describe *important packages* that were *sent* by powerful

people that contained powerful and important contents.[10] You will especially see in Chapter Three how this relates to the ministry of an apostle.

- Plato similarly used this word to depict *a huge ship that was fully loaded with cargo and manned by a specialized crew to accompany an admiral who ventured into new territory to construct a new community.*[11] When we come to Chapter Three, it will become clear how this also relates to the ministry of an apostle.

- Aristotle used *apostolos* to picture *the seeing off* or *sending away* of important individuals.[12] This powerful meaning of *apostolos* has great significance when we discuss New Testament apostles, which you will understand when we come to Chapter Three.

- Lysias, Demosthenes, Lucian, and Plutarch each respectively used forms of this word to depict *a fully equipped large fleet sent on an expedition to a new territory* or *the sending away of a trade ship filled with cargo.*[13] In Chapter Three, I will show you how this meaning of *apostolos* relates to New Testament apostles.

- Polybius used this word to depict *a huge ship that was fully loaded with cargo and manned by a specialized crew to accompany an admiral who ventured into new territory to construct a new community.*[14] As in the aforementioned notations, you will see how this powerful meaning of *apostolos* relates to New Testament apostles when we come to Chapter Three.

Jesus Himself stood in all the fivefold gifts, or ministry offices, and Hebrews 3:1 says that He is, in fact, the *first* apostle. But all these Greek meanings, nuances, and usages — combined with how the word *apostolos* is used in the New Testament — provide amazing insights into the past, contemporary, and last-days ministry of apostles in the Church. I will reserve further commentary on apostolic ministry for Chapters 3-6. You will see how all of these meanings are important to understanding an apostle's role in the Church for all time. However, if you desire to skip ahead to Chapter Three, my comments on apostolic ministry can stand alone in those chapters. I do recommend that you return to these "building" Chapters One and Two for insight into God's intention for His Body — His Temple — the *Church.*

The Meaning of the Word 'Prophet'

Second, Ephesians 4:11 says, "And he [Christ] gave some, apostles; and some, ***prophets....***"

The ministry of the prophet will be covered in Chapters Seven and Eight, but as an introduction, the word "prophet" is a translation of the Greek word *prophetes*, which is a compound of the words *pro* and *phemi*. The word *phemi* means *to say* or *to speak* and lets us know the prophetic gift is a *speaking* gift or a *saying* gift. The first part of the word "prophet" is the prefix *pro* — and this adds a wide range of meanings, and all of it is critical to understanding a prophet's role in the past, contemporary, and last-days Church.

You will learn more fully later in this book that the Greek word for a "prophet" projects four primary ideas that describe the function and responsibility of a prophet by portraying his position:

- First, *before* God.
- Second, *in front of* people.
- Third, *on behalf of the* Lord.
- Fourth, this word even depicts one with the ability to speak *in advance of something that is to occur.*

But just as the word *apostolos*, from which we get the word "apostle," predates the New Testament, the word prophet — the Greek word *prophetes* — was also used by various ancient writers. Since the word *prophetes* and its various forms was used by illustrious Greeks before it found its way into the Greek version of the Old and New Testaments, we must see how those notable figures used it.

- Herodotus and Plato both used the word *prophetes* to describe *those possessed with the ability to interpret the will of the gods*, such as oracles at pagan temples.[15] You will see in Chapters Seven and Eight how this relates to a prophet's role in the past, present, and last-days Church.

- Euripides and Aristotle both used the word *prophetes* to picture *a divine expounder*, *divine interpreter*, or *a mouthpiece for the gods and the spirit realm.*[16] In Chapters Seven and Eight, you will understand how this relates to a prophet's role in the Church historically and today.

- Sextus Empiricus used *prophetes* to picture one who was *a divine commentator.*[17] As in the aforementioned notations, you will see how this powerful meaning of *prophetes* relates to the prophet's role in the Church for all time.

In multiple verses in the Gospels, we read that Jesus Himself stood in the office of a *prophet* (for a small sampling of these verses, *see* Matthew 21:11,46; Mark 6:15; 8:28; Luke 4:24; 7:16; John 4:19; 6:14; 7:40,52; 9:17).

But historical writers also used the Greek word *prophetes*, and when we combine how they used it with how it was used in the Greek version of the Old and New Testaments, we can discover remarkable insights into the past, present, and future ministry of prophets in the Church.

Because I will deal extensively with the ministry of prophets later in this book, I will delay further commentary on prophetic ministry until we come to those chapters.

The Meaning of the Word 'Evangelist'

Third, Ephesians 4:11 says, "And he [Christ] gave some, apostles; and some, prophets; and some, ***evangelists***...."

Many are confused about what an evangelist is and what he does. I understand, for having grown up in a denominational church, we called nearly every guest speaker in our church an "evangelist," whether he was scripturally an evangelist or not. The term "evangelist" was simply a label we used to describe anyone who wasn't a pastor and who publicly preached as an itinerant minister.

Complicating it even more was the fact that, back in those days, if you had a preaching itinerant ministry and wanted to legally incorporate it, it was usually incorporated as an "Evangelistic Association." This was true of any ministry other than that of a pastor. The result of this was a lot of people were called evangelists who were not evangelists. Few in those days embraced the possibility of an apostle or prophet in contemporary times, and because of the accepted tradition of the day, it was rare for someone to travel as a full-time teacher. So anyone with an itinerant ministry was almost automatically called an "evangelist."

This book will not go into deep detail about the Christ-given gift of "evangelist," but the word "evangelist" is a translation of the Greek word *euangelistes*. It is a compound of the word *eu*, which describes *something that is really good, pleasant, or swell*, and the word *angelos*, which is the New Testament word for *a messenger*. When these words are combined, they form the word *euangelistes*, which describes *a bringer of good news.* That is the New Testament word for an "evangelist."

But, remarkably, one of the earliest uses of the word "evangelist" — translated in the New Testament from the Greek word *euangelistes* — was found in a non-Christian inscription etched on an ancient stone marker to commemorate a pagan *oracle* or *medium.*[18] By "oracle" or "medium," I am referring to a person who is allegedly *a voice* or *channel* or *medium* for the spirit realm — a *human conduit* through whom the spirit realm spoke or supernaturally operated.

The Importance of 'First Usages'

First usages of words are very important and bear an impact on the future use of a word. Because this Greek word *euangelistes* was used early to depict a *medium* of the spirit world, or one who channeled the voice of the spirit world to the world of the living, we need to see the impact of this historical use on the future usage of the word "evangelist" in the New Testament. A New Testament evangelist is one who speaks for God and supernaturally operates in signs and wonders, so it is clear why such a word would be used to picture this Christ-given fivefold ministry gift.

Indeed, God's call on an evangelist is to be the *clearest channel* possible for the Holy Spirit to proclaim the Gospel and to manifest God's power in the natural realm. So in early New Testament times, in addition to being a bearer of the Good News of the Gospel, if a person described himself as an evangelist — taken from the Greek word *euangelistes* — it could have meant he was saying, "I'm a channel through whom God speaks and through whom His supernatural power flows."

If you study evangelists in the book of Acts, you will see they were each proclaimers of the Good News and operated in miraculous signs and wonders.

In fact, there is no record of any evangelist in the New Testament whose ministry was not accompanied with signs and wonders.

Many who are called evangelists in contemporary times do not operate in signs and wonders and, therefore, fail the test of being authentic New Testament evangelists. It is likely they are prophets or teachers who have been mislabeled because of a lack of understanding concerning the real function of New Testament evangelists. A real New Testament evangelist divinely proclaims the Gospel, but also always comes with miraculous manifestations to fulfill Gospel promises to those who are in need.

But as the words *apostolos* and *prophetes* predate the New Testament, the word evangelist — in Greek, *euangelistes* — was also used in the ancient world by many Greek writers who were superlative in their use of the Greek language. So to more thoroughly understand the ministry calling and function of the New Testament evangelist, we must see how they used it.

- Xenophon, used *euangelistes* as meaning *to make a thanksgiving sacrifice at the hearing of good news.*[19]
- Demosthenes, Plutarch, and Lucian each used this word to depict *good news* or *one who reports good news or congratulates good news.*[20]
- Plutarch separately used this word to depict *a reward that accompanied good news.*[21]

It's interesting that Plutarch used *euangelistes* to depict a reward that accompanied good news. If those who hear an evangelist's message choose to believe it, there is definitely a reward for those who release their faith to embrace the message of a New Testament evangelist!

Just as Jesus stood in the office of the apostle and the prophet, He likewise stood in the office of the evangelist, and He was, in fact, the *first* evangelist. In Luke 4:16-19, we read Jesus' announcement of His ministry.

It says, "And he came to Nazareth, where he had been brought up: and, as his custom was, he went into the synagogue on the sabbath day, and stood up for to read. And there was delivered unto him the book of the prophet Esaias [Isaiah]. And when he had opened the book, he found the place where it was written, The Spirit of the Lord is upon me, because he hath anointed me to preach the gospel to the poor; he hath sent me to heal the brokenhearted, to preach deliverance to the captives, and recovering of sight to the blind, to set at liberty them that are bruised, to preach the acceptable year of the Lord."

Beyond this section, this book will not go further into the ministry of the evangelist, but let's look briefly at what Jesus said about a true evangelist's ministry. The first thing Jesus said about Himself as an evangelist was that, "The Spirit of the Lord is upon me to preach the gospel..." (Luke 4:18).

The phrase "to preach the gospel" is a form of the Greek word *euangelistes,* which, as we've seen, is the New Testament word for *one who announces good news, preaches good news, or channels good news* or *one who evangelizes.* In essence, Jesus proclaimed, "*I've been anointed with the Holy Spirit to do the work of an evangelist!*" And, of course, there was never a clearer channel for the Holy Spirit to work through than Jesus. He was a divine conduit through which the Gospel was proclaimed and through which the supernatural activity of the Holy Spirit flowed into the natural realm.

Good News for the Financially Poor

In Luke 4:18, Jesus went on to describe the things that become visible when the evangelist's anointing is allowed to operate. He began by saying He was anointed to evangelize the "poor." The word "poor" is the Greek word *ptochos,* and it pictures *abject poverty* or *those who are impoverished.* This tells us the Gospel is good news for the poor. When an evangelist carries the Gospel to people in abject poverty, that good news is an economic game-changer that causes their financial status to change. Indeed, the Gospel is good news for the poor because if it is believed and embraced, it will change their economic status.

Good News for the Brokenhearted and Those Crushed by Others and by *Life*

Next, Jesus said He was anointed as an evangelist to heal the "brokenhearted." The word "broken" is a form of the Greek word *suntribo* — a word that is used throughout the New Testament and the writings of the First Century. It was used to describe *the crushing of grapes with the feet* or *the smashing and grinding of bones into dust*. It depicts *people who have been walked on by others, those who have been crushed by others, or those who feel they have been smashed to pieces by life or relationships*. Thus, the word "brokenhearted" describes those who are emotionally shattered, tattered, and smashed by life.

Jesus said this particular anointing would "heal" them. The word "heal" is a translation of the Greek word *iaomai*, a word that literally means *to cure*. It usually points to *a progressive cure* and often depicts *healing power that progressively reverses a condition over a period of time* — a sickness that is *progressively healed* rather than healed instantaneously.

This means that when an evangelist preaches, the Gospel he or she preaches and the power of God that is released in his or her ministry does not only heal the physically ill, but it even heals the brokenhearted.

If people's hearts have been smashed or crushed by others, the power of God discharged through the Good News an evangelist preaches can touch them and then keep progressively working until those who are brokenhearted are brought into a place of healing and wholeness. Indeed, the Gospel is good news for the brokenhearted because if it is believed and embraced, it will make them whole again.

Good News for Those Who Are Captive and in Bondage

Then Jesus announced that as an evangelist, He was also sent to preach "deliverance" to the "captives."

The word "deliverance" is from the Greek word *aphesis*, which describes *a release* or *a dismissal*. It means *to set free* or *to permanently loose*, and this *release* or *permanent freedom* is for the "captives." The word "captives" is a translation of the Greek word *aichmalotos*, which describes *those taken captive at the point of a spear, those who are dragged into bondage* or *those manipulated by bondage*. This is important, so let me help you understand what kind of captives Jesus is describing in this verse.

Imagine for a moment if your hands were bound and a person behind you pressed a sharp spear between your shoulder blades. With one push of that spear, he could force you to go wherever he directed you to go. This Greek word "captives" is used to picture *an outside force directing, manipulating, and forcing a person into bondage*. It represents any kind of outside force — including abusive relationships or addictions that enslave and control a person's life. But when an evangelist shows up to proclaim the Good News, and the Gospel message is released, the liberating power of God begins to flow. As a result, people who have been bound by abuse or addictions are permanently set free. Indeed, this is a miraculous work of God that happens through the evangelist.

Good News for the Blind

Next Jesus said that a true evangelist's anointing also gives "recovering of sight" to the "blind." The words "recovering of sight" are a translation of the Greek word *anablepsis*, which literally means *the returning of one's sight, the restoration of sight*, or *to see again*.

The word "blind" is very significant because in Greek, it is the word *tuphlos*, which doesn't just depict a person who is unable to see — it depicts a person who has been *intentionally blinded* by someone else. It pictures one whose eyes have been *deliberately removed* so that he is *blinded*. Because of this, he has *no eyes* with which to see.

In Second Corinthians 4:4, Paul told us that Satan "...hath blinded the minds of them which believe not...." This word "blinded" is the same Greek word, *tuphlos*, and it tells us that those who don't believe may not even have spiritual eyes to see. That's why when someone tries to share the Gospel with them, they just can't seem *to see* what is being said. The reason is, they *don't* see, because they have *no spiritual eyes to see*.

But, miraculously, when an evangelist begins to preach, the Holy Spirit begins to work and the power of God is released to create spiritual eyes in those who are spiritually blind, and for the first time, they begin *to see* and understand the truth.

Good News for Those Who Are Fractured and Bruised

Jesus said that a real evangelist's anointing will "set at liberty" those who are "bruised." The phrase "set at liberty" is, again, the Greek word *aphesis*, which describes *a release* or *a dismissal*. But in this case, it indicates *a permanent release from the detrimental effects of a shattered life*. We know that because of the word "bruised," which in Greek means *to crush* or *to break down*. This word depicts *a person who has been shattered or fractured by life* or *those whose lives have been continually split up and fragmented*. It is the exact same Greek word from which we get the word "trauma." Thus, this anointing to evangelize "sets at liberty" — *gives a permanent release* — to people who have been traumatized by life. Indeed, when a genuine evangelist shows up to declare the Gospel and its promises, divine restoration and freedom come to those who are hurting.

The Acceptable Year of the Lord

Finally, Jesus said the anointing to evangelize is also to "preach the acceptable year of the Lord" (Luke 4:19).

The word "acceptable" is the Greek word *dektos*, and it means *favorable* or *accepted*; it describes *a favorable time to receive*. This means when an evangelist comes on the scene, it is a *divine moment* and *a favorable time* to receive from the Lord. A true New Testament evangelist comes with a supernatural message and supernatural power to bring freedom, healing, and restoration to the poor, broken, blind, and anyone that has been traumatized by life. These are the manifestations that accompany the ministry of a true evangelist. You can see why he is called a bearer of Good News!

Jesus Himself is the best example of an evangelist. In addition to Jesus, there are other examples of New Testament evangelists in the book of Acts who were human conduits, and each of them was a human conduit for the proclamation of the Gospel and for the power of God to work signs and wonders in the natural realm.

In Acts 6:5, we read that although Stephen was first chosen as a deacon, he emerged as one of the earliest evangelists in the New Testament. His evangelistic ministry is described in Acts 6:8, where the Bible says, "And Stephen, full of faith and power, did great wonders and miracles among the people."

Notice Stephen's evangelistic preaching was a divine proclamation that was simultaneously accompanied with supernatural wonders and miracles. In every respect, Stephen was a picture of a human conduit through whom God operated to bring the message and promises of God to those who were in need.

In Acts 8:5-8, we also read about the evangelistic ministry of Philip: "Then Philip went down to the city of Samaria, and preached Christ unto them. And the people with one accord gave heed unto those things which Philip spake, hearing and seeing the miracles which he did. For unclean spirits, crying with loud voices, came out of many that were possessed with them: and many taken with palsies, and that were lame, were healed. And there was great joy in that city."

In both of these New Testament examples, we see that evangelists are Gospel proclaimers and divine channels through whom the power of God flows to do miraculous signs and wonders.

Furthermore, Acts 8:8 tells us when Philip preached, there was "great joy" that erupted as he preached with the manifestations of healings, miracles, and deliverances from unclean spirits. This speaks to the eruptive joy that manifests in the ministry of a true Christ-given evangelist.

Dressed for the Part!

Another very early use of the word "evangelist" portrayed *an official messenger-announcer who carried joyful news of victory in a war or joyful news of some other event — and the celebration that accompanied his arrival.* I remind you that Xenophon said the word *euangelistes* meant *to make a thanksgiving sacrifice at the hearing of good news.* That definition describes the joyous celebration that comes with the declaration made by such a news carrier.

When such a historical messenger-announcer arrived with joyful news of a victory in war or with joyful news about some other kind of event, such a messenger lavishly decked his weapons and apparel with celebrative decorations to accentuate the wondrous news he was about to announce. A celebration was about to occur, so these messenger-announcers dressed the part! They not only announced the joyful news, but they dressed to look like the news they were heralding.[22]

This is something to consider in observing modern-day evangelists who, to some, are a bit "flashy" in appearance or present themselves flamboyantly.

In light of what you just read, you might now see such ministry gifts in a different light. What you may think is a presentation that's a bit ostentatious could simply be their "calling card," as it were, to stir listeners to the spiritual celebration that is about to take place!

The arrival of those good-news messengers in ancient history was so exciting that when a city heard such a messenger-announcer was coming, they prepared by adorning the city itself with festive decorations in eager anticipation of his arrival. When the *euangelistes* messenger finally showed up to announce his glad news, everyone was ready for him and burst into celebratory expressions of joy when he arrived because they knew the delivery of his message would be such a joy-filled occasion.[23]

When I think of authentic New Testament evangelists that I have known over the years, they are indeed celebrative, joyful proclaimers who bring such joy as they preach. They impart faith, release miraculous signs and wonders, and joy is the result as lives are instantaneously changed by their ministries. Indeed, when a real New Testament evangelist shows up, it often looks and feels like a divine party has erupted as sick people are healed, the demonized are set free, and the brokenhearted and traumatized are restored.

Indeed, when a real New Testament evangelist shows up, it often looks and feels like a divine party has erupted as sick people are healed, the demonized are set free, and the brokenhearted and traumatized are restored.

In Acts 8:8, we read that "there was great joy in that city" when Philip the evangelist carried out his ministry among them. Likewise, the ministry of a Christ-given evangelist will be accompanied with a celebrative eruption of joy.

The Church today needs Christ-given fivefold ministry evangelists! How vital it is that we see how they operated in the past, how they are to operate in the present, and how they are to operate in the last days of the Church so we can embrace the gift that they are and stir ourselves to receive from their ministry in our midst.

Next, we'll look briefly into the calling of a "pastor," another ministry gift or office in Paul's list of fivefold ministries in Ephesians 4:11.

The Meaning of the Word 'Pastor'

Fourth, in Paul's enumeration of ministry gifts, he wrote, "And he gave some, apostles; and some, prophets; and some, evangelists; and some, ***pastors***..." (Ephesians 4:11).

The word "pastor" is a translation of the word *poimen*, a Greek word used to depict *a shepherd*. It pictures one who *feeds*, *guards*, *guides*, *governs*, *protects*, and *tends* a flock. And just as the words *apostolos*, *prophetes*, and *euangelistes* — "apostle," "prophet," and "evangelist" — predate the New Testament, the word "pastor" was also used by many well-known early Greek writers.

Since *poimen* was used by various historical figures, let's see how some of them utilized this important word in their writings.

- Homer notably used the word *poimen* to picture *a shepherd of sheep*[24]
- Aeschylus used the word *poimen* to describe *a chief* or *a leader of people*.[25]
- Euripides used *poimen* to picture one who was *a shepherd of sheep* or *a shepherd of people*.[26]

- Plato used the word *poimen* to mean *to cherish, to surround with tender care* and to depict a *coach, mentor, ruler,* or *trainer.*[27]
- Theocritus used the word *poimen* as meaning *to sooth, calm down,* or *comfort.*[28]
- Lucian also used *poimen* to describe *a shepherd of sheep.*[29]

These uses of *poimen* tell us that a pastor is to be a shepherd of people. As their shepherd/pastor, he is called to feed, guard, guide, govern, protect, and tend his congregation. All of these concepts need examination and explanation, but that is not the purpose of this book. However, this does show us that the ministry of a pastor is one with the Christ-given role of being the chief leader in a local congregation — who is to cherish his flock and provide tender care for them and whose pastoral charge is to provide coaching, mentoring, and training, along with ruling, and to pastorally, supernaturally provide comfort and a soothing, calming effect on his flock as needed.

Just as Jesus stands in the offices of apostle, prophet, and evangelist, He also stands in the office of a pastor — and you can readily see all the characteristics of a pastor in the ministry of Jesus. In John 10:11, Jesus made the stunning declaration: "I am the good shepherd...." The Greek translation of this phrase "the good shepherd" *ho poimen ho kalos,* importantly repeats the definite article *"ho"* twice — it was done for the sake of emphasis to show us something very important.

The use of a definite article in the words *ho poimen* means it should be translated that Jesus is *THE Shepherd* — pointing to the fact that there is none more superior than Him as a pastor. However, the Greek phrase doesn't stop there. It continues to say *ho kalos,* which also includes a definite article. And it means Jesus is declaring that He is not just *THE Shepherd,* but that He is *THE Good One*!

Jesus is the Most Excellent Shepherd, the Supreme Example of a shepherd of the sheep. The word "shepherd," again, is the Greek word *poimen*, which describes *one who feeds, tends, guards, guides, and protects a flock or congregation*. So in John 10:11, when Jesus declares that He is *the Superior Example* of what a shepherd should be, He is setting the example for all other pastors.

An Exhortation for Pastors

While this book primarily focuses on the ministry of apostles and prophets, let's briefly cover Peter's exhortation to pastors in First Peter 5:1-4. There are many texts in the New Testament we could use to describe a pastor's ministry, but Peter's words in this text succinctly summarize God's word to pastors.

In First Peter 5:1-4, the apostle wrote, "The elders which are among you I exhort, who am also an elder, and a witness of the sufferings of Christ, and also a partaker of the glory that shall be revealed: Feed the flock of God which is among you, taking the oversight thereof, not by constraint, but willingly [according to God]; not for filthy lucre, but of a ready mind; Neither as being lords over God's heritage, but being ensamples to the flock. And when the chief Shepherd shall appear, ye shall receive a crown of glory that fadeth not away."

In First Peter 5:1, Peter began by saying, "The elders which are among you I *exhort*...." The word "exhort" is a form of the Greek word *parakaleo*, a compound of the word *para* and *kaleo*. The word *para* means *alongside*, and the word *kaleo* means *to call*. When compounded, it forms the word *parakaleo*, which pictures *one who comes alongside someone else to encourage him, exhort him, plead with him, or console him in some way*.

But there is also something very important to understand about the word *parakaleo*. This word was often used by military leaders or commanding officers before they sent their troops into battle. Rather than hide from the reality of war, the commanding officer would summon troops together to speak straightforwardly with them about the potential dangers of the battlefield. The soldiers were soberly assured by their leader that bloodshed, injury, and even death could be encountered as they fought their battles. A good commander wouldn't ignore these dangers or pretend they didn't exist because he knew it was his job to prepare the troops for war. So he would urge, exhort, encourage, and beseech his troops to stand tall, throw back their shoulders, look the enemy straight-on and eye-to-eye, and face their battle with steadfast courage.

Peter used this word *parakaleo* because he knew pastors are on the frontlines of battle and wage warfare to bring salvation, restoration, and wholeness to their congregations. As frontline warriors, they deal with constant attacks against their sheep and even against their pastoral posts. Peter used the word *parakaleo* and spoke to them like a commander to urge them to stay at their posts regardless of the challenges and spiritual conflicts they may find themselves in from time to time.

In First Peter 5:2, Peter wrote, "*Feed* the flock of God which is among you...." We already saw that the word "feed" is a form of the Greek word *poimen*, and it is a direct command to pastors *to do the full work of a shepherd*. That includes everything we have already seen, but above all else, the primary meaning of *poimen* is *to feed* a flock. This tells us that the chief duty of a pastor above all else is to feed his congregation with the teaching of the Bible that will cause them to grow personally, spiritually, and numerically.

Today pastors are pulled in many directions to provide all types of supplementary things for the church. There is the pull to provide music, great sound, and entertainment, which is very unique to a modern church in the Western world. There is nothing wrong with any of this unless it takes away from the pastor's chief charge to feed the flock. As we saw in the word *poimen*, the word "pastor" is very connected to the idea of "feeding" and, in fact, is translated *to pastor* or *to feed.*

This charge for pastors to "feed" the flock of God is found in Paul's specific exhortation to pastors in Acts 20:28 and to Timothy in Second Timothy 4:1-5. In all these texts about pastoral ministry, the Bible makes it abundantly clear that the chief call of a pastor is to provide the teaching of God's Word to his congregation. If he does not do this, he is failing at the most basic level, as the most basic meaning of the word "pastor" is *to feed.* It is imperative for pastors to never be sidetracked by other things or forget that it is the anointed exposition of the Bible that will bring spiritual health, healing, and numerical and spiritual growth to their flocks.

In First Peter 5:2, Peter added, "Feed the flock of God which is among you, taking the *oversight* thereof...." The word "oversight" is a form of the Greek word *episkopos,* a compound of the word *epi,* meaning *over,* and the word *skopos,* meaning *to look.* When these words are compounded, the new word *episkopos* means *to look over, to administrate,* or *to manage.* It pictures *one in a supervisory position whose responsibility is to guide, direct, and give oversight to the local congregation.*

Pastors Are To Serve Willingly and Soberly According to God

In First Peter 5:2, Peter also urged pastors not to serve "...by *constraint,* but *willingly....*" The word "constraint" is a translation of the Greek word *anagkastos,* which describes *someone who is doing something by compulsion, by force,* or *against his will* — or *with a bad attitude.* Instead, Peter said pastors are to do their ministry "willingly."

The word "willingly" is a translation of the Greek word *hekousios,* which means *of one's free will* or *of one's own accord.* Interestingly, the original Greek includes a phrase with the word "willingly" that was unfortunately not included in the *King James Version*. The original includes the phrase *kata Theon*, and it literally means *according to God.* It gives the sense of being *answerable to God.* The implication is that, because every pastor has been set in position by the Lord, he will be held *accountable, or answerable, to God* for his pastoral duties and the attitude in which he did them.

Peter then went on in First Peter 5:2 to say pastors are not to serve "...for *filthy lucre*, but of *a ready mind.*"

The words "filthy lucre" are a translation of the Greek word *aischrokerdos*, and it describes *a shameful gain made from a dirty game of cards* or *shamefully throwing the dice to make a gain of someone else*. The use of this word implies that *the task of pastoring is more than a game to be played for financial gain.* There is nothing wrong with receiving a good salary, and churches and ministry organizations *should* generously compensate those in ministry positions. But Peter was saying that those in ministry must never see it as a game to be played for financial gain.

The other part of that phrase in verse 2 says that pastors are to serve with *a ready mind.* The words "ready mind" are a translation of the Greek word *prothumos*, which means *to be enthusiastic, willing, eager*, or *ready*. The role of a pastor is a special assignment entrusted to a person by Heaven, so pastors must fulfill their roles in ministry enthusiastically and see it as a privilege to serve God's people as a shepherd (*poimen*) or overseer (*episkopos*). Those called to serve in this capacity should be eager and enthusiastic about it.

Then in First Peter 5:3, Peter added, "Neither as *being lords* over God's heritage, but being ensamples to the flock." The phrase "being lords" is a translation of the Greek word *katakurieuo*, which is a compound of the words *kata* and *kurieuo*. The word *kata* carries the idea of *a force that is dominating or subjugating*, and the word *kurieuo* pictures *the force of a lord or master.*

When these words are compounded to form *katakurieuo*, it means *to completely conquer, to master, to quash, to quell, to crush, to subdue, to defeat, to force into a humiliating submission, or to bring one to his knees in surrender*. It denotes *a domineering influence* and pictures *a tyrant-type of person*. Thus, when Peter said, "Neither as being lords over God's heritage," he was in essence saying, "Don't be domineering tyrants that crush your congregations."

A Pastor Preaches With His Life

Instead, First Peter 5:3 says pastors are to be "...*ensamples* to the flock." The word "ensamples" is a translation of the Greek word *tupos*, and it describes *an example, a permanent impression, an image, a model for others to follow*, or *a pattern others can see and duplicate*.

A pastor must come to grips with the fact that he is preaching at all times. Whether he or she recognizes it or not, people watch how pastors speak to their spouse, how they react in difficult situations, how they give and spend money, how they pray, and how they worship. Pastors are on full display to people who are watching all the time. Peter's charge was for pastors to live so godly, stable, strong, and faith-filled — as "ensamples," or examples — that those in the congregation want to duplicate the life they see in their pastor.

And, finally, in First Peter 5:4, Peter promises, "When the chief Shepherd shall appear, ye shall receive a crown of glory that fadeth not away." The phrase "chief Shepherd" in Greek is *archipoimen*, and it describes *the Chief Shepherd, the Head Shepherd*, or *the Arch-Shepherd*.

Make no mistake, Jesus *is* the Chief Shepherd — the Arch-Shepherd of all God-called shepherds. One day when pastors stand before Him, Jesus will reward those pastors who have executed their ministries faithfully, and He will give them a special crown. This should be the greatest motivation for obediently serving Jesus in pastoral ministry.

Pastors are uniquely selected by the Holy Spirit to be shepherds and spiritual overseers for the Church, which is comprised of the most prestigious group of individuals on the face of the earth. As such, pastors are entrusted with the care of people, and their specific task is to help *guide, direct, and give oversight* to them, with a special emphasis on *feeding* the flock — the greatest mandate God has entrusted to them.

The Meaning of the Word 'Teacher'

Finally, Ephesians 4:11 says, "And he gave some, apostles; and some, prophets; and some, evangelists; and some, pastors and ***teachers***."

The word "teacher" in this verse is a translation of the Greek word *didaskalos*. It is the word primarily translated as "teacher" throughout the New Testament. It describes *a fabulous and masterful, gifted teacher*. So this is not talking about a person who likes to occasionally comment on a scripture; rather, it is a person with a masterful grip on the Scriptures.

The word *didaskalos* is used 47 times in the gospels and the verb form of *didaskalos* is used more than 200 times in the Septuagint version of the Old Testament and in the Greek New Testament. Any word used with such frequency is well-established with a clearly defined meaning.

But as we saw with the words *apostolos, prophetes, euangelistes,* and *poimen* — apostle, prophet, evangelist, and pastor — the word "teacher," or *didaskalos*, was used by other ancient Greek writers. Hence, in addition to what we know from the Septuagint and the Greek New Testament, we need to see how this word was used historically.

- Aeschylus used the word *didaskalos* to describe *a teacher* or *a mentor*.[30]
- Herodotus used *didaskalos* to depict *a subject of study* or *scientific research*.[31]

- Aristophanes (c. 450-386 BC), a comic playwright from ancient Athens who is known as the father of comedy, used a form of *didaskalos* to depict *the activities of a theatrical director who directed the goings-on in a stage performance.*[32]

All these insights are crucial to understanding the Christ-given gift of *teacher.* These combined historical insights tell us that a *didaskalos* is:

- A *teacher* so committed to his subject or field of expertise that he delves deeply into his studies to explore his subject almost *scientifically*. He takes it apart piece by piece to understand all the elements under study — then reassembles it and compares it to other data to arrive at a correct conclusion that he can *teach* in an understandable way to others.

- A *mentor* who takes students to his side so he can impart truth to them and show them how to apply it to their lives. The verb form of *didasklaos* can describe the side-by-side relationship between a teacher and a pupil or a master and apprentice. *The New International Dictionary of New Testament Theology* says, "What is taught may be not only knowledge, opinions, or facts but also artistic and technical skills, all of which are to be systematically and thoroughly acquired by the learner through the activity of a teacher."[33] Thus, we see that a teacher is a *mentor* who teaches his apprentice not only information, but skills for living. For a pupil to obtain such skills requires a committed and submitted relationship so the teacher can *mentor* the student directly and build those skills into the student.

- A *commanding director*, like a theatrical director who knows every line in a performance because he has rehearsed and rehearsed every line until he has every word, nuance, and movement memorized.

Thus, a Christ-given teacher is one who knows his subject and possesses an *astute* and *a masterful grip* on it.

TEACHER, RABBI, MASTER

The word *didaskalos* is also the Greek equivalent for the Hebrew word "rabbi." The word "rabbi" depicts *a teacher-scholar who is respected for his accumulation of facts and knowledge.* If translated literally from the Hebrew language, the word "rabbi" means *great in number,* but when used as a title, it pictures the great number of facts and plethora of knowledge possessed by a well-versed rabbi.

A good example of the use of this word is recorded in John 3 to describe the moment Nicodemus came to Jesus secretly. John 3:1,2 tells us on that memorable night, "there was a man of the Pharisees, named Nicodemus, a ruler of the Jews: the same came to Jesus by night, and said unto him, *Rabbi,* we know that thou art a teacher come from God: for no man can do these miracles that thou doest, except God be with him."

Nicodemus was theologically trained, so it was indeed remarkable that he called Jesus "Rabbi." This leader would never have used this title unless he had already heard Jesus handle the Scriptures and had been impressed by Jesus' knowledge and grip on the Scriptures. That Nicodemus called Jesus by this privileged title that was attributed only to those who were viewed as the greatest theologians tells us that Nicodemus was impressed with Jesus' masterful grasp of the Scriptures.

In the gospels, we actually find that the words *teacher, rabbi,* and *master* are often used interchangeably. For example, Matthew 8:19 says, "And a certain scribe came, and said unto him, Master, I will follow thee whithersoever thou goest." The word "master" in this verse is the Greek word *didaskalos,* meaning *a masterful teacher*. When people called Jesus *didaskalos*, it emphatically meant they recognized Him as *One with a mastery of knowledge*.

Then in John 13:13, Jesus said, "Ye call me Master and Lord: and ye say well; for so I am." The word translated "Master" in the *King James Version* is the Greek word *didaskalos*, which, again, is the word for *a masterful teacher*. This shows the interchangeability of the words "teacher" and "master."

Notice also that Jesus said, "Ye call me Master and *Lord*...." This is very important because if one was a *didaskalos* (teacher) or a *rabbi* (rabbi), he was also considered to be a "lord" — that is, *one who exercised authority in the lives of his students*. In essence, Jesus said, "When you call Me *didaskalos* (teacher), you are acknowledging I have authority to speak into your life. As My students, you are to listen to Me, internalize what I say, and do what I instruct you to do. I'm your Master, your Teacher, and your Rabbi, and not only do I have scriptural authority, but I also have spiritual authority in your lives."

Then John 20:16 says, "Jesus saith unto her, Mary. She turned herself, and saith unto him, Rabboni; which is to say, Master."

In this verse, we read that Mary Magdalene was in the garden just after Jesus' resurrection. In that moment, she called Him "Rabboni." In Greek, it is the word "rabbi," meaning *great one*. But then the Bible immediately clarifies: "...And [she] saith unto him, *Rabboni*; which is to say, *Master*."

Immediately we find that the meaning of "rabbi" is explained in Greek by the word *didaskalos*, which means *a masterful teacher*. Both words "rabbi" and "master" are used side by side in this verse to demonstrate their interchangeability.

The following are several more verses in the gospels that show the interchangeability of the words "teacher," "rabbi," and "master" — all from the Greek *didaskalos* — that I encourage you to read and study.

- Matthew 9:11
- Matthew 19:16; 26:25,49
- Mark 9:5; 11:21; 13:1; 14:45
- Luke 10:25; 19:39; 20:21,39; 21:7
- John 1:38,49; 3:2; 4:31; 11:8

Again and again in Scripture, the word "teacher" — translated from the Greek word *didaskalos* — is interchanged with the words "rabbi" and "master." Each of these three words describe *an outstanding, masterful, great teacher*. While these words clearly describe Jesus, they can also be used interchangeably to describe those who operate in the fivefold ministry gift of *teacher*.

Since a teacher is not really a teacher without someone to teach, every rabbi and teacher in the First Century had students. Such *rabbis* would gather a group of students around them and take those students everywhere they went.

Students would listen to their rabbi, follow him, and emulate his life. Virtually every moment they were together became a teaching moment. Each student or apprentice would submit to his teacher or master, and there was a close relationship between them. The teacher had the right to speak into the lives of his pupils. The pupil's job was to hear his teacher, internalize what he said, and put it into practice. The student or apprentice was also to help his teacher or master with his ministry or business. You can see all of this clearly in the relationship between Jesus and his disciples.

What Is a Disciple?

This brings us to the word "disciples" — a translation of the Greek word *mathetes*, which describes *a pupil*, *a student*, or *a learner*. It would be better to say Jesus' 12 "disciples" were actually the 12 "learners" because this is a literal translation of the Greek word *mathetes.*

In Mark 3:14, we read that Jesus "...ordained twelve, that they should be with him, and that he might send them forth to preach...." This verse perfectly illustrates the relationship that existed between *a teacher* and *his pupils* — or between *a master* and *his apprentices.*

As we have seen, the word *didaskalos* can picture a teacher that stays at the side of a pupil to teach him. Jesus chose the disciples to be "with" Him, and He literally stayed at their side to teach them as a true teacher, master, or rabbi would do. And as His disciples, they *received* Him as *Teacher, Master,* and *Rabbi.*

We must never forget that titles are very important, as they often define relationships. An example can be found in the words "Daddy" and "Mother." These words each define the unique relationship between a child and a parent. The word "boss" defines a relationship between an employee and his employer, a relationship much different than the one that exists between the employee and his fellow employees. In a nation, the words "Mr. President" define the relationship between a nation and its leader. Likewise, the word "pastor" defines a relationship between a congregation and their pastor.

Titles are crucial because they help provide clarity to relationships and define who people are in our lives. In fact, titles are so important that a world without titles would be a world with confusion, because titles give rank, order, and definition to relationships.

I tell you this because Jesus told the disciples, "Ye call me Master and Lord: and ye say well; for so I am" (John 13:13). Jesus affirmed that it was correct that they called Him by the title "Master." That title defined *who He was* to them and *who they were* to Him. Although they were in one spiritual family, they were not equal in terms of mastery and authority. Every time they called

Jesus "Master," they recognized who Jesus was and who they were. Jesus was the One with *a masterful grip* on the Scriptures, and they were the learners who were to follow, obey, and explicitly do what He told them to do. Every time they called him Teacher, Rabbi, or Master, it reaffirmed His leadership position where they were concerned — and their submissive position as learners in the relationship.

As Jesus stood in the office of an apostle, prophet, evangelist, and pastor, He also stood in the office of a *teacher.* But there are other examples of Christ-given fivefold teachers in the New Testament. For example:

- In Acts 13:1, we read that in the church at Antioch there were two fivefold ministry teachers named *Manaen* and *Saul,* who was later renamed *Paul.*
- In Acts 18:24,25, we read of *Apollos* who was "an eloquent man, and mighty in the scriptures." The Greek word for "eloquent" tells us Apollos was *educated* and *well-versed* in the Scriptures. He was *a gifted and masterful teacher* of the Word of God.
- In Acts 18:26, we read of two more fivefold ministry teachers named *Aquila* and *Priscilla.* This husband-and-wife team served with Paul for years, but there are some scholars who assert with merit that Priscilla may have had the greater teaching gift in this husband-wife team.
- In First Timothy 2:7, we read that Paul wrote of himself, "Whereunto I am ordained a preacher, and an apostle (I speak the truth in Christ, and lie not;) a *teacher* of the Gentiles in faith and verity." So in addition to being an apostle, even Paul recognized he was also a fivefold ministry teacher — one of the greatest teachers of Scripture the world has ever known and whose epistles became books of the New Testament.

The Seriousness of the Title — Words Have Consequences

The God-given role of fivefold ministry teachers is so consequential in the Church that James 3:1 warns: "My brethren, be not many *masters*, knowing that we shall receive the greater condemnation." The word "masters" in this verse is the plural form of *didaskalos*, which is actually the word for teachers. Here it is translated "masters" to convey the understanding that fivefold ministry teachers are those who have *a masterful grip* on the Scriptures.

But in this verse, the Holy Spirit goes on to warn about the great responsibility laid on fivefold teachers. Their role is so influential in the lives of others that this verse warns that anyone who claims to stand in this office will ultimately be subject to "greater condemnation."

James wanted those who were legitimate fivefold teachers to understand that their position was so influential that it would bring them under the scrutinizing gaze of God. This means that claiming a teaching gift should be done cautiously and with the full understanding about the seriousness of this position. James warned that one should not boast of this gift unless he is willing to be subject to divine scrutiny, which he calls the "greater condemnation."

I'll explain. The word "greater" is a translation of the Greek word *meidzon*, and it means *far greater by comparison.* The word "condemnation" is the Greek word *krima*, and it depicts *a verdict* or *judgment* that is the result of a formal investigation. In this verse, the Holy Spirit forewarns those with spiritual influence that they will ultimately be scrutinized by God Himself, who will watch to see if what they endorse or teach is in agreement with the entire body of Scripture. This clearly means that every word, every phrase, and every nuance that is spoken in a public forum by a spiritual leader is significant to God.

We can see just from the witness of this one verse why it is so important for Christian leaders to always remember that *words have consequences.* James 3:1 categorically declares teachers will be held to a higher standard because of their influence on hearers.

A tremendous example of a well-versed teacher in the Bible is the scribe Ezra. The Bible says, "This Ezra was a scribe, [who] was well versed in the law..." (Ezra 7:6 *NLT*). The *New King James Version* of this verse says that Ezra "...was a skilled scribe in the law...."

But what exactly did Ezra do that made him such a skilled teacher of the Scriptures? I think the answer can be found in the following various translations of another verse, Nehemiah 8:8.

- The *New International Version* says, "They read from the Book of the Law of God, *making it clear* and *giving the meaning* so that the people could understand what was being read."
- The *New Living Translation* says, "They read from the Book of the Law of God and *clearly explained the meaning of what was being read,* helping the people understand each passage."
- The *New American Standard Bible* says, "They read from the book, from the law of God, *translating to give the sense* so that they understood the reading."
- The *New King James Version* says, "So they read distinctly from the book, in the Law of God; and *they gave the sense,* and helped them to understand the reading."

Notice Ezra saw it as his responsibility to make the Word of God clear and to give its meaning to listeners. He knew his God-given assignment was to clearly explain the meaning of what the Word of God was communicating. To help his listeners, he translated the original text to give the sense of it in words that listeners could understand.

It is also important to note what Ezra did was *text-related.* He focused entirely on truth concealed inside the text and saw it as his task to "mine" it and share its deep treasures with God's people. This should ultimately be the aim of every Christ-given fivefold ministry teacher today.

A significant portion of a fivefold ministry teacher's task should be focused on *translating* and *explaining* the meaning of the Scriptures. Just as Ezra's ministry was *text-related* fivefold teachers are also to be *text-related.* Of course, inspiration is important, but their God-given task has more to do with exploration and study than a momentary gust of inspiration. One of their chief tasks is to delve as deeply as possible into the original Hebrew and Greek so they can communicate the essence of its meaning in common language so people can understand. This may sound daunting, but with all the Greek and Hebrew study tools readily available today, this is possible even for those who do not read original biblical languages.

At the time Ezra was teaching, he was keenly aware that because he was speaking to Jews who had been in captivity for 70 years, they had lost so much scripturally. To help them, he took the deeper meanings of the Scripture and did all he could to make it clear and to help his listeners understand each passage. The Bible plainly says Ezra *translated* and *explained* its original meaning to help them more easily understand the Scripture.

We are likewise living in a day when the Church has lost so much biblically that much of the Church has become biblically illiterate. As in the days of Ezra, fivefold ministry teachers are desperately needed who are willing to mine truths from the Scriptures and help those who have become biblically illiterate in this age to understand what God is communicating in His Word.

True fivefold ministry teachers must study, pray, and prepare — and once preparation is complete, they must depend on the anointing and inspiration of the Holy Spirit as they speak from their spirits and souls — processing, elaborating, and incorporating human experience to convey what God has shown them in the Scriptures. The teacher must fill his inner being with the Word of God and let it affect him completely, for only then can he step into the pulpit and publicly deliver a word from God with authority and power.

The need to ingest and digest God's Word is vital for an authentic Christ-given teacher, which I refer to in the following excerpt from my book entitled, *No Room for Compromise*.

> For a messenger to hear God's Word and deliver it without *first* tasting and digesting every part of it himself is strictly forbidden. This includes both the pleasurable parts *and* the bitter parts, the commendation and the correction, and so forth. Before he can deliver that message in power to others, he must become intimately aware of its every nuance and meaning.
>
> This divine expectation places great responsibility upon ministers who are called to teach frequently in public settings. Considering the myriad distractions of modern life, it can be a real challenge for them to find time to fully devour, consume, and digest the words God gives them to impart before their next meeting. As a result, many sermons are delivered without the power of the Holy Spirit, even though they are delivered in a professional and timely manner. For a word to be preached in the power of the Holy Spirit, one must fill his inner being with the Word that God has imparted and let it affect him completely. Only then can one step into the pulpit and publicly deliver a word from God with authority and power.
>
> In fact, one who preaches a message that he hasn't first internalized is like a chef who heartily recommends a dish he has never even tasted. Such a chef may know all about the cuisine he is recommending; he may possess all the right ingredients to produce that dish; and he may even know how to cook and prepare it for others. But if he has never actually tasted that dish

himself, everything he knows about it is merely head knowledge. He cannot truly speak about that food with authority because he hasn't had a tangible, firsthand experience with it.

This explains why so much teaching in the Church today lacks the power of the Holy Spirit. Feeling the pressure to produce spiritual meal after spiritual meal, ministers rush to their Bibles and take out scriptures, like recipes pulled from a cookbook, to cook up something new and different. Trying to keep up with the schedule, they rush from the kitchen to the table to serve meals they have never tasted themselves. And because they never took the time to digest these truths on their own, they merely dish out sermons that may be interesting, but they are rarely life-transforming.

Each spiritual leader is to read the message, meditate on it, memorize it, and deliver it as Jesus expects. Even if the message contains truths that are unpleasant to hear, difficult to consume, and painful to digest, Christ expects those who speak for Him to yield to Him and deliver the message in the power of the Holy Spirit.

Remember that even in Jesus' day, scribes were masterful "Scripture-lawyers," but they lacked the power of the Holy Spirit. Paul referred to the deadness of the letter without the anointing in Second Corinthians 3:6 where he wrote that "the letter killeth," but "the Spirit giveth life." It was the anointing of the Spirit and divine authority that set Jesus apart from the scribes. This is why Matthew 7:28,29 says, "And it came to pass, when Jesus had ended these sayings, the people were astonished at his doctrine: for he taught them as one having authority, and not as the scribes."

It wasn't that scribes couldn't teach, because they were masters at doctrine, but they did not teach with the authority and anointing of the Spirit. Just as Jesus taught "as one having authority," this is what Christ-given fivefold teachers are also called to do.[34]

In summary, a Christ-given fivefold ministry teacher is to be a *didaskalos* — a *masterful teacher-scholar* or like *a rabbi who possesses a great accumulation of facts and knowledge* and who delivers it in the power of the Spirit.

Why the Fivefold Ministry Gifts?

In short, the ultimate goal of every fivefold ministry gift is to *preach, warn,* and *teach* as found in Colossians 1:27 and 28, where Paul wrote, "To whom God would make known what is the riches of the glory of this mystery among the Gentiles; which is Christ in you, the hope of glory: whom we preach, warning every man, and teaching every man in all wisdom; that we may present every man perfect in Christ Jesus." In this section, we're going to discuss the common purpose of these ministry gifts where the building of the Church is concerned.

After Paul listed the fivefold ministry gifts, he went on to state in Ephesians 4:12 that they were given by Jesus "for the perfecting of the saints, for the work of the ministry, for the edifying of the body of Christ."

These fivefold ministry gifts were not given to the Church randomly, purposelessly, or as an afterthought. The word "for" at the first of this phrase is a translation of the Greek word *pros*, which points to *an express purpose*. Paul used it to underscore that fivefold ministry gifts *are explicitly given for an express purpose*, and he went on to enumerate those divine purposes.

'For the Perfecting of the Saints...'

First, Paul said, "For the perfecting of the saints, and for the edifying of the body of Christ" (Ephesians 4:12). When Paul said these gifts were *explicitly given for the express purpose* of "perfecting" of the saints, the Holy Spirit wanted to convey an important point. This "perfecting" work was and is so critical to the health, well-being, power, and effectiveness of the Church in the earth *then* and *for the remainder of the Church Age*. And while the saints of God have been reborn of the Spirit of God and have become "the spirits of just men made perfect" (Hebrews 12:23), there is a subsequent, ongoing work of "perfection" or transformation that must occur in the lives of true New Testament followers — learners, or disciples — of Jesus Christ.

Because there are varied teachings on the word "perfecting," let's go to the original Greek to find what the Greek word "perfecting" meant to those who read and heard it in the First Century.

The word "perfecting" is a form of the Greek word *katartidzo,* which is a compound of *kata* and *artidzo.* The prefix *kata* gives the impression of something moving *downward*, and the basic meaning of *artidzo* is *to adjust.* The word *kata* is an intensifier and pictures a movement from the top to the bottom. But when compounded with *artidzo*, it pictures an *adjustment or tweak that is being made from the top to the bottom.* It implies that due to these adjustments and tweaks, whatever has been adjusted and tweaked is in good working order and can now function correctly.

As we have found with other key words in the New Testament, the word "perfecting" — the Greek word *katartidzo* — was also used by many famous Greek writers in a variety of ways. Seeing how they historically used it will help us see why Paul chose to use this exact word in Ephesians 4:12 to communicate the important purpose of the fivefold ministry gifts.

- Herodotus used *katartidzo* to describe *something being put in order, to complete*, or *to restore.*[35]
- Plutarch used *katartidzo* to describe something *soothing* or *calming* and also to picture *a leader who led or guided the way for others.*[36]
- Polybius used *katartidzo* to picture *correcting something* or *fixing something* and to convey the ideas of *equipping* or *preparing* either a person or an object for some specific use.[37]

- Diodorus (c. 90-30 BC), an ancient Greek historian who was known for his monumental work called *Bibliotheca historica,* used *katartidzo* to describe *connecting* or *assembling* something, such as stones, materials, ligaments, joints, etc.[38]

So when believers in the First Century heard this word *katartidzo,* it likely carried a wide range of meanings that included *adjustments* or *tweaks* being made *to put something in order, to complete it,* or *to restore it.* It also pictured leaders who *led* and *guided* in an *adjustment* and *tweaking process.* The purpose of the *adjustments* and *tweaks* was to bring *correction* or *to fix* something in need of repair. And the objective of these *adjustments* was to *equip, outfit,* and *prepare* a person or object to be *fully operational.*

This word also pictured people doing their parts *to connect* and *to assemble* various elements, like stones, materials, ligaments, or joints. So when people in the early New Testament heard the word "perfecting," or *katartidzo,* they could easily envision leaders doing what they were called by God to do to connect and assemble the various elements of teaching, and doctrine in the life of the believer. But they also understood that leaders anointed roles were additionally to connect and assemble *other believers* — "lively stones" (*see* 1 Peter 2:5) — those who needed to be joined as various "joints" in the Body so that each joint could render his or her *supply* to the Body of Christ (*see* Ephesians 4:16).

In the word *katartidzo,* we see the "perfecting" purpose of the fivefold ministry gifts for building the Church, and we see this building of the Church as both building a *temple* and a *body.*

Paul used *katartidzo* to tell us that if the Christ-given fivefold ministry gifts of apostle, prophet, evangelist, pastor, and teacher *understand* their roles and *are allowed* to operate in those roles as God designed, God's Spirit will use them to bring *adjustments* and *tweaks* to the Church that will result in *order, completion,* and *restoration* where the Church is in need of it. God will use them *to lead and guide* as the Church is *adjusted* and *tweaked* on the way to maturity.

Christ will use His fivefold ministry gifts to assist in bringing *correction* where it is needed, to *fix* what is broken, and *to equip* and *to prepare* the Body of Christ for works of ministry so that it is not hindered by issues that have not been dealt with along the way. Another crucial part of their God-given roles is to help each member of the Body become *connected* and *assembled* into right places, which will result in the Body of Christ becoming *fully operational* and *fully functional.*

Paul used *katartidzo* to tell us that if the Christ-given fivefold ministry gifts of apostle, prophet, evangelist, pastor, and teacher *understand* their roles and *are allowed* to operate in those roles as God designed, God's Spirit will use them to bring *adjustments* and *tweaks* to the Church that will result in *order, completion,* and *restoration* where the Church is in need of it.

'Perfecting' To Teach, Correct, and Prepare

But there are other uses of *katartidzo* — "perfecting" — that also need consideration. For example, the word *katartidzo* is used in Luke 6:40 to depict a young disciple who is being *worked over* by a master-teacher so that disciple can be *equipped* and *prepared* for what is ahead of him.

The benefits of such a master are indeed remarkable, but only realized *if* a pupil submits to the guidance and correction of the master-teacher. If a pupil is willing to recognize the authority of a master and submit to and obey his instruction, it will result in his being equipped and prepared for his future endeavors.

In like manner, the Church must recognize, submit to, and obey the instruction provided by godly Christ-given fivefold ministers so that the full benefit of these Christ-given gifts will be realized inside the Church — and *outside* the Church to a lost and broken world.

'Perfecting' To Arrange and Connect in Order To Strengthen and Build

The word *katartidzo* was also used in a construction sense to picture professional builders who put forth effort *to strengthen a building that was under construction.*

To construct a building, materials must first be brought to the construction site, where specialists *arrange* and *connect* the materials to be *framed together.* So in a construction sense, the word *katartidzo* pictures materials being *arranged* with builders subsequently *assembling* and *connecting* — *joining* — them in the right places so a building can emerge. Paul clearly used *katartidzo* with this in mind to depict how Christ-given fivefold ministry gifts help *arrange* and *connect* God's people in their God-assigned places in the Body of Christ.

'Perfecting' To Repair or Restore

The word *katartidzo* was also used in the ancient fishing industry. We find it used this way in Matthew 4:21, where James and John have just finished fishing and are pulling up their nets. The verse says they were "mending" their nets. The word "mending" is a form of *katartidzo*, and in this context pictures them *meticulously going over every inch of their nets to adjust and tweak them* as needed. After a long day of fishing, they *arranged* their nets in *proper order* and examined them *from top to bottom* to see if they needed to be *repaired* or *restored*. A significant part of the process involved *untangling* the nets where they had become tangled. They did whatever was necessary to *adjust*, *tweak*, *mend*, or *fix* their nets so they would be *fully operational* for the next day of fishing.

Hence, Paul used *katartidzo* (the word "perfecting") in Ephesians 4:12 to also show the meticulous effort the fivefold ministry gifts provide in looking over the Church to determine its real condition. Once problems are identified, it is the task of the fivefold ministry gifts to assist in *untangling* what is tangled in the Church. A large part of their task is *to lead* and *to guide* in bringing *correction*, *mending*, or *restoration* to whatever is broken, defective, or malfunctioning. God uses them to enable the Body of Christ to be *fully operational* and to operate at *maximum capacity* as God intends.

'Perfecting' To Calm and To Heal

There is yet another use of the word *katartidzo* in the ancient world. In a medical sense, it was used by the Greek's most famous medical doctor, Galen, an accomplished physician, surgeon, and medical researcher in antiquity. As a physician, Galen succeeded where others had failed in treating a diversity of patients that ranged from wounded gladiators to the Emperor Marcus Aurelius himself.[39]

Galen resided in Pergamum, where he was director of the vast healing center located there. In his medical documents, Galen specifically used *katartidzo* to illustrate how a medical doctor could make *physical adjustments* to the human body to cause joints and limbs *to work together with greater ease* and thus bring *a soothing* and *a calming* to parts of the body that were previously in a state of distress and pain.

No doubt this medical use of *katartidzo* was also in Paul's mind when he used it in Ephesians 4:12. It portrays the task of Christ-given fivefold ministry gifts to make *spiritual adjustments* to the Body of Christ so *its various parts can work together with greater ease.* And when fivefold ministry gifts are permitted to operate as God designed. They bring *a soothing* and *a calming* to parts of the Body that were once distressful and painful.

All these meanings of *katartidzo* give significant meaning to Ephesians 4:12, where Paul says Christ-given fivefold ministry gifts are given for "perfecting" the saints. When all of these meanings are taken into account, it tells us God intends to use the fivefold ministry gifts of apostle, prophet, evangelist, pastor, and teacher to assist:

- In *bringing order* to the Church.
- In *bringing completion* and *maturity* to the Church.
- In *equipping, furnishing,* and *preparing* the saints in the Church.
- In *assembling* and *connecting* the saints in their correct places in the Body of Christ.
- In *mending* and *restoring* that which needs repairing and restoring.
- In *making adjustments* and *tweaks* so the Body of Christ can work with greater *ease.*
- In *bringing a soothing* and *a calming* to what was once painful and distressful in the Body.

'...For the Work of the Ministry...'

In Ephesians 4:12, Paul then elaborated, stating that fivefold ministry gifts are "for the work of the ministry." This no doubt means that when these gifts fulfill their Christ-given roles without hindrance, God's Spirit uses them to release a lot of ministry into the Church. However, another important point is derived from the fact that the word "work" is a translation of the Greek word *ergon,* a word that especially denotes *a person's line of work*, *career*, *occupation*, *labor*, or *profession.*

In addition to depicting the release of a lot of ministry into the Church, Paul also used this word to tell us it is best when those fivefold ministry gifts do it as their *full-time profession.* There may be times when those who stand in the fivefold ministry must work at other jobs until they can work full time in the ministry, but the use of *ergon* strongly implies God's best is that they do these ministries in the Church as *a full-time line of work.* Fulfilling their role as Christ-given fivefold ministry gifts requires concentration and hard work. For them to do what Christ has called them to do, it is the responsibility of the Church to financially support those called into these positions so they can do it with no financial stress and provide the full benefit of their ministries to the Body of Christ.

We know that Paul *worked hard* in his ministry, and he referred to this *very hard work* in First Corinthians 15:10 when he said, "But by the grace of God I am what I am: and his grace which was bestowed upon me was not in vain; but I laboured more abundantly than they all: yet not I, but the grace of God which was with me."

The word "laboured" is a translation of the Greek word *kopiao*, and it depicts *the most difficult, exhaustive type of work*. Because Paul used this word to describe his own work ethic, it tells us that Paul was a hard worker and was willing to do anything and everything to accomplish the task God had given him. Although there were times when Paul worked on the side to support himself as he performed his ministry assignment, he implied in Ephesians 4:11-13 that doing it full time and with no distractions is best.

The word "ministry" is a translation of the word *diakonia,* a specific Greek word used to depict *high-level servants who provided high-level service.* A vivid example of *diakonia* would be *highly trained servants* whose primary responsibility was to professionally serve food and to wait on the tables of high-class, high-level people, such as kings, royalty, or others deemed to be the upper crust of society. The Greek word *diakonia* pictures these particular highly trained, highly skilled, professional servants who painstakingly attended to clients so professionally that it made those being served feel as if they were nobility.

Paul used *diakonia* both to state the assignment and the privilege of being called as a fivefold ministry gift. Serving the Body of Christ in any capacity is an honor, and each Christ-given fivefold gift is expected by Christ to carry out his or her role as *excellently* and as *professionally* as possible.

There is no greater honor than to serve those seated around God's table, and Christ expects high-level service from those whom He has called to serve them. So regardless of your position — whether you are a Christ-given fivefold ministry gift who stands in a full-time position or a member of the Church who volunteers in some position — Christ expects each of us to be high-level servants. Paul uses *diakonia* to express that *no less than the best* is satisfactory when it comes to how the Body of Christ is to be served.

'...For the Edifying of the Body of Christ...'

In Ephesians 4:12, Paul went on to say that Christ-given fivefold ministry gifts are specifically given for the "edifying" of the Body of Christ: "For the perfecting of the saints, for the work of the ministry, for the *edifying* of the body of Christ." This leaves no wiggle room or second-guessing about the purpose of fivefold ministry gifts, for Paul categorically stated they are given expressly for the "edifying" of the Body of Christ.

But what does "edifying" mean in this context? The word "edifying" is a form of the word *oikodomeo*, and it is a compound of *oikos and demo.* The word *oikos* is the Greek word for *a building, a house*, or even *a temple.* The second part of the word is *demo,* a word borrowed from the world of construction to depict the careful process of *constructing a new building, house, or temple* — or to describe actions taken *to physically enlarge an already existing building, house, or temple.* In the New Testament, the word *oikodomeo* is usually translated as the word "edifying," but the Greek word portrays the whole process of *new construction* or of *enlarging an already existing building.*

This word was also used by well-known ancient Greek writers, so let's see how some of them used it in addition to how we find it in the Greek version of the Old and New Testaments.

- Herodotus used this word to picture *the construction or erection of a building, house, or temple* and *the whole building process needed to bring it from its beginning to its completion.*[40]
- Plato used it to depict *the acquired art or professional skills* that any builder needed to carry out construction.[41]
- Aristotle likewise used it as Plato did to describe *the acquired art or professional skills* that any builder needed to carry out the construction of something.[42]

It must be underscored that the word "edifying" in Ephesians 4:12 is connected to *construction* and involves the whole building process. For example, it can include:

- Removing debris to build a new structure on a newly chosen site.
- Developing an architectural plan.
- Laying a foundation.

- Everything from building new walls and putting on a roof to installing interior works and decorative items.

It pictures the whole process involved to build a new building, house, or temple.

Some years ago when my family and I lived in Riga, Latvia, we led the charge for our church to construct a new church building — the very first to be built in that city for 55 years due to the rule of socialistic communism in that part of the world.

In the process of constructing that church building, first a site was chosen and debris was removed. Then bulldozers removed dirt that was carried away in hundreds of truckloads. The foundation was poured, the walls went up, the roof was put in place, and, finally, the interior was finished out. It was a long, elaborate, expensive process — and that entire process could be described by the word *oikodomeo* in Greek, which is the word "edifying" in Ephesians 4:12.

It is important to repeat that the word "edifying" can also picture taking action to physically enlarge an already existing building, house, or temple to make it substantially bigger. To do it requires careful planning as well as the tearing down of existing walls in order to push them out to make more space; reinforcing foundations and walls; and putting on a larger, stronger roof, etc. We could say that the word "edifying" in Ephesians 4:12 also means *to amplify, augment, broaden, enhance, expand, develop, grow, improve, increase, supplement, or to swell to a larger size.* It pictures the step-by-step actions needed to bust out the walls and expand outward to amplify a space. In Greek, the whole process is called *edification.*

When God later led us to build a facility for our church congregation in Moscow, Russia, we purchased an abandoned building that had to be completely renovated and enlarged to accommodate the growth God wanted to give us. As we began to expand that space, the process was so difficult and involved that I often thought it would have been easier to build something from scratch. The foundation and walls had to be reinforced, the floors strengthened, and so on. For us to "edify" that space required a plan and the focused attention of multiple people who worked nonstop to increase the size and maximize the space. All of that is pictured in the Greek word *oikodomeo* that Paul used in Ephesians 4:12. That work was a living illustration of this Greek process of *edification.*

Paul used the word *oikodomeo*, translated "edifying" in Ephesians 4:12, to give us multiple meanings, as we have already seen. First, the use of this word lets us know the fivefold ministry gifts of apostle, prophet, evangelist, pastor, and teacher are God-given builders who are anointed to do their respective parts in building Jesus Christ's Church. Together they remove spiritual debris so the Church can be established in a new location. They follow an apostolic plan to lay spiritual foundations, build walls, put on the roofs or coverings, etc. And God uses them to install interior spiritual works and fortifications — and spiritually decorative items, too, as the Lord continually adorns and beautifies the saints.

In regard to the comparative work of physically starting brand-new churches, these Christ-given fivefold ministry gifts are anointed to help construct the Church as a collective "holy temple" in the Lord — a subject we will soon return to in Chapter Two.

Second, since the word "edifying" can picture an expansion project as well as a building project from scratch, it lets us know that fivefold ministry gifts are to assist in the spiritual and numerical amplification of the Church at large and in the growth of local churches. This involves implementing divine plans, tearing down hindrances and barriers, reinforcing spiritual foundations, pushing spiritual walls outward to make more space, and raising the spiritual ceiling of the Church higher.

If they understand their roles and are freed to operate as God designed, these Christ-given gifts assist in the Church's being *amplified, augmented, broadened*, *enhanced*, *expanded*, *developed*, *grown*, *improved*, and *increased* until the Body is *edified* — *built* or *enlarged* and *increased* — as God intended. God's long-term plan is to see the Body of Christ "edified." His heart is and has always been to see the Body of Christ become an enormous, powerful Body of believers on the earth.

'...Till We All Come in the Unity of the Faith...'

Paul then added in Ephesians 4:13 that the Christ-given fivefold ministry gifts of apostle, prophet, evangelist, pastor, and teacher are to exist in the Church "till we all come in the unity of the faith, and of the knowledge of the Son of God, unto a perfect man, unto the measure of the stature of the fulness of Christ."

The use of the word "till" does away with any notion that any of the fivefold ministry gifts passed away at the end of the Apostolic Age. The word "till" is a translation of the Greek word *mechri.* A better rendering would be "until," and it points to the end of the age when the Body of Christ reaches full maturity. The use of *mechri* expresses that apostles, prophets, evangelists, pastors, and teachers will continue "until" the Church has "...come in the unity of the faith, and of the knowledge of the Son of God, unto a perfect man, unto the measure of the stature of the fulness of Christ."

Paul furthermore stated in Ephesians 4:13 that God's plan is for the Church to "come" to the unity of the faith. The word "come" is a translation of the word *katantao*, a rarely used word that typically depicts *one who arrives at a new destination* or *a ship that lands at a never-before visited shore.* Paul used *katantao* to forecast a time in the future when the Body of Christ will reach a new frontier. Paul identified that *never-before visited shore* as the "unity of the faith." He wrote futuristically because when he wrote, this "unity" he forecasted had not been attained. But by faith, Paul could see the "unity" on the horizon and was convinced God's plan was for the Church to "come" to its shore.

What Is 'Unity'?

The word "unity" is a word that means different things to different people. Ask any crowd what "unity" means to them and you'll hear all kinds of responses. So we must put away preconceived ideas about what "unity" is in order to see what Paul meant when he used the word "unity" in Ephesians 4:13 by the inspiration of the Holy Spirit.

The word "unity" is translated from the Greek word *henotes*, which depicts *oneness*, *accord*, *agreement*, or *harmony*. But because the Greek has a definite article, it means this is not just any ol' unity, but it is a very *specific* kind of unity. Before we discuss the kind of unity Paul was forecasting, let's delve deeper into the Greek word *henotes* to see why Paul used this specific word in Ephesians 4:13 to describe this long-awaited "unity" that God desires for the Body of Christ.

The word *henotes* was a specific term used by historical writers Plato and Aristotle to express the ideas of *unanimity* or *agreement*.[43]

In addition to these meanings, the Greek word *henotes* — translated "unity" in Ephesians 4:13 — also conveys the following ideas:

- oneness
- coherence
- cohesion
- singleness
- solidarity
- accord
- agreement
- camaraderie
- commonality
- harmony
- synchronization
- congruence

Hence, Paul forecasted a time in the future when the Body of Christ will experience *oneness, coherence, cohesion, singleness, solidarity, accord, agreement, camaraderie, commonality, harmony, synchronization,* and *congruence.* Indeed, such a state or condition throughout the Body has not been reached, but Paul said that in the future, the Body of Christ will come into such a oneness in regard to "the faith."

The phrase "the faith" in Greek has a definite article, which remarkably means it is referring to *the* faith — or the *doctrines* and *tenets* of the Christian faith. But since the Body of Christ has never been united on the basis of doctrine — and it is unlikely the many doctrinal branches of the worldwide Church will ever come into oneness, accord, agreement, or harmony on every doctrinal point — what kind of "unity" could Paul have been referring to in this verse?

'...And of the Knowledge of the Son of God...'

Even among my most cherished friends in the ministry, sometimes we see things differently and have various opinions about certain minor doctrinal matters. Yet I experience amazing unity with them because our focus is not on our differences, but on the lordship of Christ over the Church. And when we focus on Him, these differences fade and melt away as God's Spirit miraculously blends our hearts and minds in worship of Him, and we are reminded of our unified effort to carry out the all-essential Great Commission in the earth.

When the Body of Christ focuses on doctrinal differences, we remain divided, but when we gaze upon Him, often minor differences evaporate in His glory and we are divinely melded into a supernatural unity that is indeed remarkable. Some doctrinal differences are very important, and I am not negating this reality. But the new destination and final frontier that Paul forecasted concerning the future was the shifted focus by the Body of Christ, as much as possible, to come into "the knowledge of the Son of God."

The word "knowledge" is a translation of the Greek word *epignosis,* which is a compound of *epi* and *gnosis.* The word *epi* means *upon* and the word *gnosis* is the Greek word for *knowledge.* Compounded into the word *epignosis*, it pictures *one who is so on top of his subject that he knows it like a professional.* This is a person who possesses an *in-depth knowledge of an object, person, or truth.* As a result of his dedication, devotion, and focus, this person has attained *a masterful and professional knowledge* of his subject. This is not a person with minimal insight, but one who is so acquainted with his subject that he is considered *an expert at the top of his field.*

When the Body of Christ focuses on doctrinal differences, we remain divided, but when we gaze upon Him, often minor differences evaporate in His glory and we are divinely melded into a divine unity that is indeed remarkable.

To affirm the meaning of this word "knowledge" in Ephesians 4:13, let's again see how historical Greek writers used this word in their various works. As you will see, the word "knowledge" — translated from the word *epignosis* — was used by many legendary Greek figures in history.

- Plato used *epignosis* to depict *one who professionally knows a subject inside and out* and also to depict *something so important that it must be known.*[44]

- Demosthenes used the word *epignosis* to depict one who is *an expert* at a given subject.[45]

- Polybius used *epignosis* to depict *one who conducts serious research.* [46]
- Plutarch used the word *epignosis* to depict *a very close acquaintance* and *intimate familiarity.*[47]
- Sextus Empiricus used the word *epignosis* as Plato did to depict *one who professionally knows* a subject. [48]

All of this cumulatively tells us that the "knowledge" Paul prophetically forecasted in Ephesians 4:13 does not describe a shallow or superficial knowledge, but rather pictures the Church becoming so acquainted with Christ that *we come to know Him inside and out.* Like a researcher who commits and focuses himself to serious exploration and research of a certain topic, Paul cried out for the Body of Christ to never stop its search of Christ until we are *intimately acquainted* with Him. God's call is for the Body of Christ to engage in a lifelong exploration of researching of the riches of Christ and His Word until we have mastered professional knowledge of Christ — to know Him so intimately that we are *on top of this subject* and know Christ *inside-out*, as *experts.*

In Philippians 3:10, Paul wrote of his own passion to know Christ as an expert. He wrote, "That I may *know* Him...." Paul had seen Christ on the road to Damascus and already possessed so many revelatory insights concerning Christ. But he was determined that he would not stop his pursuit until he had mastered Christ with the highest level of expertise. Indeed, he was on a lifelong venture to search out the unsearchable riches of Christ until he mastered his knowledge of Him.

In Ephesians 4:13, Paul clearly stated that God's plan is for the Church to finally come to a new spiritual destination, where it is so consumed with Jesus that all doctrinal differences melt away and we come into a supernatural harmony as we focus on Christ. This lets us know that God will never be satisfied with the Body of Christ living on a superficial level, and He is still calling the Church to set itself on Christ Himself and to move upward into higher realms of the knowledge of Him.

'...Unto a Perfect Man...'

In Ephesians 4:13, Paul states that God's longing is for the Church to become "a perfect man." The word "perfect" does not mean *perfection* in the sense of never making a mistake. The word "perfect" is a translation of the Greek word *teleios*, a word that pictures *a full-grown adult who has transitioned from being youthful and immature to become full-grown and mature.* It even portrays the image of *one who is progressively graduating upward from one grade to the next* or *one who is moving upward in a continued progression of growth.*

The word *teleios* pictures one so mature that he is *stable, settled, seasoned, fully grown,* and *able to handle adult responsibilities.* It is the opposite of a young, immature child or teenager, who is easily moved, easily influenced, easily led astray, and unable to be entrusted with making mature decisions or handling adult responsibilities.

The word *teleios* is yet another word frequently used by historical Greek writers, hence, its meaning is indisputable. For example, Plato, Aeschylus, Xenophon, and Polybius each used *teleios* to depict *one who is full-grown, an adult,* or *one who is of full age* and, therefore, *mature.*[49]

Because *teleios* gives the picture of one who is progressively graduating upward from one grade to the next — or who is moving upward in a continued progression of growth — it means there are many levels of spiritual maturity. The Body of Christ must never be content to stop at a lower level when God is calling us even higher into the highest attainable level of "the excellency of the knowledge of Christ Jesus" (*see* Philippians 3:8).

In Ephesians 4:11-13, Paul metaphorically likened the Church to the "Body of Christ." Now we see that God is not pleased for the Church to remain a child, but in verse 13, we see that God is calling on the Body of Christ to become a perfect "man."

To understand what Paul meant by "man," we need to understand that ancient Greeks were very age-specific when they described a person's level of maturity. Consider the following:

- The word *nepios* can depict *a baby* so young that *he or she is still at a breastfeeding stage.*
- The word *brephos* can depict *a toddler who is learning to walk and to communicate.*
- The word *paidion* can depict *a child who is old enough to be disciplined and to start his education.*
- The word *neotes* can picture *a younger person between the age of 20 to 40 years of age.*
- The word *presbutes* gives the image of *one who is considered older* or *elderly.*
- The word *andros* in Ephesians 4:13 depicts *an adult male.*

From a linguistic point of view, *andros* is not so fixated on a man's age as much as on *a status of mature manhood.* In fact, Herodotus used *andros* to describe *a true man, a man full of courage and determination*, or *a valiant man.*[50]

The word *andros* would generally be used to picture *a man* with sufficient maturity to work, to own a company, to manage personal property, to marry and give responsible oversight to children, to provide a living and to care for his family, and to bear arms and defend his family or land. And, if needed, he is mature enough to rise to the moment when he needs to fight for his people — his city, state, or nation — and to rule and reign. This word *andros* does not describe a male child, a boy, or teenager who is still growing, but rather pictures one who is a responsible and trustworthy man that has attained manhood.

When Jesus reached the end of His earthly ministry, He was 33 years of age. At that point, He was the perfect example of a fully mature man. Today Christ sits enthroned above all as the Head of the Body of Christ, and God's plan is for the Church to catch up to the maturity that is inherent in the Head of the Church.

By using the word *andros* in this verse, Paul told us God's plan and revealed another purpose for the Christ-given fivefold ministry gifts of the apostle, prophet, evangelist, pastor, and teacher: to bring the Body of Christ from infanthood to the spiritual manhood — that is, to become a Body mature enough to manage, to rule, and to reign.

Paul told us God's plan and revealed another purpose for the Christ-given fivefold ministry gifts...to bring the Body of Christ from infanthood to the spiritual manhood — that is, to become a Body mature enough to manage, to rule, and to reign.

In the past, the present, and the last-days Church, God's goal has been, and still is, for the Church to become a mature body of believers permeated with the overflowing life of Christ.

'...Unto the Measure of the Stature of the Fulness of Christ'

Paul made the unequivocal declaration that God will not be satisfied until the Body of Christ has grown beyond youthfulness and immaturity to reach "...the measure of the stature of the fulness of Christ" (Ephesians 4:13).

The word "fulness" in this verse is from a form of *pleroma*, the same word for "fulness" that we saw in Ephesians 1:23. In antiquity, this word described a container so completely full that it was bulging and overflowing. Thus, we see God's intention is that the Church *be filled to the point of overflowing* with Christ's presence in the earth. In both Ephesians 1:23 and Ephesians 4:13, we read that it is the Father's plan for the *superabundant presence of Christ* to completely pervade every part of the Church.

But reading further in Ephesians 4:14-16, Paul added, "That we henceforth be no more children, tossed to and fro, and carried about with every wind of doctrine, by the sleight of men, and cunning craftiness, whereby they lie in wait to deceive; but speaking the truth in love, may grow up into him in all things, which is the head, even Christ: from whom the whole body fitly joined together and compacted by that which every joint supplieth, according to the effectual working in the measure of every part, maketh increase of the body unto the edifying of itself in love."

Ephesians 4:14-16 is very important, and we will cover this passage in more detail in the last chapter of this book. But verse 15 clearly says that God's aim is for the Body of Christ to "...grow up into him in all things, which is the head, even Christ." The words "grow up" give the vision of spiritual maturity that God longs to see in the Body of Christ.

As we saw in Ephesians 1:22, the word "head" — referring to Christ — is a translation of the Greek word *kephale*, and it describes *a physical head* or *a capstone* that connects two sides of an arch in the center. As noted previously, Christ is the physical Head of the Body, and He is the Center of the Church upon whom everything leans on for its existence. But because the word "head" is also the word for a physical capstone in a building, in addition to describing Christ as the physical Head of the Body, Paul here pictured Christ as the Capstone in a mighty Building — a Temple, or *naos*.

This marvelously leads us to the next chapter, where we will see clearly that the primary metaphor used in the New Testament for the Church is that of *a holy Temple* in which Christ is the Capstone. You are about to learn that God's intention is for the Church to become a holy Temple and a glorious habitation of the Holy Spirit in the earth today. Christ has given fivefold ministry gifts — *apostle*, *prophet*, *evangelist*, *pastor*, and *teacher* — to aid in the construction of this Temple, and that construction is happening *right now.*

QUESTIONS FOR DEEPER CONSIDERATION

Chapter 1

1. In this chapter, you read that Paul metaphorically compared the Church to *a vineyard, a body,* and *a temple* in various texts throughout the New Testament. Can you, in your own words, explain why Paul used these various metaphors to depict the Church?

2. In the preceding pages, you have read substantial material about the original meanings, and all the nuances, of the Greek word *ekklesia*, the New Testament word for the Church. In what ways did this material affect your view of the Church and your privileged role in it?

3. Against all odds and societal norms, Galatians 3:12 and Colossians 3:11 state that in Christ, a single, united Body comprised of people with different skin colors, ethnicities, and societal statuses — male and female — who have been supernaturally baptized by one Spirit into the Body of Christ. As a result, we are supernaturally, "mystically" blended — joined, fused, intermingled, amalgamated, and divinely melded — into a single Body of believers. In your experience, does today's Church reflect this divine diversity and lack of barriers, or does it need to reflect it better?

4. This chapter gave a brief description of the God-given roles and functions of apostles, prophets, evangelists, pastors, and teachers. After reading this

material, what are the newest insights you have received about the fivefold gifts that you had never read or heard before? Which of these descriptions was the most meaningful to you? In what ways does it change your view of these fivefold gifts and how they are to operate in the Church?

5. Ephesians 4:12 states that the Christ-given fivefold ministry gifts of apostle, prophet, evangelist, pastor and teacher are given "for the perfecting of the saints, for the work of the ministry, for the edifying of the body of Christ." After reading the section in this chapter about this important verse, how would you explain to someone else what the "the perfecting of the saints" means?

6. Based on Paul's words in Ephesians 4:13, can you confidently express how long God intends for all the Christ-given fivefold gifts of the apostle, prophet, evangelist, pastor, and teacher to be operational in the Church?

CHAPTER 2

BUILDING THE TEMPLE OF GOD

Now therefore ye are no more strangers and foreigners, but fellowcitizens with the saints, and of the household of God; and are built upon the foundation of the apostles and prophets, Jesus Christ himself being the chief corner stone; in whom all the building fitly framed together groweth unto an holy temple in the Lord: in whom ye also are builded together for an habitation of God through the Spirit.

— Ephesians 2:19-22

In the previous chapter, we looked at Paul's words about the Christ-given fivefold ministry gifts of the *apostle*, *prophet*, *evangelist*, *pastor*, and *teacher*. We also studied their roles in building the Body of Christ until it becomes the mature Body that God longs for it to be at the culmination of the Church Age.

As we've already seen, in the New Testament, there are other metaphors besides the word "body" to describe the Church. Each of these metaphors illustrates different aspects of the Church, but Paul gave his apostolic vision of the Church most clearly in Ephesians 2:19-22, where he wrote that the Church is a "*Holy Temple*" that's being progressively constructed by God to become a habitation of the Holy Spirit in the earth today.

In this chapter, we will focus on this illustration of the Church as a building, or "temple," and see how this relates to God's plan for the Church and *all* its members. I warn you in advance that this is a serious chapter that contains information about what I believe is the foremost apostolic vision of the Church and what it is to grow into and become in the days ahead.

As I said in Chapter One, if you feel you need to skip ahead to Chapter Three, you will not miss the importance of the foundational ministry of the apostle, which I begin covering in that chapter. But please do return and study these first two chapters, for in them lie God's very vision for His Church — and its purpose — and you will be enriched by your careful study of these truths.

Throughout the New Testament, Paul repeatedly used the Greek word *naos* — "temple" — to describe the Church. We learned in Chapter One that the word *naos* was a word used by both Jews and Greeks to describe *a temple where a god dwelled*. For example:

- Pindar used the word *naos* to describe *any habitation of a god.*[1]
- Herodotus used the word *naos* to depict *the innermost part of a temple where a god reputedly dwelled.*[2]

By using this Greek word *naos* over and over again in his inspired New Testament writings, Paul imparted the vision that God is building a Body of believers into *a Temple* for the habitation of the Holy Spirit in the earth.

By using this Greek word *naos* over and over again in his inspired New Testament writings, Paul imparted the vision that God is building a Body of believers into *a Temple* for the habitation of the Holy Spirit in the earth.

Paul's Audience and Language — His Message Was Unmistakable

I want to draw your attention to Romans 11:13, where Paul wrote, "For I speak to you Gentiles, inasmuch as I am the apostle of the Gentiles...." Paul knew he was called as an apostle to the Gentiles and, therefore, his primary audience was Greek-speaking believers who were pagans before they came to Christ. So Paul used words and examples that native Greek-speakers could easily relate to and understand. Paul often used metaphors from the Greek world because that was the focus of his apostleship, as already noted.

Paul, who was raised in a wealthy, prestigious home in the city of Tarsus, and who later became the primary writer of the New Testament epistles, had received a marvelous education. When it came to language and literature, he was brilliant. In fact, this may be one of the reasons God chose him to author so much of the New Testament. When it was time for Paul to pen his timeless epistles, the Holy Spirit reached deep into the apostle's vast repertoire of language, literature, and history and used his knowledge to convey incredible spiritual truths. Because there was no precedent for Christian vocabulary at the time, it had to be established. And since Greek was the foremost language of the First Century, the extensive Greek vocabulary was the perfect source from which to draw.

The fact is, as a result of the conquests of Alexander the Great and his generals who succeeded him, Greek became the first international, worldwide language. For the very first time in human history, a large swath of the civilized world could speak and read a single form of verbal and written communication. Greek had become the common language of the day.

Consider how English is read and spoken around the world today, and it will help you understand the role the Greek language played in the First Century. It was spoken almost everywhere in the Roman Empire, irrespective of other, native languages and dialects that might have been used in the privacy of people's homes. Even highly educated Jewish scholars of Alexandria — men who were very advanced in Hebrew studies — spoke Greek in their daily lives. In fact, Jewish scholars of Alexandria translated the Old Testament into Greek in the Third Century BC, a translation called the *Septuagint* that is an invaluable resource for biblical studies today.

Scholars generally agree that Paul's words in Galatians 4:4, "But when the fulness of the time was come, God sent forth his Son...," was likely a reference to this unprecedented event in time when the Gospel could be preached in a single language and many people would be able to understand it, regardless of their ethnic identity.

Prior to this time, spreading the Gospel would have been much more difficult, to say the least, because no single, unifying tongue existed to unite mankind. The task of learning every language in order to reach every group would have been impossible for any preacher. But precisely when the Roman Empire was finally united in one language — *in the fullness of time* — God sent forth His Son. By using the Greek language, which was known far and wide, almost everyone in the far-flung empire could hear and understand the Gospel and then choose to accept or reject it.

It is simply a fact that if the New Testament had been written in Hebrew, it would have been difficult for its message to penetrate the worldwide audience that Jesus came to redeem. The use of Hebrew would have simply limited the availability of the message. On the other hand, Greek opened the door for the message of Christ to spread to the far reaches of the Roman Empire and the known world.

Furthermore, if even the *imagery* used in the New Testament was solely borrowed from the Old Testament, pagans would have missed the significance of most of the illustrations since they were unfamiliar with Hebrew culture. Therefore, God in His wisdom chose to use the imagery, symbolism, and figures of speech that even the pagan world would understand. Of course, the New Testament draws many images and concepts directly from the Old Testament, but the overwhelming majority of the words and images in Paul's epistles could be understood by the Greek world.

One clear example is the Greek word *naos*, a word that interestingly was used by both Jews and pagans, and understood in both cultures to depict their respective temples. So when Paul used the word *naos* to metaphorically depict the Church, he was brilliantly using a Greek word that the worldwide audience at that time could easily understand.

The theme of the Church as a "Holy Temple" recurs in Paul's writings again and again. Although this book is about the roles of apostles and prophets in the building of that Temple, we must first begin with Paul's apostolic vision of the Church itself, for this is foundational to everything else you will read in this book. Paul's writings make it clear that he viewed the Church as a "Holy Temple."

Because this illustration is foundational to everything else, if you don't understand his portrayal, or *vision*, of the Church, you will be unable to understand the various roles of the Christ-given fivefold ministry gifts of *apostle, prophet, evangelist, pastor*, and *teacher*, which are all involved in helping construct and expand this Temple for God's Spirit in the earth today.

The Prominence of God's New Testament Temple, the Body of Christ

When Paul wrote his New Testament epistles, it was at a time when the Temple in Jerusalem was still standing and was in full use by the Jewish people, and the word used to describe the Temple was the Greek word *naos.* Pagans had their own temples as well that were scattered by the thousands all over the Greek and Roman world, and they were likewise referred to as *naos* temples.

For this reason, when Paul used the word *naos* to depict the Church as a Temple for God in the earth, Jews could easily comprehend Paul's metaphorical illustration because the Temple was still standing and was so prominent in their culture. Pagans likewise could easily comprehend Paul's metaphorical illustration of the Church as a temple because the pagan world was *plastered* with *naos* temples.

The 'Why' of Temples

But to *really* understand why Paul described his apostolic vision of the Church as a "temple" over and over again, it is vital to delve into the significant roles that temples held in the ancient Jewish and pagan worlds. From the Old Testament, we know, for example, that the Shekinah glory of God was held inside the Holy of Holies — that is, deep inside the physical Temple in Jerusalem.

Pagans likewise believed that their various gods dwelt in the "holiest," most sacred part of their own temples. But in Paul's epistles, he clearly expressed that it was God's intention for the Church to be a new "spiritual Temple" — His habitation in the earth — a Holy Temple superior to any physical temple ever constructed.

Ephesians 3:10 and 11 communicates that God's eternal plan was always to dwell in the hearts of mankind and not in a physical temple constructed by man. This is why Paul wrote in these verses, "To the intent that now unto the principalities and powers in heavenly places might be known *by the church* the manifold wisdom of God, according to the *eternal purpose* which he purposed in Christ Jesus our Lord."

In fulfillment of God's eternal plan, He has supernaturally moved into the hearts of born-again believers, and the Church has now become the "Temple" of God in the earth today.

So the idea of a temple was not new to Jewish *or* pagan audiences — they knew full well the meaning and nuances connected with the word "temple," or *naos.* Even Jews knew this word *naos* because scholarly Jews in Alexandria who translated the Hebrew Scriptures into the Septuagint Greek version of the Old Testament used the word *naos* over and over to refer to the physical Temple in Jerusalem with the Holy of Holies and the Shekinah glory of God inside.

In fulfillment of God's eternal plan, He has supernaturally moved into the hearts of born-again believers, and the Church has now become the "Temple" of God in the earth today.

But because Paul was sent primarily as an apostle to the Gentiles, the majority of his readers were Greek and had been raised as pagans in their past. Being from that background, they knew the word *naos* because it was a well-known and common word used to depict *a pagan temple*, *a house for a god*, or *a highly decorated shrine* where a god was worshiped, where prayers could be offered, and where sacrifices were made.

To Greek-speakers, the word *naos* immediately gave the impression of a grand temple with vaulted ceilings and marble, granite, gold, silver, and highly decorated ornamentations. Such pagan temples were prevalent in inestimable numbers at that time in the Greek and Roman worlds. So regardless of whether or not one was Jew or Greek, they each comprehended the word *naos* as Paul used it in his letters. Both Jews and Greeks used the word *naos* to describe in their respective cultures *a temple, a house for God (or a so-called god)*, or *a shrine.*

However, pagans used it mostly because of the incalculable number of pagan temples of all sizes and sorts that were scattered all over the Greek and Roman worlds. Pagans were so devoted to their plethora of gods that they constructed tens of thousands of such temples — some small, others massive, but most of them magnificently built and lavishly decorated.

So as we have established in the first section of this chapter, whenever Paul used the word "temple" in his writings, translated from the Greek word *naos,* he was using a familiar word that was well-known and widely used by both Jews and pagans.

The Significance of *Naos* as 'the Holy Place'

In the ancient Greek language, there were actually two primary words for *a temple.* One was *hieron* and the second was, of course, *naos.*

The word *hieron* referred to *any sacred location or sacred place*, and it usually included *an entire sacred compound or complex* in addition to the temple that was constructed in the middle of it. The word *naos* pictured the actual *temple* inside the *hieron* — the sacred compound — which we know was the very place where a god reputedly dwelled. It was the inner sanctuary or *holiest place* inside a temple. So when Paul referred to a *temple,* he repeatedly used the word *naos,* which categorically pictures *a temple*, *a house of God*, or *a shrine* where prayers, sacrifices, and worship were offered to God or to a so-called deity. Of course, we understand it as God's vision for the Church — to live in a Holy Temple, the Body of Christ, as His House, where prayers, sacrifices and worship would be offered to Him there.

I ask you to forgive me if you think I'm belaboring a point or if it seems I'm strictly giving you a lesson in ancient pagan religions and temples. My purpose is that you *see* what Paul's readers saw when they read the word *naos* in his epistles that later comprised much of the New Testament. The use of this word was *not* accidental; it was extraordinarily important. Therefore it is necessary to grasp the role that *naos* temples held in the ancient world to see why Paul used this word over and over in his New Testament writings.

So now, let's dive deeper into the word *naos* to see how it was used in the ancient world at the time of the Early Church.

Ancient Temples in Antiquity

In antiquity, cities were *filled* with pagan temples (as can be seen in the illustrations in the center of this book). Pagans believed the gods needed a "house" to live in among humans. Each temple constructed and dedicated to that purpose was a consecrated place where these gods could allegedly dwell, be worshiped and experienced, and where prayers and sacrifices could be made to them. With this belief fixed in their minds, pagans enthusiastically constructed infinite numbers of *naos* temples for a pantheon of gods they worshiped in every part of the far-flung ancient world.

Greeks called each of their temples a *naos*, a magnificent structure that contained a central idol inside the inner sanctuary. Because they believed in the importance of these types of temples, pagans spared no expense in building ornate, magnificent architectural structures — mysterious places — where supernatural and often eerie spiritual activities took place. Pagans offered sacrifices, consumed wine, and committed fornication in the various precincts as a part of their worship ceremonies. And as far-fetched as it seems, they even believed it was possible for the idols they worshiped to be empowered by their faith to come to life for those who worshiped them.

To accommodate this plethora of gods, the Greeks built huge colonnaded temples laden inside with extravagant riches — massive moldings, mosaics, frescoes, and sculptures carved from expensive marbles to look like their respective gods. These sculptures resembled angelic-like creatures, giants, monsters, and animals — all of which were elaborately and meticulously painted to look life-like. The ancient statues viewed in museums today have lost their original color, but originally they were fabulously painted to look like living beings: Eyes looked like real eyes, flesh looked like real flesh, and garments looked like real flowing fabric.

The task of building such temples was so great that only the most renowned architects and builders were employed to design them, build them, and decorate them with the finest, most durable materials that were intended to last thousands of years. There was little thought of economizing as artists and sculptors embellished the interiors with exquisite adornments and decorations that included precious stones, gold and silver gildings, and garnishings that were nearly beyond description.

Of course, the cost for building such temples was astronomical, but it was a *naos* — that is, a *temple*, *a house for a god*, or *a shrine* — so no expense was considered too exorbitant for the construction of such a structure. These were intended to be sacred structures to stand for millennia, so whatever sum was required to build the best for their various gods was deemed the appropriate thing to do.

It is impossible to know exactly how many *naos* temples were built across the vast Greek and Roman worlds because so many have been covered by thousands of years of dirt. But as excavations of the ancient world unfold, the vast number of such temples that are being discovered is mind-boggling. There are literally thousands of smaller, lesser known *naos* temples that have survived from the pagan world — far too many to list in any single catalog of ancient temples. In addition to this myriad of lesser-known temples, there are hundreds of famous, bigger examples. Eventually we will discuss the Temple in Jerusalem, but we'll begin with four pagan temples that I have noted in the following paragraphs: The Temple of Artemis; the Altar of Zeus; the Parthenon; and the Pantheon.

The Temple of Artemis in Ephesus

The *Temple of Artemis* in Ephesus was a *naos* situated in a massive *hieron* complex that was so magnificent in antiquity that it was listed by ancient Greek writers as one of the Seven Wonders of the Ancient World. (*See* Philo of Byzantium, Herodotus, Callimachus of Cyrene, and Antipater of Sidon.)[3]

This *naos* temple in Ephesus was 425 feet long and 220 feet wide, and it had 127 marble columns, each of which was 60 feet high. For those who walked the length of the temple, as they meandered through its massive columns, it must have felt as if they were walking through a forest of marble.

In addition to being lined with marvelous columns of marble, the *naos* Temple of Artemis itself was garlanded with statues of lions and bulls that posed as massive, intimidating guards at the doorways. Gorgons (mythological monsters that served as protective deities) were positioned on either side of the "god" Artemis inside the temple pediments, while winged, gold-gilded female messengers of stone were gracefully positioned as if they were ready to fly away at any moment.

The gargantuan idol of Artemis stood inside the inner *naos* sanctuary and was depicted wearing a turret-shaped crown on her head, which indicated she was both a goddess and the official protectress of the city of Ephesus. Each of her arms rested on a twisted column, and she was served on either side by carved priests as well as lions, whose respective roles were to minister to her and to defend her. Her torso was disgustingly lined with multiple rows of bulls' testes, which were sacrificed to her because pagans believed semen from bulls was holy, especially in regard to Artemis' role as the goddess of fertility. Her lower body from her waist down was covered with sculpted rows of lions, rams, and bulls.

The colossal *naos* of Artemis was located at a vantage point where passengers who arrived at Ephesus by ship could see it as their ship approached the harbor. The temple's enormous size alone made it an impressive sight to people viewing it for the first time. Elated worshipers could even see the massive idol of Artemis facing them from the temple grounds, looming larger and larger in their view as the ships approached the port. The worship at the Temple of Artemis in Ephesus was so involved that one historian suggested there were no less than 6,000 priestesses who served the goddess and her worshipers.

There were several versions of the *naos* of Artemis in Ephesus constructed over a period of a thousand years, but the final version was badly damaged by the Goths who raided Ephesus in 268 AD and set it on fire. Later, stones from the temple were hauled away to be used in the construction of other buildings, and some of the columns were allegedly transported to Constantinople (modern-day Istanbul) to become a part of the decorations of the Hagia Sophia. But when the Temple of Artemis was first built, unthinkable sums of money went into its construction because the builders intended to construct it as a *naos* — *a temple*, *a house for a god*, or *a shrine* — to stand forever.

The Great Altar of Zeus in Pergamum

The *Great Altar of Zeus* in ancient Pergamum was another *naos* where pagan celebrations and sacrificial rituals occurred in honor of the "god" Zeus.

Because of its immense size and its artistic value, this magnificent *naos* — *temple, house for a god*, or *shrine* — became one of the most renowned pagan altars in the history of mankind. In antiquity, it was so magnificent that it also was listed by ancient Greek writers, as we've seen, as one of the Seven Wonders of the Ancient World. (*See* Philo of Byzantium, Herodotus, Callimachus of Cyrene, and Antipater of Sidon.)[4]

The Great Altar of Zeus was revered as one of the most magnificent architectural masterpieces in the entire world. It was constructed like a mighty throne where Zeus sat and ruled the region. Pergamum's citizens offered sacrifices on this altar to express their thanksgiving to Zeus for giving them victory over their enemies. The *naos* temple of Zeus in Pergamum sat on the upper rim of the city approximately 1,000 feet above the valley below. Because of its location on the edge of the upper district of Pergamum, as well as its enormous size, this *naos* was visible to visitors who approached the city from the valley below. The extensive gold gildings of this huge altar gleamed ubiquitously in the sunlight — and what seemed like an eternal cloud of smoke from the offering of sacrifices billowed continually into the sky.

Dimensions for the Great Altar of Zeus were 118 feet by 111 feet, and a 65-foot-wide stairway of 24 steps led to its upper level where a double colonnade enclosed the open-air sanctuary on three sides and was showcased with fabulous sculptures. The central altar in this *naos* was used for burnt sacrifices and stood in a roofless interior court. It had 88 Ionic columns, and 50 more marvelously scrolled and decorated columns lined the top of the platform where the sacrificial rituals were performed. Fittingly, the altar was flanked by projecting wings and many sculptures, among them the 371-foot-long sculptural frieze that depicted the fighting between giants and gods.

The greatest architects and builders of the age decorated this *naos* temple with the finest, most expensive and durable materials, and artists and sculptors embellished and garnished the entire site. Eventually, the Great Altar of

Zeus in Pergamum fell into ruin and was dismantled, *and* elements of it were transferred to various museums around the world mostly to the Pergamum Museum in Berlin, Germany. But this magnificent *naos* stood for epochs of time in testimony to the fact that the builders constructed this *naos* — *temple, house for a god*, or *shrine* — to last forever.

The Parthenon in Athens

In Athens is situated one of the most famous *naos* temples of the ancient world. *The Parthenon* is a *naos* that sits atop the Acropolis. In antiquity, it was rebuilt several times, but the final version that has mostly remained to the present day was adorned with 46 massive outer columns and 19 inner columns and embellished with multi-colored, lavishly decorated sculptures that were trimmed with precious metals. The exterior frieze was a high-relief sculpted zone — more prominently three-dimensional — surrounding the cella of the temple (similar to a sanctuary) that was almost 525 feet long and contained 378 human and god figures and more than 200 animal depictions.

The inner *naos* sanctuary was surrounded with a double Doric colonnade, and in the center was a massive 40-foot tall idol of the goddess Athena made of wood and veneered with exquisite ivory for skin. The gargantuan idol of Athena held a massive shield made of bronze in her left hand, a six-foot-high statue of the goddess Nike in her right hand, two griffins (fabled Greek monsters) and a sphinx on top of her helmet, and a giant snake could be seen behind her shield. The massive idol was draped in a garment that was fabricated of 220 pounds of pure gold, and the idol's base was adorned with a marvelous gilded relief. A reflective pool stationed in front of the idol of Athena provided an awe-inspiring view for worshipers as they entered the door of the temple.[5]

Those who constructed the Parthenon temple invested massive sums of money in the construction of this *naos* temple because they intended to construct a *naos* — *a temple*, *a house for a god*, or *a shrine* — that would last for generations. Again, the most renowned architects, builders, artists, and sculptors were sought out to design it, build it, and embellish its lavish exteriors and interiors.

The Pantheon in Rome

In the heart of Rome is another ancient *naos* temple that is amazingly still in use today. The *Roman Pantheon* was built of Roman brick, and its exterior and interior were veneered with precious marble gathered from the lands conquered by the Roman Empire. Most scholars believe the Pantheon was first commissioned by consul Marcus Agrippa in approximately 27 BC in the wake of Augustus' victory over Mark Antony and Cleopatra at the Battle of Actium. At Marcus' order, 732 craftsmen began construction of the massive edifice, and in only three short years, it was completed. Considered an architectural masterpiece today, it remains one of the most magnificent *naos* temples ever built.[6]

The word "Pantheon" is derived from the Greek words *pan* and *theos.* The word *pan* means *all*, and the word *theos* means *god*. When compounded, they form the word *pantheon*, which tells us this staggeringly large structure was built to be a *naos* to the worship and veneration of *all gods*. And because it was intended to be the greatest tabernacle for all gods in Rome, no expense was spared in its construction.

The Pantheon's exterior entrance was adorned with granite columns, the largest of which stood 50-feet tall and weighed 100 tons, and each of them were made of Egyptian granite, mined from quarries in Aswan (in Egypt), transported by ship down the Nile and then across the Mediterranean, finally arriving in Rome to become the main columns of the portico to the temple. Exquisitely carved Corinthian capitals crown the pillars and support the pediment of the roof.

In antiquity, a worshiper entering this *naos* temple would have been awed by the outer architectural features before he ever reached the richly decorated interior. The roof and pediments were decorated with striking, gold-gilded bronze reliefs where iron clamps once held a gigantic, gold-gilded bronze sculpture of an eagle perched on a wreath. Gold ribbons once extended from this wreath to the corners of the pediments. In addition, ornate reliefs and sculptures of gods and goddesses adorned the exterior of the building so pagans could pay homage without actually setting foot in the sanctuary.

The vaulted dome ceiling overhead was the most visually striking element of the Pantheon. Even today this ceiling holds the distinction of being the largest unreinforced concrete dome ever constructed in the world. It is 142 feet high, 142 feet wide, and weighs approximately 4,535 metric tons. At its base, the dome is approximately 21 feet thick and tapers to a mere 3.9-foot thickness near its center. At the dome's center is a 3-foot-wide *oculus* (the Greek word for an eye) that provided light for the entire building — along with the front entrance, where 40-foot high, gilded bronze doors were left open to allow worshipers to enter the sanctuary.

As worshipers strolled through the Pantheon, they also walked among large, intricately carved idols nestled between the columns of the inner walls and the towering statues representing the foremost deities of the Roman pagan religion. The second floor contained handsomely carved niches that held the images of a host of lesser gods to ensure that no deity was ignored.

Again we see that those who designed the Pantheon fully intended to construct a *naos* — *a temple*, *a house for a god*, or *a shrine* — that would stand forever. Remarkably, it does still stand in Rome where it has been converted into a Catholic church called *St. Mary of the Martyrs* and is visited by millions of people annually. When people walk into this site, they are actually entering what was originally an ancient pagan temple with its original marble veneers, floors, niches, and many other original embellishments.

In-Home Temples for a Sundry of Gods

The idea of having a *naos* — *a temple, a house for a god,* or *a shrine* — for one's own personally venerated god to dwell in was so common in the Greek and Roman worlds that it was common for even a private residence to feature an in-home *naos* — *a small temple, house for a god,* or *a shrine.* The historian Herodotus specifically used the word *naos* to depict such miniature temples that were commonly used as in-home shrines for the veneration of ancestral gods.

These small temple-shrines were placed right inside people's homes where they could privately pray and offer sacrifices. To make their particular god feel accommodated and honored, they decorated these small in-home *naos* temples lavishly with painted sculptural detail and trimmed them with precious stones and even gold and silver. Each day, pagans paused at home to pray and to offer sacrifices at these small in-home *naos* temples, where they believed their particular god resided in their midst.

It was customary for a residential *temple, house for a god,* or *shrine* to be positioned near the main entrance of a home, in a central hallway, or in a courtyard where residents or visitors could have easy access to pray and make daily sacrifices to their gods.

This practice was so common in pagan homes that it is clear the worship of so-called gods and goddesses was indeed an integral part of daily life for the great majority of people living in the Roman Empire. Many in-home *naos* temples and shrines have been found in excavations of homes in ancient cities, where large numbers of these small temple shrines have been uncovered from 2,000-plus years of dirt and ash from volcanic eruptions that preserved them. These residential *naos* temples and in-home shrines were dedicated to a variety of so-called gods or ancestral deities that had been venerated by families for generations. On a visit to Pompeii, it is easy to see what I am describing because many of these small, in-home *naos* temples have survived and you can view them for yourself.

From city to city and province to province, the number of gods and goddesses varied, as did their names and functions. By early New Testament times, the list of so-called gods and goddesses became so huge that compiling a complete list of them would have been impossible. I listed many of the deities worshiped in the Greek and Roman worlds in my book *No Room for Compromise.*[7] But even that long list falls short of enumerating all the gods and goddesses that were revered and worshiped in those ancient societies.

Ancient pagans really believed that a family's favorite venerated god needed an in-home *naos* — *temple, house,* or *shrine* — in which to live among them and be worshiped.

The Temple in Jerusalem — A Temple for the One True God of Israel

All the aforementioned *naos* temples were impressive in one way or another, but no temple in the ancient world could compare to the *Temple* that Solomon constructed in Jerusalem. It was a magnificent and splendorous *naos* — *temple, house,* or *shrine* — for the One True God of Israel. All other *naos* temples in the ancient world simply paled in comparison. In truth, there was no *naos* ever constructed anywhere that could be compared to the splendor of the Temple that Solomon constructed for God's presence in the heart of Jerusalem.

Scriptures show that King David loved the presence of God so much that for a time, he kept the Ark of the Covenant in a small tent near the place where he lived. But David knew it was unfitting for the glory of the One True God to reside in a tent, so he longed to build a glorious and stunning house for Him, a *naos* — *temple, house,* or *shrine* — to accommodate the presence of

God in Jerusalem. And it would need to be superior to any *naos* temple *ever* built anywhere else in the world for any other so-called god.

To fulfill this dream, David began to set aside the resources needed to build the most magnificent temple ever constructed. Although David never saw the fulfillment of his desire, Solomon followed through on His father's plans and used David's contributions, along with his own, to construct the most expensive building that ever existed in the history of the world. There was no physical structure in antiquity — or even in the present day — to compare to the associated costs of constructing the *naos* Temple for God in Jerusalem. There were other temple complexes that were physically larger in terms of size, such as Karnak on the banks of the Nile in Egypt. But no temple complex constructed in human history has come close to the financial sum invested to construct and adorn the *naos* Temple and its sacred *hieron* complex in Jerusalem.

Biblical records tell about David's financial contributions for the building of the Temple — namely First Chronicles 22:1-5 and First Chronicles 29:2-5. In these passages, we read in detail what David gave *personally* for the building of the *naos* — *temple, house,* or *shrine* — for the Lord in Jerusalem.

The following sums do not include the associated costs of manpower or the artistic value of what was created by the finest craftsmen who lived at that time. These figures are based only on the raw weight of the materials, the information for which is provided in the Bible, as we will see. The totals are conservative, as all the materials used in Solomon's Temple are not listed. If the costs of manpower, artistry, and technology were included in the following list, the total would far exceed what you are about to read.

Let's begin by looking at the calculated raw-weight value of what David and his leaders contributed for the building of the Temple. In First Chronicles 22:1-5 and First Chronicles 29:2-5, we read that David *personally* gave the following to this momentous project:

- 103,000 talents of gold, which is approximately 99,345,807 troy ounces of gold. At the time of this writing, that amount of gold is valued at approximately $174,108,493,877. (That's more than one hundred and seventy-four *billion*, one hundred and eight *million*, four hundred and ninety-three *thousand* dollars!)

- 8,000 talents of silver, which is approximately 7,716,179 troy ounces of silver. In today's market, at the time of this writing, that amount of silver is valued at approximately $173,768,355. (That's more than one hundred and seventy-three *million*, seven hundred and sixty-eight *thousan*d dollars!)

This is actually not all that David contributed, but these figures *alone* tell us that in today's currency, David's personal contributions for building a *naos* — *a temple*, *house*, or *shrine* — for God would be approximately $174,282,262,232. (That's more than one hundred and seventy-four *billion*, two hundred and eighty-two *million*, two hundred and sixty-two *thousand* dollars!)

However, First Chronicles 29:7 also tells us what David's *leaders* contributed toward the building of this magnificent temple:

- 5,000 talents of gold, which is approximately 4,822,612 troy ounces of gold. In today's market, that amount is valued at approximately $8,451,868,635. (That's more than eight *billion*, four hundred and fifty-one *million*, eight hundred and sixty-eight *thousand* dollars!)

- They also gave 10,000 talents of silver, which is approximately 9,645,224 troy ounces of silver. At the time of this writing, that amount is valued at approximately $217,210,444. (That's more than two hundred and seventeen *million*, two hundred and ten *thousand* dollars!)

- 18,000 talents of brass/copper, which is approximately 17,361,403 troy ounces of *brass/copper*. In today's market, this amount of brass would be valued at approximately $5,203,213. (That's more than five *million*, two hundred and three *thousand* dollars!)
- 100,000 talents of iron, which is 96,452,240 troy ounces of iron, which today would be valued at approximately $390,728. (That's more than three hundred and ninety *thousand* dollars!)

Combining what we know David and his leaders contributed of these specific materials only, the calculated amount comes to approximately $182,956,935,252. (That's more than one hundred and eighty-two *billion*, nine hundred and fifty-six *million*, nine hundred and thirty-five *thousand* dollars!)

But it is also helpful — and astonishing — to include other items that David gave besides the value of the silver and gold I just calculated. First Chronicles chapters 22 and 29 tell us that there were also precious stones, jewels, ivory, and many other valuable things that David personally contributed in addition to silver and gold. Some scholars estimate these "other things" amounted to at least another $100,000,000, in today's market, added to the previous sum he'd contributed for building this *naos — a temple*, *house*, or *shrine* — in Jerusalem.

Thus, if everything is calculated from the biblical record that David and his leaders contributed for the building of a *naos* Temple for the One True God in Jerusalem, we can roughly estimate that the cost for the Temple's construction in today's currency would be approximately $183,056,935,252. (That's more than one hundred and eighty-three *billion*, fifty-six *million*, nine hundred and thirty-five *thousand* dollars!)

We do not know the exact square footage of the entire massive Temple complex, but we do know that the original *naos* Temple itself was approximately

6,000 square feet. So if you take the total construction cost of $183,056,935,252 and divide it by 6,000 square feet, you will see that the cost for the Temple in Jerusalem was about $30,509,489 per square foot (more than thirty *million*, five hundred and nine *thousand* dollars per square foot!).

This is why we can confidently say the Temple in Jerusalem was categorically, *emphatically* the most expensive building to be constructed in human history.

Again, these figures do *not* include the manpower or artistic value of the items that were marvelously created and used to embellish the interiors of the Temple and its complex. Furthermore, if you add the additional fortune that Solomon invested from his own treasury, the amount escalates until the cost of building the Temple was, and is, simply mind-boggling beyond imagination.

The walls and floors of the Temple were lined with gold sheets ornamented with intricately carved palm trees and cherubim, and inside the Temple were ten solid gold lampstands. Beside each golden lampstand was a golden table for displaying showbread (the showbread was ever-present as a covenantal symbolic offering to God), and at the end of the room was the altar of incense made of cedar wood that was covered in pure gold.

Behind the altar of incense was the doorway that led to the Holy of Holies, which was the inner *naos* sanctuary that held the Ark of the Covenant. The Ark was made from a special wood that was covered with pure gold and had two golden winged cherubs on top of it. The way leading to the Ark was filled with fabrics and tapestries made with golden thread and colored with expensive dyes in rare hues.

We're told in First Kings 8:13 that once the Ark of the Covenant was placed in the Temple, Solomon dedicated it and declared, "I have surely built thee *an house* to dwell in, a settled place for thee to abide in for ever." Afterward, Solomon prayed a lengthy prayer for God's blessings to reside upon *the house* he had built for the presence of the Lord and for God's people in Jerusalem. Second Chronicles 6:40,41 tells us that Solomon said, "Now, my God, let, I beseech thee, thine eyes be open, and let thine ears be attent unto the prayer that is made in *this place*. Now therefore arise, O Lord God, into *thy resting place*, thou, and the ark of thy strength: let thy priests, O Lord God, be clothed with salvation, and let thy saints rejoice in goodness."

Second Chronicles 7:1,2 also tells us, "Now when Solomon had made an end of praying, the fire came down from heaven, and consumed the burnt offering and the sacrifices; and the glory of the Lord filled *the house*. And the priests could not enter into *the house* of the Lord, because the glory of the Lord had filled *the Lord's house*."

In that divine moment, the Temple supernaturally became a *naos* — *a temple*, *a house for God*, or *a shrine* — where God's presence came to rest in Jerusalem and where the people of God came to pray to, sacrifice to, worship, and experience God.

In antiquity, the entire world regarded the Temple at Jerusalem as the grandest *naos* ever built for any god. Those in the Jewish *and* pagan worlds were stunned, as you no doubt are, by the astronomical sum of money and priceless materials that were used in the construction and adornment of the Temple. Indeed, it was the most expensive building ever constructed, such a magnificent *naos*, where God's presence resided. Again, in the Greek Septuagint version of the Old Testament, it is this word *naos* that is used to describe *the Temple* and *the Holy of Holies* where the Shekinah glory of God dwelled.

Later Herod the Great rebuilt and expanded the Temple Mount and built the Second Temple (after Solomon's Temple had been destroyed in 586 or 587 BC by King Nebuchadnezzar II). Herod's version of the Temple was also fabulous, although but a shadow compared to the glory of Solomon's Temple. But the Second Temple was so magnificent that when the Roman emperor

Titus laid siege to the city of Jerusalem in 70 AD and destroyed the Temple, he first entered it to plunder its treasures to carry them back to Rome. Today at the Arch of Titus in the Roman Forum (*Forum Romanum*), there is a carved relief on the interior of the arch that pictures the golden menorah from the Temple being carried into Rome in a triumphal procession along with other treasures taken from the Temple — *naos* — in Jerusalem.

Most people do not realize the incalculable value of what Titus plundered from the Temple. It is so immense that once it was converted into cash, the sales of the Temple treasures were sufficient to rebuild parts of Rome after the Great Fire of 64 AD. The profit was even enough to pay for the construction of the Roman Colosseum, the largest construction in the Roman world. All those government projects in Rome were financed by cash produced from vast treasures taken from the second Temple in Jerusalem in 70 AD. In fact, right after Titus plundered the Temple, so much gold was flooded into the market that the price of gold significantly dropped — as much as 50 percent in some parts of the Roman Empire.[8]

Perhaps these insights help you fathom the inestimable wealth and treasure that were once held inside even the second Temple in Jerusalem before it was sacked and plundered by the Roman army. It is mind-bending to contemplate how vast were the treasures inside the second Temple during Jesus' day, and it explains why professional treasure hunters are still looking for hoards of its treasures today.

An End to God Dwelling in Physical Temples — '*Ye* Are the Temple'

As glorious and splendid as the first and second Temples in Jerusalem were, they were not the ultimate temple God longed to dwell in among man. In Old Testament Scriptures, God had long expressed that His greatest desire was not to dwell in buildings made by human hands, but that He longed to live in the hearts of His people. This is why in Acts 7:48, Stephen said, "...The most High dwelleth not in temples made with hands...." And in Acts 17:24, Paul said, "God that made the world and all things therein, seeing that he is Lord of heaven and earth, dwelleth not in temples made with hands."

In Second Corinthians 6:16, Paul referred to God's fulfilled promise of old that He would one day make human hearts His temple. Paul told the Corinthians, "...For *ye* are the temple of the living God; as God hath said, I will dwell in them, and walk in them; and I will be their God, and they shall be my people" (2 Corinthians 6:16). In this verse, Paul quoted a composite of Old Testament verses to affirm that God's intention had always been to live in the hearts of His people *individually* and, therefore, *corporately* as the Church — the new *naos* Temple of God. Paul quoted from Exodus 29:45, Leviticus 26:12, and Ezekiel 37:27 to remind his readers that God longed for a day when He would come to *literally* live inside the hearts — the reborn spirits — of His people.

But notice Paul wrote, "...Ye are the *temple* of the living God..." (2 Corinthians 6:16). Paul amazingly used the word *naos* in this verse where it is translated "temple." Being highly educated, Paul unequivocally knew this was the word used in the Greek Septuagint version of the Old Testament to describe the Temple in Jerusalem that had held God's presence inside the Holy of Holies. But most of Paul's readers were Greek — such as the Corinthians to whom he was writing. And as Greeks, they had grown up seeing *naos* temples scattered throughout the Greek and Roman worlds where they lived. They emphatically knew and understood the word *naos* and all its nuances and implications.

So when Paul said "...Ye are the temple of the living God...," using the word *naos*, he deliberately used an image his readers could visually imagine and actually see all around them so they could understand.

Very importantly, the Greek literally says, "...Ye are the *naos* of the living God...." This unquestionably means the Church is the new *naos* — *the temple, house of God*, or *shrine* — where God dwells in the earth today. While the members of the Church may meet in physical buildings, the Church itself — that is, the people of God — are the treasure chamber where God lives by His Spirit. This gives new appreciation for why Christ likened the Church to "golden candlesticks" in Revelation 1:12. In the mind of Christ, His Church — His *naos* Temple and place of habitation — is indeed *golden.*

While the members of the Church may meet in physical buildings, the Church itself — that is, the people of God — are the treasure chamber where God lives by His Spirit.

The word "golden" is translated from the Greek word *chrusos* — the word for "gold" used in the Greek version of the Old and New Testaments. This particular word is also used throughout ancient literature to describe the purest form of gold. The most sought-after and expensive gold in the ancient world was gold that was *absolutely pure.* Other forms were less valuable because they were mixed with silver and were, thus, a lower and less desirable grade of gold. But when Christ talks about the Church as being "golden" in Revelation 1:12, the word used in the text is *chrusos.* Thus, in Christ's view, there is nothing inferior, low-grade, or undesirable about the Church. As a matter of fact, in the eyes of God, the Church is *pure gold.*

Because of the historically high cost required to produce this grade of pure, refined gold, it became *the* metal associated with royalty or nobility. In the ancient world, only pure gold was fitting for magnificently wealthy, powerful kings or nobility and was therefore used to make their cups, bowls, plates, saucers, and platters, as well as many other items. When ambassadors or the head of a foreign state came to visit a king, they came with gifts. To bring a gift crafted of gold (*chrusos*) was a way of showing the highest respect and honor. Furthermore, *pure gold* was also the preferred metal used to fashion all the instruments for the holiest part of the Temple in Jerusalem.

Christ's use of the word "golden" in Revelation 1:12 to depict the Church conveys the *immense value* that Jesus places on His Church. Especially in our age when so much criticism is leveled against the Church and so many people focus on its failures and weaknesses, it is good for us to remember that Jesus gave His own blood to purchase His Church and that it is *valuable* and *precious* to Him. Of course, the Church is still in the process of purification and refinement, but regardless of its imperfections, Jesus still sees the Church as *pure gold*.

You may sometimes feel disheartened by what you see or know about the Church. You may feel discouraged at times because of your experiences with a local church body. You may even be tempted to think the modern Church is in such an irreversibly sad condition that it will never turn around for the better. But whenever your mind is bombarded by such thoughts, it is vital to remember that Jesus loves His Church, He bought it with His own blood, and the Holy Spirit is still actively working to purify it.

The Church's imperfections are nothing new, and as long as the Church awaits the coming of Jesus, this refining process will never end. Jesus Christ — the Head of the Church and our Great Refiner — desires His Church to reach the highest possible state of purity, holiness, and spiritual maturity.

So if you're ever tempted to feel dismayed about the carnality and powerlessness that sometimes seem so pervasive in the contemporary Body of Christ, remember that Jesus paid the highest price of all for the Church, that He loves His people, and that He still remains in the *midst* of the Church, His *naos* — *temple*, *house*, or *shrine* — where God dwells in the earth today.

It is vital to remember that Jesus loves His Church, that He bought it with His own blood, and that the Holy Spirit is still actively working to purify it. The Church's imperfections are nothing new, and as long as the Church awaits the coming of Jesus, this refining process will never end. Jesus Christ — the Head of the Church and our Great Refiner — desires His Church to reach the highest possible state of purity, holiness, and spiritual maturity.

Christ loves the Church and abides in the midst of it, and whatever Jesus loves and does, is exactly what we must also love and do. Thus, we must love the Church, abide in it, and value it, for it is the *naos* Temple of God's presence in the earth today.

The point is that the word *naos*, which Paul so aptly used in his epistles lucidly and accurately depicts *a temple*, *a house*, or *a shrine* veneered with precious stones and metals. But today God does not dwell in a man-made structure. He invested the highest price of all, the blood of His own Son, to purchase us and transform us into a dwelling place, where He lives in human hearts. He fashioned the Church to be the dwelling place of the presence of the Holy Spirit in the world today.

Jesus Prophesied the Destruction of the Second Temple in Jerusalem

In John 2:19-21, Jesus angered a group of Pharisees when He prophesied that a day would come when the second Temple built by Herod the Great would cease to exist (the second Temple, built by Herod, is pictured later in this book). In John 2:19-21, we read, "Jesus answered and said unto them, Destroy this temple, and in three days I will raise it up. Then said the Jews, Forty and six years was this temple in building, and wilt thou rear it up in three days? But he spake of the temple of his body."

The religious leaders were *aghast* at Jesus's declaration that the Temple would be destroyed and rebuilt in the space of three days and reminded Jesus that Herod the Great built the second Temple over a span of 46 years. Herod the Great was known for building everything in gargantuan style, so in his typical style, he enlarged the entire temple mount to become the largest temple complex constructed in the Roman world at that particular time.

One stone of the Temple that is still visible in the Western Wall is one of the heaviest objects ever moved by man, a single stone with an estimated weight of 517 tons.[9] These massive stones were quarried and transported to the Temple site during Herod's time, a feat difficult to do even today with advanced technology. When Jesus said it would all be destroyed and rebuilt in three days, the religious leaders were dumbfounded that anyone could assert it could be torn down and rebuilt so quickly. That vast complex was an architectural wonder, so the Pharisees were *horror-struck* that Jesus even insinuated it could be torn down and rebuilt in the space of a mere three days. To them, this idea was *preposterous.* But the Scripture explains, "But he [Jesus] spake of the *temple* of his body" (*see* v. 21). The word *naos* is used in this verse where Jesus refers to the "Temple" of His body. So when Jesus prophetically declared that God would move into a new *naos* Temple, He was saying that the new Temple would be His Body.

Jesus was saying that God's Spirit would be moving from a physical temple into His Body, that is, the Body of Christ. That glorious moment was signaled when the veil inside the physical structure of the Temple was rent, or torn, in two at the time of Jesus' crucifixion, announcing that God's presence was moving from behind the curtain in a physical temple into the hearts of born-again men and women in the corporate Body of Christ, which was the new "Temple" Jesus was referring to in John 2:21.

Matthew's gospel records that in the final moments of Christ's crucifixion, the veil of the Temple was supernaturally torn into two pieces. It says, "Jesus, when he had cried again with a loud voice, yielded up the ghost. And, behold, the veil of the temple was rent in twain from the top to the bottom..." (Matthew 27:50,51).

The word "behold" in Greek is *idou*, a very difficult word to translate, for it carries such intense feeling and emotion. The *King James Version* most often translates it as *behold.* But in our contemporary world, it might be better rendered, *Wow!* It carries the idea of *shock, amazement, and wonder*. It's almost as if Matthew was saying, *"Wow! Can you believe it? The veil of the Temple itself was ripped from top to bottom!"* Even though Matthew wrote about this event many years after Christ's crucifixion, he was still so dumbfounded by what happened that day that he exclaimed, in effect, *"Wow! Look what happened next!"*

An inexplicable, mystifying supernatural event occurred when the massive, fortified veil that stood before the Holy of Holies was suddenly split in half supernaturally, from the top all the way to the bottom. Many agree that the dimensions of the veil were 60-feet high, 30-feet wide, and four inches thick. The sound of that veil splitting must have been deafening as it ripped and tore, starting from the top, some 60 feet into the air, and going all the way down to the floor. God's invisible hands reached from eternity to grab hold of that veil separating Him from man, to rip it to shreds, and to permanently discard it from having any place between God and man.

Imagine how shocked the priests must have been when they heard the ripping sounds above and watched in astonishment as the veil was torn in half, leaving two sides of the once-massive curtain lying collapsed at their right and left. Just think what must have gone through their minds when they saw that the way inside the Holy of Holies had been opened.

But God's presence was moving from behind the veil in the Temple in Jerusalem into the hearts of born-again men and women inside the Church, and this is why Paul wrote that Jesus "...hath broken down the middle wall of partition between us" (Ephesians 2:14). When Jesus' blood was accepted on the Cross as the final payment for man's sin, it opened the way for the Holy of Holies to enter each one of us, where God would dwell by His Spirit.

This is such a mind-boggling, magnificent truth. We read in Isaiah 6:3 and Revelation 4:8 that angels and "living creatures" around God's throne cry, "Holy, holy, holy" to the Lord continually. As temples *and hosts* of His awesome majestic presence within, we should certainly do no less — and we should live our lives accordingly.

When Jesus was raised from the dead, a new era commenced when it finally was possible for the Holy Spirit to move into the hearts of His disciples. John 20:22 records that the disciples became the first in history to be *indwelt* by the Spirit of God. And as Jesus prophesied to the Pharisees, it all happened in *three days.* God supernaturally erected a new *naos* — the Church — a *new* Temple in which the Holy Spirit would dwell in the earth.

Now the Holy Spirit lives *singularly* in the heart of every individual believer, and He dwells *corporately* in the entire Church at large. We are individually the *naos* temple where God's Spirit dwells, and the Church is God's holy Temple where God dwells corporately in the midst of His people.

This is why Paul wrote in Ephesians 2:21,22, "In whom all the building fitly framed together groweth unto an holy temple in the Lord: in whom ye also are builded together for an habitation of God through the Spirit."

You *Individually* Are a Temple of the Holy Spirit

As previously noted, in his New Testament writings, Paul often metaphorically likened the Church to a *naos* Temple. A prime example we have already seen is Second Corinthians 6:16, where Paul said, "…Ye are the temple of the living God…."

For the first time ever, believers were gathering and listening to the teaching of God's spoken Word — and it let them know that when they acknowledged Jesus as the Lord of their lives, the Holy Spirit literally moved into their hearts, and they became a *naos* temple of the Living God. And throughout all of Paul's writings, he reinforces that each, *singular believer* and all the *corporate Church* at large are the Temple where the Holy Spirit dwells in the earth today.

However, right now I want to focus on the New Testament truth that you are *singularly* a temple for the Holy Spirit to indwell.

When any person confesses Jesus Christ as Lord, in a split second, God's Spirit miraculously moves inside that person and he or she instantaneously becomes a *naos* temple for the Holy Spirit. This is the miraculous work of God Himself to transform every single believer into a *naos* temple for His Spirit to indwell, and this miracle occurs at the moment of salvation. It is done by God Himself at the moment of faith and repentance and without anyone else's participation — thus the reason Paul wrote in Ephesians 2:8 that salvation is "the gift of God."

Paul asked the Corinthians, "*What?* know ye not that your body is the temple of the Holy Ghost which is in you, which ye have of God, and ye are not your own?" (1 Corinthians 6:19). The word "what" in this verse shows Paul's complete shock that believers in Corinth had never fully grasped what God had miraculously done inside them. That word "what" is the Greek equivalent of saying, *"What! Don't you get it? Have you not yet comprehended?"*

Again Paul said, "…[Have you not known and grasped] that your body is the temple of the Holy Ghost, which ye have of God, and ye are not your own?"

The word "body" in Greek is *soma*, which is the word for *the human body*. The word "temple" is *naos*, and, again, it is the word used in the Greek version of the Old and New Testaments that would normally describe *the most sacred, innermost part of the Temple in Jerusalem*. But by connecting the words "body" (*soma*) and "temple" (*naos*), Paul tells us that our human bodies have *really* become the place where God has taken up residency! Paul categorically declares that each believer washed in the blood of Jesus is born again and has become a *naos* temple where God literally dwells. After each person is born again, he or she is instantly transformed to become a *walking cathedral* where God resides.

After each person is born again, he or she is instantly transformed to become a *walking cathedral* where God resides.

'Christ *in* You' — There's More to You Than Meets the Eye!

In First Corinthians 6:19, Paul importantly said, "...Your body is the temple of the Holy Ghost which is *in* you...." The word "in" is very important in Greek, for it is the word *en*, and it identifies that the *location* of this *naos* temple is *inside* us. This means there is more to you than meets the eye!

When I was a boy, the guys in our neighborhood loved to play like we were pirates. My friends and I would draw detailed maps with palm trees, waterfalls, lagoons, and, of course, *buried treasure*! The location of the buried treasure was always specified with a huge "X" to mark the spot of the hidden prize. As we acted out our game, we pretended to search for the "X" that designated the hiding place of that treasure.

Even today, I enjoy seeing how treasure hunters scour the earth and sea in their quests for treasures and relics left by previous generations and civilizations. But think about it. The greatest treasure in the entire universe is *inside you*. I'm talking about a cache of wealth so immense that its reserves can never be completely dug out, explored, discovered, or discerned — spiritual assets beyond your wildest imagination.

In Second Corinthians 4:7, Paul wrote about this astonishing treasure when he said, "But we have this treasure in earthen vessels, that the excellency of the power may be of God, and not of us." In this verse, Paul tells us where the "X" is that marks where this treasure is concealed. He writes, "But *we have* this treasure…."

The words "we have" in Greek are a form of the word *echo*, which means *to have, to hold,* or *to possess*. It depicts what one has in his own possession. And the word "treasure" is the Greek word *thesauros*, which describes *a treasure, a treasury, a treasure chamber, or a place where riches and fortunes are kept*. The Greek word *thesauros* actually pictures *a specially built chamber, container, or room designed to be a repository for massive riches and wealth*.

Let me give you some examples of how the word *thesauros* was used by famous ancient Greek writers:

- Aeschylus used the word *thesauros* to picture *fabulous hidden treasures of gold and silver.*[10]
- Herodotus used the word *thesauros* to describe *a storehouse filled with treasure* or *a hidden treasure chamber*.[11]

- Euripides used the Greek word *thesauros* to describe something *so magnificently rich that it is immeasurable.*[12]
- Aristotle used the word *thesauros* to depict *a treasure trove* or *a hidden hoard of treasure.*[13]

Paul knew very well the meaning of *thesauros.* He intentionally used this word to gloriously declare that *each and every believer is a repository that contains treasure and riches beyond our wildest imagination.* We indeed are chambers, repositories, or treasuries where God has placed the immeasurable fortunes of His Spirit. And because the words "we have" — from the Greek word *echo* — precedes the word *thesauros* in this verse, it could be translated, *"We have and hold in our possession this unfathomable treasure-trove of wealth."* This treasure is what we already *possess* because God placed it deep within us in the moment of our conversion to Christ.

A good illustration of the word *thesauros* — that is, *a temple or treasure chamber filled with vast treasure and wealth* — can be seen in the temples and tombs of the pharaohs located in the Valley of the Kings along the Nile River. Other such *thesauros* temples are located in the Karnak Temple Complex near the Nile at Luxor, Egypt. Upon entering these temples and tombs, one can see the walls are covered with intricate hieroglyphs and paintings. In tombs that have been found still intact, archeologists have discovered riches and precious jewels nearly beyond one's imagination.

One of the better-known among those is that of King Tutankhamun, also known as *King Tut,* a tomb discovered by archeologist Howard Carter in 1922. When Howard Carter made his discovery and drilled a hole into the tomb to look inside, his assistant asked him, "Can you see anything?" When Carter got a glimpse of the 3,000-plus treasures inside the tomb, he was so stunned that all he could answer was that he saw *"wonderful things"*![14]

But let's consider again the vast wealth inside the Temple in Jerusalem in Solomon's time and again during the time of the second Temple that was built by Herod the Great. Not only did these Temples contain immense treasures, the Temples *themselves* were treasure chambers constructed with materials that were also considered to be extremely valuable.

We noted that Solomon's Temple was approximately 6,000 square feet in size, not large in comparison to other temples in the world. We also saw that — excluding the salaries paid to the workforce and the best artisans in the world who created that fabulous masterpiece — the Temple in materials alone cost roughly $183,056,935,252 in today's value. Again, if you divide that sum by the 6,000 square feet that made up the physical Temple itself, the cost to build the Temple was approximately $30,509,489 per square foot!

I remind you again that even the second Temple — the "lesser" of the two Temples — had so much treasure inside it that when the Romans plundered it, its value was sufficient to rebuild major sectors of Rome after Nero's Great Fire in 64 AD. In addition, there was enough wealth to construct the colossal Roman Colosseum. The Temple in Jerusalem overflowed with treasure beyond our ability to comprehend, but as rich as these tombs and temple treasures were, they were *dim* compared to the cache of spiritual treasure that resides in the heart of every believer.

Paul wrote in Second Corinthians 4:7 that we each, *singularly*, are *treasure chambers* where vast reserves of spiritual riches are deposited by God's Spirit indwelling us. We each *have*, *hold*, and *possess* treasure far greater than any wealth that was ever contained in any treasure chamber at any point in human history. Paul used the word *thesauros* to explain that we have more riches *inside us* than even the wealth that was stored inside the Temple in Jerusalem.

So if "X" marks the spot where buried treasure can be found, it means the "X" is marked on each of us, because God has placed His greatest treasure inside you and me!

As rich as these tombs and temple treasures were, they were *dim* compared to the cache of spiritual treasure that resides in the heart of every believer.

We Possess This Treasure in *Earthen Vessels*

In Second Corinthians 4:7, we see that Paul himself was mystified and in awe that God would put such a treasure inside our physical bodies, referring to our bodies as "earthen vessels." The word "earthen" is a form of the Greek word *ostrakinos*, a word that was used by Lucian of Samosata, a Hellenized Syrian satirist and rhetorician who was known for his superb use of Greek to describe *cheap vessels made of clay.*[15] And by the time Paul was writing his epistle, the word *ostrakinos* generally described *fragile pottery made of inferior materials that was inexpensive and usually covered with beautiful decorative paint.*

People generally loved to purchase *ostrakinos* because it was inexpensive and could be easily replaced if broken. In fact, it was so inexpensive that over time, the word *ostrakinos* represented *anything inferior, low-grade, mediocre, shoddy, second-rate, or substandard.*

What is more interesting to me is that the word *ostrakinos* came to depict the broken shards of *ostrakinos* pottery that were used for casting votes against citizens who were banished from society. Even Aristotle used the word *ostrakinos* to depict votes that were cast to condemn and banish someone to be sent away and *ostracized.*[16] Thus, the word *ostrakinos* came to be associated with *ostracizing* someone and is actually where we get the word "ostracize." So in the vernacular of Paul's time, *ostrakinos* was also used to depict a person who was ostracized for some reason.

Maybe you have been made to think you are "less" than others or not worth the time of day. Perhaps it's a self-imposed judgment that you've placed on yourself — for some reason, you feel that you do not count as compared to others. In that case, I guess you see yourself like *ostrakinos* — that is, inferior, low-grade, mediocre, shoddy, second-rate, or substandard. But take heart! Paul has gloriously revealed to us by the power of the Holy Spirit that God has placed His greatest treasure deep inside us, hidden from the human eye. For this reason, even Paul wrote with amazement that God did the unthinkable when He placed such immense treasure in such flawed receptacles. *But that is precisely what God did when He placed the Holy Spirit into each one of us in the new birth.*

Then Paul added to the word "earthen" the word "vessels" as another way of describing our bodies. In Greek, the word "vessels" is a translation of the Greek word *skeuos*. It describes *a vessel, container*, or *utensil*. It could also depict *baggage, containers, equipment of various sorts, military equipment, implements used in worship, kitchen items, or elegant articles of gold and silver put on public display.*

By the time of the New Testament, the word "vessel" was used even to depict a piece of luggage one could carry as he traveled, and this is important, for it means that wherever we go in life, we carry divine treasure along with us!

It is no accident that the Holy Spirit moved upon Paul to use the words *ostrakinos* and *skeuos* to describe our human bodies as containers of God's Spirit. Our physical bodies are like *ostrakinos* pottery. Although we decorate them with beautiful clothing and cosmetics, they are nevertheless *fragile, inferior, low-grade, mediocre, shoddy, second-rate, substandard*, and *flawed*. But, amazingly, God chose to place His "treasure" — from the Greek word *thesauros* — inside us. The inexhaustible treasure of His Spirit — wealth beyond imagination — has been deposited in us. God furthermore turned us into a *skeuos*, a vessel designed to carry this divine treasure wherever we go. God has made us each *walking cathedrals* or *walking sanctuaries*, and as such, we carry God everywhere we go!

The Greek words in Second Corinthians 4:7 communicate, *"We possess treasure within ourselves! And not only do we possess treasure, but our easily broken, inferior, temporary bodies are themselves the treasure chambers where this astonishing cache is kept...."*

By the time of the New Testament, the word "vessel" was used even to depict a piece of luggage one could carry as he traveled, and this is important, for it means that wherever we go in life, we carry divine treasure along with us!

In Second Corinthians 4:7, Paul used those two Greek words *ostrakinos* and *skeuos* to announce the truth that the body of *every individual believer* has become the residence of the Holy Spirit. That means you are a treasure hunter's greatest dream. "X" marks the spot for where the hidden treasure lies, but this time you don't have to go searching for the hidden treasure because the "X" is written on *you*. You really are the hiding place for God's greatest treasure — the Holy Spirit!

But there is more to this verse that you need to see. Paul went on to say, "...That the *excellency* of the power may be of God, and not of us." The word "excellency" in this verse is a form of the Greek word *huperballo*, a compound of *huper* and *ballo*. The word *huper* describes *something that is above and beyond what is normal* or *something that is exceeding or surpassing*. The word *ballo* means *to hurl* or *to throw*. When compounded, the word *huperballo* pictures something like an archer who aims his arrow at the target, but he shoots way over the top of it. Hence, the word "excellency" in this verse depicts *something beyond the range of anything considered normal* or *something that is unparalleled*.

Paul knew exactly what he was doing when he used this word because *huperballo* was so widely used by famous Greek writers in important ancient Greek literature.

- The word *huperballo* and forms of it were used by the Greek historian Herodotus to describe that which was *running over, overflowing, flooding,* or *conquering.*[17]
- Sophocles, one of classical Athens' three great tragic playwrights, used it to depict anything that *outran* something else.[18]
- The famed philosopher Plato and Aristotle both used forms of *huperballo* to depict anything that was *excellent, extreme, superior, preeminent,* or *unlimited.*[19]
- Xenophon and Demosthenes, used various forms of *huperballo* to depict what was *exceptional.*[20]

Knowing full well the dramatic way *huperballo* was used in history and culture, Paul chose to use this remarkable word to describe the vast riches and power resident inside every single believer. What is deposited inside us is simply *exceeding, surpassing, and beyond our wildest imagination.*

Again, in Second Corinthians 4:7, Paul said, "...That the excellency of the *power* may be of God, and not of us." The word "power" is a form of the word *dunamis*, a Greek word that describes *power* or *ability,* and it was the very word to depict *the assembled forces of an army whose combined strength enabled them to push back enemies, take new territory, and achieve unrivaled victories.*

Those military forces were so strong that they could not be resisted. Hence, Paul was telling us that the "power" we *have*, *hold*, and *possess* is so mighty that it can drive back the forces of hell and is impossible to resist or defeat.

But the word *dunamis* was also the Greek word used to describe a force of nature like an *earthquake*, *tornado*, or *hurricane*. By using this word, Paul was literally saying we have a force in us that can produce a spiritual earthquake, and its strength is even stronger than a tornado or hurricane. We are a *spiritual force* because of the Holy Spirit's power that resides in us. We have within us what is needed to spiritually shake things up and to blow away evil forces!

Oh, how we need to comprehend what God has done inside us and what He has fashioned each of us to be. We are each singularly a *naos — a temple*, *a house of God*, or *a shrine* — and every one of us *has*, *holds*, and *possesses* the cache of spiritual wealth and surpassing power of His Holy Spirit. As believers, we must tap into the rich deposits of God's Spirit in us and learn to release that surpassing power into any situation we find ourselves in so we can advance the Kingdom of God.

We have a force in us that can produce a spiritual earthquake, and its strength is even stronger than a tornado or hurricane. We are a spiritual force because of the Holy Spirit's power that resides in us. We have within us what is needed to spiritually shake things up and to blow away evil forces!

But wait...*it's about to get even better!*

The Church *Corporately* Is the Temple of the Holy Spirit

As wonderful as it is to think about what we each singularly possess, when we came to Christ we were supernaturally baptized by one Spirit into one

Body (*see* First Corinthians 12:12). In that moment, we were each joined to the conglomerate Body of Christ, which is the Church. It is wonderful to meditate on how God dwells in each of us individually, but we also need to consider what this means about us *corporately*, as the Body. By baptizing us into one Body, God divinely joined us with others who are containers of the same treasure and power — and by connecting us, together, we become a corporate Temple that is filled to overflowing with spiritual riches and power.

Think of it like a bank account. If we each have one million dollars in our bank account, that amount would give each of us tremendous ability in the financial realm. But if we *join* our accounts and investments to that of others, we would have a sum so massive, we would be able to corporately do what we could never do independent of each other.

Likewise, when we are joined to others in the Church, the vast repository of riches we each carry is divinely connected to others who are *also* repositories of spiritual riches and power. Once supernaturally joined, the combined spiritual riches and power becomes beyond anything our minds can begin to fathom.

This is why the devil works nonstop to sow seeds of strife and division in the Church. He really understands the spiritual treasure and power in us and that it becomes amplified when we are *joined together*. The devil knows that once we are connected, God's treasure and power in us *meld together* and enable the Church to emerge as a force so powerful that the gates of hell cannot stand against it.

The fact is, we possess *more* spiritual treasure and *more* spiritual power when we are joined to and co-working with others. When we are a conglomerate Body — *a holy Temple* — we "burst at the seams," packed with the unsearchable riches and power of Christ Himself.

The devil works nonstop to sow seeds of strife and division in the Church. He really understands the spiritual treasure and power in us and that it becomes amplified when we are *joined together*. The devil knows that once connected, God's treasure and power in us *meld together* and enable the Church to emerge as a force so powerful that the gates of hell cannot stand against it.

The Role of God and the Role of Fivefold Ministry Gifts in Building the Temple — the Corporate Body of Christ

So now we've seen that when we are each born again, God Himself personally transforms us *singularly* into *naos* temples where the Holy Spirit indwells. The miracle of the new birth is the greatest act of God on the earth, one that can only be performed by God Himself. Whether it occurs in one's life when he is by himself or in a meeting alongside others, the new birth is a personal act of creation carried out by God Himself in every individual believer. And as a result of that divine transaction, God has personally transformed each of us as believers to be walking cathedrals.

However, for us — for the Church — to become the corporate Temple He desires, Christ has given the fivefold gifts of the *apostle*, *prophet*, *evangelist*, *pastor*, and *teacher* to be *builders*, who are anointed to help construct the corporate House of God. For every individual believer to be properly connected to others so that we become a united, conglomerate Body requires the ministry and operation of these Christ-given fivefold ministry gifts.

For every individual believer to be properly connected to others so that we become a united, conglomerate Body requires the ministry and operation of these Christ-given fivefold ministry gifts.

Indeed, we are immediately baptized into one Body at the moment of our salvation, but these Christ-given fivefold ministry gifts have been given to help assemble, perfect, and connect the individual parts to become one functional corporate Body — a united *naos* Temple — for the Holy Spirit's habitation and the display of His splendor in the earth.

When constructing a building of any kind, various materials are needed for construction. Materials can be purchased and placed in piles on a construction site, but they remain random and disconnected until professional builders lay a foundation and then begin to assemble them by mortar, hammer, and nail. As piece by piece is joined correctly by professional *builders* into each one's respective place, we watch as a magnificent Building begins to materialize.

'Living Stones' Are To Be Transformed Into God's *'Living House'*

Keeping all this in your mind, consider Peter's words in First Peter 2:5, in which he said, "Ye also, as lively stones, are built up a spiritual house, an holy priesthood, to offer up spiritual sacrifices, acceptable to God by Jesus Christ." But first, let me give you a little background concerning Peter's choice of words here.

In Galatians 2:8, Paul acknowledged Peter's apostleship to the Jews when he wrote, "For he that wrought effectually in Peter to the apostleship of the circumcision, the same was mighty in me toward the Gentiles." So just as Paul used words, phrases, and illustrations that a Greek-speaking world would understand because he was primarily called as an apostle to the Gentiles, Peter used words, phrases, and illustrations that a Jewish world would readily comprehend because he was called to the Jews. The Jews were Peter's primary audience, and they easily understood him when he spoke.

Actually, with both Paul and Peter, we learn the important lesson of knowing exactly to whom you are called and how important it is to know how to correctly speak understandably to your God-assigned audience.

Because Peter wrote primarily to those who were from a Jewish background, as he wrote the words in First Peter 2:5, he employed the use of words, phrases, and illustrations that alluded to the Temple in Jerusalem. Nearly all scholars agree that when Peter spoke of *living stones*, *a spiritual house*, *a holy priesthood*, and *the offering up spiritual sacrifices*, he was drawing on the images that Jews would have been familiar with at the Temple in Jerusalem. But many agree that Peter wrote this epistle after the destruction of the second Temple in 70 AD. In that case, the physical temple on the Temple Mount would have already become nonexistent. But Peter declared, regardless, that God was now in the business of constructing a *new* Temple — the Church — and in this new Temple of God, every believer had individually become a "lively stone" that God would use as materials collectively to construct this new Temple.

The word "lively" is actually a translation of the Greek word *zao*, and it pictures that which is *living*, *lively*, *vibrant*, or *full of life*, which is a perfect description of a child of God who possesses the *vibrant life* of God within. But notice in this verse, Peter called each member of the Church a "stone." In Greek, this is the word *lithos,* which is plural in this verse and means *stones.* The word *lithos* is precisely the same word that would depict the "stones" used for constructing the Temple in Jerusalem. This fits perfectly into Peter's analogy of God's plan today to build a new *naos* Temple for the Holy Spirit in the Church.

But the physical stones quarried — chiseled, refined, and used in building the physical Temple in Jerusalem — were lifeless stones. Now God was building a brand-new *naos* Temple comprised of "lively stones" — represented by *each and every member* of the Body of Christ.

Since the outpouring of the Holy Spirit on the day of Pentecost, God has been progressively constructing a new *naos* Temple where His Spirit can dwell and work mightily. In this new Temple, each born-again believer is singularly *a living stone* that God is using to place side by side with other living stones to progressively construct the Temple He has always longed to indwell. Since Pentecost, God has been constructing this new Temple with redeemed souls — "lively stones" — as Christ-given fivefold ministry gifts do their respective parts as professional builders to chisel each stone into its respective God-called place in the *naos* Temple of God.

A Simple Explanation of Christ-Given Fivefold Ministry Gifts

For God's new conglomerate Temple to emerge, it requires a workforce to select a building site, to design a plan, to quarry and cut the stones, and to assemble all the materials to build a temple. With these metaphorical job descriptions in mind, let me summarize *very simply* the various roles that the Christ-given fivefold ministry gifts of *apostle*, *prophet*, *evangelist*, *pastor*, and *teacher* play as professional builders. They are each anointed to help construct God's people into a new *naos* Temple of God in the earth today.

- **Apostles** and their teams select the construction site where the Church has never been established before. When they enter a new location, they are anointed by God's Spirit to clear spiritual rubbish out of the way and to lay a foundation for the Church in that location. And as team leader, the apostle works side by side with his God-called team to lay a rock-solid foundation on which others can come along to do their parts in building a magnificent structure. We will focus on the role of Christ-given apostles in Chapters 3-5.

- Building inspectors also play a key role to make sure the construction is being carried out properly and up to code. This is where the Christ-given fivefold ministry gift of **prophets** enter the picture in regard to their part in building the House of God. Often prophets operate like anointed building inspectors who are divinely enabled to *see* what others may not see, including what is done correctly or incorrectly. With Christ-given insight, Christ-given prophets impart courage to build correctly and at times to address issues that need to be fixed in the building process.

- Peter states in First Peter 2:5 that the House of God is built with "living stones" or the souls of those who have been redeemed. This brings us to the role of the Christ-given ministry gift of the **evangelist.** Evangelists are anointed "stone collectors" who go into the field to win souls who will become the "living stones" in the construction of God's House. Once those living stones are won and collected, the evangelist's responsibility is to see them brought onsite, where they can be assimilated into the Temple of God.

- Raw stones need a specialist to chisel, cut, trim, sand, grind, buff, and polish them to snugly fit next to other stones in the building. This brings us to the Christ-given fivefold ministry gift of **pastor**. In God's great building program, pastors are specialists who are anointed to carry out the nitty-gritty business of chiseling, cutting, trimming, sanding, grinding, and polishing all the souls or "living stones" that the evangelist gathered in the field and brought to the building site. A part of a pastor's function is to prepare all those living stones to be fitted into their respective places in God's House.

- Blueprints and plans are so vital that they must be explicitly followed for any building to be constructed according to the architect's plan. This is where the Christ-given fivefold ministry gift of **teacher** enters the picture. Christ-given teachers are like master instructors who turn us again and again to the instructions and principles in God's Word to keep on target with God's objective so that each of the "living stones" will glisten where it is placed in God's House.

Peter continued in First Peter 2:5 by saying, "Ye also, as lively stones, are *built up* a spiritual house..." The words "built up" are a translation of the Greek word *oikodomeo,* a compound of *oikos* and *demoo.* The first part of the word is *oikos,* which is the Greek word for *a house.* It is the very word used in the Greek Septuagint version of the Old Testament and by Jesus in the Gospels to refer to the Temple in Jerusalem. Even though Peter didn't use the word *naos* in First Peter 2:5, his use of *oikos* means he was unequivocally describing *a Temple* or *House of God* that was being constructed with "living stones" to become a habitation of the Spirit.

The second part of *oikodomeo* is from the Greek word *demoo,* a construction term that means *to build.* It importantly is a derivative of *doma* that denotes *the roof* of a building, house, or temple. It actually pictures a complete construction process, starting from the foundation to the roof, or the process of constructing a building from start to finish. This word assures us God intends to *finish* what He has *started* as He constructs the Church to become a holy Temple.

But when *oikos* and *demoo* are compounded, this Greek word speaks of *the entire process of constructing a building, a house, or a temple from beginning to end.* It furthermore includes the plan *to intentionally enlarge* a building, a house, or a temple. This tells us God's intention from the beginning has been for the Church, his new *naos* Temple, to be *enlarged* or, as Paul said in Ephesians 2:21, to be a Body of believers that "groweth unto a holy temple in the Lord."

As we saw in the previous chapter, the word for "groweth" is the Greek word *auxano*, and it means to be *amplified*, *augmented*, or *enlarged*. It even gives the idea of *escalating* or *multiplying*, and Paul used the word *auxano* to convey God's longing for the Church to grow to become a magnificent spiritual cathedral built of living stones. It is significant that in Paul's epistles, the word *oikodomeo* is used specifically to describe the building, growing work of apostles, a point we will come back to in subsequent chapters.

But notice Peter also added in First Peter 2:5, "Ye also, as lively stones, are built up *a spiritual house*...."

The "spiritual house" Peter referred to is the new *naos* Temple that God is building in the Church as His dwelling place in the earth today.

The Priesthood 'Then and Now' — What It Means To Be a Holy Priesthood in God's New Temple

Jewish and pagan temples both had *priests* and *priesthoods* that offered up sacrifices and served the worshipers. In his writings, the apostle Peter let us know there is also a bona fide priesthood inside the Church. This is what He meant in First Peter 2:5 when he added to his discourse, "Ye also, as lively stones, are built up a spiritual house, *an holy priesthood*...."

Because the modern world is largely disconnected from the ancient world, where priest and priesthoods were active in their related ministries, much of what it meant to be a priest or a member of a priesthood has been lost. But the words "priest" and "priesthood" were familiar to readers in the time of the early New Testament. In fact, priests were of paramount importance in the ancient world as an elite, limited group of individuals who bore great responsibilities.

To help you understand the roles of priests in the ancient world, I am providing you the following glimpse into some *expected* responsibilities of those priests, the majority of which would have been true for a priest in either the Jewish or pagan world. Afterward, we'll compare ancient priests' roles to the roles of the New Testament priesthood of believers, of which we are all a part.

- **Priests were temple-keepers.**
  This means priests were *expected* to defend the temple at any cost, including giving their lives for it, if necessary. They were to protect the temple and see that it was honored.

- **Priests were oracles.**
  This means priests were *expected* to speak for the divine and to spread the reputation of the divine to others.

- **Priests were sacrificers.**
  This means priests were *expected* to offer sacrifices for themselves and to assist worshipers who brought different kinds of sacrifices to offer at the altar.

- **Priests were 24-hour-a-day worshipers**.
  This means priests were *expected* to worship the divine and to teach others how to worship.

- **Priests were academics.**
  This means priests were *expected* to attentively study ancient texts to learn more about what they believed and to impart that knowledge to others.

- **Priests were mediators.**
  This means priests were *expected* to be a connection between the earthly and spiritual realms and to help others access that other realm.

- **Priests were counselors.**
  This means priests were *expected* to help others receive help from the divine.

- **Priests were prophets**.
  This means priests were *expected* to have supernatural abilities to see into the spirit realm and to deal with deep spiritual matters.

- **Priests were supernatural.**
  This means priests were *expected* to function to some degree in supernatural powers, including prophecy and healing.

- **Priests were servants.**
  This means priests were *expected* to serve others and help the community draw nearer to the divine.

It is easy to see how all of these ancient priestly functions also apply to believers in the House of God — the Church — today. If only using the limited list we just read, we see that God expects:

- **Believers are to be temple-keepers.**
  This means believers are *expected* to defend the Church at any cost, including giving our lives for it, if necessary, and we are to do everything possible to protect the reputation of the Church and see that it is treated honorably.

- **Believers are to be oracles.**
  This means believers are *expected* to speak for Christ and to spread His Word and reputation to as many people as possible.

- **Believers are to be sacrificers.**
  This means believers are *expected* to live at the altar, offering ourselves as living sacrifices and assisting others in giving *their* lives to God.
- **Believers are to be 24-hour-a-day worshipers.**
  This means believers are *expected* to worship Jesus and to teach others how to worship Him as 24-hour-a-day worshipers.
- **Believers are to be academics.**
  This means believers are *expected* to give ourselves to the study of God's Word and to impart that life-changing knowledge to others.
- **Believers are to be mediators.**
  This means believers are *expected* to be a connection between the earthly and spiritual realms and to help others access the promises of God by prayer, faith, and obedience to the Word of God.
- **Believers are to be counselors.**
  This means believers are *expected* to always be available to assist others with any counsel we can offer to help them receive whatever they need from the Lord.
- **Believers are to be prophetic.**
  This means believers are *expected* to be a mouthpiece for the Holy Spirit and should seek to help others move into deeper spiritual realms.
- **Believers are to be supernatural.**
  This means believers are *expected* to function in the gifts of the Holy Spirit and to let His power operate through them to meet the needs of others.
- **Believers are to be servants.**
  This means believers are *expected* to serve others in the community and help them draw nearer to the Lord and to His Church.

In First Peter 2:5, Peter calls the Church a holy priesthood. In this verse, the Greek word "holy" is *hagios*, and the word "priesthood" is the Greek word *hierateuma*. Both of these Greek words are strategic, so we must consider them one by one.

In the Greek version of the Old and New Testaments, the word translated "holy" is from various forms of the Greek word *hagios*. This word describes anything that has been *separated, consecrated, made holy*, or *made sacred*. The person, place, or thing that has been declared *holy* may have been common in the past, but once declared "holy," that person, place, or thing is never to be regarded or used in a common way ever again. Once made "holy," it is *separated* into *a special category* and is to be viewed and treated as *sacred* forevermore.

Let me give you several illustrations of the word "holy" to demonstrate the meaning of this word. When the translators of the *King James Version* of the Bible first published it in 1611, they officially called it the *Holy Bible*. The word "Bible" is a Greek word that means *book*. The word "holy" is from this Greek word *hagios*, which means *separated, consecrated, made holy*, or *made sacred*. As noted, this word "holy" referred to a person, place, or thing that once declared as such, that person, place or thing was never to be regarded or used in a common way again. So anything deemed "holy" has been removed from commonality and placed into a *sacred category* that is *separate* from all else.

The name *Holy Bible* perfectly demonstrates the meaning of the word "holy." Libraries are full of books and, if you go to a library, it is likely you will find a *Holy Bible* on its shelves. But the word "holy" in its name signifies the Holy Bible is in a category by itself and no other book can be compared to it. The Holy Bible is *sacred* and *separate* from all other books. Its very name means it is *set apart* into a *consecrated, holy category* and is *different* from all other books. While it may physically look and feel like a book, the word "holy" in its name means it is *different* and unlike any other book in the world.

Another example of the word "holy" can be seen in Moses' experience with God on Mount Horeb. As Moses approached the burning bush, God told him to remove his shoes because he was standing on "holy" ground. That word "holy" in the Greek Septuagint version of the Old Testament is the word *hagios*. This tells us that when God's divine presence touched that mountain, His divine presence *consecrated* and *sanctified* that mountain.

By simply looking at Mount Horeb, it physically looked no different from any other mountain in the region. But when God's *presence* touched it, it was supernaturally *separated* from all other mountains; it was *set apart* into a *holy* category and became so *sacred* that it became known as the *holy mount*. Although nestled as one mountain in the midst of an entire mountain range of normal-looking mountains, in that moment, Mount Horeb ceased to be normal — and from that day forward after God's presence touched it, it was *separated* from all others and its status was permanently changed.

The Bible is full of examples of *hagios*, but another is the word "saints" found in Paul's letter to the Church in Rome. In Romans 1:7, Paul wrote, "To all that be in Rome, beloved of God, called to be *saints*...." The word "saints" is a form of the Greek word *hagios*, again describing a person, place, or thing that has been *separated*, *consecrated*, *sanctified*, and *set apart* for special use and is never again to be regarded or used in a common way.

When Paul called believers "saints" — using a form of the Greek word *hagios* to describe them — it let us know that the indwelling presence of the Spirit *set them apart* and made them *different*. His divine presence caused them to be *sacred* people, and that is why Paul called them "saints." Using a form of *hagios* to describe them, Paul emphatically declared that it does not matter who we were in the past — what matters is that the blood of Jesus cleansed us and the Holy Spirit lives in us, and this literally *separated* and *consecrated* us. Although we physically look like common human beings, that word *hagios* — translated as "saints" in Romans 1:7 — means we are no longer like other people. God's presence in us has made us *holy*, and we are never to be regarded or used in a common way ever again.

Let's look next at the word "priesthood" in First Peter 2:5 because Peter connected the word "holy" to the word "priesthood." The word "priesthood" is a translation of the word *hierateuma*, a rare Greek word that denoted *a priesthood with all its priestly functions.* This word was used by Herodotus and by Plutarch, who both used this word to depict an exclusive, elite caste of priests who served in pagan temples.[21] The fact that Plutarch used *hierateuma* was especially important because he was actually a member of such an elite caste of priests.

But most important is the form of this word "priesthood" used by Peter to depict *an entire royal kingdom of priests* in which every member in the Kingdom is a priest with priestly functions and priestly responsibilities.

This is a radical concept because there had never been *an entire kingdom of priests* in any kingdom anywhere in human history. In the Old Testament, certain God-chosen groups had priestly functions, but there simply had been no kingdom *ever*, in which every member in it was a priest. However, this all changed in the new *naos* Temple of God, for Peter plainly stated that God's Kingdom is, indeed, a Kingdom in which *every believer* is a God-called priest with priestly functions and responsibilities.

So not only is *every believer* a "living stone" in the new *naos* Temple of God — the Church — *every believer* is, without exception, a God-called priest with priestly functions and priestly responsibilities. How glorious it is to comprehend that believers are the "living stones" that compose God's Temple, where God dwells, and each one of us is also a God-called priest with priestly functions and priestly responsibilities in God's House.

Indeed, the Church is a "holy priesthood" in which every redeemed member has become a God-called priest engaged in offering spiritual sacrifices to God. Revelation 1:6 states so clearly that Christ "...hath made us kings and priests unto God."

The Value of a Priestly Sacrifice

I must note that when Rome authorized the destruction of the second Temple, the Jews began to negatively refer to Rome as "Babylon." As Babylon destroyed the first Temple in Israel's past, under Nebuchadnezzar's reign, Roman troops also plundered the second Temple, built by Herod, and destroyed it.

In First Peter 5:13, Peter also referred to Rome as "Babylon," and because this was a term used by Jews to describe Rome *after* the destruction of the Temple in 70 AD, a number of scholars believe Peter's use of the term "Babylon" is proof that he wrote his epistles *after* the destruction of the second Temple in Jerusalem. Because sacrificial offerings were only offered in the Temple in Jerusalem, when it was destroyed, it meant all sacrificial offerings by the Jewish people came to a grinding halt.

This makes even more important the fact that First Peter 2:5 states that *all* believers today are God-called priests who are "*...to offer up spiritual sacrifices....*" This affirms the fact that all believers are actually believer-priests in the new *naos* Temple of God. And whereas the offering of sacrifices was once only performed by priests on the Temple Mount, this privilege has divinely passed to every individual believer-priest who is now to be engaged in regularly offering up *spiritual* sacrifices in the new *naos* Temple of God in the earth, which is the Church.

What sacrifices are all New Testament believer-priests to offer up? First, the words "offer up" are a form of the word *anaphero,* a word particularly used to picture priests in a temple whose responsibilities were *to offer physical sacrifices upon an altar.* The word *anaphero* and its various forms were used by many ancient Greek writers, and looking more deeply into the historical usage of this word gives additional meaning to the value of a sacrifice.

For example, Homer used *anaphero* to depict *the hard effort required to bring something to the surface from deep inside the earth.* Herodotus used the word *anaphero* to picture *someone who dug deep into the earth to mine something from deep within.* And Pindar used the word to mean *to discover something that was deeply hidden.*[22]

Combined, all these various uses of *anaphero* picture *an individual who puts forth effort to dig deep in order to find what is precious to bring it out of hiding and to the surface.*

Just imagine the work of a miner who put forth effort, even at times endangering his life, as he digs for gold. At long last, the gold is found, mined, and brought to the surface. The entire enterprise is expensive and dangerous. This scenario conveys the truth that bringing a sacrificial offering to God is an enterprise that should never be done carelessly or haphazardly. A sacrifice should be something that is premeditated, carefully carried out, and performed with intention. When we bring sacrificial offerings to God, it should be the result of "digging deep" in our personal lives with premeditated planning and a determined intention to bring our service or offering to the Lord with the honor that is certainly due Him.

So what are the sacrifices we are to "offer up" in the new *naos* Temple of God today? We are not commanded to bring butchered animals or foods as they were brought into a physical temple in the past. Instead, First Peter 2:5 tells us we are to offer up "spiritual sacrifices." These words are translated from the Greek words *pneumatikas thusias.* The word "spiritual" is from *pneumatikos,* which means *of a spiritual nature.* This, of course, means we are to offer sacrifices of a *spiritual nature.* The word "sacrifices" is translated from the *thusia,* which means *to sacrifice* or *to give up something precious and dear as a sacrificial offering.*

The word "sacrifice" — translated from *thusia* — is so very important that it is used throughout ancient Greek literature, in the Septuagint Greek version of the Old Testament, and throughout the New Testament.

- Various forms of *thusia* were used by Homer and by Plato in the sense of *massacring, killing, slaughtering,* or *sacrificing.*[23]
- Xenophon used *thusia* to depict *prayers that were offered at the time a sacrificial burnt offering was presented in a temple.* [24]
- Aristotle used the word *thusia* to describe *the entire celebration and pageantry that occurred when a person brought a sacrificial animal to the altar of a temple.*[25]
- Herodotus used the word *thusia* to paint a picture of *a sacrifice of the highest caliber.*[26]
- Lucian of Samosata used the word *thusia* to picture *the sacrificial animal itself as it was being offered upon an altar.*[27]

So combined, we see that the concept of a *thusia* — *a sacrifice brought with celebration, pageantry, and prayers in a moment when a worshiper came to an altar to offer a burnt sacrifice* — was important in both the ancient Jewish and pagan worlds.

In fact, it was so important, I would like to give you a glimpse of the offering of such sacrifices during that early period to help you grasp the importance of the sacrifices offered by worshipers in their respective temples.

Sacrifices in the Ancient World

Bringing sacrificial offerings to God existed since the time Cain and Abel (sons of Adam and Eve) brought their first sacrifices (*see* Genesis 4:3-5). And Noah sacrificed animals to God upon leaving the ark (*see* Genesis 8:20,21). Abraham offered up various burnt offerings during his sojourning (*see* Genesis 12:7,8; 15:9,10). Then later, God stopped Abraham from sacrificing Isaac, and the Bible tells us Abraham instead offered a sacrificial burnt offering in the place of his son (*see* Genesis 22:13). And, of course, during the years Israel wandered in the wilderness, they offered sacrificial offerings and then continued that practice after they finally settled in the Promised Land.

Sacrificial offerings played an enormous role in all ancient cultures and religions. Pagans believed that offering sacrifices was a way to appease gods and therefore avoid their wrath — or a way to help them obtain divine blessings upon their various endeavors.

The Jewish idea of bringing a sacrificial offering for the atonement of sin was not a part of pagan sacrifices because pagans essentially had no concept of sin. Sin was an unknown concept in much of the ancient world and was unique to the Jewish people. This is one reason why preaching about sin or warning against a sinful lifestyle was so offensive to the pagan world — they had never viewed their activities as being sinful. For that reason, pagans found the Gospel to be very confrontational to their sinful way of life.

'Blood' and 'Bloodless' Sacrifices

We'll get to ancient Jewish sacrifices soon, but let's begin with Greek and Roman sacrifices, which could be placed into categories of *blood* and *bloodless* sacrifices.[28] These two types of sacrifices served as a system of exchange between people and the gods. Through these different kinds of sacrificial offerings, the people hoped to gain some type of divine help or some type of miraculous benevolence that was beyond their current circumstances.

In ancient Greek culture, the highest form of offering was to offer a bloody sacrifice of a bull — but a sheep, goat, or other kind of domestic animal could be used as well. *Blood sacrifices* were nearly always offered in a public ritual and were centered around the ceremonial killing of an animal, such as a bull, an ox, or a sheep. Although pigs were considered unclean to Jews, it was not uncommon for pagans to even offer slaughtered pigs as a sacrifice.

A pagan sacrifice usually began with a procession to the altar in which a participant often sang and danced to sacred music as the sacrificial animal — decorated with gold and other ornaments — was led along behind the participant. Upon reaching the altar, a circle was marked off around the sacrificial animal with water, which symbolized a separation between the sacred and the profane. Then the worshipers washed their hands in a ceremonial cleansing, and droplets of water were shaken onto the sacrificial animal.

After the purification process was complete, a participant observed a moment of silence before saying a prayer and throwing barley onto the animal's back, the altar, and the ground. A small lock of the animal's fur was shaved off and placed into the fire, and smoke ascended like incense into the atmosphere of the temple. The animal's head was forced downward onto the altar, and a knife was used to slit its neck. The animal's blood was not to touch the ground, so worshipers held a special bowl next to the incision to catch the blood, which they would then pour onto the altar.

Next the animal was disemboweled, cut into sections, and its organs were inspected for defects. If blemishes were found, a new animal would have to be procured and the ceremony restarted because it was unacceptable to offer a sacrifice that was defective. Once a sacrificial animal was inspected and approved, the organs and select cuts of meat were then offered to a god, and other parts of the animal were cooked and eaten by participants. Finally, wine was poured onto the altar and also around its base, and special sacrificial cakes were placed into the fire. The smoke from the burnt offerings swirled into the atmosphere of the temple, which pagans believed represented their prayers ascending and billowing upward to the gods.

In ancient Roman culture, animal sacrifices — blood sacrifices — typically began with a call to silence. The officiating pagan priest initiated the ceremony by burning a precursory offering of wine and incense in the altar fire and by calling on a god or goddess through a prayer. Afterward, the time came for the sacrificial animal, having been sprinkled with wine and grains of salt, to be led to the altar where the main sacrifice was to be conducted and a prayer was to be uttered.

The sacrificial animal's head was held toward the ground, struck with a mallet on the forehead to stun it, the throat was quickly cut, and the internal organs were removed to be inspected. As with the Greeks, any abnormalities or defects discovered in the organs caused the animal to be unacceptable and the process had to be repeated with a different animal. If no defect was found, the animal was butchered, and the organs along with select cuts of meat were covered in salt, placed onto the altar, and burnt to ash. Whatever remained was cooked and distributed among worshipers to eat or to take home for later consumption. And as with Greeks, Romans believed the smoke from the burnt offerings that filled the temple were prayers that ascended upward to the gods.

In both ancient Greek and Roman cultures, *bloodless sacrifices* consisted of wine, incense, barley, cakes, fruit, or other food items, and even garlands of flowers or single flowers could be offered. Sacrifices were offered on altars scattered throughout cities to make it easier for those who wished to offer a sacrifice. Pagan altars came in a wide variety of sizes and shapes, as we saw in Chapter One — tall, short, round, square, long, and hexagonal — and were conveniently placed along the sides of streets and on street corners, as well as in marketplaces, gymnasiums, bathhouses, and other public buildings.

Now that we've covered pagan sacrifices as an overview, let's consider sacrificial offerings that were brought to God by the Jewish people.

Sacrifices in the Jewish Temple

Sacrificial offerings were brought by God's people to altars in various places, but once the first and second Temples were constructed, sacrifices were only permitted there.

As we have seen, the first sacrificial offerings were brought by sons of Adam and Eve, but eventually sacrifices were offered to God by the Jewish people in Gilgal for *14 years* — then at Shiloh in the Tabernacle (the tent shrine) for *369 years*. Shiloh was one of the main centers of worship for the Jewish people during the pre-monarchic period because of the presence of the Ark of the Covenant, God's holy presence, there in the Tabernacle. Later, when Solomon's Temple was constructed signaled the moment when sacrificial offerings would be offered at the first Temple for *410 years*. And, finally, the Jewish people brought their sacrificial offerings to God at the second Temple in Jerusalem for *420 years*.

Animals were sacrificed in such huge quantities at the Temple in Jerusalem that one scholar has described the entire Temple precinct as *a massive slaughterhouse*. In fact, if you read *only* what Solomon sacrificed on a few occasions, it is almost inconceivable to try to comprehend how massive the process and expense was to corral so many thousands of animals and transport them to Jerusalem to be sacrificed. The number of hands required to slaughter them and then offer them on the altar as burnt offerings is nearly incalculable.

The process of this immense sacrificing to God was such a massive endeavor that to do it required long-term planning, complex organization, and the employing of a substantial workforce to slaughter so many animals in such a short span of time. Thus, presenting a sacrificial offering was much more than a mere casual, physical act. It was a plan conceived in the heart and mind, and carried out purposefully and worshipfully.

This brings two passages to mind that give the *astonishing* numbers of burnt offerings Solomon offered to the Lord in Jerusalem. Second Chronicles 1:6 tells us, "And Solomon went up thither to the brazen altar before the Lord, which was at the tabernacle of the congregation, and offered *a thousand burnt offerings* upon it." Later we are told in Second Chronicles 7:5, "And king Solomon offered a sacrifice of *twenty and two thousand oxen*, and *an hundred and twenty thousand sheep*: so the king and all the people dedicated the house of God."

Once when I had dinner with a man who owned one of the largest slaughterhouses in the United States, he made a comment about these verses that deeply impressed me. He and I discussed the enormous number of animals that Solomon offered, and he said, "Even with all our advanced technology, we do not have the ability today to slaughter and process that number of animals in a short span of time."

He continued, "For Solomon to bring that many animals to the Temple mount was already a major feat, but to think those animals had to be killed, cut into pieces, and offered as burnt sacrifices means thousands of people were involved in the process."

This man finally said, "Even the biggest slaughterhouses can't do it today, so for Solomon to do it, we know it cost a fortune and required thousands of hands to carry out this nearly impossible task."

You see, a sacrifice wasn't merely presenting an animal to God as an offering — it included the desire to do it properly, in an honoring, reverential way;

the long-term planning to carry it out; careful organization; a workforce to do it; and all the astronomical costs associated with carrying out such a feat. And Solomon did it *over* and *over* as an intentional act of worship. Even more, amassed millions of Jews traveled to Jerusalem over many years to offer burnt sacrifices before the Lord. There was no temple anywhere else in the world where such infinite numbers of sacrifices were offered to any other god. This explains why Romans disparagingly referred to the Jewish religion as a *bloody religion.*

If you were allowed to look into history thousands of years ago to see the activities at the Temple in Jerusalem, you would see thousands of worshipers arriving with their families and their sacrificial animals that walked alongside them. Some came great distances, so they could not physically transport their sacrifice to the site. For them, special booths lined the exterior of the temple where they could purchase unblemished animals to offer as sacrifices to God.

But before the worshipers entered the Temple platform, they had to be ceremonially cleansed, so they stood in long lines to walk down stone steps into holy water to be ceremonially cleansed before entering the Temple precincts. And as one attempted to go up the steps to the Temple platform, he would have been thronged by other worshipers who were ascending the steps to reach the Temple Mount at the same time.

Finally stepping onto the Temple Mount, the panoramic view before a worshiper would have been breathtaking. The Temple was there with the brazen altar before it, where the sacrifices would be made. The smoke of burnt offerings billowed into the air, and the atmosphere was filled with the smell of animals and the bleating of sheep and goats, the bellowing of oxen, and the cooing of pigeons and turtledoves that had been brought to be sacrificed. The aroma of death pervaded the air from the stench of slaughtered animals. If you had been there, your ears would have also been filled with music and the sound of prayers that priests were proclaiming over the sacrifices and the worshipers. The entire temple complex was filled with the nonstop activity of priests running here and there to assist worshipers as they brought all sorts of sacrifices to God.

To help the myriad of worshipers with their thousands of sacrifices, priests had to be totally focused on the task of assisting others as they offered their sacrifices. Indeed, to be a priest in the Temple was a consuming task; it required every priest to be hard-working and constant. They knew that their priestly function was to serve God as well as the worshipers who had come great distances to bring premeditated and costly offerings to God.

And God commanded the Jewish people to come to Jerusalem three times a year to do it. In Deuteronomy 16:16, God commanded, "Three times in a year shall all thy males appear before the Lord thy God in the place which he shall choose; in the feast of unleavened bread, and in the feast of weeks, and in the feast of tabernacles: and they shall not appear before the Lord empty." Thus, we see that Jewish people were commanded to make a pilgrimage to Jerusalem *at least* three times a year — once for Passover, once for Shavuot (the Feast of Weeks), and once for Sukkot (the Feast of Tabernacles).

Deuteronomy 16:16 seems to say only men were to appear before the Lord in Jerusalem, but we know women and families accompanied them, and they bore the same spiritual obligations to offer various sacrifices. And as commanded, faithful Jews made at least three pilgrimages to Jerusalem each year to present themselves before the Lord and to bring Him sacrificial offerings.

For the Jewish people, sacrificial rituals were *deeply personal* and were to be *deeply felt*. For example, if a worshiper was seeking atonement for sin, it wasn't sufficient to merely bring a physical offering. The one who brought it had to *feel remorse* for his sin as the sacrifice was slaughtered and offered on the altar. One Jewish scholar stated that to genuinely repent, the person offering a sacrificial offering for sin had to realize that what was being done to the animal essentially should have happened to *him* instead.

Sacrifices were categorized as burnt offerings, sin offerings, guilt offerings, and peace offerings. In the case of a burnt offering, the animal had to be sacrificed entirely on the altar. In the case of a sin offering or a guilt offering, the animal was partially burned on the altar with the rest of it being consumed by priests. In the case of a peace offering, the animal was cut into pieces on the altar by priests or by the individuals who brought it to be sacrificed.

Jewish sacrifices typically consisted of oxen, sheep, goats, turtledoves and pigeons, but other sacrifices could consist of wheat or barley flour accompanied by olive oil, frankincense, and wine that was poured onto the altar. If oxen, sheep, and goats were brought as sacrifices, they were required to be blemish-free, as this was a gift for God, and it had to be the best that could be given. There were also specifications regarding the age and gender of the animals that were to be offered.

When a worshiper brought an animal to be sacrificed, the giver laid his hands upon it, confessed his sins, and the animal was slaughtered. Its blood was caught by the worshiper in a container so none of it would be lost. The blood was then sprinkled or smeared onto the altar, and the remaining parts of the animal were sacrificed on the altar. If the sacrifice offering was a bird, its blood was applied to the walls of the altar while the bird was sacrificed on the altar, and the remaining parts were eaten by priests. If one brought an offering of flour, the officiating priest scooped three fingers of flour onto the altar as a sacrifice, and the rest of it was eaten by priests.

Again, sacrifices were only allowed to be offered at the Temple in Jerusalem, so after the destruction of the second Temple in the year 70 AD, sacrifices, of course, ceased there. If Peter wrote his epistles *after* the destruction of the Temple, then all the Temple activities I just described were no longer being carried out. However, although physical sacrifices in that physical Temple had ceased, sacrifices actually never ceased in God's mind, because Christ called every believer as a member of a brand-new holy priesthood to offer up sacrifices of a *spiritual* nature. Physical, bloody sacrifices ended, but other sacrifices continued and do continue. Because each believer today is simultaneously a *temple* and a *priest*, it means any believer can offer up a "spiritual sacrifice" at any time and in any place.

This section was written to help you understand that sacrificial offerings in the Greek, Roman, and Jewish worlds were serious events that were not ever to be done haphazardly or in an aloof manner. There, emphatically, was *nothing* more consequential or serious in the ancient world than offering up a sacrificial offering. It was so important that rules, regulations, and protocol be explicitly followed in order to do it correctly. The whole process required each sacrificing person to do it with forethought — and organized, intentional planning was required to bring a sacrifice that was acceptable to God.

What Are the Sacrifices of a Holy Priesthood in the Temple of God Today?

At the first of this chapter, we saw the apostolic vision Paul communicated in Ephesians 2:21 of the Church as the new *naos* Temple for the Lord in the earth today. In Peter's epistles, he built on this same concept. He informed us that, whereas the priesthood formerly consisted of a small group of exclusive and elite individuals on a Temple Mount, now *every* believer is a believer-priest and a member of a "holy priesthood" within the Church, who is to offer up spiritual sacrifices that are acceptable to God.

That means the Church is to be filled with the nonstop activity of believers offering their own spiritual sacrifices and assisting others in bringing *their* spiritual "sacrifices" to God. True apostolic vision categorically envisions the

Church as a new *naos* Temple of God where every member in it is a full-time priest. The Church is a dwelling place for God's Spirit that is to be filled with divine activity and divine service. And we're told in Ephesians 4:12 that the role of each Christ-given fivefold ministry gift of apostle, prophet, evangelist, pastor, and teacher is to prepare God's people for such works of the ministry in the new *naos* Temple of God.

There is no doubt whatsoever that Peter's use of the words "holy priesthood" in First Peter 2:5 pictures *every believer* as a priest in God's house. First, we were chosen as the "living stones" — the materials God would use to construct this *naos* Temple. Then we were each appointed to be believer-priests entrusted with priestly functions and responsibilities.

So whether you're reading the inspired writings of Paul or Peter, both apostles definitely picture the Church as the new *naos* Temple where God's Spirit dwells and where every believer is a member of a holy priesthood in which he is expected to offer up sacrifices of a spiritual nature to God.

The Church is a dwelling place for God's Spirit that is to be filled with divine activity and divine service.

Indeed, the Christ-given apostolic vision is that the Church is the new *naos* Temple of God, and it is a sacred place God longs to populate with believer-priests occupied in offering "spiritual sacrifices" to Him. It was explicitly clear what priests and worshipers were to sacrifice to God before the destruction of the Temple. And it is clear what believer-priests are to offer up to God today.

But you may ask, "What *are* the spiritual sacrifices we are to offer to God today?"

Sacrifice Number One: the Sacrifice of the Body

In Romans 12:1, Paul tells us that all believer-priests are commanded to offer up *their body as a living sacrifice* every day. A part of the role of Christ-given fivefold ministry is to call for all believers to come daily to the altar to present themselves as living sacrifices. Any minister who is remiss to do this has failed at a basic level. Paul himself wrote, "I beseech you therefore, brethren, by the mercies of God, that ye present your bodies a living sacrifice, holy, acceptable unto God, which is your reasonable service" (Romans 12:1).

Especially notice the word "beseech" in Romans 12:1. It is a translation of the Greek word *parakaleo*, a compound of the words *para* and *kaleo*. The word *para* means *alongside*, and the word *kaleo* means *to call* or *to beckon*. When these two words are compounded, the new word depicts *a person who comes alongside someone else, as close as he can get, and then begins to passionately call out, plead, beckon, or beg the other person or group of people to do something*. In fact, the sense of pleading is so strong that one expositor suggested this verse figuratively shows the apostle Paul on his knees, pleading with his readers to hear what he is saying and to do what he is requesting. For sure, this is not merely asking — Paul is *prayerfully pleading* for his readers to hear his petition and obey it.

But the word *parakaleo* holds another layer of meaning. By early New Testament times, this word was used to describe military commanders who passionately addressed troops before sending them into battle. In this way, *parakaleo* means *to exhort*, and it depicts a leader urging his soldiers to take action, prepare themselves for a fight, and to brave the imminent battle with courage and a commitment to win, regardless of the difficulties that might lie ahead. This is no suggestion — *it is an earnest command!* Paul's use of *parakaleo* in Romans 12:1 means that in addition to *earnestly pleading* with his readers, he also conveyed that what he was about to ask them to do would require commitment to obey it regardless of the battle or struggle they faced in order to do it.

But what *was* this difficult challenge Paul was urging each of them to intentionally engage in? Paul continued, "I beseech you therefore, brethren, by the mercies of God, that ye present your *bodies* a living sacrifice...."

The word "bodies" is the Greek word *soma*, which refers to *the physical body*. Paul called on believers everywhere to offer up their physical bodies as a living sacrifice to God — that is, to put their bodies on the altar, as it were, and to dedicate them as "a living sacrifice" to God.

Paul knew this endeavor would be a battle to overcome because the body by its fleshly nature does not want to be laid on the altar. Flesh desperately desires to be in full control and actively resists God's pleading for surrender. Hence, like a military commander, Paul exhorted God's believing troops to surrender their bodies to the Lord regardless of how their flesh tried to circumvent this decision.

The body by its fleshly nature does not want to be laid on the altar. Flesh desperately desires to be in full control and actively resists God's pleading for surrender.

Paul's language in this verse is peculiar because, according to history and traditions, there had been no such thing as a *living* sacrifice. When a sacrificial animal was killed on an altar, the act was final, and the animal couldn't protest or scream out after the fact that it didn't want to be sacrificed. All sacrifices were *dead*, and by the time they were laid on the altar, they had no more voice to resist.

But in Romans 12:1, God calls on us to present our bodies as *a living sacrifice.* He seeks for those who belong wholly to Him to lay themselves on the altar, to *stay* on the altar of their own free will, and to stay there as a "living sacrifice."

We are to be completely surrendered to Him, dedicated to His purpose, living entirely for Him — *24 hours a day, 7 days a week.* Just as priests in physical temples had to be focused to carry out their priestly duties, staying on that altar and remaining surrendered will require your focused attention.

Paul also importantly said, "I beseech you therefore, brethren, by the mercies of God, that ye *present* your bodies a living sacrifice...."

The word "present" is a translation of the Greek word *paristemi*, which means *to place at one's disposal, to surrender, to offer a sacrifice to God, to present as a special offering to God,* or *to dedicate once and for all.* It is the exact word used in Luke 2:22 to depict when Mary and Joseph "presented" Jesus to God in the Temple. The use of the Greek word *paristemi* explicitly tells us that when Mary and Joseph "presented" Jesus that day, they surrendered and placed Him at God's disposal. They offered Jesus as a sacrifice to God and dedicated Him once and for all. On that day, Jesus was the offering they presented, and they never backtracked on their promise.

Likewise, by using the word *paristemi* in Romans 12:1, Paul is telling each of us to *officially dedicate ourselves — once and for all, forever — to the plans and purposes of God.* It is a sacrifice never to be retracted, and one that all believer-priests are called to offer to God each day.

When Paul says we are to present our "bodies" as a living sacrifice, the context of this verse involves our *physical body* as well as all the faculties of our soul — our mind, will, and emotions. So I must ask, are you presenting your physical body *and* your mind, will, and emotions as a living sacrifice to the Lord every day? This is the beginning place for fulfilling your priestly functions and responsibilities.

Recall that in First Peter 2:5, Peter said we are to "offer up" spiritual sacrifices. Again, the words "offer up" are a translation of the Greek word *anaphero*, which pictures *an individual who puts forth effort to dig deep to find what is precious to bring it out of hiding and to the surface.* This means you'll have to put effort into bringing the sacrifice of your body to the altar. Furthermore, the prefix *ana* at the first of the word indicates it is an act to be done *repeatedly*, so presenting our bodies to the Lord is a decision to be *repeated* over and over. There are vast numbers of believers who have never officially said, "Lord, I'm giving You my body — it's Yours and it's no longer mine. My physical person is at Your disposal once and for all." But Romans 12:1 clearly tells us this is one of our foremost priestly responsibilities.

The *mind* is another area many Christians have never officially surrendered to God. They have given Him their heart, but often their thinking remains in their own control. Deuteronomy 6:5 says, "And thou shalt love the Lord thy God with all thine heart, and with all thy *soul*, [consisting of the mind] and with all thy might." So according to this verse, dedicating our mind to the Lord is not a suggestion; *it is a command.*

Are you presenting your physical body *and* your mind, will, and emotions as a living sacrifice to the Lord every day? This is the beginning place for fulfilling your priestly functions and responsibilities.

God wants you to "present" your mind to Him once and for all because the mind is the control center of your life. Proverbs 23:7 tells us that as a man

"...thinketh in his heart, so is he...." Whoever controls your mind ultimately controls everything about you — what you do, what you say, and what you believe.

Have you ever said, "Lord, I officially present to You my mind as my sacrifice to You. It's Yours and no longer mine. My memory banks and thinking capacity are at Your disposal once and for all." If you have not surrendered your mind to the Lord as a believer-priest, you need to do it so your mind will be under the full lordship of Jesus. Romans 12:1 clearly means this is your priestly function and your priestly responsibility every day.

There are multitudes of believers who have given Jesus their hearts, but they have never fully yielded the control of their *emotions* to Him. Emotions are powerful and can be very unpredictable. When your emotions are not under the lordship of Jesus, they can become a weapon that quickly leads you in the wrong direction, making you say and do things you later regret. Proverbs 25:28 (*NKJV*) confirms this saying, "Whoever has no rule over his own spirit is like a city broken down, without walls."

Romans 12:1 calls on you to "present" your emotions once and for all to God as a part of your becoming a living sacrifice. Once again, the word "present" is the Greek word *paristemi*, which means *to present once and for all.* This means God calls on every believer-priest to once and for all present his body, mind, emotions, and all that he or she is to the Lord *as a special offering to Him.*

That means *you* are to surrender yourself and all your faculties, placing yourself at His disposal. And although you're to do it *once and for all*, Paul's words in Romans 12:1 emphatically include presenting your emotions to God as another of your priestly functions and priestly responsibilities that you are to repeat, or affirm, every day.

The word "sacrifice" in Romans 12:1 is the Greek word *thusia*, which we earlier saw means *to sacrifice or give up something precious and dear as a sacrifice.*

It includes *the celebration, pageantry, and prayers that accompanied that moment when a worshiper came to an altar to offer a sacrificial offering or burnt sacrifice.* The word *thusia* also came to depict *one's surrender* or *one who gave up something that was precious and dear.*

A sacrifice was expensive because it cost a giver something to offer it. Likewise, to become a living sacrifice will require *a death to self.* Such a living sacrifice occurs when you bow your will, dethrone self, enthrone Jesus by choosing to submit to His lordship, and choose to obediently live to fulfill His commandments. This is a renewed daily sacrifice of saying *no* to self and *yes* to God.

As noted earlier, there was no such thing as a *living* sacrifice in the ancient world because sacrifices that weren't dead were not considered a sacrifice; the shedding of blood was required for a sacrifice. In other words, if a person walked off with a living animal, all he did was make a spectacle.

Likewise, we can put on a show and say a lot of impressive words about how we want to surrender our lives to God — but until we do it, it is nothing more than a spectacle. For us to be a living sacrifice, we must be willing to crawl onto the altar, surrender ourselves, yield what is precious and dear, if needed, and be willing to renounce all claims to ourselves, fully surrendering to the purposes of God.

A living sacrifice occurs when you bow your will, dethrone self, enthrone Jesus by choosing to submit to His lordship, and choose to obediently live to fulfill His commandments. This is a renewed daily sacrifice of saying no to self and yes to God.

Dying to *self* is an act of surrender we must perform *daily.* If there is no death to self, there is no sacrifice. And when we once and for all make this act of surrender, we must realize we are no longer our own, which is why Paul wrote, "What? know ye not that your body is the temple of the Holy Ghost which is in you, which ye have of God, and ye are not your own?" (1 Corinthians 6:19). From the moment we present ourselves to Him, we become holy — that is, we are set apart, consecrated, and dedicated to God and to His purposes. This is what it means to be *a living sacrifice*.

So when Paul wrote in Romans 12:1 that we are *to present our bodies as a living sacrifice*, he was beseeching us to climb onto the altar daily to present ourselves to God. As believer-priests, every one of us, *each day*, are to place ourselves on the altar and say, "God, I am presenting myself to you. I surrender to You my body and soul — including my mind, my will, and my emotions. I choose to die to what I want, what I think, and how I feel about things, and I humbly place myself at Your disposal."

When a believer in the new *naos* Temple of God presents himself or herself as a living sacrifice, it is a "holy" event. Paul uses the word "holy" in Romans 12:1 — the word *hagios* in Greek, which means *separated*, *consecrated*, *made holy*, or *made sacred*. Thus, when a believer-priest presents his life as a living sacrifice to God, that act elevates him into a *sacred* category. Although all believers are called by God to do it, many never have. But when a believer surrenders himself as an offering — a "living sacrifice" — to the plans and purposes of God, it truly moves that believer into a category that is very special in the eyes of God.

When a believer surrenders himself as an offering — a "living sacrifice" — to the plans and purposes of God, it truly moves that believer into a category that is very special in the eyes of God.

What Does 'Acceptable to God' Really Mean?

It is so impactful when a believer offers himself or herself to God as a living sacrifice. Paul said it is a sacrifice that is "acceptable" to God. The word "acceptable" in Romans 12:1 is a translation of the word *euarestos*, which is a Greek word that means *fully agreeable*, *fully pleasing*, or *fabulous*, and it depicts *a sacrifice that God has accepted and approved*. Here we discover that God is euphoric when a believer-priest in the new *naos* Temple surrenders himself or herself in this way. This is a sacrifice that is well-pleasing to God. He accepts it, "consumes" it, and subsequently fills it with His presence.

In Romans 12:1, Paul continued to say that giving ourselves as a living sacrifice is our "reasonable" service. The word "reasonable" is a translation of the Greek word *logikos,* a word that means *logical* or *rational.* Plutarch used this word to depict something that should be done *intellectually* and *rationally*, as opposed to *emotionally*.[29]

This is important because making the intellectual choice to offer up ourselves as a living sacrifice cannot be based on fickle feelings that easily change. Hence, Paul implores us to *intellectually decide* and *rationally choose* to offer ourselves as living sacrifices. God's expectation is for every believer in the new *naos* Temple to begin his priestly duties of offering up spiritual sacrifices by first offering up *himself*.

In Romans 12:1, Paul remarkably adds that this is our reasonable "service." The word "service" is a translation of the Greek word *latreia*, which is the exact word used to depict *priestly service that is rendered according to priestly protocol.* The use of this word leaves no room for misunderstanding. Paul is emphatically conveying that just as temple priests followed a protocol of offering sacrifices each day, we are to follow a *daily protocol* of offering ourselves to God. This is where priestly service begins, and it cannot be sidestepped if we are to be faithful believer-priests in the new *naos* Temple of God. Offering ourselves as a living sacrifice is a lifelong priestly occupation.

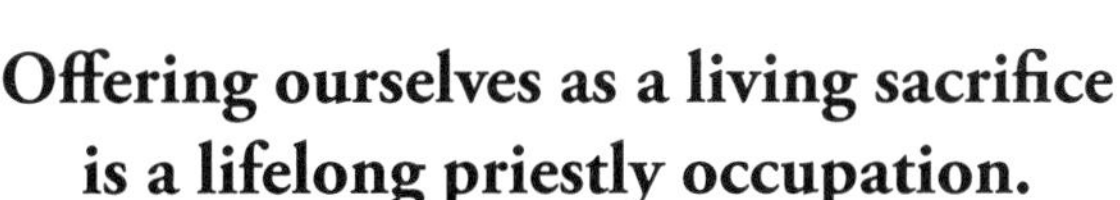

Offering ourselves as a living sacrifice is a lifelong priestly occupation.

Sacrifice Number Two: the Sacrifice of Prayer

Whether Jewish or pagan, every priest in the ancient world knew he was to offer *sacrificial prayer* as a priestly function. At the Temple in Jerusalem, priests knew they were to offer up prayers to God and that the "incense" of prayers would ascend to Heaven, where they would enter into the nostrils of God. Offering up sacrificial prayer was a paramount function of all priests, and it is likewise the honor of every believer-priest today to bring sacrificial prayer to God.

In Psalm 141:2, David refers to the sacrificial incense that is released when sacrificial prayer is offered to God. He said, "Let my prayer be set forth before thee as *incense* in and the lifting up of my hands as the *evening sacrifice*."

Also, in Revelation 8:3 and 4, we read that the prayers of the saints ascend to Heaven, where God smells *the sweet aroma* of their prayers. Those verses say, "And another angel came and stood at the altar, having a golden censer; and there was given unto him much *incense*, that he should offer it with the *prayers of all saints* upon the golden altar which was before the throne. And the *smoke of the incense*, which came with the *prayers of the saints*, ascended up before God…."

In Ephesians 6:18, Paul urges all believers to step into their priestly function of offering up prayer. He said, "Praying always with all prayer and supplication in the Spirit, and watching thereunto with all perseverance and supplication for all saints." The word "always" tells us that offering prayers to God is a chief responsibility of every believer-priest, or every born-again believer in Jesus Christ.

In this verse, Paul used a form of the word *proseuchomai* when he wrote, "*Praying* always with all *prayer....*" Both "praying" and "prayer" are a translation of the Greek word *proseuchomai*. This word is a compound of *pros* and *euchomai*. The word *pros* means *toward* and implies *closeness*; the word *euchomai* means *to offer a request*. When compounded to form *proseuchomai*, it means *to come near to offer a request*. It refers to *the prayer of consecration* that is offered at an altar of sacrifice.

Face-to-Face Intimacy With God

When we take a closer look at the word *pros* — the first part of the word *proseuchomai* — we see that it is a preposition that actually in this context means *face to face* or *eyeball to eyeball*. It is the very word used in John 1:1 to describe the intimate relationship between Jesus and the Father. That verse says, "In the beginning was the Word, and the Word was *with* God, and the Word was God." The word "with" in this verse is taken from the Greek word *pros*.

By using this word to describe the relationship between the Father and the Son, the Holy Spirit is telling us that theirs is an *intimate* relationship. One translator has translated John 1:1, "In the beginning was the Word, and the Word was *face to face* with God...." It is a picture of such close intimacy that God the Father and Jesus His Son could nearly feel each other's breath upon their faces. Nearly everywhere the word *pros* is used, it carries the meaning of *a close, up-front, intimate contact* with someone else. And when it is used in connection with prayer, it means God is calling us to a place of face-to-face intimacy with Him.

The second part of the word "prayer" in Ephesians 6:18 — a form of the Greek word *proseuchomai* — is derived from the Greek word *euche*, an old Greek word that describes a *wish*, *desire*, *prayer*, or *vow*. The word *euche* was originally used to depict a person who made some kind of vow to God because of a need or desire in his or her life. This individual would come to an altar, and instead of offering the sacrifice of an animal, the person would *vow* to sacrifice or give something of great value to God in exchange for a favorable answer to his or her prayer. Such sacrificial offerings were called "votive offerings" (derived from the word "vow").

A perfect example of this can be found in the story of Hannah, the mother of Samuel. Hannah deeply desired a child, but was not able to become pregnant. After being barren year after year, she cried out to God in great desperation and anguish of spirit. On one of her family's annual trips to worship and sacrifice to the Lord in Shiloh, First Samuel 1:10,11 says: "And she [Hannah] was in bitterness of soul, and prayed unto the Lord, and wept sore. And she vowed a vow, and said, O Lord of hosts, if thou wilt indeed look on the affliction of thine handmaid, and remember me, and not forget thine handmaid, but wilt give unto thine handmaid a man child, then I will give him unto the Lord all the days of his life, and there shall no razor come upon his head."

Notice that Hannah made a *solemn vow* to the Lord and said, in essence, "Lord, if You answer my prayer and give me a son, I will give him back to You to serve You all the days of his life."

This is a vivid picture of the word *proseuchomai*. And we see God's response to her prayer in just a few verses where First Samuel 1:19,20 tells us, "And they [Hannah and her husband, Elkanah] rose up in the morning early, and worshipped before the Lord, and returned, and came to their house to Ramah: and Elkanah knew Hannah his wife; and the Lord remembered her. Wherefore it came to pass, when the time was come about after Hannah had conceived, that she bare a son, and called his name Samuel, saying, Because I have asked him of the Lord."

You must keep in mind that the majority of Paul's readers were Greek in origin, but when they saw the Greek word *proseuchomai* in Ephesians 6:18, they, too, understood the ramifications of what was being said to them. They understood that prayer was intended to bring them face-to-face and intimately close (*pros*) to God. They also realized that prayer would bring them to an altar, where they would make a divine exchange — where they would consecrate and fully yield themselves to God and where He would respond by answering their request and providing them with what they needed.

Because the word *proseuchomai* has to do with these concepts of *surrender* and *sacrifice*, this tells us that God desires to do more than merely bless us. As believer-priests, we are called by God to the altar, where the Holy Spirit may convict our hearts concerning areas that need to be surrendered to His sanctifying power. He will never forcibly take these things from us; *we* must surrender them. Thus, we see that *prayer* points to a place of decision and consecration — it's an altar where we freely vow to give our lives to God in exchange for His life.

When we as believer-priests "come to the altar" and offer prayer to God, our prayers arise like incense to His nostrils. The new *naos* Temple of God is to be filled with believers who carry out their priestly function to lift up the incense of prayer to God. As we do, the sweet aroma produced by prayers reaches the nostrils of God as a well-pleasing aroma that invites face-to-face communion, the blessing of His presence, and a divine exchange of our lives for *His* life in the particular thing we are praying about.

Sacrifice Number Three: the Sacrifice of Praise

Hebrews 13:15 tells us of yet another sacrifice that believer-priests are to offer God in the new *naos* Temple called *the Church*. It says, "Therefore by Him let us continually offer *the sacrifice of praise* to God..." (*NKJV*). This verse clearly says all in God's house are to offer "the sacrifice of praise" and to do it "continually." Let's begin with the word "continually" in this verse.

This word is translated from the Greek words *dia pantos,* and these words literally mean *through all, through all situations, continually, at all times,* or *continually.* This is certainly not instruction to thank God *for* all situations, as we are never to accept what is evil or destructive. But herein is God's instruction for believer-priests to offer the sacrifice of praise *in* all situations.

The word "offer" is once again the word *anaphero,* the word used to picture priests inside a temple whose responsibilities were to *offer physical sacrifices upon an altar.* But it is important to note again that the prefix *ana,* means *up* and carries the idea of *repeating an action.* Thus, every believer-priest in the new *naos* Temple of God today is *to repeatedly offer up* the *sacrifice of praise.*

It should be no surprise that the word "sacrifice" is again the Greek word *thusia,* which means *to sacrifice, surrender, or give up something precious and dear.* This means that for a believer to offer a sacrifice of praise, it may cost something to do it. For example, it's a sacrifice when your soul argues that there is nothing to praise God about. It's a sacrifice when you have to overcome a bad attitude or foul mood to praise the Lord — or to praise Him in the midst of your attitude or mood. It's simply a fact that sometimes you need to deal with an uncooperative soul in order to bring a "sacrifice of praise" to God.

The word "praise" is a translation of the Greek word *ainesis,* a word that depicts *audible expressions of praise.* Because it is so connected to "sacrifice" in this verse, the message is clear that it can be very sacrificial to offer verbal — audible — praise to God at times. But if you are in a tough spot in life and do not "feel" like offering audible praise to God, you can push your soul and flesh to the side and choose to do it anyway. In such moments, your praise is indeed a "sacrificial offering" that you brought to the Lord. God knows when this is difficult for you to do, and He is honored when you bring a verbal, or *audible*, "sacrifice of praise" to Him.

Sacrifice Number Four: the Sacrifice To Serve God and Others

It is interesting that immediately after Hebrews 13:15 instructs us to offer a "sacrifice of praise," the following verse gives another sacrifice that all believer-priests are to be engaged in offering to the Lord. It says, "But do not forget to *do good* and to *share*, for with such *sacrifices* God is *well pleased*" (Hebrews 13:16 *NKJV*). Here we discover that the mere acts of "doing good" and "sharing" can be sacrificial offerings which every believer-priest is called to offer to God in His new *naos* Temple.

This verse says that when we "do good" and "share," it is a sacrifice acceptable, or well-pleasing, to God. Just as bringing a sacrifice of praise can be very sacrificial to do, we are now instructed that there are times when "doing good" and "sharing" can indeed also be very sacrificial. But these are sacrifices with which God is "well-pleased" according to Hebrews 13:16.

The words "do good" are the plural translation of the Greek word *eupoiia*, which is a compound of *eu* and *poieo*. The word *eu* means *swell, well, wonderful*, or *really pleasurable*, and the word *poieo* means *to do* and is the same word from which we get the word "poet," which depicts an individual who possesses some kind of a creative flare. Compounded, it means to creatively do good, meaning if you cannot conveniently find a way to do good, then *get creative and FIND a way to do good to others!*

The words "to share" are translated from the word *koinonias*, a word that pictures *contributory help* to others as opposed to ignoring the needs of others and refusing to help. In Hebrews 13:16, the word "sacrifice" is, again, *thusia*, which means that sharing with others may be a very sacrificial thing to do. Serving others may require us to sacrifice something precious and dear, like time and money — giving up previously planned activities or changing our plans to use money in another way in service to God or others. But if you do it with a right heart, it is a sacrifice that is *well-pleasing* to Him.

The words "well-pleasing" is the word *euaresteo*, a compound of *eu* and *aresko*. The word *eu* means *swell*, *well*, *wonderful*, or *really pleasurable*, and the word *aresko* means *enjoyable* or *pleasing*. As we saw earlier in this chapter, this word describes something *well-pleasing*, or it depicts *the intense pleasure one feels* from seeing or experiencing something *pleasurable* or *delightful*. Hebrews 13:16 says when we serve others, Heaven is thrilled with such sacrificial service. As we serve God and assist others in the Temple of God, our personal sacrifices arise like sacrificial incense to Heaven, where God receives a sweet aroma of priestly service that is well-pleasing to Him.

Sacrifice Number Five: the Sacrifice of Our Finances

Priests in the Temple at Jerusalem brought their own sacrificial offerings to God in addition to assisting others in bringing theirs. Likewise, as believer-priests in the new *naos* Temple of God, we are to be engaged in bringing financial gifts to the Lord that are sacrificial for us to give.

In Philippians 4:18, we read that the Philippian believers had sent a very sacrificial financial gift to Paul for his ministry. He told them in response, "But I have all, and abound: I am full, having received of Epaphroditus the things which were sent from you, *an odour of a sweet smell, a sacrifice acceptable, well-pleasing* to God."

Paul wrote that their sacrificial financial gift was "an odour of a sweet smell" in the nostrils of God. These words are a translation of the Greek word *euodia*, a compound of *eu* and *odzo*. As we just saw, the word *eu* means *swell*, *well*, *wonderful*, or *really pleasurable*. The word *odzo* depicts *an odor* that could be either enjoyable or offensive. However, when the word *eu* is affixed to the front of *odzo,* it emphatically depicts *an odor that is swell, well, wonderful, or really pleasurable.*

Paul knew the enormous offering they sent to him was indeed a sacrifice, so that's what he called it in this verse — a "sacrifice." Again, the word "sacrifice" is the Greek word *thusia*, which depicts *a sacrifice, a surrender*, or *a giving up of something precious and dear*. The use of the word "sacrifice" tells us that for the Philippians to send the financial gift they sent, it was a very sacrificial act. For them to give it meant they denied themselves in some way. Perhaps it was money they'd planned to use in another way, or maybe it was a sum that was simply beyond their natural ability to give. Perhaps it required a disruption of their own financial plans in order to give it. But, for sure, the use of *thusia* tells us the financial gift they sent for Paul's ministry was sacrificial; it cost them something to give it.

In Philippians 4:18, Paul teaches that when believer-priests in the new *naos* Temple of God offer up such financial sacrifices, it is "acceptable" to God. That word "acceptable" here is a translation of the word *dektos*, an infrequently used Greek word depicting a person or action that is *warmly received in an acceptable and welcomed manner*. This means God throws open the doors, rolls out the red carpet, and embraces what we bring when He knows it has required a sacrifice to give it and that giving it, therefore, was a true matter of the heart.

Then Paul concluded by saying that such financial sacrifices are "well-pleasing." The words "well-pleasing" is, again, from the Greek *euarestos,* depicting the *intense pleasure* one feels when he has seen or experienced what someone else has done. God finds it pleasurable when believer-priests give sacrificially, and He throws open the door to embrace the *giver* and the *gift*!

As Old Testament priests at the Temple in Jerusalem were continually offering up expensive burnt offerings of animals, today believer-priests in the *naos* Temple of God are to continually bring the sacrifices of our finances. But when we bring a very large financial sacrifice for God's work, Philippians 4:18 declares that it especially brings a sweet aroma to the nostrils of God that He receives, responds to, and generously blesses.

When we bring a very large financial sacrifice for God's work, Philippians 4:18 declares that it especially brings a sweet aroma to the nostrils of God that He receives, responds to, and generously blesses.

Sacrifice Number Six: the Sacrifice of Speaking for God

In First Peter 4:11, Peter speaks of another sacrifice all believer-priests are to regularly offer in the new *naos* Temple of God. Most miss what Peter meant because they don't understand the context of the verse, but in that verse, Peter wrote, "If any man speak, let him speak as the *oracles* of God...."

The Greek word for "oracle" is *logion*, a word that was used in the original Greek language to describe a person who was *a channel* or *a mouthpiece for the spirit realm*, and thus called an *oracle*. Today we would call these individuals "mediums."

- Herodotus used the word *logion* to depict anything uttered by an oracle. The word *logion* even depicted *the geographical location where an oracle was known to regularly speak and to utter prophecies.*[30]
- Euripides used *logion* to picture a prophetic utterance. But he also noted that the word *logion* was very connected to sacrificial offerings

because such offerings were given to gods or to the spirit realm to try to provoke the gods to speak.[31]

ARE ALL BELIEVERS TO BE PROPHETIC?

You'll see how this applies to every believer-priest today in just a moment, but first let me take you into the world of ancient oracles so you'll understand Peter's reason for using the word "oracle" in First Peter 4:11. In the First Century, the word "oracle" was well known, so Peter used it intentionally to convey an important message to us that would compel us to accept, as one of our priestly functions, to serve as *a mouthpiece for God* in the new *naos* Temple called the Church. This means to some degree that God intends for all believers to be *prophetic.*

The word "oracle" was mostly used in the pagan world, but before we see how they used it, let's first go to the Hebrew language to see how the word "oracle" was also used among the Jews in ancient times. In Hebrew, the word "oracle" has the basic meaning *to say* or *to speak*, and it implies *the verbal response of God* or *the place where God's voice can be heard.*

The manner in which the Jews received these forms of *divine utterances* varied greatly. That is why Hebrews 1:1 says, "God, who at sundry times and in divers manners spake in time past...."

The words "divers manners" are a translation of the Greek word *polutropos*, a compound of *polus* and *tropos*. The Greek word *polus* means *a great number* or something that is *multitudinous*, *plenteous*, or *numerous*. The Greek word *tropos* means *a way* and even depicts *twists and turns along the way* — it therefore pictures something that is *unconventional.*

Compounded, the Greek word *polutropos* in Hebrews 1:1 carries the idea of God speaking in the past *in a great number of unconventional ways.* In the Old Testament, at times God spoke face-to-face, as with Moses; at other times by dreams and visions, as with Joseph; and at still other times by signs and tokens, as with Gideon and Barak. And sometimes God spoke through a mysterious system of communication, such as the Urim and Thummim. But the writer of Hebrews states that at long last, God is speaking clearest of all through His Son (*see* Hebrews 1:2).

In the New Testament, we find that the word "oracle" appears multiple times to describe how God communicated in the past. For example, we read in Romans 3:2 that there was a time when the "oracles" — the speaking voice of God through a number of unconventional ways — was entrusted to the Jews. At that time, God spoke through angels, prophets, thunder, clouds, lightning, and a long list of ways God unconventionally communicated in the past. But the word "oracle" even in Hebrew pictures *a divine speaking* or *divine communication* that somehow transpired supernaturally between God and His people.

Ancient Pagan Oracles

However, the word "oracle" was mostly used among pagans to depict various kinds of supernatural communication connected to some form of divination. To pagans, the word "oracle" usually signified an answer given through a medium who had yielded his or her voice to gods or to the spirit realm. This was so demonic that Early Church fathers wrote that such oracles were actually manifestations of demons speaking from the realm of the spirit.

Nevertheless, ancient pagans really believed oracles were *channels* or *mouthpieces* for gods and the spirit realm, and they revered mediums who yielded their voices so the gods and those spirits could speak through them. They believed gods and the spirit realm could be consulted through these mediums and that a seeker could receive counsel, direction, and mystical prophetic utterances by consulting one.

The most famous oracle in the ancient world was the Oracle at Delphi, a female priestess called *the Pythia*, who served as *a channel* or *mouthpiece* for the spirit realm at the Temple of Apollo. In that ancient city, there was a pagan shrine located on the slopes of Mount Parnassus above the Corinthian Gulf, so close to Corinth that a person standing on the slopes of Corinth would likely see the smoke billowing into the air across the bay where ancient Delphi was located on the side of that sacred mountain.

The word *Pythia* used to describe this female medium was from the Greek word *puthon*, which is the Greek word for *a serpent* and from which we derive the word "python." An ancient legend said that the god Apollo killed a massive serpent at the site of Delphi, and that its decomposing body rotted in a crevasse on the slopes of Mount Parnassus where the Temple of Apollo was later constructed. Pagans believed this female medium, called the *Pythia*, was an oracle — that is, a medium, channel, or mouthpiece — for the spirit realm, but especially for Apollo. The Delphi site became famous and people journeyed there to consult with the medium. Pagans longed for communication with the spirit realm and spent enormous sums and traveled great distances to see this oracle, who was the most renowned in the pagan world.

The *Pythia* at Delphi postured herself astride a three-pronged, three-legged altar that sat directly inside the Temple of Apollo — on the same kind of altar that typically would have been used for offering burnt sacrifices to the gods. As she sat astride the three-pronged, three-legged metal altar, she gave herself as a living sacrifice to the gods and the spirits so they would speak through her. As she yielded to these invisible forces, she uttered riddles with supernatural answers to those who had come to her for divine counsel and prophetic direction.

The Oracle at Delphi became so legendary that seekers traveled days, weeks, and even months to reach Delphi to seek guidance. This included notable seekers, such as Croesus, king of Lydia, who resided in the city of Sardis and came to ask the oracle if he should cross the river to attack Persia. The medium mystically answered in a riddle: "If you cross the river, a great empire will be destroyed." King Croesus took it as a divine signal to proceed with the invasion, but the great empire that was destroyed was his own.[32]

It is interesting that in Acts 16:16, we read of a girl who had a spirit of divination. Talking about the apostle Paul and his companions, that verse says, "And it came to pass, as we went to prayer, a certain damsel possessed with a spirit of *divination* met us...." The word "divination" is the Greek word *puthon*, which is the same word used to describe the female medium at Delphi. It is entirely possible this girl with a spirit of divination in Philippi was considered to be an oracle in her community. Paul eventually cast that spirit out of her, but before she was freed, she had brought great gain to her masters because people paid enormous sums of money for her services as a medium.

Other oracles could be found in various places in the ancient world, including Thebes, Tegyra, Boeotia, Phocis, Thessaly, and Delos. In Anatolia, oracles could be found at Patara, Branchidae, Claros, and Grynium.[33] But no oracle anywhere in the pagan world was as revered as the Oracle of Delphi. In fact, even the name Delphi is important, for it is the Greek word for a woman's womb, and it was used to describe the city of Delphi because Greek-speaking peoples believed it was the central spiritual womb for all Greek religions. As such, the temples that were scattered up and down the slopes of Mount Parnassus at Delphi were filled with nonstop burnt offerings — sacrifices that swirled and wafted into the air above the peak of the city.

I realize all this talk of oracles seems dark, but the idea of an oracle was common in both the Jewish and pagan worlds. So when Peter said, "If any man speak, let him speak as the *oracles* of God..." (1 Peter 4:11), he was using a word that was well known both to Jews and Greeks. To both, the word "oracle" described some kind of divine communication associated with a person or a place where sacrificial offerings were made so that divine communication could occur. Peter used this word intentionally to describe the need for believer-priests to likewise become yielded vessels through which the Holy Spirit could speak and work in line with God's spoken and written Word.

Just as oracles in the past gave themselves as living sacrifices to the spirit realm, by using the word "oracles," Peter calls on each of us to yield ourselves at the altar of God and to consecrate ourselves as living sacrifices for God Himself to use. Doing this may mean sacrificing personal comfort and surrendering whatever else that may be required so you can yield to the Holy Spirit without the hindrance or distraction of the flesh.

Pagan oracles were completely surrendered, yielded individuals who gave themselves entirely as full-time vessels to become a mouthpiece for the spirit realm. Peter — knowing full well the customary usage of this word — used "oracles" to communicate the responsibility of believer-priests in the new *naos* Temple of God to possess a willingness to surrender to the *Holy Spirit* so that He and His gifts can operate through us to strengthen the Church and bless humanity.

In the past, an oracle was a person or place where divine communication occurred, and seekers had to travel great distances to the remote locations where these oracles could be found. But today *every* believer-priest has become an oracle because he is indwelled by the Holy Spirit. That means wherever we are, we can be a channel or mouthpiece through whom the Holy Spirit can speak. But to be an instrument the Holy Spirit can use, we must daily climb onto the altar of surrender to give ourselves as living sacrifices to God, yielding to the Holy Spirit's control in every area of our lives so we can be an instrument God can use to help bring answers, direction, and assistance to others.

Doing this kind of yielding as a believer-priest may mean sacrificing your personal comfort zone to yield to the Holy Spirit and to say or do what He instructs you. But as ancient oracles were completely surrendered, yielded individuals who gave themselves entirely as full-time vessels to become a mouthpiece for the spirit realm, Peter communicates that every believer-priest is to offer up himself in the *naos* Temple of God as a living sacrifice that the Holy Spirit and His gifts can operate through.

In these pages, we've seen a small sampling of the "spiritual sacrifices" that every believer in the new *naos* Temple is to offer up to God. But the fivefold ministry gifts of *apostle*, *prophet*, *evangelist*, *pastor*, and *teacher* are given to assist and equip all believer-priests in this *naos* Temple to offer up spiritual sacrifices that are acceptable to God by Christ Jesus.

Again, as the first and second Temples in Jerusalem overflowed with priests who were continually offering up sacrifices and assisting others in offering up theirs — with smoke and incense filling the atmosphere and ascending upward to Heaven — the Church today is to be a dwelling place for God, a *Temple*, that's filled with believer-priests who are occupied with carrying out priestly functions and responsibilities.

BEFORE MOVING ON...

In the first and second chapters of this book, I listed many verses and dove deeply into history and Greek word studies in an attempt to provide you with the *apostolic vision* of the Church that was communicated by Paul and Peter in their various epistles. If you feel that you have not grasped it all yet, please reread these sections because what is written in the first two chapters is foundational to everything else you will be reading in subsequent chapters.

I am aware this is not easy reading and it requires deep thinking. It is written to those who are searching for God's heart for the Church and who also long to understand the specific roles that apostles and prophets played in the Church historically and the roles they play in this present hour and in the days ahead for the Church.

So far we have seen that Jesus is the Head of the Church, which is the Body of Christ in the earth today — and that God's intention is for the Body of Christ to reach spiritual adulthood before the climax of the age. We have also established that the Church is the new *naos* Temple for God's mighty indwelling presence in the earth today — and that every believer is a priest in a holy priesthood, who is to be occupied with offering up spiritual sacrifices in this great spiritual House.

We have also seen that the function of the fivefold ministry gifts of apostle, prophet, evangelist, pastor, and teacher is to help build the Body of Christ and the new *naos* Temple, equipping and preparing every member to take his God-assigned place and to perform his sacrificial priestly ministry.

In the next chapter, we will finally begin to examine the role that Christ-given apostles are assigned to fulfill in the Church both historically and in the present. I believe you will find what God has to say about this fivefold ministry gift will be eye-opening and life-changing.

Questions for Deeper Consideration

Chapter 2

1. After reading this chapter, what would you say is the chief metaphor used by Paul in his epistles to depict the Church?

2. This chapter documented various examples of prominent temples that were constructed in the ancient world. Can you recall which of them was the largest temple ever constructed? Can you recall which of them was the most expensive temple to ever be constructed in history? And in terms of today's monetary values, do you recall what amount of money was spent to construct the most expensive temple ever built?

3. For what reason did the value of gold in some parts of the Roman Empire fall by 50 percent after the treasures inside the Temple were plundered by Titus and his Roman troops in 70 AD? How did the Roman government use the gold that Titus and his troops plundered from the Temple in Jerusalem?

4. In Revelation 1:12, Christ symbolically refers to the Church as being like "gold." Why did Christ state that the Church is "golden" in His sight? After what you have read in this chapter, how does Christ's "golden" view of the Church affect your own view of the Church?

5. In Second Corinthians 4:7, Paul stated that we have "this treasure in earthen vessels." I want to ask, What does the word "treasure" mean to you after reading this chapter? And exactly what is the treasure inside you? Furthermore, what do the words "earthen vessels" mean? How do these insights affect your own self-image and your honor for the presence of the Holy Spirit in the Church?

6. This chapter provided a simple explanation of the fivefold gifts of the *apostle*, *prophet*, *evangelist*, *pastor*, and *teacher* in construction terms. So can you now explain how the apostle is used in the building process in the Church? Or can you express the role of the prophet in the divine building process? How would you explain the role of an evangelist in the process of building the Church? How would you articulate the role of a pastor in the building of the Church. Lastly, can you explain the building role of a teacher as he works alongside the other fivefold gifts who are each doing their parts in building the Church?

7. In First Peter 2:5 we read that God is building the Church to become a Temple that is composed of "living stones." What does it mean that God is building the Church to be a Temple in the earth? And what or who are the "living stones" He is using to construct it?

8. Romans 12:1 clearly commands each of us to present ourselves to God as a living sacrifice. In this chapter, I provided five different ways we are each to offer ourselves as living sacrifices to God and to His service. What are the five ways we are each to offer ourselves to God in a sacrificial manner?

CHAPTER 3

WHAT IS AN APOSTLE?

And he gave some, apostles; and some, prophets;
and some, evangelists; and some, pastors and teachers;
for the perfecting of the saints, for the work of the ministry,
for the edifying of the body of Christ.

— Ephesians 4:11,12

Now that we've covered the apostolic vision for the Church given by Paul and Peter, let's at last turn our attention to the Christ-given fivefold ministry gifts of apostles and prophets. We will begin by focusing on what the Bible says about New Testament apostles.

We have already seen that Ephesians 2:20 says the Church is "...built upon the foundation of the apostles and prophets, Jesus Christ himself being the chief corner *stone*." Since the work of apostles and prophets is foundational to the Church, it is imperative that we have a biblical understanding of the foundational work they each perform. But in this chapter, we will begin with the Christ-given gift of *the apostle.*

The denomination to which I belonged when I was growing up taught that all apostles ceased to exist at the end of the "Apostolic Age" and that there was no such thing in our day as a living apostle. To our way of thinking, the term "apostle" applied only to a group of 12 legendary men who walked with Jesus some 2,000 years ago, and once that exclusive group of 12 died, it was the end of apostles.

The theology I grew up hearing wouldn't sanction someone in the contemporary world being called an apostle. In fact, to call someone an apostle seemed like a blasphemous insult to the original 12 apostles. Even to my own young ears, to hear someone calling a living person an apostle was tantamount to stealing a precious title that only belonged to those original 12 apostles of Jesus. In those days, it would have offended me to the core if I heard a living person being called an "apostle." But today we know that the gift of the apostle is still with us and will continue unto the end of the Church Age.

In the 1500s, scholarly Christians who spoke and read Latin, for various reasons, began to use the word "missionary" as a replacement for the word "apostle." By definition, a missionary is one who is sent by ecclesiastical authorities to labor for the propagation of the faith in a place where it has not existed before or to assist with the establishing of a Gospel work.

The word "missionary" is a wonderful word to describe those who have been dispatched on such missions; however, it is not a correct term to describe an apostle. Some people are really called and mightily anointed to be *missionaries* — those who sense a need to go on a "mission" to help the work of God. A small percentage of those whom we call missionaries are indeed apostles, but it is imperative to understand that simply being a missionary does not qualify a person as an apostle.

My own extended family has a long missionary history, and I have no adequate vocabulary to express the respect I have for the work they have done on the mission field. They are heroes for what they have done with their lives. But they are not apostles, nor would they ever claim to be apostles. They are examples of mightily anointed, God-sent missionaries, who worked to help advance the Gospel where they were dispatched to work.

However, as I've stated, this serious work of serving in places where one is dispatched — or led or called to serve — does not qualify someone to be an apostle. Over the ages, the Church has sent thousands of people into the world as missionaries to labor for the propagation of the Gospel. And, oh, how we need mission-minded people — *true missionaries* — who are sent by their local church or denomination to help on the mission field. But that work, albeit important and necessary, does not constitute an apostolic call.

Before I go any further, I also want to make it unequivocally clear how thankful I am for the denomination I grew up in because it laid a solid foundation of Bible doctrine underneath my life. But our denomination did not embrace the reality of present-day apostles or prophets, nor the present-day operation of the gifts of the Holy Spirit. We were what is called *cessationists* — which means we believed the ministry gifts of apostle and prophet, and other spiritual gifts (*see* 1 Corinthians 12:7-11), were nonexistent as present-day gifts. In other words, we believed those things *ceased* at the end of the Apostolic Age. We were selective as to what we believed *ceased* and what we believed *remained.* In other words, we absolutely believed the *evangelist*, *pastor*, and *teacher* were valid present-day ministries that transcended the Apostolic Age.

Especially since the outpouring of the Holy Spirit in the early 1900s, God began to bring correction to incorrect teaching and, thankfully, today, many understand that miracles, signs, wonders, and gifts of the Holy Spirit are very alive and well in the Church. And while no one ever debated the need for fiery evangelists, powerful pastors, and God-gifted teachers, many in the Body of Christ were finally awakened to the fact that apostles and prophets — whom many previously believed no longer existed — are also alive and well and *needed* in the Body of Christ.

In Ephesians 4:11-13, we are told by Paul that the Church cannot reach full maturity unless *all* five of the Christ-given fivefold ministry gifts are imparting their unique portions of Christ to the Church — to the building of the *"naos"* Temple of God. In this chapter and the three following chapters, we will see that, like the other fivefold ministry gifts, the gift of apostleship is an *essential element* to carrying the Church upward to Her destiny as a "...glorious church, not having spot, or wrinkle, or any such thing..." (*see* Ephesians 5:27). All of the Christ-given fivefold ministry gifts — *including the apostle* — must be active "till we all come in the unity of the faith…" (Ephesians 4:13) at the end of the Church Age.

From One Ditch to the Other Ditch

Before we proceed to see what an apostle is, I feel the need to make a statement about the correct and incorrect use of the term. Because of an insufficient understanding of the word "apostle," in recent years, it seems we have gone from not believing in modern-day apostles to jumping into the other ditch of calling *too many* people apostles — which, of course, includes many who categorically are *not* apostles. Because there has not been clear, concrete teaching about the ministry of the apostle, people seem to be confused as to what an apostle is and does.

For example, I have heard many call people *the apostle of prayer*, *the apostle of finances*, *the apostle of faith*, *the apostle of parenting*, *the apostle of praise and worship*, and so on. Although many of these individuals are indeed respectable leaders in their particular fields of ministry — amazing God-called specialists in their respective areas and groundbreaking pioneers who have helped pave a new path and lead the way for others — that does not qualify them to be called apostles. While many notable individuals — some my close, personal friends — have done groundbreaking work in areas that should be recognized and honored, being pioneering and innovative does *not* qualify a person to be an apostle.

It seems we have used the term "apostle" as a badge of respect to endorse a minister's hard work and ground-breaking, pioneering efforts, but this is an incorrect use of the word "apostle" that has created confusion.

Of course, I believe in showing honor where honor is due, but the problem seems to be that some, although they mean well, simply don't understand what the word "apostle" really means. Therefore, we are seeing the word "apostle" used very sincerely, albeit wrongly, over and over again. The result is that the *awe* and *respect* that is biblically attached to the word "apostle" has been diluted and, sadly, nearly lost altogether. I am convinced that if the apostle Paul were alive today and saw the growing list of people who are called "apostles" in magazine articles, on television, and in other media, he would be *aghast*.

Two thousand years ago at the inception of the Church, Paul was already waging warfare with some who claimed to be apostles, but were not, so this is not a new problem. However, 2,000 years ago, there was no confusion about the meaning of the word "apostle," as you will see in the pages that follow. In early New Testament times, many claimed to be apostles who were not, but they did it deliberately *because* they understood the great *weight* and *influence* that went along with the name "apostle." It seems that some *intentionally* claimed this title because they believed it would give them leverage over God's people. Those back then who misused this term did so deliberately because they believed it would give them an advantage over others, and that is why Paul took such a strong stand against them.

If the Church in its infancy 2,000 years ago was dealing with confusion about who was and wasn't an apostle — and Paul was already at that early stage trying to set the matter straight — I am sure he would be *astonished* to see the misuse of the word "apostle" today and to witness the seemingly endless list of people who are claiming to be apostles!

Do Apostles Abound in the Church Today?

Apostles are *real* and *powerful* as a fivefold ministry gift, but only a *handful* of those who claim to be apostles today are real apostles — that is, compared to an ever-growing list of those who claim to be apostles or who are incorrectly called apostles by others. By the way the word "apostle" is being used today, I am convinced that people who use this word wrongly are simply uninformed about *what* and *who* an apostle is. Anyone who really grasps what and who an apostle is, and what an apostle does, would not freely apply that title so casually to so many people.

Although the apostolic ministry was deliberately misused by many in the Early Church, I want to be *kind* to those who incorrectly call themselves apostles or who incorrectly call others apostles today because I believe the misuse of this term is largely due to *unclear teaching* on the subject of apostleship.

Words and terms are very important. When a very specific term that applies to very few people — like the word "apostle" — is used too freely or loosely, it gives the false impression that apostles abound in the Body of Christ, and this simply is not the case. But most who incorrectly use the term apostle do it out of ignorance because there is so little clarity on the subject. My purpose in this book is to help you gain a biblical grasp on the gift of apostleship.

In the First Century when the New Testament was being written and the Church was being established, the word "apostle" was an important and very well-known word that was understood and that carried great authority even in the ambassadorial, educational, governmental, military, philosophical, political, and other parts of the secular world. As you read further, you'll understand more ramifications of the word "apostle" and the powerful concepts that were instantly and automatically conveyed when people heard this word.

Do You Know What the Word 'Apostle' Means?

If Christians today were asked to provide a description of what an apostle is, most would say, "An apostle is someone who is a leader" or, "An apostle is a person who has done something new, innovative, and pioneering." Occasionally one might even answer, "An apostle is someone who starts churches." Even though that last answer comes a little closer to the truth, even *it* is an overly simplistic statement. These common answers show a great deficiency of information and understanding about *what* and *who* an apostle is.

Many people would, partly correctly, say, "An apostle is someone who starts churches!" But to illustrate how insufficient that answer is, let me ask you — how many people do you know who have started a church? Does merely starting a church make them a Christ-given apostle? If the answer is simply that an apostle is someone who starts churches, it means any person who starts a church is an apostle. But that is not the case, so there must be more to the word "apostle" than the superficial answer that "apostles start churches," even though they certainly do start churches as a part of their Christ-given calling.

Church leaders around the world — reputable people who have taught on the subject of apostleship — have expressed to me that they have often felt frustrated by their inability to articulate what an apostle is and what he does. They agree that simply saying "apostles are *sent ones* who start churches" feels like a shallow answer. Dissatisfied and feeling that surely there must be more to the word "apostle" than simply saying that apostles start churches, these leaders know this simple explanation is insufficient, yet they often don't know what else to say on the matter. I see this, again, as the result of a lack of teaching and information on a very important topic. For centuries, this subject wasn't deemed necessary or important to explain or teach about because most denominational thinking did not believe apostles currently existed.

But to show how much confusion there is in general, even today, about fivefold ministry, let me tell you about a particular event at which I was invited to be one of the speakers.

It occurred at a conference years ago at a very dynamic, exciting church. The speaker who preceded me asked the crowd, "How many of you are called into the fivefold ministry?" I turned to see how many hands were raised, and to my shock, it looked like 80 to 90 percent of the crowd raised their hands to say they were called to be either an apostle, prophet, evangelist, pastor or teacher — one of the fivefold ministry gifts. I'm talking about hundreds and hundreds of people, and this was not a ministerial meeting; it was just a regular church conference.

So I feel the need to categorically state that everyone is *not* called into fivefold ministry — and that the gifts of *apostle, prophet, evangelist, pastor*, and *teacher* are much rarer than the large conglomeration of people who today call themselves by these names or who are called these names by those who misuse the terms to describe them. The overuse of fivefold ministry names has given the incorrect impression that these Christ-given gifts can be found in large doses and that people can be self-titled and self-called. The result is the awe, respect, and weightiness that Christ intends for these authentic gifts to possess among us — so they can perform their building, equipping, and unifying function — is degraded.

However, it is important to note that a person can be *apostolic*, *prophetic*, *evangelistic*, *pastoral*, or have a heart for *teaching* without being a Christ-given *apostle*, *prophet*, *evangelist*, *pastor*, or *teacher*. For example:

- Many have *an apostolic heart* to see the Gospel advance and churches established, but having an apostolic heart and being an actual Christ-given fivefold ministry gift of *apostle* are not the same thing. Every apostle needs people who have apostolic hearts to help, but having an apostolic heart and even serving alongside an apostle doesn't mean you're an apostle. Therefore, everyone serving on an apostle's team is not an apostle. If your desire to help see the church established in new places is strong, it *could* be God's way of providing you direction to develop a fivefold ministry call — or, *more likely*, it is direction as to where you should be serving in the church or in someone else's ministry.

- Many have *a prophetic tendency* or a *prophetic leaning*, but having a prophetic leaning or tendency and being an actual Christ-given fivefold ministry gift of *prophet* are not the same. Paul even said that we can all prophesy, but he never said that prophesying made us Christ-given fivefold prophets (1 Corinthians 14:31). If you have a leaning toward prophecy that is especially strong, it could simply be God's way of providing you direction as to where you should serve in the church or in someone else's ministry.

- Many have *a heart for the lost*, as we all should, but having a heart for the lost and being an actual Christ-given fivefold ministry gift of *evangelist* are not necessarily equivalent. Shouldn't each of us have a heart for the lost? Perhaps the anointing of the evangelist is developing in you. Yet if your desire to reach the lost is particularly strong, it could simply be God's way of providing you direction as to where you should serve in the church or in someone else's ministry.

- Many have *a heart to help care for others*, but having a caring heart and being an actual Christ-given fivefold gift of *pastor* are not the equivalent. Simply having a caring heart does not mean a person stands in the fivefold ministry gift of pastor, because we should all have a caring heart for others. It's possible that the anointing of a pastor is developing in you, but if your desire to care for others is strong, it *could* be God's way of providing you direction as to where you should serve in the church or in someone else's ministry.
- Many people have *a heart for Bible teaching* and love to share insights from the Bible with others, but loving to share the Bible and being an actual Christ-given fivefold gift of *teacher* are not necessarily the same. We should all enjoy sharing the Bible with others, but if your desire to share truths from the Bible is strong, it *could* be God's way of showing you where you should be serving in the church or in someone else's ministry, where they can grow their gifts as they are being "...faithful in that which is another man's" (Luke 16:12).

As a result of confusion on these matters, multitudes of sincere believers wrongly think they are called to all kinds of things that they are not. One example is, there are so many people today who claim to be prophets that I do not know how one could possibly keep count of the growing list of names of those who claim to stand in this fivefold office. The vast majority of them are people who have a leaning toward prophetic things, but they have mistakenly taken it to mean they are actual prophets. While I praise God for their sincerity and spiritual desire that I find to be so commendable, this misunderstanding has really confused things on many fronts.

The biblical qualifications and characteristics, or *signs*, of both prophets and apostles that I share in this book can help people know whether they're called to the fivefold ministry or to some other walk of life — including serving in someone else's ministry, where they can grow their gifts as they are being faithful to their assignment.

But hang on. If you have felt you might be called to one of these two offices of *apostle* or *prophet* — or you know someone who does — this book will help you know whether you're on the right track or not. The good news is that, whether one is called to serve God in the fivefold ministry or not, God has a unique, *precise* plan for every believer on the planet — including *you*!

In this chapter, we are talking specifically about the Christ-given gift of *apostle*, so I want to say that most who incorrectly call themselves apostles, or who are incorrectly called apostles by others, err simply because they do not know the real meaning of the word "apostle." I say again that a person may be a real innovator and be good at successfully pioneering and starting things — but that alone does not qualify a person to be an apostle. As I told you earlier, the Church was once in the ditch of not believing in present-day apostles at all — but now we strangely find that many have jumped into the *other* ditch of freely calling any pioneering person an apostle simply because he is groundbreaking, innovative, or pioneering.

When the apostle Paul wrote his second epistle to the Corinthians, he was deeply concerned about people misusing the word "apostle" and even wrote about how deeply disturbed he was by "false apostles" (2 Corinthians 11:13).

I find it interesting that the words "false apostles" are translated from a single Greek word *pseudapostolos*, which is compounded of the two words *pseudes* and *apostolos*. The word *pseudes* carries the idea of *any type of falsehood*. It can picture *a person who either intentionally or unintentionally projects a false image of himself* or *someone who walks under some pretense or who projects an image that is untrue*. Whether the falsehood is intentional or unintentional, the result is the same: The person is giving a false or untrue impression about something. A more up-to-date translation of the words "false apostles" could be *pretend apostles* or *bogus apostles*.

In subsequent chapters, I will deal with the criteria necessary to prove who is and isn't an apostle — and those criteria or "signs of an apostle" are *very* telling. But right now, I want you to understand that the Greek word for "false apostles" depicts both *unintentional* and *intentional* falsehood. I think this is so important because it emphatically lets us know that some who wrongly claim to be apostles do it *innocently* — and there are others who egregiously do it *intentionally*.

It is important to note again that the Greek word *pseudapostolos* — translated "false apostles" in Second Corinthians 11:13 — definitely lets us know that some who misuse the term sincerely, but wrongly nonetheless, do not comprehend what they are saying — most likely because they do not understand what a real Christ-given apostle is.

I am careful not to accuse people who incorrectly claim to be apostles. I choose to believe (at least in most cases) that the misuse and overuse of this term is due to ignorance about who an apostle is and what an apostle does. But before we delve further into the following chapters where we will begin seeing the role of apostles in the past, present (contemporary), and the last-days Church, it is imperative that we back up to see where the word "apostle" originates. If we can understand and grasp exactly what the word "apostle" meant to believers in the First Century, it will help *us* know how and when this powerful word should be applied in this end-time age of the Church. Christ is still building His Church (*see* Matthew 16:18), and He is still using His fivefold ministry gifts to do it!

In the following pages, we will dive into the various Greek meanings of the word "apostle" to discover its diverse historical usages in the ancient world and how it all carried over into New Testament times. My intention is not to give you a history lesson, but to help you gain *a foundational understanding* of exactly what early New Testament ears understood 2,000 years ago when they heard the word "apostle." You will probably be surprised to discover all the various applications the word "apostle" had at that time, how it applied to apostles in the Early Church, and what these various meanings tell us about those in our own time who are true Christ-given apostles.

The Greek Word 'Apostle'

No one wrote more extensively about the ministry of Christ-given apostles than the apostle Paul himself. He used multiple powerful metaphors to depict apostolic ministry, which we will get to in subsequent chapters.

But for now, let's journey back in time to see where the word "apostle" came from and what it meant to New Testament ears. By going backward in time to look at these various usages and nuances of the word, you will learn how the word "apostle" was used *before* and *during* the time of the early New Testament and how it applied to the ministry of authentic Christ-given apostles then and how it still applies in our world today.

Let's begin with the Greek word that is translated "apostle" in the New Testament, which is the Greek word *apostolos*, an old word compounded from the preposition *apo* and the word *stello*. The preposition *apo* means *away* and the word *stello* means *to send*. When these two words are compounded, it forms the word *apostolos* — that is, of course, translated "apostle" — which in its simplest meaning and form depicts *one who is sent away.*

This Greek word appears more than 80 times in the New Testament, but the root of *apostolos*, which is the word *apostello*, is used more than 132 times in the New Testament and more than 700 times in the Old Testament Greek Septuagint! I give you these figures to show you that the use of *apostolos* and *apostello* is very well established in the Bible.

Again, before we dive into the specific use of this word *apostolos* (the word "apostle") in Scripture, I want to note how various writers in the ancient Greek world used this word. Since the word *apostolos* is such a notable Greek word, we must see how legendary Greeks used it, as this set the stage and painted a vivid picture for how this word would also be used in the New Testament.

- The Greek playwright Euripides and historian Thucydides used *apostolos* to describe *important packages that were sent* — special packages sent by powerful people that contained powerful and important contents.[1]
- The Greek philosopher Aristotle used it to picture the *seeing off* or *sending away* of important individuals.[2]
- The Greek historian Herodotus used it to describe *a high-powered ambassador who had been sent to represent a government or king.*[3]
- The Greek pagan priest, historian, philosopher, magistrate, and ambassador Plutarch used this word to depict *the sending away of a trade ship filled with cargo.*[4]
- The Greek philosopher Plato and historian Polybius likewise used this word to depict *a huge ship that was fully loaded with cargo and a specialized crew to accompany an admiral who was venturing into new territory to construct a new community.*[5]
- The satirist, philosopher, and speechwriter Lucian, along with the historian Lysias and Demosthenes and Plutarch all used this word to depict *a fully equipped large fleet that was sent on an expedition to a new territory.*[6]

As it is used in the New Testament, the word *apostolos*, or "apostle," depicts individuals who were *appointed*, *empowered*, or *invested with authority* — either by the leadership of the Church or by the Lord — and were *dispatched to represent leadership to do some kind of special task.*

As used by the Church in early New Testament times, the word "apostle" was *only* used to depict *individuals who were dispatched either by the Church or by Christ Himself to establish the Church in places where it had not previously existed.* The Greek word *apostolos* — "apostle" — categorically had no other application in the times of the New Testament. Therefore, the word "apostle" *never* refers to one self-appointed, but depicts an individual who was selected, empowered, invested with authority, and dispatched to accomplish a special task by *a sender.*

But let's keep digging to see how all these significant historical meanings of the word "apostle," used so heavily in ancient times, carry over into the New Testament. There were many noteworthy usages of the word, and all of them had *significance* and were carried into the New Testament's meaning of the word "apostle."

'Apostle' as a Maritime Word

Long before the word *apostolos* was ever used in the New Testament, it was a specific term that was very connected to *seafaring.* As already noted, Plato and Polybius used the word *apostolos* in this sense to depict *a huge ship that was fully loaded with cargo and a specialized crew to accompany an admiral who was venturing into new territory.* And we also saw that Lucian, Lysias, Demosthenes, and Plutarch each used this word to depict *a fully equipped large fleet that was sent on an expedition to a new territory.* Additionally, Plutarch used this word to depict *the sending away of a ship filled with cargo.*

From this very well-established usage of *apostolos* ("apostle"), it can be clearly seen that this word was used as a naval term to describe:

- The admiral of a fleet of ships.
- The fleet of ships that traveled with him.
- The specialized crew who accompanied and assisted the admiral as he sailed to locate territories where civilization was nonexistent and then construct a replica of their own life, language, and culture there.
- The supplies and cargo needed to sustain the crew and to establish civilization where it had been nonexistent.

Thus, the ancient Greek word *apostolos* — the New Testament word for an *apostle* — was used in a maritime sense to picture a highly powered *admiral* and his specialized crew who were sent off with all the cargo and belongings needed to sustain them and to establish a civilization where it had been non-existent. That admiral — called the *apostle* — along with his specialized crew, set sail to virgin lands where they disembarked and settled down to establish life as they believed it should be. Once on land after they disembarked, the admiral — *apostolos* —became the team's on-the-ground, onsite leader, who then led the entire crew as they established and constructed a new community that had never existed before. In other words, they were *colonists.*

In most cases, these ancient Greek colonists, who were led by an *apostolos*, aimed to replicate their civilization in new regions. They were so committed to expansion that they planted Greek colonies across the Mediterranean world — from the shores of the Black Sea, Crimea, Anatolia (modern-day Turkey) to Bactria in the Far East to the southern coast of the Iberian Peninsula in the West, as well as Magna Graecia (southern Italy). Colonies were also established on the Libyan coast of northern Africa, and significant Greek colonies were established on the coast of ancient Illyria on the Adriatic Sea.[7]

These specially trained colonists were dispatched under the leadership of their apostle to spread their culture and influence across the world. Because of the bravery needed to colonize a new region — often where people were considered to be barbarians — colonists were considered to be heroes, and it was common to honor these founders as such after their death.

But to fulfill this task of colonizing new territory, these admirals (called apostles) also needed in their fleets *associates*, *assistants*, *secretaries*, and all the resources needed to carry out their assignments to colonize new territories. Hence, when an admiral — an *apostolos* or apostle — disembarked from his fleet of ships to walk down the plank into a new region, he didn't walk onto the new site alone, but with other team members as a part of his apostolic crew.

Due to the nature of the *apostolos* or apostle's assignment, it was impossible for him to travel alone or to attempt to do this job by himself. So again, we see that this man who was initially an admiral of a specialized fleet of ships then became a high-powered leader once on the ground, leading the establishing of a new colony and civilization. The daunting task before him was so huge that he found it necessary to work side by side with an apostolic crew. It required him to think as a team leader and to depend on his fellow team members and associates to help him in constructing the new colony.

Once on land, the admiral — that is, the *apostolos* — along with his apostolic team immediately surveyed the new location to identify challenges, difficulties, and whatever advantages they could find there. Once this first step concluded, they began the difficult process of transforming a strange land. It required commitment to the task, endurance to withstand opposition, and stamina to brave the obstacles as they began the process of replicating life as they believed it should be.

Their purpose was total *colonization* of new and often unfamiliar, dangerous, or even uncivilized territory until it became a replica of their own culture. This colonization included teaching their language, laws, and customs to the natives in that new place. It also included the building of infrastructure, roads, buildings, houses, and of course, *temples* for the worship of their various gods. In this sense, the admiral fulfilled the position of architect, designer, foundation-layer, building director, and construction-site overseer. The task before him was huge and required many hands who worked in sync with the admiral.

To fulfill his task, the admiral had specialized workers with him who were trained to build roads, to construct buildings, and to teach uncivilized natives how to read, write, and function in a new kind of society. So when his special fleet of ships pulled up to shore, the admiral — the *apostolos* — possessed both the personnel and the resources required to establish a new culture, a new life, and a new community.

Exactly how long the admiral remained in one location with his crew depended on the challenges that arose with each new location. Some regions were easier to colonize; others were harder. But the admiral — the *apostolos* or apostle — did not move to the next location with his team until the process of colonization was well underway.

However, finally, when a new region was settled and the process of colonization was substantially underway, the admiral, along with certain members of his apostolic team, reboarded the ships to set sail again to find other uncivilized areas and new territories so they could repeat the entire colonization process all over again. Meanwhile, other members of the apostolic team remained long-term in each new colony to maintain continued oversight of what they had built and of ongoing development.

So we find one of the most important meanings of the word *apostolos* was given to us by the combined writings of Plato, Polybius, Lucian, Lysias, Demosthenes, and Plutarch. The collective insight of these ancient writers lets us know that the word *apostolos* was a term to describe an admiral who sailed the high seas looking for new regions that needed to be civilized; his specialized team that traveled with him; and the cargo and supplies they carried with them. Then once on the ground, that admiral "apostle" became the team leader to lead his team to establish new communities in new territories.[8] *Wow. That is powerful insight to the word apostle!*

The Work of an Apostle in 'Regions Beyond'

There is so much more to learn about the word *apostolos.* But if we stopped here, we would already understand how the meaning of this Greek word impacts the New Testament understanding of the apostle. To early New Testament ears, an *apostolos* — "apostle" — was a high-powered individual dispatched either by the Lord or by the Church to launch out with a team into virgin territories where the Gospel had never been preached and to establish the Church where it had never existed before.

This explains why the apostle Paul boasted that his apostolic focus had primarily been on "regions beyond," where no one had ever gone or worked before him (*see* 2 Corinthians 10:16). With his apostolic team that regularly traveled with him, Paul ventured into theretofore untouched territories. Once they arrived, he and his team embarked into that region to preach the Gospel, drive back darkness, and press forward to spiritually colonize a once dark region until the culture and life of the Church was established where it had never existed before.

From reading the book of Acts and Paul's various epistles, it is clear that in the same way those ancient admirals — "apostles" — always traveled with a team, Paul nearly always traveled with a God-called team during his own apostolic journeys. Acts 13:13 tells us that "Paul and his company" traveled together. As an *apostolos*, or apostle, who was entering new territory, Paul knew he needed God-called people who were gifted to help him, so he traveled with team members such as *Barnabas*, *Silas*, *John Mark*, *Timothy*, *Erastus*,

Sopater, Aristarchus, Secundus, Gaius, Timothy, Aquila and Priscilla, Tychicus, Trophimus, and *Luke.*

The book of Acts shows Paul traveling alone only *once* when he entered the city of Athens, and I find it interesting that Paul's time in Athens *alone* was one of the low periods of his ministry. After Athens when he traveled on alone to Corinth, he was supernaturally joined by the God-called team of *Aquila and Priscilla.* Though Paul was mightily gifted as an apostle, he could not do the task alone and thus needed the side-by-side participation of others who would help him in establishing the Church in each new location. Yes, Paul was unquestionably the admiral who led the expedition — the *apostolos*, or apostle — but he needed a God-called apostolic team alongside him to fulfill his apostolic assignments.

As was true with the historical admirals described in the preceding paragraphs, the length of time that Paul and his team remained in each region before launching out to do it again depended on the difficulty of the task in each region. A study of the book of Acts reveals that Paul and his team stayed longer in some places than others. But once the establishing of the Church was underway in each new location, it wasn't long before Paul set sail again to do it all over in the next new location.

Hence, this meaning of *apostolos* — the New Testament word for a Christ-given apostle — is one of the earliest and foremost described definitions in ancient Greek times. And as you can see from a brief overview of the apostle Paul's own experiences, those ancient descriptions have a significant bearing on the idea of apostleship in the New Testament.

So we first find that one of the earliest usages of the word *apostolos* is that it was a naval term to describe *an admiral, the fleet of ships that traveled with him, and the specialized crew who accompanied him* as he sailed into open seas to locate territories where civilization was nonexistent so he could colonize them — that is, replicate life, language, and culture there as it should be. But in the case of the New Testament apostle, his assignment is the establishing of the Church where it has never existed before. *What a perfect description of a New Testament apostle!*

'Apostle' as *a Package, a Travel Document,* or *a Passport*

There is more to learn about the word *apostolos* and its unique nuances and meanings. As we've seen, the Greek playwright Euripides and historian Thucydides also used this word to describe *important packages that were sent* — special packages sent by powerful people that contained powerful and important contents.

This lets us know that Christ-given apostolic gifts are "packages" sent by the Lord or by the Church, and that these Christ-given individuals are filled with powerful contents. This is why Paul could confidently tell the Romans, "And I am sure that, when I come unto you, I shall come in the fulness of the blessing of the gospel of Christ" (Romans 15:29). As an apostle, Paul understood that he was a divine package sent by Christ and that he carried within him the anointing of God and everything needed for everywhere Jesus was sending him. As a divine package sent by Christ that carried the anointing of God, a real apostle is a package who carries that anointing to do whatever is necessary when he shows up!

As we continue our study, we will also see the amazing fact that the word *apostolos* was closely associated with ideas connected to *travel.* In fact, it was so closely linked to travel that it even eventually became synonymous with the concept of *a travel document* or *a passport.* That's right, over time, the word *apostolos* — translated as "apostle" — became a well-known technical term to depict *a travel document* or *a passport.*

Today, if a person wants to exit a country, travel abroad, or enter a new country, he or she must present a *travel document* or a *passport* to cross a border and enter a new country. In the ancient world as well, people were also often required to possess a travel document or the equivalent of a passport to travel abroad or to enter a new country. It was essentially *a legal travel document.* That *travel document*, or *passport*, guaranteed an individual *the right of passage and the ability to move freely from one place to another.* In the ancient Greek-speaking world, these travel documents were called an *apostolos* — which, of course, is the word that is translated "apostle" in the New Testament.

As a divine package sent by Christ that carried the anointing of God, a real apostle is a package who carries that anointing to do whatever is necessary when he shows up!

Some suggest an example of such travel documents or passports can possibly be found in Romans 16:1 and 2, where Paul wrote, "I commend unto you Phebe our sister, which is a servant of the church which is at Cenchrea: that ye receive her in the Lord, as becometh saints, and that ye assist her in whatsoever business she hath need of you: for she hath been a succourer of many, and of myself also."

The city of Cenchrea was a luxurious port city situated on the Saronic Gulf, about five miles from the ancient city of Corinth. During the time Paul lived and worked in Corinth, the port city of Cenchrea was one of two major ports travelers could use to access the city-state of Corinth, and it was the primary port travelers used when they intended to sail east. Romans 16:1 informs us that in this flourishing port city, there was a local church, probably started while Paul was based temporarily in Corinth.

In Romans 16:1, Paul refers to a woman named Phebe who was "a servant of the church which is at Cenchrea." Then in verse 2, we are told in the *King James Version* that Phebe had been a "succourer" of many. This old King James word is a translation of the Greek word *prostatis*, a word that gives the image of one who gave legal assistance to others. One scholar has suggested that because Phebe lived in Cenchrea, a significant seaport on the east side of lower Greece, her job may have been to provide *travel documents* to those who entered and exited that part of lower Greece through the port at Cenchrea.

It cannot be said with certainty that this was the way Phebe had been a "succourer" of many, but knowing the legal system of that day, such travel documents *were required* for those entering or exiting at the port of Cenchrea. At such a port, arriving ships were filled with people who had to present a travel document to enter the region. And those who were departing the region to sail east, likewise, had to present the equivalent of *a travel document* or *a passport.* These documents were a requirement for movement in and out of the area, and these documents were called an *apostolos.*

It is important to understand that travel in antiquity was difficult, expensive, and required proper documentation to freely move about. Widespread travel was primarily done in the interest of warfare and diplomacy, for visiting religious sites, or for traveling abroad for health-related reasons. But regardless of why one was traveling, it would have been difficult and nearly impossible to move about freely without a *travel document* or the equivalent of a *passport* to guarantee the right of passage. These documents, called an *apostolos*, provided a person the ability to move from one region to another.

In many cases, if travelers did not have an *apostolos* document, travel was restricted, and borders were frequently even closed to those who *did* have proper documentation. Regions that were highly sensitive or considered more volatile required an even higher level of documentation with higher authorization. This meant if a person wanted to travel into a region that was highly sensitive or volatile, no admittance would be granted without that person possessing an *apostolos*-type document. Yet in those regions that were more sensitive or volatile, it was even more difficult to obtain these *apostolos* documents.[9]

I wonder if you can see how this aspect of the word *apostolos* applies to the Christ-given gift of apostle in the New Testament. Let me make sure you connect the dots to see how this applies to the Church of early New Testament times and today.

Just as *a travel document* or *a passport* is a door-opener that is needed to journey into new regions or new territories, this additional ancient use of the word *apostolos* informs us that an apostle is anointed like *a travel document* or *a passport* that opens doors for him and his ministry that may not ordinarily be open for others. That apostolic anointing enables him to have supernatural passage into new territories. Indeed, his anointing supernaturally gives him the *right of passage* into new geographical regions and territories that would be normally difficult, if not impossible, to enter. This means a bona fide apostle is graced and supernaturally anointed to cross difficult barriers into new regions so he and his team can colonize that new territory for the Kingdom of God.

I will tell you that I personally know authentic apostles, and it is my observation that they *thrive* in territories that others find difficult or nearly impossible to even penetrate. I am not implying that their task is easy. Frontline, apostolic work can be very difficult. But an apostle is especially anointed to supernaturally cross into new territory. Once there, he becomes like a divine bulldozer to clear demonic rubbish out of the way so the process can begin for the establishing of the Church where it has never existed before.

Look at the ministry of Paul and you will see he was regularly entering new territory and seizing new opportunities where the Gospel had never been preached and where the Church had been nonexistent. In Paul's letters, he even writes about "open doors" that were set before him to reach into virgin territory.

For example, in First Corinthians 16:9, Paul wrote, "For a great door and effectual is opened unto me, and there are many adversaries." It is amazing that doors that were shut to others opened for Paul — but that was because he had the anointing of God upon him like *a divine travel document* or *a divine passport* that enabled him to pass into new and often hostile territories. That anointing was a part of his God-given equipment to do the work that a genuine apostle is called to do in virgin territory.

The word "great" in the phrase "great door" in First Corinthians 16:9 is a translation of the Greek word *megale,* which describes something *enormous* or *massive*. The word "door" is a translation of the Greek word *thura,* which in history described a door that was usually locked shut with a heavy bolt that slid through rings attached to the door and the frame. This kind of door was normally sealed tight, but Paul said that what had been sealed tight for others swung wide open for him.

Paul also called it an "effectual" door, and that word "effectual" is a translation of the Greek word *energes*, which describes something *extremely powerful* and *filled with possibilities*. It was the equivalent of his saying, *"An enormous, massive door that is usually sealed shut for others has suddenly swung open for me with great possibilities."* That opened door provided Paul supernatural access into regions that had been off-limits for others. His apostolic anointing — like a spiritual travel document or a passport — supernaturally opened doors and enabled him to go where others could not go.

But Paul further went on to say, "...And there are many adversaries" (1 Corinthians 16:9). Many adversaries were standing on the other side of that open door, but Paul was unafraid, because he was anointed to cross that threshold into new territory.

In Second Corinthians 2:12, Paul also referred to open doors, when he wrote, "Furthermore, when I came to Troas to preach Christ's gospel, and a door was opened unto me of the Lord."

Paul was anointed as an *apostolos*, an apostle — therefore that apostolic anointing was opening doors so he could forge into new regions and territories where he and his apostolic crew could do their God-ordained ministry. The Greek word for a "door" is once again the Greek word *thura*, which describes *a door which normally would be bolted shut* — but Paul wrote here that another normally sealed-tight door had swung wide open for him.

Many adversaries were standing on the other side of that open door, but Paul was unafraid, because he was anointed to cross that threshold into new territory.

Repeatedly in Paul's writings, he tells us that doors swung wide open for him that would have normally been sealed tight for others. No one is smart enough to open these kinds of sealed-tight doors by himself — including Paul. Paul knew it was the anointing of the apostle upon his life that caused doors to supernaturally open to him that were closed to others.

Patient Endurance as a Sign of Apostleship

However, for Paul and his apostolic team that he led to walk through those doors — and then to stay in those territories that could be rather hostile — he also needed divine endurance to stay where those doors led him. That is one reason Paul lists "patience" in Second Corinthians 12:12 as one of the "signs" that a person is a real apostle. I'll cover this more in the next chapter, but for now, let's look at the word "patience" in this verse that Paul says is a sign of apostleship.

> **Truly the signs of an apostle were wrought among you in all *patience*, in signs, and wonders, and mighty deeds.**

That word "patience" is a translation of the Greek word *hupomone*, a powerful word with many nuances that are important to apostolic ministry.

First, this word "patience" — from the Greek word *hupomone* — depicts one's ability *to stay*, *abide*, *remain in one's spot*, or *to keep a position*, and it pictures *the inner resolve to maintain territory that has been gained*. Indeed, those who do true apostolic work in regions that are not for the faint of heart, often find that the devil launches assaults against them to push them out. But true apostles are divinely graced with the supernatural ability to *stay put*, regardless of the pressures put upon them. Paul says this ability to *stay put* in the face of hostile attacks is as supernatural as any *sign* and *wonder*.

In a military sense, the word "patience" — the Greek word *hupomone* — was used to picture soldiers who were ordered to maintain their positions even in the face of opposition. Those soldiers were ordered to defiantly stick it out regardless of pressures mounted against them. This word depicts what one Greek scholar calls *"staying power, 'hang-in-there' power, and the attitude that holds out, holds on, outlasts, perseveres, and hangs in there, never giving up, refusing to surrender to obstacles, and turning down every opportunity to quit."* The word "patience" pictures one who may be under a heavy load, but this person refuses to bend, break, or surrender because he is convinced that the territory, promise, or principle under assault rightfully belongs to him.

Genuine apostles are anointed to walk through normally sealed-shut doors and function in regions and territories that can be difficult or hostile to the Gospel. So in Second Corinthians 12:12, where Paul lists the signs of an apostle, in addition to *signs* and *wonders*, he also lists *supernatural endurance* — from the Greek word *hupomone* — as one of the greatest signs that a person is a bona fide apostle.

This means that a real apostle doesn't "tuck his tail and run" when times get tough. He is under divine orders to stay put and has been graced with *staying power*, *"hang-in-there" power*, and the attitude that *holds out*, *holds on*, *outlasts*, *perseveres*, and *hangs in there*, *never giving up*, and *refusing to surrender to obstacles*. He is divinely empowered to turn down every opportunity to quit. Though under a heavy load, he refuses to bend, break, or surrender because he is convinced that the territory, promise, or principle under assault rightfully belongs to him. Once he has walked through an open door, he is anointed to stay there even if the open door comes with adversaries.

The word "patience" pictures one who may be under a heavy load, but he refuses to bend, break, or surrender because he is convinced that the territory, promise, or principle under assault rightfully belongs to him.

A clear example of this in Paul's ministry would be his ministry in the cities of Corinth and Ephesus — two of the world's most wicked cities during the time of the First Century. To fulfill his apostolic assignments there, first, Paul experienced God supernaturally opening a door for him to be there.

Second, for Paul to *stay* there, he had to be able to resist many adversaries in both cities. His assignments in both these cities required a God-given endowment of *patience* — which is the supernatural ability to *stay put* regardless of the pressure or opposition that one encounters. This supernatural endurance gives sufficient strength and courage to keep one pressing forward when it seems as if all of hell is coming against him.

Paul testified that *hupomone*, or "patience" — the supernatural ability to hang in there and stay put no matter what forces try to stop someone — was one of the most visible proofs that he was an authentic apostle. According to Paul, this divine ability to *stay put* while laying the foundation of the Church, often in the face of intense opposition, is supernatural. This is why Paul listed it as a sign that always accompanies true apostolic ministry.

Hence, when early New Testament ears heard the word *apostolos* — "apostle" — it additionally depicted to them a person who, like *a travel document* or *a passport*, was supernaturally anointed to journey into regions that were barred from others or that were otherwise hard to penetrate. This explains why it was possible for the early apostles to travel across the world at a time when travel was very difficult. But not only did they travel, they journeyed *far* and into difficult regions of the world where doors would normally have been shut for others.

Where Did That Apostolic Anointing Enable the First Apostles To Go?

In obedience to Jesus' Great Commission in Matthew 28:19 to "go ye therefore, and teach all nations" and His command in Acts 1:8 to take the Gospel first to Jerusalem, then to Judea and Samaria, and finally to "the uttermost parts of the earth," the apostles began traveling to take the Gospel message to the ends of the earth and to establish the Church everywhere in accordance with Jesus' Great Commission.

Considering the difficulties associated with travel in the ancient world — where people primarily journeyed either by foot, by ship, or on the back of an animal — it is simply remarkable to see how far the early apostles took the life-changing message of the Gospel. These men truly had the anointing of an *apostolos* upon them. They were mightily anointed to penetrate hard-to-reach regions as they went to places almost impossible to reach.

The following is a brief recounting of where some of these apostles supernaturally traveled in order to illustrate the supernatural anointing upon them that enabled them to travel so far and wide to fulfill their apostolic mandates.

The Apostle Andrew

Besides the information provided by the Early Church theologian Origen, Eusebius is our other primary source that tells us *Andrew* went to Scythia to preach the Gospel[10] — a region that included the currently named countries:

- Kazakhstan, Russia, and eastern Ukraine (inhabited by Scythians since at least the Eighth Century BC).
- The northern Caucasus area, including Azerbaijan and Georgia.
- Ukraine, Belarus, and Poland up to Oceanus Sarmaticus, known also as the Baltic region.
- Southern Ukraine with the lower Danube River area and Bulgaria, also known as Scythia Minor.

The tradition of Andrew ministering in this part of the world is so ingrained in Church history that he is even recognized as a patron saint of the Orthodox Church in Ukraine and Russia. In addition, the following historians of the Early Church record Andrew's missionary journeys:

- Gregory of Nazianzus reported that Andrew went to Epirus (a region straddling modern-day Greece and Albania).[11]
- Jerome states that Andrew took the Gospel message to Achaia (south-central Greece).[12]

- Theodoret wrote that Andrew took the Gospel to Greece.[13]

The truth is, it is likely that all of these ancient historians are correct. The Byzantine historian Nicephorus included all of these as a part of Andrew's travels, writing that the apostle took the Gospel to Cappadocia, Galatia, Bithynia, Byzantium, Macedonia, Thessaly, Achaia, and Scythia.[14] Scholars generally agree that Andrew was crucified at the order of a Roman governor in the city of Patras, located in Achaia. Andrew was bound with ropes to an X-shaped cross, known as a *decussate* cross, where he hung for a very long time and suffered a prolonged death. Andrew's martyrdom took place during the rule of Nero near the year 60 AD.

The Apostle Bartholomew

Tradition says that *Bartholomew*, who was also known as Nathanael, took the Gospel to the region known today as Armenia. According to Eusebius, Pantaenus (who was Origen's spiritual mentor), reported that Bartholomew had made disciples in India and that he'd given his converts the gospel of Matthew[15] "India" was a term that encompassed a large region, including Arabia Felix (modern-day Yemen). Other early accounts state that Bartholomew preached in Mesopotamia, Persia, Egypt, Laconia (a southern region of Greece), Phrygia (a kingdom in central Asia Minor), on the shores of the Black Sea, and in Armenia. The tradition of Bartholomew preaching the Gospel in Armenia is so well established that he is recognized as the patron saint of that nation.

According to a very early tradition, Bartholomew was martyred in Albanopolis, an ancient city in Armenia. Some early traditions present him as being beheaded, crucified, flayed with a knife, or skinned alive, suffering a miserable death at the hands of pagans. Some others assert that he was killed in India; however, the earlier tradition of martyrdom in Albanopolis is more likely.

The Apostle James (Son of Alphaeus)

James was also known as *the son of Alphaeus* and was not the same James who was beheaded in Acts 12:1,2. According to a strong early tradition, James preached throughout Israel before traveling to minister to pagans in Egypt, where tradition states he was martyred as a result of pagan opposition.

The Apostle Jude

Tradition holds that *Jude*, who was also known as Thaddaeus, traveled to preach the Gospel in Judea, Samaria, Idumaea, Syria, Mesopotamia (modern-day Iraq), and Libya — often accompanied by Simon the Zealot. The two also traveled to Persia, known in today's world as the country of Iran, to preach the Gospel. Jude is believed to have been bludgeoned to death in 65 AD by local pagans who opposed his ministry in either Syria or Persia.

The Apostle Matthew

According to early traditions passed down to us primarily through Early Church theologians Irenaeus and Clement of Alexandria, *Matthew* (also known as Levi the tax collector) preached the Gospel among the Jews for 15 years. Eusebius reports that before Matthew took the Gospel to other nations, he first wrote his gospel in the Hebrew language for Hebrew-speaking people.[16] Other early sources indicate that Matthew then took the Gospel to the region of Ethiopia on the Caspian Sea (*not* the country of Ethiopia in Africa), then on to Persia, Macedonia, and Syria.

Although very little is known about Matthew's martyrdom, it is strongly suggested that his death occurred in Ethiopia, and one tradition states that Matthew was killed on the orders of the king of Ethiopia while the apostle was worshiping at church. Other scholars believe that Matthew was either burned, stoned, or beheaded. Matthew is most remembered for his contribution of writing the gospel of Matthew.

The Apostle Matthias

Although *Matthias* was chosen as a disciple after the death of Judas Iscariot (*see* Acts 1:26), he was recognized by the other 11 apostles as a legitimate apostle and is therefore included here in this discussion. According to early documents written by Byzantine historian Nicephorus, Matthias first ministered in Judea and then to the barbarians and cannibals in the interior of Ethiopia in Africa.[17] One tradition says Matthias was crucified and then chopped to pieces in Sebastopolis (a city in the northeastern region of Asia Minor) and was buried there. Other traditions place his martyrdom in Jerusalem. However, the strongest evidence points to his martyrdom in Ethiopia.

The Apostle Peter

Paul referred to *Peter* as an apostle to the Jews, and Peter's life certainly demonstrated that he had a special grace for ministry to the Jewish people. Eventually Peter traveled to Rome, where early tradition states he served as bishop of the Church in Rome.

Peter's first epistle was written from Rome. In it, he wrote, "The church that is at Babylon, elected together with you, saluteth you; and so doth Marcus my son" (1 Peter 5:13). This name Babylon referred to Rome and its pagan influences, because the real Babylon on the Euphrates had already been abandoned and lay in ruins. Scholars believe that this "Babylon" comment was Peter's way of describing the city of Rome and identifying Rome as the place where he wrote his first epistle.

Notice Peter also specifically stated that Mark was with him at the time he wrote his first epistle, the book of First Peter. From the writings of Bishop Papias of Hierapolis and Clement of Alexandria, it is known that Mark wrote the gospel of Mark while he was living in Rome, because Christians in Rome wanted him to write a clear presentation of the doctrines Peter had preached to them.[18] Irenaeus confirms this information,[19] and Early Church leader Clement of Rome, in his epistle to the Corinthians that he wrote sometime between 95-97 AD, places *both* Peter and Paul in Rome.[20] The following Early Church writers also confirm that Peter and Paul were martyred in Rome: Bishop Ignatius of Antioch, in a document written before 117 AD,[21] Bishop Dionysius of Corinth, in a letter written between 165-174 AD[22]; and Tertullian.[23]

Between 198-217 AD, Caius, one of Rome's Early Church leaders, wrote these words (recorded in Eusebius' *Church History*): "But I can show the trophies of the Apostles. If you care to go to the Vatican or to the road to Ostia, thou shalt find the trophies of those who have founded this Church [referring to the Roman church]."[24]

Scholars believe that Caius' use of the word "trophies" was a specific reference to the graves of Peter and Paul in Rome. This lets us know that both apostles' burial sites were known between the years 198-217 AD. According to strong early traditions, Peter was crucified upside down near the present-day Vatican either in the year 67 or 68 AD. Under St. Peter's Basilica in Rome is an ancient necropolis (cemetery), which, according to the Catholic Church, contains the burial place of Peter. This claim is most likely factual. Eusebius wrote about "the inscription of the names of Peter and Paul, which have been preserved to the present day on their burial-places there."[25]

Peter's and Paul's deaths occurred somewhere around the fourteenth year of Nero's reign, probably in the year 67 AD, a date accepted by scholars and attested to by both Eusebius and Jerome. In his writings, Jerome states that Peter came to Rome during the rule of the Emperor Claudius in the year 42 AD, and it is believed that this apostle ministered in Rome approximately 25 years before suffering martyrdom.[26] From Rome, the apostle Peter wrote the epistles that came to be known as First and Second Peter. In his lifetime, Peter's apostolic authority was widely recognized, and he was viewed as a leader among the apostles.

The Apostle Philip

When Philip began his traveling ministry, he took the Gospel to Phrygia, a region located in what is known today as central Turkey. Philip's martyrdom in Hierapolis is a well-established fact in church tradition. It is interesting to note that many early documents claim that Philip the deacon (who later became Philip the evangelist) and Philip the apostle may both be buried in Hierapolis. Today visitors to the ancient city of Hierapolis can view the ruins of an ancient church building built on top of Philip's gravesite.

The Apostle Thomas

Today India recognizes *Thomas* as the apostle to India because of a long-held tradition that Thomas brought the Gospel to the Kerala area of India, a territory located near the Indian west coast. This tradition is confirmed in the writings of Ephrem, Ambrose, Paulinus, Jerome, and Gregory of Tours, as well as other Early Church writers. Afterward, Thomas traveled further eastward to bring the Gospel to the eastern coast of India.

Tradition says that Thomas was killed near the city of Madras — speared to death by pagans who opposed his ministry. In that region today, there remains a bas-relief dating to the Seventh Century that states Thomas laid down his life in that area. It is believed that at some point, perhaps during Thomas' journey to India, he preached the Gospel in what is known today as Iraq and Iran.

The Apostle Simon

Simon was known also as *Simon the Zealot* because he was so politically zealous for Israel before Jesus called him into the ministry. Early Church fathers wrote that Simon was later compelled by that same zeal to take the Gospel to pagans along the Black Sea and in Egypt, northern Africa, and even Britain. Later Simon joined Jude in carrying the Gospel message to Persia and to ancient Armenia (a region that today is part of modern-day Iraq and Georgia), where both Simon and Jude were martyred.

Two early traditions state that Simon was sawn in half at Suanir, Persia, or in Colchis, an ancient kingdom in the Caucasus region of modern-day Georgia. The ancient Armenian historian Moses of Chorene wrote that Simon was martyred at Weriosphora in Caucasian Iberia, also a part of modern-day Georgia.[27] Simon's place of burial is unknown.

Divine Desire Grew To 'Go' and To 'Stay Put'

As apostles, these men categorically had a door-opening anointing that enabled them to journey beyond where others had ventured and into regions where no man had labored so they could fulfill their calling to preach the Gospel and to establish the Church where it had been previously nonexistent. Not only did they possess a divine grace enabling them to walk through those doors, they also were anointed with *hupomone* to supernaturally "stay put" in spite of adversaries, enemies, or the hostility they encountered.

In addition to these original apostles, those today with an apostolic calling are likewise anointed to go into difficult regions and are divinely graced to work there to establish the Church where it has not previously existed. This is a part of the supernatural equipment given to the apostles that was important in the beginning days of the Church — and it is important now and will continue to be important in the very last of the last days of the Church Age.

The fact that apostles thrive in difficult regions is one reason why the Church in comfortable parts of the world seems to be less familiar with living apostles as they are with the other fivefold ministry gifts. For this reason, in Chapter Six, I will address in greater detail why we know so few names of living apostles. You will see that although apostles are still very prevalent, they are living far from the "comfort zone" as they serve on the frontlines in territories where the church community is not as well established.

A Spiritual Messenger To Take Others Into New Spiritual Realms

As time passed, the word *apostolos,* which became our New Testament word for "apostle," took on another meaning, which further made it familiar to the ears of early New Testament hearers. The word *apostolos* became a common word in history to signify a person who was especially gifted by the gods with *special insight* and *revelation* and who was sent by them as their *special messenger.*

The ancient Greek world stood in awe of such messengers and believed that gods had endued them with *special wisdom* and *revelation* that would enable these *apostolos* individuals to take others with them up into higher realms of revelation and understanding. Knowing this well-established usage of *apostolos,* it means to the ears of early New Testament hearers, the word also depicted Christ-given spiritual leaders who possessed *special insight* and *revelation* that could lead others from one spiritual dimension into a higher spiritual dimension or level in their Christian walk.

This brings to mind Paul's words in Galatians 1:11 and 12, where he said, "But I certify you, brethren, that the gospel which was preached of me is not after man. For I neither received it of man, neither was I taught it, but by the revelation of Jesus Christ."

In this verse, Paul declared that his insights were not taught to him chiefly by man, but by the "revelation" of Jesus Christ. This word "revelation" is a translation of the Greek word *apokalupsis,* which is a compound of the preposition *apo* and the word *kalupsis.* The preposition *apo* means *away* and the word *kalupsis* depicts something that is *covered, hidden,* or *veiled.* But when compounded, forming the word *apokalupsis,* it pictures *an obstructive covering that has been suddenly and supernaturally removed*, and what was on the other side of that obstruction is now *un*covered, *un*hidden, and *un*veiled.

Let me illustrate the word *apokalupsis* for you. It can describe a moment when a person pulls a string that enables him to draw curtains out of the way so he can see what has always been there, just outside the window. The scene was always there to enjoy, but the curtains blocked the ability to see what had been hidden. However, when the curtains are pulled apart, suddenly what was always there, but hidden from the person's eyes, comes into view. The moment one sees beyond the curtain for the first time and observes what has been there all along, but wasn't evident before, *that* is what the Bible calls a "revelation" — *apokalupsis.*

If you apply this to what Paul says in Galatians 1:12 when he writes about the "revelation of Jesus Christ," it means God had supernaturally allowed Paul to see what others had not seen. This agrees entirely with what Jesus told Paul on the road to Damascus, where Jesus informed Paul that He would be repeatedly re-appearing to him during the course of his ministry (*see* Acts 26:16).

How does the believer engage this supernatural endowment of the apostle so he or she can receive and benefit from the "revelation of Christ" that the apostle is gifted to impart? The answer lies in the word "access."

But first, Ephesians 2:18 teaches that *every* believer has "*access* by one Spirit unto the Father." The word "access" in this verse is a translation of the Greek word *prosagoge,* which means *access, approach*, or even *intimate interaction.*

- Plutarch used *prosagoge* to mean *an opportunity.*[28]
- Thucydides used it to mean *acquisition* or *gain.*[29]
- Herodotus used it as a religious term to describe *a religious process en route to a temple.*[30]

In Ephesians 2:18, the use of "access" clearly means that every blood-bought believer has *access* — opportunity and ability — to approach and gain intimate interaction with God.

In addition to the access that every believer has by himself, the word *apostolos* lets us know that when a church is near a genuine apostle, the apostolic anointing on his life will not only provide *him* with supernatural insight, but that anointing will enable others to journey with him into new spiritual realms, revelations, and dimensions. Because the apostle is a special messenger sent by Christ who has special insight and revelation, if one grabs hold of his spiritual coattails and sticks with him, it will take that person along with him into new and higher realms.

Because the apostle is a special messenger sent by Christ who has special insight and revelation, if one grabs hold of his spiritual coattails and sticks with him, it will take that person along with him into new and higher realms.

Think how blessed the churches at Rome, Corinth, Galatia, Ephesus, Colossae, Philippi, Thessalonica, and other locations were because of the insights and revelations they received as a result of being in relationship with Paul. By hanging onto his apostolic coattails, those churches that were in relationship with him heard amazing revelation that other churches perhaps never heard.

As a result, those churches who had access to Paul were enabled to spiritually go places that they may have never attained by themselves. By staying close to Paul — their *apostolos* or apostle — as their God-sent messenger, they had access to special insight and revelation, and the anointing on Paul's life enabled them to venture into spiritual realms that other churches likely did not experience.

An Abundance of Revelations and a Thorn in the Flesh

Paul wrote in Second Corinthians 12:7 that his bursting into new realms of revelation was so threatening to the domain of darkness that it caused the devil to launch attacks against him to distract him. In this greatly misunderstood verse, Paul wrote, "And lest I should be exalted above measure through the abundance of the revelations, there was given to me a thorn in the flesh, the messenger of Satan to buffet me, lest I should be exalted above measure."

The words "exalted above measure" are a translation of the Greek word *huperairo*, a compound of the words *huper* and *airo*. The word *huper* means *over*, *above*, and *beyond*. It depicts something that is *way beyond measure* and conveys the idea of something that is *greater, superior*, *higher*, *better*, *more than a match for*, *utmost, paramount*, or *foremost*. It could also describe something that is *first-rate, first-class, top-notch, unsurpassed, unequaled, and unrivaled by any person or thing*. The second part of the word *huperairo* means *to lift up*, *to raise*, or *to be exalted*.

When these two Greek words are compounded to form the word *huperairo*, it speaks of *a person who has been supremely exalted*. This is *a person who has been magnified, increased, and lifted up to a place of great prestige and influence*. Although *huperairo* could be used to express the idea of a person who haughtily exalts himself, this is categorically *not* the idea Paul had in mind when he wrote this verse. Rather, Paul used the word *huperairo* to depict one who has been greatly honored and recognized due to something he has written, done, or achieved.

Because Paul was an apostle, we know that God had graced him with supernatural *special insight* and *revelation.* In Second Corinthians 12:7, Paul indeed referred to the "abundance of the revelations" God had given him. And all New Testament ears who heard the word *apostolos* knew this depicted a spiritual leader who possessed *supernatural insights* and who had the potential to lead others from one spiritual dimension into the next spiritual dimension or level.

Paul said he had received an "abundance" of such revelations. The word "abundance" is from the Greek word *huperballo*, which is a compound of the words *huper* and *ballo*, which means *to cast* or *to throw.* When these two words are compounded to form the word *huperballo*, it describes *something that is phenomenal, extraordinary, unparalleled, or unmatched.* It is like an archer who aims for the bull's-eye, but when he releases the string and shoots his arrow, he watches as his arrow flies way over the top of and beyond even the target.

Paul used this word *huperballo* — here translated as the word "abundance" — to explain that the revelations he had received were not only *unparalleled in quality*, but the vast number of them were *far beyond* what anyone else had ever received. As an *apostolos* — or apostle — we have already seen Paul was like *a travel document* or *passport* and was enabled to go into new geographical regions, but he was also able to journey into *spiritual realms, spiritual dimensions*, and to receive *spiritual truths* in a greater way than others.

Paul preached these "abundant revelations" as he traversed the regions surrounding Asia and the Mediterranean Sea. Everywhere he went, he preached what had been divinely revealed to him, and as he preached, his power, authority, and fame grew greater and greater. Those who heard Paul were enabled to journey with him into spiritual truths they probably would have never accessed if they had not been in his apostolic presence and heard his apostolic voice.

Due to these revelations and his boldness to preach them, Paul became one of the most influential apostles in history. Paul tells us in Second Corinthians 12:7, in effect, that Satan was so alarmed by the progress Paul was making with the Gospel that the enemy launched a full-scale attack to impede that progress. Satan didn't want Paul to be recognized or magnified to a greater extent, so the devil attempted to ruin him, to destroy him, and to discredit the message he preached. Paul said he was afflicted with a "thorn in the flesh."

The word "thorn" is the Greek word *skolops*, a word used to describe *a dangerously sharp, spiked instrument or tool.* However, this word was also used to describe *the stake on which an enemy's head was stuck after being decapitated.* Some have suggested that the words "in the flesh" refer to a physical sickness, but this cannot be affirmed by any scripture in the New Testament and should be taken as unsubstantiated conjecture. People have even gone so far in their imaginations as to assert that Paul suffered from malaria, epilepsy, eye disease, club feet, or a hunched back. There is nothing in any New Testament scripture to back up such speculations.

But one thing *is* clear, however, and that is, *Satan wanted Paul's head on a stake!* He wanted to eliminate this man of God and put him completely out of the picture. The words "in the flesh" most likely describe a type of event that was a constant source of irritation to the apostle Paul that caused him personal distress, and it kept occurring over and over again. This is why he referred to it as a "thorn in the flesh."

Some ridiculously argue that God sent the thorn to keep Paul from being prideful about his many revelations. But Paul plainly wrote that it was a "...messenger of *Satan* to buffet me..." (2 Corinthians 12:7). It was not a messenger from God, but a messenger of Satan sent to buffet and distract him.

The word "messenger" is the Greek word *angelos*, a word that can describe *an angel, one who is sent on a special mission*, or *a messenger who is dispatched to perform a specific assignment*. This was a "messenger of Satan" — perhaps a demonic entity — that was sent directly from Satan himself to buffet Paul and to restrict the progress of his ministry.

This thorn in the flesh categorically did *not* come from God; otherwise, Paul would have called it a "messenger of God." But Paul plainly states that this thorn in the flesh was given to him by a "messenger of *Satan*" — a special force that had been dispatched to keep Paul from gaining additional status and prestige and to prevent him from taking the Gospel further and higher into the world scene.

Paul was preaching to kings, governors, and world leaders. He was establishing churches, writing New Testament Scripture, and pushing back the forces of hell. His personal influence was growing and his impact was increasing day by day. The revelations that God had given him were about to change the course of human history. So fearing that Paul's influence would grow too great, Satan strategically sent forces that had been instructed to create disturbances to "buffet" the apostle.

The word "buffet" is the Greek word *kolaphidzo*, a Greek word that comes from the word *kolaphos*, a word that describes *the fist* or *knuckles*. When it becomes the word *kolaphidzo*, as Paul used it in Second Corinthians 12:7, it refers to *beatings with the fist*. The Greek tense describes *unending, unrelenting, continuous, repetitious beatings*. This means Paul was not telling us of a single event, but of a *series* of many events. This word *kolaphidzo* ("buffet") gives us our greatest insight into the "thorn in the flesh" Paul was writing about in this verse.

Paul endured many afflictions during his ministry, but some of the greatest afflictions he faced were due to religious leaders who so fiercely opposed him.

These religious leaders included Jewish leaders who hated him and his message, and they included false brethren who were constantly trying to displace his position of authority and to usurp his apostleship in the local churches. Paul was resisted outside the church by leaders of the Jewish faith who hated him, and he was opposed from within by those who wanted him out of the picture so they could take his place of prominence inside the church.

Paul was resisted outside the church by leaders of the Jewish faith who hated him, and he was opposed from within by those who wanted him out of the picture so they could take his place of prominence inside the church.

Thus, the biggest "thorn" in Paul's life was the fact that he had to deal with these different groups of people who covertly planned the problems and hassles he frequently faced in the ministry. A special messenger from Satan, perhaps even a demonic angel, had been sent to incite and stir up these people against Paul.

In light of these Greek words, consider this fresh *RIV* interpretation of Paul's words in Second Corinthians 12:7:

> **Because of the phenomenal revelations I have received and on account of the vast number of these revelations that God has entrusted to me — and to hinder the highly visible progress I am making in the Lord's cause — a special messenger has been sent from Satan to harass me with constant distractions and headaches. There's no doubt about it! Those whom Satan has stirred up against me want my head on a stake! Satan is using these people to constantly buffet and distract me in an attempt to keep me**

from reaching a higher level of visibility and recognition and to sidetrack me from preaching my revelations.

Paul's thorn in the flesh was his way of saying the devil was using people again and again to try to keep him distracted solving "people problems" and hindered from making significant Gospel advancements and being effective in the place God had assigned him to help build His *"naos"* Temple.

As an *apostolos* — an apostle — Paul was sent from God as *a special messenger* with *special insight* and *revelation.* Like a true apostle, he had an "abundance of revelations" because the apostolic anointing on his life opened spiritual dimensions to him and supernaturally enabled him to take others in the churches with him into greater territories of revelation. He was a true *apostolos*, or apostle, in every sense of the word.

This meaning of *apostolos* in history lets us know an apostle is *a spiritual leader who is gifted by God to lead others into deeper and higher realms*, and it has such significant bearings on the idea of apostleship in the New Testament. So now we know that when early New Testament ears heard the word apostle, they also knew it referred to one who possessed exceptional divine revelation and who was anointed to lead people into new spiritual territories.

An Envoy or Ambassador

Next, we discover that the word *apostolos* was also used to picture *powerful dignitaries*, like *ambassadors*, who were *chosen and designated to represent a government or a king.*

- The Greek philosopher Aristotle used it to picture the *seeing off* or *sending away* of important individuals.[31]
- The Greek historian Herodotus used it to describe *a high-powered ambassador who had been sent to represent a government or king.*[32]

In this very old and well-established meaning of the word *apostolos* — "apostle" — we now discover that this word was used very early to picture *an envoy who was sent to do business on behalf of the one who sent him.* Specifically, it pictured a *personal representative, emissary, messenger, agent, diplomat,* or *ambassador.*

This meaning of *apostolos* is so very important that I want to take a moment to talk to you about ancient ambassadors. I realize the following may seem like a lot of detailed information, but for those who wish to dig deeper, I want to provide more insights. So let's see how the word *apostolos* was regularly used prior to the time of the emerging Church to depict real-life ambassadors in antiquity.

In the ancient world, the word *apostolos* was used for *an ambassador* who was a high-ranking diplomat dispatched to represent a government or king who sent him on a specific mission in a foreign city or land. As the government's or king's representative, these *apostolos* individuals held the highest diplomatic rank that could be given. This, too, has relevance for the ministry of apostles, for it means Christ-given apostles hold an especially high-rank in the Body of Christ. In God's view, they are individuals who are dispatched by God as His chosen representatives and, as such, they hold an elevated rank in the Church.

The earliest-known emergence of ambassadors can be traced all the way to ancient Egypt to the capital of Amarna, a city that was constructed at the order of Pharaoh Akhenaten (died c. 1335 BC) of the Eighteenth Dynasty of the new Kingdom of Egypt, who was married to Queen Nefertiti and who was the father of Tutankhamun, otherwise known as *King Tut.* Some of the earliest records about ancient ambassadors come from what are called the Amarna tablets, which are ancient records that were discovered in archeological excavations in the ruins of Amarna in 1887. Scholars allege that those early writings may be the earliest records of *ambassadors* traveling back and forth between the pharaohs and the kings of Syria-Palestine, Babylonia, Assyria, Canaan, Hatti, Mittanni, and other kingdoms in the Near East.[33]

After that, it seems the next known records of ancient ambassadors comes from Greek antiquity, where we read and learn that Greek ambassadors were high-ranking individuals who were dispatched to negotiate business between various city-states.[34] As Greek civilization expanded, the need arose for individuals with skills of negotiation to represent governments and kings to other governments and kings abroad. Because philosophical and oratory skills were components for strategic negotiations, we are told by the Greek writer Thucydides that Greek city-states first chose philosophers and orators to represent them as ambassadors. Because their chief task was to deliver very eloquent, powerful, and persuasive speeches and to make business deals with foreign powers, it was believed that philosophers and orators would be the best for the job.[35]

But after that, the process of selecting ambassadors continued to develop, and soon ambassadors were primarily selected from among the "heralds" who had well represented a government or a king. Early governments and kings always had their eye out for those with potential to serve them as ambassadors, and their attention fell upon heralds whom they believed had done their jobs faithfully. However, even if a herald's potential was visible, and it was generally believed a certain herald would eventually be ambassadorial material, heralds would only be selected for this dignified service after proving themselves faithful.

The word "herald" is a special term used primarily to denote the official public spokesman of a government or king. It's interesting that it is a translation of the Greek word *kerux,* which is the New Testament word translated "preach" or "preacher." Of course, the apostle Paul knew the word "herald" was a special word that denoted *the official spokesman or herald of a king.* Hence, when he specially chose to use it to denote *a preacher*, he did so because *kerux* held so many connotations for those who preach the Gospel — *and*, as you will see, for those who are called to apostolic ministry.

How the Word *Kerux* — 'Herald' — Applies to Every Gospel Minister

According to Paul, any preacher of the Gospel is a *kerux* — one who is an official representative and public spokesman for the Lord. Therefore, it is imperative for every preacher to understand the nuances that go along with the word *kerux*.

Because a *kerux* — a "herald" — in history, was the official representative of a government or king, he was expected to clearly announce the desires, dictates, orders, news, policy changes, or messages that the government or king wished to convey to the people in the kingdom or to those who lived abroad.[36] Being a "herald" was the highest, most noble, privileged position in a kingdom because his position permitted him to have access to the king or to those in authority that was not afforded to many.

For example, if a government leader or king wanted to convey a special message to people in the nation or in his kingdom, he would first summon his "herald" into his private quarters. The herald then came in with writing instruments in hand to carefully pen whatever the governmental leader or king desired to express through him to others. When the king or leader finished dictating the message, if needed, the herald was permitted to ask questions and seek clarification. His job was to be sure he understood every nuance and point that he was to convey to the people.

A herald understood that his job was to speak on behalf of the king and that there was no room for misunderstanding or for mistakes in his delivery of the message. Finally, when the herald was assured he fully understood the message he had been summoned to deliver, he went to his podium to publicly announce the message given to him. It was expected that his delivery of the message be accurate, precise, and faithful to the message the king or governmental leader wanted to express.

Just as it was important for the *kerux*, or herald, to communicate the king's message very accurately, it was likewise important for him to capture the sentiment, heart, and emotions on these various issues so he could convey not only information, but also the heart and passion of the one who sent him. Thus, when the herald stood to speak, it was expected that he would deliver the correct information in a way that conveyed the heart and passion of one who sent him.

To be a herald also required professionalism. Because he was the government or king's representative, when a herald stood before people to speak, he was expected to dress professionally in order to be a good representative of the government or king. Publicly representing a government or king required that he dress accordingly. An unprofessionally, shabbily dressed herald would have been an insult to those he represented.

Because the herald represented those in authority over him, he likewise had to learn how to speak in a style that was cultured and polite. If the spokesman was deemed offensive and rude, his impolite behavior reflected negatively on people's perception of those he represented. But when a herald was deemed cultured and polite, this reflected positively on those he represented and thusly affected people's perception of those who had sent him.

In every word a herald "spoke," communicating a clear message; in every piece of clothing he wore; and in his actions both public and private, he ultimately had a huge effect on the public's opinion of those he represented. Consequently, a herald understood that to stand in such a noble position required that his life be lived honorably, honestly, and uprightly. It was understood that to the best of his ability, even his personal life was to be spotless, immaculate, pristine, and gleaming.

Because a herald had regular, substantial contact with powerful individuals, there were perhaps many opportunities when people might have attempted to use him to garner favor with those he represented. As a public figure, a herald also found himself in moments when he *could* express his personal opinions on many issues, but as a herald, he did not have the right to give his own personal commentary about the things he had been asked to communicate.

Furthermore, he was never allowed to use his public position to draw attention to himself or to use his position for personal gain. Such behavior would be considered a gross violation of his honored position. It would guarantee the loss of his cherished position and that someone else would be selected to replace him.

But if a herald was found faithful over a period of time, he could possibly be selected for a greater position — including ambassadorial duties abroad — which leads me back to the word *apostolos,* which could denote an *ambassador.*

But, first, I want to tell you how all this "herald" information applies to those who publicly preach the Gospel in any way. Remember, the word *kerux,* the Greek word for "herald," is the very word Paul used very frequently to picture *preachers* who are called to *preach* — *herald* — the Word of God.

What God Expects of His 'Heralds' Today

First, those who speak as "heralds" for God today must clearly understand that their highest priority is to come into His presence in order to hear both the message and every nuance of what God wants to communicate to His people. More than just intellectually communicating information, those who speak for the Lord must capture not only *information*, but also His *heart* that needs to be conveyed to His people — and His heralds must do this with conviction and passion.

Second, like a herald of the ancient world was required to dress appropriately, speak kindly and courteously, and be polite, it is imperative that those who represent the Lord bring honor to Jesus in their appearance and in their dealings with people. The images in the word *kerux* emphatically informs us that those who are the Lord's representatives must be professional in how they dress, how they speak to others, and in how their actions, both public and private, affect others' perception of the Lord.

Third, Paul's use of this analogy tells us that those who publicly represent the Lord must not allow others to use them for advantage, and they are to refrain from making personal commentary that is not their business to make. Speaking as the Lord's representatives means the pulpit is to be used for speaking what comes from the lips of Jesus, and as His representatives, they are authorized only to publicly speak what the Lord has directed them to say.

In ancient times, *if* a herald was found faithful in these matters, it was possible that he could be selected as an ambassador. Like ambassadors today, those ancient ambassadors were high-ranking, powerful, tested, and trusted individuals who were invested with authority to act in the stead of the one who sent them. The word *apostolos* depicted such ambassadors. This informs us that real Christ-given apostles are Christ's tried and tested ambassadors and that, as such, they possess the clout and influence to *speak* and *act* on behalf of Jesus, who sent them on assignment.

In New Testament times, people stood in *awe* of authentic apostles because they understood their weighty position. When an apostle spoke, the hearers knew they were to take his words as authoritative and weighty. In fact, the hearers would count his words as the words of Jesus — the One who dispatched him as His ambassador. Because an apostle was so connected to His Sender, when an apostle acted, those observing his actions viewed his behavior and actions as the behavior and actions of Jesus Himself. As an *apostolos,* the apostle was Jesus' spiritual ambassador, the representative of Jesus Christ, so he indeed carried spiritual clout and possessed the backing of Heaven to get a job done. And, of course, with Heaven's backing, he also carried great *responsibility*.

As an *apostolos*, the apostle was Jesus' spiritual ambassador, the representative of Jesus Christ, so he indeed carried spiritual clout and possessed the backing of Heaven to get a job done.

In ancient history, after what seemed like long years of waiting, a herald could finally be selected to become an ambassador. Please understand that even if those in authority over him knew from the beginning that he had the potential to become an ambassador, they allowed time and tests to prove the readiness of the candidate before laying hands on him for such a powerful position. And the same holds true of one called as a New Testament apostle — he will be required to pass many tests to prove his readiness to fill that God-called role in a way that is befitting of the One who called him.

Paul knew from the time of his salvation that God had called him to be an apostle. He testified of this in Acts 26:17,18 when he wrote the words that Jesus had spoken to him on the road to Damascus. In that event, Saul (later called Paul) heard Jesus say He would protect him, "delivering thee from the people, and from the Gentiles, unto whom now I *send* thee, to open their eyes, and to turn them from darkness to light, and from the power of Satan unto God, that they may receive forgiveness of sins, and an inheritance among them which are sanctified by faith that is in me."

But notice right at the moment of his salvation, Paul heard Jesus say He would "send" him to the Gentiles and that he would become an apostle to the Gentiles. The word "send" in Greek is *apostello,* which not only means *"I send,"* but it is the New Testament word to describe apostolic ministry. Even though Paul knew right from the start that his would be an apostolic ministry, like all others who are called, he would need to be prepared and proven ready before actually stepping into his apostolic calling.

God Tests the Sincerity of Our Hearts

Many years passed before Paul was separated unto his apostolic calling to begin fulfilling it. During those waiting years, Paul served in the church at Antioch, and I'm sure he must have passed many tests as he learned how to be a *kerux* — a herald — of the Lord in those years. In First Thessalonians 2:4, Paul referred to this long and tedious process when he said, "But as we were allowed of God to be put in trust with the gospel, even so we speak; not as pleasing men, but God, which trieth our hearts."

In this verse, Paul reflected on those years during which he waited for God to trust him with the bigger assignment of launching out into his apostolic ministry. Recalling those days of waiting, he wrote these amazing words: "But as we were *allowed* of God...."

The *King James Version* really doesn't give the full impact of the original Greek text. In Greek, the word "allowed" is a translation of the Greek word *dokimadzo*, a daunting word that *means to test, to examine, to inspect, to scrutinize, or to apply a test to determine the quality or sincerity of a thing.* Only after the object has been scrutinized and has passed the test can it be viewed as *genuine* and *sincere.*

Significantly, this word "allowed" — the Greek word *dokimadzo* — was also the very word used to illustrate the test used to determine real and counterfeit coinage. After a scrutinizing test was performed, the bona fide coinage would stand up to the test, and the counterfeit would fail.

The word *dokimadzo* also pictured the act of refining metal by fire to remove its impurities. First, the metal was placed in a fire that burned at a certain degree of heat; then it was placed in a fire burning at *an even higher* degree; and finally, it was placed in a blazing fire that burned at the highest degree of all. Three such tests were needed in order to remove from the metal all the unseen impurities that were hidden from the naked eye.

From the viewpoint of the naked eye, the metal looked strong and ready to be used even prior to those tests. But unseen defects were resident in the metal that would have shown up later as a break, a fracture, or some kind of malfunction. To be assured the metal was free of defects and ready to be used effectively, with no breakdown, these three purifying tests at three different degrees of blazing hot fire were required. The fire was hot and the process was lengthy, but the tests were necessary in order to achieve the desired result.

Furthermore, in ancient Greece, a form of *dokimadzo*, the word *dokimasia*, was used in Athens to describe the process of testing the character of individuals before they were permitted to be installed into any public office.[37] Being a public officer was so serious that to find out if an individual possessed the right inner character for a notable position, he was thoroughly examined to see if he could pass a character test. This intense examination was carried out by a supreme council, and its purpose was to determine if a candidate was worthy to hold a public office. If a candidate was approved, he could be chosen for public leadership, but if he failed a character test, he would be eliminated from any public leadership in society.

Because Paul used the word *dokimadzo* to describe the way God tested him to see if he was ready for a bigger assignment, his words actually meant: *"It was a lengthy process and I went through a lot of refining fires to get to this place, but finally I passed the test and God saw that I was genuinely ready...."*

Although God had called Paul to be an apostle right from the start and Paul even *knew* it, he was not *ready* right from the start. Years passed as he was refined and prepared before he could finally step into his apostolic calling. The preparation process was a serious test that literally lasted for years. During Paul's years serving in Antioch, as it is true concerning all "heralds" with potential, God already had a plan for Paul, and His eyes were fixed on him. In all those years, Paul no doubt was being refined as he learned how to be all that a representative for Jesus should be. When he was finally ready, the Holy Spirit quickly spoke and separated him unto his calling, which is recorded in Acts 13:2,3.

How All These Meanings of *Apostolos* Were Understood in the Minds of New Testament Believers

So by the time of the New Testament, the word *apostolos* — the word for "apostle" — had a lengthy history and carried a whole range of important meanings, all of which overlapped and interrelated to the other meanings. To sum it up, when early New Testament believers heard the word *apostolos,* as Greek-speakers who knew just how this word had historically been used, they understood the many connotations and implications inherent in it. They were readily able to associate its usage to Paul's teaching on the apostolic ministry.

To those believers, an *apostolos* — or an apostle — was like:

- An *admiral* who traveled with a specialized fleet of ships and a specialized crew who accompanied and assisted him as he sailed into open seas to locate territories where civilization was nonexistent. There, he and his crew were to replicate the life, language, and culture as it should be and to construct infrastructure, roads, buildings, houses, and temples in a new territory.

- A *travel document* or *a passport* that enabled the apostle and his team to journey into new geographical areas to preach the Gospel, to drive back darkness, and to replicate the life, language, and culture of the Church.
- A *spiritual package* that was packed with God's powerful anointing to do whatever was needed onsite — and also *a spiritual messenger from God* who was gifted with *special insight* and *revelation* and whose function was to lead others upward into new spiritual realms and territories.
- An *ambassador* who represented Christ in the same way an ambassador would represent a king or government. He was a tried and tested emissary, messenger, governmental agent, high-ranking diplomat, or as we have seen, an *ambassador.* As apostles, they were hand-chosen, powerful individuals who had spiritual clout and the backing of Heaven to fulfill an assignment or mission.

While all of this may be new information and insights for you, most of Paul's readers were Greek-speakers and understood the word "apostle" and its various usages and nuances as they pertained to New Testament apostolic ministry. This is probably why Paul never stopped to elaborate extensively on the meaning of the word *apostolos* — or "apostle" — in his writings. To a large degree, his readers needed no explanation. Most likely, they already had an understanding of much of what we have covered so far in this chapter.

How Many People Does the New Testament Identify as Apostles?

As already noted, there are some denominations that insist the original 12 men that Jesus called to serve with Him were the only true apostles. Conversely, others believe that the ministry of apostles has extended beyond the original 12 and has continued throughout Church history for 2,000 years. So I'd like to provide you a biblical answer to this question, not based on conjecture, but on the use of the word *apostolos* in the New Testament.

Jesus Was the First Apostle

Hebrew 3:1 affirms that Jesus Himself was the very first apostle. It says, "Wherefore, holy brethren, partakers of the heavenly calling, consider the Apostle and High Priest of our profession, Christ Jesus." In this verse, the word *apostolos* is used to describe Jesus as the Chief Apostle of the Church. As the Chief Apostle, He set the standard for those who subsequently are Christ-given apostles.

A careful study of Jesus' ministry reveals that He fulfilled all the meanings of the Greek word *apostolos* that we have studied so far.

- He was God's *admiral*, going into new territory where the Kingdom of God had never before existed, and with the help of His specialized, apostolic crew (the disciples), He brought Heaven to earth.
- He was God's *Passport* that brought the disciples and countless others into deep spiritual dimensions they could have never gone to on their own.
- He was God's *Special Package*, and He was God's *Special Messenger* with unprecedented supernatural insights and power given to Him by the Father that was vital for the growth and the building up of the Church.
- He was, and is, God's Ambassador that is equipped with all power and all authority and is authorized to speak and act on God's behalf.

As the first Apostle, Jesus selected and trained a team of 12 men to be a part of His apostolic team, and He led them to drive back the forces of darkness and establish truth in people's hearts. He was, and is, the supreme example of what an apostle is to be. A study of Jesus' ministry shows that, as an apostle, He could operate in all of the fivefold ministry gifts. He was an Apostle, a Prophet, an Evangelist, a Pastor, and a Teacher. In every respect, He was, and is, the *perfect example* of all five offices.

But to carry out the advancement of the Kingdom of God, Jesus indeed chose 12 men to become His first apostles to establish and lay the first foundations of the Church. In Revelation 21:14, the first apostles Jesus chose are called "the apostles of the Lamb." For our purposes in this book, I will call the original 12 apostles *foundational apostles* because they were the first, and there will never be any other like that first group. Their calling is described in Luke 6:13 and Matthew 10:1-4, where the Bible tells us Jesus called the 12 men. Again, I refer to them as *foundational apostles* because they were the first Jesus chose to set not only the foundation for the Church, but also to set the standard as examples for all future apostolic ministry.

Matthew 10:1-4 identifies the original 12 apostles, "And when he had called unto him his twelve disciples, he gave them power against unclean spirits, to cast them out, and to heal all manner of sickness and all manner of disease. Now the names of the twelve apostles are these; The first, Simon, who is called Peter, and Andrew his brother; James the son of Zebedee, and John his brother; Philip, and Bartholomew; Thomas, and Matthew the publican; James the son of Alphaeus, and Lebbaeus, whose surname was Thaddaeus; Simon the Canaanite, and Judas Iscariot, who also betrayed him."

These were the 12 whom Jesus selected and appointed to establish and lay the foundation of the universal Church and to set in place its non-negotiable doctrines. Luke 6:13 says, "And when it was day, he called unto him his disciples: and of them he chose twelve, *whom also he named apostles.*"

Luke additionally tells us that Jesus sent these original 12 to preach the Gospel, heal the sick, cast out demons, and to preach the Kingdom of God. Those verses say, "Then he called his twelve disciples together, and gave them power and authority over all devils, and to cure diseases. And he sent them to preach the kingdom of God, and to heal the sick.... And they departed, and went through the towns, preaching the gospel, and healing every where." (Luke 9:1,2,6).

Judas Iscariot eventually committed suicide due to his unresolved inner conflict that resulted from his mishandling and betrayal of Jesus. The Bible tells us in Acts 1:15-26 that Matthias was chosen as Judas Iscariot's replacement among the 12 foundational apostles. Those verses say, "And they prayed, and said, Thou, Lord, which knowest the hearts of all men, shew whether of these two thou hast chosen, that he may take part of this ministry and apostleship, from which Judas by transgression fell, that he might go to his own place. And they gave forth their lots; and the lot fell upon Matthias; *and he was numbered with the eleven apostles*" (Acts 1:24-26).

If one simply looks at the use of the word *apostolos* as it is used in these mentioned verses, in addition to the original 12 apostles, we see Matthias also became an official apostle. So if we count everyone who is called an *apostolos* so far — including Jesus as the first apostle, along with the addition of Matthias as a replacement for Judas Iscariot — it means the New Testament has already named 14 apostles.

But are there others in the New Testament who are also called apostles? The answer is, unequivocally, *yes*.

Other Apostles Named in the New Testament

In addition to Jesus, the original 12 foundational apostles, and Matthias, there are numerous other people in the New Testament who are referred to by the Greek word *Apostolos* — "apostles." These are certainly not in the same classification as the first *foundational apostles* — nevertheless, they were Christ-given apostles in a broader sense that were also given as gifts to help establish churches in conjunction with the other fivefold ministry gifts of prophet, evangelist, pastor, and teacher.

The following is a list of other apostles specifically named in the New Testament:

- **Paul** (Romans 1:1; 1 Corinthians 1:1; 2 Corinthians 1:1; Galatians 1:1; Ephesians 1:1; Colossians 1:1)
- **Barnabas** (Acts 13:2,3,50; 14:14; 1 Corinthians 9:5,6)
- **Apollos** (1 Corinthians 4:6-13)
- **Epaphroditus** (Philippians 2:25; the word *apostolos* is translated here as "messenger")
- **Andronicus**, a relative of Paul (Romans 16:7)
- **Junia**, the wife of Andronicus (Romans 16:7)
- **Titus** (2 Corinthians 8:23; the word *apostolos* is translated here as "messenger")
- **An unnamed brother** who traveled with Titus (2 Corinthians 8:18,23)
- **Another unnamed brother** with Titus (2 Corinthians 8:22,23)
- **Timothy** (1 Thessalonians 1:1; 2:6)
- **Silvanus** (1 Thessalonians 1:1; 2:6)
- **James**, the Lord's brother (Galatians 1:19)

If we count all those in the New Testament to whom the word *apostolos* is specifically applied, we discover that there are *at least* 26 people who were described using the word *apostolos* and who did apostolic work. I say, "at least" because there are actually a few more who could potentially be added to this list.

Indeed, there were the original foundational apostles, the exceptional case of Paul, and others who were sent apostolically by the churches. This means that contrary to what many denominations have taught, real apostolic ministry was not limited to the original 12 *foundational* apostles, nor did this Christ-given fivefold ministry gift cease with the close of what is called the Apostolic Age.

Ephesians 4:11-13 clearly says, "And he gave some, apostles; and some, prophets; and some, evangelists; and some, pastors and teachers; for the perfecting of the saints, for the work of the ministry, for the edifying of the body of Christ: till we all come in the unity of the faith, and of the knowledge of the Son of God, unto a perfect man, unto the measure of the stature of the fulness of Christ."

Paul states that these Christ-given fivefold gifts will be needed in the Church until we've "...come in the unity of the faith, and of the knowledge of the Son of God, unto a perfect man, unto the measure of the stature of the fullness of Christ" (v.13). So until that time comes, all five of these Christ-given ministry gifts will be in operation.

Apostles, prophets, evangelists, pastors, and teachers have continued to operate for 2,000 years. Although apostles have been less recognized — often called missionaries or called by some other name — they have nonetheless always functioned in God's Church and will continue to do so until we have reached the fullness of Christ. Since that fullness and maturity will truly be ultimately reached at the time of the glorious rapture of the Church, we can be assured that all these Christ-given fivefold ministry gifts will operate among us until we reach that long-awaited maturity.

In the next chapter, we will examine the criteria given in Scripture and used by the Early Church to determine who *is* and *is not* an authentic apostle.

Questions for Deeper Consideration

Chapter 3

1. After reading this chapter, can you explain the important theological difference between a cessationist and a continuist. Do you now understand the difference between a cessationist and a continuist? Can you verbalize the difference between these two terms? And now I ask: Are you a cessionatist or a continuist?

2. This chapter demonstrated clearly that the word "apostle" is being misapplied by many today. Can you explain in what ways the word "apostle" is being wrongly used? After reading this chapter, can you explain the consequences of using an important biblical term in an incorrect way? Please explain how the overuse or wrong use of the word "apostle" has diluted its powerful meaning.

3. Can you explain the difference between an apostle and a missionary, or are they one and the same? Based on what you read in this chapter, can you now say why the word missionary came to be used in the Church? What roles do missionaries play in worldwide evangelism and how would you define the role of a missionary after reading this chapter? Additionally, what is the difference between a missionary and an apostle?

4. The word "apostle" is translated from the Greek word *apostolos*, which is a compound of the preposition *apo* and the word *stello*. When these two components are joined, they form the word *apostello*, which is transformed into the word *apostolos*. Can you explain the meaning of the word *apostolos* and how the components *apo* and *stello* work together in the word *apostolos*?

5. We have seen that the word "apostle" is an old Greek word with various meanings and applications in the ancient world. But based on what you have read in this chapter, what historically was the earliest meaning of the word "apostle?" After you have answered that question, please express other subsequent meanings of the word "apostle" that were discussed in this chapter.

6. In Second Corinthians 12:7, Paul states he had to continually deal with a "thorn" in the flesh. What new insights did you get from this chapter about Paul's "thorn" in the flesh? Based on what you read in this chapter, can you now express what was Paul's "thorn" in the flesh? Was it different from what you've heard from other sources? What have others said about Paul's "thorn" in the flesh that he had to battle from time to time?

7. Can you now say how many people in the New Testament are identified as apostles? What is the difference between *foundational apostles* and *other apostles*?

CHAPTER 4

WHAT ARE THE AUTHENTICATING SIGNS OF A GENUINE APOSTLE?

Truly the signs of an apostle were wrought among you in all patience, in signs, and wonders, and mighty deeds.

— 2 Corinthians 12:12

We saw in the last chapter that although there was the original group of *foundational* apostles — and no one else will ever be added to that original group — there were indeed others who were Christ-given apostles in the broader sense of the word. In fact, by the end of the First Century, so many people were claiming to be apostles that the church at

Ephesus had to develop criteria based on Scripture to determine who *was* and *wasn't* a real apostle.

I find it interesting that the Early Church never questioned that others in addition to the original 12 disciples could be apostles. The Early Church knew this was an essential fivefold ministry gift that extended beyond the original group of the 12 foundational apostles. But as noted already, there were so many people showing up who were claiming to be apostles that the leadership in the Early Church, particularly in Ephesus, felt the pressing, urgent need to develop scriptural criteria to determine who *was* and *wasn't* an apostle.

The special efforts by the leadership of the church at Ephesus to discern who *was* real and who *wasn't* real was so impressive that Jesus commended them for it. During the First Century, the church at Ephesus was the largest church in the world and seemed to have been the most developed in terms of organization, doctrine, and ministry. And in Revelation 2:2, Jesus told the church at Ephesus, "I know thy works, and thy labor, and thy patience, and how thou canst not bear them which are evil: *and thou hast tried them which say they are apostles, and are not....*"

The word "works" at the first of this verse is a word that denotes *deeds* or *actions*. But the sentence structure is actually different in Greek. The word "works" in Greek is *followed* by the word "thy" and should therefore be interpreted, "I know the works *of you*." The emphasis is on that phrase *"of you"* — in other words, Christ implicitly knew about the works of *this* particular church. It lets us know that Christ knew specific details about the works — deeds and actions — that were unique to this local body of believers.

But Jesus didn't say that He knew *generally* about the Ephesian believers' works. He proceeded to explain *precisely* what He knew about them. In the rest of Revelation 2:2 and 3, Christ spoke words of commendation about: their hardworking attitude; their endurance against the many forces arrayed against them; their devotion to ministry; their intolerance of doctrinal impurity; their desire to protect the flock from apostolic pretenders; and their steadfast refusal to give in to fatigue or weariness.

As Jesus opened His heart and spoke to His church in Ephesus, He applauded and saluted them for the things they had done correctly. First, He said, "I know thy works, *and thy labour...*" (v. 2). By naming "labor" as the first item on His list of the Ephesian believers' many commendable works, Jesus drew attention to what might have been the *chief characteristic* of this church: They were a hardworking congregation.

The word "labor" in this verse doesn't refer to a normal level of work; rather, it describes *the most difficult, exhausting, and wearisome kind of labor*. It is the Greek word *kopos* — a word often used to depict a farmer who works in his field during the hottest season of the year with sweat pouring down his face. Enduring the extreme temperatures of the afternoon sunshine, the farmer strains, struggles, and toils to push that plow through the hardened ground. Although the work is strenuous, the farmer keeps laboring. After he finishes plowing one row, he turns and starts all over again on the next one. By the end of the day, the farmer is physically exhausted, mentally drained, drenched with perspiration, and covered with dirt. His labor (*kopos*) has required his total concentration and devotion.

Jesus' use of this Greek word *kopos* to describe the church of Ephesus lets us know that these believers gave the best physical, mental, and spiritual energies they had to offer. Because this word describes *exhausting* and *wearisome* work, it allows us to see into the life of the Ephesian congregation. These believers gave themselves over to the work of the ministry with no limitations, laboring (*kopos*) to the point of *exhaustion*.

Jesus said, "I know thy *labor*." Again, the sentence structure in the Greek is different in a very important way. The word "labor" in Greek is *followed* by the word "thy," and the emphasis is on "thy," or "you." It should literally be interpreted, "I know the labor *of you*" — implying that this type of labor was a unique characteristic specifically demonstrated by the church of Ephesus. In the next paragraphs, we will see exactly what labor impressed Jesus the most.

The Leadership at Ephesus

The Ephesian leadership labored intensely because it was the largest church of its time. This fact alone demanded a high level of investment from its leadership and all its members. Because Ephesus was the largest city in all of Asia, this brought many visitors to the city, including Christians who were passing through Ephesus en route to other places. Hosting a constant flood of Christian visitors required the highest level of hospitality and organization — which was, in itself, a very difficult assignment.

Paul himself apostolically started the church of Ephesus with the help of his team members Aquila and Priscilla, and people came from across Asia to hear the apostle's teaching, especially during the years he resided there. Ships arrived at the massive harbor of Ephesus carrying visitors from around the world. This was strategic, as Ephesus had become the headquarters for Paul's explosive ministry that was expanding throughout Asia — and this, too, attracted Christians to the city. People looked to the church of Ephesus for leadership and direction and considered it to be the center of spiritual oversight for the region. This brought a continual stream of spiritual leaders and believers into the city who were seeking counsel regarding problems they were facing back home.

The Ephesian congregation was a missions-oriented church that sent many Christian workers to assist in the pioneering of other churches in Asia during the First Century. For instance, neighboring churches were launched in *Aphrodisias, Colossae, Hierapolis, Laodicea, Miletus, Pergamum, Philadelphia,*

Sardis, and *Smyrna*, as well as in many other cities of that region. Teachers and workers were dispatched from the Ephesus church to every part of Asia where churches were being established. Each time workers were dispatched, replacements had to be trained and prepared. Thus, this cycle of preparation and reassignment continued nonstop in the church of Ephesus — requiring a high level of focus, diligence, organization, and manpower in the work of God's Kingdom.

Jesus' use of the word *kopos* clearly depicts a congregation in Ephesus that was extremely hardworking — yet in Revelation 2:2, no hint of complaint can be found. The congregation of Ephesus carried out this work with joy, year after year. Christ *commended* them for their obedience, their willing attitude, and their readiness to do whatever was required for the good of their church, the salvation of the lost, and the building up of the saints.

But Jesus went on to stress the next characteristic that was unique to the church of Ephesus. He said, "I know thy works, and thy labour, and *thy patience...*" (Revelation 2:2).

Although the *King James Version* says, "and thy patience," the Greek sentence structure actually positions the word "patience" first, followed by the word "thy," or "you." In other words, the emphasis is on the *believer's* patience. Therefore it should be interpreted to say, "I know the patience *of you*" — implying a type of patience that was uniquely characteristic of the Ephesian believers.

The word "patience" comes from the same Greek word we saw in the last chapter, which is the Greek *hupomone*, a compound of the words *hupo* and *meno*. The word *hupo* means *under*, as to be *underneath* something that is very heavy. The word *meno* means *to stay* or *to abide*. As noted before, it describes *a resolute decision to remain in one's spot, to keep a position*, or *to maintain territory that has been gained*. But when the words *hupo* and *meno* are compounded to form the word *hupomone*, the new word portrays *a person who is under some type of heavy load, but who refuses to stray from his position because he is committed to his task.* Regardless of how heavy the load, how fierce the opposition, how intense the stress, or how much weight is thrown against him, the person exercising this kind of patient endurance has inwardly resolved that he is not going to move. He is committed to stay put, and he will never surrender for any reason.

One scholar has described *hupomone* as *staying power*; another contemporary translator has said it could be described as *"hang-in-there" power.* Both of these interpretations correctly express the concept behind *hupomone* because it is the attitude that *hangs in there, never gives up, refuses to surrender to obstacles, and turns down every opportunity to quit.* Apparently, the Ephesian believers' "patience" was one of their most outstanding features. This *staying power* was such a unique characteristic among them that Christ commended them for it.

As Jesus continued to speak to the Ephesian leadership and church members, He proceeded to commend them for their intolerance of religious imposters — including large numbers of people who were claiming to be apostles, but who were not. He said, "I know thy works, and thy labour, and thy patience, *and how thou canst not bear them which are evil...*" (Revelation 2:2).

The phrase "canst not" is a form of *dunamai*, which is the word for *ability* or *power.* However, in this verse, it is used with a negative, which changes the word to mean *intolerance*, *inability*, or *powerlessness.* Although intolerance would normally be perceived as a negative quality, this was a correct type of intolerance for which Christ commended this church. It was an intolerance of spiritual imposters who attempted to creep into this church for the sake of self-promotion or self-advantage. The church of Ephesus had no tolerance for pretenders. This is the reason Christ went on to say, "I know thy works, and thy labor, and thy patience, *and how thou canst not bear them which are evil....*"

The word "bear" comes from the Greek word *bastadzo* — a word that means *to suffer, to carry, to lift up*, or *to bear something* — as in *to bear* a responsibility. It is used 27 times in the New Testament, and in each instance, *bastadzo* denotes a person or group of people who are responsible for *carrying* or for *bearing* some type of responsibility. But as used in Revelation 2:2, this word *bastadzo* denotes the Ephesian congregation's absolute *intolerance* for those who were "evil." These believers emphatically refused *to carry, endorse, bear responsibility for, lift up*, or *publicize* any person they believed to be "evil."

The word "evil" is from the Greek word *kakos*, a word that is used 50 times in the New Testament and always describes something that is *bad, destructive, evil, foul, harmful, hurtful, injurious*, or *vile*.

At that time, Ephesus was called "The Light of Asia" — a term that describes the enormous effect this intellectual and sophisticated city had on all of Asia. For hundreds of years, Ephesus was an attraction for anyone with a new concept, new religion, or new god. If something new found acceptance in Ephesus, it was easy to extend its influence to other parts of Asia via the many roads that led from the city. As a result, Ephesus became a testing ground of new ideas and a magnet for ambitious new thinkers, as well as for pretenders and charlatans. They all descended on the city to try their luck to see if their new ideas could win popular approval.

Protecting True Apostolic Ministry From the Taint of 'Pretend' Apostolic Ministry

The pagan population in Ephesus had long grown accustomed to the fact that their city was an attraction to these glory-seekers. And after it became clear that the church at Ephesus was the primary spiritual leader in Asia, the city also began to attract a wide range of people who attempted to gain notoriety by trying out their new doctrines and revelations in Ephesus. It was generally felt that if one could "make it" in Ephesus and receive that church's endorsement, the door would then potentially open to *all* the churches in Asia. As a result, false apostles were constantly descending on the city to try to make a name for themselves there.

But the Ephesian church leadership had *no tolerance* for these people who tried to infiltrate the church with hidden and selfish motives. The Ephesian believers understood their church's pivotal role in the entire region, and they understood that what they endorsed would be carried into all the other churches. Therefore, they didn't quickly assume responsibility for newcomers.

Instead, Revelation 2:2 implies that the church set up a system whereby they could test new arrivals to see if they were really what they claimed to be. The leadership at Ephesus loved their church so much that they had no tolerance for anyone who twisted the Word to create a new, popular doctrine, nor did they have any stomach for those who selfishly wished to use the Ephesian church for their own advantage.

The phrase "and how thou canst not bear them which are evil" also gives us insight into how Jesus Himself feels about those who try to use the Church for selfish gain, self-promotion, or for self-glory. Jesus said these people are "evil." As we already saw, this word for "evil" always describes something that is *bad, destructive, evil, foul, harmful, hurtful, injurious*, or *vile*. In this case, people were claiming to be apostles who were not, and it was damaging to the true apostles when false apostles gained a public foothold and stained or ruined the reputation of apostolic ministry. This situation was so destructive that Jesus *commended* the Ephesian leadership for refusing to tolerate or endure false apostles, or pretenders. The leaders' desire to uphold the honor of public ministry was one of the characteristics about this local-church leadership that made it commendable in the eyes of the Lord.

In Revelation 2:2, Jesus went on to say, "I know thy works, and thy labour, and thy patience, and how thou canst not bear them which are evil: *and thou hast tried them....*"

Here we discover that the leadership in Ephesus developed scriptural criteria to "try" those many newcomers who claimed to be apostles. The word "tried" is the Greek word *peiradzo*, which means *to put to the test, to test in order to prove, to test a person or object in order to expose the truth*, or *to witness concerning the quality of a substance.* This word was often used to describe the testing of people to determine if they really were what they claimed, boasted, or advertised about themselves.

'Tried' by Fire

As I shared earlier, the word *peiradzo* was used to describe the purifying fires placed underneath metal to bring impurities to the surface. As the metal was put through ever-increasing degrees of blazing heat, the fire caused impurities to rise to the surface that otherwise would have remained undetected to the naked eye. The multiple degrees of blazing fire caused all the impurities to rise to the surface. Once exposed, the impurities were scraped off and removed — but without the test of fire, they would have remained undetectable.

However, when the word *peiradzo* is used to describe testing *people*, it depicts *a calculated, premeditated test or an investigation that is deliberately designed to expose any deficiency or falsehoods.* The questioner stokes the flames again and again in an attempt to expose the impurities or defects in an individual that otherwise are unseen. If the person is free of defects, the fire will reveal nothing and will prove his or her quality. But if hidden motives are present, the heat of the flames are designed to bring any defects and impurities to the surface.

This is how the word "tried" is used in this case to describe the process by which the church leadership at Ephesus tested those who claimed to be apostles. This church was being inundated with people who claimed to be apostles with new, outstanding revelations.

The Ephesian church leaders were serious about protecting the reputation of real apostles and about sparing the church from the assault of pretenders. The use of the word "tried" — *peiradzo* — tells us that those leaders aggressively tested people who boasted about being apostles, closely examining them to see if they could pass the scriptural criteria to authenticate they were truly what they claimed to be. During that testing, the church leadership applied criteria that enabled them to determine who did and who didn't have a genuine apostolic call.

The word *peiradzo* implies that the recipients of this testing were so thoroughly examined that they must have felt as if they were being *put through the fire*. During an unspecified amount of time, the flame of examination was turned up again and again until the church leadership was able to obtain an accurate picture of these individuals and determine whether they were *genuine apostles* or *deceptive pretenders*.

The church leadership in Ephesus was serious about protecting the name of Jesus and authentic apostolic ministry. Jesus referred to this in Revelation 2:2, saying, "I know thy works, and thy labor, and thy patience, and how thou canst not bear them which are evil: *and thou hast tried them which say they are apostles, and are not....*"

The issue of apostleship was extremely important to the First Century Church. This was evident in Ephesus, where the church leadership "tried" those who claimed to be apostles. These leaders clearly believed that the apostolic ministry was crucial and that its role in the Church needed to be protected and honored. In fact, the problem of false apostles was so serious in the Ephesian church that the leadership became equally serious about correcting it. This prompted Jesus to tell the Ephesian believers, "...Thou hast tried them which say they are apostles, and are not, and hast found them liars" (Revelation 2:2).

As noted earlier, the word "tried" points to *a thorough and serious investigation*. It means *to try*, *to examine*, *to inspect*, *to investigate*, *to scrutinize*, or *to put to the test*. The leadership of the church at Ephesus wanted to guard the reputation of the true apostolic gift and protect the members of their congregation from pretenders who sought to lead them astray.

Apostolic Criteria

The church of Ephesus was *birthed* in the power of true apostolic ministry, and the Ephesian believers were noted for their relationship with Paul and his team. Because of that close association, they were very familiar with the signs that should accompany genuine apostles. Therefore, developing a test — *a series of criteria* — to determine the veracity of people who claimed to be apostles was not a difficult task for these spiritually experienced believers.

We know from Jesus' words in Revelation 2:2 that many of the individuals who came to Ephesus and claimed to be apostles failed the test. Jesus went on to say, "I know thy works, and thy labour, and thy patience, and how thou canst not bear them which are evil: and thou hast tried them which say they are apostles, and are not, *and hast found them liars*."

The word "found" is from the Greek word *heurisko*, a word that primarily means *to discover as a result of intense research*. In this word is a sense of exhilaration that accompanies such a discovery — it is a facet of meaning that's found in our word *"eureka,"* which is derived from *heurisko*. The Greek word paints the picture of a researcher who, after a long and diligent search, succeeds in digging up, uncovering, and ferreting out the hidden information he inwardly knew was there all along. In that moment, he strikes it rich as he exposes a "mother lode" of information. He exclaims exultantly, *"Eureka, I found it!"*

The use of the word "found" the Greek word *heurisko* — depicts the great exhilaration the spiritual leadership in Ephesus felt when they exposed a false apostle who had masterfully masqueraded as a real one. Because of the church's strategic location and its leading role in Asia, the Ephesian believers understood their accountability to God regarding the endorsement of ministers. They knew if they got it wrong in this matter, their error in judgment would affect not only their church, but other churches throughout the region as well. Thus, the spiritual leaders of Ephesus made it a priority to carefully test and try people *before* they endorsed them as true apostles and ministers of the Gospel.

The word *heurisko* meaning "found" — in Revelation 2:2 seems to suggest that the church leaders in Ephesus refused to be swayed by the outward appearance of a person claiming to be an apostle — even if that newcomer looked, sounded, and acted right. If these church leaders inwardly sensed something was amiss, they persistently searched and continued to stoke the flame of questioning higher and higher until *finally* the impurity bubbled to the surface and the dishonesty or impurity was exposed.

This was a "eureka" moment — the result of a staunch commitment and a thorough search in order to preserve the integrity of the true apostolic gift and to protect the Church. It was for this steadfast commitment that Jesus commended the leadership at the church of Ephesus. In the phrase, "hast found them liars," the word "liars" is the Greek word *pseudes* — the same word Paul used in Second Corinthians 11:13 to describe *false* apostles. It denotes *a person who misrepresents the truth, twists the facts, projects untrue images, or deliberately misleads others by giving them false information.*

These pretenders, if they could convince others that they were genuine apostles, could possibly gain leverage in people's lives. But the Ephesian church leadership refused to be easily swayed, and their commitment to integrity helped protect their own church, as well as churches throughout Asia, from being misled by these bogus apostles.

In Revelation 2:3, Jesus expounded further on these points by saying, "And *hast borne*, and hast patience, and for my name's sake hast laboured, and hast not fainted." The words "hast borne" are, again, a translation of the Greek word *bastadzo*, the same word used in verse 2, where it is translated, "canst not *bear* them which are evil." It conveys the idea of the Ephesian believers' *intolerance* or *inability* to endorse or bear responsibility for anyone they found to be questionable or evil. The Greek tense used also implies that they *had always been intolerant* of evildoers in the past and they *remained intolerant* in the present.

The spiritual leadership in the church of Ephesus had no tolerance for those who falsely called themselves apostles. This had been and continued to be the believers' pattern over the years since the church began. For the second time in two successive verses, Jesus commended them for this important quality, demonstrating the high value He places on integrity in the ministry.

The words "hast patience" are a repetition of what Jesus already said in Revelation 2:2, but the tense used here again implies that *they had been patient in the past* and *they remained consistently patient in the present.* Then Jesus continued in Revelation 2:3, saying, "And hast borne, and hast patience, *and for my name's sake....*" The phrase translated "and for my name's sake" actually means *on account of my name*. This is important because it tells us the church of Ephesus endured all their challenges and hard work for the right reasons.

In Revelation 2:3, Jesus continued to speak to the church of Ephesus, "And hast borne, and hast patience, and for my name's sake *hast laboured, and hast not fainted.*" The word "labored" comes from the Greek word *kopos*, which was also used in Revelation 2:2 where Jesus told the Ephesian believers that He was aware of the *strenuous labor* they had carried out for the Gospel. In Revelation 2:3, Jesus once again emphasized this quality, revealing the high value He places on those who work hard and consistently for the sake of the Gospel. Just as they *had been* intolerant of evildoers and *remained* intolerant — and just as they *had been* patient in the beginning and *remained* patient — they also *had always been* and *remained* a hardworking church. The Ephesian church had worked extremely hard for many years, bearing continual responsibility in producing spiritual leadership for all of Asia.

It is significant that Jesus went on to tell these believers, "And hast borne, and hast patience, and for my name's sake hast laboured, and *hast not fainted.*" The word "fainted" is *kekopiakes*, a form of the word *kopos*, the Greek word for *extreme labor* or *exhausting work*. The Greek tense used here means that in spite of the difficulties the Ephesian believers faced, *they never gave in to exhaustion or weariness*. The work they accomplished could have brought the church or group to their knees in exhaustion. Yet their spirits remained strong, and they refused to relax their work ethic as they strove to serve their Lord and Savior.

Additionally, the issue of apostleship was so extremely important in the minds of the leadership in Ephesus that they "tried" those who claimed to be apostles because they believed the apostolic ministry was important and its role in the church needed to be protected and honored.

If they were able to develop *a series of criteria* to determine who was and wasn't a true apostle, it means God does not leave us to guess who *is* and *isn't* a genuine apostle. The fact is that Paul was such a mighty apostle that he penned nearly half of the New Testament and apostolically founded churches across the Roman Empire in the First Century. And through this mighty apostle's epistles, the Holy Spirit established criteria that we need even today to determine true apostleship.

In his writings, Paul provided six biblical proofs of apostleship. So let's proceed to see the six criteria Paul gave us to determine who is and isn't a true apostle.

Proof Number One:
An Apostle Is Marked by a Supernatural *Vision of Jesus*

After Judas Iscariot committed suicide, the remaining apostles took serious steps to carefully pick someone to replace him. It was Peter who said *the first criterion* to be a replacement among the foundational apostles was that one had to have personally seen Jesus' ministry with his own eyes and to have personally witnessed His resurrection. Matthias met this qualification, among others (*see* Acts 1:15-26) — thus, he was chosen to be Judas Iscariot's replacement.

But it appears that Paul took it a step further, describing his own proof of apostleship, when he wrote to the church in the bustling city of Corinth. In First Corinthians 9:1, Paul wrote, "Am I not an apostle? am I not free? have I not seen Jesus Christ our Lord? are not ye my work in the Lord?" So it is logical to ask, "If Paul himself wrote that seeing the Lord was a criterion for being an apostle, when did Paul see the Lord?"

While there is no biblical evidence to support it, Paul was in the city of Jerusalem during the time of Jesus' ministry, and it is within the realm of possibility that Paul had personally witnessed Jesus at some point during that time. However, in First Corinthians 9:1, Paul is not referring to that possibility. He is referring to multiple *supernatural* visions in which he had personally seen the Risen Lord.

The first of these visions occurred when Paul was traveling on the road to Damascus (*see* Acts 9:1-6) at the time of his dramatic salvation. But other visions followed when Jesus appeared over and over again. We know from

Jesus' own words to Paul recorded in Acts 26:16 that Jesus said he would be appearing to Paul in visions multiple times. So we can say confidently that through multiple visions, Paul had indeed seen the Risen Lord. In these visions, Jesus gave him direct and personal revelation of the Gospel (*see* Galatians 1:11,12). Apparently, Paul believed these visions of Jesus qualified him to pass the first criterion for being a true apostle — to have personally seen the Risen Christ.

But in addition to having these supernatural visions, we also know that Paul had a clear apostolic "vision" of the Church — the *naos* Temple of God, the Body of Christ — and this perhaps also qualified as Paul's "seeing" the Lord.

One thing is sure: For an apostle to do his work, he must have a clear understanding and vision of Christ and His lordship and headship in the Church. All apostolic work is built around this vision. Today there are undoubtedly people called to apostolic work who have never had a literal vision of Jesus Himself, but they have had, and *have*, a burning vision of Christ in His Church that compels them to do what they do.

But it is certain that as a part of their apostolic criteria, Early Church leaders who tested those who claimed to be apostles would have asked, "Has this individual who claims to be an apostle seen the Risen Christ? Do they really have a bona fide, burning vision in them of Christ in the Church?" The Bible makes the first criterion plain — that any person who is a genuine Christ-given apostle *must* have had a supernatural encounter with Jesus Christ, and he *must* have a burning vision of Christ expressing Himself in His Church.

Proof Number Two: An Apostle Is Marked With Supernaturally *Proven Fruit*

In First Corinthians 9:1, Paul also stated, "Am I not an apostle? am I not free? have I not seen Jesus Christ our Lord? *are not ye my work in the Lord?*"

Paul added that the churches he had started were additional proof that he was a bona fide apostle. As we saw in the last chapter, an authentic apostle is not just a pioneer or innovator of new ideas. In the New Testament, the word "apostle" is never used except to describe those who start and lead churches. This is why Paul refers to the Corinthians themselves as proven fruit of his apostleship.

Of course, this church was one of the churches he had started. Thus, Paul made it clear that if a person has *not* started churches, *plural*, he simply does not qualify to be called an apostle — *period.* That person may have tremendous biblical insight and indeed be a pioneer and innovator in his respective field and worthy of great honor. But if an individual has not driven back the forces of hell and planted churches where the Church in those localities previously did not exist, he simply does not scripturally qualify to be called an apostle.

It's interesting that today, many who are working apostolically are not recognized as bona fide Christ-given apostles, though they fit the criteria and their ministries exhibit all the authenticating signs. By the same token, many who are called apostles *don't* pass the scriptural muster as a fivefold ministry gift of apostle. So some are apostles in deed, but not in name — while others are apostles in name, but not in deed.

A Brief Word About 'Hidden Apostles'

There are true "hidden apostles" who are called to certain groups of people in much the same way the apostle Paul was called to the Gentiles and Peter was called to the Jews. But the target groups those "hidden apostles" are called to reach don't have to be a certain nationality or ethnicity. For example, there are men and women assigned in the Body of Christ to rescue sex-trafficked people, bring them to Christ, and even establish churches among them. These "apostles" establish works from the ground up where transformation can occur in people's lives and these apostles move to other localities — including various countries of the world — to do it all over again. People functioning in this role in the fivefold ministry could accurately be called *apostles.*

Apostles are sent to lay the foundation of the Church where it has not existed before. So even if a person possesses all the other following criteria listed in this chapter, but he has no record of ever starting churches or leading churches, he is categorically not an apostle. It may even be true that the person is blessed with supernatural activity and wonderful insights, but the fact that he has not started or led churches means he simply does not qualify as an apostle.

I am confident that as a part of their scriptural criteria for apostleship, the Early Church leadership would have asked, "Does the individual before us who claims to be an apostle have the proven track record and fruit of churches he has started and leads?" Any person who is a genuine Christ-given apostle *must* have the proof of churches that he has started and leads.

Proof Number Three: An Apostle Is Marked With Supernatural *Patience*

The apostle Paul wrote further in Second Corinthians 12:12 about signs — or *criteria* — that are to be used to discern whether or not a genuine apostle is in our midst. In that verse, Paul wrote, "Truly the signs of an apostle were wrought among you in all *patience*, in signs, and wonders, and mighty deeds." In this verse, Paul gives the next sign to help us recognize a true apostle: *patience.*

First, Paul says, "Truly the *signs* of an apostle..." (2 Corinthians 12:12). Paul remarkably says the signs of an apostle were wrought *right there among them*, possibly even in the very center of the wicked city of Corinth. The word "signs" informs us that there are *recognizable signs* you'll see if a person is a genuine Christ-given apostle. The word "signs" is a translation of the Greek word *semeion*, a word that was used to describe *the official written notice that announced a court's final verdict*. This word *semeion* also described *the signature or seal applied to a document to guarantee its authenticity* or *a sign that marked key locations in a city*. This significant word was carried into New Testament language — and Paul used it in Second Corinthians 12:12 as he described the signs of an apostle.

By using this Greek word *semeion*, Paul declared that certain signs will always exist as *the final verdict* to prove a person's apostleship. He says these accompanying signs are like a *signature* or *seal* that *authenticates* and *guarantees* a person is a real apostle. There are many more signs than these, but Paul says these particular signs provide authentication — verifiable proof — and they will accompany every person who genuinely carries an apostolic mantle. Thus, Paul tells us that if the "signs" he lists are evident in a person's ministry, those signs should be seriously considered as a possible *announcement*, *guarantee*, or *proof* that a particular person is a Christ-given apostle.

The signs Paul lists in this verse are certainly not all-inclusive; however, they serve as good indicators to point to a bona fide apostolic call. Similar to the way a highway sign lets you know you are coming closer to a particular city or destination, these signs in a person's life and ministry may be evidence that a person has a genuine apostolic call.

In Second Corinthians 12:12, Paul wrote, "*Truly* the signs of an apostle were wrought among you in all patience, in signs, and wonders, and mighty deeds." The word "truly" comes from the Greek phrase *ta men*, a phrase that means *emphatically* or *indeed*, and it could be translated, *"Of a certainty!"* By using these exact words, Paul was declaring that if a person is truly apostolic, you will *categorically* see these particular signs in his life or ministry.

Paul wrote, "Truly the signs of an apostle were wrought among you in all patience, in signs, and wonders, and mighty deeds." The very first "sign" Paul listed in this passage as an authenticating marker to alert someone that he is seeing a real apostle is that the person will exhibit the quality of *patience.*

To list *patience* as a supernatural sign may seem strange at first, but anyone who understands apostolic ministry knows that genuine apostolic ministry often takes place in difficult and uncomfortable conditions. For sure, it is real frontline ministry — it is a spiritual military expedition to push into new territory, to fight against the powers of darkness, and then to bulldoze demonic opposition out of the way so the foundation of the Church can be established where it never existed before. If there was ever a virtue that an apostle needs, it is this divine element that Paul calls *patience.*

As noted in the last chapter and earlier in this chapter, the word "patience" is a form of the Greek word *hupomone.* Forgive me for repeating it again, but this important word bears repeating. It is a compound of *hupo* and *meno.* The word *hupo* means *under* and the word *meno* means *to stay* or *to abide.* Compounded into the word *hupomone,* it means *to remain in one's spot regardless of how heavy or hard the situation, to keep a position, to resolve to maintain territory gained.*

And again, in a military sense, it pictures *soldiers ordered to maintain their positions even in the face of opposition.* It depicts *one that defiantly sticks it out regardless of pressures mounted against it.* It can also be described as *staying power* or *"hang-in-there" power*; *the attitude that holds out, holds on, outlasts, perseveres, and hangs in there, never giving up, refusing to surrender to obstacles, and turning down every opportunity to quit.* It is a picture of *one who is under a heavy load but refuses to bend, break, or surrender because he is convinced that the territory, promise, or principle under assault rightfully belongs to him.*

This means if a person is called to be a genuine apostle, that call will be evidenced by a supernatural endurance *to stay put* and not to "abandon ship" when things get tough. In fact, by placing *patience* first on this list, Paul forcefully lets us know this *supernatural patience* — or, better, *endurance* — is one of the chief signs of one's real apostleship. Only a douse of this supernatural patience and endurance can give sufficient strength to an apostle to keep pressing forward when it seems all of hell is raging against him. Paul lists this kind of patience and endurance as a supernatural evidence of real apostleship.

As already noted, individuals with a real apostolic call live on the frontlines and do frontline work in environments that are difficult and often hostile to the Gospel. In order to fulfill this divine call, they have to resist the demonic powers and all the other forces arrayed against them. This assignment requires a special God-given endowment of patience — *endurance* — or the supernatural ability to *stay put* regardless of the pressure or opposition one encounters.

When Paul listed the signs of an apostle in Second Corinthians 12:12, remember that he wrote, "*Truly* the signs of an apostle were wrought among you in all patience..." That word truly was Paul's way of saying that *emphatically* and *categorically*, one of the signs of a real apostle is the supernatural ability to stay put when everyone else abandons ship and heads home. Paul knew that his ability to remain steadfast in the midst of the intense resistance he consistently faced was supernatural. Paul was so impacted by this divine grace that enabled him to *stay put* in hostile environments that he included it as one of the signs of legitimate apostolic ministry.

Only a divine endowment of this supernatural patience and endurance can give one the sufficient strength and stamina to keep pressing forward when it seems as if all of hell is raging against him. Paul testified that the apostle's *hupomone* ability to *stay put* while laying a foundation and then building upon it which includes establishing divine order and strengthening the saints — often in the face of discouragement or intense opposition — is remarkable and supernatural. Thus, Paul listed it as a sign that *always* accompanies true apostolic ministry.

The Supernatural Power To Endure Attacks

Although the following section may at first seem to be a bit of a diversion, I want you to see Paul's words in Second Corinthians 11:23-27, where he described some of the difficulties and hassles he encountered as he preached the Gospel, drove back darkness, and began to apostolically replicate the life, language, and culture of the Church where it had never existed before. As he wrote to the Corinthians, they would have remembered some of those ferocious attacks, like when Paul was dragged before the court in Corinth to be condemned, but was miraculously delivered.

Paul was *not* glorifying what he had been through, but was rather using these nearly unimaginable events to demonstrate what a great and supernatural endurance was working in him and making him tougher than any of these resolve-breaking circumstances and situations. As Paul pressed forward to fulfill his apostolic anointing, he encountered events that would have shattered a normal man — but, regardless, he pressed onward, divinely empowered by the Spirit to go where no man had gone and to do what no man had ever done.

Paul candidly told his testimony in Second Corinthians 11:23-27 as he chronicled *some* of Satan's attacks against him and his apostolic assignments. He lucidly recounted the kind of staggering strength that was required to resist each attack and do whatever level of work was necessary to finish his Christ-given assignments in the various virgin territories where the Holy Spirit had sent him.

In that account, Paul wrote that he was "… in labours more abundant, in stripes above measure, in prisons more frequent, in deaths oft." He continued,

"Of the Jews five times received I forty stripes save one. Thrice was I beaten with rods, once was I stoned, thrice I suffered shipwreck, a night and a day I have been in the deep; in journeyings often, in perils of waters, in perils of robbers, in perils by mine own countrymen, in perils by the heathen, in perils in the city, in perils in the wilderness, in perils in the sea, in perils among false brethren; in weariness and painfulness, in watchings often, in hunger and thirst, in fastings often, in cold and nakedness" (2 Corinthians 11:23-27).

Let's look at this list for a moment so you can see what Paul faced as he carried out his ministry as an apostle. You will see that regardless of the cost, and regardless of the roadblocks Satan tried to set before him, none of these nearly unimaginable difficulties knocked him out of the race. As an apostle, Paul knew that a part of his divine equipment was his being endued with *a supernatural endurance* that enabled him above and beyond his own natural strength and ability to outlast them all.

We'll begin with Paul's "labors more abundant."

'In Labours More Abundant'

In Second Corinthians 11:23, Paul writes that he had been "in labours more abundant." He uses the Greek word *kopos* to describe the kind of "labor" he put forth in the fulfillment of his apostolic call. This word *kopos*, as we've seen, represents the *hardest, most physical kind of labor*. It is often used to picture a farmer who works in the field, enduring the extreme temperatures of the afternoon sunshine. He strains, struggles, and toils to push that plow through the hardened ground. This effort requires his total concentration and devotion.

This word *kopos* is the same word Paul used to describe the kind of worker he was in his ministry. In fact, he went on to say, "In labours more abundant" (v. 23). The word "abundant" is the Greek word *perissos*. It is used here in the superlative sense, meaning *very abundantly.* It would be best translated, *"I worked more abundantly than most men"* or, *"I worked more than you could even begin to comprehend."* Paul was empowered and sustained by *a supernatural endurance* that literally enabled him to do more than others could do.

'In Stripes Above Measure'

Next in Second Corinthians 11:23, Paul said he'd experienced "stripes above measure." This clearly tells us that he had been physically beaten as he fulfilled his God-given apostolic calling. The word "stripes" is the Greek word *plege*, and it means *to smite*, *to hit*, *to wound*, or *to violently strike.*

There are many examples of this word in the New Testament. For example, in Luke 10:30, Jesus tells us, "…A certain man went down from Jerusalem to Jericho, and fell among thieves, which stripped him of his raiment, and *wounded* him, and departed, leaving him half dead." The word "wounded" is this Greek word *plege.*

Notice that the man's wounds were so devastating that when the thieves departed, they assumed he was dead. They were *mortal wounds.* Now Paul uses this same word to describe the kinds of beatings he received as he sought to fulfill his God-given assignment in life.

This very word *plege* is used in Acts 16:33 to describe the kind of beating Paul and Silas received in Philippi. After God's power shook the prison walls and set Paul and Silas free, the keeper of the prison came to them and asked how to be saved. This verse tells us that once the prison guard was saved, he "...took them the same hour of the night, and washed their *stripes*...." This word "stripes" is the same Greek word *plege.* Here we see an example of the physical beatings Paul endured. But this incident in Philippi was just one example of Paul being physically knocked around.

In Second Corinthians 11:23, Paul went on to say that he experienced "stripes above measure." The words "above measure" is a form of the Greek word *huperballo*, which is a compound of the words *huper* and *ballo*. The word *huper* means *above and beyond what is normal.* The word *ballo* means *to throw.* When these two words are joined together, they paint a very powerful picture. Picture an archer who takes his bow and arrows to the field for target practice. He aims his arrow at the bull's-eye, pulls back on his bow, and shoots that arrow! But he misses his target and shoots *way over the top* or *exceedingly out of range.* The arrow flies *way beyond the range of anything considered normal.* This is a picture of the word *huperballo.*

This tells us that Paul was beaten way beyond the range of what we could even begin to imagine. The word *huperballo* describes both the *frequency* and the *intensity* of his beatings. The beatings Paul received occurred frequently. They were cruel, severe, merciless acts of brutality, and what Paul's enemies did to his body was *way over the top*. But Paul was sustained by a divine endowment of *supernatural endurance* to keep going.

'In Prisons More Frequent'

In Second Corinthians 11:23, Paul added that he had been "in prisons more frequent." The word "prison" is a translation of the Greek word *phulake*, which describes *a place of custody*, *a prison ward*, or *a place heavily guarded by keepers and watchmen*. Such a prison was usually a small, dark chamber in which the most hardened, dangerous, menacing prisoners were confined. The prisoners who were put into this particular kind of chamber were considered so risky that they were usually accompanied by prison guards who guarded them 24 hours a day.

Paul was imprisoned numerous times, but when I read this verse, I particularly think of when he and Silas were imprisoned for a short period in the city of Philippi. Rather than throw in the towel and quit, Acts 16:25,26 says, "And at midnight Paul and Silas prayed, and sang praises unto God: and the prisoners heard them. And suddenly there was a great earthquake, so that the foundations of the prison were shaken: and immediately all the doors were opened, and every one's bands were loosed."

Because they refused to give in and give up and offered a sacrifice of praise to God in that horrible place, God sent an earthquake that supernaturally shook only that one particular building and opened the prison doors for Paul and Silas, causing their shackles to fall off so they could walk free. What began as an attack ended as the birth of the church in Philippi, as the Philippian jailer and his family came to Christ that night.

But Paul was kept in this kind of extreme confinement many times during his ministry, and that is why he says he was in "prisons more frequent" (2 Corinthians 11:23). No one wants to go to jail, but if going to jail meant that Paul would accomplish his apostolic calling along the way, then that's what he would do. He was willing to undergo any inconvenience, pay any price, and go to all lengths to do what God had commissioned him to do. Even jail would not stop him. It is clear that Paul truly was sustained by a *supernatural endurance* that empowered him to keep going regardless of these assaults.

'In Deaths Oft'

In Second Corinthians 11:23, Paul continued to say he was "in deaths oft." The word "deaths" is from the Greek word *thanatos*, but here, Paul uses the plural form, *thanatoi,* which is literally translated "deaths."

We know that Paul frequently wrote about dying. We tend to spiritualize it, but the fact is, Paul faced actual physical death on a regular basis. When he wrote, "...I die daily" (1 Corinthians 15:31), he meant, *"I am constantly confronted with the prospect of death."*

Paul faced death so often that he learned how to face it bravely. He wrote in Romans 14:8, "...Whether we die, we die unto the Lord...." In First Corinthians 15:55, we see that he learned to meditate on victory rather than on mortality and fatality. He wrote, "O death, where is thy sting? O grave, where is thy victory?" These are not allegorical verses about death. They are the thoughts of a man who faced the prospect of death almost on a daily basis.

In First Corinthians 15:32, Paul said he "...fought with beasts at Ephesus...." The Greek word *theriomacheo* is used in this verse, a compound of *therion* — which means *wild beasts, dangerous animals, vicious killers* — and *machomai* — which means *to fight, usually with weapons.* Compounded, *theriomacheo* means *to fight wild, dangerous animals, possibly with weapons.*

Some have tried to say these verses allegorically refer to difficult people that Paul had to contend with, but Paul was saying that there was a literal moment in Ephesus when he was thrust into the theater or stadium to fight ferocious beasts. When Paul wrote First Corinthians 15:32, that event was no doubt still very vivid in his mind. Again, Paul was empowered by a *supernatural endurance* that empowered him to keep going regardless of the attacks that were waged against him.

'Five Times Received I Forty Stripes Save One'

In Second Corinthians 11:24, Paul added that "of the Jews five times received I forty *stripes* save one." This refers to a Jewish method of punishment, which Paul suffered on five different occasions. After being repeatedly beaten in this terrible manner, Paul would get up and go right back to what he was doing before he was beaten. Paul was so committed to fulfilling his God-given call that he wouldn't let anything stop him. *He would not stop until his mission was complete!*

Because Paul was sustained by a *supernatural endurance,* he never allowed himself to let this experience become a permanent roadblock to his ministry. In fact, he pushed the event out of the way, got up, and went on.

'Thrice Was I Beaten With Rods'

In Second Corinthians 11:25, Paul added, "Thrice was I beaten with rods...." In the ancient world, a beating with rods was a horrible, ugly form of torture. It's interesting that the book of Acts never gives us a specific example of Paul being beaten with rods in such a manner. However, as we continue to look at this list in Second Corinthians 11, we'll see that many events occurred during Paul's ministry that Luke never recorded in the book of Acts. But Paul never forgot any of them, and he was telling us here in his second epistle to the Corinthian church about some of those events into which the book of Acts gives us no insight.

It is evident that rather than throw in the towel and quit because of this experience, Paul again grabbed hold of the power of God and went on his way to keep doing what God called him to do. This was a man the devil couldn't keep down!

No wonder Paul wrote about the resurrection power of God! He was writing from personal experience when he said, "But if the Spirit of him that raised up Jesus from the dead dwell in you, he that raised up Christ from the dead shall also quicken your mortal bodies by his Spirit that dwelleth in you" (Romans 8:11).

'Once I Was Stoned'

This event in the life and ministry of Paul occurred in Acts 14:19. After a successful campaign among the Gentiles in Lystra, Jewish opposers came from Iconium to stir up trouble for Paul's ministry. They were so effective in spreading bad information about Paul that the entire city turned against him. In a moment of fury, the people of Lystra stoned him and "...drew him out of the city, supposing he had been dead" (Acts 14:19).

It may well be that Paul *was* dead. In the practice of stoning, the stoners would aim their sharp rocks at the victim's head in order to deal a fatal blow. To assure the victim's death, the stoning didn't usually stop until his head was crushed. When it was apparent that there was no possibility of survival, the remaining rocks were dumped, and the victim's corpse was dragged out of the city and left for the dogs and wild beasts to eat. So when Acts 14:19 says the people of Lystra "supposed" Paul was dead, there is no reason to think he was *not* dead at that moment.

Acts 14:20 tells us that as the disciples came and stood near Paul's corpse, "he rose up." Is it possible that these disciples joined hands and prayed for Paul's resurrection? This is precisely my view. Later Paul gave testimony of a visit he made to Heaven (2 Corinthians 12:1-4). He explained that he heard and saw things that he had never been given permission to speak. When did Paul make this visit to Heaven? This could have possibly been at the time he was stoned in Lystra.

No wonder Paul could write with such conviction: "For I am persuaded, that neither death, nor life...shall be able to separate us from the love of God, which is in Christ Jesus our Lord" (Romans 8:38,39). Even death cannot stop a man who is determined to keep going!

Paul could have resigned himself to his fate as the people were stoning him and thought, *Well, I guess this is the end of the road. I guess I'll give up and die now.* If he had done that, I'm sure stoning would have been the end of him. But I'm just as certain that as they stoned Paul, he thought, *I'm not dying now! My job isn't done! If they kill me, I'll just have to be resurrected!*

Being stoned was an unexpected event that the devil orchestrated to try to stop Paul from fulfilling his call. But although the experience stole time and delayed Paul's plans a little, it did not permanently hinder him from going on, because he was sustained by a *supernatural endurance* that empowered him to keep going.

'Thrice I Suffered Shipwreck'

In Second Corinthians 11:25, Paul further said, "...Thrice I suffered shipwreck...." This statement is a bit of a mystery because there is only one recorded shipwreck in the book of Acts. Yet we have already seen from this list that too many significant events occurred during Paul's ministry for all of them to be recorded in Luke's account of the Acts of the Apostles.

Traveling by sea in those days was a perilous and risky undertaking. Ships were not always reliable. The routes often took them through waters cluttered with sharp rocks, reefs, and debris. Even if the vessel was guided by strong and skilled leadership, currents were so strong that even the best ships could be carried directly into rocks and other dangerous obstacles.

In Acts 27:41-44, we read that Paul was traveling aboard a ship that ran into rocks and broke into pieces. A prisoner on that ship, Paul perceived by God that danger lay ahead, and he warned the ship's crew and the Roman soldiers who were guarding him. His warnings were not heeded and, later, in their moment of crisis, Paul became God's man on board the ship! Being later encouraged by "the angel of God" (Acts 27:23), Paul spoke the word of faith to the crew and passengers — that there would be no loss of life — and soon he was in charge of the entire situation.

Once marooned on the island of Melita, Paul worked with the other crew members to collect wood for a fire. Apparently a venomous viper was hidden in the sticks Paul was carrying to lay on the fire. When he dropped his wood onto the flames, that snake charged out of the pile of wood and bit Paul on the hand. This type of snake was extremely venomous. In fact, when the barbarian inhabitants of the island saw "the venomous beast hang on his hand," they superstitiously said among themselves, "…No doubt this man is a murderer, whom, though he hath escaped the sea, yet vengeance suffereth not to live" (Acts 28:4).

But Acts 28:5 says, "And he shook off the beast into the fire, and felt no harm." By the end of verse 6, the barbarian crowd was so shocked Paul didn't die that they assumed he was a god. Paul used the situation to the advantage of the Gospel, and in just a short time, he had the whole island gathered for a crusade!

Publius, the chief of the island, was so impressed, he took Paul into his own home for three days. While there, Paul laid hands on Publius' father, who "...lay sick of a fever and of a bloody flux..." (Acts 28:8). The man was miraculously healed, and soon the entire island was in revival! The Bible tells us, "So when this was done, others also, which had diseases in the island, came, and were healed" (Acts 28:9). By the time Paul departed from Melita, he was so respected and honored that they "laden" him with everything necessary for the remainder of his journey (v.10)!

Paul's attitude enabled him to be sustained by a *supernatural endurance* that kept him in the midst of revival everywhere he went. Just like you and me, Paul had the opportunity to give in to his flesh and throw a pity party. But because he chose to keep going and never stop, God's power was always available to him in every situation.

These "impasses" were definitely inconvenient and painful — and some were quite disastrous — but they were unable to permanently hinder him from getting to his appointed destination.

'A Night and a Day Have I Been in the Deep'

In Second Corinthians 11:25, Paul adds "…A night and a day I have been in the deep." This clearly refers to a 24-hour time period in which Paul was in the "deep." The word "deep" is the Greek word *buthos*, and it refers to *the deepest parts of the sea.* Because Paul mentions this event immediately following his recollection of three shipwrecks, we assume that this "night and a day" in the deep was the result of one of the other shipwrecks of which we have no knowledge.

It is not possible to make much commentary on this, as we know only what Paul says in this verse. But whenever and however it occurred, the Greek tense shows that the experience was still fresh and vivid in Paul's mind as he wrote about it. Indeed, Paul spent a 24-hour period treading water in the deepest parts of the sea. Yet it didn't scare him away from getting on the very next ship to continue his trip and go where God had ordered him to go. It was just another *impasse* on the journey, but it didn't stop his trip because he was sustained by a *supernatural endurance* that empowered him to continue making forward progress.

'In Journeyings Often'

In Second Corinthians 11:26, Paul said that he had been in "journeyings often." The word "journey" in Greek is *hodoiporia*. This word describes a *walking journey*. The word "often" is the word *pollakis*, and it refers to *many times*, *often*, or *frequently*. Paul used this phrase to tell us that he had walked to most destinations where he had been called upon to preach.

- For instance, the apostle Paul *walked* from Antioch Pisidia to Iconium (Acts 13:51); he *walked* from Iconium to Lystra (Acts 14:6); and he *walked* from Lystra to Derbe (Acts 14:20). From Derbe, he *walked* back to Lystra (Acts 14:21); and from Lystra he *walked* back to Iconium (Acts 14:21). From Iconium, he *walked* back to Antioch Pisidia (Acts 14:21); from Antioch Pisidia, he *walked* throughout the whole region of Pamphylia (Acts 14:24); and then he *walked* all the way to Perga (Acts 14:25).

- For a brief period, Paul and his team traveled by ship to Antioch (Paul's home base). But then they *walked* to Phenice and Samaria (Acts 15:3). From there, they *walked* to Jerusalem (Acts 15:4); and from Jerusalem, they *walked* back to Antioch (Acts 15:22). From Antioch, the apostle *walked* throughout the regions of Syria and Cilicia (Acts 15:41). He *walked* back through the cities of Derbe (Acts 16:1) and Lystra (Acts 16:1). Then he *walked* to Phrygia (Acts 16:6) and *walked* throughout the regions of Galatia (Acts 16:6). After that, he *walked* to Mysia (Acts 16:8) and then *walked* all the way down to Troas (Acts 16:8).

- After seeing a vision of a man in Macedonia calling to him for help (Acts 16:9), Paul took a ship from Troas (Acts 16:11). His ship ported in the city of Samothracia (Acts 16:11) but departed the next day to Neapolis (Acts 16:11). From there, Paul and his associates sailed to Philippi (Acts 16:12), a chief city in that part of Macedonia. From Philippi, Paul *walked* through Amphipolis and Apollonia (Acts 17:1); then he *walked* to the city of Thessalonica (Acts 17:1). From Thessalonia, Paul *walked* to Berea (Acts 17:10).

- Paul took a ship from Berea to Athens (Acts 17:14,15). From Athens, he *walked* to Corinth (Acts 18:1). He sailed from Corinth to Syria (Acts 18:18). Then from Syria, he *walked* to Ephesus (Acts 18:19). From Ephesus, he sailed to Caesarea (Acts 18:22); but from there, he *walked* to Antioch (Acts 18:22). From Antioch, he *walked* all over the regions of Galatia and Phrygia (Acts 18:23), and then he

> *walked* along the upper coastlines to Ephesus (Acts 19:1). The list of places where Paul traveled to fulfill his calling is amazing. Paul did a lot of *walking* during the course of his ministry!

If you add up all the miles or kilometers Paul walked, he probably spent more time *walking* than he did *preaching.* No wonder he could say, "I thank my God, I speak with tongues more than ye all" (1 Corinthians 14:18)! He had a lot of time to pray in tongues as he walked across the east and northeast sides of the Mediterranean countries to preach the Gospel and establish the Church.

Paul had no car, no train, and no airplane to get where he needed to go. Traveling that far by foot meant he had to face incredible hardship and difficult circumstances along the way. But nothing was so hard to bear that it was going to stop him from fulfilling the call on his life. Paul had made up his mind and was sustained by a *supernatural endurance.* Even if it meant he had to walk around the world by foot in order to fulfill his call, that is precisely what he would do.

'In Perils of Waters'

In Second Corinthians 11:26, Paul tells us some of the things he encountered as he traveled by foot across the countries of the Mediterranean world. He tells us that he was "in perils of waters."

The word "perils" is the word *kindunos,* a Greek word for an *extremely dangerous* or *highly volatile* situation. Paul used this word eight times in this chapter to tell us that the majority of his ministry was marked by extremely dangerous situations. Danger isn't something Paul sought, but it often went with the territory God gave him.

The word "waters" is the Greek word *potamos*, which is the word for *a river*. By using these two words *kindunos* and *potamos*, Paul told us that as he traveled, he was occasionally forced to cross extremely dangerous rivers to get to the places where the Holy Spirit sent him.

Crossing rivers was a very serious act in the ancient world. It's a vivid example of the hazards a traveler encountered in Paul's time. Bridges were few and far between, especially in remote areas. This presented awkward problems, especially during times of floods and flash-flooding, which were frequent occurrences.

Although Paul did not mention the exact rivers he had to cross, we know they would have included the *Jordan River* (Judea), the *Orontes River* (Syria), the *Cydnus River* (Cilicia), the *Meander River* and *Cayster River* (Asia), and the *Strymon River* and *Axios River* (Macedonia).

During Paul's journeys, he passed through some of the most dangerous rivers of his time. We don't usually think of these kinds of hazards when remembering Paul's ministry. But regardless of what he faced to fulfill God's plan, Paul was equipped with a *supernatural endurance* that enabled him to get across the hurdles Satan tried to put in his way.

'In Perils of Robbers'

In Second Corinthians 11:26, Paul used the Greek word "perils" for the second time in this text. As noted previously, it is the Greek word *kindunos,* which pictures something that is *extremely dangerous*. But this time he said he had been "in perils of robbers."

One danger Paul constantly faced was the threat of robbers. The word "robbers" is the Greek word *lestes*. It refers to *a plunderer*, *robber*, *highwayman*, *bandit*, or *rapacious imposter*. This word pictures a bad breed of bandits who used weapons, cunning, and violence to steal from others.

In the ancient world, robbers and thieves hid in the ditches and caves along roads that led from city to city — particularly along main routes of travel. This is why some Greek expositors translate the word "robbers" as "highwaymen." This term especially applied to bandits who ambushed those who traveled by roads. Considering how frequently Paul and his companions walked, we can easily see why Paul faced "perils of robbers."

Imagine traveling to the farthest ends of the earth by foot and carrying everything you need for that journey. You know that pillaging, predatory plunderers are hidden in the ditches and caves along the roadside as you walk along, just waiting for the right prey to pass by. You also know that these bandits are famous not only for stealing, but for wounding and killing their victims. Yet there's no other road for you to take if you are going to get where you need to go.

We can be sure that Paul and his traveling companions were alert the whole time they traveled on those roads. Because Paul used the word *kindunos* ("perils"), we know this was an extremely dangerous predicament. Yet even this predicament was not strong enough to stop Paul from doing the will of God because he was sustained by a *supernatural endurance.*

'In Perils of Mine Own Countrymen'

Now for the third time, the apostle Paul used the word "perils" (from the Greek word *kindunos,* meaning *extremely dangerous*). In Second Corinthians 11:26, he said he had been "in perils by mine own countrymen." The word "countrymen" comes from the Greek word *genos*, which is where we get the word "genes."

This word would be used *only* to denote *someone with whom one shares a common ancestry.* Paul was referring to the Jewish people who constantly opposed him everywhere he went. They opposed him in Salamis (Acts 13:8), Antioch Pisidia (Acts 13:45,50), Iconium (Acts 14:2), Lystra (Acts 14:19), Thessalonica (Acts 17:5-9), Berea (Acts 17:13), Corinth (Acts 18:12-16), and so on.

Paul told us that what he faced from his own natural kinsmen was extremely dangerous. They persecuted and hunted him down everywhere he went and were a tool Satan used to resist him — at times, viciously. But in spite of their endless persecutions, Paul pressed onward and was sustained by a *supernatural endurance*. He wasn't going to let any group of angry religious people keep him from doing what he was assigned to do.

'In Perils of the Heathen'

Then in Second Corinthians 11:26, Paul used the word "perils" for a fourth time when he testified that he had been "in perils of the heathen." Again, the word "perils" is the Greek word *kindunos,* which denotes something that is *extremely dangerous*. The word "heathen" is the Greek word *ethnos*, and it specifically refers to *Gentiles* or to *anyone not Jewish.*

The Gentile world was a strange and curious world. It was filled with wild religious beliefs, customs, and a pagan culture opposed and averse to the knowledge of a righteous and holy God. The religion of the Gentile world promoted the grossest, most depraved, and most perverted sort of sexuality. Thousands of different gods were worshiped in pagan temples, each with its own particular style of worship. Most of these religious orders involved the use of wine and drugs to induce the worshiper into wild, mindless debauchery as a part of his or her act of "worship" to the gods.

These religions were filled with demons. As the wine, drugs, music, drum-beating, and sexual perversion of temple worship intoxicated those participating in the pagan ceremony, demonic activity became stronger and stronger in the temple. During a moment of such intensity, anything could have happened, and things could have easily gotten out of control. At such moments, an act of aggression against Gospel preachers could have freely occurred. This environment was extremely dangerous, especially to Paul and his team as they confronted the powers of darkness and commanded these idol worshipers to repent.

The travels of the apostle Paul took him to some of the world's most pagan and demonic cities. In fact, Thessalonica, Athens, Corinth, and Ephesus are listed among some of the most pagan, demonic cities in the history of mankind.[1] Yet this is where the Holy Spirit led Paul. It was also where Paul experienced his most successful periods of ministry.

Going places where it is safe and secure is not always where God sends people who have an apostolic calling on their lives. The Gospel must go to every country, every city, and every village in the world. If we go only where it's comfortable and safe, none of us will ever go very far from where we live right now. Thank God for those who went before us and who pushed the powers of darkness out of the way so we can now know the glorious light of the Gospel!

Paul was called as an apostle to the Gentiles (Romans 15:16), but no danger in the Gentile world was so terrifying that he couldn't conquer it with the power of God. Paul was so sustained by a *supernatural endurance* that he was empowered to challenge and push his way through the most wicked and spiritually dark conditions to do exactly what God had called him to do.

'In Perils in the City'

In Second Corinthians 11:26, Paul used the word "perils" for a fifth time when he wrote that he had been "in perils in the city." Again, the word "perils" is from the Greek word *kindunos,* and it depicts something that is *extremely dangerous.*

Paul labored especially in larger cities that were dark and devious places filled with evil. Ephesus, Athens, Corinth, Antioch — the list goes on and on. You would think a city would be a little more civilized, but some of Paul's worst confrontations occurred right in the heart of the world's most advanced and cultured cities. Paul often labored in larger metropolitan areas. As an apostle, his primary calling was to establish the Church in every place he went. Therefore, the Holy Spirit usually sent Paul into large population centers, where there were many people and the potential for a huge harvest. But as is true in large cities today, there were dangers in the ancient cities that didn't exist in the smaller towns and villages.

Paul faced these challenges courageously with the *supernatural endurance* the Holy Spirit imparted to him. Some of these challenges were financial and political, not to mention the normal stress that a person faces when he attempts to do business in a big city. But Paul pressed forward and completed his responsibility in every place to the best of his ability.

'In Perils in the Wilderness'

Then in Second Corinthians 11:26, the apostle Paul used the word "perils" for a sixth time when he said he had been "in perils in the wilderness." The word "perils" is used again to explain dangerous situations he faced in the wilderness. The word "wilderness" is the Greek word *eremia,* which describes *a remote, isolated location* in the middle of nowhere.

Paul's travels no doubt took him through remote areas where thieves and plunderers could have easily victimized him and his companions. I'm also certain that wild beasts confronted them as they walked from place to place. Just as they faced certain dangers that were unique to the city, they also faced dangers unique to the wilderness as well. Yet Paul faced these challenges with assurance and *supernatural endurance* that enabled him to conquer each peril successfully.

'In Perils in the Sea'

For a seventh time, Paul used the word "perils" in Second Corinthians 11:26 when he wrote that he had been "in perils in the sea." The word "perils" is again the Greek word *kindunos*, which means Paul had faced *extremely dangerous* experiences traveling by sea.

As we've already seen, Paul survived three different shipwrecks, but only one of these is recorded in the book of Acts. But in addition to what Luke tells us in his account in Acts, Paul said here that there were two other catastrophes at sea that he encountered.

These sea catastrophes were just as dramatic and memorable as other events Paul faced. It was surely a horrible experience for someone to be adrift at sea, not knowing if he'd be rescued and survive. Paul says he went through this type of ordeal three separate times.

I'm sure these devilish attacks at sea were designed to put in Paul such a fear of sailing that he would never get back on another ship. But if he was going to get to the various places where God had called him to minister, he had no choice. Therefore, Paul didn't allow these occurrences to stop him from getting back on another ship to sail through dangerous waters again. If that is what he needed to do, a *supernatural endurance* given to him by the

Spirit would enable him to do whatever was needed to successfully fulfill his God-given assignment in life.

'Among False Brethren'

For the eighth time in this passage, the apostle Paul used the word "perils" in Second Corinthians 11:26 to say he had experienced "perils among false brethren." Of course, we know that the word "perils" is the Greek word *kindunos,* meaning *extremely dangerous*, and Paul used it here to describe the danger he had experienced with "false brethren."

The Greek word for "false brethren" is *pseudadelphos.* The first part of the word is *pseudes* and carries the idea of something that is *untrue.* It could be translated *pretend*, *phony*, *fake*, or *bogus.* The second part of the word, *adelphos* is simply the word for a *brother.* Compound these two words, and the new word describes *pretend, phony, fake, bogus brethren.*

"False brethren" no doubt refers to those who had hidden agendas that they kept to themselves as they tried to worm their way into the Church leadership. Whoever these "false brethren" were, Paul said they created a situation that was *extremely dangerous* and *highly volatile.*

Imagine how paranoid this situation could have made Paul, knowing that pretenders were out there constantly trying to secretly hurt him and those he loved. It could have driven Paul into a pattern of fear, suspicion, and retreat. Paul could have chosen either to retreat in insecurity or to take hold of the Spirit's help to press forward. Paul chose to lay hold of a *supernatural endurance* the Holy Spirit gave him to keep pressing ahead. Thus, these disappointing experiences couldn't stop him from going on to work with people, nor from establishing the Church in various locations.

'In Weariness'

Paul added in Second Corinthians 11:27 that he had experienced a state of "weariness" in the course of his apostolic ministry. The Greek word for "weariness" is *kopos*, which refers to *the hardest kind of work*, and it is the same word Paul uses in verse 23 when he said that he experienced "labours more abundant." By repeating this word two times in this chapter, Paul is drawing our attention to the fact he was *an extremely hard worker*.

Paul carried out hard work, as his whole life was wrapped up in his calling. But regardless of what was required for him to advance the Kingdom of God, he was able to do it because he was sustained with a *supernatural endurance* to do it.

'In Painfulness'

To make sure we comprehend how far Paul was willing to go when it came to hard work, he added in Second Corinthians 11:27 that he had experienced times in "painfulness." This word "painfulness" describes the incredible effort, toil, or physical exertion he put forth to fulfill God's calling on his life.

The Greek word is *mochthos*. This word has to do with the idea of *struggle*. But this isn't a physical struggle with pain resulting from sickness. The word *mochthos* is the picture of *a person who has worked so hard that he is about to collapse* and it pictures *one who is exhausted from physical labor.*

Paul used this word to further amplify how he worked in his ministry. The *King James Version* calls this type of hard work "painfulness," but a better translation of *mochthos* would be *to work yourself into a frazzle* or *to work yourself until you are physically depleted of strength*. This is the picture of an individual who is drained and who feels like his physical strength is nearly used up. But God's power gave him *supernatural endurance* to push beyond the normal capacity of human strength. God's power came upon him and empowered him to do what other men and women could not physically do.

'In Watchings Often'

In Second Corinthians 11:27, Paul said he had been "in watchings often." The word "watchings" is the Greek word *agrupnia* and it depicts *sleeplessness.* It is probably a reference to the long nights Paul lay awake to defend himself and his team against bandits and robbers who waited to attack them in roadside ditches and caves. The word "often" is the Greek word *pollakis,* which means *many times*, *often*, or *frequently*.

It was very common for a traveling group to take turns at "watching" during the night. If no one stayed awake and alert, plundering robbers would come and steal all the belongings of the traveling company while they slept. This phrase "in watchings often" reinforces the fact that traveling was extremely dangerous back then, especially at night. And because Paul used the word *pollakis* ("often"), we know it wasn't rare for him to take his turn guarding the camp at night. It happened "often" as his team traveled from place to place.

Paul was a team player, and like everyone else on his team, he took his turn at watching the campfire while others slept. This may not sound like a spiritual part of ministry, but it was a necessary part of his job if he was going to get where he needed to go so he could preach.

During the course of Paul's ministry, he had to do many things that seemed unspiritual and unconnected to ministry, but that had to be done so he could minister. They were often mundane, boring, time-consuming, and uncomfortable obligations. Yet without them, the real spiritual ministry could never have occurred.

If you know God has called you to do something special, don't be so high and mighty that you can't do a mundane, boring, time-consuming, or undesirable task along the way. It may not be something you relish doing. But if you don't do it, you might fail to achieve the real dream God has placed on your heart. The fact that Paul wrote "in watchings often" emphatically tells us that he had a *supernatural endurance* that enabled him to do anything required to preach the Gospel message God had entrusted to him.

'In Hunger and Thirst'

In Second Corinthians 11:27, Paul said he had known times of "hunger and thirst" as he fulfilled his ministry. The word "hunger" is the Greek word *limos*, and the word "thirst" is the Greek word *dipsos*. These words refer to *being hungry from a lack of food* or *thirsty from a lack of drink*.

This means there were times when Paul didn't have sufficient food to eat. He recalled times of inconvenience when food may not have been available. He no doubt traveled occasionally through inhospitable, barren terrain where food was not abundant. Also, because of the great distances between some of the cities Paul and his team walked, they sometimes simply ran out of food because it wasn't always possible for them to carry enough for their journey. Yet this lack of food and drink did not affect Paul's desire to go onward to the next town. It was only an inconvenience — not enough to hinder him — because he had a *supernatural endurance* to keep pressing ahead.

'In Fastings Often'

Paul added in Second Corinthians 11:27 that he has also been "in fastings often." The word "fastings" is the Greek word *nesteia*. It refers to *skipping or foregoing meals voluntarily* — in this case, probably because there was no time to eat. The word "often" is *pollakis*, and it means *many times*, *often*, or *frequently*.

The apostle Paul kept a rigid routine and busy schedule, and eating food was not a high priority on his list of things to do. First and foremost, he wanted to accomplish his God-given objectives each day in each city where he labored. The words "in fastings often" tell us Paul didn't take his trips to taste and experience the local menu. He went to get a job done. Whether the food was good or bad, Paul went where the Lord told him to go. Whether there was time to eat or no time to eat, he was determined to succeed at the job he was given to do. Because Paul was endued with *supernatural endurance*, nothing as insignificant as food had the power to knock this man out of his race.

'In Cold and Nakedness'

In Second Corinthians 11:27, Paul also testified that he had known "cold and nakedness." This phrase could refer to many incidences in Paul's life. For instance, he may have been remembering the "cold" he felt as he treaded seawater during one of his times adrift at sea.

Paul may have also been remembering the "cold" he felt during one of his many imprisonments. Ancient prisons were notorious for being damp and cold. Prisoners often contracted terrible cases of lung disease and died prematurely on account of these damp conditions. To make a prisoner's stay in prison even more miserable, the captor would often strip him almost naked before throwing him into the cave-like cell.

Another expositor suggests the phrase "in cold and nakedness" may be Paul's recollection of times when bandits successfully robbed him and his team as they traveled from city to city. It isn't possible to state definitively what Paul was referring to in his statement about "cold and nakedness." But whatever event he was remembering, it's obvious that it was *not* a pleasant experience.

I'm telling you about Paul's experiences because I want you to know that *everyone* runs into obstacles and difficulties on the pathway of obeying God — even the apostle Paul with all his God-given revelation and anointing. However, Paul was able to keep going because he was empowered with a *supernatural endurance* that enabled him to press through all of it.

I guarantee you that if you freeze every time the devil throws a roadblock in your path, you'll spend most of your life frozen. Perfect circumstances are terrific if it's possible to line them up. But perfect circumstances or not, Paul decided to grab hold of God's power, move full-speed ahead, and let God show him how to get around every *impasse* so he could finish the job. By God's grace, Paul endured and outlasted every attack of the enemy.

Do you see how important *patience* and *endurance* were as a part of the supernatural equipment God gave Paul along with his apostolic office? That is why Paul said, "*Truly* the signs of an apostle were wrought among you in all patience..." (2 Corinthians 12:12).

Again, this word "truly" in Greek is a translation of the word *ta men*, which means *emphatically*, *indeed*, or *of a certainty*. In other words, Paul said a person's supernatural ability to stand strong and steadfast as he fulfills his divine call to establish the Church, regardless of the opposition that comes against him, is truly — *emphatically* — one of the evident, undeniable signs in the life of someone with an apostolic call.

And as a part of their *apostolic criteria,* the Early Church would have asked, "Does the individual who claims to be an apostle demonstrate the supernatural patience and endurance that marks a real apostle?" Any person called to stand in an apostolic position *must* show the supernatural ability to stick it out on the frontlines even when the going gets tough.

Proof Number Four:
An Apostle's Ministry Is Marked With Supernatural *Signs*

Paul wrote, "Truly the signs of an apostle were wrought among you in all patience, in *signs*..." (2 Corinthians 12:12). In addition to supernatural patience to endure and outlast every attack and difficult circumstance, Paul added the word "signs" to the list of criteria for an apostle.

When Paul wrote to the Corinthians, he knew they would recall the miraculous signs that he worked among them, which were such an impetus in birthing the Church in Corinth. Although these specific miracles are not mentioned in Acts 18, Paul referred to them in First Corinthians 2:4 and 5 when he said, "And my speech and my preaching was not with enticing words of man's wisdom, but in demonstration of the Spirit and of power: that your faith should not stand in the wisdom of men, but in the power of God."

The word "signs" in Second Corinthians 12:12 is once again a translation of the Greek word *semeion,* which describes *a proof* or *an authenticating marker*. Because Paul wrote that miraculous signs were also a proof of apostleship, some people erroneously get the impression that Paul's ministry was continually visited with nonstop miracles. But if you carefully and honestly examine the book of Acts to determine the regularity of these types of supernatural signs, you will find they didn't occur nonstop in Paul's ministry. They occurred at pivotal and crucial moments when miracles were needed to open the door for the Gospel even wider. For example:

- In the city of Lystra, strength was restored to the limbs of a lame man (Acts 14:8-10).
- In Philippi, demons were cast out of a woman (Acts 16:16-18).
- In Ephesus, healing power was transferred through aprons or napkins taken from Paul's body to those who were bedridden and who

couldn't attend his meetings because of their physical conditions (Acts 19:11,12).

- In Troas, a young man was raised from the dead (Acts 20:9-12).
- In Melita, the sick were healed (Acts 28:8,9).

All of these signs and many others were miraculous proof that the Gospel message was true, and they were also proof of Paul's apostleship. While they didn't occur constantly, miracles did faithfully occur at just the right moments when they were needed.

So as a part of their *apostolic criteria*, the Early Church would have asked, "Has the individual who claims to be an apostle had miraculous signs at pivotal moments in his ministry?" Any person called to stand in an apostolic position *must* be able to show that miraculous signs have occurred at some junction in the course of his ministry.

Proof Number Five: An Apostle Is Marked With Supernatural *Wonders*

In Second Corinthians 12:12, Paul added, "Truly the signs of an apostle were wrought among you in all patience, in signs, *and wonders....*" Along with *supernatural patience* and *miraculous signs*, Paul said that *wonders* will also accompany true apostleship.

The word "wonders" is the Greek word *teras*, which describes *an event that leaves one baffled, bewildered, or astonished*. It depicted *the shock, surprise, or astonishment felt by bystanders who observed events that were contrary to the normal course of nature*. Such occurrences were viewed as miracles, and people believed they could only take place through the intervention of divine power. These miraculous events left spectators speechless, shocked, astonished, bewildered, baffled, taken aback, stunned, awestruck, and in a state of wonder.

The Greek word *teras* for "wonders" describes occurrences so out of the ordinary that people are left in a state of *perplexity*, *amazement*, and *wonder* as a result. When an individual has an authentic apostolic calling on his life, there will be moments in his ministry when baffling "wonders" take place.

An example of a wonder occurring in Paul's life can be found in Acts 28:3, when Paul was shipwrecked and marooned on the island of Melita. On that rainy day as Paul was gathering sticks to build a fire, "...there came a viper out of the heat, and fastened on his hand."

When the barbarians saw the deadly, venomous viper hanging from the apostle's hand, they expected Paul to swell up and suddenly fall down dead (*see* v. 6). But instead, verse 5 tells us that Paul "...shook off the beast into the fire, and felt no harm."

The deadly poison of that snake should have killed Paul. But as the powerful venom surged through the apostle's circulatory system, God's power intervened, overruling and nullifying the venom so that it had no adverse effect on Paul whatsoever! On the other hand, this "wonder" had a *huge* impact on those who were standing nearby, watching in amazement. Instead of seeing Paul fall dead, these people saw "...no harm come to him..." (v. 6). The Barbarians were so shocked by this miraculous event that a major revival erupted, through which many people from every quarter of the island came to Christ. This would therefore definitely qualify as a "mighty deed" occurring in the life of the apostle Paul.

As mentioned previously, in Second Corinthians 11, Paul tells of being shipwrecked three times, severely beaten on five different occasions, traveling on dangerous roads and across treacherous rivers, and so forth. If it hadn't been for God's power sustaining Paul and intervening on his behalf, many of these experiences would have ended the apostle's life.

We must note again that there was a time when Paul was stoned in Lystra and left for dead. Religious Jews were professionals at stoning people to death, so it is unlikely they would have stopped stoning him if they thought he was still alive. We are told in Acts 14:19 that certain Jews "...having stoned Paul, drew him out of the city, supposing he had been dead."

After pummeling Paul's body with stones, these Jews dragged him out of the city and left him there to be eaten by animals. But Acts 14:20 goes on to tell us, "...As the disciples stood round about him, he rose up...." This was a *wonder* — a special working of God's miraculous power that seems to have actually raised Paul from death itself.

As a part of their *apostolic criteria,* the Early Church would have also asked, "Has the individual who claims to be an apostle had mind-boggling wonders at key moments in his ministry?" Any person who is called to stand in an apostolic position *must* have had wonders occur in the course of his ministry.

Proof Number Six: An Apostle Is Marked With Supernatural *Mighty Deeds*

Paul finally added, "Truly the signs of an apostle were wrought among you in all patience, in signs, and wonders, *and mighty deeds*" (2 Corinthians 12:12). In addition to supernatural patience and miraculous signs and wonders, Paul stated that "mighty deeds" were another mark of apostleship.

When thinking of mighty deeds, my mind goes to the nonstop flow of "mighty deeds" that occurred in the seaside city of Capernaum during the time of Jesus' residency there. Paul says that such miraculous manifestations are an attestation to anyone who has true apostolic ministry. That is why Paul went on to say "*and* mighty deeds." The word "and" is the Greek word *kai*, which could — and probably should — be translated *even*, causing the phrase "mighty deeds" to actually *amplify* the word "wonders." Thus, the phrase could be translated "wonders, *even mighty deeds*." In other words, Paul was saying that these "wonders" were so amazing, they were truly "mighty deeds."

The phrase "mighty deeds" is a translation of the word *dunamis*, the Greek word for *power*. It is from this word that we derive the English word "dynamite," which is a very appropriate use of this Greek word. Indeed, *dunamis* power carries the idea of *explosive, superhuman power that comes with enormous energy and produces phenomenal, extraordinary, and unparalleled results*. It is also the word for a force of nature, like a *hurricane, tornado,* or *earthquake*. The word *dunamis* depicts "mighty deeds" that are impressive, incomparable, and beyond human ability to perform — denoting events that, like *a spiritual hurricane, tornado, or earthquake*, really shake people up and leave them reeling in their minds.

Keep in mind that "wonders" refers to people being stunned by events that don't occur in nature or by experiences that are out of the flow of normal life. Because Paul connected "wonders" to the phrase "mighty deeds" — the Greek word *dunamis*, referring to *superhuman or miraculous powers that leave people reeling* — we know that, among other things, he was referring to instances when the laws of nature are overruled or suspended by the supernatural power of God. In some way, God Himself intervenes in the laws of nature and does something that could never occur in the natural realm.

Whenever God's power intervenes to reverse a physical condition that medical science defines as incurable, this can technically be defined as *a miracle*. There were many instances of "mighty deeds" in Paul's ministry pertaining to miraculous healings that could never have occurred naturally or even with the assistance of medicine.

In addition to the supernatural power that flowed from Paul to others to work healing miracles, there were also some truly amazing instances when God's power intervened on *Paul's* behalf. We find an example of this in Acts 16, when

Paul was miraculously released from his jail cell in Philippi after a remarkable earthquake shook the prison and set him free. This was truly a *mighty deed.*

Acts 16:24 tells us of this time when Paul and Silas were in an "inner prison" and their feet were "fast in the stocks." As the two apostles began to pray and sing songs of praise to God in the middle of the night, "...suddenly there was a great earthquake, so that the foundations of the prison were shaken: and immediately all the doors were opened, and every one's bands were loosed" (v. 26).

Consider how strange the occurrence was that night as this earthquake shook the prison, opened all the doors, and caused the chains to fall off the prisoners. Yet it seems not one brick fell, for there is no record of any damage to the actual building. In fact, this appears to have been such a "regional," or location-specific, earthquake that it affected only one building in the entire city. Only the prison where Paul and Silas were confined apparently felt the impact of this particular earthquake!

When people heard about this landmark event, the news left them in a state of *wonder*. In other words, they were left *speechless*, *shocked*, *astonished*, *bewildered*, *baffled*, *taken aback*, *stunned*, and *awestruck*. Certainly this earthquake would qualify as a "mighty deed" — a miraculous event — that occurred in the life of the apostle Paul.

Those who have an apostolic call on their lives serve God on the frontlines of His Kingdom, facing challenges and difficulties beyond what others might encounter. These individuals must forge their way and make significant inroads into the enemy's territory. Therefore, there are *undeniable moments when God's power intervenes in the natural course of events.* These "mighty" moments will always be evident in the lives of those whom God has called to be apostles.

I must tell you that the word *dunamis* — here translated "mighty deeds" — is also the Greek word that was used to depict *the full advancing force of a mighty army that drives back enemies and takes new territory.* Part of the "mighty deeds" Paul refers to in this verse could, in fact, include the forceful advancement of the Gospel in dark and hostile locations where it would have naturally been impossible to do God's work. When Paul looked back on his own apostolic ministry, he could see that God's power had apostolically advanced him into new regions to drive back darkness and to establish the Church where it never existed before, which is a *mighty deed.*

Throughout an apostle's assignment, God's power will show up when needed to perform signs, wonders, and mighty deeds — not only to follow the anointed preaching of His Word, but also to ensure the divine assignment is completed. As a result, people's lives are transformed to the glory of Jesus Christ and the building of His Church!

So as a part of their *apostolic criteria*, the Early Church would have asked, "Has the individual who claims to be an apostle experienced *mighty deeds* at moments in his ministry?" Any person who is called to stand in an apostolic position *must* have had mighty deeds occur in his ministry.

Again, at the end of the First Century, such a large number of people were professing to be apostles that the Ephesian church developed certain criteria — *a paradigm* or *model* — to determine who *was* and who *was not* an authentic New Testament apostle. When the church at Ephesus tested individuals to see if they were apostles as they claimed to be, these six proofs were among the criteria they would have used to determine whether they were dealing with a real apostle.

This testing was *not* intended to promote suspicion, but to encourage *discernment* and to protect real Christ-given apostolic gifts. The apostolic call is important for building up the local church; therefore, those who imitate this call for the sake of personal gain should not be tolerated in a congregation. And if a person has an authentic apostolic call, a test or a little scrutiny won't hurt or diminish it. In fact, it will only *prove* that the call is genuine and authentic, which will then open the way for people to open their hearts and receive the rich benefits of the apostolic anointing whenever it is present in their midst.

Why Would Anyone Claim To Be an Apostle if He Wasn't?

In the First Century, those who spoke and read Greek as their native tongue knew much of what I have shared in this book so far, and they knew well that the word *apostle* depicted a position that held enormous authority and that those who carried this title could obtain leverage in the lives of those in the Church. Therefore, some coveted this title and intentionally claimed it as a way to gain control and exert power over God's people.

It is a fact that what an apostle said carried great weight within a church or even within an entire group of churches, so whoever laid claim to the apostolic title would potentially be able to influence what happened in the lives of many people. For a genuine Christ-given apostle, this was a very serious responsibility exercised with holiness, fear, and prudence. But for a person with impure motives, such an authoritative position represented an opportunity to use power for all types of selfish gain.

In the First Century, Paul had to confront the fact that many false apostles moved on the scene like predators, just waiting for the opportunity to seize a fledgling church and claim it for themselves. In fact, false apostles frequently followed Paul from city to city, lying in wait until he left town. After his departure, they would begin implementing a plan to try to discredit Paul and his reputation so they could claim his work and territory for themselves.

Apostolic Authority and Ministry Is Relational, Geographical, Territorial, and Ethnically Related

Please understand that although Paul was universally respected in the Early Church as an apostle, he was *not* an apostle to every First Century church. He was an apostle only to those with whom he had an *apostolic relationship*. The apostolic call is relational, geographical, and territorial.

For example, churches in other cities and regions acknowledged Paul's apostleship, but he was not *their* apostle. Other believers respected Paul as an excellent minister, a beloved brother in the Lord, and an able leader. But he only had apostolic responsibility for the churches he had helped start and for those whom he served as mentor, teacher, and father in the faith.

Thus, Paul's apostleship was limited to those for whom he bore direct spiritual responsibility and with whom he had a unique relationship. This would have included the churches of *Ephesus*, *Colossae*, *Corinth*, *Galatia*, *Hierapolis*, *Laodicea*, *Pergamum*, *Philadelphia*, *Philippi*, *Sardis*, *Smyrna*, *Thyatira*, and others. Paul's relationship with these churches is the reason we have the books of First and Second Corinthians, Galatians, Ephesians, Philippians, and Colossians. Paul wrote these letters because he was directly responsible for the spiritual well-being of these believers and because he had a unique *apostolic relationship* either with them or with their local leadership.

One example of Paul's apostolic relationship with local leadership was the church in Colossae. Paul may have visited Colossae when he took the interior road to Ephesus on his way back from Jerusalem (Acts 19:1), but there is no clear record of it in the Bible, nor is there any record that says Paul personally founded the Colossian church. It appears that he sent Epaphras as his *personal emissary* to fulfill that assignment. It seems that under Paul's orders and spiritual covering, Epaphras was dispatched to Colossae to start the church there. But once the Colossian church was established, that congregation received and related to Paul as the apostle to that church based on his spiritual relationship with Epaphras.

Even Paul was very aware that he wasn't an apostle to everyone. That is why he wrote, "Not boasting of things without our measure [or out of our territory]...not to boast in another man's line of things made ready to our hand [for example, not to take credit for another person's apostolic work]" (2 Corinthians 10:15,16).

In this passage, we find that Paul was respectful of the work of others and was careful not to cross over into another man's territory if it might produce confusion about who was supposed to give direction to certain churches or to whom those churches were accountable (*see* 2 Corinthians 10:13,14). This tells us that Paul not only *possessed* authority, but he also *respected* the authority and territory of others.

This explains why Paul told the Corinthians, "If I be not an apostle unto others, yet doubtless I am to you..." (1 Corinthians 9:2). The word "doubtless" is actually the Greek word *gar,* and it means *indeed.* It is an affirmation of his apostolic relationship to them. A better translation would be: "*Indeed I am to you!*" Paul knew that his own apostleship was *territorial*, *geographical*, and *relational*, so he concentrated on those with whom he knew he "*indeed*" had this special, God-given relationship.

It must also be remembered that Paul and Peter were called to two different ethnic groups — Paul as an apostle to the Gentiles and Peter as an apostle to the Jews. In both cases, these audiences were scattered all over the lands of the Roman empire, and Paul and Peter were both uniquely graced by the Spirit to reach these different groups. Just as interesting is that neither one seemed very successful when he tried to cross into the other's ethnic audience. Jews had little patience for Paul, and Gentiles were put off by Peter, so learning to stay in their respective callings, assignments, and anointings was very important.

You can study this more thoroughly in my book called, *The Will of God — The Key to Your Success.*

Although Paul and Peter understood the perimeter of their apostleship, Paul frequently had to defend his apostleship because of deceitful workers who were attempting to exert their authority over entire regions of churches that he and other apostles had established and to which those founding apostles had imparted their lives. Even pretenders understood that to claim apostleship equaled influence and power — as we have already seen — but those with impure motives sought to invade Paul's territory to claim his fruit and to exploit his work for themselves.

These fraudulent workers used every imaginable method to attract, tempt, lure, entice, and seduce the churches who were under the authority of genuine apostles. In Paul's case, they couldn't find a legitimate reason to accuse the apostle, so they used slanderous and even stupid accusations as they tried to persuade the churches to reject Paul and submit to *their* authority instead. For example, these false apostles:

- Accused Paul of being unimpressive in appearance and a poor public speaker (*see* 2 Corinthians 10:10; 11:6).
- Accused Paul of financially taking advantage of the churches (*see* 1 Corinthians 9:14,15).
- Endeavored to lure churches back into the noose of legalism by accusing Paul of being loose in his doctrine of grace (*see* Galatians 1:6,7).
- Asserted that Paul's revelations weren't as deep as theirs, prompting Paul to remind his readers that he was the one who actually had a direct revelation of Jesus Himself (*see* 1 Corinthians 9:1).

These usurpers of apostolic authority were after Paul's territory — and in order to get what they were after, they attempted to *discredit* Paul. This is another reason why Paul frequently started his letters by saying, "Paul, an *apostle* of Jesus Christ" (*see* Romans 1:1; 1 Corinthians 1:1; 2 Corinthians 1:1; Galatians 1:1; Ephesians 1:1; Colossians 1:1).

When Paul's apostleship was being questioned or threatened by false apostles whose intent was to usurp, Paul was determined not to allow those deceivers to destroy his credibility or steal the sheep under his care.

WHAT WAS PAUL'S THORN IN THE FLESH?

As we saw earlier, in Second Corinthians 12:7, Paul wrote that there was assigned to him "...a thorn in the flesh, the messenger of Satan to buffet me...." People have debated what this "thorn" was but Paul answers this question very clearly in this verse.

In the last chapter, we saw that the word "thorn" is the Greek word *skolops* and it could refer to either a *thorn* or a *splinter* that gets under the skin and causes *a constant irritation.* Paul specifically identified these "thorns," or *splinters*, as "the messenger of Satan." We earlier identified this "thorn" as irritating individuals that were used to constantly hassle Paul, insomuch that he even called them Satan's messengers.

Paul endured many afflictions during his ministry, many as a result of false ministers who constantly tried to displace his position of authority over the flock of God in the local churches. They wanted Paul out of the picture so they could usurp his position. Therefore, they attempted to discredit him, hoping to shift the spotlight to themselves. Paul alluded to these sheep-stealers in Second Corinthians 11:5 (*NIV*) when he sarcastically referred to them as "super apostles" and scoffed at their claims of hyper-spirituality.

Paul Had To Constantly Guard Against 'Pretend Apostles'

Those who coveted Paul's apostolic position used every imaginable method to attract, tempt, lure, entice, and seduce the churches under the realm of authority of his genuine apostleship. They used slanderous and even ridiculous accusations to try to persuade the churches to reject Paul and submit to *their* authority instead because they were after his relational and geographical territory.

Again, this is why Paul opened so many of his letters by saying, "Paul, an apostle of Jesus Christ...." Paul opened his epistles this way in Romans 1:1; First Corinthians 1:1; Second Corinthians 1:1; Galatians 1:1; Ephesians 1:1; and Colossians 1:1. In fact, there are only three letters that don't begin with this apostolic introduction — Philippians and First and Second Thessalonians. But in the churches at Philippi and Thessalonica, it seems Paul's apostleship was never contested and, therefore, he felt no need to defend his apostleship in writing to those churches.

The Problem of False Apostles

I believe that most people who call themselves apostles, *but who are not*, don't do it intentionally. Rather, they do it because they don't understand what the word "apostle" really means. However, in Second Corinthians 11:13,14, Paul did address the issue of outright false apostles, who understood they were being deceitful in their claims. He said, "For such are false apostles, deceitful workers, transforming themselves into the apostles of Christ. And no marvel; for Satan himself is transformed into an angel of light."

The phrase "false apostles" in verse 13 comes from the Greek word *pseudapostolos*, a compound of *pseudes* and *apostolos*. The word *pseudes* carries the idea of *any type of falsehood*. It can picture a person who *projects a false image of himself*, someone who *deliberately walks in a pretense that is untrue*, or someone who *intentionally misrepresents facts or truths.*

In every instance where this word is used in the New Testament, it portrays *someone who misrepresents who he is by what he does, by what he says, or by the lie or misrepresentation that he purports to be true.* The second part of the word *pseudapostolos* is *apostolos* — which, of course, is the word for "apostle." Therefore, the word *pseudapostolos* actually describes *a pretend apostle* or *someone who intentionally represents himself to be an apostle even though he knows he is not.*

Paul called these false apostles "deceitful workers." The word "deceitful" comes from the Greek word *dolios*, which is derived from a root word used to describe *bait that is put on a hook to catch fish*. It conveys the idea of *craftiness, cheating, cunning, dishonesty, fraud, guile, and trickery intended to entrap someone in an act of deception*. Like a fisherman who carefully camouflages a hook with bait, these counterfeit apostles lured sincere believers closer and closer until those believers finally "took the bait." And once the hook was in their victims' mouths, the false apostles "pulled the hook" and took congregations, even entire groups of churches, captive.

Paul said these individuals were deceitful "workers." This word "workers" is taken from the Greek word *ergates*, a word that denotes *someone who actively works at what he is doing*. This indicates that nothing was accidental about this act of deception and that these false apostles put forth great effort to impersonate genuine, authentic apostolic ministry.

Paul said these deceitful workers were so skilled at the art of deception that they were able to "transform" themselves into the apostles of Christ. The word translated "transform" in this verse is the Greek word *metaschematidzo*, which means *to disguise oneself, to deliberately change one's outward appearance*, or *to masquerade in clothing that depicts a person as different than he really is*. Paul was referring to individuals who intentionally attempted to pass themselves off as apostles, knowing full well that they were not. He was describing a blatant act of deception.

As we will see in the next chapter, at that time in the Church, such a large number of people were professing to be apostles that the Ephesian church had to develop certain criteria — *a paradigm* or *model* — to determine who *was* and who *was not* an authentic New Testament apostle. The problem was serious in the Ephesian church, and that church was serious about correcting it. This prompted Jesus to commend the Ephesian believers, "...Thou hast tried them which say they are apostles, and are not, and hast found them liars" (Revelation 2:2).

The leadership of the church at Ephesus wanted to guard the reputation of the true apostolic gift and protect the members of their congregation from pretenders who sought to lead them astray and get something from them for greedy, personal gain. This leadership was so serious about correcting this error before it became widespread that they developed a "test" to prove whether or not a person really had an apostolic calling. This should show how powerful the apostolic call is — for if the church at Ephesus was testing people to see if their call was real, it meant they felt a need to protect those who had a *bona fide* apostolic calling.

This discourse is *not* intended to promote suspicion, but rather to encourage discernment. The apostolic call is so important in building up the local church that those who imitate this call for the sake of personal gain should not be tolerated in a congregation. If a person has an authentic call, a test or a little scrutiny won't hurt or diminish it. In fact, it will only *prove* that the call is genuine and authentic, which will then open the way for you to open your heart and receive the rich benefits of the apostolic anointing whenever it is present in your midst!

In the Next Chapter...

In the next chapter, we will look at important metaphors Paul used to describe apostolic ministry. But thus far, we've established that even in early New Testament times, there was an emerging problem of those who claimed to be apostles, but were not — and that Jesus specifically applauded the church at Ephesus for using *apostolic criteria* to determine who *was* and *wasn't* a real apostle. Likewise, God expects us to use our heads and be wise about whom we call an apostle in our own day.

As we recognize and esteem Christ-given apostles operating throughout the earth in this hour, we will help the Body of Christ receive the full benefits of this part of *the Perfect Gift*, which is Christ Himself expressed to the Church through fivefold ministry. And as we embrace all five of these Christ-given expressions, we will become more equipped to do all that the Church is called to do before the return of the Lord (*see* Ephesians 4:11-14).

But now let's move on to study the important foundation-laying responsibilities of apostles enumerated by Paul in the New Testament, which will impart to us powerful insights into the work of authentic apostles.

QUESTIONS FOR DEEPER CONSIDERATION

Chapter 4

1. In Revelation 2:2, we discover that the spiritual leadership in the Church at Ephesus was so concerned about false apostles that they developed *criteria* to determine who *was* and *wasn't* a real apostle. Why was it so important "to test" those who claimed to be apostles? Based on what you have read in this chapter, can you conjecture the kind of test they were using to determine who *was* and *wasn't* an apostle?

2. In Paul's writings throughout the New Testament, he describes "signs" that should be evident in the life and ministry of a genuine apostle. Can you express what the word "signs" mean? Can you now name the specific "signs" that Paul stated should accompany a true apostle?

3. In Second Corinthians 12:12, Paul provides a very specific list of various "signs" he said should accompany the ministry of an apostle. There is one "sign" that most people overlook, but Paul considered it to be one of the powerful evidences that a person is a true apostle. What is the sign most people overlook in Second Corinthians 12:12?

4. Again in Second Corinthians 12:12, we read that Paul mentions signs, wonders, and mighty deeds that should be evident in the ministry of a true apostle. Can you now explain the difference between a sign, a wonder,

and a mighty deed? According to the record that we have in the book of Acts, with what kind of regularity do these supernatural events occur in the ministry of an apostle?

5. People in early New Testament times, and in our age as well, have claimed to be apostles, but often it is a false claim. After reading this chapter, can you explain why a person would claim apostleship if he is not an apostle? What type of leverage would an apostolic claim give someone in the Church?

6. Genuine apostolic authority and ministry is relational, geographical, territorial, or ethnically related. Can you express in your own words what this means?

7. We find in Romans 1:1, First Corinthians 1:1, Second Corinthians 1:1, Galatians 1:1, Ephesians 1:1, and Colossians 1:1 that Paul began each of these epistles by stating that he was "an apostle of Jesus Christ." Why did Paul begin each of these particular epistles by affirming his apostleship, and why did he not do it in other epistles?

CHAPTER 5

WHAT PAUL SAID ABOUT THE FOUNDATION-LAYING MINISTRY OF APOSTLES

According to the grace of God which is given unto me, as a wise masterbuilder,
I have laid the foundation, and another buildeth thereon.
But let every man take heed how he buildeth thereupon.

— 1 Corinthians 3:10

As the coming of the Lord draws nearer and nearer, the Body of Christ — God's Temple — desperately needs authentic apostles like never before to start new works of God and to make certain the last-days "*naos* Temple" of God is established on a strong spiritual and doctrinal foundation. (If you haven't read Chapter 2, I encourage you to read it in order to understand the fullness of the Greek word *naos* as it pertains to the Temple of God — Christ's Church — today.) Ephesians 4:11 and 12 says the gift of the apostle is needed in the Church *until* the Church reaches the fullness Christ intends for it to possess. As long as we are short of that fullness, we will need *every* fivefold gift, and that includes the ministry of the apostle.

In this chapter we are discussing the role of apostles, and in doing so, it is important to note Hebrews 3:1 specifically states Jesus is the "Apostle" of our faith. In fact, we already saw He is the first Apostle, and He fulfills every meaning and nuance contained in the Greek word *apostolos* we studied in Chapter Three. It is also important to repeat that each of the fivefold ministry gifts enumerated in Ephesians 4:11 is an expression of Jesus Christ, who is the perfect Apostle, perfect Prophet, perfect Evangelist, perfect Pastor, and perfect Teacher.

As the perfect Apostle, Christ has given the gift of apostleship to the Church to continue His apostolic ministry of building the House of God throughout the Church Age. So in the gift of the apostle, we actually see the continuing apostolic work of Jesus Christ as He builds His Church (*see* Matthew 16:18).

In the gift of the apostle, we actually see the continuing apostolic work of Jesus Christ as He builds His Church

In this chapter, we are discussing the exact role of apostles as they help build the Church. So, again, please note Hebrews 3:1 says Jesus is the "Apostle" of our faith. That will be important as we proceed in this explanation of an apostle's foundation-laying ministry in the Church today.

We have seen the gift of apostleship is listed first in the fivefold ministry gifts enumerated in Ephesians 4:11. In that verse, Paul wrote, "And he [Christ] gave some, apostles; and some, prophets; and some, evangelists; and some, pastors and teachers." I must note the original text adds a Greek word that simply means "indeed." In other words, "And Christ *indeed* gave...." It is used nearly like an exclamation mark to indicate something that is categorically a fact.

Thus, Ephesians 4:11 should be taken to mean, "And he [Christ] indeed and of a surety gave some, apostles; and some, prophets; and some, evangelists; and some, pastors and teachers." The use of the Greek word that's translated "indeed" is very important, for by using it, Paul made an exclamatory statement that Christ *indeed* gave these gifts to the Church — and in so doing, Paul was stating a fact that never needed to be questioned.

But the ministry gift of the apostle is listed first in Ephesians 4:11 because of the apostle's *foundational role* in starting churches. For example, in the process of building a temple or a house — or any similar structure — the laying of the foundation is the critical first step in that massive undertaking. Similarly, the role of the apostle is to lay a solid foundation underneath a God-assigned work so what is built upon that foundation will glorify God and stand the test of time.

In First Corinthians 12:29, Paul gave a *partial* list of fivefold ministry gifts again, but in that verse, he uses different words to describe them. For example, He said, "Are all apostles? are all prophets? are all teachers? are all workers of miracles?"

The words "apostle," "prophet," and "teacher" clearly denote the ministry of apostles, prophets, and teachers as enumerated in Ephesians 4:11. But in First Corinthians 12:29, Paul used the phrase "workers of miracles" to depict evangelists, who are especially, divinely equipped with miracles as a part of their ministries.

But notice in this partial list in First Corinthians 12:29, Paul again listed the apostle *first* in the great scheme of things concerning God's Temple, or House. This is done deliberately to show the apostle is the first to show up in the establishing of a local church. The apostle's role is foundational, and the other fivefold ministry gifts eventually build on top of the foundation laid by an apostle.

While prophets, evangelists, pastors, and teachers tend to be more focused in their respective God-given fields of expertise, an apostle does the foundation-laying for a new congregation in a new location —and while he waits for the other fivefold ministry gifts to appear, an apostle, by necessity, is gifted to function in all the fivefold ministry gifts. He is the *apostle* who lays the foundation, and he is the *prophet* who speaks the mind of God. He is the *evangelist* who preaches to the lost in a new vicinity, and he becomes a *pastor* and *teacher* to tend to that flock and establish them in biblical truths.

So by necessity, an apostle to some degree must also serve prophetically, evangelistically, pastorally, and even instructionally. Until the other fivefold ministry gifts are raised up in the new congregation or come to join him, the apostle is anointed to uniquely minister in all five of these Christ-given ministries, and he is the only one of the five who, if needed, can stand in for all five of these ministries.

While the apostle is called to lay a foundation in the Church, eventually he stands side by side in participation with the other fivefold ministry gifts. All the fivefold ministry gifts are vital, and without the input of them all, the Body of Christ will lack the fullness God intends for it to possess, as each of the fivefold ministry gifts expresses a different aspect of Jesus Himself.

But because Paul was one of the most impacting apostles to ever live, what he wrote in First Corinthians 3:10-17 about apostolic ministry is perhaps the most comprehensive teaching found in the New Testament on the subject of apostleship. As we proceed, we will cover this passage verse by verse, because every point in these verses is filled with so much revelation. But you will see that each of these many points will intersect with this chapter's theme: *what the apostle Paul said about the foundation-laying ministry of apostles.*

Paul's Description of His Foundation-Laying Ministry

In First Corinthians 3:10, Paul gave a description of his own apostolic work in the city of Corinth. His work in Corinth was monumental because prior to that, Paul traveled extensively and preached, which was a part of his apostolic call. But while he was in Corinth, he mightily experienced the foundation-laying aspect of his own apostolic ministry over an extended period of time. Remembering it well, in First Corinthians 3:10 he wrote, "According to the grace of God which is given unto me, as a wise masterbuilder, I have laid the foundation, and another buildeth thereon. But let every man take heed how he buildeth thereupon."

We will dissect this verse into the following segments to analyze Paul's words and more fully understand what he wrote about apostolic ministry. Then we will study the meaning of the following words and phrases in this paramount verse on apostolic ministry.

- "According to"
- "the grace of God"
- "given unto me"
- "a wise masterbuilder"

- "I have laid the foundation"
- "another buildeth thereon"
- "every man"
- "take heed how"

Although Paul did not explicitly use the word *apostolos* in this verse, he used the words "wise masterbuilder" — a very powerful metaphor — to illustrate his work as an apostle. The use of this metaphor is so critical to the ministry of Christ-given apostles that any book on the ministry of an apostle would be incomplete without considering its profound meaning in the context of apostolic ministry. So in the next pages, we will extensively cover First Corinthians 3:10 to see why Paul referred to himself apostolically as a "wise master builder."

'According To...'

Paul begins the verse by saying, "According to the grace of God which is given unto me..." (1 Corinthians 3:10). The words "according to" are a translation of the Greek word *kata,* which can indeed be translated "according to." However, the use of *kata* in this particular verse gives a sense of something that is *dominating*. It could be taken to mean, "*Being dominated by the grace of God given unto me...*" Here, Paul describes a specific grace so heavy on his life it has come to *dominate* his life and ministry. The subjecting force of *kata* suggests it may have been a struggle for Paul to surrender to the particular grace God placed on his life to not only be an apostle, but, as we shall see, an apostle *to the Gentiles*.

When Paul stood before King Agrippa, it is recorded in Acts 26:16,17 that he testified what Jesus had said to him when he was conquered by Christ on the road to Damascus. In that experience, Jesus told Paul (then called Saul), "...Rise, and stand upon thy feet: for I have appeared unto thee for this purpose, to make thee a minister and a witness both of these things which thou hast seen, and of those things in the which I will appear unto thee; delivering thee from the people, and from *the Gentiles, unto whom now I send thee.*"

The word "send" in this passage is a form of the Greek word *apostolos*, which is the word for *an apostle*. Thus, from the outset of his conversion, Paul was supernaturally informed that Christ was calling him to be an apostle and was going to apostolically send him *to the Gentiles*. This was so well understood by Paul that he confirmed this specialized assignment on his life numerous times throughout his epistles, where he wrote about his unique calling and apostleship to the Gentiles.

In Romans 1:5, Paul wrote, "By whom we have received grace and apostleship, for obedience to the faith among all nations [Gentiles]…" This clearly states Paul understood his unique apostleship was to the Greek-speaking world, or to *the Gentiles*.

In Romans 1:13 and 14, Paul again specifically described His Christ-given call to be an apostle to the Gentiles. He wrote, "Now I would not have you ignorant, brethren, that oftentimes I purposed to come unto you, (but was let hitherto,) that I might have some fruit among you also, even as among other *Gentiles*. I am debtor both to the *Greeks* [Gentiles], and to the Barbarians; both to the wise, and to the unwise." Again, Paul's words make it plain he knew his apostleship was to the Greek-speaking world, or to the Gentiles.

In Galatians 1:13-16, Paul also testified, "For ye have heard of my conversation in time past in the Jews' religion, how that beyond measure I persecuted the church of God, and wasted it: and profited in the Jews' religion above many my equals in mine own nation, being more exceedingly zealous of the traditions of my fathers. But when it pleased God, who separated me from my mother's womb, and called me by his grace, to reveal his Son in me, that I might preach him among the *heathen* [Gentiles]…." Again and again,

Paul confirmed his apostleship was to the Greek-speaking world, or to the Gentiles.

Then Paul wrote in Galatians 2:7-9, "But contrariwise, when they [the spiritual leadership in Jerusalem] saw that the gospel of the *uncircumcision* [Gentiles] was committed unto me, as the gospel of the circumcision was unto Peter; (for he that wrought effectually in Peter to the apostleship of the circumcision, the same was mighty in me toward the *Gentiles*:) and when James, Cephas, and John, who seemed to be pillars, perceived the grace that was given unto me, they gave to me and Barnabas the right hands of fellowship; that we should go unto the *heathen* [Gentiles], and they unto the circumcision."

In these three verses in Galatians chapter 2, Paul confirmed his apostolic calling to the Greek-speaking world *three times*.

Even though Paul explicitly knew his calling was to the Gentiles, for him to be *sent* to the Gentiles was a radical idea that was difficult for him to embrace. He had been reared as a religious Jew and was taught to loathe Gentiles, whom he would have found to be disgusting and repulsive on many levels. Although he heard these instructions from the mouth of Jesus Himself, he must have inwardly thought, *I'm a Jew. How could God send me to low-level Gentiles?*

The book of Acts doesn't explicitly say Paul struggled with this aspect of his assignment; however, if you closely study Paul's travels in the book of Acts, you will see that *going to the Gentiles* wasn't his natural inclination. Making the Gentiles the first priority of his thoughts, prayers, and actions wasn't his natural inclination, even though they were the audience God primarily had called him to reach. (If you're interested in learning more, I recommend you read my book *The Will of God — The Key to Your Success*, in which I extensively cover Paul's struggle to accept his apostolic calling to the Gentile world.) Nevertheless, Paul was called by Christ to be an apostle *to the Gentiles*.

It is important for you to comprehend that because Paul was raised a strictly religious Jew, he only had *limited interaction* with Gentiles before his conversion. In Philippians 3:5, he wrote he was "circumcised the eighth day, of the stock of Israel, of the tribe of Benjamin, an Hebrew of the Hebrews; as touching the law, a Pharisee."

This verse emphatically affirms that Paul had been raised in a strict, religious Jewish home, and as such, he had a very Jewish worldview. He grew up in Tarsus, a very pagan and Gentile city, but he and his family were cloistered in the small Jewish community there. At a young age he had relocated to Jerusalem to study theology under the renowned pharisee Gamaliel (*see* Acts 22:3), the son of Simeon ben Hillel — identified by many scholars as the identical Simeon who prophesied over Jesus at the time of his dedication in the temple (*see* Luke 2:25-28).[1] Gamaliel was, importantly, the grandson of the great Jewish theologian Hillel. Gamaliel was so revered as one of the greatest Jewish scholars of his day that he was not called Rabbi, but *Rabban*, which meant *the most masterful of all*, and for this reason, he also became the chief leader of the Great Sanhedrin in Jerusalem.

In Acts 22:3, Paul affirms that "...at the feet of Gamaliel, [he was] ...taught according to the perfect manner of the law...." The words "at the feet" are translated from *para tous podous*, a Greek phrase that literally means *alongside the feet* of Gamaliel, indicating that Paul was such a dedicated disciple of Gamaliel that he studied as a submitted student at his feet and followed in his footsteps — that is, in his doctrine and in his strict manner of life. It was a life so sequestered in the strictest of all Jewish communities that the law allowed little room for anything non-Jewish.

Paul furthermore says that from a young age, Gamaliel theologically trained him according to "...the perfect manner of the law..." (Acts 22:3). The word "perfect" is a form of the Greek word *akribeia,* a word that pictures *strictness, scrupulousness to every detail*, and one so rooted in the law that he *never wandered from it or tolerated any other way of thinking.*

It was his strict, scrupulous adherence to the Jewish law and traditions that drove Paul (then named Saul) to persecute Christians, as his training would have caused him to view them as being deviant, error-ridden, disease-spreading converts that needed to be eliminated before they infected others. Acts 7:58 records that Saul was present at the bloody execution of Stephen, and in Acts 26:9,10, Paul testified that he did *many* things to resist Christians. As one totally committed to his Jewish beliefs and completely intolerant of Jews who were non-Orthodox, Saul was chosen by the Jewish leadership in Jerusalem to lead a special brigade to purge Israel of this "Christian plague." By his own admittance in Acts 26:10, we know he had been authorized to arrest them, to imprison them, and to cast his vote for their executions, as we find in the case in Stephen, who became the first martyr in the Church (*see* Acts 7:58-60).

If prior to his conversion, Paul felt this repugnance toward wandering Jews, whom he thought did not "toe the line" theologically, then perhaps you can begin to understand the repulsion he would have felt toward *Gentiles* who were even *more repulsive* to him. This is who Saul — who later came to be called Paul — was at the time of his conversion. And because he had grown up in the strictest, most cloistered Jewish environment of the day and had little interaction with Gentiles, what he did know of them and their manner of life was stomach-turning to him.

Let me reiterate what was noted in Chapter One about what religious Jews felt toward pagans, their beliefs, and their lifestyles. What religious Jews felt toward pagan Gentiles was so acute, they kept a distance between themselves and pagans, whom they judged to be idol-worshipers with no moral law and who were sexually deviant and perverse in their lifestyles. A devout religious Jew — like Paul and his sequestered religious community — found pagan Gentiles so reprehensible that he would not even permit one to cross the threshold of his house. Even if a Jew felt that a particular Gentile seemed better than others, to a devout religious Jew, he was nevertheless an impure, contaminated person to be avoided if possible. In the Jewish mind, Gentiles were uncircumcised idol-worshipers whose lands were filled with drunkenness, debauchery, and sexual immorality — and in this regard, Jews were actually entirely correct.

So try to imagine the mental earthquake Paul — then called Saul — experienced as he struggled to grasp that Jesus had told him he was going to be sent as an apostle to the Gentiles. *I'm a Jew, and these Gentiles are morally filthy. Why would You send a Jewish man like me to minister to heathens?* Saul's mind must have gone *"tilt, tilt, tilt"*! But Christ indeed had chosen him to be an apostle to the Gentile world.

Paul's calling to the Gentiles had been confirmed over and over, but the book of Acts shows the apostle's soul nonetheless naturally gravitated toward the Jews. To focus on Gentiles and to connect with them from his heart was such a huge leap of faith for Paul that it would take several years for him to fully engage this aspect of his call and to adjust accordingly.

Paul's Surrender to the Unique Grace God Had Placed on His Life

Because the word *kata* in First Corinthians 3:10 carries the force of something that is *dominating* or *subjugating*, it gives the impression that for his apostolic ministry to blossom, Paul first had to hoist a white flag and *surrender* to this aspect of his calling. But when he finally capitulated, God's grace conquered him, and he became divinely empowered to fulfill his calling as an apostle of Jesus Christ *to the Gentiles*.

That moment of surrender seems to have occurred as Paul journeyed toward the vile and pagan city of Corinth. Corinth was "life in the gutter" — as low as low could get — a city world-famous for its sinfulness, sexual perversions of all sorts, and a plethora of pagan temples dedicated to what possibly felt like an endless sundry of pagan gods. It was so renowned for debauchery that pagans in other parts of the Greek and Roman world used the term "Corinthian" disparagingly to describe any person, *anywhere*, who lived a life of drunkenness and debauchery.

The city had two harbors, one on the west that received ships from western Roman provinces, and one on the east that received ships from eastern Roman provinces. As a result of the two ports, large numbers of travelers and sailors traveled in and out of Corinth's ports on a frequent basis, coming from all over the world for the purpose of imbibing themselves in the city's world-famous sex business and party spirit.

Before Paul arrived there, he already knew of Corinth's wicked reputation, and it is likely that going there would have never been his personal preference. But as abhorrent as Corinth was to a man like Paul, his arrival there marked the dawn of a new day and a new way of doing ministry. (To understand more about the wicked environment in Corinth, I advise you to read my book *Why We Need the Gifts of the Holy Spirit*, in which I extensively cover the historical background of the city of Corinth and its environment during the First Century when the Church was established there.)

In Acts 18, we read when Paul first arrived in Corinth, he went to the synagogue to try to reach the Jewish community there. But in Corinth, Paul began to come to terms with his apostolic calling to the Gentiles, and soon he redirected his energies to the Gentile community. As Paul focused more than ever before on Gentiles, he witnessed God's power erupt with signs, wonders, and mighty deeds. As a matter of fact, Paul himself was so impressed with the miraculous activity he observed in his ministry in Corinth that he personally wrote more about it than about any other miraculous activity anywhere else in his ministry (*see* First Corinthians 2:1-5; Second Corinthians 12:12).

It seems that finally, in Corinth, Paul hoisted that "flag of surrender" to his apostolic calling to the Gentiles. It was there that he stopped allowing his repugnance of pagans to stop him, and he capitulated to the grace that God had assigned to his life to become an apostle to the Gentiles. Of course, he also attempted to reach Jews as he traveled to new cities, as they were his own natural people and he deeply longed to see them converted. But a general overview of Paul's actions *after* Corinth demonstrates his chief focus had finally shifted to the Gentile world.

Because Paul used the Greek word *kata* in First Corinthians 3:10, it suggests an intense struggle that Paul experienced until he finally succumbed and embraced the unique grace God assigned to his life. This was not a calling he naturally relished, but once Paul surrendered, divine grace flowed into his life — *dominating* and *subjugating* him (*kata*) — transforming him to become the unlikely apostle to the Gentiles.

But there is another possible tug-of-war that may have gone on inside the apostle Paul that must also be considered.

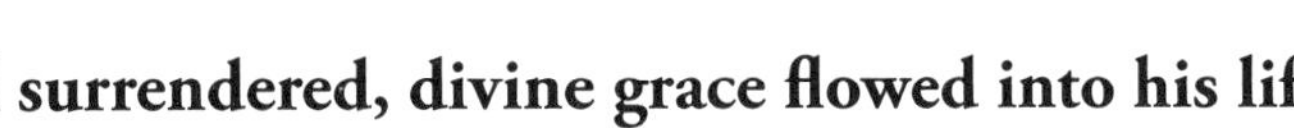

Once Paul surrendered, divine grace flowed into his life, transforming him to become the unlikely apostle to the Gentiles.

The Transitory Nature of Apostolic Ministry

In Chapter Three, we saw the various meanings of the Greek word *apostolos* — the New Testament word "apostle" — and learned that the Christ-given gift of the apostle is a *transitory* and *mobile* gift. Unlike a pastor or teacher who may remain in a single location for many years at a time, the transitory and mobile nature of an apostle's gift means an apostle doesn't often stay relatively long in a single place. Certainly there are exceptions to this rule, but most often, apostles move from one location to another location during the course of their ministry to continue the frontline ministry of establishing the Church where it has never existed before.

The apostle arrives in a new and potentially hostile region with his apostolic team to do what they are specially anointed to do. As they preach the Gospel and shine its glorious light into a dark region, they begin to spiritually bulldoze demonic powers so they can then begin the work of establishing the life, language, and culture of the Church in a brand-new location. Unfathomable amounts of power and grace are needed to repeat this over and over in various locations, along with divine endurance to outlast all the devil's attempts to stop them.

That divine endurance is so paramount, as we saw in the last chapter, that Paul lists it as a part of a *true apostle's* spiritual equipment. He even listed it as a sign of an apostle *before* he listed signs, wonders, and mighty deeds (*see* Second Corinthians 12:12). This may seem strange to a non-apostle, but anyone who moves in apostolic ministry completely understands the level of supernatural endurance required for this gift to operate in difficult frontlines.

Once this mind-boggling power has been released and powers of hell have been pushed out of the way, the Church is established and a pastor is raised up to lead the work, and that is often when that apostle and his apostolic crew launch out to repeat this foundation-establishing work all over again somewhere else. As they take their journey to do it all over again, they wave farewell to the work that has sprung up as a result of their anointing and hard work — and they watch as a newly raised up pastor whom they set in place remains behind to lead the work into its next exciting phase in God's plan of building and growth.

As that apostle and his apostolic crew start this process all over again in a new location, try to fathom the radiant reports they no doubt keep hearing of all the marvelous things that are happening in their last location. Can't you just imagine an apostle thinking...

Oh, how good it is to hear all these reports. It's everything I prayed for and believed to happen there, but I'm not there to see and experience it. How wonderful it would be if I could stay in one spot long enough to enjoy the long-term fruit of my labor. But every time a new work is established and is in good hands, God reassigns me to do it all over again in another location while the pastor we left behind enjoys the fruit of my labor. Oh, how I wish I could stay long enough to see and enjoy the full fruit of my ministry in the last location. But...my calling doesn't accommodate that longing because I'm a starter, not a prolonger, which means I am to keep following where the call leads.

A time truthfully comes when every apostle, prophet, evangelist, pastor, or teacher must come to terms with the specific grace God has given to him or her. For example, an apostle must come to terms that the grace on his life means he and his family are going to be mobile in their life and ministry. Although he may long to stay longer in one location, being transitory and mobile is part of the territory that goes with an apostolic calling.

Prophets, on the other hand, often feel disregarded as weird or strange and think how wonderful it would be to be a teacher who seems respected for his or her intellectual acumen. But while prophets may dream of how wonderful it would be to be like a teacher, teachers, on the other hand, dream they could be more like prophets, whom they perceive to be more spontaneous compared to a teacher's rather predictable ministry.

Or how about the wishful thinking of evangelists who move from place to place and preach to brand-new faces nearly every week, often inwardly struggling that they don't stay anywhere long enough to see people spiritually grow. How they dream they could be like pastors, who get to stay in one place long enough to see people grow in their faith. But pastors, on the other hand, frequently become weary of seeing the same people and dealing with the same problems week after week, and think about how wonderful it would be to be mobile, like an apostle, a traveling teaching minister, or an evangelist, who sees new faces nearly every time he or she preaches.

The truth is, it doesn't matter who we are or what we are called to do, we each have to come to a moment when we accept what God has called us to be. We must each hoist the white flag of surrender to do exactly what God has graced us to do and quit wishing we could stand in the grace on someone else's life. That final moment of surrender — when we stop resisting and finally begin to embrace our unique grace and accept what that means — is usually when the unique God-given grace we have received *engages* and we become more productive than ever before.

That final moment of surrender — when we stop resisting and finally begin to embrace our unique grace and accept what that means — is usually when the unique God-given grace we have received *engages* and we become more productive than ever before.

Whether one is called to be an apostle, prophet, evangelist, pastor, or teacher, a moment usually comes when each Christ-given fivefold ministry gift must come to terms with the unique grace God has given to him or her — to accept what it means to be what God has called that person to be. And not only must a minister come to terms with it, he or she must surrender to it and embrace the grace God has assigned to his or her life from the foundation of the world.

The use of *kata* in First Corinthians 3:10 may mean Paul had to come to terms not only with the fact that he was called to the Gentiles, but that his unique God-given grace meant he would live a transitory and mobile life. The truth that mobility is inherent in the gift of apostleship cannot be denied. It is also entirely possible the word *kata* in First Corinthians 3:10 is Paul's way of testifying that rather than fight against this mobile aspect of his ministry and the fact he would be constantly moving on to the next location, he had surrendered to it and had allowed that unique grace to conquer him. As a result, he was empowered supernaturally to become the great apostle we remember him to be.

Paul learned to embrace his grace. He boldly marched forward with the grace that was on his life, and in city after city, he pushed the powers of hell out of the way in order to lay the foundations of the Church where it never existed before. Someone had to do it, and that was the anointing God assigned to Paul, so he remained mobile and lived to establish new churches until the end of his life. Indeed, that was the grace assigned to him.

I want you to see that the word *kata* in First Corinthians 3:10 implies Paul may have struggled with his life assignments, just as many of us have struggled with ours. But he finally came to a place where he quit struggling, started embracing, and that is when God's unique grace on his life began to dominate and cause him to blossom as the apostle to the Gentiles.

I want to say that if *you* will stop resisting your God-given grace and embrace it, it will put an end to your feeling threatened by or envious of the grace that belongs to someone else. You will be able to confidently say, "This is my grace. Other people can't do what I do, and I can't do what they do. They are in their grace, and I am in mine!"

Never forget that God's grace defines your place. Every person must discover his or her unique grace, embrace it, and allow it to dominate. When Paul did just that, it transformed him into the legendary apostle we know him as today. That is what will happen to you *if* you'll *stop resisting* and *start embracing* the unique grace God has given you for *your* life assignment.

I want to say that if *you* will stop resisting your God-given grace and embrace it, it will put an end to your feeling threatened by or envious of the grace that belongs to someone else.

'...The Grace of God...'

In First Corinthians 3:10, Paul said, "According to the *grace* of God...."

So far, I've written extensively about Paul's unique grace — that everything he did so successfully in his ministry was "according to" the grace of God. But it is imperative for us to understand what the word "grace" meant to those who heard it in the time of the early New Testament. We use it as a theological term — and it *is* a very supernatural New Testament word — but it did not originate in the New Testament. The word "grace" was in use a long time before the New Testament was written. In fact, it was borrowed from the Greek-speaking world and carried into the New Testament. But why?

The truth is, most people — perhaps even *you* — wrangle verbally when trying to explain just what "grace" is. So it's important for us to see where this word came from, how it was most frequently used before it found its way into the New Testament, and how believers in the First Century understood the word "grace."

The word translated "grace" in Greek is *charis* — a word notably used outside the New Testament among Greek-speaking pagans to describe a transaction when *the gods conferred a special touch on an individual or group of individuals.* Once *charis* — the word translated "grace" in the New Testament — was conferred on a person (or group of people), he was instantly *transformed* and endowed with *superhuman abilities* he previously did not possess.

The contrast of who people were *before* and *after* this divine touch was conferred upon them was so *stark* that some ancient Greek writers surmised such individuals or groups of individuals had been placed under some kind of a "magic spell" by the gods.[2] Observers had no other explanation for how their personalities were so instantly altered or how they could be suddenly in possession of so many supernatural abilities. Bystanders were so stunned by the stark change, they alleged that the gods had put them under *charis* — a "magic spell" — and that was the reason they were so vastly different from what they had previously been.

This is the background of the word *charis*, which, of course, is the word "grace" in the New Testament. So when early New Testament ears heard the word *charis*, they exactly understood it to be a divine touch that God graciously confers upon an individual (or group of individuals) to supernaturally transform and empower them. Indeed, they saw "grace" as a divine impartation and touch from God Himself to transform an individual and give him the ability to do or be what he could never have done or been on his own.

It is so important to understand what the ears of those New Testament hearers heard and understood about the word *charis.* Let me give you a famous example of *charis* as it is used in Ephesians 2:8. In this verse, Paul writes, "For by grace are ye saved through faith; and that not of yourselves: it is the gift of God." The Greek says, "For by *charis* are ye saved through faith; and that not of yourselves: it is the gift of God."

Now that you see what New Testament believers understood when they heard the word "grace" — the Greek word *charis* — it becomes clear that this verse carries the idea, *For you are saved only because of the divine and supernatural touch of God that was conferred upon you. You could never have been saved on your own; it was received by your faith. Your salvation is the sole result of God's divine touch that empowered you to be saved; it is entirely the gift of God.*

Our salvation is so *entirely* the result of God's divine *charis* — that is, His divine touch — that, *alone*, opened our ears and eyes to hear the truth, see our need for salvation, and empower our faith to be ignited to believe.

Ephesians 1:6 says, "To the praise of the glory of his grace, wherein he hath made us accepted in the beloved." The *RIV* (*Renner Interpretive Version*) of that verse says, "Talking about all of this makes me want to stop to give God a standing ovation for this incredible, extraordinary grace that shines so resplendently in our lives. This fabulous grace has been liberally poured out on us, like grace on top of grace. I'm talking about so much grace and favor that it just keeps proliferating more and more and more! Oh, there's no end to it! And it was this grace and favor that made us to have a place inside His Own Beloved Son!"

Another example of *charis* is found in First Corinthians 15:10, where Paul writes, "But by the grace of God I am what I am...."

When you understand the meaning of *charis* as believers heard and understood it in the First Century, this verse emphatically means Paul was declaring, "Everything I now am is a result of God's transformative touch of grace (*charis*) on my life. When that divine touch of God came upon me, it entirely changed and transformed me — so much so that I am now completely different from what and who I used to be."

I remind you that those who received a touch of *charis* were so transformed that observing Greek-speaking pagans could possibly have said, "Wow...that person must be under a magic spell because he is so different from what he used to be. That person is obviously under some kind of spell because he could have never before done what he is doing now. He's clearly, obviously under grace [*charis*]."

If you look at your own life and see how you have changed since the grace of God touched you, isn't the change stark compared with who you used to be? Can you think of a greater compliment than someone looking at you and saying, "He must be under the divine spell of God because he and his behavior are so different. The only way he could be so transformed is because he is under "the divine spell of God" — His *grace*!"

It's easy for me to understand this concept. As a young man, I was an inhibited, embarrassed, and shy person. The original Rick Renner would have never sought to stand before people or to sit in front of a TV camera or agree that my face and teachings be shared around the world in various media. Before God "graced" me, I could have never even *imagined* it. Even now, my natural tendency when I am in a crowd of people is to gravitate toward the door to make an exit. Except for the *charis* of God upon my life — that is, God's grace — I would run from all of it. But when God's *charis* — His divine and empowering touch — came on my life, I became like a man operating under "the divine spell of God."

Just as the apostle Paul exclaimed in First Corinthians 15:10, I, too, am what I am by the grace of God — which means, I am nothing like I used to be. What I am now is because of God's grace that so completely transformed me, and I am now doing what I could have never done previously.

If you had known Rick Renner before the grace (*charis*) of God came on my life, it would *flabbergast* you to see how different I am now in comparison. You might even be tempted to say (and many *have* said), "He must be under a divine spell because he is nothing like he used to be. The Rick Renner I knew earlier in life could have never done or become what he has done and become. Something has happened to him because he is so different." Your observation would be a testament of God's grace on my life. *To God be the glory!*

In Romans 1:5, Paul remarkably connected the words "grace" and "apostleship" in a single verse. He wrote, "By whom we have received *grace* and *apostleship....*"

Notice the order in this verse is "grace" and *then* "apostleship." In this statement, Paul affirmed that all the glory went to God for his apostolic ministry because the bestowal of God's grace is what empowered and transformed him. He received "grace" — *charis* — that enabled him to stand in the office of an apostle.

'...Given Unto Me...'

After Paul explained the working of the grace of God in his life, he then added in First Corinthians 3:10, "According to the grace of God which is *given unto me....*"

The words "given unto me" tell us once again that Paul had to come to terms with his own grace-given assignment — he had to accept and embrace it. In Romans 12:6, Paul acknowledged that there are a myriad of manifestations of grace and that each person differs in his or her expression of Christ by the unique grace each individual has received. In that verse, Paul wrote, "Having then gifts differing according to the grace that is given to us...."

An example of differing graces is found in Galatians 2:8, where Paul also wrote, "For he that wrought effectually in Peter to the apostleship of the circumcision, the same was mighty in me toward the Gentiles."

In this remarkable verse, Paul doesn't give a hint of feeling either inferior or superior to Peter's apostolic grace to the Jews. Instead, he celebrated the fact that the grace that "wrought effectually" in Peter to be an apostle to the Jews was also "mighty" in him toward the Gentiles. Paul understood that each of them had received a special and unique grace that they needed for their respective assignments. But notice Paul knew *exactly* what grace had been given to him, and he also knew and acknowledged it was different from the grace given by God to Peter.

In First Corinthians 1:10, we find believers in the Corinthian church were comparing ministers to other ministers, alleging one was better than the other, and this comparison became so robust it brought division into the church. Paul was the founder of the church there, but later Apollos assumed an important pastoral role in that church. Some in the church who were saved under Paul's ministry liked Paul's style better. Others liked Apollos' intellectual style better. And an unthinkable wrangling erupted inside the church over whose style was most preferred.

When Paul heard of these divisions inside the church at Corinth, he wrote in First Corinthians 3:6 and said, "I have planted, Apollos watered...." The word "planted" is translated from the Greek word *phuteuo*, which is a form of *phuton*, the Greek word for *a plant*, and it simply refers to *the act of planting a plant*. By using this word, Paul was metaphorically describing *his role* in Corinth as *a planter*. His grace-given task, like planting a seed beneath the soil's hard surface, was to apostolically penetrate the darkness of the city and plant a church there.

Like a neglected garden overrun with pests and weeds, Corinth had been infested with demonic powers. In order to plant the Gospel in people's hearts and firmly establish the Church in that tough environment, Paul had to press forward and till the ground with the power of God; then he had to get on his hands and knees and *pull* the spiritual weeds. *That was hard work!* Yet for one and a half years, Paul poured his life into this pioneering job. When he finally left Corinth to pursue his apostolic call in another city, the Corinthian church had not only been planted — it was *deeply rooted* and *producing good fruit.*

Paul described his God-given role in Corinth as a planter. But he was fully aware where his responsibility ended and another's equally important responsibility began. That is why he went on in First Corinthians 3:6 to say, "I have planted, *Apollos watered....*"

The word "watered" is a form of the Greek word *potidzo*, which most often means *to water* or *to irrigate.* It is the very word that would have been used to depict a farmer watering his garden to provide nourishment to his plants so they could grow. It can also be translated *to imbibe*, which in this context would convey the act of a field becoming *soaked* or *saturated* in water.

By describing Apollos' role in Corinth with the Greek word *potidzo*, Paul actually gave Apollos *a great compliment.* It is as if Paul said, "Apollos didn't just water you; he *saturated* you...." In other words, Paul acknowledged what a wonderful, equally important job Apollos was doing in the Corinthian church!

God's grace divinely empowered Paul to pull the weeds, chase away the pests, plant the seed, and establish the new growth of the young plant. God's grace divinely empowered Apollos to nurture that plant, watering it regularly with the Word of God and thus contributing equally to the great increase that happened in that church. The God-given roles of both ministers were absolutely vital. One was not better than the other; rather, each played a significant role in the spiritual development of that church.

Paul continued in First Corinthians 3:6 by saying, "I have planted, Apollos watered; but God gave the *increase.*" This word "increase" is the Greek word *auxano*, which means *to cause to grow*, *to cause to increase*, or *to cause to become enlarged.* Here Paul states we can each carry out our different roles of planting and watering, but only God can provide the sunshine and weather that allows it to grow. If God doesn't provide His part, all of our planting and watering is in vain.

In his inspired discourse, Paul passed up the opportunity to say, *"How DARE you like Apollos' ministry better than mine! After all I did for you — starting the church, teaching you, and pastoring you — how is it possible that you would like him more than me?"*

Instead of entering the fray about who was greatest among them, Paul recognized and celebrated the fact that he and Apollos had very different graces. Both needed to be valued and appreciated and not to be held up side by side. This shows us that Paul was secure in the grace given to him, and he did not feel threatened by the grace of another. In fact, he was able to celebrate the other person's grace!

The problem of comparing one minister to another continued for a long time, so in Second Corinthians 10:12, Paul urged those who were at the root of the problem to stop it. He wrote, "...But they measuring themselves by themselves, and comparing themselves among themselves, are not wise."

The word "comparing" is a form of the Greek word *sunkrino*, and it pictures *two or more who stand side by side to thoroughly examine themselves in comparison to each other and then to critically judge who is superior among the candidates.* One group is classified as superior, and the other is classified as inferior. It elevates one and puts another down, and it fails to recognize the many diverse graces that exist within the Church. Because the Corinthians had infighting among themselves to prove who was the greatest among them, Paul rebuked them for making such comparisons.

The point I want you to see is that God has given each of us different kinds of grace and intentionally made us each different from one another. We are each actually a result of God's divine design. Our mannerisms, insights, and style that are different from others are the very qualities that make each of us uniquely positioned to fulfill a specific need.

I'll tell you that when I was young in ministry, I struggled with the fact that I was so different from other ministers. But when I finally understood that *God* was the One who made me different, and I began to embrace the unique grace He explicitly gave to me, I began to see that I could shine His light in ways others could not. What I thought would hold me back is actually what gave me my place in His plan. When I began to accept the unique grace God gave to me, I was able to *embrace* my grace that makes me shine differently from others.

We are each actually a result of God's divine design. Our mannerisms, insights, and style that are different from others are the very qualities that make each of us uniquely positioned to fulfill a specific need.

Paul's words in First Corinthians 3:6 that one plants, another waters — and his words in First Corinthians 3:10, where he writes that he knows exactly what grace has been given to *him* — tell us emphatically that Paul learned to enjoy and even "frolic" in the grace God had given him. Paul did not struggle with comparing his grace to the grace of others. He knew what his grace was, and he accepted and embraced it.

That is why Paul wrote in Romans 12:6, "Having then gifts differing according to the grace that is given to us...." Paul learned the secret of finding, accepting, embracing, and learning to flow in the marvelous grace committed unto him. As a result, it shined brightly in his life, and just *how* it shined is what we find next in First Corinthians 3:10.

'...A Wise Masterbuilder...'

In summary, so far we have seen what Paul meant when he told us, "According to the grace of God which is given unto me..." (1 Corinthians 3:10).

As we've seen, this verse tells us Paul quit struggling with the grace God assigned to his life. A pivotal moment came when he finally hoisted the white flag of surrender to accept and embrace God's unique grace on his life. After Paul came to terms with that grace and surrendered to it, it flowed mightily into his life, and that grace began to dominate him and miraculously transform him into a great apostle.

When that grace touched Paul and he surrendered to it, it divinely gave him abilities he could have never naturally possessed. It was that divine touch of God's *charis* upon him that enabled Paul to supernaturally become "a wise masterbuilder." This is why Paul continued in First Corinthians 3:10 to say, "According to the grace of God which is given unto me, as a wise masterbuilder..."

The metaphor of a "master builder" is power-packed, so let's pause to understand why Paul used this phrase and how it relates to roles of apostles in the past, present, and last-days Church.

The word "wise" is a translation of the Greek word *sophos*, a well-known word that pictures *insight* or *wisdom.* If *sophos* is used to describe those who are "wise" in the eyes of the world, it depicts *ultra-smart* people. In fact, the word *sophos* was often used in ancient Greek culture to portray *highly educated people*, such as scientists, philosophers, doctors, teachers, and others who were considered to be the *super-intelligentsia* of the day. These belonged to a class of individuals the world would have called *clever*, *astute*, *smart*, or *intellectually brilliant.* The term *sophos* was reserved only for those considered to be *a cut above* the rest.

But Paul used *sophos* to say God's grace had explicitly given *him insight*, *revelation*, or *wisdom* that is *not* attained by education or life experience. He was describing supernatural revelation, a *divinely bestowed wisdom*, given to him by God Himself that enabled him to brilliantly know what to do every step along the way in his apostolic ministry.

In this sense, God's grace caused Paul to be spiritually *brilliant.* But because the word *sophos* was reserved for those considered to be *super-impressive* or *a cut above* the rest, it means Paul's insights, given to him by God's grace, were *super-impressive* and *a cut above* what others claimed to possess. And because Paul connected "wisdom" — the Greek word *sophos* — to God's grace in His life, he gives God all the glory for all his divine insights. Paul knew his mind was *not* the source for these insights and he possessed them only as the result of a special grace working in his life.

Paul then adds that the grace operating in his life enabled him to become a "wise *masterbuilder.*" Because "wise" is translated from *sophos,* Paul in humility acknowledged he wasn't just gifted as a masterbuilder, but he was so mightily gifted by God's grace in this respect that he was indeed a *super-impressive masterbuilder.* But what is a masterbuilder?

The word "masterbuilder" is a poor *King James Version* translation of the Greek word *architekton*, the actual Greek word for an ancient *architect,* and it is, of course, from where the English word "architect" is derived. The word *architekton* is a compound of two words, *archo* and *tekton.* The word *archo* means from *the beginning*, and the word *tekton* describes *a highly trained technician.* But when compounded, it forms *architekton*, the Greek word that pictures an architect who is responsible to begin a project and lead it to its completion. The *architekton* in the ancient world was invested with the responsibility:

- To envision what needed to be constructed.
- To assist in selecting a site for construction.
- To provide an architectural design and plan.
- To develop a budget for the entire project and ensure the project stayed on budget.
- To meticulously oversee all workers on-site who, under his guidance, were building what he had envisioned.

Paul used the metaphor of an architect to describe his apostolic ministry. But it is important to comprehend exactly *why* he chose this metaphor to describe the work of an apostle. So to make sure we are on solid footing regarding Paul's use of this exact word — the only time it was used in the New Testament — we must turn to historical sources to see how this word *architekton* was used by notable writers in antiquity. How ancient writers used it will explain why Paul chose this word in First Corinthians 3:10 to describe apostolic ministry.

Historical sources inform us that:

- Herodotus and Plutarch both used the Greek word *architekton* to depict an architect and all his *numerous* responsibilities.[3]
- Plato used the word *architekton* to depict *a ruler of workmen* who contributed his knowledge specifically to a construction project. His task was to draw up plans and give instruction to the workers about how to build. However, he was not actually counted among the workman themselves, but was the *project manager* or *leader of the work.*[4]

- Plato and Euripides both also used the Greek word *architekton* to picture *a masterful organizer* or *manager of large projects*, including *building projects*.[5]
- Demosthenes used the Greek word *architekton* to illustrate the work of *a theatrical director* whose function included *overseeing*, *managing*, and *directing theatrical performances* — a task that included managing and overseeing hundreds of performers and stagehands so a coordinated and flawless performance could be produced and enjoyed.[6]

When all these meanings are taken into consideration, we find that an ancient *architekton* was not only an architect, but an on-site director or leader of a building project, tasked with all the responsibilities of an ancient architect. He contributed advanced knowledge to a construction project by drawing up plans and giving instruction to all the workers on-site. He had to possess masterful organizational skills, and like a theatrical director who directed and oversaw hundreds of people on and off stage to produce a flawless theatrical production, an ancient *architekton* was to provide vision, guidance and leadership from the beginning to the end of a project and to see that the whole endeavor was carried out flawlessly.

If you'll recall, in Chapter Two, I gave an abridged history of famous temples that were constructed in the ancient world. What I did not say then, but will say now, is that each of those temples were envisioned, designed, and constructed under the guidance of world-renowned architects of that time. These architects were so renowned, we still know their names today. To this day, their names are commemorated due to their groundbreaking and monumental architectural work in their respective ages. As a painter signs a masterpiece, the names of these architects are like *eternal signatures* on the historical structures they conceived and constructed. (In a few pages, you'll understand why this point about their *signatures* is so significant.)

For example:

- Although the *Temple of Artemis* in Ephesus was reconstructed several times in its multi-thousand-year history, the longest-standing and most grandiose version of it was designed by a world-renowned Cretan architect named *Chesiphron* who designed and oversaw its construction with the help of his son *Metagenes.* Together this father-son team led the project from beginning to end with thousands of workers whom they guided through the entire process.[7] As a result, the names *Chesiphron* and *Metagenes* have been repeated again and again throughout history as scholars have discussed, studied, or taught about the *Temple of Artemis* at Ephesus. Their names are forever etched in history as the architects of that project which became one of the Seven Wonders of the Ancient World.

- *The Altar of Zeus* in Pergamum was ordered by King Eumenes II of the Attalid dynasty. The structure is believed to have been designed by *Phyromachos,* the last of the greatest architects and sculptors from ancient Greece. With him was an entire team of under-architects that included *Kresilas, Myron, Phidias, Polykleitos, Callimachus, Skopas, Praxiteles,* and *Lysippos.*[8] Today large sections of this breathtaking altar are on display in the Pergamon Museum in Berlin. In antiquity, it was listed among the Seven Wonders of the Ancient World. But now, thousands of years later when scholars discuss it, they still reverentially speak the name *Phyromachos* when referring to its chief creator.

- On the Athenian acropolis sits the world-famous *Parthenon,* a colossal structure designed in antiquity by two world famous architects named *Ictinus* and *Callicrates,* who were handpicked by Pericles — the Greek statesman and general during the Golden Age of Athens — to conceive, design, and lead the construction of it.[9] The enormous task required talent, skill, and the enormous undertaking of orchestrating the coordinated efforts of thousands of workmen and craftsmen needed to produce this architectural wonder. Due to the combined efforts of these two architects, *Ictinus* and *Callicrates*, their names have reverberated throughout history for this glorious temple they constructed in the heart of Athens.

- In a marshy sector of ancient Rome, the Emperor Marcus Agrippa dreamed to totally transform that swampy region to make it the domicile of the *Pantheon,* a massive temple to all the Roman gods. The structure was to have the largest non-reinforced dome ever constructed in human history. The undertaking was so gargantuan that Marcus Agrippa conscripted the brilliant services of an architect named *Apollodorus* from Damascus.[10] Apollodorus would eventually be executed by the emperor, but what he designed became a marvel of architecture that stuns architects and engineers even by modern standards. The name Apollodorus will forever be memorialized as the architect who conceived the *Pantheon* in Rome.

- Unlike the aforementioned temples, the *Temple in Jerusalem* was designed by God Himself, who gave instructions to King David about how to build and decorate it. Years later, David's son, King Solomon, fulfilled God's command to his father and constructed it according to God's design. Solomon had many great achievements, but the *Temple* in Jerusalem was the crowning achievement of King Solomon's reign. However, if one attempts to name a single architect accredited as the one who conceived the *Temple* in Jerusalem, he would be frustrated, as the only conclusion that can be reached is God Himself was the Architect of the *Temple* — and, as such, *God's name* is eternally associated from beginning to end with the design, construction, and furnishing of the *Temple.*

Paul used the word *architekton* metaphorically in First Corinthians 3:10 to picture apostolic ministry because it is a word that depicts a gifted architect with the ability to visualize whatever was needed to be constructed, including designing it and putting it on parchment so others could see it and follow every phase of the plan as the building process commenced. The *architekton* was the *visionary*, the *designer*, and the *leader* who started and finished the project with the help of thousands of workers he led through every phase of the process.

Paul knew all the nuances of this word, and he remarkably used *architekton* in First Corinthians 3:10 to describe his own apostolic ministry. As an apostle, he knew God had entrusted him with the task of envisioning whatever needed to be built and then orchestrating the work of other Christ-given fivefold ministry gifts as well as overseeing God's people who worked under his authority onsite.

While I do not want to belabor the point, the following paragraphs are included to help you better understand the nuances of the word *architekton* so you can see how this metaphor figuratively applies to apostolic ministry in the beginning of the Church Age, in contemporary Church history, and also in the last-days of the Church Age.

The Numerous Responsibilities of an Ancient Architect

Again, Paul, a brilliant scholar, used the word *architekton* to describe apostolic ministry because all the nuances connected to this word so aptly describe the work of an apostle. For a few paragraphs, let me take you on a journey to an imaginary building site in past history in order to help you see the various responsibilities connected to an architect in the ancient Greek and Roman worlds. We will use the illustration of a hypothetical architect commissioned to build a *temple*, as this was one of the most common assignments given to ancient architects.

Before going further into the responsibilities of an ancient architect and how those nuances relate to the work of an apostle, I must point out that world-class architects in the ancient world were highly paid and well-rewarded for their services. Few could do what they were gifted to do, and as a result, they were remunerated very well, both in terms of money and with honor by society for the projects they conceived and constructed. In a few pages, you will see how this also applies to apostolic ministry.

But first, at the start of any project, before any work commenced, selecting the site where a temple was to be built was very important. The architect performed investigative work to locate, in most cases, a conspicuous site where the temple to be constructed would be most visible. Usually it was an outcropping where the architect imagined it would have great visual attention. To find the best site for the temple, the architect scouted the environment until the most appropriate location was identified.

Every religious temple had a specific purpose, and that purpose was critical in the architect's selection of a temple site. For example, some pagan religions were wide-open to receiving as many visitors as possible, while other pagan religions were secretive and required a less approachable location. For an architect to choose the appropriate site, he had to understand the purpose and all the associated nuances for the temple and then customize a location perfect for that temple's need.

Once a location had been located, it was the job of the architect to hire ground-levelers to come on-site to chip away at the ground's surface until it was level and smooth enough for a massive stone foundation to be placed on top of it. Because laying a temple foundation was so significant, the architect invited pagan priests on-site to consecrate the site with a festive opening before any construction commenced. Today this would be called a groundbreaking ceremony, but this was a ceremony "on steroids" that was attended by frenzied worshipers, musicians, and priests who offered burnt offerings to the spirit realm before construction work began.

Because a temple needed to look glorious, the architect searched for the finest stone materials to be used in construction. Once such stone was located, the architect was tasked with hiring and overseeing all the manual laborers who worked at quarries to chisel the massive stones that would be used in the foundation, walls, columns, pillars, pediments, and even portions of the roof. To do this monumental job, thousands of workers were hired to quarry the massive stones and then transport them to the construction site under the watchful eye of the architect who was responsible for organizing all the work.

Once the massive stones were on-site, the architect hired stone-carvers to come and begin the process of chipping away at every piece of stone until near-perfect measurements were achieved. The stone-carvers began the elaborate and painstaking process of carving all the architectural elements, including pillars and cylindric columns of different styles. Once each stone for a column was carved and it was time for it to be erected, each piece of stone (weighing many tons each) was hoisted carefully by ropes until a tall column of stacked stones reached a crowning apex. Then ironsmiths, whom the architect also hired, came to pour molten iron into the grooves in the stones, pillars, and columns to reinforce the temple so it could withstand movement caused by earthquakes. And like all other phases of the project, this was carried out under the watchful eye of the architect.

It wasn't long until stone-polishers arrived on-site to begin the laborious process of grinding and polishing every individual stone so each piece would fit snugly into place with other stones. And because the temple was to gleam in the light of the sun and moon, the exterior of the stones were polished brilliantly until they became reflective of the light of the heavens.

Once each polished stone was ready, the architect meticulously oversaw the process of seeing each stone so snugly set in place the seams between them were nearly imperceptible. All of this, too, was done under the guiding hand of the architect.

Then as the walls of the temple towered upward, carpenters contracted by the architect arrived to construct gargantuan scaffolding that roof workers scaled as they put massive timbers in place for the beams of the roof — huge beams that could hold the weight of thousands of terracotta roof tiles that would rest on top of them. Then the scaffolding was reassembled at different sections of the exterior so highly paid professional artisans — carvers, painters, and special metal workers — could use them to create elaborate reliefs and friezes around the upper exterior of the temple and pediments.

Once the reliefs and friezes were carved, masterful painters scrambled up the scaffolding to paint each detail to look life-like. Before disassembling the scaffolding, metal workers inserted bronze and copper elements into the reliefs and friezes where needed, such as actual bronze bridles in the mouths of carved horses that protruded from the friezes and reliefs and realistically appeared ready to run fiercely into the distance.

Simultaneously, work was being carried out inside the inner sanctum of the temple. Artisans designed magnificent floors with inlaid granite, marble, and mosaics in a fusion of coordinated colors and hues. Other painters painted richly colored frescoes, and sculptors masterfully carved statues to commemorate local heroes and idols of the gods who would soon adorn the niches in the interior and exterior walls of the temple. Reflective pools of waters were positioned in key interior locations to reflect the roof, interior walls, and the image of the temple's patron god or goddess. And before the whole process was completed, the architect arranged for weavers and dyers to come on-site to hand-produce richly dyed draperies that would be positioned around the walls of the sanctuary's interior parts.

Before finalizing the project, more exquisite marble and granite ordered by the architect were transported to the site to be cut into thinly sliced panels. The veins in the stone were fabulously pieced together as if they were unending veins of natural marble, and the panels were polished until they glistened. At that point, stone experts used the panels to veneer exterior portions of the temple as a masterful finishing touch, also under the ever-watchful eye of the architect.

In addition to all this oversight, the architect had to interact with pagan temple priests who regularly interrupted the work to offer sacrifices as every phase of the building project continued. Their interaction was required to affirm to the architect that what was being constructed would meet all the needs of their religious rituals. Finally, for such a temple to be built to such high expectations, it meant the architect's name — like the *signature* of a famous painter on a masterpiece — would be memorialized for all ages as the architect who constructed it.[11] You can understand why, then, an architect on such a project would be so well-compensated for his multifaceted, painstaking work.

How This Metaphor Applies to the Ministry of an Apostle

What you have just read may be new information to you, but as a scholar and master of the Greek language and history, Paul knew very well everything that was included in the word *architekton*. And he used this word *architekton* — again, it's the only time this word is used in the New Testament — to specifically describe his apostolic work in Corinth.

As I pointed out previously, ancient architects were highly paid and rewarded for their services. Few could do what they were gifted to do, and as a result, they were compensated very well, in terms of both money and acclaim. Likewise, those who serve apostolically on the frontlines should be well-supported. In First Corinthians 9, where Paul wrote extensively to defend his apostleship, he candidly wrote about the need for those on the frontlines to be well supported financially.

Then in First Corinthians 9:7, Paul rhetorically asked, "Who goeth a warfare any time at his own charges? who planteth a vineyard, and eateth not of the fruit thereof? or who feedeth a flock, and eateth not of the milk of the flock?"

In verses 11-14, he continued, "If we have sown unto you spiritual things, is it a great thing if we shall reap your carnal things? If others be partakers of this power over you, are not we rather? Nevertheless, we have not used this power; but suffer all things, lest we should hinder the gospel of Christ. Do ye not know that they which minister about holy things live of the things of the temple? and they which wait at the altar are partakers with the altar? Even so hath the Lord ordained that they which preach the gospel should live of the gospel."

In these verses, Paul taught (and kindly scolded) the Corinthian church for not financially supporting his work among them. He let them know that he had every right to receive financial support as he labored among them. But they did not do well in supporting his ministry. That is why he continued in verse 15 to say, "But I have used none of these things…."

Think how unreasonable it would be to engage an architect to build a building and to require him to personally pay for the honor of building your project. That is precisely what happened to the apostle Paul while he ministered in Corinth. He went there by faith, and because he had little financial help from the church while he was there, he also worked to pay the bills. The Corinthians had money to support him, but did not, and there was nothing right about that situation. Yet Paul was so committed to his call and so determined to obey God that he worked a job at the same time he ministered to them. It did not have to be that way, and Paul wrote these verses to teach them and, to a degree, to "shame" them, or call them to account, for how they had provided such little financial support.

I currently know some who are called to the frontlines to preach — to push back the powers of darkness and to establish the Church where it has never existed before. To do such a task is monumental and requires *a thousand-percent* focus. Yet so often because of a lack of financial support, they are distracted by trying to find ways to pay for the ministry they were dispatched to do. Instead of staying on the frontlines where they need to be, they find the need to run back and forth to their former country in an attempt to find financial support. So often these brave heroes accepted the call to go where no one else goes or even wants to go, only to discover a lack of financial support from those who laid hands on them and sent them. That is when they discover they were sent and are now expected, rightly or wrongly, to foot by themselves the bill for all ministry expenses.

It is imperative to understand Paul was figuratively comparing apostles to world-class architects in the ancient world who were highly rewarded for their services. Likewise, the Church must come to grips with its need to generously support those whom they send abroad. Those *sent-ones* need to be supported financially so they can stay where they are called to serve without undue burdens. In fact, in First Corinthians 9:7,11-14, we find it is God's plan for anyone sent to the frontlines to be supported well as they contribute to the growth of the Church. This remuneration should include money and honor from others in the Church, especially the sending church or sending organization, for their work to establish churches where others have not gone before them.

All these nuances in the aforementioned paragraphs suggest so many points about apostolic ministry. For example, they let us know that when Paul arrived in the city of Corinth, he was like an *architekton* who scouted the city for the right site upon which to establish the new church. He analyzed the city's particular spiritual needs, and then he went about to establish a new church with the help of all the God-called workers who labored alongside him under his watchful eye. He was the leader who imparted the *sophos* wisdom he had received by the grace of God about how to establish the new church in the new location.

As the apostolic team leader, Paul needed to provide direction and guidance to those who would help him establish the church, but he needed God-called individuals who possessed skills he didn't possess. Most importantly, he needed to take heed to "how" he established the church, because Christ, the Head of the Church, was the One who had dispatched him there, and Christ was the One to whom he would answer for what sort of church had been established.

As an apostle, Paul's task was always to establish a glorious habitation for the Spirit of God that would *glisten*. And if he did his task well, the churches he established would bear his *apostolic signature* upon them forever. Thus, we know today who founded churches in Galatia, Ephesus, Philippi, Colossae, Thessalonica, and others, including churches scattered all over ancient Greece, Macedonia, and the Roman Province of Asia. We know because Paul's *apostolic signature* is forever etched into the history of those churches.

Furthermore, Paul had to provide leadership to the project of laying a foundation for the Church in a new place, understanding that the eye of Jesus Christ was upon him and his endeavor, and, hence, it was essential he follow through on every point of the plan to ensure the new church was being built according to the divine blueprints Christ had given him.

An apostle who works alone will never build much, for it doesn't matter how much he can visualize in his head or put onto paper — if he has no fellow team members, his vision will remain in the mental realm and never become a reality. In order to bring his vision to reality, cooperation with others who are gifted differently than him is essential. The apostle is indeed the unquestionable visionary, the designer, and the leader of the project, but his vision will only come to pass *if* he engages strategic partners at his side to do their parts.

As we discuss the subject of all of us doing our various parts in building the House of God, I am reminded of the words of Charles Spurgeon, who said, "We need to have a Church in which all the members do something, in which all do all they can, in which all are always doing all they can; for this is what our Lord deserves to have from a living, loving people bought with His precious blood! If He has saved me, I will serve Him forever and ever. And whatever lies in my power to do for His glory, that shall be my delight to do, and to do at once!"[12]

By using the word "masterbuilder" — translated from the Greek word *architekton* — Paul let us know he visualized himself as an apostolic architect: *the apostolic visionary*, *the apostolic designer*, and *the apostolic leader* in seeing the Church established in a new territory. But as I just noted, what Paul divinely visualized could only become a reality *if* he worked alongside others who were called to assist him in the building process by doing what he could not do. Paul metaphorically used the word "masterbuilder" to illustrate that for apostolic ministry to be successful, apostles *must* cooperate with other God-called people to build the Church in any new location.

An example of this cooperation is seen in Acts 18 when Paul first arrived in Corinth. As an apostle, he was gifted to see how God's House needed to be spiritually built in the city of Corinth. He was *an apostolic architect*, but for that vision to come into reality, God called other team members alongside Paul to add their parts and to supply what he was lacking. In this case, God graciously brought him Aquila and Priscilla (Acts 12:2). In that team of three, Paul was the undisputed apostolic visionary, apostolic designer, and apostolic leader — the "wise masterbuilder" — who had the final say in how things proceeded. Yet he needed others with him in the building process.

If you study Paul's overall apostolic ministry recorded in the book of Acts, you will discover he rarely traveled or ministered alone. He was accompanied by Barnabas, Silas, John Mark, Timothy, Erastus, Sopater, Aristarchus, Secundus, Gaius, Tychicus, Trophimus, and Luke — crucial members of his apostolic team who each worked with their leader, Paul, as he led them apostolically wherever they journeyed to establish a new church. By using the word *architekton* in First Corinthians 3:10, Paul thereby acknowledged that as the spiritual architect of a new church, he was to lead the whole project with an anointed spiritual construction team at his side.

You may recall reading in Chapter Two that for God's *naos* Temple to emerge, a God-assembled workforce is required. In addition to all the members of the Church who serve with their various gifts, God has also set the various roles of *apostles*, *prophets*, *evangelists*, *pastors*, and *teachers* in the Church to serve as professional builders in the *naos* Temple of God. Let me summarize again how they could be described as a part of an apostolic-architectural team.

- **Apostles** and their teams select the "construction" site where the Church has never been established before. When they enter a new location, they are anointed by God's Spirit to clear spiritual rubbish out of the way and to lay a foundation for the Church. As team leader, the apostle works side by side with his God-called team to lay a rock-solid foundation on which others can come along to do their parts in building a magnificent structure or work. The apostle is the overall team leader charged with responsibility from God to oversee the project from its beginning to its conclusion.
- Building inspectors also play a key role to make sure the construction is being carried out properly and up to code. This is where the

Christ-given fivefold ministry gift of the **prophet** enters the picture in regard to his or her part in building the House of God. Often prophets operate like anointed building inspectors who are divinely enabled to *see* what others may not see, including what is done correctly or incorrectly. With Christ-given insight, Christ-given prophets impart courage to build correctly and, at times, to address issues that need to be fixed in the building process.

- Peter states in First Peter 2:5 that the house of God is built with "living stones" or the souls of those who have been redeemed. This brings us to the role of the Christ-given ministry gift of the **evangelist.** Evangelists are anointed "stone collectors" who go into the field to win souls who will become the "living stones" in the construction of God's House. Once those living stones are won and collected, the evangelist's responsibility is to see them brought on-site where they can be assimilated into the Temple of God.

- Raw stones need a specialist to chisel, cut, trim, sand, grind, buff, and polish them to snugly fit next to other stones in the building. This brings us to the Christ-given fivefold ministry gift of the **pastor.** In God's great building program, pastors are specialists who are anointed to carry out the nitty-gritty business of chiseling, cutting, trimming, sanding, grinding, and polishing all the souls or "living stones" that the evangelist gathered in the field and brought to the building site. A part of a pastor's function is to prepare all those living stones to be fitted into their respective places in God's House.

- Blueprints and plans for a project like this are so vital that they must be explicitly followed for any building to be constructed according to the architect's plan. This is where the Christ-given fivefold ministry gift of the **teacher** enters the picture. Christ-given teachers are like master instructors who turn us again and again to the instructions and principles in God's Word to keep us on target with God's objective so each of the "living stones" will continue to glisten where it is placed in God's House.

By using the work *architekton* to describe apostolic ministry, Paul wrote that he understood much of the role of an apostle in architectural terms. *First,* he knew the heartbeat of a true apostle must be to see a spiritual structure raised that is so magnificent the Holy Spirit will be honored to dwell there. *Second,* he knew the heartbeat of a true apostle is to see a *naos* Temple emerge where God's people, a new spiritual priesthood of believers, can carry out their functions in the temple with no hindrances (*see* Chapter Three). *Third,* Paul knew the heartbeat of a true apostle is to be mindful of those who are "without" — unbelievers whom we either appeal to or drive away from the Gospel.

'...I Have Laid the Foundation...'

Throughout the New Testament, Paul used construction metaphors regularly and understood that God's people were being built together as a holy Temple for the habitation of the Spirit in the earth. In the Old Testament, God's presence was in the Temple, but by divine revelation, Paul understood *the Church* had become the House of God — or the Temple of the Holy Spirit — a new dwelling-place for God's presence in the earth. This Temple had become a permanent replacement for the Holy of Holies in the Old Testament, and the apostle Paul knew God now dwelled in the hearts of born-again people both individually and corporately as the Church.

It is amazing that Paul, who would have likely not chosen to live and minister in a city like Corinth, was so immensely proud of the church in Corinth he joyfully wrote about his time there, "...I have laid the foundation" (1 Corinthians 3:10).

Let me give you a little history of the church at Corinth so you can gain a better understanding of why Paul was so proud of what God had done in this church from the time he and his God-called team first arrived there to establish a new church.

The city of Corinth was a very old city that had previously rebelled against the authority of Rome. As a result, Rome attacked and destroyed the city in 146 BC, and its ruins lay in waste and were uninhabited for many years. Then in 44 BC, Julius Caesar decided to reestablish Corinth as a Roman colony because of its advantageous position on the narrow isthmus that served as a "land bridge" linking central and southern Greece.[13]

Rebuilding Corinth proved to be a challenge because few people wanted to relocate to these old, devastated ruins. So Julius Caesar offered the incentive of a new life to veteran Roman legionnaires (soldiers), as well as to the poor and freed slaves of Rome. Caesar promised free land if these people would relocate to Corinth, help reconstruct it, and become the new city leaders. As a result of this offer, large numbers of these groups of people moved to Corinth and became the founding fathers of the newly emerging city.

The Greek goddess Aphrodite was prominent in the older version of Corinth, and because Julius Caesar actually believed he was a direct descendent of the goddess, he decided to dedicate the new Corinth to Aphrodite. Since Aphrodite was revered as the goddess of sex and of prostitutes, the sex industry came to play a major role in the reconstructed city of Corinth, just as it had in the Corinth of centuries earlier. Among many other pagan temples, a significant temple was built for the worship of Aphrodite, and the sex industry flourished in a new city that was filled with a large population of lower-class freedmen and tough, seasoned legionnaires.

The city was also located between two ports, one on the west coast to receive ships from Rome, and another on the east coast to receive ships from

Asia and beyond. Because of the city's sex industry, it became a tourist stop for sailors and travelers who arrived at these ports and made their way into Corinth to indulge in sexual pleasures.

In addition, Corinth was widely known for its culture of drunken debauchery. The excessive use of alcohol by Corinthians was so notorious that if a person lived in the Roman world and was a drunkard, it is likely that person would have been referred to as a "Corinthian." In fact, the term "to Corinthianize" came to refer to engaging in debaucheries of all types — sexual sin as well as drunkenness. The portrayal of actors as drunk Corinthians was widely practiced throughout the Roman Empire. Such was the reputation of Corinthians across the Roman world in the First Century. They were generally thought of as lower-class, crude, fornicating drunkards.

Furthermore, not far from Corinth were the Panhellenic Games of ancient Greece that were conducted every other year and attracted hordes of visitors to the region. Because Corinth was the city closest to the site of these games, it benefited from revenue generated from people who came from all over the Roman world to participate in or to view the games. Of course, the large numbers of visitors to the games contributed to the growth of the sex industry, the sale of alcohol, and to the tourist business in general. These Panhellenic Games were highly competitive games, and as a result, a prevailing spirit of competition also affected the mindset of Corinthian society and helped build the city's reputation as one marked by fierce competition.

Because the city was filled with people seeking a new future, Corinth unfortunately also attracted a large number of fortune hunters who wanted to make a quick and easy buck. Professional swindlers saw this as a great opportunity, so they, too, arrived in large numbers.

In addition to all of this, the city was famous for its plentiful number of pagan temples. It's hard to fathom for tourists of these ancient ruins today, but when Paul arrived in Corinth, the city was *engulfed* with temples to various gods. As a result, smoke billowed into the air continually from the sacrifices offered to false gods in these temples. Sounds of "wrangling," eerie music could be heard on the streets coming from inside the temples where pagan practices were being carried out. These practices included slitting the necks of bulls offered at the altars positioned on the steps of these temples, where blood flowed profusely. In fact, so many sacrifices were being offered to pagan gods in Corinth that Paul dedicated significant space in First Corinthians to deal with the issue of meat that was offered to idols (*see* 1 Corinthians 8:1-13; 10:19-32).

All these components of life in Corinth paint a realistic picture of the city when the apostle Paul first arrived there. It was a city of strategic location that offered unrestricted sex and limitless consumption of alcohol, and that boasted a fierce spirit of competition. It was a city largely populated by coarse, immoral soldiers, sailors, and freedmen, with a large dose of charlatans, swindlers, and cheaters added to the mix. It was a cesspool of dark religious practices, and demonic powers abounded there. When all of these ingredients are resident in a single location with all restraint thrown to the wind — the result is a city like the ancient city of Corinth.

This is the reason for Paul's description of the Corinthian believers before they came to Christ: "Know ye not that the unrighteous shall not inherit the kingdom of God? Be not deceived: neither fornicators, nor idolaters, nor adulterers, nor effeminate, nor abusers of themselves with mankind, nor thieves, nor covetous, nor drunkards, nor revilers, nor extortioners, shall inherit the kingdom of God. And such were some of you..." (1 Corinthians 6:9-11).

Paul's words describe precisely who the people in the church at Corinth were before they came to Christ. It was a congregation full of individuals with a morally lurid past.

When Paul first started preaching to the Corinthians, who were deeply pagan and immersed in gross darkness, he knew words alone would never do the job. To reach them, he knew it would require a demonstration of God's power. In First Corinthians 2:4, he wrote about what happened when he first preached to them. He said, "And my speech and my preaching was not with enticing words of man's wisdom, but in demonstration of the Spirit and of power."

Then Paul continued to explain the reason he wanted them to see a demonstration of God's power. He wrote, "That your faith should not stand in the wisdom of men, but in the power of God" (1 Corinthians 2:5). Paul knew that miracles, healings, and other displays of power would have a great impact on these particular listeners. If all he offered them were "enticing words of man's wisdom," they could argue, disagree, or debate with him and remain in their calloused, darkened state. But if an unquestionable miracle happened right before their eyes — *a demonstration of supernatural power that knocked them off their feet* — they would know God Almighty was behind the message Paul was delivering to them.

Paul knew a display of God's power would have a great influence on the Corinthians, so in addition to carefully crafting a message that would touch their hearts, he took it one step further and made the choice to allow the power of God to do its unparalleled work. Paul knew the power of God would melt away every doubt and put an end to all debate, so he stepped aside and allowed God's power to show off and thus confirm the message he preached was indeed the truth!

He later told the Corinthians the reason he took this approach was "that your faith should not stand *in* the wisdom of men, but in the power of God." The word "in" in this verse is the little Greek word *en*, which simply means *in*. As used here, it describes the medium in which faith is *rooted*. It could be translated, "I took this approach so your faith would not be rooted *in* the wisdom of men...." Then Paul continued, "...but *in* the power of God," where he used the word *en* again. This lets us know Paul wanted his Corinthian listeners' faith to be rooted deeply *in* the power of God.

The word "power" in this verse is the Greek word *dunamis*. This well-known, often-used word denotes the *mighty power of God*. In this verse, it denotes not merely power, but *tremendous power*. It signifies God's supernatural power, which is *explosive*, *mighty*, and *awe-inspiring* to those who see or experience it. In fact, Paul's words in First Corinthians 2:5 could be paraphrased, *"I took this approach so your faith would not be rooted in the wisdom of men, but so your faith would be steadfastly rooted in the power of God."*

This was indeed a church that was called from darkness into light — birthed in the supernatural power of God and then apostolically established in that same divine power. When Paul recalled that amazing beginning in Corinth — the divine power that manifested there — his heart overflowed with gratitude to God for what he witnessed among the people God had sent him to reach. Recalling how once lost and dark the Corinthians were before they came to Christ made the work there sparkle all the more with God's grace. Thus, when Paul wrote his first epistle to the Corinthian church, he proudly stated, "…I have laid the foundation…" (1 Corinthians 3:10). Paul was elated that his apostolic signature was upon the church there!

The words "I have laid" show that Paul was still elated and "reveling" in his personal involvement in laying the foundation of the church in Corinth. While modern scholars often try to portray the church in Corinth as a carnal church, Paul explained vividly in First Corinthians 1:4-9 that it was a church overflowing with the transformative *grace* of God. His words "I have laid" in First Corinthians 3:10 are translated from a form of the Greek word *tithemi*, which is used here to depict one who architecturally *lays* or places a foundation for a building. But Paul personalized it to make sure every reader forever understands he is the one who personally laid or placed the foundation under the Corinthian church. This pictures the foundation-laying aspect of an apostle's ministry.

As we have seen, when the apostle Paul first entered Corinth, the city was utterly consumed with idolatry and heathenism. It is no exaggeration to say that Corinth was one of the most wicked, perverted cities on the face of the earth at that time. Therefore, for Paul to establish a church in that evil environment, he had to push like a spiritual bulldozer in the Spirit to shove those demonic powers out of the way. Once the spiritual rubbish had been cleared from his path, he then preached the Word in order to establish a firm foundation under the feet of these newly saved Corinthians. Paul's enormous efforts and intense focus produced a foundation under them that would withstand any attack of the enemy — including horrific persecution — and would last for generations!

Because of Paul's hard work, along with his God-called team, and his cooperation with the power of God, the church in Corinth was set on a firm spiritual foundation that enabled it to become one of the most influential congregations of the Early Church. Although other spiritual leaders followed Paul and contributed their part, a large part of the fruit produced in the Corinthian church can be directly attributed to the talents, energy, and gifts Paul used to establish the foundation for that congregation.

The word "foundation" Paul used in First Corinthians 3:10 is the Greek word *themelios*, a compound of the words *lithos* and *tithemi*. The word *lithos* is Greek for *stone*, and *tithemi* means *to lay something down*. When these words are compounded, they form the word *themelios*, which describes *a foundation set in stone that is strong, stable, enduring, and not easily moved.*

In addition to describing a physical foundation, the word *themelios* was also used metaphorically to denote the *laying of a moral, theological, or educational foundation in a person's life*. These figurative foundations, just like an actual physical foundation of a building, are all built with enormous effort, intense concentration, and great expense.

The word "foundation" — *themelios* — in First Corinthians 3:10 is so important in understanding the foundation-laying aspect of an apostle's ministry. But once again, we must refer to ancient historical sources so we can establish how this word was used in antiquity. A scholar himself, Paul was familiar with the use of *themelios*, and he carefully selected this word to describe the foundation-laying aspect of apostolic ministry because of all the nuances connected to its meaning.

- The word *themelios* was used by Homer to describe any kind of foundation, including a foundation for building, a moral or ethical foundation, an educational or religious foundation, or a foundation for society — hence, any kind of foundation strong enough to hold up something significant.[14]
- Interestingly, Pindar used the word *themelios* to depict the deepest parts of the bottom of the ocean.[15]

Thus, the word *themelios* is not just a foundation, but a deeply-laid foundation intended to be an everlasting support for whatever is constructed on top of it. With this knowledge, Paul's word in First Corinthians 3:10, in effect, meant, "*I personally set the foundation deeply in place, and it is an unmovable, unshakable, solidly-fixed foundation that is strong and stable, and it will endure the test of time.*"

The Foundation-Laying Aspect of an Apostle's Ministry

The foundation-laying ministry of an apostle is so important that Paul also wrote about it in Ephesians 2:20. In that verse, he said, And "[you] are built upon the foundation of the apostles and prophets, Jesus Christ himself being the chief corner stone."

Ephesians 2:20 and its following verses are so important to comprehending the apostle's ministry to lay foundations in the House of God in the earth, it is imperative to understand Paul's words when he said the Church is "... built upon the foundation of the apostles and prophets, Jesus Christ himself being the chief corner stone" (v. 20).

Paul used the word "foundation" in this verse in obvious connection with the foundation-laying ministry of an apostle. The word "foundation" is again a translation of the Greek word *themelios* — the same word Paul used in First Corinthians 3:10 to describe the "foundation" he had personally laid under the church in Corinth. Once again, it describes *a foundation that is set in stone and is so solid it is unmovable, unshakable, solidly fixed in place, and will endure the test of time.*

Paul said the Church is *built upon* the foundation of the apostles and prophets (*see* Ephesians 2:20). The words "built upon" are a translation of the Greek word *epoikodomeo,* which is a compound of *epi* and *oikodomeo.* The word *epi* means *upon,* as *on top* of something. The second part of the word is *oikodomeo* — which is a compound of *oikos,* the word for *a house*, and *demoo,* a word for *construction.* When these two words, *epi* and *oikodomeo*, are compounded, it describes the *enlarging of a house*, as well as all that is entailed in the building process. To add to a house or building, one must plan ahead, implement ideas, use instruments, and make a sizable investment. Basically, this word describes a deliberate decision, as enlarging a house doesn't normally occur accidentally. For a building to be built correctly, it has to be built with a plan.

So these words "built upon," translated from the word *epoikodmeo,* picture the combined efforts of architects who work hand in hand with foundation-layers and builders who bring into physical reality a concept that previously only existed on a blueprint. For that concept to leave the *dream realm* and enter the *real realm* requires the mutual effort of all the contributors who do their parts to turn the concept into a reality.

This lets us know that God, who is the Great Architect of the Church, has a plan for the Church to become a mighty Temple in the earth for His presence. But for that divine plan to come into reality, Christ has given gifts — fivefold ministry specialists — who are each anointed to do their respective parts to bring the Church into the reality God dreams for it to be. And Ephesians 2:20 lets us know Paul clearly states that apostles are called to do the foundation-laying in the Church.

Paul said we are built upon the "foundation" of the apostles and prophets. Now Paul uses this word "foundation" — from the Greek word *themelios* — to tell us that the chief role apostles play is laying *unmovable, unshakable, solidly fixed foundations* for the Church. This was emphatically true of the first 12 foundational apostles, who in addition to starting local churches also laid the foundation of the universal Church with unshakeable, non-negotiable doctrines. Everything they did was apostolic, or foundation-laying, as they forged into the "territory" of spiritual darkness with the light of the glorious Gospel and drove back those dark powers to establish the Church from the foundation upward.

However, this word "foundation," or *themelios*, also depicts the ministry of subsequent and modern-day apostles who are God-sent and supernaturally anointed to go into new territories, to preach the Gospel of Christ, to drive back forces of darkness, to establish doctrine, and to lay the foundation of the Church by beginning local churches with the help of an apostolic team.

Paul categorically used this word "foundation" to depict the work that Christ-given apostles do to lay unshakable foundations in the Church. In early

New Testament times, apostles spent a lot of time teaching correct doctrine and correcting false doctrines that were spreading like wildfire in the newly emerging Church. As a part of their foundation-laying ministry, they understood they needed to address doctrinal problems, and so serious was this issue of erroneous teaching that, at times, they even found it necessary to call out the names of those responsible for spreading false teachings in the Church.

It was incumbent upon the apostles to speak up when they sensed error was attempting to penetrate the ranks and spiritually weaken the flock of God. These leaders loved the Church too much and believed the Gospel too fully to stay silent when someone twisted God's eternal message of truth. That's why they stepped forward to boldly address it. These early leaders firmly believed it was God's charge to them to guard the Church and to contend for the faith, and it is our charge as well (*see* Jude 3). For this reason, those leaders could not sit idly by and do nothing when error tried to creep into the ranks of the Church. They were compelled to speak up and guard the flock over which the Holy Spirit had made them overseers (*see* Acts 20:28).

These leaders loved the Church too much and believed the Gospel too fully to stay silent when someone twisted God's eternal message of truth.

Error-ridden leaders were gradually leading the Church off track doctrinally, forcing the Early Church to combat the infiltration of doctrinal error and spiritual extremes. This led Early Church leaders to come together at certain key times to write a fixed doctrinal statement of non-negotiable New Testament truths. Such early creeds were established to bring order to the theological madness that was erupting throughout the Christian world.

These fixed doctrines were viewed as the most important tenets of the Christian faith and were never to be modified. Based on New Testament Scripture and the historical teachings of the Church, early apostolic leaders developed creeds, composed to put forth the non-negotiable doctrines of the Christian faith for every church and every Christian.

Just as early apostles placed great emphasis on a correct doctrinal foundation, in the late hour of this age, it's important that apostolic leaders in the last-days Church accept the responsibility to speak accurately and clearly for God as His spokesmen and to call the Church back to the authoritative voice of the Bible. We must dig our heels into Scripture and resolve to *receive* nothing, *believe* nothing, and *follow* nothing that cannot be found in or proved by the Bible. A crucial role of apostles is not only the laying of an *organizational* foundation for the church, but also making sure a strong *doctrinal* foundation is put in place.

So we see in every way that the apostolic task is to lay a foundation so *solid* that it will endure the test of time — *an unmovable, unshakable, solidly fixed foundation* that is strong, stable, and enduring. Paul uses this word "foundation" (*themelios*) to depict the work that Christ-given apostles do to lay such unshakable foundations in the Church.

In subsequent chapters, we will also look at the relevance of prophets in securing the Church foundationally, but here Paul unquestionably stated that apostles are foundation-layers in the Church. Then he added in Ephesians 2:21,22 "In whom all the building fitly framed together groweth unto an holy temple in the Lord: in whom ye also are builded together for an habitation of God through the Spirit."

The word "building" in Ephesians 2:21 is translated from the Greek word *oikodome,* an architectural term that means *to build, enlarge, or amplify a house.* Inherent in this word is the idea of *enlargement*, *amplification*, and *growth,* which already tells us God's plan is for the Church to become *enormous.* But Paul then added, "In whom all the building *fitly framed together* groweth unto an holy temple in the Lord."

The words "fitly framed together" in this same verse are from the Greek word *sunarmologeo,* a triple compound of *sun, harmos,* and *lego.* The word *sun* means *together with,* the word *harmos* depicts *a joint that is used to connect various building materials together,* and the word *lego* means *I say.* When these three words are compounded, it forms the word *sunarmologeo,* which emphatically pictures different building materials that have been connected and joined together by a spoken word. It pictures a chief architect who gives the *final word* about which parts go where or how to "frame together" all the parts that must come together in order to construct a building.

Here, Paul pictures Jesus as the Architect and Great Director who alone knows where each person in the House of God should fit and what roles each of them is called to fulfill in His great building program as He builds His *enormous* Church.

Paul then added, "In whom all the building fitly framed together *groweth* unto an holy temple in the Lord" (Ephesians 2:21). The word "groweth" is important because it depicts the *enlargement, amplification,* and *growth* God longs for His Church to experience. It is a translation of the word *auxano,* a word that denotes *enlargement, amplification, augmentation, enhancement, and growth.*

At the outset of the Church Age, remarkable and supernatural growth was experienced at the very beginning, and it has continued throughout the centuries. By using this word "growth" — from the Greek word *auxano* — Paul pictures the Church over the ages becoming larger and larger as God's Spirit augments it with power, truth, and doctrine. In fact, Paul accurately forecasts that it will grow to become a *"Holy Temple"* in the Lord (*see* Ephesians 2:21).

APOSTLES & PROPHETS

1) Depicted here are builders resting who were helping to construct Solomon's Temple. Paul and Peter both compared the Church to a Temple that God is building today. This Temple is to be filled with believers who each are members of a Church-wide holy priesthood (*see* pages 7, 10-12).

2) This illustration depicts the apostle Paul speaking to an early body of believers who are meeting together. In Paul's epistles, he imparted an apostolic vision of the Church as the "Body of Christ" (*see* pages 12-13).

3) This illustration shows a fisherman throwing his nets into the Sea of Galilee. As noted on pages 78-79, the word "perfecting" in Ephesians 4:12 is the same word used in the fishing industry to depict fishermen meticulously going over every inch of their nets to adjust them as needed after a long day of fishing.

1

2

3

APOSTLES & PROPHETS

1) The *Temple in Jerusalem* is depicted in this illustration. As noted on pages 99-100, Ephesians 2:19-22 states that the Church today is being progressively constructed to become a new *naos* "Temple" for the Holy Spirit in the earth.

2) In antiquity, pagans believed the gods needed a "house" to live in among humans. Such pagan temples were consecrated places where they believed gods could dwell and be worshiped and experienced — and where prayers and sacrifices could be made to them (*see* pages 107-116).

3) The *Temple of Artemis* in Ephesus was a massive temple complex so magnificent that even in antiquity, it was listed by ancient Greek writers as one of the "Seven Wonders of the Ancient World." (*See* pages 109-110.)

1

2

3

1) The *Great Altar of Zeus* in ancient Pergamum was a temple where pagan celebrations and sacrificial rituals occurred. Because of its immense size and its artistic value, this magnificent *naos* — a *temple*, a *house for a god*, or a *shrine* — became one of the most renowned pagan altars in the history of mankind (*see* pages 110-111).

2) The *Parthenon in Athens* in ancient Athens sat atop the Acropolis. The final version of this temple was adorned with massive outer and inner columns, embellished with lavishly decorated, multi-colored sculptures trimmed with precious metals, **hundreds of sculpted figures, and an exterior frieze with a high-relief. And** in the inner sanctuary was a 40-foot tall idol of the goddess Athena draped in a garment made of 220 pounds of pure gold (*see* page 112).

3) The *Roman Pantheon* was an ancient temple that is still in use today. This architectural wonder was filled with large and intricately carved idols that were nestled between the columns of the inner walls and also housed towering statues representing the foremost deities of the Roman pagan religion. Those who designed it intended to construct a *naos* — a *temple*, a *house for a god*, or a *shrine* — to stand forever (*see* pages 113-114).

APOSTLES & PROPHETS

1) Pagans were so obsessed with accommodating their so-called gods, especially the particular god their family venerated above all the others, that private residences often had a small *naos* — a *temple,* a *house for a god,* or a *shrine* — right inside their homes where they could privately pray and offer sacrifices (*see* pages 115-116).

2) No temple anywhere in the ancient world could compare to the Temple that Solomon constructed in Jerusalem. It was a magnificent and splendorous *naos* for the One True God of Israel. No *naos* was ever constructed anywhere that could compare with the Temple in the heart of Jerusalem (*see* pages 116-117).

3) The Temple in Jerusalem, built for the One True God, was the grandest ever built for any god. Both the Jewish and pagan worlds were stunned by the astronomical sum of money and priceless materials that were used in the construction and adornment of it (*see* pages 118-122).

3

1) Titus laid siege to the city of Jerusalem in 70 AD, plundered the Temple, and carried many of its treasures back to Rome. At the Arch of Titus in the Roman Forum, there is a carved relief on the interior of the arch that pictures the golden menorah from the Temple being carried into Rome (*see* page 122).

2) This illustration pictures the second Temple built by Herod the Great. Jesus prophesied it would cease to exist and declared that God would move into a new *naos* Temple, which would be His Body. Now the Spirit lives *singularly* in the heart of every individual believer and *corporately* in the entire Church at large (*see* pages 126-127).

3) The Holy Spirit literally moved into the hearts of believers, and they became a *naos* Temple of the Holy Spirit. In Paul's writings, he reinforces that each *singular believer* and the *corporate Church* has become the Temple in which the Holy Spirit dwells in the earth today (*see* pages 129-137).

APOSTLES & PROPHETS

1) Other temple complexes were physically larger in terms of size, such as Karnak on the banks of the Nile in Egypt (illustrated here). But no temple complex in human history came close to the sum invested to construct and adorn the Temple and its sacred complex in Jerusalem (*see* page 117).

2) This illustration shows a father and son using pieces of pottery called *ostrakinos*. Paul used this word *ostrakinos* to describe our human bodies as containers of God's Spirit. Although our bodies remain *fragile*, *inferior*, *low-grade*, *mediocre*, *shoddy*, and *flawed*, God has chosen to place His Spirit inside us (*see* pages 135-137).

3) This illustration shows skilled builders constructing a temple in the ancient world. As noted on pages 142-144, now God is constructing a new Temple — the Church — and in this new Temple every singular believer has individually become "a lively stone" that God is using collectively to construct this new Temple.

1

2

3

1) This illustration depicts an ancient stonemason chiseling a stone to become an element in a temple. For God's conglomerate Temple to emerge in these days requires a workforce composed of the fivefold ministry gifts of *apostle, prophet, evangelist, pastor,* and *teacher* who are anointed to help construct His people into a new *naos* Temple of God in the earth today (*see* pages 144-146).

2) The Temple in Jerusalem was filled **with *priests* who offered up sacrifices and served worshipers who were there to worship the One True God. Today believers are priests in a Church-wide spiritual priesthood, who are called to serve in God's new *naos* Temple called the Church (*see* pages 147-154).**

3) At the brazen altar before the Temple, the smoke of the burnt offerings billowed into the air, and the atmosphere was filled with sounds and smells of oxen, sheep, goats, turtledoves, and pigeons being brought to be sacrificed. The Temple complex was filled with the nonstop activity of priests who assisted worshipers as they brought sacrifices to God (*see* pages 162-163).

APOSTLES & PROPHETS

1) God commanded His people to make a pilgrimage to Jerusalem at least three times a year — once for Passover, once for Shavout (the Feast of Weeks), and once for Sukkot (the Feast of Tabernacles). This illustration depicts Jews coming to Jerusalem on one of the required pilgrimages (*see* page 163).

2) Just as the Temple in Jerusalem was filled with nonstop priestly activity, the Church today is to be filled with nonstop activity of believer-priests offering their own spiritual sacrifices and assisting others as they bring spiritual sacrifices to God (*see* page 165).

3) As Jewish priests offered up worshipful sacrifices to God in the Temple, believer-priests today are entrusted with priestly functions in the new *naos* Temple. The Church is a sacred place that should overflow with believer-priests who are occupied in offering up spiritual sacrifices to God (*see* pages 165-184).

1

2

3

1) This illustration depicts Paul teaching the Word of God to believers in the Early Church. Ephesians 4:11-13 states that the Church cannot reach full maturity unless *all* the Christ-given gifts are imparting their unique "portions" of Christ to the Church, and that all these fivefold ministry gifts, including the apostle, will be active "till we all come in the unity of the faith" at the end of the Church Age (*see* page 196).

2) Jesus is portrayed here at the Last Supper with the 12 original apostles. The word "apostle" was a powerful title in the First Century, and if we understand what the word "apostle" meant to believers in the past, it will help us know how this word should be applied in this end-time age of the Church (*see* page 205).

3) The ancient Greek word *apostolos* — the New Testament word for an "apostle" — was used in a military and maritime sense to picture a highly-powered *admiral* and his specialized crew who were sent off by ship with all the cargo and belongings needed to sustain them and to establish a civilization where it hitherto had been nonexistent (*see* pages 207-211).

APOSTLES & PROPHETS

1) To colonize new territories, admirals needed fleets, associates, assistants, secretaries, ship hands, and all the resources needed to carry out his assignment to colonize a new territory. When these admirals disembarked from their fleet of ships to walk down the plank into a new region, they walked onto the new site with other team members as a part of their apostolic crew (*see* pages 209-211).

2) After the process of colonization was well underway, the admiral reboarded the ships to set sail again to find other uncivilized areas and to repeat the entire colonization process all over again while other members of the team remained in the new colony to give oversight to the development (*see* page 210).

3) Portrayed here is Phebe (*see* Romans 16:1-2), who may have processed *travel documents* called *apostolos*. The word *apostolos* was synonymous with the concept of *a travel document* or *a passport* (*see* pages 213-216).

1

2

3

1) Illustrated here is an ancient ship port that would have been similar to one to which the early apostles arrived when they traveled by ship. It is remarkable to see how far the apostles took the life-changing message of the Gospel. These men were mightily anointed to penetrate hard-to-reach regions and went to places almost impossible to reach (*see* page 222).

2) As time passed, the word *apostolos* signified a person especially gifted by the gods with *special insight* and *revelation* and who was sent as a *special messenger*. Just as apostles are dispatched to break into new geographical areas, the word *apostolos* depicts the apostolic anointing to access new spiritual territories and revelations in order to lead others into spiritual truths (*see* pages 229-248).

3) The word *apostolos* was also used very early to picture *an envoy who was sent to do business on behalf of the one who sent him*. It pictured a *personal representative*, *emissary*, *messenger*, *agent*, *diplomat*, or *ambassador*. These individuals held the highest diplomatic rank that could be given (*see* page 238).

APOSTLES & PROPHETS

1) This illustration shows Jesus speaking to Jewish leaders at the Temple in Jerusalem. Hebrew 3:1 says Jesus was the very first apostle. A careful study of Jesus' ministry reveals that He fulfilled all the meanings of the Greek word *apostolos*. And as the Chief Apostle, Jesus set the standard for all apostles (*see* page 249).

2) Illustrated here is Jesus and the original 12 apostles walking in the Kidron Valley. In addition to those original 12 apostles, there were numerous other people in the New Testament who are referred to by the Greek word *apostolos* (*see* pages 250-251).

3) Depicted here is Curetes Street in Ephesus. The church at Ephesus felt the need to develop a *scriptural criteria* to determine who *was* and *wasn't* a real apostle. The special efforts by the church at Ephesus to discern who *was* real and who *wasn't* real were so impressive that Jesus commended them for it (*see* page 258).

1

2

3

1) With the help of his team members, Paul entered Ephesus through the Harbor Gate (portrayed here) when he first arrived. He established the Church there, and it became a headquarters for Paul's *explosive* ministry in Asia. Believers in Asia looked to the church of Ephesus as an example (*see* page 260).

2) Because the church at Ephesus had such influence, false apostles were descending on the city to try to make a name for themselves, but the church leadership there had *no tolerance* for these people who tried to infiltrate the church with hidden and selfish motives (*see* page 264).

3) This illustration gives a wide view of the ancient city of Ephesus, where the issue of apostleship was so extremely important that church leadership "tried" those who claimed to be apostles. They believed apostolic ministry was crucial and that its role in the church needed to be protected (*see* pages 266-270).

APOSTLES & PROPHETS

1) Depicted here is the ancient city of Corinth where Paul and his team established the Corinthian church. Paul wrote to Corinthian believers about the "signs" of an authentic apostle. In Paul's writings, he provided at least six biblical proofs of apostleship (*see* pages 271-310).

2) Paul established the church at Corinth (illustrated here). In his second letter to them, he wrote that there were certain signs (like a *signature* or *seal*) that *authenticate* and *guarantee* that a person is a real apostle if these "signs" are evident in a person's ministry (*see* page 275).

3) In the center of this illustration is the judgment seat where Paul was put on trial in Corinth. Paul encountered events that would have shattered a normal man, but he pressed onward — divinely empowered by the Spirit to go where no man had ever gone and to do what no man had ever done (*see* page 278).

1

2

3

1) In the ancient city of Philippi (depicted here). Paul and Silas were imprisoned after casting a spirit of divination out of a fortune-teller (*see* Acts 16:16-24). Paul was imprisoned frequently, but was sustained by a *supernatural endurance* that empowered him to keep going regardless of assaults (*see* page 187).

2) Depicted here is the heart of ancient Corinth. Some of Paul's worst confrontations with evil occurred in the heart of the world's most advanced and cultured cities. Paul faced these challenges courageously with the *supernatural endurance* the Holy Spirit imparted to him (*see* page 220).

3) This illustration pictures a gathering of believers in Corinth in a typical setting in which Paul would have ministered during his tenure there. In First Corinthians 2:4-5, he reminded them that he came to them with a supernatural demonstration of the Spirit and of power. (*See* page 303.)

APOSTLES & PROPHETS

1) This illustration depicts the Peirene Fountain in Corinth. Paul told the Corinthians, "Truly the signs of an apostle were wrought among you in all patience, in signs, *and wonders*...." Hence, another proof that a person is an apostle is "wonders" (*see* page 299).

2) The city of Capernaum (depicted here) was filled with "mighty deeds" during the time of Jesus' residency there. However, Paul says "mighty deeds" and miraculous manifestations are also an attestation of anyone who has a true apostolic ministry (*see* pages 304-306).

3) Thessalonica is depicted in this illustration. Paul's apostolic relationship with churches is why we have the books of First and Second Corinthians, Galatians, Ephesians, Philippians, Colossians, and First and Second Thessalonians (*see* page 311).

1) We see builders in this illustration being directed by architects as workers constructed an ancient temple. In First Corinthians 3:10, Paul uses the words "wise masterbuilder" — from the Greek word *architekton* — to picture apostolic ministry (*see* pages 347-350).

2) In this illustration, Abraham is illustrated greeting three divine messengers (*see* Genesis 18:2). Abraham is revered as the prophet to whom God chose to reveal Himself and with whom God initiated a covenant (*see* Genesis 26:3-4). **Ancient sources refer to Abraham as a prophet, as the friend of God, and as the father of the walk of faith (*see* pages 542-545).**

3) After Moses encountered God on Mount Sinai (depicted here), God dispatched him as a prophet to speak to Pharoah and to bring deliverance to the children of Israel. **Moses is traditionally regarded as the author of the first five books of the Bible, and according to Jewish tradition, he was *the greatest prophet* who ever lived (*see* pages 549-551).**

APOSTLES & PROPHETS

1) The prophet Samuel is portrayed in this illustration anointing David to be king of Israel. Samuel was a prophet and seer from a young age (*see* 1 Samuel 3:4-19) and became a national prophet after the death of Eli (*see* 1 Samuel 7:15). It is impossible to overstate the importance of Samuel's prophetic role, and **ancient sources refer to Samuel as one of the most significant *prophets* to ever live (*see* pages 558-559).**

2) Scripture identifies Deborah as a significant prophetess, one of the 12 judges of Israel, and one of the seven women whom ancient rabbis referred to as *prophetesses* (**the others were** Sarah**, Miriam, Hannah, Abigail, Huldah, and** Esther). Her role was great in the Old Testament, and ancient sources refer to Deborah as a prophetess of God **(*see* pages 555-556).** In this illustration, the prophetess Deborah is discussing military strategy.

1) This illustration depicts John the Baptist baptizing Jesus at the Jordan River. **John the Baptist's ministry predated the actual period belonging to the New Testament, which commenced only after the resurrection; hence, John the Baptist is considered to be an intertestamental prophet (*see* pages 616-620).**

2) Jesus' death, burial, resurrection, and ascension started the period of the New Testament. Until that moment, He functioned as an intertestamental prophet and spoke on behalf of God. In this illustration, Jesus is portrayed overthrowing the money-changers' tables in the Temple in Jerusalem (*see* pages 621-625).

3) Prophets stirred the hearts of God's people about the need to resume building the Temple in Jerusalem. In Ezra 5:1, we read, "Then rose up Zerubbabel the son of Shealtiel, and Jeshua the son of Jozadak, and began to build the house of God which *is* at Jerusalem: *and with them were the prophets of God helping them*" **(*see* pages 595, 596, 631).**

APOSTLES & PROPHETS

1) In this illustration, the prophets and teachers in Antioch are depicted. Acts 13:1 says, "Now there were in the church that was at Antioch certain prophets and teachers; as Barnabas, and Simeon that was called Niger, and Lucius of Cyrene, and Manaen, which had been brought up with Herod the tetrarch, and Saul" (*see* pages 638-644).

2) The prophet Agabus, Philip the evangelist, and the apostle Paul, are illustrated here. When the prophet Agabus arrived at the house of Philip, he prophesied about what awaited Paul in Jerusalem. As a result of Agabus' gift, God's Spirit provided information for the apostle Paul (*see* pages 647-652).

The original Greek text says *naos hagion*, and this "Holy Temple" indeed pictures *a holy shrine*, *a holy dwelling place*, or *a holy temple* where God Himself lives. The first part of the phrase is from *hagios*, which portrays something that is holy and set apart, while the word *naos* was used by both Jews and Greeks to describe *a temple where a god dwelled*. By using this Greek word *naos,* Paul gives the apostolic vision that God is building a Body of believers into *a holy and set-apart Temple* for the habitation of the Holy Spirit in the earth. Because the entire phrase is "Holy Temple," it lets us know this is a temple unlike any other temple ever constructed — it is in its own consecrated, separated, set-apart, *unique* category.

In Ephesians 2:22, Paul added, "In whom ye also are *builded together* for an habitation of God through the Spirit."

The words "builded together" are from the Greek word *sunoikodomeo* — a compound of the words *sun* and *oikodomeo.* The word *sun* means *together with*, and *oikodomeo* is the word we saw in verse 21 to describe architectural plans and the building process used to bring an architectural concept to reality. However, because Paul uses *oikodomeo* in conjunction with *sun* in this context, it pictures an architectural plan designed by God Himself and executed by apostolic builders, who marvelously join a host of building materials together — that is, God's people, or living stones — so they can jointly be connected and form a collective "habitation" for God's Spirit.

The word "habitation" is the Greek word *katoiketerion*, which is derived from *katoikeo* — a compound of *kata* and *oikeo.* The word *kata* means *down*, and *oikeo* is from *oikos*, which is the Greek word for *a house*. But as *oikeo*, it means *to dwell or to reside in a house*. When the words *kata* and *oikeo* are joined, it pictures one who is so satisfied with his new residence that he settles down there and never, ever intends to leave it. This is an indweller who has settled down, taken up permanent residency in a home, and who is so comfortable there that he plans to stay there perpetually. Ephesians 2:21, 22 pictures God being so thrilled with a glorious Church that *He has settled down into it as a permanent resident and has made Himself a home there.*

Here we discover that while authentic apostolic vision is indeed about planting new churches, it is about much more. Although starting new churches is the major thrust of an apostle's work, his heartbeat is to lay a spiritual foundation that is strong enough to support the ever-growing *naos* Temple that God desires the Church to become in the earth. A true apostle's goal is to see a holy Temple emerge so marvelous that God's Spirit will reside in it and make it His place of habitation forever. *This* speaks of the divine order an apostle brings to a local congregation to help build that "habitation of God." God will indwell in power that which *He* designs, authenticates, and plans. And He has planned from the beginning to indwell not only the individual believer in the new birth, but also the corporate Temple — His enormous Church, the Body of Christ — one local-church congregation at a time.

'...Another Buildeth Thereon...'

In First Corinthians 3:10, after Paul talked about the apostle's ministry as a foundation-layer — and his own ministry, in particular — he talked about *building upon* that apostolic foundation. Paul knew where his grace started and also when it ended and it would become time for another person to move on-site to continue his work. As an apostle, once Paul and his team laid the foundation, and other ministries were raised up to lead the work, he and his team embarked on doing all over again somewhere else what they had just established in that particular place. Of course, he maintained an apostolic relationship with each church, but Paul knew that whoever he raised up would continue to build on top of his foundation, and that is why he added in First Corinthians 3:10 that "another buildeth thereon."

The word "another" is the Greek word *allos*, which simply means *someone else.* The word "buildeth thereon" is a form of the word *epoikodomeo,* a compound of the words *epi* and *oikodomeo*, as we have seen. The word *epi* means *upon*, as *on top of something already existing*, and *oikodomeo* is an architectural term that pictures the enlarging or increasing of an existing facility. Here Paul logically describes the normal process of others who arrive on a building site to carry on the work of building upward once a well-laid foundation has been set in place.

Let's see again how ancient writers used the word *epoikodomeo*. By looking at how it was used by the ancient world's most illustrious writers, we learn much about this word. Paul certainly knew of its use by these writers, and he especially selected this word due to its many meanings in connection with apostolic ministry. For example:

- Plato used the word *epoikodomeo* to depict *building on top of something that is already existing.*[16]
- Xenophon and Demosthenes also used *epoikodomeo* to picture *building on top of something that is already existing*, but they additionally used it to picture *rebuilding*, *reconstructing*, or *restoring* something that had fallen into ruin or into a state of waste.[17]
- Aristotle used *epoikodomeo* to illustrate *strengthening* something already in existence.[18]
- Polybius used *epoikodomeo* to picture something being built, like a *fortress*, that was constructed to provide defense, protection, and safety.[19]

All of these meanings are so important to the work that continues after an apostle has laid a foundation for a local church congregation. Those who follow in his steps must see their God-given roles to build on top of what the apostle has laid and to strengthen it. At times, apostles have laid grand foundations in place and set leadership in position to follow their work, but the newly appointed leadership, for various reasons, failed to build correctly on the foundation that was laid. As a result, although the foundation was set in place, what was built on top of it became ruinous, which meant an apostle must then come on-site to begin the process of apostolically rebuilding, reconstructing, or restoring what should have never fallen into a state of ruin.

In the end, the goal of every subsequent leader should be to build on an apostle's solid foundation a spiritual structure that provides defense, protection, and safety for the saints so they can do their work as priests in the *naos* Temple of God that is called the Church.

The goal of every leader should be to build on an apostle's solid foundation a spiritual structure that provides defense, protection, and safety for the saints so they can do their work as priests in the *naos* Temple of God that is called the Church.

'...Every Man...'

Paul continued in First Corinthians 3:10 to give a warning to everyone who builds "subsequently" in the House of God — to those who build upward and onward upon an apostolic foundation. He said, "...But let every man take heed how he buildeth thereupon."

The words "every man" are a translation of the Greek word *hekastos,* an all-encompassing term meaning *everyone, with no one excluded.* It is a general and robust apostolic warning that is issued to everyone, but specifically to any person who would ever assume a leadership role in the Church in subsequent years or generations.

Everything with a good foundation is eventually built upon, expanded, or upgraded, so Paul logically knew that someone else — perhaps the next generation of leaders — would build on top of his work. He accepted that, as we all must, but he issued a warning to anyone who would build on top of his foundation. He told them they must "take heed how" they build on top of what God had graced him to establish apostolically in order to spiritually undergird each local body of believers God had called him to reach so that they could flourish and grow.

'...Take Heed How...'

The words "take heed" are a form of the Greek word *blepo*, a word Paul used here in First Corinthians 3:10 that is intended to jar or jolt a listener. Speaking to those who would build on his apostolic foundation, Paul warned them to really pay attention and listen to what he was about to tell them: "...Let every man take heed *how* he buildeth thereupon."

The word "how" in Greek means *how* or *in what way* — and in this verse, it was Paul's way of pleading with the next generation of leaders that would follow in his steps. He was urging them to pay attention to *how* they proceeded and to do all they could to ensure they used good and not inferior spiritual materials as they built the *naos* Temple of God upward from its apostolic foundation.

This was Paul's apostolic heart's cry for those who would follow in his steps after he was gone from the scene. He pled with them to carry the work forward with quality and carefulness and to build the House of God with moral, ethical, and doctrinal purity.

As the apostolic visionary, designer, leader, and overseer who started the church at Corinth, Paul felt apostolic responsibility for it. Therefore, he challenged the next spiritual leaders to be careful *how* they carried on the work — *how* they built upon it — and he urged them to build with spiritual materials that would enable the church congregation to have longevity. By using the word "how," Paul also admonished those following him not to get in too big a hurry, not to build sloppily, and not to resort to using carnal tactics or inferior spiritual materials as they continued the work of augmenting the church by building up the people that made up that local congregation.

After taking a closer look at these words and phrases, First Corinthians 3:10 could be interpreted, "My life has become dominated by a specific grace of God, a divine touch that has totally transformed me and given me supernatural abilities I did not originally have. This divine impartation has given me insight and wisdom that cannot be naturally attained, and it has enabled me to become like a fabulous architect who envisions, designs, and leads a project. Now someone else is currently building on top of the foundation I laid. But let me be emphatically clear that whoever is taking it to the next level must pay careful attention to how he builds on top of my foundation."

A Natural Illustration of Sloppy Building

It is sad to say, but many people have been turned off by the Gospel, not because of the message itself, but because of the sloppy and less-than-excellent behavior they have observed in a local church. Because they see things being done unprofessionally or in a less-than-wise manner, they cease to take the church seriously because they don't see anything that looks serious to them. Let me give you an example of something physically constructed that illustrates what I mean by unprofessional, non-serious, sloppy building.

As Denise and I drive back and forth from our home to Moscow every day, I am always perplexed by a particular house along the main road that seems to have been built with *no plan* whatsoever. It is no exaggeration to say it is the most outlandish, weirdest looking house I've ever seen anywhere. Because it sits on the main road, everyone who drives past it wags their head in disbelief that someone would build something so monstrous in such a conspicuous location. If the owner decided to put that house on the market to sell it, I am certain there would be no buyers because it is so *bizarre.*

I once commented to a fellow traveler, "With all the money that man spent building that wacky-looking house, can you imagine what a gorgeous home he could have built with the same money *if* he'd had a plan to follow when he started."

The problem wasn't a lack of money, because that house is huge and cost a fortune to build. Instead of building with a plan, it is a "hodgepodge" house that is a *complete embarrassment.* It is obvious the owner randomly put up a wall here, then added a weird angled roof over there, then put in a strange-looking staircase that leads to nowhere, and then added multiple crooked-looking towers all around the roof. It is so strange that everyone who sees it *knows* it was built with *no plan.*

Let me give you another very vivid example of a catastrophic construction project that took place in a city where the city leaders decided to build a spectacular building to impress — foreign guests who came to visit them. The site for the building was chosen in the most prime and visible location in the city, and the architect finalized his plans for what he declared would be an outstanding architectural achievement. The city was soon filled with people's continual chatter about the many benefits this new building project would attract to the city.

Eager to have the project finished, the city leaders announced an opening date for the hotel that was unrealistic, considering the amount of work that had to be done. It soon became apparent that the project was taking longer than expected. Impatient and fearful they wouldn't meet their own hurried-up deadline, the city leaders urged the architect to go faster, even though rushing the construction could jeopardize the integrity of the structure. Bulldozers began to move dirt, and concrete trucks began to pour concrete in great volumes. It wasn't long until a towering building was erected on the site — so tall that it could be seen from a great distance.

You can imagine the horror it was to city leaders and to the entire city when they realized the building began to lean dangerously to the side. The foundation had been poured so quickly and with such inferior materials that it wasn't able to hold up the weight of the structure. Eventually the building leaned so much that the entire project had to be abandoned. It is an uninhabitable building to this day because it was built so incorrectly.

What had been intended as a great architectural achievement became the city's greatest public embarrassment. That enormous building still stands leaning *and abandoned* in the very spot where it had been hastily built by leaders who refused to take the necessary time to ensure it was built properly. Instead of becoming the pride of the city as they had hoped, today it is a permanent reminder of how buildings should *not* be built.

Similarly, apostles — masterbuilders, or *architects* — are anointed to arrive on-site with an apostolic team to preach the Gospel, drive back darkness, spiritually level the ground, bulldoze demonic forces out of the way, and lay a rock-solid foundation for the church in every new location where they are dispatched by the Holy Spirit. Likewise, those who follow them must be serious in how they *continue* the work. Getting in a hurry and building with inferior spiritual materials leads to catastrophic spiritual results.

I shudder to think of the people who got in too big of a hurry and did not continue a well-started work correctly. A big noise was perhaps made to announce that something fantastic was happening until it became the talk of the town. But, soon, what started with a bang ended with a fizzle. "Time and fire" (*see* 1 Corinthians 3:13) revealed there were serious flaws made in the process, and all the big talk followed by faulty workmanship produced an embarrassment.

This is why Paul urges *everyone* — from the Greek word *hekastos*, meaning *everyone, with no one excluded* — to be careful *how* they build upward upon an existing work. Many fabulous foundations today have shanties built on top of them, when the foundation was sufficiently constructed to hold up something fabulous. *Don't let this be your story!*

Anyone called to establish a new church, in any new location, or to subsequently become the leader after the previous leadership has moved on, must ask:

- Am I building a *naos* Temple of God's people so wonderful that God will want to occupy it and bless it with His mighty manifested presence?
- Am I building in a way that will bring glory to God?
- Am I moving so hastily and building with such inferior materials that this work could produce an embarrassment for the Kingdom of God?

We are called to construct a *naos* Temple so magnificent that it becomes a glorious habitation for the Spirit of God. But I must pose the question: Is it possible that some churches have been built so hurriedly and sloppily, and are so ill-built, that it is an "embarrassment" for God to occupy them with His presence and stamp of approval? In Christ, we are all approved, but in some cases, churches or organizations build shabbily in His name, in a way that makes it difficult for Him to bless those works as He desires to do. To Christ, this question of "how" we build is of paramount importance.

Paul added in First Corinthians 3:11, "For other foundation can no man lay than that is laid, which is Jesus Christ." This was Paul's confident declaration that he was sure the foundation he laid in the church was so strong it would never need to be replaced with a better foundation. He was assured that his work was done correctly.

Anyone with an apostolic call must accept that his anointing is to lay a strong, long-lasting foundation and do the best he possibly can to raise up subsequent leadership who will continue to build wisely on top of it. But, ultimately, every man will be judged or rewarded individually for the phase of the work he carried out. Paul was confident in the Lord that his foundation-laying work was impeccable and would never need to be uprooted or replaced with a better foundation. But he nonetheless warned those who followed in his footsteps, and placed before them the following question.

Gold, Silver, Precious Stones, Wood, Hay, or Stubble — *Are You Building To Pass the Test of Time?*

In First Corinthians 3:12, Paul made a very important statement that cannot really be understood without understanding its historical context. He said, "Now if any man build upon this foundation gold, silver, precious stones, wood, hay, stubble." In this verse, Paul was talking about the long-term effects of building *carefully* and with *good materials* as opposed to *inferior materials.* And to make the point, he uses the illustration of gold, silver, precious stones, wood, hay, or stubble.

Now let me give you some context concerning building materials used in the ancient world. For example, in the modern city of Rome, many ancient buildings still stand and are usable to this day because they were correctly constructed of *stone.* Because ancient Romans wanted their greatness to be etched forever into human history, they intentionally constructed their buildings to last for millennia. Government buildings, palaces, streets, monuments, columns, and statues — all of these were intended to tell future generations about how great the Romans were. Although the *gold*, *silver*, and *precious stones* that once adorned these buildings have since been stripped away, scores of these structures remain intact because they were constructed with durable, time-tested materials.

But not all of Rome was made of stone, gold, silver, and precious stones. There was another part of Rome that, sadly, was comprised of flimsy, poorly made wooden shanties, which were the dwellings for poorer people. Wealthy Romans didn't like to do manual labor, so they imported foreigners from across the empire to build their buildings for them. As a result, wealthy Romans retreated from manual labor and grew fat, while this massive importation of foreign slaves grew larger and larger until it became the largest single sector of Rome. The city was so inundated by foreign immigrants and slaves that some scholars estimate the slave population outnumbered the free population by three to one.[20]

As significant as the slave sector was within the city of Rome, the ancient shanties where the slaves lived have not survived the past 2,000 years. Over centuries, due to weather, decay, and fires that ravaged Rome, those flimsy wooden structures where poorer people lived have long ago vanished. Whereas the wealthy lived in homes made of durable, time-tested materials like stone, the shanties were constructed cheaply with wood, hay, and stubble as their primary building materials. That is why nearly nothing remains of those shabby dwellings. The poorer sectors of the city were never intended to last like the magnificent stone structures that have remained for more than 2,000 years.

As Paul traveled throughout the vast lands of the Roman Empire, he witnessed the disparity between the rich and the poor. He could see the massive stone structures and also the flimsy homes where slaves lived. It was easy to see that one structure was built to last *forever*, while the other was so rickety, it probably wouldn't even last a *lifetime*. This is exactly what Paul saw in his mind when he wrote First Corinthians 3:12, "Now if any man build upon this foundation gold, silver, precious stones, wood, hay, stubble."

Paul was rhetorically asking the next generation of leaders that would follow him, *Are you using spiritual materials that will stand the test of time — or are you building a work so rickety it won't last very long? Are you building hastily and cheaply only for today — or are you building with durable materials that will pass the test of time?*

Let's look again at the kind of building materials the apostle Paul listed in First Corinthians 3:12. In that verse, he wrote, "Now if any man build upon this foundation *gold, silver, precious stones....*"

Notice that Paul first mentioned "gold," translated from the Greek word *chrusos*, which means *gold* and describes the most valuable material in the Roman Empire. Gold was extremely *rare* — and it was therefore *highly prized*. If a building was extremely important, gold was used ornamentally on the reliefs and on the decor of its exteriors and interiors. When gold was used on the interior or exterior decor of a building, it was indicative of the significance of that structure, even as it is today.

The word "silver" is from the Greek word *arguros,* which depicts actual *silver*. Architecturally, silver was used inside buildings for ornamentation and decoration, similar to the way gold was used. Anything in the ancient world made of silver was considered *expensive* and *precious*. Both gold and silver would only be found in the ornamentations of extremely important buildings that were intended to last a long time.

Paul then added the word "precious stones," which come from the word *lithos*, the Greek word for *stone*, and the word *timios,* a word meaning *honorable, costly*, or *precious*. When Paul mentioned "precious stones," he was not alluding to diamonds, rubies, emeralds, sapphires, or other gemstones.

Rather, he was referring to expensive building materials, such as *marble* or *granite*, that were considered top-of-the-line building materials because they could endure *weather*, *fire*, and *time*. Any building fashioned of marble or granite was intended to stand a long time.

The words gold, silver, and precious stones (marble and granite) signify the most expensive and highest quality materials used in the construction of a building in Paul's day. *These were durable, long-lasting, resilient materials.* This is the reason why many buildings that were constructed of those materials 2,000 years ago still stand strong today.

Paul then added, "Now if any man build upon this foundation gold, silver, precious stones, *wood, hay, or stubble*" (1 Corinthians 3:12). Paul moved on to describe another category of building materials that he called *wood, hay,* and *stubble.*

Let's look at these words to see why Paul mentioned them in this verse. You are about to discover that Paul was making a very dramatic comparison in the way one should and should *not* build the House of God — the Church — and he was, of course, referring to the building of *people.*

The word "wood" is from the Greek word *zulos*, which depicts *wood, wooden timbers, branches of a tree, boards*, or *anything made of wood.* This word was also used to depict *fuel for a fire.* It describes building materials that are *cheap, temporary, perishable*, or *burnable.* Although one may quickly build such a building of these materials, a house made of wood was not built to last for ages. This type of cheap material was used for the construction of the shanty slave dwellings in Rome that didn't last very long. And if these wooden houses were touched by fire, they quickly went up in a puff of smoke.

Next, Paul mentioned "hay," which was another building material used in the construction of poorer slave dwellings. The word "hay" is from the Greek word *chortos*, and it depicts *grass* or *hay* — materials that should never have been used as construction material. This material was meant to be food for animals and was often used as *fodder*. Because of its fragile, transitory nature, it was considered to be *the poorest material* to use in construction. However, in the ancient slave homes in Rome, this type of *hay* was commonly used for the *roofs* of the shanties in poorer districts.

Paul then mentioned "stubble." This is a translation of the Greek word *kalame*, and it means *straw* or *stubble*. This material was so inferior that even animals wouldn't eat it. Yet in the homes of slaves, it was used as a *floor covering*, as *insulation*, and as *stuffing for beds*. It was cheap, disposable, and replaceable. In essence, these slave dwellings were made of wood and sticks; the roofs were made of grass; and the walls were insulated with straw. *No wonder these dwellings didn't last and went up in a puff of smoke if accidently touched by fire.*

So we see in First Corinthians 3:12 that one type of building was built to last *forever*, whereas the other was so rickety that it wouldn't even last a *lifetime*. By using this stark comparison, Paul confronted every generation of spiritual leaders with the questions: *Are you building hastily and with perishable materials? Or are you building carefully and with materials that will last not only in this present generation, but also in generations to come?* A minister of the Gospel must seek the Lord for His divine wisdom and directives, with which that minister will then build. What a minister receives from God in the process is costly and precious — it is invaluable to the building assignment to which he or she has been called.

The Raging Effects of Fire

Living in the First Century and ministering in multiple large cities all over the Roman Empire, Paul had no doubt seen the tragic effects of what fire could do to buildings that were constructed of cheap, perishable materials.

Those slave dwellings were made of wood and sticks, covered with a roof of grass, and insulated with straw. *Imagine how quickly those flimsy structures went up in smoke when a fire touched them!* When fire struck one of those little houses, it ignited like a box of matches and started a chain reaction. Pieces of burning wood, grass, and straw whirled upward into the air as hot embers fell on the surrounding slave dwellings. One after another, every little house made of wood, hay, and stubble burst into flames and began to burn like an inferno. Wood, hay, and stubble fueled the fire!

When these fires ran their course and died out, everything that *could* be burned *was* burned. Everything made of wood, hay, and stubble was *gone*! This is one reason important buildings were made of stone. The builders knew that if a fire ever raged through the city, a stone building might get scorched, but it would survive. Although it might be stained with smoke, the building would endure the worst of a fire and be fixable!

Knowing that hardships, tests, and trials eventually come to every work, Paul used the natural example of raging fires as a backdrop when he wrote First Corinthians 3:13. It says, "Every man's work shall be made manifest: for the day shall declare it, because it shall be revealed by fire; and the fire shall try every man's work of what sort it is."

Notice Paul said, "Every man's work shall be made manifest...." By using the words "every man," the apostle informed us that eventually a time comes when *every work* is tested. The words "every man" are translated from the Greek word *hekastos* that, again, means *everyone, with no one excluded*. Hence, Paul was telling us that no one is completely exempt from fiery situations that arise to test a person and his works. Those fires reveal the true quality of what that person has done or built. When these fires come, it is the moment when each person discovers if his works were made of *gold*, *silver*, and *precious stones* — or if he has been building with *wood*, *hay*, and *stubble*.

Works Tested by Fire

The word "work" in First Corinthians 3:13 informs us of *what* will be tested. The Greek word "work" in Greek is *ergon*, which refers to *the work* or *the output* of one's life. It signifies *some kind of action, deed, or activity*. Very often it referred to *a person's occupation, a person's labor*, or *the things produced by a person's effort or life*. Paul warned that eventually a time comes when our *works* are tested. At that time, the true quality of our work — what we have built and what kinds of materials we have used — and the real motive, intention, and reason behind our work will become evident.

Paul went on to say, "Every man's work shall be made *manifest....*" The word "manifest" is the Greek word *phaneros*, and it describes something that is *visible, observable, obvious, clear, open, apparent*, or *evident*. It means a day eventually comes when what we have built — and the motives behind it — are exposed and visible for all to see. That is why Paul went on to say, "Every man's work shall be made manifest: for the day shall declare it, because it shall be *revealed...*" (1 Corinthians 3:13).

The word "revealed" is a form of the Greek word *apokalupto*. It is a compound of two Greek words, *apo* and *kalupto*. The word *apo* means *away*, and the word *kalupto* means *to cover or hide* and pictures *a curtain* or *a veil*. But when these two words are compounded, the new word describes *something that has been veiled or hidden for a long time, but is now clear and visible because the veil has suddenly been removed.* It's like pulling the curtains out of the way so you can see what has always been just outside your window. The scene was always there for you to see, but the curtains blocked your ability to see the real picture. But when the curtains are drawn apart, you can suddenly see what had been hidden from your view. In that moment, you can see beyond the curtain for the first time and observe what was there all along, but had not been visible to you or to anyone else.

Paul said, "Every man's work shall be made manifest: for the day shall declare it, because it shall be revealed *by fire...*" (1 Corinthians 13:13). The words "by fire" can either be translated *by fire* or *in the midst of fire.* The language makes it a thousand-percent clear that *fire* is the medium that exposes the truth about what we have built or what we are currently building.

Many wrongly assume that this verse is describing a fiery test that comes from God. But I assure you that life by itself will send many tests your way. Your ministry, your church, your relationships, your job, your finances — all of these will be *tested* along the path of life, and God's participation is not needed to make these tests happen. They are just part of the package of life. In addition, the devil will try to find a way to bring destructive fires into your life or ministry. He would love to set fire to your ministry, church, relationships, job, finances, or anything else you hold dear.

Often we see things on the surface, but we don't know the real motivations of a person's heart or the hidden reason why people do what they do. However, a day will inevitably come when our works and the works of others will suddenly come into view. On that day, the curtains will be drawn apart, and the picture will become clear both to ourselves and to others. On that day, Paul said *fire* will pull the curtains apart so the real picture becomes clear.

By using our faith and listening to the Holy Spirit, we can avoid many catastrophes and demonic attacks in life. But as long as we are in this world where the devil operates, there will nonetheless be moments when fire comes to test our *works*. When these fires come, that is the golden moment when we discover if our works are made of *gold, silver*, and *precious stones* — or if we have been building our lives with *wood, hay*, and *stubble.*

Be assured that between life and the devil, you *will* encounter fiery tests in the course of life. I'm trying to help you see *why* it is so important that you build correctly so that you and what you have built with your life or ministry can withstand every test. If you have built your work right with "gold, silver, and precious stones" — that is, with durable materials that pass the test of time and that can survive life's fires — you and your works will pass the test. But if you have built with "wood, hay, and stubble" — that is, sloppily, hastily, and with perishable materials — when the tests come along in life, they will ignite what you have built like a match set to hay.

Regardless of why the fire comes, Paul said a time will come to every man's work to test them. And he went on to say, "...And the fire shall *try* every man's work of what sort it is."

The word translated "try" is a form of the Greek word *dokimadzo* and it means *to test*, *to try*, or *to scrutinize*. It was the very word used in the First Century to describe the testing of metals or other materials to see if they could stand up under pressure. If these materials had a flaw of any kind, the pressure of this test was so intense it would cause that object to crack or to break into pieces. The purpose of the test was *not* to hurt the object, but to *expose* the flaws that, if ignored, could later do greater damage to many people.

If you have built with "wood, hay, and stubble" — that is, sloppily, hastily, and with perishable materials — when the tests come along in life, they will ignite what you have built like a match set to hay.

Putting materials through such *dokimadzo* tests was intended to point out weak, dangerous, hidden flaws before these materials were used. It was simply a fact that later when these materials were used, they would be put under tremendous stress. If hidden flaws remained undiscovered, it could prove disastrous. Moving too quickly or using materials that were inferior could result in the loss of an entire project, in the loss of money, and even in the loss of life.

I think of several times when our own ministry experienced hardships that revealed important things to us. Sometimes, the pressure that came to do damage actually proved we had built so well that the ministry could survive that fiery test. Other times such tests revealed hidden flaws in our organization that we were unaware of at the time. We never relish the experience, but I am not only thankful that the fires affirmed where we had built well, I am also thankful for fire that showed where weaknesses existed that we were unaware of but needed attention. If a situation revealed an area of weakness, we acknowledged the defects and repented for the areas where we had been incorrectly building our ministry, and we corrected those areas. Although God Himself was not the instigator of those fiery situations, they exposed the truth we *needed* to see!

That is why Paul concluded by saying, "Every man's work shall be made manifest: for the day shall declare it, because it shall be revealed by fire; and the fire shall try every man's work of *what sort* it is" (1 Corinthians 3:13).

You see, fire always reveals what "sort" of materials have been used. In the ancient world, fire consumed everything made of wood, hay, and stubble, but what was made of gold, silver, and precious stone survived. When the fire had finished raging, what had been built cheaply, hastily, and with perishable materials became evident because it was consumed in the fire. But fire also revealed what had been built with *right* materials and by *right* methods, because what was built correctly and with durable materials survived the blaze.

Paul explained that fire is the medium that reveals *what sort* of thing we've been building! An interpretive version of First Corinthians 3:13 could read as follows:

Regardless of who you are, it is just a fact that a day will eventually come when the true nature of what you have built will be exposed by fiery situations. When the fire comes, you'll be so thoroughly tested that you'll have a clearer picture afterward of what you have been building right and what you have been building wrong.

On What Basis Will We Be Rewarded?

Paul then added in First Corinthians 3:14, "If any man's work *abide* which he hath built thereupon, he shall receive a reward."

The word "abide" in this verse comes from the Greek word *meno*, which means *to stay*, *to remain*, *to continue*, or *to permanently abide* and is so profoundly important. It gives the idea of something that *lasts, remains*, *persists*, or *endures.* It speaks of something that has *lasting power.*

In this verse, Paul actually proclaimed that we are not going to be primarily rewarded for activity, but we will be rewarded for what "abides" — that is, for what we build that lasts, surviving all the tests and fires that come to our lives and ministries.

Man measures success by activity and earthly achievement, but God measures success by how well we build our works and by the longevity of our works. As impressive as our works may be at the moment, if they don't pass the test of time, they will not merit a reward. That is why the Bible declares, "If any man's work *abides* which he hath built thereupon, he shall receive a reward." Works that were built incorrectly will burn, and works that were built correctly will endure. And Paul assured us that we will be rewarded only for the works that endure, or *abide.*

Paul then promised, "If any man's work abide which he hath built thereupon, he *shall receive....*" These words "shall receive" point to a *future moment* when we will stand before Jesus. At that moment, the books will be opened, and Jesus will carefully examine our lives. He will look to see if our works survived or if they failed in the fires of life. By looking at His ledger, He will know if we built thoughtfully and in a manner that brought honor to His name — or if we built "shacks" on top of a glorious foundation.

If our works were built correctly and endured the tests of life, Paul wrote in First Corinthians 3:14 that we will receive a "reward." Because the word "reward" — the Greek word *misthos* — is also so very important, we'll return to the ancient writers to see how it was used so we can know exactly what Paul had in his mind when he used *misthos* to describe *a reward.*

- The writers Homer, Euripides, Herodotus, Aristophanes, and Xenophon each used the word *misthos* to denote a *salary* or *wages* that one has due to him for his work.[21]
- Hesiod and Herodotus also used the word *misthos* to describe *a sum of money that was owed to a worker based upon a previously agreed-upon written contract.*[22]
- It is very interesting that Euripides used *misthos* to describe *retaliation* rendered to an enemy.[23]
- The writer Plato used *misthos* in a more general way to depict *any kind of reward.*[24]

This means the word "reward" — the Greek word *misthos* that Paul used in First Corinthians 3:14 — denotes *pay, salary,* or *reward* that one has coming to him for what he has done and for how he has performed. Paul's use of *misthos* also means God has clearly stated in advance that if we work professionally for the name of Jesus, He makes a guarantee to us that He will see to it we are well-rewarded for a job well-done. And because Euripides used *mithos* to depict a form of *retaliation,* it means we can rest assured that even if the enemy has tried to attack us along the way or steal from us, if we stay on track with God's assignment to us, God will pay us well as a retaliatory act against the enemy. God always has the last word, and if we each do what God has asked us to do, He will see to it that we are paid and reimbursed for all expenses. *God will see to it that we each get exactly what we have coming to us!*

God has clearly stated in advance that if we work professionally for the name of Jesus, He makes a guarantee to us that He will see to it we are rewarded well for a job well-done.

In other words, Jesus will make sure every person who carried out his or her God-given assignment correctly will be *well-compensated* and *rewarded.* If your works were built right, when you stand before Jesus and He sees that your life and works survived every test, you will receive *full remuneration* for every sacrifice you made. This clearly means if you build your works correctly, you'll get a *bonus* that will last for all eternity!

As important as we think all our activities are, God's measuring stick by which He determines rewards is not measured by how busy or active we are in life. His measuring stick is how well we built and whether or not what we built was able to "abide" and survive the test of fire. Why would God reward us for building so sloppily that our works go up in a puff of smoke? He never promises to reward us for works that go up in smoke because of shoddy workmanship or because we built with wrong motives — including self-promotion, fame, financial gain, and hastily giving leadership positions to wrong people that jeopardizes the Lord's work.

Since we will only be rewarded for what "abides," we must ask the Holy Spirit to help us take an honest look at what we are building to see what has been built right and what has been built wrong. It's never too late to start doing it right.

If you've built your life on a solid foundation and in a way that it can pass any test, you should throw up your arms and rejoice! But if you know you have not built works to survive, it is time for you to let the Spirit of God help you build long-term with long-lasting materials. And if your works have already burned, the good news is, there is still a well-laid foundation under the ashes. Because Jesus Christ is the foundation, with God's help, you can build again and do it correctly this time!

The Devastating Results of Sloppy Building

In First Corinthians 3:15, Paul wrote, "If any man's work shall be burned, he shall suffer loss: but he himself shall be saved; yet so as by fire."

The word "burned" in Greek is *katakaio* — a compound of *kata*, meaning *down*, and *kaio*, meaning *to burn*. Compounded, the word means *to burn down*, such as a building that burns all the way to the ground. In other words, this is a fire that completely devours a building so that nothing remains *except* for the foundation. The word *katakaio* in this verse means *to burn down until nothing remains but the foundation.*

Such a consuming fire can cause great loss, and that is why Paul went on to say, "If any man's work shall be burned, he shall suffer loss...." The word "loss" is from the word *zemioo*, which means *to suffer loss*, *to experience damage*, or *to forfeit one's reward.*

Thucydides, Xenophon, and Lycius used the word *zemioo* to depict *tragic damage* or *loss, while* Herotodus and Aeschines (a Greek statesman and one of ten famous Attic orators) used the word *zemioo* to describe *punishment* given to offenders for wrong actions and behaviors. Plato and Plutarch used the word *zemioo* to describe *a penalty* or *a fine* for something done wrong.[25]

Paul now uses this *zemioo* to graphically portray the *tragic damage* and *loss* that a person experiences when he does not carry out his God-given assignments correctly. Although building correctly may take longer, it is far better than the consequences of building wrongly and with inferior materials that leads to tragic results.

Historically, the word "loss" — translated from the Greek word *zemioo* — likewise speaks of a fine or punishment given to those who did something incorrectly. When the fires of life come and burn down anything that is hastily and ill-built, the one who suffers tragic loss feels that sense of a "fine" or even punishment as a consequence of not doing what was right from the start.

Without a doubt, the word *zemioo* pictures *injury*, *harm*, and *loss of property*. It is the sad image of a person standing in the burned-down, charred remains of a house or building — but in this case, he is standing in the midst of his own works that are now *burnt to a crisp* because he used the wrong materials and was sloppy in the building process. As a result, nothing remains but a pile of rubble.

'Saved, Yet So as By Fire'

In First Corinthians 3:15, Paul announced that even though such a person may have suffered temporal loss, "...he himself shall be saved; yet so as by fire."

The phrase "yet so as by fire" comes from the Greek words *dia puros.* The word *dia* means *through*, and the word *puros* is the Greek word for *fire.* When these words are used together, as in this verse, most commentators agree that the Greek phrase means, "...He shall be saved, but like one who is escaping through the flames." One person has even translated it, *"...He is saved, but as one escaping through the flames and with the smell of smoke on his clothes."*

These verses were written for our admonition and to encourage us to build our lives and what God has called us to do in a way that glorifies Him and in a way that will stand up against life's fires and tests. Paul went into all this detail because he had poured his life into the church at Corinth, and now others were building on top of his apostolic endeavors. This was to be expected, because he wanted those who followed him to take heed *how* they built on top of his pristine foundation.

Paul wanted them to know that if they moved carefully and built wisely with long-lasting materials, they would be greatly rewarded. But if the next generation of leaders built hastily and with shoddy spiritual materials, it would become catastrophically evident, as some test would eventually come to reveal "what sort of work" they had built substandardly.

What If Your Work Has Already Gone Up in a Puff of Smoke?

Jesus Christ is the Chief Apostle and He is, ultimately, the Foundation underneath the Church that is immovable. What we build on top of that foundation depends on our level of personal commitment and the level of excellence we require of ourselves as we continue leading the work of God onward with time. But I need to again ask you: Are you building what will be enduring, or are you building so hastily and poorly that what you've built will eventually go up in a puff of smoke?

For some people, fire comes early — *quickly* — to reveal mistakes, while others experience fire later, but those experiences nonetheless reveal flaws that could have been avoided if those people had moved more carefully early on and listened to the Holy Spirit. The good news is that even when leaders have poorly stewarded their responsibilities in the Church and their works are consumed as a result, there is a long-lasting Foundation under the Church that cannot be consumed. That is why Paul said in First Corinthians 3:11, "For other foundation can no man lay than that is laid, which is Jesus Christ."

An apostle is a foundation-layer, and as such, he *could conceivably* lay a faulty one. While Paul was confident of the foundation he had laid in Corinth, this doesn't mean every apostolic foundation-layer has done his assignment accurately. In First Corinthians 3:10, Paul issued a warning not only to all who come behind an apostle to continue the work, but also to all apostolic foundation-layers — *and to each one of us concerning how we build our lives* — to do it *carefully*.

Never forget that Jesus is the ultimate Foundation of the Church! And as we have seen, that word "foundation" pictures *a foundation set in stone* that is *strong*, *stable*, and *enduring*. This thankfully means that anyone who has made the mistake of building incorrectly or with inferior materials or wrong motives — and everything built on top of it burned down as a result — can rest assured the fire will not affect the foundation. In fact, the Foundation of Jesus Christ remains completely, faultlessly intact.

In these situations of devastation, once repentance is made for errors along the way and there is submission to someone with authority to help get things back on track, it becomes clear the Foundation is still there to build on top of again. Fire may have affected the flimsy structure that burned down, but fire does not affect stone. And when the ashes are removed, you'll see the Foundation is still there waiting for you or someone else to build correctly on top of it this time.

Throughout 2,000 years of Church history, many have built cheaply, with wrong motives, with bad doctrines, or with man-made traditions on top of the foundation of Jesus Christ that apostles laid so deeply 2,000 years ago. That foundation was put in place so correctly, it remains to this very moment in spite of every sabotage imaginable that has been waged against the Church.

We are speaking metaphorically of building in haste, with wrong motives and faulty materials. But in the same way, if a person has built *any* area of his life incorrectly, and it puts him on a spiritual "ash heap" — once the ashes are cleared away — he can begin to build again because the Foundation of Jesus Christ underneath Him is still gloriously intact. So even if that person has been selfishly ambitious, has obtained things prematurely by cutting corners, or has made a moral mistake, if Jesus is his foundation, there is always hope of recovering and starting again.

If a person has built *any* area of his life incorrectly, and it puts him on a spiritual "ash heap" — once the ashes are cleared away — he can begin to build again because the Foundation of Jesus Christ underneath Him is still gloriously intact. So even if that person has been selfishly ambitious, has obtained things prematurely by cutting corners, or has made a moral mistake, if Jesus is his foundation, there is always hope of recovering and starting again.

What It Is All Leading Up to — You Are the *Naos* Temple of the Holy Spirit

Finally, after his inspired discourse in First Corinthians 3:10-15, in verse 16, Paul resoundingly affirmed that all along in this text, he has been talking about apostolically constructing the Church as the *naos* Temple of God. He asked, "Know ye not that ye [plural] are the temple of God, and that the Spirit of God dwelleth in you?"

In this verse, Paul wrote that in addition to each believer being a temple of the Holy Spirit, the Church is *corporately* a sanctuary for the Spirit of God.

The phrase "know ye not" is the Greek words *ouk oidate*, which are from the words *ouk* and *oida*. The word *ouk* is *an emphatic no*, and the word *oida* means *to see, perceive, understand, or comprehend*. Taken together, the phrase "know ye not" is the equivalent of Paul saying, "Don't you get it? Have you not yet comprehended it? Do you not realize that, as a church, you are corporately the Temple of God?"

The word "temple" is again the Greek word *naos*, and it describes *a temple or a highly decorated shrine*. As we have seen before, it portrays the image of vaulted ceilings and beautiful marble, granite, gold, and silver, as well as highly decorated ornamentation. It is the same word used to describe *the most sacred, innermost part of a temple*; *the Holy of Holies*. Paul said that collectively — as a universal Church Body — we are a *naos* Temple for God's Spirit to dwell inside in the earth.

The word "dwelleth" is the Greek word *oikeo*, a word we have already seen, that means *to dwell in a house*, *to settle into a home*, or *to be at home*. It is the picture of *a person who takes up permanent residency* and becomes *a permanent indweller* in a specific place. Herein Paul tells us that God's Spirit has permanently moved into the Church, and God's intention is for us to corporately be a magnificent dwelling place for Him. That is the foremost apostolic vision of the Church given in the New Testament.

Be Careful Not To 'Defile' God's Temple

Paul went on in First Corinthians 3:17 to say, "If any man defile the temple of God, him shall God destroy; for the temple of God is holy, which temple ye are [plural]."

This is a sobering warning that everyone who ever labors in the *naos* Temple of God must understand. First, notice Paul said, "If any man." The word "any" is the Greek word *tis*, which means *any one* or *any person*. This Greek term is gender-neutral, including any male or any female. It is all-inclusive of anyone who ever adds his or her part in building the Church of Jesus Christ in any respect.

Paul then added to this somber warning, "If any man *defile*…." (1 Corinthians 3:17). The word "defile" is a form of the Greek word *phtheiro*, and it means *to waste, corrupt*, or *deteriorate*. Figuratively, it means *to cause a moral deterioration*. It pictures *a decomposition or breakdown that causes something to move from a higher level to a lower level*. Thus, Paul was saying, "If any person in the Church is a contributor to defiling the Church — causing it to deteriorate, become corrupt, or break down and move from a higher level to a lower level — him shall God destroy." This means no one called to ministry should be casual or cavalier toward that holy calling, and one might also want to think twice about corrupting an individual "temple" who makes up the broader Church.

Paul was saying, "If any person in the Church is a contributor to defiling the Church — causing it to deteriorate, become corrupt, or break down and move from a higher level to a lower level — him shall God destroy."

It is important to note that the words "destroy" and "defile" in this verse are from the same identical Greek word — the word *phtheiro*. So when Paul wrote, "Him shall God destroy," it literally means, "Him will God *waste, corrupt*, and *deteriorate*." Thus, any person — man or woman — who corrupts or causes the Church to break down and move from a higher level to a lower level, God will Himself cause that person to decompose and break down. In other words, God will do to him what he did to the Church. Remember, the Church is corporately the Temple — *naos* — of the Holy Spirit of God, and He is highly protective of it.

The Church is corporately the Temple — *naos* — of the Holy Spirit of God, and He is highly protective of it.

Two 'Corrupting' Sons in Ministry — a Lesson and an Admonition

A great example of what happens when a person defiles the House of God is found in the book of First Samuel. As the book opens, we discover Eli is serving as the judge and priest in Israel, and his sons, Hophni and Phinehas, were serving under him. But Hophni and Phinehas did not have a relationship with the Lord, and they brought great dishonor to the House of God. They were abusing the people who came to worship God by stealing God's offerings. To make matters worse, they were having sexual relations with the women who came to the door of the tabernacle.

First Samuel 2:17 says, "Wherefore the sin of the young men was very great before the Lord: for men abhorred the offering of the Lord." Because of Hophni and Phinehas' actions, the people grew to detest coming to the tabernacle to worship God, and many of them simply stopped coming altogether because they were tired of being abused. These young men were wasting and corrupting the House of God and negatively affecting God's people.

A careful reading of the story reveals that God patiently tolerated the destructive behavior of Hophni and Phinehas for a long time. Even though they were doing wrong, God did not quickly bring judgment. The truth is, God is never in a rush to judge and dole out punishment, but when behavior becomes so foul that it detrimentally affects His people, God steps in to bring judgment. The way Hophni and Phinehas dealt with God's House is the way God dealt with them — *and* with their father Eli. First Samuel 4:11-18 tells us that in one day, all three of them died. This historical account is a strong warning that we must be careful how we treat God's Temple and the people who corporately *are* that Temple.

In First Corinthians 3:17 Paul went on to say, "If any man defile the temple of God, him shall God destroy; for the temple of God is holy, which temple ye are [plural]." The word "holy" is the Greek word *hagios*, which describes *something that is holy, consecrated, different, separate*, or *special.* This tells us the house of God is different and special, a consecrated and separated place that is to be holy unto God.

Then Paul concluded this text on the foundation-laying ministry of apostles in First Corinthians 3:17 by saying, "...Which temple ye are." In this verse, he was speaking to the entire Church, saying that, corporately, we are the Temple of the Holy Spirit.

If Not Intentionally Remembered, the Foundation-Laying Work of Apostles Can Be Forgotten

It is important for an apostle to be secure in who he is in the Lord, because if an apostle lays a good foundation, a time may eventually come when his work will nearly be forgotten — *unless* it is intentionally memorialized. Let me give you another example from our ministry in the former USSR.

In the 1990s, after the collapse of the Soviet Union, God led me to lead our team and congregation to construct a large physical church building. Of course, one of the most important steps in that complex process was laying *a physical foundation* that was strong enough to support the church building. Since the planned structure was massive, the foundation would have to be *immense*, and this also meant it would be *very expensive*!

The land we purchased for the building was ideal in terms of its location, but the ground itself was composed of a type of soil very similar to peat moss. Peat moss is a beautiful, rich, dark soil, but structurally, it is unsound. And this soil on our property was so unsound to build upon that, if we *had* built on top of it, our building would have sunk down into the soil. So before we could start laying the foundation, bulldozers had to come on-site and remove that rich, dark soil *by the hundreds of truckloads.*

Day after day, I watched as the crew dug deeper and deeper, trying to find hard ground beneath all that "peat moss." At long last, they found hard soil *12 feet deep* in the earth! When it was all said and done, 12 feet of that flimsy soil had to be removed — it was an area nearly the size of a football field. Every day I went to the site to watch as dump trucks loaded with porous, lightweight soil drove away to dump that soil into the river!

When the huge depression for the foundation was finally dug, I climbed down into it and walked from one end to the other. I was so proud of that big hole in the ground that had cost more money than any other project I had ever carried out in my life. But once the soil was excavated, it was time to fill the hole with copious amounts of heavy sand and gravel so the foundation could be laid. Over the course of the next few months, the same dump trucks that had previously carried soil away returned to pour layers upon layers of sand and gravel into that big, expensive hole. By the time the hole was refilled with rock and sand, the preparatory work for the foundation had already cost a fortune.

The next step was to lay the actual *foundation* for the physical building. The workers built a wood frame around the perimeter of the building site and then laid steel to reinforce the concrete once it was poured. Once the frame was secure, concrete trucks arrived and began pouring concrete. For weeks, cement trucks churned sand, water, and cement into concrete, and workers poured it onto the site. The newly poured concrete was then carefully smoothed before it dried, and the laborers worked quickly and efficiently to complete each new section before moving on to the next. Everyone involved worked meticulously with an observant eye to ensure no mistakes were made in this important process.

Finally the day came when all the trucks left, and I could examine our new foundation. At 306 feet long and 108 feet wide, that foundation was huge. In fact, it was so big that it took several minutes for me to walk from one end to the other. But it wasn't long until the next part of the construction crew arrived with their noisy grinding machines and they literally ground the surface of that foundation until it was nearly as smooth as silk. Then it was finally time for the next phase — the construction of the building's steel frame.

But before that steel frame was put in place, I would drive to the site early each morning to walk around the foundation and look at it in wonder. I would think about how it began as an abandoned field of "peat moss," and then through a lengthy, elaborate, *expensive* process, it became our rock-solid foundation. *I loved that foundation!*

When we started to build it, we didn't have the money needed to complete it. Day by day, I prayed and believed God for the money to dig that hole, buy the sand and rock, and purchase the concrete to lay the foundation. No one appreciated the foundation as much as I did because no one else knew what a miracle it was that we had been able to pay for it. That foundation had been built by faith. *It was my miracle foundation!*

When it was time to lay the tiles and carpet, it almost broke my heart because the tiles and carpet were laid over that foundation that I loved so much. After all the work and money that had gone into building that foundation, now I watched as the tiles and carpet began to completely hide it. It was so well concealed that no one would ever think of the foundation as they walked over it. No one entering that building would ever realize the fortune of sand, rock, and concrete that was beneath his or her feet, yet it was there whether people realized it or not. Although that foundation was no longer visible to anyone's sight, it was *essential nevertheless* to keeping that building standing strong for years to come. And that building is still standing strong decades later, and the church work there is also strong!

Think about it — how often do you walk into a building and say, "Wow, what an awesome foundation this building has!" When you walk into a new building, you see carpet, tile, wallpaper, light fixtures, and other beautiful cosmetic work, but you don't see the foundation. You don't even think of the foundation *unless* the foundation has a problem — then everyone talks about that poorly placed foundation! A bad foundation results in crooked floors and walls. But if a foundation was properly laid, people probably don't even think about the foundation. However, if the foundation isn't properly put in place, that building won't last very long. *The longevity of the whole building depends on the foundation.*

Building a foundation is a hard, elaborate, lengthy, expensive process, but it is *extremely important.* I remind you again that when Paul entered Corinth, the city was utterly consumed with idolatry and heathenism. It is no exaggeration to say that Corinth was one of the most wicked, perverted cities on the face of the earth at that time. For Paul to establish a strong and long-lasting church in that evil environment, he had to put a firm foundation under the church there — under the spiritual feet of those newly saved Corinthians. Paul's enormous effort and intense focus produced a foundation under them that would withstand any attack of the enemy — including horrific persecution — and would last for generations!

But Paul was an apostle, so a time always came when he raised up a new pastor and sailed away into another new territory to apostolically establish a church in another new region. But the foundation that the apostle Paul set beneath that church was rock-solid and needed *no improvements.* That is why he confidently stated to the Corinthians, "For other foundation can no man lay than that is laid, which is Jesus Christ" (1 Corinthians 3:11). From the ground up, Paul had faithfully and diligently built that church on the Foundation of Jesus Christ, which cannot be imperfect or shaken. But Paul's concern was that subsequent leaders could potentially continue the work by building shabbily, absent of the faithfulness and diligence Paul had invested in his own holy calling.

Never forget that the longevity of a building greatly depends on the foundation.

Although the apostolic work of envisioning, designing, leading, overseeing, and helping to lay the foundation is a hard, elaborate, lengthy process that can come at great cost, it is nevertheless *extremely important.* If an apostolic foundation is laid correctly, a church will be well-supported and will be able to pass the fires of life and the tests of time, providing that others build upward and onward in the same careful manner. On the other hand, if a foundation is built too hastily or on *shifting soil,* it will not have a firm footing and will suffer loss.

You see, the foundation is very important — and laying a solid spiritual foundation underneath the lives of believers is part of an apostle's work. And if an apostle, like Paul, has done a good job, a time will naturally come when someone else will come along to put "tiles and carpet" on top of it, and it may feel like the foundational work he did is forgotten. But if it is forgotten, it's actually a sign that an apostle did a very good job at laying the foundation — for a flawed foundation that was built shabbily would become apparent, and no one would ever forget the disastrous effect of doing something hastily and in a substandard manner, with inferior "materials."

Because an apostle's work is done at the very beginning and can be unintentionally displaced or forgotten by years of activity and subsequent generations who are unfamiliar with a church's beginnings, it is wise to document how and who started a church and celebrate its beginning. Commemorating those who paved the way by faith and who started it is important, and we must always revel in the memories of the divine power God put forth to produce its birth! Never forget those who started a work and the miraculous power that manifested in the beginning.

As the psalmist said in Psalm 77:11, "I will *remember* the works of the Lord surely I will *remember* thy wonders of old." In Psalm 111:4, the psalmist said, "He hath made his wonderful works to be *remembered....*" And Psalm 143:5 added, "I *remember* the days of old; I meditate on all thy works; I muse on the work of thy hands." An apostle's God-assigned job of foundation-laying in the Church is performed by grace and in cooperation with God's power and plan — and it is right to commemorate it, giving thanks to God for that effectual, long-lasting work.

In the next chapter, I'll answer specific questions I've received over the years concerning apostolic ministry. I believe you'll find the answers very practical — and some of them very surprising.

Questions for Deeper Consideration

Chapter 5

1. There is a lot of talk about grace in our times. But after reading this chapter, how would you define "grace" if someone asked you to help them understand it? How would you capsulize the meaning of the word "grace" and how would you now describe its effects when it touches a person's life?

2. By studying the New Testament, we find that Paul's and Peter's apostolic ministries were directed to different people groups. To whom was Peter primarily sent as an apostle? To whom was Paul primarily sent as an apostle?

3. This chapter covered the transitory nature of apostolic ministry and the possible frustrations it could present to an apostle. Can you explain why an apostle's ministry is transitory? Can you explain why the transitory nature of an apostle's ministry could possibly present a frustration to him?

4. Paul refers to himself as a "wise masterbuilder" in First Corinthians 3:10. Because these words are so pivotal to understanding the ministry of an apostle, take a moment to express in your own words what the words "wise" and "masterbuilder" mean in this verse. Can you explain how the words "wise masterbuilder" depict the ministry of an apostle?

5. Paul rarely traveled alone and worked with an apostolic team who helped him start churches in various locations. Why did Paul nearly always travel

and work with a team? And in those teams, what was Paul's specific role? What is the principal role of any apostle in any apostolic team?

6. In First Corinthians 3:12, Paul stated that some build the Church with "...gold, silver, precious stones, wood, hay, stubble...." Why did Paul specifically describe these materials? What is the implication? Can you now describe the difference between buildings that are built with gold, silver, precious stones — and those that are built of wood, hay, and stubble?

7. In First Corinthians 3:13, Paul warned, "Every man's work shall be made manifest: for the day shall declare it, because it shall be revealed by fire; and the fire shall try every man's work of what sort it is." Can you explain what "day" Paul was forecasting in this verse? Was this a fire sent by God or from some other source? What type of "fire" is Paul describing and how will "fire" reveal the sort of works that have been built?

8. By looking at First Corinthians 3:17, we find a solemn warning to anyone who intentionally mishandles and defiles the temple of God. By looking at that verse, what will happen to one who intentionally mismanages or abuses the temple of God?

CHAPTER 6

TEN QUESTIONS ABOUT APOSTOLIC MINISTRY

Study to shew thyself approved unto God, a workman that needeth not to be ashamed, rightly dividing the word of truth.

— 2 Timothy 2:15 KJV

In this chapter on Christ-given apostles before we move on to the subject of prophets and their role in the Body of Christ — I will answer the following 10 questions that have been asked of me over the years. Even with the following questions answered, there is still more material on apostolic ministry than I can cover in one book. But in this chapter, we will answer each of the following as succinctly as possible to provide biblical answers to these important questions.

- What is the highest calling of an apostle?
- What role does divine revelation have in the ministry of a true apostle?
- What kind of authority does a true apostle possess?
- Do all apostles operate similarly in their ministries and have the same identical gifts and ministries?
- Can a true apostle also stand in the other fivefold ministry gifts?
- What attitude should a true apostle possess about himself?
- Why did Paul write that he was "born out of due season"?
- Why is it so difficult to name more living apostles today?
- Why did Paul write that apostles were "set forth" as "last" and "appointed to death?"
- What is the glory and crown of a true apostle?

What Is the Highest Calling of an Apostle?

Before Jesus ever sent His apostles out to do the work of ministry, He called them "unto Him" to be "with Him." Mark 3:13-15 says, "…[Jesus] goeth up into a mountain, and calleth *unto him* whom he would: and they came *unto him*. And he ordained twelve, that they should be *with him*, and that he might send them forth to preach, and to have power to heal sicknesses, and to cast out devils."

As would be true with any of the Christ-given fivefold ministry gifts of apostle, prophet, evangelist, pastor, or teacher, anyone who is called to a Christ-given fivefold ministry office must know, first and foremost, he or she is called "unto Him" to be "with Him." Of course, eventually, Christ sent

His apostles forth to preach, to have power to heal sicknesses, and to cast out devils. But before any of this activity began, they were called "unto Him" to be "with Him."

Likewise, a person called into apostolic ministry must burn with a passion to be *with Christ*, and his desire to know Him must be so all-consuming that he will be willing to forsake all to know Him better. This is the very kind of passion Paul wrote about in Philippians 3:7-10. In that famous text, Paul wrote:

> **But what things were gain to me, those I counted loss for Christ. Yea doubtless, and I count all things but loss for the excellency of the knowledge of Christ Jesus my Lord: for whom I have suffered the loss of all things, and do count them but dung, that I may win Christ, and be found in him, not having mine own righteousness, which is of the law, but that which is through the faith of Christ, the righteousness which is of God by faith: that I may know him, and the power of his resurrection, and the fellowship of his sufferings, being made conformable unto his death.**

An apostle is the representative of Christ, and as such, an apostle must know the transformative power of the risen Christ. He must understand that even before he does the job he is called to do, his foremost need is to come "unto Him" and to be "with Him" so that the Lord can teach and mature him. Flowing from that relationship in his ministry, an apostle will then have the insight and power to proclaim Christ in fullness to those he leads.

Paul referred to such a proclamation of Christ in Colossians 1:28 when he clearly stated that he was to preach Christ with the intention to present every man perfect in Him. That powerful verse says, "Whom we preach, warning every man, and teaching every man in all wisdom; that we may present every man perfect in Christ Jesus."

Hence, the highest calling for an apostle is to come "unto Him" to be "with Him" as we read of Jesus and the first apostles in Mark 3:13-15. Afterward,

Christ will dispatch the apostle to preach, to have power to heal sicknesses, to cast out devils, and to lay the foundation of the Church where it has never existed before — or possibly where it once existed, but has fallen into ruin and needs to be restored.

What Role Does Divine Revelation Have in the Ministry of a True Apostle?

Paul answered this question unequivocally in Galatians 1:11 and 12, where he wrote, "But I certify you, brethren, that the gospel which was preached of me is not after man. For I neither received it of man, neither was I taught it, but by the revelation of Jesus Christ."

But before we get into the role divine revelation plays in the ministry of an apostle, it is important to remember that learning from every available, reliable source is critical to one's spiritual growth. The apostle Paul played a *major* role in the founding of the early Church. God used him to write almost two thirds of the New Testament, and his epistles have guided the Body of Christ for nearly 2,000 years. However, Paul — then Saul — had to go somewhere entirely unexpected early in his Christian life to learn from mentors and come to an accurate understanding of God's vision for the Church.

Soon after his life-changing conversion on the road to Damascus, Paul traveled to Jerusalem, eager to connect with the disciples there and begin his ministry. Given his background as a former rabbi who spoke fluent Hebrew, it's easy to understand why Jerusalem would be the natural choice for Paul to focus his efforts on. After all, he was intimately acquainted with the Jewish culture, tradition, and religious thought that permeated that city. However, God had called Saul (Paul) first and foremost to bring the Gospel to the Gentile world. Although God did use key parts of Paul's past to equip him for his call, Jerusalem's predominantly Jewish environment could not adequately prepare him to fulfill this ministry.

Through a series of events, God eventually led Saul to the church in the city of Antioch, a city located approximately 250 miles north of Jerusalem in modern-day Turkey. It was also in Antioch where he would begin to be called Paul. Antioch was the third largest city in the Roman Empire during early New Testament times; only Rome and Alexandria exceeded it in size.[1] Situated on a crossroads between the East and West, it was a thriving commercial center and a true melting pot of cultures and peoples. The city's population was also composed primarily of Gentiles, which was a very important factor for Paul, given the nature of his calling as an apostle to the Gentiles.

The Gospel was first brought to Antioch in the wake of Stephen's martyrdom, and many who resided there warmly received the message. In fact, this city experienced a revival as pagans and Jews alike left behind their old lives and accepted Jesus as their Lord and Savior. Before long, a thriving church had been established in Antioch, and the believers began to actively evangelize their city and the surrounding region. During his time with this congregation, Paul regularly ministered alongside Gentiles and learned to communicate effectively with them. These experiences would do much to equip him for the epic apostolic journeys he would later embark upon across the Roman Empire.

Antioch's rich, diverse environment was God's "right place" for Paul in that season so he could become equipped and fully prepared for ministry. A brand-new move of the Spirit was taking place in that city, and — by following God's calling to move there — Paul put himself in a position to receive a completely fresh perspective of the Body of Christ. During his time in Antioch, he learned important lessons from what he saw and experienced that he could never have learned if he had stayed in Jerusalem.

In Antioch, Paul learned how to minister alongside Gentiles. He likely could have never received this special revelation of the Church if he had stayed in Jerusalem. The congregation in Jerusalem was very proud of their Jewish roots, and their wrong beliefs prevented them from readily acknowledging that God could work through people of all types and backgrounds. Paul was called to minister to the Gentile world, and if he had based his ministry in Jerusalem — which, as we've seen, was primarily a Jewish church filled with Jewish people and Jewish thinking — he likely would have been unprepared to minister to the Gentiles.

Consequently, God orchestrated events that led Paul to the church of Antioch, where a diverse congregation provided him with an environment in which he could learn how to minister to the Gentile world. There in Antioch, Paul was able to see firsthand the grace of God working through people of many different nationalities, ethnicities, and social classes. This experience engrained in him a multiracial mindset that allowed him to see believers of every background just as Jesus does: *All* are equal partners in the Body of Christ.

In Antioch, Paul was able to see firsthand the grace of God working through people of many different nationalities, ethnicities, and social classes. This experience engrained in him a multiracial mindset that allowed him to see believers of every background just as Jesus does: All are equal partners in the Body of Christ.

God placed Paul into this ripe environment for a reason. By being constantly surrounded by fervent, open-minded believers during a crucial stage of his spiritual development, Paul grasped a Christian worldview that he could not have experienced in an environment where the old Jewish mindset was more prevalent. If he had remained in Jerusalem, it is likely that his growth would have been stifled by the narrow-minded, religious vision of the Church that had taken root in that city. In Jerusalem, he could not have openly taught the type of new revelations he received in Antioch because many of the believers in Jerusalem would have dismissed them outright as being too radical. However, in Antioch, Saul was free to develop his teaching gift in a supportive, non-threatening environment.

Antioch became a spiritual training ground for Saul and countless other believers during the First Century. When God moved the hub of His Spirit's activity to that city, He imparted to the believers there His new vision of a worldwide, expansive Body of Christ that would become enormous as He built His Church. It was in that environment that God was able to impart to Paul the revelation of what the Church of Jesus Christ was actually supposed to look like.

Antioch was a proving ground for Saul where he received ministerial training that he could never have received in the Jewish congregation of Jerusalem. This part of God's divine plan was instrumental in furthering Saul's spiritual development and transforming him into the mighty man of God he grew to be in Christ.

It is imperative for each one of us to be in the right place at the right time to receive revelation from mentors and from a right spiritual environment. But while all of this indeed occurred in his life, in Galatians 1:11,12, Paul categorically and emphatically declared that he was additionally taught by the supernatural revelation of Jesus Christ. Although he had been trained rabbinically earlier in his life, the revelation of Christ and of the Church that He preached was not the result of past scholarly training. This revelation was the result of divine revelation imparted to Him by Christ Himself, and it gave Paul his vision of the Church and enabled him in his role to help lay its foundation.

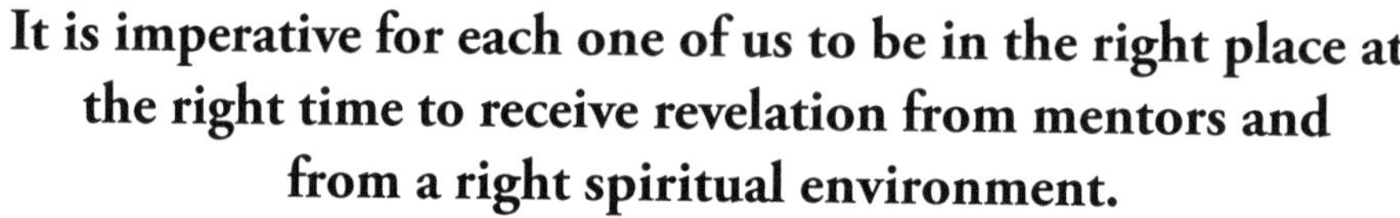

It is imperative for each one of us to be in the right place at the right time to receive revelation from mentors and from a right spiritual environment.

The moment Paul was converted on the road to Damascus, he was informed by Christ that he would be a recipient of divine revelation. Though the full narrative of what Jesus said to Paul in that experience is not recorded in Acts 9, Paul quotes the actual words he heard Jesus speak to him on the road to Damascus when he was testifying to King Agrippa in Acts 26:12-18. In that passage, Paul quoted verbatim what He heard Jesus say to him at the moment of his conversion. He told King Agrippa:

> **Whereupon as I went to Damascus with authority and commission from the chief priests, at midday, O king, I saw in the way a light from heaven, above the brightness of the sun, shining round about me and them which journeyed with me. And when we were all fallen to the earth, I heard a voice speaking unto me, and saying in the Hebrew tongue, Saul, Saul, why persecutest thou me? it is hard for thee to kick against the pricks.**
>
> **And I said, Who art thou, Lord? And he said, I am Jesus whom thou persecutest. But rise, and stand upon thy feet: for I have appeared unto thee for this purpose, to make thee a minister and a witness both of these things which thou hast seen, and of those things in the which I will appear unto thee; delivering thee from the people, and *from* the Gentiles, unto whom now I send thee, to open their eyes, *and* to turn *them* from darkness to light, and *from* the power of Satan unto God, that they may receive forgiveness of sins, and inheritance among them which are sanctified by faith that is in me.**

Paul told King Agrippa that Jesus supernaturally appeared to him, called him by name, and told him he was being "sent" as an apostle to the Gentile world. Paul vividly remembered how Jesus told him that He was sending him to the Gentiles "to open their eyes, and to turn them from darkness to light, and from the power of Satan unto God, that they may receive forgiveness of sins, and inheritance among them which are sanctified by faith that is in me" (Acts 26:18). But Jesus also importantly told him, he would "make thee a minister and a witness both of these things which thou hast seen, and of those things in the which I will appear unto thee" (Acts 26:16).

In his first experience with Christ, Paul had a divine revelation and heard Christ say that he would continue to "appear" to him in the future to teach him even more. Paul affirmed his apostleship was supernatural in Galatians 1:1, where he wrote, "Paul, an apostle, (not of men, neither by man, but by Jesus Christ...)." From the very outset of his new life in Christ, Paul was informed that Jesus would be appearing to him regularly, and he knew that he was an apostle, not by the choice of man, but by Jesus Christ Himself.

This leads us back to Galatians 1:11,12, where Paul wrote, "But I certify you, brethren, that the gospel which was preached of me is not after man. For I neither received it of man, neither was I taught it, but by the revelation of Jesus Christ."

The word "certify" in verse 11 is a translation of the Greek word *gnoridzo*, and here it means *to make something so clearly known that the point being made cannot be misconstrued.* In essence, Paul said, "I will make it known to you so clearly that you cannot misconstrue what I am saying...." Then Paul added that "the gospel which was preached of me is not after man." The word "after" in Greek is *kata*, a preposition which means *after*, *according to*, or *it was not passed down to me by any man.*

Then in verse 12, Paul robustly adds, "For I neither received it of man, neither was I taught it, but by the revelation of Jesus Christ." The word "received" is a form of the Greek word *paralambano*, a compound of *para* and *lambano*. The preposition *para* in this event means *alongside* and the word *lambano* means *to take* or *to receive*. Compounded, the word *paralambano* depicts one who *takes something* or *receives something* from another human being. But in this case, Paul certifies that he did not receive his revelation from any human being. The Greek clearly means his revelation of the Gospel and the Church did not originate in a human source.

He then said, "...Neither was I taught it..." (Galatians 1:12). The word "taught" is a form of the Greek word *didasko*, which means *to teach, to instruct*, or *to prescribe*. In Greek literature, this word was primarily used to describe the relationship between a teacher and a pupil or a master and apprentice. What is taught may be not only knowledge, opinions, or facts, but also artistic and technical skills, all of which are to be systematically and thoroughly acquired by the learner through the activity of a teacher. Thus, the word *didasko* refers not only to *teaching*, but *how to apply teaching*, and it is the same word used to describe *a masterful teacher who would teach his knowledge to an apprentice*. But in Galatians 1:12, Paul said, "I did *not* learn what I know, nor how to apply it, from any human source."

No doubt Paul learned much from his environment in Antioch, but he did not arrive at the core of his revelation by listening to human sources. Paul told us he received his revelation of the Gospel and the Church supernaturally. That is why he added in Galatians 1:12, "...but by the revelation of Jesus Christ."

The word "but" in Greek is *alla*, which means *on the contrary*. Thus, he says, "On the contrary, I received it *by* the *revelation* of Jesus Christ." The word "by" is a translation of the Greek word *dia*, which means *by* or *through* and specially describes the way he received his divine insights. According to Paul, he received it directly from Jesus Himself, which agrees with the vision

Paul had on the road to Damascus in which Jesus foretold that He would be appearing to Paul again and again over the course of his apostolic ministry.

To make it clear, Paul was not talking about human insight — he called his insights "revelation." The word "revelation" is translated from the Greek word *apokalupsis*, a compounded of *apo* and *kalupto*. The word *apo* means *away*, and *kalupto* depicts *a veil that hides* or *a veil that conceals*. When compounded, it denotes something that was veiled or hidden, but then the veil is suddenly removed, what was previously hidden becomes clear and visible to the mind or eye. It is an unveiling — a sudden revealing — it means to uncover something that was once veiled or hidden. In a split second, the veil is suddenly removed and what was hidden comes into plain view. It refers to *something that has been veiled or hidden for a long time and then suddenly, almost instantaneously, it becomes clear and visible to the mind or eye.*

It is like pulling the curtains out of the way so you can see what has always been just outside your window. The scene was always there for you to enjoy, but the curtains blocked your ability to see the real picture. But when the curtains are drawn apart, you can suddenly see what has been hidden from your view. The moment you see beyond the curtain for the first time and observe what has been there all along but not previously evident — *that* is what the word "revelation" means in Galatians 1:12.

This means Paul's revelations were not obtained from a human source, but they came directly from Jesus Christ Himself, who appeared to him again and again in the course of his ministry. The truths Paul received were always there, but they were *hidden*. Because it wasn't the time for these truths to be revealed, they remained obscured from his sight. But when the right time arrived for them to be revealed, Paul said the Lord Himself pulled the concealing veil apart that had obstructed his view, and *instantly* his mind *saw* — he *understood*, or he *had a revelation*.

Apostolic individuals move in various levels of divine revelation. But when I say that apostles move in revelation, I am not talking about extra-biblical revelation, but rather revelation and insights concerning what is already revealed in the New Testament. Specifically, apostles possess divine revelation that burns in their heart and mind about the Gospel and the Church as the Body of Christ and the *naos* Temple of God. The level of revelation may vary from one apostle to the next, but nonetheless, an apostle will possess insights and revelation that especially concern the Gospel and God's vision for the Church.

What Kind of Authority Does a True Apostle Possess?

All the Christ-given fivefold gifts move in divine authority that is given to them by Christ Himself to perform their respective roles. A Christ-sent apostle is no different — *however*, he is marked with authority to carry out his function in building *from the ground up* the *naos* Temple of God. As such, this fivefold ministry gift can operate in *all* the Christ-given ministry gifts as enumerated in Ephesians 4:11 and as we saw in Chapter Five. Therefore, the authority of the apostle in the realm of the Spirit is a unique level of divine authority — and this authority is bestowed upon him so he can perform his deep *uprooting*, *pushing back*, *establishing*, and *building* function in the Body of Christ, as we will see in greater detail in this chapter.

We saw in the previous section that different apostles move in various levels of revelation. In the same manner, different apostles move in various levels of *authority*, depending on the scope of their assignments. Some may experience more authority and others less authority. But a true apostle moves in Christ-given apostolic authority that enables him and his team to preach the Gospel, to push back the power of darkness, to bulldoze demonic strongholds, to understand how to lay the foundation of the Church in a new location, to supernaturally lay that foundation and begin solidly building that work, and to raise up other ministry gifts to lead the church once the apostle is called by Christ to move on and do it all over again in another new location.

In fact, a true apostle is recognizable by the authority given to him by Christ or by the authority that has been delegated to him by those who commissioned and sent him. In other words, that an apostle is supernaturally commissioned and is supernaturally fulfilling his divine assignment should be obvious and recognizable — *evident* — as he sets about to do the work of his God-called ministry.

The Christ-given authority of an apostle is different from the other five-fold ministry gifts. He is part of the government of God, and as part of that government, he is endued with special apostolic authority. We saw in Chapter Four that apostles are *relational, geographical,* and *demographical*, and we will review and expound on this in this chapter. A careful study of Paul's New Testament writings reveals that apostolic ministry and the authority that an apostle possesses is based upon apostolic relationships. This means a person who is an apostle is not an apostle to everyone, but is rather an apostle only to a church or group of churches *with whom he or she has a relationship.*

Relational

For example, we saw that while Paul was universally respected in the Early Church as an apostle, he was not an apostle to every First Century church. He was an apostle only to those with whom he had an apostolic relationship. *This means no one who purports to be an apostle has the right to automatically claim authority in every church.*

Using Paul as an example, churches in other cities and regions — like the church in Jerusalem — acknowledged Paul's apostleship, but he was not their apostle. Although other believers respected Paul as an excellent minister, a beloved brother in the Lord, and an able leader, he only had apostolic responsibility for the churches he had helped start and for those whom he'd served as mentor, teacher, and father in the faith. Thus, Paul's apostleship was limited to those for whom he bore direct spiritual responsibility and with whom he had a unique *relationship*.

This would have included the churches in: *Ephesus*, *Colossae*, *Corinth*, *Galatia*, *Hierapolis*, *Laodicea*, *Pergamum*, *Philadelphia*, *Philippi*, *Sardis*, *Smyrna*, *Thessalonica*, *Thyatira*, and others. Paul was personally involved in starting all of these churches. Therefore, he had an apostolic relationship with them and bore the responsibility for overseeing the spiritual growth and well-being of the believers there. His relationship with these churches is the reason we have the books: *First Corinthians*, *Second Corinthians*, *Galatians*, *Ephesians*, *Philippians*, *Colossians*, *First Thessalonians*, and *Second Thessalonians*.

Paul wrote letters to these churches (which we've come to know as books of the Bible) because he was directly responsible for the spiritual well-being of these believers and because he had a unique apostolic relationship either with them or with their local leadership. His relationship and investment in them gave him the right *and the authority* to speak into their lives.

This explains why Paul told the Corinthians, "If I be not an apostle unto others, yet doubtless I am to you: for the seal of mine apostleship are ye in the Lord" (1 Corinthians 9:2). Paul knew that his apostleship was relational, so he concentrated on those with whom he knew he had this special, God-given relationship.

Geographical and Demographical

Not only is apostleship relational, it is also *geographical*. Understandably, apostles can't go everywhere on the planet and build relationships with everyone. They tend to be limited geographically, as the very nature of apostleship is limited to certain territories an apostle can access and to the people with whom he can build a relationship.

But apostles can also be demographical, as we clearly see in the case of Paul and Peter. In Galatians 2:8, Paul wrote, "For he that wrought effectually in Peter to the apostleship of the circumcision, the same was mighty in me toward the Gentiles." In this verse, Paul plainly states that Peter's apostleship was primarily to the Jews, and his own apostleship was primarily to the Gentiles. This would represent a "territory" or demographic sphere to which an apostle may be particularly called — and, thus, receive a unique grace to work among a certain nationality, ethnicity, language, or even an age group that has little or nothing to do with geography. But, certainly, there are apostles who are called to work in various nations of the world.

In all of the above cases, an apostle possesses authority to start churches in these respective realms and to speak with authority into the lives of those with whom he has an apostolic relationship. This would include starting churches, training leaders, setting doctrine in place, helping to set new leadership in place when needed, bringing correction if needed, and maintaining an ongoing apostolic-pastoral relationship with the leadership of the church, at least for a period of time.

But in addition to the authority in these above stated realms, another kind of apostolic authority is referred to in First Corinthians 5:4 and 5. In those verses, Paul confronted a sin problem in the church at Corinth and told the leaders of that church to deliver a brother committing dishonorable, immoral acts over to Satan "for the destruction of the flesh." We find no other fivefold ministry gift in the New Testament with the power and authority to carry out such an act. Paul knew the authority he possessed as an apostle, and he said, "In the name of our Lord Jesus Christ, when ye are gathered together, and my spirit, with the power of our Lord Jesus Christ, to deliver such an one unto

Satan for the destruction of the flesh, that the spirit may be saved in the day of the Lord Jesus" (1 Corinthians 5:4,5).

In these verses, Paul said, "In the name of our Lord Jesus Christ, when ye are gathered together, and my spirit, with the power of our Lord Jesus Christ...." Paul connected his own authority to the presence and power of the Lord, and he knew that if his authority was there, the Lord's authority was there too. He clearly understood that apostles in such cases stand in the stead of Christ and act as His spokesman. As Christ's commissioned ambassador, Paul was empowered to speak and to act on Christ's behalf, and his words were to be taken as the Lord's words. Thus, an apostle carries a weighty position in the house of God — and a weighty responsibility to know when he is being led and commissioned by the Head of the Church to exercise this level of spiritual authority.

We see in Scripture that an apostle also has the authority — that is, the "spiritual clout" — to charge individuals or churches with specific responsibilities. For example, Paul charged Timothy in Second Timothy 4:1-5:

> **I charge thee therefore before God, and the Lord Jesus Christ, who shall judge the quick and the dead at his appearing and his kingdom; preach the word; be instant in season, out of season; reprove, rebuke, exhort with all longsuffering and doctrine. For the time will come when they will not endure sound doctrine; but after their own lusts shall they heap to themselves teachers, having itching ears; and they shall turn away their ears from the truth, and shall be turned unto fables. But watch thou in all things, endure afflictions, do the work of an evangelist, make full proof of thy ministry.**

So powerful, in fact, was Paul's authority to charge Timothy with these responsibilities that what Paul was directing Timothy to do has become *our* charge, too, as believers.

Through apostolic authority, a church with an apostolic relationship can potentially receive direction, correction, and guidance. Because most Western believers are connected to churches and denominations that have existed a long time, they no longer have apostolic oversight and are usually led by Christ-given pastors. But in the areas of the world where the church is still being established in new places, apostolic relationship and authority is still desperately needed.

Do All Apostles Operate Similarly in Their Ministries and Have the Same Identical Gifts and Styles?

Just as every prophet is not the same in his or her style of delivery and ministry — and the same is true about every evangelist, pastor, and teacher — individual apostles also carry different styles and "flavors" in their giftings and ministries. This means one style does not fit all. In First Peter 4:10, Peter referred to the various flavors of God's grace that operate in His people when he wrote, "As every man hath received the gift, *even so* minister the same one to another, as good stewards of the *manifold* grace of God."

The word "manifold" is a translation of the Greek word *poikilos,* which carries the idea of something that is *diverse, variegated, of different colors,* or *manifold.* It is the identical word used in the Septuagint version of the Old Testament to describe Joseph's coat of many colors (*see* Genesis 37:3,32). As used in that text, it tells us that Jacob gave Joseph an unusual outer garment to be worn as a robe that was *diverse, variegated,* or *of different, manifold colors.* This was quite unusual at a time when most garments were spun of materials made of a single color.

By using this word *poikilos,* Peter was telling us that God gives variety to the gifts He imparts to His people. We are not all the same, and we each carry a distinctive blend of the grace of God that makes us look and shine differently from others.

Think of the light that is refracted by the cuts on a diamond. A diamond is a diamond, but when lights falls upon its various cuts, each of them refracts the light in a different way. In this way, we also see that when the grace of God shines brilliantly in each of our lives, we each refract that grace and glory in a different way and thus collectively reflect the multifaceted grace of God. As a result, every believer has been supernaturally favored with unique giftings. This could refer to an entire range of enablements, styles, and flavors of the grace of God — and this also includes the way God's grace manifests in the various fivefold gifts of the apostle, prophet, evangelist, pastor, and teacher.

God intends for the church to enjoy all the styles and flavors of His grace, yet people tend to compare one person's gifting or style to that of another, and such comparisons always create troubles. This happened in the church at Corinth, and that is why Paul wrote in First Corinthians 1:11 that there were "contentions" among them. Sadly, contentions developed among them *exactly* because of preferred styles, flavors, and personalities of various ministers.

The word "contentions" is the Greek word *eris*, and it is a word that most often depicted a *political party* and thus it is frequently translated as *a party spirit.* It pictures an individual or group of people who are fighting fiercely over preference — or a person or group of people who are jockeying for the advancement of something they prefer. Paul stated in First Corinthians 1:12 that they were wrangling over the styles and personalities of different ministers. He said, "Now this I say, that every one of you saith, I am of Paul; and I of Apollos; and I of Cephas; and I of Christ."

To make the point, let's focus only on the different styles between Paul and Apollos. As an apostle called to the city of Corinth, Paul was responsible for starting the church in that city. However, he also served as their first pastor until God raised up another pastor to take his place. This replacement was a well-respected, highly educated man from Alexandria in Egypt named Apollos — and soon after Paul's departure, he became the senior pastor of the Corinthian church. History tells us that Apollos was a gifted orator who was renowned for his eloquence.

In Paul's absence, the church at Corinth began to compare the different speaking styles of Paul and Apollos. Some who had been in the church from the beginning and were extremely affectionate toward Paul apparently didn't like the style of the new pastor. There were others in the church who loved Apollos and asserted that his preaching was superior to Paul's. Yet the message Paul and Apollos preached was the same — *they merely had different flavors and styles.*

In the same way, none of the fivefold gifts can be expected to be identical in their flavors, styles, or personalities. In respect to apostles, you should expect them to each shine differently. Some may be more greatly gifted with teaching skills while others are more gifted with administrative skills — and still others with organizational skills. Some may be louder, others may be quieter. Some may be more showy, while others seem less spectacular. While their apostolic purpose is the same, we can expect each of them to carry a distinctive blend of the grace of God that makes them shine differently from others.

Furthermore, there are various blends of fivefold ministry gifts. For example, some prophets also have the ability to teach; there are pastors who tend to be very evangelistic; there are teachers who are also prophetic. The various blends and mixes can seem limitless, showing again the vast, multifaceted grace of God that operates in fivefold ministry gifts.

Can an Apostle Also Stand in Other Fivefold Ministry Offices?

We saw in Chapter Two that for God's conglomerate Temple to fully emerge, it requires a divine workforce to assemble all the materials to continue to build and maintain the *naos* Temple of God. We also saw that apostles and their teams arrive to establish the Church where it has not yet been established. As they enter a new location, they are anointed by God's Spirit to clear spiritual rubbish out of the way and to lay a foundation for the Church in that locality. And as team leader, the apostle works side by side with his God-called team to lay a rock-solid foundation on which others can come along to do their parts in building a magnificent structure that has longevity.

In the early beginnings of building a church, an apostle is accompanied by his apostolic team to begin establishing a work from the ground up. Although other ministry gifts can arrive with an apostle as a part of his apostolic team, it is often not until later that the other Christ-given gifts appear as needed to put their respective hands to the task of building up that local church work. That's why an apostle is uniquely gifted to function in all the fivefold ministry gifts *if* needed until the other gifts arrive "on the site" — or are raised up by the apostle — to stand in these positions.

Let's take the example of the apostle Paul, who operated from time to time in all the fivefold ministry gifts. In Paul's epistles, he acknowledged over and over that he was "an apostle of Jesus Christ" (*see* Romans 1:1; 1 Corinthians 1:1; 2 Corinthians 1:1; Galatians 1:1; Ephesians 1:1; Colossians 1:1; 1 Thessalonians 2:6; 1 Timothy 1:1; 2 Timothy 1:1; Titus 1:1) — *and* that Christ chiefly called him to be an apostle to the Gentiles (*see* Acts 9:15,16; 26:15-18; Romans 1:5; 11:13; 15:16).

But while Paul stood in the office of an *apostle*, he acknowledged that he additionally stood in other fivefold ministry offices. In First Timothy 2:7, he wrote, "…I am ordained a *preacher*, and an *apostle*…." In Second Timothy 1:11 he added, "…I am appointed a *preacher*, and an *apostle*, and a *teacher* of the Gentiles." In both of these verses, the word "preacher" is the Greek word *kerux* and could possibly be referring to the office of a *prophet*. Regardless,

Paul acknowledged that as an apostle, he stood in *multiple* Christ-given fivefold ministry offices.

In these verses, Paul also uses the words "ordained" and "appointed" to describe his standing in these gifts. The word "ordained" and "appointed" in both cases is a form of the word *tithemi*, a Greek word meaning *to set in place, to firmly fix in place, to establish in place*, or *to appoint in place*. The use of *tithemi* tells us that his calling to be a fivefold gift of *prophet* and *teacher* was as authentic as his calling to be an *apostle*. He stood in all three of these fivefold gifts, and as you will see, he actually operated in all five of them, as all apostles are anointed to do *if* needed.

We first find that Paul operated in multiple giftings in the record that is provided by Luke in Acts 13:1. It says, "Now there were in the church that was at Antioch certain *prophets* and *teachers*; as Barnabas, and Simeon that was called Niger, and Lucius of Cyrene, and Manaen, which had been brought up with Herod the tetrarch, and Saul [Paul]." In this verse, Luke lists Paul among *prophets* and *teachers*.

But in Acts 13:2 and 3, Luke continued his narrative by telling us that while the elders in Antioch "...ministered to the Lord, and fasted, the Holy Ghost said, Separate me Barnabas and Saul for the work whereunto I have called them. And when they had fasted and prayed, and laid their hands on them, they sent them away." The words "sent them away" indicate the moment when Paul and Barnabas were released into their apostolic ministries. In these verses, we see again that Paul was an *apostle, prophet,* and *teacher*.

As one reads through Luke's meticulous account in the book of Acts, it is clear that when Paul preached in a new city, he also did the work of an *evangelist* to collect "living stones," or the souls of those who responded to the Gospel's message. Until a Christ-given fivefold evangelist arrived on site or was raised up among them, the apostle, by necessity, stood in the office of the *evangelist* to go into the field to win souls who would become the "living stones" in the construction of God's House. Once those living stones were won and collected, they were brought on site where they could be assimilated into the Temple of God.

After those "living stones" had been saved, a pastor was needed to take those raw stones and chisel, cut, trim, sand, grind, buff, and polish them to snugly fit next to other stones in the church. But until the Christ-given fivefold ministry gift of pastor arrived or was raised up among them, Paul the apostle, by necessity, also stood in the office of a *pastor* to carry out the nitty-gritty business of chiseling, sanding, and polishing all the souls or "living stones" that had been gathered and brought to the building site. In this sense, Paul was the "pastor" to feed God's flock and to guide the members of the church.

But wait…there's still more. In addition to all the preceding work that Paul did, the new congregation needed to be taught the Word of God. The fivefold ministry gift of teacher does this masterfully, but until a teacher, or a pastor with a teaching gift, arrived on-site or was raised up to take his position in the new church as a teacher, it was necessary for Paul to also stand in the position of a *teacher* to establish the new believers and the church in the principles of God's Word. Warning, exhorting, encouraging, comforting, and at times, rebuking, all played a role in the teaching ministry of an apostle.

Ephesians 2:20 says the Church is built on the foundation of apostles and prophets, so it is clear that prophetic ministry is also essential to the establishing of the church. But until a prophet arrives on-site or is raised up, an apostle can also stand in the position of a prophet to speak the mind of God to the church. If needed, apostles, indeed, can stand in the office of the prophet to impart courage to build correctly and at times address issues that need to be fixed in the building process to avert future disaster that could occur if those issues are not corrected.

While Paul's primary gifting seemed to be that of an apostle, until a prophet, evangelist, pastor, or teacher arrived on-site or was raised up, he had the ability to operate in all the Christ-given fivefold ministry gifts. Due to the nature of apostolic ministry of breaking into new territory and starting new churches, this would likely also be true of anyone who stands in the gift of apostle.

What Attitude Should a True Apostle Possess About Himself?

Paul was repulsed by some who claimed to be what he called "super apostles" (*see* 2 Corinthians 11:5; 12:11 *NIV*). These "super apostles" were arrogant pretenders whom Paul called "super" in a disparaging manner. Not only were they claiming a title that did not belong to them, but their arrogant attitude was a *far cry* from the attitude that should be demonstrated by a true apostle.

These "super apostles" were attacking Paul in an attempt to dislodge him from his role in certain churches so they could seize his apostolic relationships and territory. Like a panther leaping upon its prey, they feverishly worked to take Paul down and to capture control of the churches that he started and led. In an attempt to dislodge Paul, these "super apostles" boasted about how great they were while publicly accusing Paul of being weak and inferior to them.

When they launched their attack upon the Corinthian church in an attempt to capture it for themselves, they unthinkably accused Paul — the apostle who started the church at Corinth and who sacrificed so much of his life for them — of being "base" in comparison to them. Paul referred to their negative attempts to discredit him in Second Corinthians 10:1, where he wrote, "Now I Paul myself beseech you by the *meekness* and *gentleness* of Christ, who in presence am *base* among you, but being absent am bold toward you."

Notice Paul said that he was meek and gentle, and then added, "...who in presence am base among you...." He used the word "base" because he knew this was how the "super apostles" were depicting him.

The word "base" is a form of the Greek word *tapeinos,* which here depicts something that should be minimized or belittled, but Paul fully says who "in presence" am "base" among you. The words "in presence" is a translation of the Greek word *prosopon*, which means *countenance* but more specially describes *the appearance of one's face*. This means Paul's accusers were making fun of his personal appearance and particularly sneering at the appearance of his face.

Why they made fun of Paul's face is not known, but it may be that his face bore the scars of multiple floggings he had endured during the course of his ministry. But regardless of *why*, they *were* laughing at Paul's face, and it was inappropriate to behave in such a way toward someone who had paid such a price as Paul had paid to fulfill his ministry call. Rather than appreciate and honor him for what he had done and had endured for the Church, they unthinkably mocked him, saying that he didn't look good enough to be a leader.

In Second Corinthians 10:7, Paul asked the super apostles, "Do ye look on things after the outward appearance?" The words "outward appearance" are also a translation of the Greek word *prosopon*, which especially describes *the appearance of one's face*. It seems Paul was saying, "After all I've done, is it possible that you are really judging me by the mere appearance of my face?

But in Second Corinthians 10:10, Paul additionally quoted what else the "super apostles" were saying about him. He actually quoted them in part when he wrote, "For his letters, say they, are weighty and powerful; but his bodily presence is weak, and his speech contemptible."

The word "weighty" is the Greek word *barus*, and it means *substantial* and *heavyweight* as opposed to something considered inconsequential or lightweight. The word "powerful" is the Greek word *ischuros,* and it means *mighty* or *strong* and pictures a man with *muscles.* As a phrase, it could be interpreted to mean, "For his epistles are substantial, heavyweight material that can really put muscles on you...." However, they then sarcastically added, "...But his bodily presence is weak, and his speech contemptible."

The words "bodily presence" is a derogatory way of describing Paul's physical body. Early Christian writers tell us that Paul was physically unimpressive and small in stature. From his own words in Galatians 6:17, we know that he bore "marks" in his body from the beatings he had received at various times as the devil tried to stop his ministry. The word "marks" in Galatians 6:17 is the Greek word *stigma,* a horrible word that depicts literal scars that Paul bore in his physical body from the rods he was beaten with at Pisidian Antioch, the stoning at Lystra, and other multiple beatings Paul refers to in Second Corinthians 11:23-25.

But the word *stigma* is also where we get our English word "stigma," which describes something that disgraces or humiliates. Due to the lashes laid on Paul's physical frame, it is entirely possible that Paul's face and body caused some to see him as a *stigma.*

The "super apostles" went about boasting and gloating about how impressive and great they were as so-called "superstars" of the Early Church. But Paul who seemed to admit he perhaps wasn't the greatest of orators — or as physically enjoyable to look at as others — did have the true signs of an apostle, and among those signs was a Christ-like attitude of humility and meekness.

In Matthew 20:25-27, Jesus called His apostles to him and told them, "... Ye know that the princes of the Gentiles exercise dominion over them, and they that are great exercise authority upon them. But it shall not be so among you: but whosoever will be great among you, let him be your minister; and whosoever will be chief among you, let him be your servant." Hence, a person who is truly great must have an attitude of humility and be willing to serve as Jesus did.

While an apostle indeed moves in great apostolic authority, he is to understand that his authority is to be marked with humility and that it was given to him, not to dominate, but to help build up others. This is why Paul wrote that "...the Lord has given me for edification and not for destruction" (2 Corinthians 13:10 *NKJV*).

Thus, because an apostle has been entrusted with divine revelation and spiritual authority and has been dispatched as the Lord's emissary to assist in building the Body of Christ and the *naos* Temple of God, he is required to be willing to do whatever Christ asks him to do to fulfill his role in seeing the Church established. While the apostle indeed carries authority and "spiritual clout," Christ expects him to demonstrate the attitude of a true servant as was exemplified in the life and ministry of Jesus Himself.

Paul reprimanded those who were arrogant and went about boasting that they were "super apostles," and he reminded every apostolic individual that he is to be given without reservation to the fulfilling of God's purposes for the Church. Hence, the required attitude of a Christ-given apostle is one of humility, not boasting, bragging, or going about to prove what a great apostle he may purport himself to be.

Why Did Paul Write That He Was Born 'Out of Due Season'?

Many people are bewildered by Paul's words in First Corinthians 15:8,9, where he wrote that he was "...as of one born out of due time." Because people ask the question in connection with Paul's apostleship, I will share expositorily what this statement means.

In the above-mentioned verses, Paul fully wrote, "And last of all he [Christ] was seen of me also, *as of one born out of due time*. For I am the least of the apostles, that am not meet to be called an apostle, because I persecuted the church of God."

Notice the intriguing statement Paul made in verse 8 where he said that he was "...as of one born out of due time." In this text, Paul stated that Christ appeared to the original apostles after His resurrection, but was last of all seen by Paul much later. Recalling that Paul was a member of the inner religious circle in Jerusalem — the most cloistered and strictly religious Jewish leaders of the city — it is entirely possible that Paul (then called Saul) had physically seen Jesus when He was in the city of Jerusalem. It is hard to fathom that a man as deeply entrenched in the religious system as Saul had not been aware of a radical Teacher from Galilee who was making "big noise" in Jerusalem.

Some scholars even suggest the possibility that Saul was among the religious leaders who treated Jesus contemptuously and slapped, spat, and cursed Jesus the night He was betrayed. Whether this is true or not, we know from Luke's account in Acts 9:1-8 that Jesus did, in fact, appear to Saul on the road to Damascus. We furthermore have Paul's own testimony of that event in the words of Acts 26 where Paul testified of his encounter with Christ to King Agrippa.

But regardless of these divine appearances of Christ to Paul (then called Saul), Paul writes that his "seeing" Christ was different from the other, original apostles who walked with Jesus, physically visited with Jesus on multiple occasions after His resurrection. Indeed, other of the apostles had physically seen and touched Christ.

But in First Corinthians 15:8, Paul states that Christ appeared to him "last" in this particular group of appearances. This does *not* mean it was Christ's all-time last appearance to people after His resurrection. We know that Christ appeared later to Stephen at the time of martyrdom (*see* Acts 7:54-56), and the apostle John testified that Christ appeared to him on the island of Patmos (*see* Revelation 1:9-20). Paul testified in Acts 26:9,22-24 that Christ would appear to him again to give him divine revelation. And, indeed, throughout the ages, Christ has appeared to many people.

But concerning the sequence of appearances to apostles after the resurrection, Paul wrote that he was *the last* to see him — Christ's appearance to him was the last appearance in this particular sequence of appearances Paul was describing (*see* 1 Corinthians 15:7,8).

Paul then described himself "as one born out of due time" (1 Corinthians 15:8). The word "as" is the Greek word *hosperei,* which means *just as, just like,* or *similar to,* and the words as "one born out of due time" is a translation of the single Greek word *ektroma.* This unusual word *ektroma* — used only here in the New Testament — is the Greek word for *a sudden and unexpected birth* and the word used among Greeks for *an abortion.* Paul does not elaborate on what he means by using the word *ektroma,* but in this verse, the word carries two possible meanings.

First, it could depict *a sudden, unexpected, violent birth of a baby,* like an infant that is born before its expected time for delivery. The birth occurs so quickly that no one is prepared and it takes everyone involved off guard. Some scholars assert that Paul used *ektroma*, which means *an untimely birth,* as his way of describing the abrupt manner in which he came to Christ on the road to Damascus.

Certainly, Paul did not anticipate calling Jesus the lord of his life on that day, yet in a split second, he was born again, passing from the deep darkness of spiritual death into the blazing light of God's glory. In this sense, the word *ektroma* really could describe his conversion.

But, *second*, there is another possibility that is also quite glorious. The word *ektroma* was the well-known word used for an abortion — and Paul, a linguistic scholar, certainly knew of its normal usage. It is a fact that Saul was a religious zealot dispatched with a religious police force provided to him by the religious leaders in Jerusalem to persecute Christian believers. This is clearly stated by Luke in the book of Acts who even tells us that Saul was present and casted his vote for the execution and martyrdom of Stephen as recorded in Acts 7:57-60.

Luke wrote even more about Saul's aggressive and demon-inspired hunt against the Christian believers in Jerusalem. In Acts 8:1-3, he recorded, "And Saul was consenting unto his death. And at that time there was a great persecution against the church which was at Jerusalem; and they were all scattered abroad throughout the regions of Judaea and Samaria, except the apostles. And devout men carried Stephen to his burial, and made great lamentation over him. As for Saul, he made havock of the church, entering into every house, and haling men and women committed them to prison."

There is no arguing with the fact that Satan intended to use Saul as a menace to persecute and kill many early believers. But that demonically inspired plan changed abruptly when Christ appeared to an unsuspecting Saul on the road to Damascus. In a split second, the demonic scheme that Satan had planned for Saul to be a notorious Christian killer was abruptly interrupted — *aborted* — by the power of God.

Paul referred to that *abortive moment* in Philippians 3:12 when he writes that he was "apprehended" very suddenly by Christ Jesus on the road to Damascus. The word "apprehended" in Philippians 3:12 is the Greek word *katalambano,* a compound of *kata* and *lambano.* The preposition *kata* means *down*, and the word *lambano* means *to take*. Compounded, it means *to seize, to grab hold of, to pull down, to tackle, to conquer, to master, to take down, or to hold under one's power.* Paul uses the word *katalambano* to declare that Christ literally laid hold of him, seized him, took him down, and mastered him. His conversion was carried out abruptly as Christ intervened in his life and *aborted* the devil's plans for him.

But delving further into First Corinthians 15:9, we find that Paul added, "For I am the least of the apostles, that am not meet to be called an apostle, because I persecuted the church of God." The word "least" is a translation of the Greek word *elachistos,* which means *the least* — and in this particular case, it carries the idea, *"I am the last and most unexpected one to be an apostle of Christ."*

When he recalled how he had been the instrument Satan intended to use in shutting down the Church, Paul was completely stunned by the grace of God on his life. Instead, Paul remarkably became an apostle, or *an architect*, for the same Church he once tried to destroy.

All of this was so unlikely and far-fetched, and Paul continued his recollections, saying, "...Because I persecuted the church of God" (1 Corinthians 15:9). The word "persecuted" is a translation for the word *dioko*, a word that means *to hunt, to chase, or to pursue.* It denoted the actions of a hunter who strategically followed in hot pursuit of an animal in order to apprehend it, capture it, or kill it.

So like a hunter who strategically follows an animal until is it captured or killed, Paul's intention had been to capture and kill Christians. But instead, Christ reached in to gloriously capture *him* on the road to Damascus. In the flash of a moment, Saul was *ektroma* — suddenly and abruptly — born again. And in that moment, Satan's demonic plan for Saul's life was terminated — *aborted* — by the power of God.

I pray this answer provides some insight as to why Paul said in First Corinthians 15:8 that he was "as of one born out of due time."

Like a hunter who strategically follows an animal until is it captured or killed, Paul's intention had been to capture and kill Christians. But instead, Christ reached in to gloriously capture *him* on the road to Damascus.

Why Is It So Difficult To Name More Living Apostles Today?

Most Christians living in a Western environment are familiar with names of notable Christian leaders in their Western society, and they are *less* familiar with those who live off the beaten track in regions far away — *where most apostolic people are located.* Simply because Western Christians live in sections of the world where churches abound, they are familiar with Christians who nearly have celebrity status, such as best-selling authors, songwriters, musicians, TV hosts, and prophets, evangelists, pastors, and teachers, who often have large ministries and can be seen in various media.

But we have seen in preceding chapters that apostolic work is a ground-breaking, foundation-laying work that occurs foremostly on front lines and in territories where the presence of the Church is negligible or perhaps even nonexistent. Thus, who apostles are, and the work they do, is usually unobservable and far from the eyes of Western believers. As a result, apostles' work is often less known, unless they have learned to communicate what they are doing with those who commissioned them and who financially support their front-line work.

A modern-day example is an apostolic brother in the far east of Russia who lives in the tundra where he ministers to the indigenous people. Because the indigenous people of that region are "closed" to outsiders, it is practically impossible to observe his work among them. Hence, his monumental apostolic work is not widely known among Westerners even though he has a powerful work in the territory of those indigenous people, in which he has laid the foundation of the Church among them. Due to the remoteness of his work, his apostolic endeavors are practically unknown except to those who commissioned and sent him and to his very small handful of financial supporters.

Certainly, apostles can work in Western countries, cities, and sectors of society where the Church is already existent, but perhaps is minimally present. For example, in large cities like New York, Paris, London, Rome, Moscow, and so on, there are large neighborhoods and geographical areas that are completely unreached, where the church as yet needs to be established. Especially in larger cities of millions of inhabitants, it is a fact that churches may flourish in some parts of the city, but be nearly absent in other parts of the city. And, indeed, sometimes modern-day apostles work in nations or places where the historical church over time has become ritualized and irrelevant and needs to be re-established in the power of the Holy Spirit.

But apostles do not normally flourish where the Christian community is well-established. So it is likely that even if Christ calls them to apostolically minister in a larger Western city, their calling will lead them far from the exciting church-filled meetings where most Christians congregate. Instead, their calling will lead them to unreached sections of that city. But because apostles minister off the beaten track, it is a fact that the very nature of their ministry means what they do is far from the gaze of Christians who live in the Western world where the Church is well-established. Therefore, who apostles are and what they do may be much less known than other Christ-given ministry gifts.

In Second Corinthians 10:16, Paul stated that his apostolic ministry took him to regions "beyond," whereas other believers lived in their already established Christian communities. Paul affirmed that the apostolic calling led them to regions that were usually beyond the sight of Western believers.

There are some apostolic individuals who *are* known because they make trips to the West to report what God is doing in their ministries in the remote regions where they serve. Some have communicated professionally and often with the churches, organizations, and Christians who support their ministries — thus, their work is more well-known. But for the most part, what most active apostles do is unknown simply because of where they are called to serve on the front lines.

Furthermore, there are fewer apostles in the world today than are reported in various media by many who call themselves apostles, yet who are not. As stated in Chapter Three, I do not question the sincerity of those who mistakenly call themselves apostles. I choose to believe that those who mistakenly call themselves apostles — or who are mistakenly called apostles by others — do it because they lack understanding concerning who an apostle is and what an apostle does. The purpose of this book is intended to help bring clarity to that question.

Why Did Paul Write That Apostles Were 'Set Forth' as 'Last' and 'Appointed to Death'?

In First Corinthians 4:9, Paul wrote about the challenges that apostles encounter due to the front-line nature of their ministry. He wrote, "For I think that God hath set forth us the apostles last, as it were appointed to death: for we are made a *spectacle* unto the world, and to angels, and to men." These words are written by one of the most powerful and legendary apostles to ever live, so let's consider the words in this verse and what they tell us about the challenges that accompany the front-line ministry of apostles.

Paul began in verse 9 by saying, "For I think that God hath set forth us the apostles last...." Notice Paul said "I think" God has "set forth" us apostles as "last." The words "I think" are a form of the Greek word *dokeo,* which here means *in my personal opinion* or *in my personal estimation.* Herein, Paul provided his own personal view — based on his own experience of being an apostle — that it seemed God "set forth" apostles as "last."

Those who do not grasp the front-line nature of apostleship — and the difficult territory that goes along with apostolic ministry — tend to focus on the supernatural signs and wonders of an apostle, thus glamorizing it and not comprehending the difficulties that can accompany apostolic ministry. While Paul embraced his apostolic calling, he did not glamorous it — but, in fact, he stated that in his personal view, it seemed God "set forth" apostles as "last." But what do the words "set forth" and "last" in this verse mean?

The words "set forth" are translated from a form of the word *apokeinumi.* This Greek word indisputably means *to vividly portray*, *to point out*, *to illustrate*, or *to make a vivid presentation.* Paul then added the word "last," which is a form of *eschatos*, a word that points to *the extreme end of a thing*, like the *very ends of the earth* or *the last stopping point on a long and distant journey.*

As Paul used it in this verse, the word "last" describes *the far-off nature of apostolic ministry at the ends of the earth.* It also implies that apostles are called to minister in places that others might see as a *dead-end* and *end-of-the-road.* These are, of course, locations where others have never gone, where others would never choose to go, and where it is not clear what exists in the next part of their journey because it is beyond where others have gone before them.

Then Paul continued in verse 9 to add, "For I think that God hath set forth us the apostles last, as it were appointed to death…."

These words "appointed to death" are powerful and must be understood. These words "appointed to death" are a translation of the Greek word *epithantios*, which is so rare that it is only used in this verse in the entire New Testament. The word *epithantios* is a compound of *epi* and *thanatos.* The preposition *epi* means *for* and is an *intensifier* in this compound word. It means *exactly for* and it applies to *thanatos*. But what is *thanatos?* It is the Greek word for *mortal danger* or *a dangerous circumstance*, and it was used to denote *a death sentence* issued by a court of law.

In First Corinthians 4:9, Paul is clearly expressing: *"Based on my personal experience, it seems God has made it abundantly clear that apostles are to be dispatched to the ends of the earth — to the dead-end places where no one else wants to go and where no one has a clue what lies beyond. And their unique calling means they will live and work in mortally dangerous circumstances where the reality of death accompanies them in that territory."*

It is not always the case that apostles are called to areas that are dangerous, but due to the nature of their calling to go where no man has gone before, apostles do encounter situations that other ministry gifts may never encounter. However, as we have seen in previous chapters, one of the major spiritual tools God has given to the apostle as a part of his spiritual equipment is *supernatural endurance*. And it is a fact that true apostles are divinely enabled to endure and press through what would normally be shattering to other people.

But Paul furthermore added in First Corinthians 4:9, "…For we are made a *spectacle* unto the world, and to angels, and to men."

The word "spectacle" is translated from the word *theatron,* a word that is derived from the Greek *theaomai,* a word that means *to observe, to watch, to study, to scrutinize, or to bring upon the stage for all to see.* It pictures spectators in a Roman theater who are watching a scenario being played on a stage before them. The spectators sit on the edge of their seats, often with anticipation for the performers onstage to make a mistake or to forget a line so they can *scorn, ridicule*, and *make fun* of them. In Hebrews 10:33, the same word is used, but it is correctly translated *gazingstock.* Thus, the word *theatron* that Paul used in First Corinthians 4:9 means to bring onto the stage for all to see and to scorn, to scoff and sneer at, to shame, to publicly humiliate, and to make a laughingstock. This word means, in effect, *to disparagingly make a humiliating spectacle of someone.*

It is a fact that true apostles are divinely enabled to endure and press through what would normally be shattering to other people.

In ancient Greek theaters, drama was performed and lectures were given for sophisticated audiences. But by the time of the First Century when Paul wrote his epistles, the Roman theater had become a place of incivility, and riotous crowds laughed at, mocked, and scorned those onstage. The theater was filled with such offensive behavior that Christians generally avoided attending any events held there. The audience was so vulgar that Christ-loving people deemed it an inappropriate location because they knew that the scornful, scoffing, shaming, sneering, and humiliating behavior was reprehensible in the sight of God.

And then Paul, a brilliant linguist who understood all the nuances associated with the word *theatron*, selected this word to express the world's lack of appreciation for what he and other apostles were doing for the cause of Christ to establish the Church in new locations. Rather than appreciate the ministry God entrusted to him and other apostles, Paul states that based on his experience, his estimation was that the world scorned, scoffed and sneered at, shamed, publicly humiliated, and even made them out to be a laughingstock.

He added that apostles were "...a spectacle unto the world, and to angels, and to men." The word "world" is a translation of the word *kosmos*, which in this case depicts every spectrum of *society*. The word "angels" is the plural form of the Greek word *angelos*, which in this verse includes *angels* and other *spiritual beings* in the spirit realm. The word "men" is the plural of *anthropos*, and here it depicts all of mankind.

In essence, Paul was saying, *"We are made a spectacle to every spectrum of society, to angels, to all spiritual beings in the spirit realm, and to all mankind. We are on the stage for all three of these audiences to watch us, and they are all giving it their best efforts to scorn, scoff at, shame, sneer at, and publicly humiliate us. We have become a laughingstock and a spectacle to each of these realms."*

Paul amplified these words by adding, "...We are made as the filth of the world, and are the offscouring of all things unto this day" (1 Corinthians 4:13). This verse requires a study of the original Greek to fully understand the message contained in it. Not only does this verse give us a glimpse into the challenges Paul and other apostles faced, but it lets us know how they emotionally felt when these things happened to them.

The exact phrase Paul used in First Corinthians 4:13 is "the filth of the world." It is translated from the Greek word *perikatharma*, a compound of the words *peri* and *kathairo*. The word *peri* means *around*, and the word *kathairo* means *to cleanse* or *to purify*. The latter word depicts the removal of disgusting grime, like the dirty ring left on the sides of a bathtub when dirty water is drained. If that filth is allowed to remain on the bathtub very long, it becomes hard, crusty, and difficult to remove. At that point, getting rid of that hardened "ring around the tub" requires determination and a lot of hard work. It means someone has to get on his hands and knees and *scrub*. Only after a lot of persistent, nonstop scouring can that hardened, grimy ring around the tub be eliminated.

This is the idea Paul conveyed when he said that he and other apostles had been treated like "the filth of the world." Instead of appreciating these apostles for all they had done to bring light into darkness, the unbelieving world had repeatedly tried to wipe them out. In the world's view, these ministers of the Gospel were *the scum of the earth*.

The words "the filth of the world" was also one of the lowest, crudest, derogatory statements that could be made about someone in the First Century. To call someone "the filth of the world" was a *terrible* insult. It was a specific phrase used to describe low-level people in society, such as criminals deemed unworthy to live. If a city had a chain of bad fortune, public officials would give the order for the "filth of the world" — low-level criminals — to be rounded up and publicly sacrificed. They believed that if this societal *scum* could be exterminated, it could reverse a city's bad fortune.

When Paul said that he and other apostles were treated like "the filth of the world," he let us know that they had been blamed for many things that had nothing to do with them. Over and over again, when something wrong happened, someone would likely cry out, *"It's the preacher's fault!"* Rather than thank Paul and other apostles for the many sacrifices they had made, the world treated them with the same disdain they would a dirty ring around a tub that needed to be wiped out. In addition to leveling terrible insults at them, large segments of the pagan population believed if they could just get rid of Christians, it would somehow bring good luck to them once again.

But Paul went on to say that they were treated like the "offscouring of all things." The word "offscouring" is a translation of the Greek word *peripsema*, which depicts *the ardent and ferocious process required to remove filth and grime*. No one wants to live in the middle of filth, and no one wants to take a bath in a tub covered with grime. When the situation gets sufficiently distasteful, someone will eventually step forward to say, "Let's do something about this sickening dirt! Let's get rid of it." The word "offscouring" depicted that moment when the world cried out, *"Enough of these Gospel preachers! Let's get rid of this filth!"*

From time to time, publicly elected officials gave the order for low-level people, criminals, and societal "scum" to be rounded up and executed. Their intention was to *scrub out that scum* from society. Paul used these same vivid phrases to tell us what the world was saying about him and other apostles. Although they were preaching and doing the good works of Jesus, Paul wrote that the world viewed them as scum that needed to be removed. The unsaved world actually believed they would be better off if these light-bearers were exterminated.

When Paul wrote that he and the other apostles were the "filth of the world" and the "offscouring of all things," this verse could be interpreted, *"The world views us like dirt that needs to be wiped off, and they are doing everything they can to scrub us out of society. We have become the scapegoats for everyone's problems. They point their fingers at us and blame us for everything wrong in the world. What they would really like to do is permanently get rid of us!"*

In First Corinthians 4:9,13, Paul used these extremely vivid words to express his own appraisal of the special challenges those with an apostolic calling may experience as they take the Gospel to the ends of the earth and lay the foundation of the Church where it has never existed before.

Then in Second Corinthians 12:12, Paul writes, "Truly the signs of an apostle were wrought among you in all patience, in signs, and wonders, and mighty deeds." As noted in Chapter Four, the first "sign" or authenticating marker to alert someone that he is seeing a real apostle is that the person will be accompanied by *patience.*

For sure, apostolic ministry is real front-line ministry — it is a spiritual military expedition to push into new territory, to fight against the powers of darkness, and then to bulldoze demonic opposition out of the way so the foundation of the Church can be established where it never existed before. If there was ever a divine virtue that an apostle needs, it is this divine element that Paul calls *patience.*

As noted earlier, the word "patience" is a form of the Greek word *hupomone*, which is a compound of *hupo* and *meno.* The word *hupo* means *under* and the word *meno* means *to stay* or *to abide.* Compounded into the word *hupomeno,* it means *to remain in one's spot regardless of how heavy or hard the situation; to keep a position; to resolve to maintain territory gained.* In a military sense, it pictures *soldiers ordered to maintain their positions even in the face of opposition.* It depicts *one that defiantly sticks it out regardless of pressures mounted against him.* It can also be described as *staying power* or *"hang-in-there" power* or *the attitude that holds out, holds on, outlasts, perseveres, and hangs in there, never giving up, refusing to surrender to obstacles, and turning down every opportunity to quit.* It is a picture *of one who is under a heavy load but refuses to bend, break, or surrender because he is convinced that the territory, promise, or principle under assault rightfully belongs to him.*

Indeed, if a person is called to be a genuine apostle, that call will be evidenced by a supernatural endurance *to stay put* and not to abandon ship when things get tough. In fact, by placing *patience* first on this list, Paul forcefully let us know that this *supernatural patience* — or better, *endurance* — is one of the chief signs of one's real apostleship. Only a douse of this supernatural patience and endurance can give sufficient strength to an apostle to keep pressing forward when it seems all "hell" is raging against him. Paul listed this kind of patience and endurance as supernatural evidence of real apostleship.

What Is the Glory and Crown of an Apostle?

First, Jesus' original apostles, in addition to receiving a regular apostle's reward (*see* Matthew 10:41), will sit as judges of the 12 tribes of Israel as recorded in the gospels and the book of Revelation.

The calling and work of an apostle is difficult. As noted in the previous section, people without a deeper understanding of what it means to be an apostle tend to glamorize this gift, but those who are genuine apostles especially have a more realistic view of what it means to stand in this Christ-given office.

So what is the reward that both temporarily and eternally awaits those who have served apostolically throughout history? We can approach the answer to this question several ways, but let's begin more generally with a promise that Christ makes to *anyone* who pays a price to obediently follow His call.

Matthew 19:28,29, "And Jesus said unto them, Verily I say unto you, That ye which have followed me, in the regeneration when the Son of man shall sit in the throne of his glory, ye also shall sit upon twelve thrones, judging the twelve tribes of Israel. And *every one* that hath forsaken houses, or brethren, or sisters, or father, or mother, or wife, or children, or lands, for my name's sake, shall receive an hundredfold, and shall inherit everlasting life."

In verse 28, Jesus promised the original apostles He chose that they would one day "sit upon twelve thrones, judging the twelve tribes of Israel." This is a unique promise made only to the original apostles. But Jesus broadens the promise in verse 29 to say, "And every one that hath forsaken houses, or brethren, or sisters, or father, or mother, or wife, or children, or lands, for my name's sake, shall receive an hundredfold, and shall inherit everlasting life." In Mark 10:30, Jesus clarifies that every person who has followed Him obediently "…shall receive an hundredfold *now* in this time, houses, and brethren, and sisters, and mothers, and children, and lands, with persecutions; and in the world to come eternal life."

The word "now" in Greek is *nun* and it means *now*, as in *right now*. In the Greek text, it then says *en to kairo touto* — which as a complete phrase meaning *now, right now, in this present time*. Thus, we see that the original apostles will sit upon twelve thrones and will judge the twelve tribes of Israel, but *anyone* who has left all to obediently follow Jesus will be rewarded *now* — that is right now, in this present time. Jesus expounded that they will have a hundredfold reward of everything they have left or sown — including houses, lands, brethren, sisters, mothers, children, lands — *and* persecutions. And in the world to come, they'll have eternal life. This is a promise made to anyone who obediently follows the call of Christ.

The apostle Paul also wrote that in this lifetime — during the time of their ministries — anyone who serves in full-time ministry should be supported and compensated for their service. In First Corinthians 9:13,14, he wrote, "Do ye not know that they which minister about holy things live *of the things* of the temple? and they which wait at the altar are partakers with the altar? Even so hath the Lord ordained that they which preach the gospel should live of the gospel."

The Greek word translated "even so" in verse 14 means *so also* or *in the same manner*. Then Paul added that the Lord has "...ordained that they which preach the gospel should live of the gospel."

The word "ordained" is the Greek word *diatasso*, a unique word that means *to prescribe*, *to arrange*, or *to fix*, and it depicts *a command made with authority that the giver, or issuer, of that command expects to be carried out and obeyed.* It is an order that comes to us from God and one that He expects to be fulfilled. Furthermore, the word "live" in this verse depicts one's livelihood.

So Paul was saying, in essence, "Even so, those who are prescribed by God's authoritative command to preach the Gospel should make their livelihood from the Gospel." This is a reward that belongs in this present life to anyone who serves full time in the ministry. Paul stated that anyone who serves full time has a right to be compensated for what that individual does in his or her work for the Lord, and this would include the ministry of apostles.

But there is another reward in this life for those who are apostles. Paul refers to it in Philippians 4:1, where he writes, "Therefore, my brethren dearly beloved and longed for, my joy and crown…."

In Acts 16, Paul and Silas traveled to Philippi where they encountered a group of women at the river. Among them was a woman named Lydia, who originally came from Thyatira, who sold purple and had become immensely wealthy. After Lydia's conversion, with her household, things went well in Philippi in Paul and Silas' ministry until Paul cast a spirit of divination of out of a woman in the central market. Because the woman with a spirit of divination had brought great income to her owners, those owners were infuriated that she had lost her ability to practice divination.

At the end of a long and difficult day, Paul and Silas were thrown into jail to await their trial and possible execution. But at about midnight, they began to praise and worship God, and as they did, God sent an earthquake that shook the chains off them and also shook open the door to the prison so they could go free. When the jailor saw that the prison doors were opened and prisoners were going free, he pulled out his sword to kill himself. But before he could do it, Paul stopped him from committing suicide and then preached the Gospel to him. That night the jailor and his household were converted, and Paul baptized him and his whole family.

I give you this brief history to remind you that Paul apostolically started the church in Philippi, and as the apostle to the Philippian church, he had a precious, long-standing relationship with them, and the congregation in Philippi regularly supported Paul's ministry as his financial partners. So when Paul told them, "You are my crown and joy," these were very precious, heartfelt words for him to speak.

When Paul thought of the Philippians, his heart probably leaped for joy because they were such solid fruit from his labors among them. They themselves were such a reward to him that he called them his "joy" and "crown." The word "joy" is translated from the Greek word *chara,* a derivative of *charis,* which is translated in the New Testament as *grace*. When Paul considered the Philippians, his ministry to them, and the long-lasting fruit of his endeavors among them, he saw God's mighty grace outwardly manifesting — and it gave him joy. In this sense, when an apostle has given his life to lay the foundation of a church and that church functions well over many years, it brings a reward of joy to the foundation-layer. This is a present reward that blesses the heart of any apostolic individual.

Paul also calls the Philippian believers his "crown." The word "crown" is translated from the Greek word *stephanos*, and it is the word for a literal diadem or crown that a mighty ruler would wear upon his head. Fabricated of gold and other precious metals and decorated with spectacular gems, such crowns were breathtaking and represented power and glory for the wearer. But now Paul stated that the Philippians were not only his joy — that is, an expression of God's grace in his life — but they were also a *present* reward to him, like a regal crown on his brow. They are proof of his apostleship and a garland that graced his life!

Paul made a nearly identical statement to the church in Thessalonica, another church that he apostolically started. In First Thessalonians 2:19,20, he told them, "For what is our hope, or joy, or crown of rejoicing? Are not even ye in the presence of our Lord Jesus Christ at his coming? For ye are our glory and joy."

While Paul and all who serve full time in ministry are to be financially compensated correctly for their ministries, and this is certainly the right thing to do, there is no better reward for an apostle than to know the church he established is doing well — that it is prospering, growing in the grace of God, and staying on track with God's Word and the vision of the Great Commission. Just as the church in Philippi was doing well, the church in Thessalonica was thriving. Just hearing of it caused Paul to say that they were his crown of rejoicing, indeed — his glory and joy.

When we come to Second Timothy 4:6-8, we find that Paul's life was coming to an end, and he knew that it would soon be time for him to see the Lord and be eternally rewarded for his labor. In those verses, he said, "For I am now ready to be offered, and the time of my departure is at hand. I have fought a good fight, I have finished my course, I have kept the faith: henceforth there is laid up for me a crown of righteousness, which the Lord, the righteous judge, shall give me at that day: and not to me only, but unto all them also that love his appearing."

The apostle's reward — his ultimate glory — is the crown that the Lord will give him on the day he sees Jesus. Along the way, there are other rewards, as we have seen, including *financial compensation*, *seeing churches established*, *experiencing the power of God*, *knowing that one's work is thriving*...all of these are apostolic rewards. But the ultimate reward for apostolic work will be received on the day that an apostle looks into the eyes of the Perfect Apostle, who is Jesus.

All earthly and temporal honors and rewards eventually pass away, but *that* reward will endure for all eternity. It is the ultimate glory, or reward, that apostles receive from the hand of the Lord. This is the reward of all rewards — the praise that comes from God. After the good fight has been fought, the race has been run, and the faith has been kept, the apostle will receive his eternal reward. And what greater reward could be laid up for him than this?

In Summary

There is much more we could cover on the subject of apostolic ministry. I do not suggest this book has comprehensively covered the breadth of this important topic, but it is my prayer that what you have read has helped to fill in empty spaces where you perhaps didn't fully understand the meaning and foundational role of apostles.

In this last hour of the Church Age, it is vital that we clearly understand the role of apostles in the past, present — contemporary, or modern-day — and in the last-days Church. We must get our bearings straight on this issue to avoid confusion in the ranks. But until the Church reaches the maturity Christ dreams for it to possess, each of the Christ-given fivefold ministry gifts is so vitally needed to help perform this maturing function, and that includes the present-day ministry of *the apostle.*

In the following chapter, we will move on to examine what the Bible tells us about Christ-given fivefold prophets and the unique roles they held in the past, their roles in present, and their prophetic roles in the last-days Church. Just as apostles are needed until the church reaches maturity, God-called individuals with prophetic voices will be operating in the earth and in the Church until the end of the age.

Let's get started on our discussion of the gift of the prophet.

Questions for Deeper Consideration

Chapter 6

1. People tend to focus on the foundation-laying aspect of an apostle's ministry or perhaps on the signs and wonders that accompany his ministry. But from what you read in this chapter — and based on Mark 3:13-15 — what is the highest calling of an apostle?

2. Apostles possess spiritual authority. But what kind of authority does a true apostle possess and do all apostles have the same level of authority? How would you describe the authority of an apostle after reading this chapter? With whom does an apostle have authority?

3. Most God-called ministers have different styles. Similarly, different apostles have different styles and flavors in their ministries. Do all apostles operate similarly and have the same types of gifts and ministries? Are they "cookie-cutter" in their approach to ministry, or do they have characteristics that make each of them unique? In what various ways can one apostle's ministry be distinct from another's?

4. After reading this chapter, what would you say to this question: Is it possible for an apostle to also operate in the other fivefold ministry gifts? If you look at Paul's writings and his example in the New Testament, did

Paul operate in other fivefold ministry gifts? If yes, what were the other offices Paul operated in?

5. In First Corinthians 15:8 and 9, Paul wrote a phrase that has perplexed scholars for ages. He stated that he was "as one born out of due season." This mystifying statement has baffled many commentators who try to make sense out of what Paul said. In this chapter, it has been demonstrated clearly what the Greek text means. After what you have read in this chapter, can you now explain what Paul meant when he wrote he was "as one born out of due season"?

6. It has been established that apostles are still active in the Church today — so why is it so problematic to name very many current-day apostles? Ephesian 4:11-15 clearly teaches that apostles will be functional until the end of the Church Age. Since this is the case, where are they and why it is hard to specifically name authentic apostles?

7. Paul wrote vividly in First Corinthians 4:9 about challenges that apostles encounter due to the frontline nature of their ministry. He wrote, "For I think that God hath set forth us the apostles last, as it were appointed to death: for we are made a spectacle unto the world, and to angels, and to men...." After reading this material in this chapter, do you now understand why Paul used such words to describe apostolic ministry?

CHAPTER 7

WHAT IS A PROPHET?

Surely the Lord God will do nothing, but he revealeth his secret unto his servants the prophets.

— Amos 3:7

And he gave some, apostles; and some, prophets; and some, evangelists; and some, pastors and teachers; for the perfecting of the saints, for the work of the ministry, for the edifying of the body of Christ.

— Ephesians 4:11,12

We have established that Christ intends for all the fivefold ministry gifts of *apostle*, *prophet*, *evangelist*, *pastor*, and *teacher* to be operational in the Church *for a specific purpose* and *for all time* until the conclusion of the Church Age.

In Ephesians 4:11 and 12, Paul listed all of the fivefold ministry gifts when he wrote, "And he [Christ] gave some, apostles; and some, prophets; and some, evangelists; and some, pastors and teachers; for the perfecting of the saints, for the work of the ministry, for the edifying of the body of Christ."

We saw in Chapter One that Paul importantly repeats the word "some" in verse 11 in order to emphasize a point. In each instance where the word "some" is used in this verse, it's a translation of a Greek word that should be taken as an *emphatic*, *categorical*, or *exclamatory* remark.

Thus, verse 11 could be translated: "And He gave *indeed*, apostles; and *indeed*, prophets; and *indeed*, evangelists; and *indeed*, pastors and [it is understood to mean *indeed*,] teachers...."

Or it could be translated, "And He gave *emphatically*, apostles; and *emphatically*, prophets; and *emphatically*, evangelists; and *emphatically*, pastors and [it is understood to mean *emphatically*,] teachers...."

Or it could be translated, "And He gave *categorically*, apostles; and *categorically*, prophets; and *categorically*, evangelists; and *categorically*, pastors and [it is understood to mean *categorically*,] teachers...."

The Greek word for "some" in this verse tells us that Paul wanted us to know that Christ has *indeed* — *categorically* and *emphatically* — given the Church the fivefold ministry gifts of *apostle*, *prophet*, *evangelist*, *pastor*, and *teacher*. And the repetitive use of the word "some" — better translated *indeed* — means the perpetual operation of these fivefold gifts should not be in question.

Christ has *indeed — categorically* and *emphatically* — given each of these for the work of the ministry and for the edifying of the Body of Christ, or the constructing, augmenting, and building up of His Temple. And in Ephesians 4:13, Paul stated that these gifts will be operational "till we all come in the unity of the faith, and of the knowledge of the Son of God, unto a perfect man, unto the measure of the stature of the fulness of Christ."

In preceding chapters, we studied extensively about the ministry of the apostle. Now we will see what the Bible tells us about the Christ-given fivefold ministry gift of the prophet. Ephesians 2:20 says that the Church is "...built upon the foundation of the *apostles* and *prophets*...." Since prophets are listed in this verse along with the foundation-laying ministry of apostles, we must understand who a prophet is and what a prophet does in the *naos* Temple of God.

What Does the Word 'Prophet' Mean to You?

In Chapter Three, I shared that when I was growing up in our particular denominational church, we didn't believe in the present-day ministry of apostles. Likewise, we did not believe in the present-day ministry of *prophets*. Our denomination laid a strong doctrinal foundation under my life and taught me how to serve God faithfully in the local church. I am so thankful for what I learned there. But doctrinally, we were what is called *cessationists*. A *cessationist* is one who believes that many aspects of the Holy Spirit's supernatural work *ceased* with the death of the apostles at the end of the Apostolic Age.

Due to the fact that cessationists believe much of the supernatural work of the Holy Spirit has ceased, the following verses demonstrate what cessationists eliminate. First Corinthians 12:6-10, 28-30 and Ephesians 4:11 lists the following as supernatural manifestations given to the Church: prophecy, serving, teaching, exhortation, giving, leading, mercy, the word of wisdom, the word of knowledge, faith, gifts of healings, the working of miracles, discerning of spirits, different kinds of tongues, the interpretation of tongues, apostles, prophets, evangelists, pastors, and teachers.

The following deliberately crossed-out words and phrases are provided to demonstrate what true cessationists believe no longer exists for our age and time: ~~prophecy~~, serving, teaching, exhortation, giving, leading, mercy, ~~the word of wisdom~~, ~~the word of knowledge~~, ~~faith~~, ~~gifts of healings~~, ~~the working of miracles~~, ~~discerning of spirits~~, ~~different kinds of tongues~~, ~~the interpretation of tongues~~, ~~apostles~~, ~~prophets~~, evangelists, pastors, and teachers.

Of all the gifts Christ gave the Church, true cessationists believe that only serving, teaching, exhortation, giving, leading, mercy, evangelists, pastors, and teachers are still in operation today. This demonstrates how a faulty belief can result in the elimination of the supernatural work of the Holy Spirit in many churches.

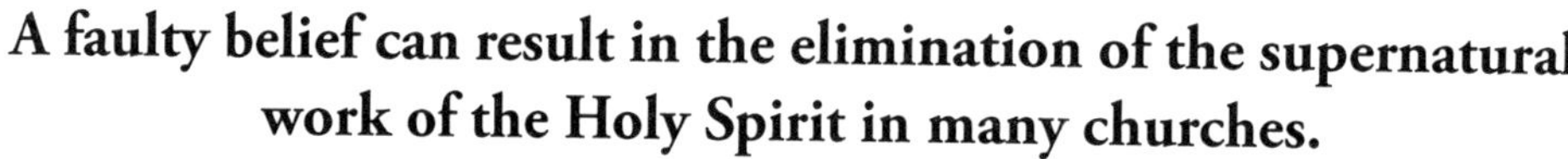

A faulty belief can result in the elimination of the supernatural work of the Holy Spirit in many churches.

The Position of Continuationism

A *continuationist* is a person who believes that all gifts of the Holy Spirit and each of the fivefold ministry gifts have *continued* without interruption from the beginning of the Church Age and will continue to be operative until the end of the Church Age. For clarification, I am a full-fledged believer that all of God's gifts are operative and *will remain* operative until the end of the Church Age. Hence, I am a *continuationist*, and so are you if you believe all the Christ-given gifts are still in operation.

It is important to state that although cessationists believe in a *cessation* of many of the Holy Spirit's manifestations, some cessationists operate in certain supernatural manifestations *unknowingly*. For example, as I said in a previous chapter, some have functioned apostolically in ministry, but were never called apostles. Others have operated in the gifts of the Holy Spirit as enumerated in First Corinthians 12, such as the word of wisdom and the word of knowledge, unaware from a biblical standpoint of what they were doing. Perhaps they called such manifestations an inexplicable "knowing" while remaining cessationist in their doctrine nevertheless.

As I was growing up in our denomination, we dogmatically believed the gifts of the Holy Spirit and the ministries of apostles and prophets ceased at the end of the Apostolic Age. We deemed that whatever it was that Pentecostals and Charismatics were claiming to experience, those experiences were merely foolish, made-up works of the flesh based on bad doctrine and a mishandling of Scripture. In fact, the impression I received was that Pentecostals and Charismatics were simply uneducated and foolish Christians who believed in silliness.

In our doctrinal view, the possibility that the gifts of the Spirit and apostles and prophets could exist in our time and age was ridiculous. But we were very *selective* about what we believed ceased at the end of the Apostolic Age, for we certainly believed in the present-day ministry of evangelists, pastors, and teachers. But apostles and prophets were off the table and relegated to a past age — thus, we believed they were no longer in existence. To us, apostles and prophets were only people who lived in biblical times, and there was no such thing as a living apostle or prophet. In fact, if anyone had dared to call himself or herself a prophet or prophetess, it is likely that we would have laughed and alleged that the person making such a claim needed psychiatric help.

In retrospect, I can see that we were confused about *who* and *what* a prophet is. As I look back at it now, I can see that, in reality, we regularly experienced the ministry of many prophets, but instead of calling them *prophets*, we called them *evangelists*. Back in those days, the term "evangelist" was used to describe nearly anyone who publicly preached in an itinerant ministry, so we lumped every itinerant ministry gift into the category of an evangelist whether he was an evangelist or not. As a result, many Christ-given gifts — including prophets — were wrongly labeled — so much so that many of them even formed "Evangelistic Associations" as a legal umbrella for their ministries.

The likelihood of prophetic ministry was so far removed from the realm of possibility in our minds that even those who were actually functioning as prophets did not know they were prophets because they had never been taught that prophetic ministry still existed.

In Chapter One, I briefly summarized the ministry of an evangelist and showed from the New Testament pattern that a true Christ-given evangelist comes with signs and wonders as a part of the spiritual equipment God has given for his or her ministry. But the fiery preachers we called evangelists in our denomination had no signs and wonders that would be typical of a real New Testament evangelist. Instead, like a New Testament *prophet*, they delivered a powerful word from the heart of God and spoke prophetically to call the Church to a higher standard.

Nevertheless, we called those prophets evangelists — and they even called *themselves* evangelists — because none of us understood that the prophetic ministry gift was still in operation in contemporary times. Hence, there were *many* Christ-given prophets who functioned in the name of evangelists and, as noted, even had evangelistic associations as a legal covering for their ministries.

Stop and think for a moment about the well-known preachers you remember being called evangelists, but who never had the signs or wonders in their ministries that should accompany a New Testament evangelist's ministry. They called sinners to repentance and they called the Church to a higher standard, but the supernatural evidence that follows the ministry of a true Christ-given evangelist was nonexistent. However, they did have the traits of a prophet as they powerfully communicated the heart and mind of God to sinners and saints who gathered to hear their powerful messages.

What Did the Word 'Prophet' Mean in Antiquity?

Historically, the word prophet was a *general term* used by all religions — pagans, Jews, and Christians — to describe any person who served as *a conduit, channel,* or *voice* for the spirit realm. That is the reason why there were prophets of God in the Old Testament who spoke by the Spirit of God, but there were also prophets of *Baal* as well as prophets for other pagan gods.

For example, in First Kings 18 we read about the prophets of Baal that Elijah encountered and defeated on Mount Carmel. Notice they were called *prophets* of Baal. Again, the point is that the word "prophet" was not only a term to describe one of God's prophets, but it was a term used in every ancient religion to depict any person who served as *a conduit, channel,* or *voice* for the spirit realm.

A biblical example of a pagan prophet is *Balaam* (*see* Numbers 22-24). Many who do not understand the tactics that Balaam used in the biblical account have mistaken him for a misled prophet of God. He indeed was a prophet, but everything in the story of Balaam affirms that he was *not* a prophet of God. But because the word "prophet" is used to describe Balaam, many have mistakenly supposed it meant he was a prophet of God, howbeit, a *backslidden* prophet. They failed to understand that the term "prophet" can describe *both* God's prophets and pagan prophets.

The story of Balaam shows clearly that the term "prophet" can depict anyone who is a conduit, channel, or voice for the spirit realm, so let's take a few minutes to look closer at the story of Balaam.

Balaam — A Backslidden Prophet of God or a Pagan Prophet?

Ancient sources contain alternate versions of the story of Balaam, but one thing they have in common is that all of them affirm Balaam was well known in his time as a *pagan prophet*, a *diviner*, and a *soothsayer*. The following paragraphs are adapted from my book *No Room for Compromise,* which I recommend you read if you want to study the subject of Balaam more deeply.

> The first mention of Balaam in the Old Testament is found in Numbers chapter 22. In that chapter, we read that Balak, king of the Moabites, heard of Israel's many victories against other neighboring kingdoms. Because Israel was approaching his territory, Balak feared that his kingdom would also be defeated by Israel's army. Numbers 22:4 states that Balak's first step was to seek an ally against Israel in Midian: "And Moab said unto the elders of Midian, Now shall this company lick up all that are round about us, as the ox licketh up the grass of the field...." Next, Balak "...sent messengers therefore unto *Balaam* the son of Beor at Pethor, which is by the river of the land..." (v. 5). This is the first time Balaam's name appears in the Old Testament.
>
> Exactly which river Numbers 22:5 is referencing cannot be stated with absolute certainty, but most Bible scholars believe that it was the Euphrates River in ancient Mesopotamia. Supporting evidence of this view comes from the 1933 archeological excavation at the site of the ancient city of Mari, which was located on the banks of the Euphrates. During this excavation, cuneiform tablets were unearthed that described in detail the activities of *a cult of soothsayers* and *pagan seers* in that area that reflect much of what we know about Balaam's activities. Given this interesting parallel, it is possible that Mari was in close geographical proximity to Balaam's home. Furthermore, Numbers 22:5 and Deuteronomy 23:4 both state that Balaam lived in a city named "Pethor." The identity of this ancient Mesapotamian city is also shrouded in uncertainty, but the prevailing view is that it was located relatively close to the city of Mari.

In addition to the references in the Old Testament, information about Balaam also comes from an array of other ancient sources. Perhaps the most extraordinary of these is a series of fragmentary inscriptions excavated in 1967 at a site known as *Tell Deir' Alla* in modern-day Jordan — an area that the Bible calls *Succouth* (*see* Genesis 33:17; Judges 8:8; 1 Kings 7:46; Psalm 60:6, 108:7). When pieced together, this incredible archeological find, officially called, "The Balaam Inscriptions" testifies of *a pagan seer* whose name was "Balaam, son of Beor." There is no doubt that the Balaam referenced in these inscriptions is the same man spoken of in the Bible. Thus, they hold particular importance as the most ancient source outside the Bible to affirm that Balaam was known in his time as a notorious *soothsayer.*

The best insights to this Old Testament pagan prophet come to us from ancient Jewish commentaries, especially those written by Jewish scholars in the city of Alexandria. Alexandrian Jews were highly educated and renowned for their ability to keep detailed historical records. From these commentaries, it is evident that educated Jewish historians took Balaam very seriously as a pagan prophet and historical figure. In ancient rabbinic literature, Balaam is essentially viewed as being the pagan equivalent to Moses and it is written about Balaam that he was widely known for his abilities to interpret dreams, practice witchcraft, and foresee the future.

Perhaps most telling is what *Philo*, one of the leading Jewish intellectuals of Alexandria who lived from 20 BC-50 AD wrote about Balaam. Philo wrote that Balaam was "a man renowned above all men for his skill as *a diviner* and *a prophet*, who foretold to the various nations important events, abundance and rain, or droughts and famines, inundations or pestilence." The city of Alexandria was a long-time center of Egyptian witchcraft, sorcery, wizardry, enchantments, incantations, magic, and spells, and the educated Jewish scholars from this city were very familiar with these practices and their descriptions. They had seen occult practices during their sojourning in Egypt, and they knew the difference between a *mere apprentice* and a *master of sorcery*. Thus, for an Alexandrian Jew to write that Balaam was "renowned above all men for his skill as a diviner" indicates Balaam possessed a profound level of skill as a *master sorcerer.*

Probably the most famous Jewish scholar was *Josephus*, whose writings are still considered the most accurate extra-biblical historical account of Jewish history ever written. Josephus wrote that Balaam was among "the greatest of the *prophets* at that time." This is a remarkable statement, since Balaam lived concurrently with the prophet Moses. Yet whereas Moses was an instrument for the power of God, Balaam was an instrument through which the kingdom of darkness found access to the earthly realm.

The use of the word "prophet" in the writings of both Philo and Josephus should not be misunderstood. In these contexts, the word "prophet" does not just refer to a spokesman of God, such as Moses or Elijah. It is clear that Balaam and his practices were diametrically opposed to God's prohibitions regarding the occult in Deuteronomy 18:10-12 and Leviticus 19:26.

Philo and Josephus used the word "prophet" in a general sense to denote *one who was able to foresee the future.* As noted earlier, pagans often used this word "prophet" to denote anyone who was *a conduit, channel*, or *a vocal instrument* for the spirit realm. In this sense of the word, Philo's and Josephus' descriptions were very much in line with what the Bible tells us about Balaam. According to Scripture, Balaam was a *diviner* who operated with powers of *divination* (*see* Numbers 22:7; 23:23). Other common names for "diviners" include *foretellers, seers, soothsayers, consulters of familiar spirits, enchanters, necromancers, wizards, witches* (such as the "witch of Endor"; *see* 1 Samuel 28:3-25), *mediums, clairvoyants*, and *voices through which the spirit realm speaks.*

Ancient diviners used a variety of occult practices to foresee the future, but one especially common practice was to slaughter an animal, spread its entrails on an altar, and attempt to "read" the future by analyzing the strewn organs. Numbers 23 tells us that Balaam accompanied King Balak to multiple mountaintops to offer animal sacrifices *before* this false prophet attempted to curse Israel. This fact has led scholars to speculate that Balaam was using an occult technique to try to read the entrails of these slain animals before he tried to curse Israel.

The ancient world was full of diviners and soothsayers, but none was more notable than Balaam during his time. Balak's own kingdom of Moab certainly had a plethora of diviners, but because Balaam was so renowned as a pagan prophet and sorcerer, Balak sent emissaries nearly 400 miles to plead with Balaam to come and curse the people of Israel on his behalf.

If diviners had a past record of success, they could demand high prices for their divination, and Balak knew that hiring a sorcerer as notable as Balaam would be very expensive. However, the distraught Moabite king was prepared to pay whatever sum was required to coax Balaam to come and curse Israel. Therefore, he sent his emissaries to Balaam, offering to "promote" him with "great honor" (*see* Numbers 22:17). Verse 18 implies that Balak was willing to pay Balaam a great fortune — perhaps even "a house full of silver and gold" — to perform this service.

Balaam was revered as a great *diviner* and *soothsayer* and known far and wide for his supposed abilities to bless or curse. For instance, in Numbers 22:6 (*NKJV*), Balak told Balaam, "...For I know that he whom you bless is blessed, and he whom you curse is cursed." However, despite his reputation, there is not a single biblical record that confirms Balaam actually possessed the ability to bless *or* curse anyone, much less God's people!

After trying to curse Israel three times, Balaam finally was forced to tell Balak, "How shall I curse whom God hath not cursed? Or how shall I defy whom the Lord hath not defied?" (Numbers 23:8). It was simply impossible for Balaam to pronounce a curse where God had pronounced a blessing.

Balaam accompanied King Balak to several mountaintop altars in order to offer pagan sacrifices and to attempt to practice divination against Israel. By doing this, he hoped to open a door to the spirit realm that would give him access to new spiritual power and enable him to speak a curse on Israel (*see* Numbers 23:2,13,27). These attempts quickly proved to be futile, yet Balaam persevered because he had become seduced by the promise of promotion and the large sums of money that Balak had offered him if he could successfully curse Israel (*see* Numbers 22:7,17,37; 23:11; 2 Peter 2:15; Jude 11). Every attempt proved futile, yet Balaam continued to follow Balak to offer sacrifices in the vain hope that a curse could eventually be spoken against Israel.

But no matter how many sacrifices were performed, how much blood was shed on pagan altars, or how much divination was employed, no door to the spirit realm was opened and no power to curse the entire nation of Israel was effective. In fact, Scripture tells us that every time he opened his mouth to speak a curse, a blessing came out (*see* Numbers 23:10). Finally, after failing repeatedly to place a curse on Israel, Balaam conceded that *divination* was no match for the power of God. It was at this point that he told Balak, "Surely there is no *enchantment* against Jacob, neither is there any *divination* against Israel..." (Numbers 23:23).

Balaam — one of history's most famous sorcerers — was unable to penetrate God's protective shield about His people with the inferior powers of Satan!

However, when Balaam finally conceded that he was unable to curse Israel with acts of divination, he took an even more insidious approach to destroy God's people. He might not have been able to curse them, but he knew how to lure Israel into sin and defeat. Therefore, Balaam devised a plan to appeal to the carnal nature of the Israelites — a plan that would lead to *a self-imposed judgment and destruction* based entirely on the works of the flesh. The powers of divination could not harm God's people, but their opening the door through sin provided the access the devil needed to pull them into defeat.

This leads us to "the doctrine of Balaam" that Jesus referred to in Revelation 2:14. Balaam's doctrine was one of *moral surrender*. He sought to lure the men of Israel out of their tents by dangling before their eyes the visual image of scantily clad, perhaps even naked, Moabite women. Then it would simply be a matter of allowing the women to lead the Israelite men to the nearby altar of Baal-peor. Once there, the men would willingly surrender their minds and bodies to sexual abandonment and spiritual defilement of the worst sort, simply for the sake of sensual gratification. Balaam knew that God would not tolerate this act of disobedience among His people. The soothsayer's plan was to get the men of Israel to willfully walk into this trap so their actions would be met with divine punishment. And once the Israelites brought judgment upon themselves, Balaam could receive the handsome fee promised to him by Balak.

At the false prophet's instructions, King Balak sent Moabite women into the Israelite camp to be sensuously displayed before the men of Israel. The Israelite men quickly succumbed to temptation and followed these women to the altar of Baal-peor, where they offered sacrifices, committed fornication, and partook in dark occult rituals. Their actions not only dishonored God, but also opened the door that gave access to their enemies, allowing them to be dragged into defilement, spiritual slavery, defeat, and ultimately into divine chastisement.

The men of Israel let down their guard and were defeated as a result of their own careless attitude toward sin. This biblical account stands as a warning to us that although God protects His children, we must still take a vigilant attitude that guards against sin, or we will be ill-affected in spite of His merciful protection.

When Balaam taught Balak to seduce Israel, Balaam was very aware that God would not overlook spiritual and moral compromise and that the actions of the Israelite men would result in divine punishment, thus ridding Balak of the impending threat of Israel's armies. What Balaam did *not* count on was that God would hold him and Balak responsible for their own devious actions.

God refused to overlook the Moabites or their allies, the Midianites, who participated in this downfall. He instructed Moses to dispatch 12,000 troops to slaughter every male child and every woman who had ever lain with a man from among the Moabites and Midianites because they "...caused the children of Israel, through the counsel of Balaam, to commit trespasses against the Lord in the matter of Peor, and there was a plague among the congregation of the Lord" (Numbers 31:16).

When the apostle Peter wrote about Balaam in Second Peter 2:15 and 16, he said that Balaam "...loved the wages of unrighteousness; but was rebuked for his iniquity: the dumb ass speaking with man's voice forbad the madness of the prophet."

The word "mad" is a form of the Greek word *paraphronia,* which is a compound of the preposition *para* and the word *phren.* The word *para* in this case means *beside* and the word *phren* is the Greek word for one's *mind* or *intelligence.* Compounded, it pictures an individual who is *beside himself mentally, who is out of his mind,* or *who is mentally deranged.* Thus, Peter tells us that Balaam was *a deranged prophet* who was *mentally reprobate* and *mentally twisted* due to the dark powers that he cooperated with in his soothsaying practice. To be certain, the Greek word *paraphronia*, translated as "mad," is not a word Peter would have used to describe a true prophet sent by God.

Before the last page of this dark chapter of history was closed, God saw to it that every person who had cooperated with Balaam's evil doctrine against Israel was judged — both the Moabite and Midianite women who initiated it and the men of Israel who compromised their conviction and followed the bait right into the trap. And what Balaam *sowed*, he eventually *reaped.* When Moses and his troops began to slay the Moabites and Midianites who had participated in this trap, they discovered that *Balaam* was among them. So along with everyone else who was killed, Moses' troops executed Balaam with the sword as well (*see* Numbers 31:8). Thus, we see that the law of sowing and reaping held true in the life of Balaam — which stands as an eternal warning to *any* of those who falsely believe they can ensnare God's people without suffering consequences for their actions.[1]

Despite his dark works and spiritual miscalculations concerning the cursing of God's people, Balaam *did* remarkably prophesy one important word. In Numbers 24:17, it is recorded that Balaam curiously spoke a Messianic prophecy when he stated that a "star" would arise out of Jacob. In this word of prophecy, which was truly odd for Balaam to speak, he foretold that a star would arise that would lead the Magi to see the young child Jesus. From time to time throughout history, God spoke through the mouths of wicked men — and that is the case here with Balaam's accurate word about Jesus the Messiah.

But in addition to the example of Balaam being a pagan prophet, antiquity was filled with other so-called prophets who were *conduits*, *channels*, and *mouthpieces* for the demonic realm. There is another biblical example of pagan prophets in history — and that is the Egyptian prophets — *sorcerers* — named *Jannes* and *Jambres.*

Who Were Jannes and Jambres?

The apostle Paul wrote about two pagan Egyptian "prophet sorcerers" who are recorded as opposing Moses in Exodus 7-9. In Second Timothy 3:8, Paul wrote, "Now as *Jannes* and *Jambres* withstood Moses...."

What do we know about these two Egyptian pagan prophets named *Jannes* and *Jambres*? To answer that question, we must turn again to the Jewish intellectuals who lived in the ancient city of Alexandria, Egypt. As residents of Alexandria, these Jewish thinkers had access to Egypt's historical records — and by studying the ancient archives, they identified and wrote about Jannes and Jambres as the pagan prophets and sorcerers who attempted to "withstand" Moses in a battle of supernatural signs and wonders (*see* Exodus 7:11,22; 8:6,7).

Jannes and Jambres were so well known in the ancient world that even Pliny the Elder wrote about them.[2] The historian Eusebius also wrote about these two men,[3] and the noted theologian Origen wrote about them as well.[4] In addition to these sources, "the names Jannes and Jambres appeared frequently in other Jewish, Christian, and pagan sources in Arabic, Aramaic, Greek, Hebrew, Latin, Old and Middle English, and Syriac."[5] Thus, we know the pagan prophets Jannes and Jambres were renowned sorcerers for the dark, occult realm that was entrenched in Egypt at the time of the Exodus.

But as I noted earlier, the ancient world had a plethora of pagan prophets. I wrote previously about the oracle of Delphi, who was a female pagan prophetess and priestess called *the Pythia*, who famously served as a *channel* or *mouthpiece* for the spirit realm at the Temple of Apollo in Delphi. Pagans believed this female priestess and prophetess, or medium, was an oracle for the spirit realm, but especially for the god Apollo. The Delphi prophetess became so legendary that seekers traveled days, weeks, and even months to reach Delphi to seek her guidance.

But because the ancient world had many pagan prophets of this type, oracles with pagan prophets and priests could be found in Thebes, Tegyra, Boeotia, Phocis, Thessaly, and Delos in Greece. And in Anatolia (modern Turkey), pagan oracles could be found at Patara, Branchidae, Claros, and Grynium. The list of pagan prophets in antiquity was so long that, to cover this subject fully, I would need to write an entire book on this topic alone.

In Chapter Eight, I will provide a list of names of God's prophets in the Old Testament, and we will also look at New Testament prophetic ministry. But for now, we must delve deeper to see the meaning of the Hebrew and Greek words for a prophet.

The Hebrew Word for a 'Prophet'

Before we look at the Greek word for "prophet" that is used in the Septuagint Greek version of the Old Testament and in the New Testament, let's look at the Hebrew meaning of the word "prophet." To assist me in providing special insight for this Hebrew meaning, I called upon a scholar who is well versed in Hebrew. My friend, Keith Trump, an American Bible Society scholar, who has been awarded the highest awards for his studies in Hebrew and Greek, shared the following insights regarding the Hebrew word for *a prophet*:

> Hebrew employs the word נָבִיא to signify both *a spokesperson commissioned by one much higher in stature, resources, and purpose than the speaker* and *a submitted person who, with a supernatural unction on his or her words, reveals what God is about to do in the earth.*
>
> Note that the word carries within itself the concept of humility. A true prophet (Hebrew, *navi*) speaks only while inspired by God. The Hebrew understanding of such prophetic inspiration concerns "the hand of God" being placed upon the spokesperson. God places his hand upon the prophet and, in so doing, transfers the divine authority from which the prophet draws credibility to speak.
>
> The term *navi* also signifies *one called to bring people to remembrance* or *one calling people back to a particular juncture in the road from where they first moved off course.* Thus, in the Old Testament, the prophets relentlessly admonished wandering Israel to return to their covenant with the Lord. The prophets set before Israel two choices: 1) repent and embrace your covenant identity, or 2) with cowardly resignation, retreat into mediocrity and accept the chains of deception. Thus, God often utilized the preaching of prophets as fuel for revival fires by calling Israel to bend in unison toward the necessary destruction of rebellion that always proceeds renewal.[6]

**The prophets set before Israel two choices:
1) repent and embrace your covenant identity, or
2) with cowardly resignation, retreat into mediocrity
and accept the chains of deception.**

Categories of Prophets: Hearers and Seers

In the Old Testament, there were two Hebrew words to describe each of the two categories of prophets. The first word is *navi*, which was discussed briefly in the preceding paragraphs, and it was used to describe *speaking prophets*, who largely receive, or *hear*, words and impressions from the Lord that they must then articulate to an audience of hearers.

The second word is *ra'ah*, and it was used to describe *seeing prophets* or *seers*. The way these two categories are described seems to describe *the manner in which* the "data" was received by the prophet. One *received words*, the other *saw images and visions*. The prophetic end result was the same, but the *manner* in which the information was imparted was different. Of course, we know that one can be used by God to receive both words *and* images or visions and to communicate them to a person or a group of people. All prophets — whether *navi* or *ra'ah* — are eventually expected by God to speak what they have either heard or seen.

But let's focus on the Hebrew word *ra'ah* that is used to depict *a prophetic seer* who has the divine ability to see things in the spirit realm that natural eyes could never see.

The first prophets to be called "seers" appeared during the time of the prophet Samuel. In First Samuel 9:9, we read, "Beforetime in Israel, when a man went to enquire of God, thus he spake, Come, and let us go to the *seer*: for he that is now called a *Prophet* was beforetime called a *Seer*." But other references to prophetic seers can be found in multiple verses from the Old Testament. The following is a list of some of the verses that refer to more well-known seers in the Old Testament.

- Second Samuel 15:27 says, "The king [Saul] said also unto Zadok the priest, Art not thou a *seer*...." So Second Samuel 15:27 tells us that Zadok the priest was a *prophetic seer*.

- Second Samuel 24:11 says, "For when David was up in the morning, the word of the Lord came unto the prophet Gad, David's *seer*...." According to Second Samuel 24:11, the prophet Gad was a *prophetic seer.*
- First Chronicles 9:22 speaks of "Samuel *the seer.*" So this verse tells us that the prophet Samuel was a *prophetic seer.*
- First Chronicles 25:5 says that Heman was "...the king's *seer* in the words of God...." Hence, according to First Chronicles 25:25, Heman was a *prophetic seer* who interpreted messages of God to King David.
- First Chronicles 26:28 also speaks of "Samuel the seer." This verse also affirms that the prophet Samuel was a *prophetic seer.*
- First Chronicles 29:29,30 speaks of "Gad the *seer.*" Hence, this passage tells us that the prophet Gad was a *prophetic seer.*
- Second Chronicles 9:29 speaks of "the visions of Iddo the *seer.*" Therefore, Second Chronicles 9:29 informs us that the prophet Iddo was a *prophetic seer.*
- Second Chronicles 19:2 refers to "Hanani the *seer.*" So according to this verse, Hanani was also a *prophetic seer*.
- Second Chronicles 29:30 speaks of "Asaph the *seer.*" While most think of Asaph as a musician, Second Chronicles 29:30 tells us that in addition to being a musician, Asaph was a *prophetic seer*.
- Second Chronicles 33:18 speaks of "the *seers*" (plural) that spake "in the name of the Lord God of Israel." This insight from Second Chronicles 33:18 means there was a whole group of *prophetic seers* in the land of Israel.
- Amos 7:12 additionally tells us that Amos was a *seer.*

Again, the reason the prophets in this category were called "seers" was, they'd been given an uncanny, supernatural ability *to see* into the spirit realm and to observe things that could not be naturally known, such as the content of men's hearts, invisible forces at work behind the scenes that could not be naturally discerned, and they even saw future events.

Like pulling the curtains out of the way so one can see what is outside a window, the seers in the Old Testament could supernaturally *see* into other realms to view what other eyes could not see. When the Holy Spirit moved those invisible veils apart, suddenly a seer could see what had been hidden from view and observe what was not evident to others. When the timing was appropriate, the Spirit removed obstructions from a seer's view so he could see, perceive, and understand what God wanted him to see and comprehend.

An Old Testament seer often saw pictures or scenes in his mind's eye, in dreams, in visions, or even in "open visions" with his natural eyes. Once a seer had "seen" what God wanted to reveal to him, it was then his responsibility to elucidate and interpret what he had seen as clearly as possible for the intended listener.

This makes me think of Hebrews 1:1, which says, "God, who at sundry times and in *divers manners* spake in time past...."

The words "divers manners" are a translation of the Greek word *polutropos*, and it is a compound of *polus* and *tropos*. The Greek word *polus* means *a great number* or something that is *multitudinous, plenteous*, or *numerous*. The Greek word *tropos* means *a way* and even depicts *twists and turns along the way* — it therefore pictures something that is *unconventional.* Compounded, the Greek word *polutropos* in Hebrews 1:1 carries the idea of God speaking in the past *in a great number of unconventional ways.*

In the Old Testament, at times, God spoke face to face, as with Moses; at other times by dreams and visions, as with Joseph; at still other times by signs and tokens, as with Gideon and Barak; and even at times through a mysterious system of communication, such as the Urim and Thummim. We also see that there were times when God *showed* things to prophetic seers. Indeed, God spoke to His people through a variety of means, including through "seer" prophets, who had a God-given ability to see into the spirit realm. Such seers in the Old Testament were visited with dreams, visions, and divine sight to be able to understand what God was saying — to interpret the divine will of God — by the things they were supernaturally enabled to see.

Thus, we discover that an Old Testament "seer" was one who was given the supernatural ability to *see* into people's hearts, to *see* hidden motivations, to *see* invisible forces at work, to *see* hidden agendas, to *see* secrets, to *see* mysteries, and to *see* different time frames, seasons, eras, dispensations, and various ages. Through the eyes of a seer, the secrets of the human heart were unlocked as the seer prophesied what he saw hidden there. And one writer has rightly noted that there was also a navigational dimension to the ministry of a prophetic seer because God at times used them to provide direction and guidance.

Naim Collins' book called, *Realms of the Prophetic* (Destiny Image) contain the following modified points concerning the seer that I find to be insightful.

> There were four dimensions of the Old Testament seer's vision in the prophetic realm:
>
> **1. Prophetic Insight**
>
> Old Testament *prophetic seers* had the divine ability to understand the root issues in situations and circumstances and people's motivations, agendas, and plans. They had the keen vision to see into a matter, evaluate the problem, and understand it in-depth. Prophetic seers had extraordinary insight to counsel and provide wisdom, as well as to bring divinely inspired solutions. They had insight to puzzle together critical, hard, or obscure cases.

2. Prophetic Foresight

Old Testament *prophetic seers* had the divine ability to see into the future — to see things before they happened. They had the visual acuity to predict events that would occur in the near or far future.

3. Prophetic Oversight

Old Testament *prophetic seers* had the divine ability to understand prophetic context, ecosystems, service roles, functions, and perspectives.

4. Prophetic Hindsight

Old Testament *prophetic seers* had the divine ability to also see things in the past. Indeed, they had the ability to comprehend things that had occurred in someone's past or events that consequently affected the present and could potentially alter the future. These seers had eyes to read the writing on the walls of a person's history and a powerful prophetic ability to see and read someone's personal and spiritual "background check."[7]

Prophetic seers were so respected in the Old Testament that some even served as counselors and advisors to the kings of Israel. An example is found in Second Samuel 24:11, where the Bible tells us, "For when David was up in the morning, the word of the Lord came unto the prophet Gad, David's *seer....* " We read again in Second Chronicles 29:25 that Gad was "the king's seer," and it informs us that Gad was a seer who served in the court of King David. Indeed, there were times when *speaking prophets* and *seeing prophets* were called upon to offer divine insights — according to what they'd heard or seen — to kings they served.

I want you to understand that in the Old Testament, there were various levels of prophets — major prophets, minor prophets, well-known prophets, unknown prophets, speaking prophets, and seeing prophets. But there were primarily two categories: *navi*, or *hearing prophets*, and *ra'ah*, or *seeing prophets.*

The Use of the Word 'Prophet' by Greek Writers in Antiquity

But just as the word "apostle" (*apostolos*) predates the writing of the New Testament, the word "prophet" — translated from the word *prophetes* — was also used outside the Bible by various ancient Greek writers who used the word *prophetes* and its various forms before it found its way into the Septuagint Greek version of the Old Testament and, even later, in the New Testament. So let's review how some of those notable figures used it.

- Herodotus and Plato both used the word *prophetes* to describe *those possessed with the ability to interpret the will of the gods*, such as oracles at pagan temples.[8]
- Euripides and Aristotle both used the word *prophetes* to picture *a divine expounder*, *divine interpreter*, or *a mouthpiece for the gods and the spirit realm.*[9]
- Sextus Empiricus, a noted Greek philosopher and physician, used *prophetes* to picture *one who was a divine commentator.*[10]

What is clear is that whether one is reading Hebrew or Greek, the basic meaning of the word "prophet" in both languages is essentially the same.

Four 'Pictures' of *All Prophets* for *All Time*

The word "prophet" that is used in the Septuagint Greek version of the Old Testament and in the New Testament is a translation of the Greek word *prophetes*, which is a compound of *pro* and *phemi*, which is the preposition *pro* that is compounded with the word *phemi*. The word *pro* carries a wide range of meaning, which you will see in the following paragraphs, but the second part of the word, *phemi*, explicitly means *to say*, *to speak*, or *to communicate.*

The word *phemi* can also signify *the shedding of light on a subject.* Thus, this word tells us that when a prophet delivers a prophetic message, he gives light on the message God wishes to communicate.

The use of the word *phemi* immediately lets us know that a prophet is a *speaking* or *saying* ministry or one who is intended *to communicate.* As noted, the preposition *pro* — the first part of the word "prophet" — adds a wide range of meanings that are all critical to understanding the meaning of the word "prophet," which we will study in the following pages.

There are four primary pictures conveyed to us in the Greek word *prophetes.* All four of the following points are true about all prophets in the Old Testament, early New Testament, current times and in the days to come.

Number One: The Word *Prophetes* Pictures a Prophet's Position *Before the Presence of God*

We find that the preposition *pro* means *before*, but when compounded with *phemi*, it becomes the word *prophetes,* which in its most basic sense means *to speak before* and it primarily tells us that a genuine prophet is to be *before* the Lord.

This pictures a prophet who stays *before* the Lord and sensitizes his spirit to hear the Lord's voice so he can receive the message God intends for him to deliver. In pages to come, you will see that the apostle Peter powerfully likens a prophet to a *sail* that has been hoisted on a ship that is specially designed to catch the wind for forward movement. By using this illustration, Peter will make it clear that a prophet cannot prophetically operate *unless* the wind of God's Spirit moves upon him and empowers him to speak.

Thus, we see that a prophet's foremost occupation and function — before ever speaking to an audience of listeners — is to be *before* the Lord so he can prepare his spirit to hear whatever the Spirit of God would say to Him and to catch the movement of God's Spirit.

The word *phemi* — the second part of the word *prophetes* — means that in addition to spending time before God, eventually a time comes when a prophet is dispatched *to speak* or *to communicate* God's message. After he spends time seeking the face of God for clarification about the message God wants him to deliver, a true prophet will be dispatched to speak on behalf of God to a specific person or group of people. But his first task is to linger in God's presence to ensure he correctly understands the exact message that God wants him to deliver to His people.

In Ezekiel 3:1-3, we see a scriptural precedence for this principle that God communicates first with his messengers *before* delivering a message through them to His people. Ezekiel wrote, "Moreover he said unto me, Son of Man, eat that thou findest; eat this roll [or "scroll" — i.e., God's message], and go speak unto the house of Israel. So I opened my mouth, and he caused me to eat that roll. And he said unto me, Son of man, cause thy belly to eat, and fill thy bowels with this roll that I give thee. Then did I eat it; and it was in my mouth as honey for sweetness."

According to *Gill's Exposition of the Whole Bible*, this passage was meant to demonstrate that God communicates with His messenger first. He then expects His prophets to fully digest every part of that word before imparting it to others. Gill states that God was instructing His messenger, "...Devour and consume, that is, concoct and digest; do not cast it out of thy mouth as, soon as thou has tasted of it; but let it go down into the stomach, and there digest it; and from thence into the belly, that so, upon the whole, virtue may be received, and nourishment come by it: and fill all thy bowels with this roll that I give thee...."[11]

For a prophet to hear God's Word and deliver it without *first* tasting and digesting every part of it himself is strictly forbidden. This includes both the pleasurable parts *and* the bitter parts, the commendation and the correction, and so forth. Before he can deliver that message in power to others, he must become intimately aware of its every nuance and meaning.

This divine expectation places great responsibility upon anyone called to speak on behalf of God frequently in public settings. Considering the myriad distractions of life, it can be a real challenge for God's spokesmen to find time to fully devour, consume, concoct, and digest the words God gives them to impart before their next meeting. As a result, many messages from God are delivered without the power of the Holy Spirit, even though they are delivered in a professional and timely manner. For a message from God to be preached in the power of the Holy Spirit, a prophet must fill his inner being with the word that God has imparted and let it affect him completely. Only then can he step into the pulpit and publicly deliver a word from God with authority and power.

Of course, this principle and practice of "lingering" before God in preparation for public ministry is true about every ministry gift. But the Greek word *pro* contained in the word for "prophet" makes it abundantly clear that a chief occupation and characteristic of a prophet is his waiting before God in His presence — it's as if a prophet's ministry calling is both private and public.

In fact, a prophet who speaks a message that he hasn't first internalized is like a chef who heartily recommends a dish he has never even tasted. Such a chef may know all about the cuisine he is recommending; he may possess all the right ingredients to produce that dish; and he may even know how to cook and prepare it for others. But if he has never actually tasted that dish himself, everything he knows about it is merely head knowledge. He cannot truly speak about that food with authority because he hasn't had a tangible, firsthand experience with it.

So the first divine assignment for prophets is to be *before* God's presence, to hear His message, to capture His heart, and to devour, consume, and digest what God speaks to them. Each prophet is to allow God's words to go down deep into his belly — his spirit man — that he might be changed, corrected, and nourished by them. And as a prophet, he is to swallow the *entire* message given to him. He has no right to eat of it selectively.

Because someone is called as a prophet, God expects him to put aside his own feelings and thoughts so God's words can be fully ingested, assimilated, understood, and then delivered in power. There is no doubt that certain parts of the message may be hard to swallow; — but nonetheless, each God-called prophet must digest *all* that is said to him, regardless of how painful it is to consume. As the *Jamieson-Fausset-Brown Bible Commentary* says, "...Eating the roll and finding it sweet, implied that, divesting himself of carnal feeling, he made God's will his will, however painful the message that God might require him to announce...."[12]

Gill's commentary on Ezekiel 3:1-3 continues to provide helpful insight. Gill quotes the *Targum*, an ancient Jewish commentary, regarding verse 3:

> "Son of man, thou shalt satiate thy soul, and fill thy belly, if thou receivest what is written in this roll, which I give thee." Then it states: "This was sufficient to qualify the prophet for prophesying and furnish him with materials enough; and these fit and proper for the discharge of his office; and so such who study the word of God with application become scribes well instructed in the kingdom of heaven; and being filled themselves, are able to bring forth things to the comfort and satisfaction of others...." [13]

This scholarly commentary should be taken to heart by anyone who is called to publicly speak as a prophetic voice. It clearly states that one cannot powerfully bring forth spiritual truths that he hasn't been filled with himself. The business of hearing God accurately was so important in the Old Testament that there were "schools of the prophets" that specialized in teaching prophetic individuals to sensitize their spirits and where trainees studied prophetic ministry under the mentorship of established prophets, spending endless hours studying the Scriptures.

In First Samuel 19:18-24, we read of a "school of prophets" that was comprised of prophetic students who were being mentored by the prophet Samuel. In Second Kings 2:7, we read that Elijah and Elisha encountered a group of 50 in-training prophets. It seems that in Second Kings 4:38-41, this school of prophets is mentioned again as a school where upcoming prophets lived, worshiped, studied, and learned prophetic ministry together. In Amos 7:14, Amos also writes about a prophetic school where prophets were training for prophetic ministry. So it seems there were at least three schools for prophets and possibly more. But the point is, prophetic ministry was deemed so serious that many who felt called to this ministry spent time training and preparing for it.

But please understand that the Greek word for a prophet — the word *prophetes* — categorically tells us that spending substantial time *before* God in order to hear His message and to capture His heart was and is the first and foremost role of a true prophet. Hence, a prophet is one who lingers *before* God to make sure he knows God's heart and God's message.

Bystanders generally do not understand the substantial time a prophet has spent before the presence of God. It may appear to them that a prophet dramatically speaks in what seems to be spontaneous movement, but they don't understand the hours, weeks, months, or years that preceded that movement. Some may innocently assume prophetic ministry is always spontaneous because that is how it may *appear* to their eyes when a prophet stands to minister.

While it is absolutely true that there are times when God's Spirit moves upon a prophet to speak spontaneously, the *"before the Lord"* preparation of a prophet for ministry is anything but spontaneous. If you thoughtfully study the Old and New Testament prophets and how they operated, you will discover that they spent substantial time *before* God's presence *before* they were ever dispatched to speak. Once a prophet understood God's message and had captured His heart and digested the message in his own spirit and soul, *that* was usually the moment when a prophet was ready to be dispatched to deliver God's message in the power of the Holy Spirit.

But…it all begins with a prophet who spends time *before* the presence of God. Hence, the Greek word for a prophet — the Greek word *prophetes* — speaks of a prophet's foremost task of spending time *before* the presence of God to hear His message and to accurately capture His heart.

Number Two: The Word *Prophetes* Pictures a Prophet's Public Position To Speak *in Front of Others*

As we have seen, the word for a prophet in the Septuagint Greek version of the Old Testament and in the New Testament is the Greek word *prophetes* — a compound of the preposition *pro* and the word *phemi*. We saw in the previous section that the preposition *pro* has varied meanings, but primarily, for our purposes, it means *before*. And again, the word *phemi* means *to say* or *to speak* and its use in this compound word automatically alerts us to the fact that a prophetic gift is a *saying* or *speaking* or *communicating* gift.

Before the Lord and *in Front of* Others

But now we will also see that the preposition *pro* additionally means *in front of*, and it pictures a prophet's role *in front of* people where he or she is *to say, to speak,* or *to communicate* to the intended audience. But the use of *pro* compounded with *phemi* emphatically tells us that real prophetic ministry eventually occurs *in front of* people where the divine insights a prophet receives are delivered to those whom God asks him or her to stand *in front of*.

Once a prophet has heard and understands God's message and heart and has tasted and internalized that message himself, he is dispatched from his solitary place *before* God to stand *in front of* people *to speak* the message God has authorized him to speak as a *mouthpiece* for God.

Those who speak on behalf of God are required to study, pray, and prepare — and once preparation is complete, they must then depend on the anointing and inspiration of the Holy Spirit as they speak from their spirits and souls to convey what God has spoken to them or shown them. A prophet is a prophetic voice, and he must stand strong on the side of truth, even if the audience he is addressing does not agree with the truth he is commanded to speak.

Thus, every prophetic voice is to hear or see the message, meditate on it, memorize it, and deliver it just as God expects. Even if the message contains truths that are unpleasant to hear, difficult to consume, and painful to digest, God expects prophets to yield to Him and to deliver His message in the power of the Holy Spirit. If a God-called prophet is willing to fully embrace, fully obey, and fully deliver God's message in the power of the Spirit with no mitigation — and if those who listen are willing to fully receive what God wants to communicate — powerful results will be forthcoming.

Think of the time when God sent Jonah to Nineveh to be His messenger on assignment to convert that heathen city. What happened there as the people received the word of the Lord was a powerful example of a holy outcome occurring from the message of a prophet — in this case, a prophet who didn't even want to be there. Just imagine the *magnitude* of transformation that can occur when God's messenger is faithful to follow and abide by the prophetic process.

It is of paramount importance that every prophet accept responsibility to speak God's message clearly as God wants it to be communicated. And always remember that prophetic ministry never veers from the authoritative voice of the Scriptures. To make this important point about speaking correctly in front of God's people and assuring we are speaking God's life-transforming and health-imparting words, I include the following modification from my book *How To Keep Your Head on Straight in a World Gone Crazy.*

> All of this about bringing a clear word from God makes me think of cupbearers in ancient times. These highly trusted servants were charged to taste the drink served at the tables of prominent individuals to whom they were assigned. A food-taster had a similar role regarding the food prepared for the individual, and often the cupbearer and the food-taster roles were combined into the same position.
>
> Although the settings for such meals were fabulously designed and beautifully executed, and the food and drink were of the finest quality, the fact remained that some with sinister motives could clandestinely mix the rich fare with concealed poison. Because of this, a highly trusted man who would risk his life to protect such an individual was appointed as "cupbearer." His responsibility was to personally sample the food or drink himself before it was served to see whether it was safe for consumption.
>
> After consuming a portion of the food or drink to be later offered to the person of prominence, these professional tasters were observed to see how they fared. If the food or drink had negative results, it was withdrawn from the menu and tested to determine what ingredients had caused ill effects to the cupbearer — or to determine if poison had been possibly mingled with what was to be served.
>
> If a cupbearer fell ill or died, this news was brought to the attention of those who prepared the food to see what they had mingled into the food or drink to produce such serious or even catastrophic results. Although the cupbearer had been negatively affected, his heroic sampling of the food and drink *before* it was served to people at the table spared the lives of those who would have ignorantly consumed the sickening or deadly ingredients.
>
> Of course, every person who got sick or who died from consuming deadly food or drink wasn't always intentionally poisoned. Sometimes poisoning

occurred unintentionally because ingredients were not inspected before adding them into the mix to make sure they were not tainted in some way. But food poisoning can typically be prevented. If the kitchen is made sanitary, if spoiled ingredients are removed from the mix, and if the menu is tested before being served, most cases of poisoning can be avoided.

In these last days when toxic spiritual influences abound, it is imperative that spiritual leaders remember that there is no one more prominent, noteworthy, or beloved in God's eyes than His blood-bought people. Therefore, what His ministers — those He gives charge over the spiritual welfare of His people — offer the saints for their spiritual diet is of paramount importance.

There is no greater violation of duty that a spiritual leader could commit than to serve poisonous spiritual fare that produces a sickening or "fatal" result in Christ's beloved Church. Hence, it is essential that spiritual leaders are willing to first sample the food they're about to offer to know if its effects are going to be healthy or unhealthy.

As end-time leaders, every prophetic voice must provide safe spiritual meat to those seated around the table. And as mentioned previously, just as historical cupbearers not only tested solid food before it was eaten, those who stand in spiritual leadership must be willing to test not only the *spiritual meat* being offered to the people, but also the *spiritual wine* that people are being persuaded to drink.[14]

Caution: Prophets Must Be Careful About What They Present in the Name of the Lord

I share the following biblical story to demonstrate the serious role of a prophet who stands *in front of* people to tell them he has a word from God that they need to consume.

In Second Kings 4:38-41, we read a remarkable story concerning a group of men who were studying under Elisha to be prophets. The Bible tells us that

Elisha commanded these younger prophetic disciples to go into the field to collect ingredients to make stew, and one of the young prophets inadvertently gathered ingredients from a wild, poisonous vine that looked very similar to a vine that produced good fruit. Because he was unskilled at choosing ingredients, the young prophet unintentionally gathered deadly fruit and mixed it with other healthy vegetables in a pot of stew.

To the untrained eye, the fruit the young prophet collected looked delicious — but if ingested in large quantities, that wild fruit would result in violent vomiting, terrible ulcerations in the bowels, and finally death. An experienced gatherer would have known the difference between the healthy and the deadly fruit. But because of the young prophet's inexperience in selecting ingredients, he accidentally selected the poisonous variety and mixed it into a pot full of otherwise good vegetables. This produced a deadly brew that could have proven fatal to those who consumed it.

When the young prophet returned with large quantities of this poisonous fruit, he shredded it into a large pot; then he mingled it together with meat cut into small pieces and the other vegetables. Finally, he put the pot on the fire to cook, and a stew began simmering that contained hidden death. There is no indication the young prophet intended to hurt anyone, but due to a lack of experience, He was simply incapable of selecting the correct ingredients.

Once the stew was ready, the young prophets poured it into basins and served the others. But Second Kings 4:40 (*NKJV*) says, "Then they served it to the men to eat. Now it happened, as they were eating the stew, that they cried out and said, 'Man of God, there is death in the pot!' And they could not eat it."

Those eating the stew recognized the bitter taste and knew it was deadly, so they cried out, "Death is in the pot!" To remedy the problem, Elisha said,

"...Then bring meal. And he cast it into the pot; and he said, Pour out for the people, that they may eat. And there was no harm in the pot" (2 Kings 4:41).

The word "meal" in this verse refers to "wheat." In Scripture, wheat is sometimes used to represent the Word of God. We can therefore see symbolically in this biblical account an example of how dangerous spiritual error can be that is insidiously mingled into a pot of otherwise good teaching. Those who mingle the poisonous ingredient into the mix may have done so inadvertently, as did the young prophet in this instance.

As a result of spiritual immaturity, a lack of experience, or insufficient knowledge, any spiritual leader may mingle poisonous influences into messages that would be otherwise beneficial to hearers. Some do it unintentionally because they are not mature enough to discern the sometimes subtle danger of certain spiritual ingredients. That was true of that inexperienced and perhaps very sincere disciple of Elisha, who did not understand that the ingredients he had chosen had bad long-term, even fatal consequences. Thus, he inadvertently prepared a deadly concoction.

To bring correction to the deadly brew, Elisha knew that they needed to add significant amounts of wheat to the stew to remedy the situation. This is symbolic of what happens when the Word of God is brought into a situation to counteract the effect of poisonous influences that are not healthy for consumption. When the "wheat" of the Word is injected in large doses into an otherwise dangerous situation, those life-giving words of truth have the power to nullify the poisonous spiritual influence and turn the situation around. The Word of God — scriptural truth injected into situations by the power of the Holy Spirit — can correct and reverse any ill effect of spiritual poison, whether intentionally or unintentionally introduced, that has negatively impacted God's people.

According to James 3:1, those with spiritual influence over others will be held accountable for what they say, what they endorse, and what they serve to saints who are gathered at their table. Those who speak prophetically in front of people must never forget the warning of those Spirit-inspired words in James 3:1: "My brethren, be not many masters, knowing that we shall receive the greater condemnation."

The word "masters" is the Greek word *didaskalos*, and it is the Greek equivalent for the Hebrew word *rabbi*. But here, it actually carries the idea of *a masterful revelator*. It would definitely include any person who publicly stands in front of others to say he is called to deliver a revelatory or prophetic word from God. Speaking in front of people is so serious that James adds that such individuals "will receive the greater condemnation."

The word "condemnation" is a form of the Greek word *krima*, and it depicts *a verdict* or *judgment* that results from a formal investigation. In this verse, the Holy Spirit forewarns those who claim to speak on behalf of God that they will ultimately be scrutinized by God Himself, who will watch to see if what they endorse or teach is correct and in agreement with the entire body of Scripture. That means every word, every phrase, and every nuance that is spoken in a public forum by a prophetic voice is significant to God. From the witness of this one scripture, we see it is so important for Christian leaders to always remember that *words have consequences*.

Like spiritual cupbearers, every prophetic voice must know with certainty that no tainted ingredients are being mixed into the pot that might bring eventual harm. They must be willing to sample the spiritual food and wine themselves to provide assurance to the saints gathered at the table that they can eat with a sense of safety. When God's people "sit around the table" to listen to prophetic voices that stand in front of them to speak as a mouthpiece for God, they must understand that those prophets' words have consequences and therefore they must stick closely to what they have been instructed to speak and make sure it is in agreement with the whole body of Scripture.

To be clear, a prophet should not stand in front of people to speak until God has clearly spoken and he has internalized the message himself. So we see again that a prophet's first occupation is to be *before* the Lord to hear Him, to converse with Him, and to wait for the Spirit to move upon him to speak. Once God has spoken to his heart and given him a message, and once he has been released by the Spirit of God to speak, then *finally* he is to move into the next phase of his prophetic ministry *in front of* people to speak God's message.

Number Three: The Word *Prophetes* Pictures a Prophet's Responsibility To Speak *'on Behalf of'* the Lord

Forgive me for reiterating what we have already covered, but it is important for you to understand that the New Testament word for a *prophet* is translated from the Greek word *prophetes.* I remind you again that it is a compound of the preposition *pro* and the word *phemi.* As we have seen, the preposition *pro* has varied meanings, and the word *phemi* means *to say* or *to speak* and it alerts us to the fact that a prophetic gift is a *saying* or *speaking* or *communicating* gift.

Thus far, we've seen that a prophet is one who first and foremost spends substantial time *before* the Lord to ascertain the message and heart of God for a particular time and for a particular person or group of people. Once a prophet has heard and internalized the message God wants him to deliver, he is dispatched by the Holy Spirit to stand *in front of* those intended by God to hear that particular message.

But now we see that the preposition *pro* also means *on behalf of.* And again, the word *phemi* means *to say, to speak,* or *to communicate.* So compounded, it can mean a prophet is *one who speaks, says, or communicates a message on behalf of God.*

The preposition *pro* underscores the fact that a prophet does not speak on his own behalf. Indeed, his function is *to speak*, but a true prophet does not have the right to speak his or anyone else's views. He is to speak *on behalf of* the Lord and to accurately represent His message. Thus, God expects a prophet to be a clear channel with a clear message given to him by the Lord. Thus, as an official spokesman of the Lord, a prophet's job is to announce with clear and unquestionable articulation the desires, dictates, orders, or the message that God wishes to express to the people. And because a prophet is dispatched from the presence of God to speak on God's behalf, he is required to be accurate, precise, and faithful to the message God wants him to express.

An individual entrusted to speak prophetically on God's behalf must let God's message go down deep into his belly — his spirit man — that he might be changed, corrected, and nourished by it. Such a leader must swallow the *entire* message given to him with no right to eat of it selectively. And as Christ's spokesman, he must put aside his own feelings and thoughts so the Word can be fully ingested, assimilated, understood, and then delivered in power. There is no doubt that certain parts of these messages will be hard to swallow; nonetheless, one of the requirements of spiritual leaders is to digest *all* that God's message says.

As God's spokesmen, prophets are expected to be prophetic voices to the Church, and as such, they must adhere to the message God has entrusted to them, even if the spiritual atmosphere does not seem to agree with the truth they are commanded to speak. It must also be underscored very strongly that Old Testament prophets were also *preachers* who were assigned the task of regularly preaching God's Word to His people.

I encourage you to reread the section in Chapter Three in which I wrote at length about the New Testament word "herald," translated as *preacher* or *to preach*, from the Greek word *kerux*. In antiquity, a *kerux* — or *herald* — was the official representative of a government or king. As such, he was expected to clearly announce, or herald, the desires, dictates, news, or any other type of message a government or king wished to convey to those in the kingdom, or *territory*, and even to those who lived abroad.

In order to deliver that message, this herald was first summoned into the private quarters of the king or government leader, ready to hear, receive, and write down the message he was to announce. When the king or leader finished dictating the message, if needed, the herald was permitted to ask questions and seek clarification. His job was to be sure he understood every nuance and point that he was being tasked to accurately convey.

A herald understood that his job was to speak on behalf of the king and that there was no room for misunderstanding or for mistakes in his delivery of the message. Finally, when the herald was assured he fully understood the message he had been summoned to deliver, he went to his podium to publicly announce the message given to him. It was expected that his delivery of the message be accurate, precise, and faithful to the message the king or leader wanted to express.

Just as it was important for the *kerux*, or herald, to communicate the king's message very accurately, it was likewise important for him to capture the sentiment, heart, and emotions on these various issues so he could convey not only information, but also the heart and passion of those who sent him. Thus, when the herald stood to speak, it was expected that he would deliver the information correctly, in a way that conveyed not just the information, but the heart and passion of those who sent him.

As a public figure, a herald also found himself in moments when he *could* express his personal opinions on many issues, but as a herald, he did not have the right to give his own personal commentary about things he had been asked to communicate. He was to refrain from making personal commentary that was simply not his business to make. Similarly, speaking as the Lord's representative means the pulpit is to be used for speaking what comes from the lips of Jesus, and as His representatives, we are authorized only to publicly speak what the Lord has directed us to say.

Those who speak as "heralds" for God must clearly understand that their highest priority is to come into His presence in order to hear both the message and every nuance of what God wants to communicate to His people. More than just intellectually communicating information, those who speak for the Lord must capture not only *information*, but also His *heart* that needs to be conveyed to His people — and they must do it with conviction and passion.

As a part of the prophet's preaching ministry, a crucial aspect of speaking *on behalf of* God includes addressing hot social topics and cultural issues that need to be addressed from the viewpoint of Scripture. This is part of the responsibility of the prophetic person. The answers, solutions, and principles to deal with societal dilemmas are found in the immutable truths of God's Word, and a true prophetic voice who speaks on behalf of God will always redirect people to the answers contained in the Bible.

It is simply a fact that if God's prophetic voices will not address these issues, the vacuum will be filled with the voice of the world, which will inevitably lead countless multitudes astray. It is *essential* for God's spokesmen to speak up and communicate what He says on controversial cultural issues in order to help God's people stay anchored in truth in spite of a world that is morally wobbling *and even free-falling* all around them.

We live in an age when true prophetic voices are often vilified as being narrow-minded, critical, judgmental, or negative. There *are* times when God's message contains truths that are corrective and therefore possibly unpleasant to hear, difficult to consume, and painful to digest. But never forget that there is a supernatural, anesthetizing effect of the Holy Spirit when He speaks difficult truths to His people's hearts. His correction does not discourage, condemn, or leave hearers in a downtrodden condition. Instead, He speaks truth in a way that protects and soothes as it corrects so that the end result is comfort, encouragement, hope, and strength. True prophets can depend upon the anesthetizing effects of the Holy Spirit to help listeners receive the correction without feeling like they are being "bludgeoned" by truth.

His correction does not discourage, condemn, or leave hearers in a downtrodden condition. Instead, He speaks truth in a way that protects and soothes as it corrects so that the end result is comfort, encouragement, hope, and strength. True prophets can depend upon the anesthetizing effects of the Holy Spirit to help listeners receive the correction without feeling like they are being "bludgeoned" by truth.

Before moving to the next point, I must add that we cannot overlook the fact that there are moments when the Holy Spirit wants to speak — and a prophet has not had time to fully digest the message, yet the prophet feels an urgency to immediately speak. In those cases, perhaps the Lord does not want the mind of the deliverer, or messenger, to complicate or process the message fully in his mind. Or with too much time to process what the Lord is imminently saying, maybe a prophet would be fearful to deliver it, or he might add his own interpretation to it.

So there are divine moments when a prophet feels like a "heavenly spigot" and he has the inner urge to speak immediately. It is as if he needs to release a *"divine discharge"* to get the word out. As the prophet releases it, it takes faith for his mouth to fully engage with his spirit, and sometimes a prophet will declare things by the Spirit that are beyond his own study and preparation, and he will afterward feel the need to process what he uttered.

It is vital to understand that God expects His prophetic voices to speak on his behalf and to deliver His message as He intends with the power of the Holy Spirit.

Number Four: The Word *Prophetes* Pictures a Prophet's Responsibility To Foretell or To Speak in Advance

As we have seen, the Greek word for a prophet is *prophetes,* a compound of the preposition *pro* and the word *phemi.* In preceding paragraphs, we have seen that the word *pro* can mean *before, in front of,* or *on behalf of.* The word *phemi* means *to speak, to say,* or *to communicate.* So we have seen thus far that a prophet is called:

- To spend substantial time *before* the presence of God.
- To stand *in front of* people to speak or *communicate* God's message.
- To speak *on behalf of* the Lord without using his position to speak on his own behalf or promote his own or some other minister's message or agenda.

But there is another important element of the word *prophetes* that must be discussed. The preposition *pro* can also carry the idea of *foretelling* or *speaking about something in advance*, which pictures a true prophet's gift at times to speak with a certain *predictive ability* or to describe events *in advance* of their happenings. Certainly, this is not what a prophet does all the time, but the Greek word *prophetes* means that a true prophet's ministry will at times include *the supernatural ability to foretell events — to hear or see what the Spirit of God is showing him in advance.*

The ability to prophetically foretell events is seen throughout the entire Old Testament. God Himself set the prophetic wheel in motion in Genesis 3:15 when He prophetically foretold that the Seed of the woman — that is, the

Messiah — would one day crush the serpent's head through the Messiah's death and resurrection.

As time progressed, God gave His prophets the charge to speak His mind on a long list of social and political issues, public morality, public *immorality*, social justice and injustice, religious idolatry, right and wrong use of power, and prophetic encouragement of a hopeful future. Prophets became so powerful that when they uttered the words, "Thus saith the Lord," it caused kings and nations to tremble, as it *should*. And the use of those words "thus saith the Lord" should be used reverently by the prophets themselves, in "fear and trembling" (*see* 1 Corinthians 2:3).

Of course, there have always been (and always will be) those who stubbornly refused the word of the Lord spoken through the prophets and who even sought to deride, persecute, and derail God's spokesmen. But on the other hand, it's a *really* sad day when men and women who are called prophets use the phrase, "Thus saith the Lord" rashly, casually, or in an almost cavalier fashion while many of them are prophesying out of their own souls or their *wishful thinking* — *or* they're adding their own interpretations to what they're truly picking up in the realm of the spirit.

I am certain that many, or most, who make these kinds of mistakes very sincerely and really do want to help, encourage, and be a blessing to those who listen to them. But because of the lack of time taken to really "percolate" what the Lord is trying to download into their hearts, error is often mixed with truth that causes the word of the Lord to become less precious, valued, and esteemed by the intended audience, because people begin to look upon those ministers' words with suspicion and misgiving.

That's why it is ever so important to note and never forget that a seasoned prophet spends more time *listening* — before the Lord (*pro*) — than he does *speaking*.

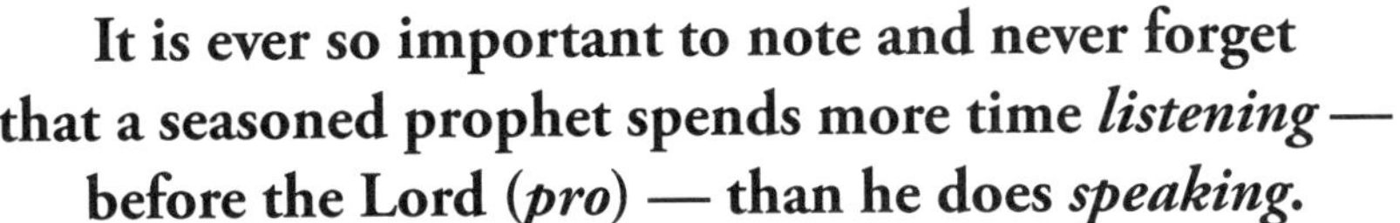

It is ever so important to note and never forget that a seasoned prophet spends more time *listening* — before the Lord (*pro*) — than he does *speaking*.

While Old Testament prophets prophetically pointed to the future coming of the Messiah, they also foretold events about:

- Israel and its various captivities and final restoration to the land.
- The rise and fall of kings and kingdoms, or empires.
- Invading armies, defeated foes, and times of both captivity and freedom.
- Economic blessings and also, at times, hardships.
- Weather, including rain and drought.
- Different ages and dispensations.
- The very end of the ages and events that still lie before us.

These foretellings of events were revealed to Old Testament prophets through dreams, visions, and revelations. Those men and women discerned the voice of God in light of natural events, such as earthquakes, winds, and storms, and they learned to discern with greater clarity God's voice as it was spoken to them through the mouths of other prophets who were speaking in their times.

As early as the days of Enoch, God began to prophetically foretell events through the mouths of His prophets. Enoch is a remarkable example of such a prophet. In that age — at the very beginning of time, in fact — Enoch was enabled to prophetically see the end of the world. Although he was the seventh from Adam and lived in the earliest beginnings of the Old Testament, Enoch was so precise in his foretelling of events that he accurately foretold the Second Coming of Christ and of the judgment that will be dispensed to the ungodly at the very end of the age. What Enoch prophesied became congruent with what was later written in New Testament Scripture.

In fact, Enoch's words were so inspired and trustworthy that millennia after God miraculously took him to Heaven (*see* Genesis 5:24), Jesus, Paul, Peter, John, James, and, most notably, Jude, quoted Enoch's prophesies. In Jude 14 and 15, we read, "And Enoch also, the seventh from Adam, prophesied of these, saying, Behold, the Lord cometh with ten thousands of his saints, to execute judgment upon all, and to convince all that are ungodly among them of all their ungodly deeds which they have ungodly committed, and of all their hard *speeches* which ungodly sinners have spoken against him."

At least to some degree, all Old Testament prophets foretold future events. You will discover in the next chapter that this divine ability to prophetically see futuristic events was not limited to Old Testament prophets, as New Testament prophets were also gifted to prophetically see and address future occurrences.

The Apostle Peter Explains How Real Prophets Do and Do *Not* Operate

Because a prophet was such a powerful force in both the Old and early New Testament periods, at times, frauds masqueraded as prophets in order to gain advantage over God's people. They knew that when they said, "Thus saith the Lord," it caused people to stand to attention, and some false prophets feigned prophetic words to gain a following and to take advantage of the people's hunger and respect for the voice of God.

In Second Peter 2:3, Peter wrote, "And through coveteousness shall they with *feigned* words make merchandise of you...."

The word for "feigned" is a translation of the Greek word *plastos*, and as you might guess, it is where we derive the word "plastic." It tells us there were some — and there *still* are some — who concocted prophetic words to meet the whims of their listeners. The purpose was not to speak on behalf of God, as true prophets should; instead, they were molding their words like plastic to fit the ears of their listeners. Peter boldly stated that the aim of some of those so-called prophets was to gain a following and to make "merchandise" of God's people.

The word "merchandise" is a form of the Greek word *emporeuomai*. The word *emporeuomai* is where we get the word "emporium," which is a place of commerce, a market, or a retail outlet. But in the First Century when Peter was writing this verse, it also denoted a place where charlatans outwitted naïve buyers with sham products.

The burgeoning problem of false prophetic ministry was growing rapidly in the Early Church, and by the end of the First Century, Peter felt compelled to address the problem and bring correction to it. So under the inspiration of the Holy Spirit, Peter articulated two amazing verses in Second Peter 1:20,21 that explicitly inform us how real prophets *do not* operate — and then how they *do* operate.

Before we unlock the truths about how prophets *do* and *do not* operate, let me give you additional background on why Peter's words in these verses were very important at the time he was writing. The importance of Peter's words is fitting for our own season, as we have seen some prophetic abuse in modern times as well.

In early moments of Church history, false revelators were propagating far-fetched prophesies and revelations that they molded like plastic to fit the ears of listeners. Elated crowds were dazzled with prophetic utterances that were *self*-manufactured by those with ulterior motives. Because so many were *self*-generating prophetic utterances at that time, Peter elected to address the problem and to elaborate on how authentic prophets *do not*, and *do*, operate.

'Knowing,' 'First,' 'No,' 'Prophecy,' 'Scripture,' and 'of Any Private Interpretation' — Here's What You Need To Know

In Second Peter 1:20,21, Peter wrote, "Knowing this first, that no prophecy of the scripture is of any private interpretation. For the prophecy came not in old time by the will of man: but holy men of God spake as they were moved by the Holy Ghost."

Peter begins this text by saying, "*Knowing* this...."

In Greek, the word "knowing" is a participle of the word *ginosko*. The word *ginosko* means *to really know*, *to really grasp*, or *to really comprehend*. Since it is a participle, it depicts *a never-ending type of knowing* or something that should *be* known, *always be* known, and *never be forgotten*. It carries the idea, *"Knowing, knowing, always knowing, and never forgetting...."* Whatever Peter was describing was so important that he said we are *to know it, always know it, never forget it, and keep it at the forefront of our minds as something of utmost importance*.

Peter then added, "Knowing this *first*...."

The word "first" in this verse is a translation of the Greek word *proton*. Here, it means *first*, *foremost*, or *above all else*. It depicts something that explicitly must be known *first, foremost, and above all else* because it is foundational to everything else Peter is about to discuss. So thus far, the verse means, *"You need to categorically know this and never forget what I'm about to tell you. First, foremost, and above all else, you need to know and never forget...."* What was it that we are to know and never forget? That "...no prophecy of the scripture is of any private interpretation" (2 Peter 1:20).

Many misinterpret this verse to mean no one should ever interpret one verse all by itself, but, rather, that every verse should be compared with other verses to arrive at a correct scriptural conclusion. Although this law of Bible interpretation is absolutely true, and it's how I study the Bible myself, Peter was *not* discussing Bible interpretation in this verse.

The original Greek in this verse is quite different from how it reads in the *King James Version* of the Bible. For example, the phrase "of any private interpretation" is a translation of the Greek phrase *idias epiluseos ou genetai.* Because this Greek wording is so important, we will examine these words piece by piece so you will understand precisely what Peter was saying in this verse.

But first, let's look at the word "no" in this verse: "Knowing this first, that *no* prophecy of the scripture is of any private interpretation."

The word "no" is a translation of the Greek word *ou* and it means *emphatically not,* alerting us that Peter is raising his voice to sound an alarm about something that is categorically *prohibited.* What is prohibited is explained by the words "of any private interpretation." This complicated and unusual phrase is the key to this verse, and we will look at it in detail in the next section.

Next in Second Peter 1:20 is the word "prophecy," a translation of the Greek word *propheteia,* a word that depicts *a supernaturally given utterance.* It can be translated as *prophecy* or *a divine utterance*, and it can refer to *one who supernaturally speaks the mind of God on a matter.*

Because the word *propheteia* is so important in this text, let's see how it was used in antiquity by well-known and respected Greek writers.

- The notable Greek poet Anacreon (582-485 BC) used the word *propheteia* to denote *one who could sing* or even to describe *a herald.*[15]
- Euripides and Pindar used the word *propheteia* to describe *one who could interpret and express the will of the gods.*[16]
- Plato used the Greek word *propheteia* to denote those who had the ability to interpret *prophetic utterances that were offered in a temple,* and he used it to describe prophets who spoke while they were under the power of a trance.[17]
- Sextus Empiricus used the word *propheteia* to describe a commentator or interpreter of holy things.[18]

If we take all these various meanings as a whole, we learn that *propheteia* conveys the idea of *one who was fluent with prophetic utterances as a professional singer*. Particularly, the one giving the utterance was called to herald and interpret the will of the god. Such utterances were made while the speaker was under the control of a supernatural power who guided his words.

Since Peter borrowed this word from the contemporary language of the day to convey the meaning of the word "prophecy," we know from Scripture that prophetic utterances flowed like music from Heaven through prophets who boldly heralded what they heard and who gave themselves to express and interpret the word and the will of God, especially when the Spirit moved upon them and they were under the direct, manifest influence of the anointing of God.

Next we'll look at the word "scripture." Second Peter 1:20 says, "Knowing this first, that no prophecy of the *scripture* is of any private interpretation." This word "scripture" is translated from the word *graphes*, the plural form of *graphe*, which refers to God-inspired *writings* or *the Scriptures*.

Thus far, we can interpret this verse to mean, *"You need to categorically know this and never forget what I'm about to tell you. First, foremost, and above all else, you need to know and never forget that all the divine utterances written in Scripture...."*

Remember, the word "no" is a translation of the Greek word *ou* that means *emphatically not* and tells us that Peter is raising his voice to sound an alarm about something that is categorically *prohibited*. What is that "something" that is prohibited? It is explained by the next words in the text "of any private interpretation." In fact, this complicated and unusual phrase is the key to this verse.

'Of Any Private Interpretation'

Our text is Second Peter 1:20, which reads, "Knowing this first, that no prophecy of the scripture is *of any private interpretation*." First, the words "of any private" are translated from the Greek word *idios*, a word that means of *one's own self*.

Next, we find that the word "interpretation" is a translation of the word *epilusis*, which is a compound of the Greek words *epi* and *lusis*. The word *epi* means *upon* and *lusis* means *to loose*, *to set free*, or *to release*. When these words are compounded to form the word *epilusis*, it depicts a *loosing* or *releasing* that occurs *at one's will*. Hence, the words "of any private interpretation" depict something that is *loosed or released by one's own self — at will*. It pictures something that is *self*-loosed, *self*-produced, *self*-propelled, or *self*-generated by one's own will.

Peter used *epilusis* with the word *ou* earlier in the verse (the Greek word for "no," meaning *emphatically not*) to inform his readers that true prophetic utterances — including the ones given to us in the Scriptures — were *not* self-loosed, self-produced, self-propelled, or self-generated by one's own will.

Because Peter used the word *ou*, which we saw is a prohibition, it tells us that Peter was raising the tone of his voice to really make his point.

There's one more word in this verse to note before we move on: "Knowing this first, that no prophecy of the scripture *is* of any private interpretation" (2 Peter 1:20). Peter used the word "is," *genetai* in Greek — a form of *ginomai* — which pictures *something that comes to pass over a period of time.* But as a whole, the phrase *ou ginetai* — "...*no* prophecy of the scripture *is*..." — means *it empathically does not happen that way* or *it just doesn't happen like that.*

The *Renner Interpretive Version* (*RIV*) of Second Peter 1:20 would read as follows:

> **You need to categorically know this and never forget what I'm about to tell you about true prophetic utterances. First, foremost, and above all else, you need to know and never forget that, emphatically, no prophecy of the Scripture is *self*-loosed, *self*-produced, *self*-propelled, or *self*-generated by one's own mere will.**

This is a profoundly important verse to teach us how real prophetic ministry *did not* operate in the Old Testament — and to show us how it is also not to operate in the New Testament. According to Peter, no true prophet in the Old Testament *self*-loosed, *self*-produced, *self*-propelled, or *self*-generated prophetic words or any prophetic movement. Peter unequivocally states that real prophetic utterances are not *self*-loosed, *self*-produced, *self*-propelled, *self*-generated, and they do not come "by the will of man." Thus, true prophets do not *self*-loose, *self*-produce, *self*-propel, or *self*-generate prophetic utterances.

This message was important at that early moment in the Church when so-called prophets were feigning prophetic words *at will.* Again, the word "feigned" in Second Peter 2:3 is a translation of the Greek word *plastos* — it is where we get the word "plastic." Peter used it to tell us that some so-called prophets were simply concocting prophetic words to appeal to their brand of listeners.

We will discover from other New Testament verses that there were some individuals and groups who were also trying *to pry their way* into the spirit realm at will. But the record of Scripture shows that this is not the way God-given supernatural experiences and prophetic utterances are imparted by God to His people. Trying *to pry one's way* into another realm is, instead, exactly how the occult primarily operates.

The Occult — Secret Knowledge, But From the Wrong Realm

The word "occult" is associated with *secret knowledge*. And nearly all occult practices are designed to enable one *to pry his way* into the spirit realm and, apart from God's help, access the spiritual world in order to obtain information and knowledge. In short, the occult is man's attempt to obtain insights about the future or to access the spirit realm on his own initiative.

But one should never forget that if you cross a threshold that is not opened by the initiative of God, it will likely open the door to evil dimensions. If one chooses to open the door to another realm by his own volition, he needs to know that the devil is happy to provide him with an experience that is diametrically opposed to the teachings of the Bible.

There is an example in Colossians 2:18 of believers who tried to pry their way into the spirit realm. In the city of Colossae, there was a group of leaders and believers who were infatuated and obsessed with angels, so they attempted to barge into other spiritual realms to interact with all sorts of angelic creatures. Paul referred to this when he wrote Colossians 2:18. In that verse, he wrote that they were engaged in the "…worshipping of angels [and] intruding into those things which he hath not seen…."

The word "intruding" is key in this verse. It is a translation of the Greek word *embatauo*, and it literally means *to force one's way into* or *to pry into* or *to intrude into* a place where a person has not been invited. In the case of some in the city of Colossae, they were attempting to intrude or barge their way into spiritual realms that God did not open to them. As a result, a flood of deception came pouring through that open door and deception came into their midst.

For this reason, I urge you to be cautious of anyone who encourages you to willfully barge into realms that have not been opened to you by a gracious act of God. You need to understand that if you are willing to go into those places by your own volition, the devil will provide false experiences that enslave you with falsehood and deception. If you study the origin of most cults, you will find this is precisely how they got started.

Yes, God wants to supernaturally visit His people and give them divine encounters, but these will be events set in motion by His will and not produced by one's own volition. In fact, if you study the entirety of Scripture, one fact will become clear to you by the stories of men and women who experienced divine encounters with God. In all of those experiences, there is one constant factor: In every instance — *without exception* — it was God's initiative to invade that person's world to give him a word, a revelation, or life-transforming experience. There is not a single example anywhere in Scripture in which any believer was encouraged *to forcibly pry his or her way* into another realm by himself.

But as believers live godly lives, keep their hearts open, and listen to the Holy Spirit, it prepares the soil of their spirit for God to supernaturally invade their world when an appropriate moment for it arrives. Our task is to follow Christ, live in obedience to God's Word, pray in the Spirit, and thus enlarge our spiritual capacity to keep our spirit alert and sensitive to spiritual things. Our part to stay spiritually alert cannot be overestimated. We are to set our heart upon Him, but divine encounters and "heavenly invasions" are always initiated by God upon the hearts of those who are open to God's movement upon them.

A wonderful example of how God initiates such divine encounters can be found in Revelation 1:10 where the apostle John writes about how he supernaturally saw Christ on the island of Patmos and how he received the vision of the exalted Christ and later wrote the book of Revelation. In that verse, John writes, "I was in the Spirit on the Lord's day...."

The word "was" is a translation of the Greek word *ginomai*. In this verse, this word describes *something that happens unexpectedly* or *something that catches one off guard*. This categorically tells us that John was not expecting this divine encounter, and when it occurred, it took him completely by surprise and caught him off guard. In a way he never could have anticipated or predicted, John suddenly found himself "in the spirit."

The word "spirit" is capitalized in the *King James Version*, but in the original Greek, the phrase "in the Spirit" is actually a translation of the Greek words *en pneumatic*. Because the phrase lacks a definite article, it should therefore be translated, "*In a way I never could have planned, predicted, or anticipated, I suddenly found myself IN SPIRIT on the Lord's day*." In this context, the phrase "in spirit" is a term to describe *another realm*, *another dimension*, or *a spiritual realm far different from the natural world* that surrounded John.

The word *ginomai* depicts an element of *surprise* and gives a clear picture of what John experienced and how he felt when this event occurred. It is clear that when John experienced this divine encounter, he did *not* know it was about to happen. The apostle was going about his business, following Christ faithfully where he was, when suddenly — *out of nowhere, taking him completely off guard and by surprise* — he abruptly found himself no longer in the same physical place, but was, rather, standing in *another dimension*. He had somehow passed from the natural realm into the realm of the spirit and was now "in spirit," or in a totally different realm.

Another vivid example of how God invades the lives of surrendered believers can be found in Acts 10:9,10. In those verses, we read that Peter went up to a rooftop to pray as he awaited lunch one day. It says, "On the morrow, as they went on their journey, and drew nigh unto the city, Peter went up upon the housetop to pray about the sixth hour: and he became very hungry, and would have eaten: but while they made ready, he fell into a trance...."

Peter didn't go onto the rooftop to forcibly pry his way into the spirit realm that day so he could have a supernatural experience. He was simply waiting for lunch, and as he prayed, suddenly, something happened that completely took him off guard and by surprise. The words "fell into" in verse 10 is a remarkable translation of the Greek word *ginomai*, which is the same identical word the apostle John used in Revelation 1:10 to explain the surprising way Christ invaded his cave on Patmos and how he unexpectedly stepped into the spirit realm to see the exalted Christ and to receive what became the book of Revelation.

Now Acts 10:10 uses the word *ginomai* to describe the surprising way this supernatural vision came to Peter on the rooftop. It describes *something that happens unexpectedly* or *something that catches one off guard*. It could be translated, "*In a way that could have never been planned, predicted, or anticipated, Peter fell into a trance.*"

Think about it. While Peter prayed and awaited lunch, he had an experience that totally took him off guard as he *slipped* into a trance. The word "trance" is the Greek word *ekstasis*, a word that by itself means *to stand outside of* something. In this case, Peter found himself *standing outside of his body* in another dimension. But Peter did not forcibly pry his way into that realm. As is always the case when God moves supernaturally upon His people, it was God's initiative to invade Peter's world.

Peter found himself *standing outside of his body* in another dimension. But Peter did not forcibly pry his way into that realm. As is always the case when God moves supernaturally upon His people, it was God's initiative to invade Peter's world.

The reason this point is important is, Second Peter 1:20 states that no true prophet *self*-loosed, *self*-produces, *self*-propels, or *self*-generates prophetic words and prophetic movements *at will.* Peter stated clearly and adamantly that real prophetic experiences and genuine divine utterances are not *self*-loosed, *self*-produced, *self*-propelled, *self*-generated, nor do they come by the mere will of man. Although Peter was specifically referring to the prophetic utterance of Old Testament Scriptures, the principle of how God *does not* move — by the will of man — is true for all prophetic ministry.

We have seen earlier that the foremost task of a true prophet is to be *before* the Lord, and as he humbles his heart and sensitizes his spirit and mind, he does his part to prepare for spiritual movement *if* and *when* the Holy Spirit chooses to move upon him to communicate a message that he is to give to God's people.

We've been studying in Second Peter 1:20 how true prophetic utterances *do not* come — they are never *self*-loosed, *self*-produced, *self*-propelled, or *self*-generated. They do not come by man's whim or will. Now that we've discussed how prophets *do not* operate, we'll look at how they *do* operate.

The Example of Old Testament Prophets

In Second Peter 1:21, Peter proceeded to powerfully explain how genuine prophetic utterances *do* come. Peter said, "*For* the prophecy came not in old time by the will of man: *but holy men of God spake as they were moved by the Holy Ghost.*"

The word "for" at the beginning of this verse is a translation of the Greek word *gar*, and it is a conjunction to link two statements together — in this case, it links verses 20 and 21. A better translation would read, "*But, emphatically, the prophecy came not by the will of man....*" The word "prophecy" can describe the scriptures that were uttered or written by past prophets, and it can also describe the general behavior of Old Testament prophets. It is, again, the Greek word *propheteia*, which depicts *a supernaturally given utterance, a prophecy, a divine utterance* — and it can refer to *one who supernaturally speaks the mind of God on a matter.*

But notice Peter says, "For the prophecy *came* not in old time by the will of man...." The word "came" is a form of the Greek word *phero* that pictures something that is being carried along — perhaps like a leaf being *carried* by a gust of wind or like the current in a river that *carries* something, like a fallen branch, downstream. The leaf and branch have no inherent ability to move by themselves and will only be moved if wind or current *carries* them along.

This of course means the leaf or branch is *dependent* upon wind or current. If the wind suddenly stops blowing, it will mean the leaf will fall to the ground. Likewise, if the current suddenly stops flowing, the branch will lay motionless in the water, for it has no ability to move without the current. Hence, all movement for the leaf or the branch depends *entirely* on the wind or current that *carries* each of them along. Please hold onto this illustration, for you will soon understand the significance of it.

Peter then added in Second Peter 1:21, "For the prophecy came *not* in old time by the will of man...." The word "not" is the Greek word *ou*, and it means *categorically not.* The words "in old time" are from the Greek word *pote*, and it should be translated *at any time.* The words "by the will of man" means *by the will or initiative of man*. So as a phrase, this part of the verse means, *"But emphatically know that divine utterances were not produced by the force of man's willpower, wits, or initiative...."*

Peter finally said, "...But holy men of God spake as they were moved by the Holy Ghost." The word "but" is the Greek word *alla*, and it is used as a conjunction to mean *on the contrary*, *on the other hand*, or *on the complete opposite side of the spectrum*. Thus, Peter was making a drastic comparison for his readers that could be translated, *"But on the contrary and clear on the other side of the spectrum...."* Then Peter finished, "...*Holy men* of God spake as they were moved by the Holy Ghost."

The words "holy men" are Peter's description of Old Testament prophets. In Greek, it says *hagioi*, the plural form of *hagios*. Here it means *holy ones*, and it can refer to either *men* or *women* or *anyone* who is *holy*. The Greek word *hagios* describes anything that, although it was once very common, has now been divinely *separated*, *consecrated*, *holy*, and made *sacred* — never again to be regarded or used in a common way.

It's the same word Paul used when he wrote to the Christians in Rome (as well as to all believers everywhere) and called them "saints" (*see* Romans 1:7). The word translated "saints" is a form of *hagios*, which again describes something that has been *separated*, *consecrated*, *sanctified*, and *set apart* for special use. Paul used the word *hagios* to describe Christians who, although they were previously just regular human beings like everyone else, were cleansed by the blood of Jesus and the Holy Spirit moved into their hearts — that divine act *set them apart* and made them so *different* that God now sees them as being *holy* and *different* from unsaved people.

Peter was now using the plural form of *hagios* to picture multiple prophets in the Old Testament, men or women, whom God chose, set apart, moved upon, and through whom He spake. Although they were once simply common people, God's call came to them, touched them, and they were *separated* from what they had previously been. They became *consecrated,* deemed *holy* and *sacred* — never to be regarded or used in a common way again — for they were now permanently *separated* unto the purposes of God.

Preparing themselves to be used by studying, preparing, and making every adjustment needed for them to become vessels *through whom* and *upon whom* God would move, they became fitting mouthpieces for the Holy Spirit. Some were trained in schools of the prophets or were mentored by other senior prophets who taught them the disciplines necessary for God to pluck the strings of their spirits so they could hear His messages and deliver His word to others in the power of the Spirit when He moved upon them to do so.

So we see that Second Peter 1:21 actually means, *"But on the contrary and clear on the other side of the spectrum, divine utterances were not produced by man's mere willpower, wits, or initiative, but common people whom God touched, set aside and consecrated for His own special purposes, spake as they were moved by the Holy Ghost."*

Setting a Prophet's Prophetic Sails To Catch the Wind

But now let's return to the example of the leaf and the branch carried, respectively, by a gust of wind or a current in a stream. Pay special attention to the words "as they were moved" in verse 21.

This phrase "as they were moved" is a translation of the word *pheromenoi*, a technical word that was used in ancient times to denote *a ship whose sails were set to catch the wind.* Peter was a fisherman by profession, so he chose an illustration that was clear to him and that well conveyed the truth he wanted to communicate about how real prophets *do* operate.

This word *pheromenoi* — translated "as they were moved" in Second Peter 1:21 — is the very word used in Acts 27:15 to describe an event when much-needed wind blew into the sails of Paul's ship to move it along. Similarly, as we've already seen, for either a fallen leaf or fallen branch to move, they are both dependent upon some outside source to move them along.

In the same way, ancient ships were dependent upon wind to be carried along in a forward movement. If the wind stopped blowing, the ship became immobile. Often sitting in sweltering sea temperatures, sailors were forced to wait for the wind because without it, there was nothing they could do to make the ship move. *No wind meant no movement.* However, the moment the wind began blowing again, the already hoisted sails caught the wind, and the ship once again was carried across the sea. But the movement of the ship depended upon the wind.

Sailors understood their total dependence on wind, so to prepare for movement, they hoisted huge sails above the ship to catch the wind the moment it began to blow. Even with the sails hoisted into place, the ship nonetheless remained motionless *until* the wind began to blow. Then, because workers had prepared for the wind by raising the ship's sails, the ship was ready to move *the moment* the wind began to blow again.

Of course, the ship workers were unable to produce wind themselves, but they *were* able to *prepare* — to do what was necessary to hoist those sails to catch the wind when it finally did begin to blow again. And because preparation was made and the sails were hoisted, once the wind began to blow, those sails caught the wind and the ship was moved along by it.

Peter uses this illustration to explain how God moves upon His prophets. According to Peter's illustration, the possibility of true prophetic utterances without the movement of the Holy Spirit is impossible. If the Spirit is not moving — yet people are still attempting to prophesy — it becomes nothing but the contrived utterances of man, like sailors trying to move a ship with no wind. The prophesies that were uttered or written by Old Testament men and women were not *self*-willed or *self*-projected. They were the result of holy people spiritually hoisting their prophetic sails to catch the wind of the Spirit when He chose to move.

This is why Peter said that no prophecy of the Scripture was given "by the will of man." Prophetic utterances are not self-willed, but are spoken by prophetic individuals who make it their occupation to set their spiritual sails so they are prepared to catch the movement of God's Spirit when He is ready to supernaturally move upon them so they could hear, see, and prophesy. Thus, the prophets of old could only supernaturally hear, see, and write or communicate as God's voice or mouthpiece as the Spirit moved them to do so.

As long as the Spirit was moving, they were able to prophetically operate. But if the wind of the Spirit ceased to blow upon their prophetic sails, they were unable to function prophetically. Like ships with sails hoisted to catch the wind, Old Testament prophets depended on the wind of the Holy Spirit because if the Spirit stopped moving upon them, there was no prophetic movement. And it's true today that real prophetic movement can only occur when the Spirit is "moving upon the sails."

Preparing for Spiritual Movement Today

There are vital lessons to learn from this illustration. For example, by making ourselves spiritually sensitive — that is, by hoisting our spiritual sails — when God wants to speak to us or through us, we will spiritually be in a position to catch the wind of the Holy Spirit and be "carried along" and empowered to do what we could never do by ourselves.

Just as an ancient ship could not move without wind, there is not much we can do without the movement of the Holy Spirit upon us. Even Jesus said,

"The Son can do nothing of himself..." (see John 5:19). Jesus recognized His need for the Father and the power of the Holy Spirit. And no one ever born on this earth knew the Holy Spirit better than Jesus. After all, Jesus:

- Was with the Holy Spirit at the creation of the universe.
- Was conceived by the Holy Spirit in the womb of the virgin Mary.
- Was baptized by the Holy Spirit at the Jordan River.
- Was empowered to minister by the Holy Spirit.
- Was crucified in the power of the Holy Spirit.
- Was raised from the dead by the power of the Holy Spirit.

Once Jesus was raised from the dead and had ascended on High, one of the first things He did was pour out the promised Holy Spirit on the Church.

Jesus knew the Holy Spirit inside and out and, in His earthly ministry, He was dependent upon the Holy Spirit and knew that He could do nothing of Himself — independent of the Spirit's power. Since that was true of Jesus, how much more is it true of all of us today. Therefore, if we have not prepared our hearts and minds to catch the wind of God's Spirit, it is just a fact that we will not see much divine activity in our lives. Our task must be to hoist our spiritual sails so we are in a position to be "moved by the Holy Ghost" when He wants to speak to us or through us to others — or use us in some other way. We must do our part to prepare to catch the wind. This is a God-given honor and our responsibility as believers.

When most people think of a prophet, they frequently focus on his or her ability to prophesy. But as we have seen, the word "prophet" can be translated *to speak before* — and it primarily portrays a prophet's role *before* the Lord. That position *before* the Lord is a necessary part of the process for a prophet when he hoists his spiritual sails. Hence a prophet must find himself or herself poised at the feet of Jesus, and in that position, that individual will sensitize his or her heart to hear the Lord's voice and do His will.

If we have not prepared our hearts and minds to catch the wind of God's Spirit, it is just a fact that we will not see much divine activity in our lives. Our task must be to hoist our spiritual sails so we are in a position to be "moved by the Holy Ghost" when He wants to speak to us or through us to others — or use us in some other way. We must do our part to prepare to catch the wind. This is a God-given honor and our responsibility as believers.

Never forget that a prophet — like a ship — is dependent on the wind of the Spirit. There is nothing he can supernaturally *self*-produce — by himself — and he cannot even accurately speak with power until the Spirit moves across his spirit. Therefore, he positions himself *before* God's presence and waits.

By staying before the Lord, the prophet sets his spiritual sail to catch the wind of the Holy Spirit, and once he is aware of the Spirit's moving across his spirit, then — finally — he is in a position to turn toward the people and move into the public phase of his prophetic ministry.

The *RIV* of Second Peter 1:20 reads:

> **You need to categorically know this and never forget what I'm about to tell you about true prophetic utterances. First, foremost, and above all else, you need to know and never forget that, emphatically, no prophecy of the Scripture is self-loosed, self-produced, self-propelled, or self-generated by one's own mere will.**

The *RIV* of Second Peter 1:21 reads:

But on the contrary and clear to the other side of the spectrum, authentic divine utterances were not carried or produced by man's mere willpower, wits, or initiative, but they were spoken by common people whom God touched, set aside, and consecrated for His own special purposes, those who learned to hoist their sails to catch the wind of the Holy Spirit. As the Holy Spirit moved upon them, they caught His wind and were enabled to speak and to move prophetically.

Warnings About Prophets Who Prophesy Things That Don't Happen

In addition to genuine prophets in the Old Testament, there were also false prophets, and the Old Testament gave strong warnings about prophets in that time period who prophesied events and dates for those events that didn't come to pass. Those clearly spoken warnings against that which was false were intended to be heeded by the people as a way of knowing when a false prophet was in their midst — or when a prophet was prophesying wrongly, or mistakenly.

Let's look at some of these warnings, and, afterward, I wish to add an important comment about judging prophetic utterances that may provide a helpful perspective that will be important to remember.

In the Old Testament, God uttered many warnings about false prophets, but in Deuteronomy 18:22, He said, "When a prophet speaketh in the name of the Lord, *if the thing follow not, nor come to pass*, that is the thing which the Lord hath not spoken, but the prophet hath spoken it *presumptuously*: thou shalt not be afraid [reverence or respect the words] of him."

In this verse, God states that if a prophet speaks in the name of the Lord — claiming that God has sent him with a prophetic word — but the thing he prophesies does not come to pass, then it is to be taken as a sign that he spoke presumptuously. Perhaps that person intended to do well; perhaps that person spoke out of his own heart, motivated by what he wanted to hear or to see. But because it did not come to pass as he foretold, God says he did not speak by the Spirit of God. Thus, in the Old Testament, if the thing a person spoke did not occur as foretold, God urged His people to be untrusting of that prophet and to keep a distance from him.

In the Old Testament, if the thing a person spoke did not occur as foretold, God urged His people to be untrusting of that prophet and to keep a distance from him.

It is important to understand that saying, "Thus saith the Lord" had great consequences — and it still does today. For one to speak so authoritatively, but *wrongly,* negatively affected people's ability to hear God speak through *genuine* prophets. Bad experiences with prophetic prognosticators caused many people to turn a deaf ear to *all* prophetic utterances because of disgust with and distrust of failed prophesies.

'Despise Not Prophesyings'

Let me divert to the New Testament for a moment, where we find in Scripture that believers in early New Testament times were also being negatively affected by failed prophesies they had heard. For example, believers in Thessalonica were so disheartened by people who said, "Thus saith the Lord" — but their words never came to pass — that they were tempted to throw *all* prophetic ministry out. But Paul knew they *needed* the true prophetic ministry and that throwing *all* prophetic utterances out was the wrong response. So in First Thessalonians 5:20, Paul told them, "Despise not prophesyings."

The word "despise" is a translation of the word *exoutheneo*, which means *to minimize*, *to reduce to nothing*, or *to utterly despise*. It depicts *utter contempt* for something and a desire to rid it from one's life. The use of this word tells us the church in Thessalonica was so weary of prophecies that didn't come to pass that they were beginning to feel *utter contempt* for anything that smacked of prophetic ministry. That is why Paul exhorted them in First Thessalonians 5:21, "Prove all things; hold fast that which is good."

Let me tell you a story to demonstrate the point I wish to communicate about this verse. I once bought a violin that I thought almost of a certainty was an authentic Stradivarius violin. Before I purchased it, I even studied how to recognize a real Stradivarius compared to a well-made copy. After convincing myself that I had found a real Stradivarius in an antique shop, I purchased that violin. But after an examination by a violin expert, that violin proved to be nothing more than a very old, fabulous fake. Only an experienced eye would have been able to discern that it wasn't authentic. Today that fake Stradivarius hangs on the wall in one of my offices as a reminder that everything that looks real *isn't necessarily real.*

I share this example because it is pertinent to what the congregation in Thessalonica was dealing with as they became so disheartened by false prophecies. One or more persons in that church claimed to be prophetically speaking, but time and again, the words proved to be incorrect.

As we have seen, perhaps those prognosticators were speaking out of their own hearts or from the soul realm. Theirs was an imitation that resembled the real gift so closely that people in the church had embraced it. The person or persons demonstrating this so-called gift must have also been fairly influential, because the congregation as a whole had, at first, taken the false demonstrations very seriously. But when those believers realized the prophecies were false, they were so distressed by the *inaccuracy* of those prophetic words that they were tempted to turn a deaf ear to *all* prophetic utterances. But closing their hearts to prophetic utterances would have been a wrong response.

Even though the congregation had indeed been exploited by bogus prophecy, the value of *genuine prophetic utterances* hadn't changed. Prophecy was, and is, a true gift from God that the people needed. If the Thessalonian believers had chosen to keep their hearts closed to that divine gift because of their negative experiences, they would have been robbed of fresh words from the Holy Spirit that were a part of their necessary supply from Heaven. Many believers in our own time have been negatively affected by unfulfilled prophetic utterances, but that doesn't mean all prophets and prophetic utterances cannot be trusted.

If the Thessalonian believers had chosen to keep their hearts closed to that divine gift because of their negative experiences, they would have been robbed of fresh words from the Holy Spirit that were a part of their necessary supply from Heaven.

We must consider and never forget that there are *many* things that are used inaccurately or inappropriately in life. For example, a car can be driven in such a reckless manner that it results in a collision — but that doesn't stop the rest of us from traveling in *our* cars. The recklessness of others simply makes us more aware of our need to drive carefully and responsibly. But if we decided to never drive a car again because someone caused damage or was wounded in a car accident, that would be an irrational response.

When Paul addressed the issue of this gift of prophecy with the Thessalonians, he didn't put a "ban" on all prophecies because of a series of false prophetic experiences. He simply told them to *test* spiritual manifestations before embracing them. Paul told them, "*Prove* all things..." (1 Thessalonians 5:21). In other words, "*Keep your head on straight when it comes to what you're about to spiritually consume!*"

The word "prove" that Paul used is translated from the Greek word *dokimadzo*, which means *to approve after testing.* This word was used in various ways, but it was significantly used to describe the process of testing coins to see if they were real or counterfeit.

Counterfeit coins look very authentic —- and there were so many counterfeit coins in circulation in ancient times that it became an accepted practice to test coins to determine if they were real or counterfeit. If tested and proven as fake or counterfeit, they were rejected. Only if the coins were tested and proven authentic were they approved for public circulation and accepted for payment.

That is where the word "prove" comes from that Paul used in First Thessalonians 5:21. He didn't tell the Thessalonian believers to reject prophetic utterances; instead, he instructed them *to test* or *to prove* them. God's people are instructed to test both *written* and *spoken* spiritual utterances before fully embracing their substance. But Paul continued in verse 21, "Prove all things; hold fast that which is good."

The words "hold fast" are a translation of the Greek word *katecho*, a compound of the words *kata* and *echo*. The word *kata* means *down*, and the word *echo* means *to hold* or *to embrace*. When these two words are compounded to form *katecho*, the new word means *to hold firmly* or *to hold down lest the desired object slip away from you*. It is the picture of figuratively wrapping one's arms around an object and *refusing* to let it go.

Therefore, Paul was urging the Thessalonian believers not to reject all prophecy simply because of a few bad experiences. They needed *to embrace* and *to hold on to* that which was "good." The word "good" denotes something that is *sound* and *in order* — something that has been tested, proven, and shown to be *authentic*.

Like a coin that has been tested and proven as worthy to be put into public circulation, Paul is commanding us to *hold fast to* what has been attested to be dependable, genuine, reliable, and true. Therefore, the Spirit of God is exhorting us to "wrap our arms around" and *hold fast to* those in prophetic ministry who are tested and proven to be *authentic* and *legitimate*, esteeming them as gifts coming directly from *Him* for our good.

Warnings From Jeremiah

In the previous section, I began by talking about the strong warnings given in the Old Testament about prophets in that time period who prophesied events, and dates for those events, that didn't come to pass. Some of the strongest Old Testament warnings about false prophets were written by the prophet Jeremiah. It is certain that those who prophetically "missed it" must have despised Jeremiah's words, which were an indictment against anyone who wrongly prophesied. In Jeremiah 14:14, he wrote, "Then the Lord said unto me, The prophets *prophesy lies* in my name: I sent them not, neither have I commanded them, neither spake unto them: they prophesy unto you *a false vision* and *divination*, and *a thing of nought*, and *the deceit of their heart*."

In this verse, God states that these prophetic pretenders speak lies, false visions, and things that come to nothing. What they prophesied may have sounded powerful, but because those things never came to pass, God tells Jeremiah that they were prophesying out of the deceit of their own hearts. We can surmise that they perhaps prophesied what *they* wanted to happen or hoped would come to pass — or they prophesied their own agendas or desires. Perhaps they simply wanted to give a word that would fall on the ears of thrilled listeners.

God also uses the word *divination* to describe the activities of these false prophets. Divination is a spiritual force, albeit an evil one. It may be that some false prophets indeed operated in a spiritual dimension, but a *wrong* dimension. If the prophetic utterance missed the target and didn't come to pass, God emphatically stated that the prophet's words should be dismissed. The bogus speaker may have given the impression that he was moving in a powerful spiritual dimension, but God warned that if what he said never came to pass, it is likely that so-called prophet was functioning in an operation of *divination*.

In all fairness, not all cases of inaccurate prophecy are a result of divination. It may be that a prophet is deeply disturbed about something he sees happening morally in society or about a political, cultural, or social issue that deeply distresses his prophetic character — his deep sense of right and wrong. He may feel a divine obligation to address it, and, indeed, addressing moral or national issues falls within the scope of his calling. But to say, "Thus saith the Lord" without the wind of the Spirit blowing upon his prophetic sail may cause him to speak presumptuously in the name of the Lord on his own initiative. No prophet is allowed to use those words, "Thus saith the Lord" unless he is quoting Scripture or is certain that the Lord has instructed him to prophetically address a matter.

In regard to prophetic insight, Paul wrote in First Corinthians 13:9, "For we know in part, and we prophesy in part." This means that even the most astute prophets did not entirely see the whole picture. Hence, if they *saw* "in part," it was important that they *spoke* "in part" — only speaking the part they saw without yielding to the temptation to fill in the blanks concerning what they did *not* see. Although the temptation to speculate is enormous, the prophetic mandate requires that a prophet speak only what he hears or sees and not move into the realm of presumption.

This brings to mind the words of James 3:1, which says, "My brethren, be not many *masters*, knowing that we shall receive the greater condemnation." As we've seen, the word "masters" is a translation of the Greek word *didaskalos,* and it is a word that depicts *a master revelator*. According to James 3:1, anyone who claims to speak on behalf of God in this way will come under "condemnation." I covered this word earlier in this chapter, but keep reading as I explain again briefly what that word means.

The word "condemnation" in this verse is a translation of the Greek word *krima*, and it depicts *a verdict* or *judgment* that results from a formal investigation. As we saw before, the Holy Spirit in this verse forewarns that those who claim to speak divine revelation will ultimately be scrutinized by God Himself, who listens to every word, every phrase, and every nuance that is spoken by His *master revelators*.

Continuing in James 3:15, we are warned that not everyone who claims to have divine revelation is moving in a right spirit. That is why James soundly warned us about the "wisdom that descendeth not from above, but is earthly, sensual, devilish."

Because this verse is so pivotal about right and wrong revelation, let's look at it more closely. In this verse, James was communicating that there can be moments when someone who claims to be moving divine revelation may in fact be moving in a low-level, earthly realm. The word "earthly" that James used in James 3:15 is a translation of the Greek word *epigeios* and it describes wisdom that is from *a mere earthly realm*.

Furthermore, this verse adds that sometimes what appears to be supernatural "wisdom" is in fact "sensual." The word "sensual" is a key to understanding the activity of those who operate from a wrong spiritual dimension.

It is translated from the Greek word *psyuchikos,* and it is a word that actually means something that is *soulish* or that *belongs to the soulish realm.* The soul has latent powers that are impressionable and that can be mistaken for spirituality. James herein warned believers that there may be moments when a person seems to be moving in a spiritual realm, but in fact, he is functioning out of *soul power* so persuasive that those who are listening perceive it to be from a spiritual source. In Jeremiah 14:14, this is referred to as those who speak *from the deceit of their own hearts.*

But James 3:15 adds there are times when this kind of activity may even be "devilish." The word "devilish" is a translation of the Greek word *daimoniodes,* a word that clearly means *influenced by demons.* This word is used by James to let us know that it is not only wrong to prophesy out of one's own heart or soul, but that doing so is dangerous, for the "soul realm" is where demons operate and mislead people. Thus, James was clearly saying that operating out of the soul realm can possibly open the door to demonic activity, and the one speaking may be wrongly convinced that he is speaking correctly when, in fact, he is operating under the influence of a wrong spirit.

James 3:15 could be interpreted, *"This is emphatically not the wisdom that comes down from Heaven, but on the contrary, it is emphatically from a low-level earthly realm; it is pure soulish activity, and anyone speaking like this is clearly under the influence of demonic activity."*

Unauthorized Utterances

In Jeremiah 23:16, God tells Jeremiah that if a so-called prophet speaks prophetic utterances that do not come to pass, it meant the prophets who gave the utterances were not sent by God. This applies both to false prophets who aren't sent by God and to prophets of God who aren't "sent" in certain situations, but who prophesy anyway, sending *themselve*s. In Jeremiah 23:16, the prophet says, "Thus saith the Lord of hosts, Hearken not unto the words of the prophets that prophesy unto you: they make you vain: *they speak a vision of their own heart,* and not out of the mouth of the Lord."

Commenting further on the egregious behavior of such prophets, verse 21 records that God told Jeremiah, "I have not sent these prophets, yet they ran: I have not spoken to them, yet they prophesied." In verse 26, God then adds, "How long shall this be in the heart of the prophets that *prophesy lies*? yea, they are *prophets of the deceit* of their own heart."

In these verses, God reveals that some run to and fro among God's people claiming to have prophetic words and visions from God, but God, in fact, never sent them or authorized them. These words may sound harsh, but they are God's words, and *He minced no words* as He called them prophets of deceit.

Certainly, those who were guilty of these charges must have despised these words, for such warnings would cause others to listen to them with discerning scrutiny. But to speak in the name of God is of such paramount importance that those who do it must be *absolutely certain* they are truly speaking a word God gave them and that they are not speaking from their own hearts, desires, or imaginations.

Just as Jeremiah explained that some prophets and so-called prophets — unintentionally or intentionally — speak from the deceit of their own hearts, or out of their soulish realm, the prophet Ezekiel wrote similarly in this vein. God also told Ezekiel that there was a category of so-called prophetic individuals who followed their own spirits and whose prophetic utterances were either an outright lie, the work of an imagination, or simply a manifestation from the soulish realm to influence those who were listening.

In Ezekiel 13:3, the prophet wrote, "Thus saith the Lord God; Woe unto the foolish prophets, that *follow their own spirit, and have seen nothing.*" In verse 6, he added, "They have seen *vanity* and *lying divination*, saying, The

Lord saith: and the Lord hath not sent them: and they have made others to hope that they would confirm the word." *The Amplified Bible* says, "...Yet they hope and make men to hope for the confirmation of their word."

An Important Observation About Unfulfilled Prophetic Utterances

There is another important aspect of judging prophetic utterances that adds another perspective, and we should consider it carefully. I'm talking about the factor of *time*.

If all the rules about prophetic utterances were strictly applied — especially whether or not something that was uttered came visibly to pass — Moses, Jeremiah, and Ezekiel, who penned them, would have failed the prophetic test. All of these God-called prophets prophesied about many long-range and long-term events that only occurred many years later — even thousands of years later — and many of them are *still* awaiting fulfillment. The vast majority of their written prophesies and utterances were not about immediate or near events, but about the long-range, long-term plan of God.

Thus, the concern of God and the indictments He spoke in these verses were not aimed at prophets who prophesied the long-range plan of God, but it was for those who predicted immediate events, perhaps even setting dates to accompany them, that did not happen as forecasted. Everyone waited, and nothing happened as predicted. This is so disheartening to the people of God and it is "discrediting" of true prophets. Remember, God said if anything doesn't occur that a so-called prophet foretold *would* occur within a short time frame, then it is right to be untrusting of that prophet and to keep a distance from him.

As we continue looking at the ministry of prophets in the Old Testament, we'll find that there were *hundreds* of God-sent prophets in the Bible. And if one considers the many "up and coming" prophets who attended various schools of the prophets but who were never named, the list becomes quite enormous. In the following chapter, I provide a list as an *overview* that shows God speaking prophetically through all kinds of various people throughout the years spanning the time of the Old Testament.

This is so disheartening to the people of God, and it is discrediting of true prophets. Remember, God said if anything doesn't occur that a so-called prophet foretold *would* occur within a short time frame, then it is right to be untrusting of that prophet and to keep a distance from him.

Questions for Deeper Consideration

Chapter 7

1. In this chapter, we saw that in recent Church history, the only widely recognized fivefold gifts were the evangelist, pastor, and the teacher. Regardless of what office others with a traveling ministry were actually called to, they tended to be "automatically" called an evangelist or a teacher by default. As a result, many Christ-given fivefold prophets were called evangelists because the Church did not embrace the possibility of a current-day prophet. Can you think of prophets in the last century who were called evangelists? Can you name an example of a prophet being mislabeled as an evangelist?

2. The word "prophet" was a name used both by pagans and by God's people in the Old Testament. Why was this word commonly used by both groups? And can you now express the meaning of the word "prophet" in the ancient world?

3. The Old Testament tells us of a prophet named Balaam. After what you have read in this chapter, would you say Balaam was a backslidden prophet of God or an outright false prophet? If you say he was an outright false prophet, what is the primary biblical proof to cause you to arrive at this conclusion about Balaam?

4. In this chapter, I extensively dealt with two Hebrew words for a "prophet." One is the Hebrew word *navi* and the other is the Hebrew word *ra'ah*. These two words describe two different kinds of prophets who receive their insights from God in different manners. Can you explain the differences between a *navi* and a *ra'ah* prophet of God?

5. The Old Testament refers to prophetic "seers." What is a seer, and how did he or she function in the Old Testament. After reading this chapter, can you name any well-known prophets in the Old Testament that functioned as seers?

6. The Greek word for a "prophet" is *prophetes*, and this word conveys four different ideas that are connected to a prophet's ministry. Can you now list the four different aspects of a prophet's ministry based on the meaning of this word *prophetes*?

7. First Peter 1:20,21 elucidates how real prophets do and do not operate, specifically stating that genuine prophets only speak as they are "moved" by the Holy Ghost. The word "moved" is a Greek word that was borrowed from a particular part of the ancient world in order to convey an image about how bona fide prophets operate. Can you recall how the word "moved" was first used in the ancient world and explain how it is used to describe the genuine operation of the prophet?

CHAPTER 8

AN OVERVIEW OF SOME OF THE OLD TESTAMENT PROPHETS

Knowing this first, that no prophecy
of the scripture is of any private interpretation.
For the prophecy came not in old time by the will of man:
but holy men of God spake as they were moved by the Holy Ghost.
— 2 Peter 1:20,21

As we have seen, there were hundreds of God-sent prophets in the time of the Old Testament. Because there are too many to list, I give the following prophetic summaries as examples of some of the more well-known prophets from that period. You may be *surprised* to see that some of these individuals were called prophets. But among ancient rabbinical circles, every person discussed in the following pages was considered to be a prophet or prophetess for various reasons.

You will see in this chapter that I have included more information about some prophets and less information about others. This is due to the fact that there is more information available about some prophets and prophetesses and less information concerning others whose prophetic activities the Bible doesn't give much detail about. Nevertheless, all the prophets included in this chapter were added because they played such important prophetic roles in the plan of God. Again, this is not an exhaustive list, but it is given as a sample of prophets, listed in approximate chronological order, whom God used throughout the timespan of the Old Testament.

In some way, these individuals hoisted their prophetic sails to catch the movement of God's Spirit, and when God was ready to speak or to reveal something to them, they were prepared to supernaturally move by the Holy Spirit, as we saw in the last chapter. As a result of their various prophetic functions, both ancient and contemporary rabbis, as well as Scripture, referred to them as *prophets.*

As you read through these pages, remember these were not born-again individuals with inwardly changed characters due to the presence of the Holy Spirit continually living in them. They were moved by the Spirit as He temporarily moved *upon* them, but that divine presence did not remain upon them at all times. When that presence lifted, some of these men and women behaved in less than expected ways. In this respect, New Testament prophets — and all New Testament believers — have a more powerful standing than any Old Testament prophet.

But let's begin our list of specially named prophets spanning the time of the Old Testament.

- ***Enoch*** lived from approximately 3384 to 3019 BC, and he was the "seventh from Adam" (*see* Genesis 5:9-14; Jude 14). He was the son of Lamech and father of Methuselah (*see* Genesis 5:22), who was the longest-living person recorded in biblical history. As one of the first prophets in the Old Testament, Enoch played a significant role and walked so closely with God that "God took him" (*see* Genesis 5:24; Hebrews 11:5), and he did not experience natural death.

  Although Old Testament references about Enoch are minimal, he was so respected as a prophetic voice that his writings were quoted by Jesus, Paul, Peter, James, Jude, and John. In addition to what we know of Enoch from Genesis 5:18-24 and Hebrews 11:5, scholars generally believe Enoch penned the oldest parts of the non-canonical *Book of Enoch*. He was so accurate in his prophetic abilities that he even saw a vision of the Second Coming of Christ in the very beginning of time. Jude refers to that prophecy that is quoted from the most ancient sections of the non-canonical *Book of Enoch*.

  Jude 14 and 15 says, "And Enoch also, the seventh from Adam, prophesied of these, saying, Behold, the Lord cometh with ten thousands of his saints, to execute judgment upon all, and to convince all that are ungodly among them of all their ungodly deeds which they have ungodly committed, and of all their hard speeches which ungodly sinners have spoken against him."

  Due to this prophetic role at his early stage in history, ancient sources refer to Enoch as a *prophet* of God.

- ***Noah*** lived from approximately 3078 to 2147 BC. He was the tenth and last of the pre-flood patriarchs. According to the Genesis account (*see* Genesis 6-11), Noah was prophetically warned by God that a flood would destroy the earth. After hearing from God, he and his family moved with urgency to build the Ark at God's command (*see* Hebrews 11:7), and his obedience ultimately saved not only his own family, but mankind itself and all land animals.

Noah is recognized by Jewish rabbis as a prophet of God who was instructed to warn people who were plunged into depravity and sin to repent. Even the apostle Peter wrote that Noah was a preacher of righteousness (*see* 2 Peter 2:5) — but, nevertheless, people of that time refused to give heed to God's message and thusly perished in the flood. After the flood, God made a covenant with Noah and promised that He would never again destroy the earth with a flood (*see* Genesis 8:21).

Ancient sources refer to Noah as a *prophet* of God.

- ***Abraham*** lived in the Second Century BC (c. 1813-1638 BC).[1] Originally named Abram (*see* Genesis 11:26; Genesis 11-12; Genesis 17:5), he became the common patriarch for all Abrahamic religions. In the Jewish tradition, he is called "our father Abraham." Abraham is revered as the *prophet* to whom God chose to reveal Himself and with whom God initiated a covenant (*see* Genesis 17:1-7; Hebrews 6:13,14). The apostle Paul wrote that all who are Christ's are the seed of Abraham and are inheritors of the promise made to Abraham" (*see* Galatians 3:29).

  Throughout history, believers have looked to Abraham as the spiritual father of all Christians. Augustine of Hippo wrote that all Christians are "children [or the seed] of Abraham by faith," and Saint Ambrose wrote that "by means of their faith, all Christians possess the promises made to Abraham."[2]

  But Abraham's walk of faith started one day when God supernaturally appeared to Abraham in a cloud of glory (*see* Acts 7:1-3) and

God preached the Gospel to him, thus making him the first man to ever hear the Gospel (*see* Galatians 3:8). At the age of 75, Abraham turned from paganism to follow God's call for him and his wife Sarah (Sarai at that time) to leave luxurious Ur of the Chaldees — and also to leave his father Terah's household (Terah was the ninth descendant from Noah) so that he and his wife could settle in a new land God specifically promised to give to him and to his descendants forever. In Genesis 12:1-3, God promised Abram that he would make of him a great nation, bless him, make his name great, bless them that blessed him, and curse them who cursed him.

Although Abraham experienced many twists and turns and mistakes in his walk of faith, he persistently and obediently followed the call of God. Leaving what was comfortable, dealing with nonstop challenges and problems along the way, enduring difficult and tragic separations with relatives, experiencing angelic visitations, judgments upon entire cities, negotiating with foreign kings, and later losing Sarah to death, Abraham nevertheless journeyed onward in obedience in his walk of faith. Over time in this faith-filled journey, God changed Abram's name to *Abraham,* which means *father of many nations,* and God likewise changed Sarai's name to *Sarah,* which means *an exalted woman* (*see* Genesis 17:5,15).

In the ancient world, a new name represented a new status or an entry into a higher level of society, and with a new name came rank, privilege, and, frequently, the right of inheritance. It marked a distinct change in an individual's status — one that might affect not only him, but also subsequent generations after him. This bestowal of a new name normally accompanied a person's advancement, elevation, ennoblement, or promotion.

When God changed Abram's name to *Abraham*, it marked a new beginning in his life — a spiritual advancement or elevation. The name *Abram* meant *father* — a name that for years must have struck chords of both tenderness and torment for a man who seemed unable to produce children. Then in Genesis 17:5 when Abram entered into a covenant with God, that covenant was accompanied by a modification to his name, marking a shift upward in his life. His name was changed to signify the promise God had given him and to reflect his new God-ordained status. Although he was still childless, his name was changed to *Abraham*, which means *a father of many nations*.

If Abram's previous name seemed unfitting for a man with no children, imagine how much *more* unfitting the name Abraham must have seemed. But the change of Abraham's name marked a pivotal change in his relationship with God and in his character. It was a point in his life from which there was no turning back.

When God affirmed His covenant to Abraham, this transformation also brought a change of status to Sarai. This event is recorded in Genesis 17:15 and 16, which says, "And God said unto Abraham, As for Sarai, thy wife, thou shalt not call her name Sarai, but Sarah shall her name be. And I will bless her, and give thee a son also of her: yes, I will bless her, and she shall be a mother of nations; kings of people shall be of her."

The new names God gave Abraham and Sarah did not in themselves change them — rather, the new names reflected the change God was performing *in* them. It marked the end of one chapter and the beginning of a new life. Abraham was 99 years old when God gave him a new name, and Sarah was 90. If anyone demonstrated that it's never too late to change, it was *Abraham* and *Sarah*.

In Genesis 20:7, we read that God called Abraham a *prophet* and instructed King Abimelech to treat Abraham well because he was a *prophet*. Then in Second Chronicles 20:7, Isaiah 41:8, and James 2:23, we find that Abraham was not only a *prophet*, but he was also the *friend* of God.

Ancient sources refer to Abraham as a *prophet*, as the friend of God, and as the father of the walk of faith.

- ***Sarah***, of course, lived concurrently in the time of her husband Abraham. She is considered one of the four matriarchs of the Old Testament and is recognized as one of the seven women whom ancient rabbis referred to as *prophetesses* (the others were Miriam, Deborah, Hannah, Abigail, Huldah, and Esther).

  In Genesis 11:30 and Hebrews 11:12, we're told that Sarah was so infertile that she was as "good as dead" and completely incapable of bearing children. But miraculously, she later gave birth to a son at the age of 90 and named him Isaac. At the age of 127, Sarah died and was buried next to Abraham's grave plot in the cave of Machpelah.

  Ancient sources refer to Sarah as a *prophetess* because of her walk of faith and for the prophetic role she played in the plan of God.

- ***Isaac*** lived approximately at the same time as Abraham and Sarah. He was the son of Abraham and Sarah, the father of Jacob, the grandfather of the 12 tribes of Israel, and one of the three primary patriarchs of Israel. Isaac was the son God had promised to Abraham and Sarah (*see* Genesis 17:16), and he became the subject of the most difficult test of Abraham's faith when God commanded Abraham to offer Isaac as a sacrifice upon Mount Moriah (*see* Genesis 22:2). Not only was it a test for Abraham; it was also a test for Isaac, who was old enough at that time to resist being offered as a sacrifice. But due to his own trust in God, Isaac did not resist. Then at the last moment, the angel of the Lord appeared from Heaven, who stopped the sacrifice, and God miraculously provided a sacrificial lamb (*see* Genesis 22:11-13).

Then in Hebrews 11:20, the writer of Hebrews referred to Isaac's prophetic words when it says, "By faith Isaac blessed Jacob and Esau concerning things to come."

Because God spoke numerous times to Isaac and for the prophetic role he played in the history of Israel, ancient sources refer to Isaac as a *prophet* of God.

- ***Jacob*** (c. 2006-1859 BC) was the son of Isaac and Rebekah. He fathered 12 sons who became the 12 tribes of Israel, and their names were Reuben, Simeon, Levi, Judah, Zebulun, Issachar, Dan, Gad, Asher, Naphtali, Joseph, and Benjamin. The Old Testament tells us of a night in which Jacob wrestled all night with an angel, and as the dawn broke, Jacob demanded a blessing and the angel blessed him and gave him the new name "Israel," which means *one who wrestled with God* (*see* Genesis 32:24-30).

  Hebrews 11:21 says, "By faith Jacob, when he was a-dying, blessed both the sons of Joseph, and worshipped, leaning upon the top of his staff." This verse portrays Jacob prophesying a blessed future upon the sons of Joseph, who were his grandsons.

  Because God spoke significant prophetic revelation to Jacob that included many future events, ancient sources refer to Jacob as a *prophet* of God.

- ***Joseph*** lived from approximately 1561 to 1451 BC. He was the eleventh son of Jacob, born to Jacob's favorite wife Rachel. Joseph fathered two sons, Ephraim and Manasseh, who became two "half tribes" of the 12 tribes of Israel.

  The story of Joseph is found in Genesis 37-50. From a young age, he was shown dreams and visions. His brothers were moved with envy because of their father's intense love for Joseph (*see* Acts 7:9). And as a result of that and their anger concerning his prophetic dreams that they would one day bow before him and serve him, they sold him into slavery for 20 pieces of silver (*see* Genesis 37:28). His new owners took him into Egypt where a high-ranking Egyptian officer named Potiphar purchased him. Joseph was so trustworthy that he became Potiphar's personal attendant and was placed in charge of Potiphar's household (*see* Genesis 39:1-6).

  Potiphar's wife tried to seduce Joseph, but he refused her each time, reminding her that he would be loyal to God and to Potiphar. But eventually Potiphar's wife tried to force herself upon Joseph, and he fled from her. But before he fled from her, she grabbed his garment, tore a piece of it, kept it, and falsely used it as evidence to allege that Joseph tried to sexually assault her (*see* Genesis 39:7-19). Hearing this from his wife, Potiphar had Joseph arrested and imprisoned (*see* Genesis 39:20).

  In prison, Joseph found such favor that he was put in charge of all the other prisoners. Among the other prisoners were Pharaoh's butler and baker, who had both dreamed dreams that disturbed them deeply. Because Joseph had the prophetic ability to interpret dreams, he correctly interpreted the dreams (*see* Genesis 40:8-22). Two years later Pharaoh himself had disturbing dreams that his sorcerers could not interpret. But Pharaoh heard of Joseph's ability to correctly interpret dreams, so he summoned him to hear his dreams, and God gave Joseph the correct interpretation (*see* Genesis 41:1-36).

As a result, Pharaoh released Joseph from prison, gave him his own signet ring, dressed him in robes of linen, put a gold chain around his neck, and promoted him to the second highest position in all of Egypt (*see* Genesis 41:37-44). In Acts 7:10, we read that God "...delivered him out of all his afflictions, and gave him favour and wisdom in the sight of Pharaoh king of Egypt...." And we know that Pharaoh made him governor over all of Egypt and over all of Pharaoh's house.

As the second in command in Egypt, Joseph managed the vast hoard of grain during a terrible famine, and he saved his father and brothers from starvation. Then Joseph relocated his family to the fertile lands of Goshen near the ancient Egyptian city of Avaris, and he cared for his father, his brothers, and their families (*see* Genesis 45:10,11). Before he died at approximately the age of 110, Joseph prophesied that God would bring the children of Israel out of Egypt and back into the land that God promised to Abraham. And Joseph was so certain of their eventual return that he gave the order for his bones to be carried out of Egypt with them when they departed (*see* Genesis 50:25).

Hebrews 11:22 says, "By faith Joseph, when he died, made mention of the departing of the children of Israel; and gave commandment concerning his bones." And as he commanded, when the children of Israel later departed from Egypt, they carried Joseph's bones with them, and he was buried in Shechem on a piece of land that his father Jacob had purchased (*see* Exodus 13:19; Joshua 24:32).

Because of Joseph's ability to hear God's voice, to see visions, and to interpret dreams — and because he significantly prophesied the return of the children of Israel to the Promised Land — ancient sources refer to Joseph as a *prophet* of God.

- ***Moses*** lived approximately 1391–1271 BC according to Jewish sources,[3] although, as is true about many of the Old Testament patriarchs, the exact dates are unclear. Moses is considered to be the most important prophet for Israel and Judaism. The name "Moses" is not Hebrew, but was a name given to him by Pharaoh's daughter when she retrieved him from his basket in the Nile River (*see* Exodus 2:5). It seems the name Moses is connected to the name Thutmose, which was most likely the name of the Pharaoh's ruling family at the time that Moses was born.

  The story of Moses is so well established that in addition to the biblical account, it was referred to by Philo[4] and Josephus.[5] According to the book of Exodus, Moses was born during the time that Israel was enslaved in Egypt. The Pharaoh at that time feared that the rapidly multiplying Israelites might join a revolt against his authority, so a harsh period of treatment was enacted to break the will of the children of Israel and to drive them deeper into slavery (*see* Exodus 1:9-14). Among the harsh edicts was one that demanded all Hebrew boys be killed at birth (*see* Exodus 1:15,16).

  So Moses' parents hid him as an infant for a time (*see* Exodus 2:2 and Hebrews 11:23), but when Moses could no longer be concealed, his mother placed him into a basket, trusting that the currents of the Nile would carry him safely to the will of God. Those currents divinely led him directly into the arms of Pharaoh's daughter, who took him from the Nile, adopted him as her son, and saw to it that he would be reared to become a leader in Egypt.

Moses was educated "in the wisdom of the Egyptians" (*see* Acts 7:20-22) and had risen to such a position of power in Egypt that Josephus and other ancient writers recorded that Moses even victoriously led Egyptian forces against the Ethiopians in a crushing defeat. But eventually Moses began to be awakened to his true identify, and he fled Egypt (*see* Exodus 2:15) and found himself serving as a shepherd alongside the priest of Midian, whose name was Jethro (*see* Exodus 2:16-21; 3:1). After Moses served as a shepherd for 40 years, God spoke to him from a burning bush on Mount Horeb and instructed him to return to Egypt. There, God would use him to set the people of Israel free from slavery (*see* Exodus 3:1-10).

Because Moses had not spoken Egyptian fluently for 40 years, he was embarrassed by his lack of eloquence in speech (*see* Exodus 4:10), so God allowed his elder brother, Aaron, to become his spokesman (*see* Exodus 4:14-16). God instructed Moses to warn Pharaoh of 10 plagues that would come upon the land if he did not willingly let the people of Israel go free (*see* Exodus 4:22-11:8). As Pharaoh hardened his heart, the plagues came one after the other in a decimation of Egypt, and Pharaoh finally agreed to let the people of Israel go (*see* Exodus 12:29-33).

But as the children of Israel drew nigh to the Red Sea and Pharaoh feared he was losing his workforce, he reneged on his decision to let them go and sent his armies to pursue them. After the Red Sea miraculously parted and the children of Israel passed to the other side, Pharaoh's armies rode into the supernatural opening in the water in pursuit of them, but the sea closed upon them and they were drowned (*see* Exodus 14:23-28).

Moses eventually led the children of Israel to Mount Sinai, where God gave him the Ten Commandments that were written on stone tablets by the finger of God (*see* Exodus 31:18; 32:15,16). Moses delivered the laws of God to Israel, instituted Aaron and his sons as priests, and in his final act at Mount Sinai, Moses gave the instructions that God had given to him for the Tabernacle (*see* Exodus 25:1-40).

From Sinai, Moses led the Israelites to the border of Canaan, where he sent 12 spies into the land, who returned with samples of the land's fertility and richness, just as the Lord had described. But 10 of the spies warned that its inhabitants were giants that make the Israelites look like grasshoppers in comparison (*see* Numbers 13:28-33). Because the people believed the report of the disbelieving spies and rebelled against God's plan for them, it was then that God prophetically declared through Moses that this particular generation would wander the wilderness for 40 years until the generation died off that had rebelled. Their children would later enter the land to possess it under the leadership of Joshua (*see* Joshua 6:20).

At last, Moses climbed to the summit of Mount Nebo to see a panoramic view of the Promised Land spread out before him. His prophetic role was so momentous that the Bible says, "...There arose not a prophet since in Israel like unto Moses, whom God knew face to face" (Deuteronomy 34:10). Moses was still so physically strong at the time of his death that "his eye was not dim, nor his natural force abated," and he died at the age of 120 (*see* Deuteronomy 34:7).

Moses is traditionally regarded as the author of the first five books of the Bible. Most of what we know about Moses is derived from the books of Exodus, Leviticus, Numbers, and Deuteronomy, but there is a wealth of additional information about Moses that was written by rabbis in ancient Jewish literature.

According to Jewish tradition, Moses was *the greatest prophet who ever lived.*

- ***Aaron*** lived concurrently at the time of Moses, but died earlier than Moses. Aaron was the elder brother of Moses and younger brother to Miriam. Aaron was chosen by God to became the founder of the priesthood in the Old Testament, and his sons continued in the priesthood after him (*see* Numbers 20:26).

  Moses had lost his eloquence in speech while living in the wilderness, so Aaron, who was a good communicator, was chosen to become Moses' spokesman. As such, Aaron was present when signs were performed for the leaders of Israel before Moses went into Pharaoh (*see* Exodus 4:30). And as Moses' spokesman, Aaron spoke to Pharaoh on Moses' behalf (*see* Exodus 4:10-16). He was at Moses' side when the staff was cast before Pharaoh and it became a serpent (*see* Exodus 7:10-12), and he was present when the plagues were prophesied to come upon Egypt (*see* Exodus 7:19,20; 8:1,2,12,13,16,17; 9:3,8,9,15,18; 10:4,5,21; 11:4-6). At the age of 123 years, Aaron died in the wilderness before the children of Israel entered the land of promise (*see* Numbers 20:28).

  Because of his prophetic role alongside Moses and because he was a mouthpiece for the word of God, ancient sources refer to Aaron as a *prophet* of God.

- ***Miriam*** lived concurrently in the time of Moses and Aaron, and she was the older sister to the prophets Moses and Aaron. Miriam is recognized as one of the seven women whom ancient rabbis referred to as *prophetesses* (the others were Sarah, Deborah, Hannah, Abigail, Huldah, and Esther).

In addition to playing a role in preserving the life of baby Moses, Exodus 15:20 states that Miriam was a *prophetess*, and she was the first woman in Scripture to be identified that way. Exodus 15:20,21 says that Miriam led Israel in prophetic song, dance, and celebration of Pharaoh's army being drowned in the Red Sea.

Like Aaron and Moses, Miriam died before the children of Israel entered into the Promised Land (*see* Numbers 20:1). Though Miriam made substantial mistakes during the course of her life, she nevertheless in Scripture and by ancient sources is called a *prophetess* of God.

- ***Joshua*** lived from approximately 1355 to 1245 BC. He was the son of Nun and of the tribe of Ephraim. He was Moses' assistant (*see* Joshua 1:1), he was full of the spirit of wisdom (*see* Deuteronomy 34:9), and Moses laid his hands upon him to replace him as the next leader of Israel (*see* Deuteronomy 34:9). Joshua finally assumed the leadership role before the people of Israel after the death of Moses (*see* Joshua 1:1,2).

  Earlier in Numbers 13 and 14, the Scriptures tell us that Joshua was selected as one of the 12 spies who were sent to spy out the land of promise (*see* Numbers 13:17-20). When the 12 spies returned, they all reported that the land overflowed with milk and honey (*see* Numbers 13:26,27), however, 10 of the spies gave an evil report and said the giants of the land were insurmountable and impossible to overcome (*see* Numbers 13:28-33). Joshua and Caleb were convinced that the people of Israel were well able to overcome the challenges there (*see* Numbers 13:30; 14:6-9). Because the people of Israel believed the evil report of the 10 faithless spies, God forbade that generation to go into the Promised Land, with the exception of Joshua and Caleb.

When Moses died at the age of 120 (*see* Deuteronomy 34:7), Joshua stepped forward as a prophet of God and leader who led the new generation of the children of Israel into the Promised Land, where they witnessed the miraculous intervention of God time and again as enemies were driven back, and they took the land that God promised to their forefathers. Joshua 24:29 records that Joshua died at the age of 110 years and was buried in the Land of Promise. Verse 30 says Israel served God all the days of Joshua.

Ancient sources refer to Joshua as a *prophet* of God, and according to the Jewish tradition, the prophets Jeremiah and Huldah are descendants of Joshua.

- ***Phinehas*** was the son of Eleazer and the grandson of Aaron, and he served as priest during Israel's wandering in the wilderness. According to First Chronicles 6:4-8, Phinehas begat Abishua, who begat Bukki, who begat Uzzi, who begat Zerahiah, who begat Meraioth, who begat Amariah, who begat Ahitub, who begat Zadok the priest.

  But Phinehas is noted for his godly position against the heresy of Peor when the men of Israel spiritually and morally defiled themselves with the Moabite and Midianite prostitutes who dangled their bodies in front of the men and enticed them into idolatry and sin (*see* Numbers 25:1-9). Once when an Israelite man and a Midianite woman were caught in the very act of fornication in a tent, Phinehas, in a holy rage, ran a spear through both of their stomachs. He thus "stayed the plague" that had broken out among the people (*see* Numbers 25:6-9) and which had already killed 24,000 of them.

  Because Phinehas showed loyalty to God, God saw his action as an atonement for sin and decided not to destroy all of the children of

Israel in anger. Phinehas took a stand against sin, and his dramatic action brought an end to a plague that God sent to punish the Israelites for engaging in idolatry and for their intermingling with the Moabite and Midianite woman (*see* Numbers 25:10-12).

In Numbers 25:10-13 and in Psalm 106:28-31, Phinehas is commended for his action to stop Israel's fall into idolatry and fornication, as well as for stopping the desecration of God's sanctuary. Due to his strong moral position, Phineas was eventually appointed the third high priest of Israel and served at the sanctuary of Bethel (*see* Judges 20:28). Later, Moses charged Phinehas to lead a 12,000-strong Israelite army against the Midianites to avenge them for participating in the heresy of Peor.

In addition, Phinehas was the chief adviser in the war with the Benjamites, but according to some rabbinic sources, Phineas was eventually removed as high priest due to his not following instructions at the time of the battle of Gibeah and for failure on several other points. Due to these failures, the high priesthood was taken from him and temporarily given to the offspring of Ithamar, which then passed on to Eli and his sons Hophni and Phinehas.

Ancient sources refer to Phinehas as a *prophet* of God.

- ***Deborah*** (c. 1107-1067 BC) is identified by Scripture as a significant prophetess and one of the 12 judges of Israel. Deborah is recognized as one of the seven women whom ancient rabbis referred to as *prophetesses* (the others were Sarah, Miriam, Hannah, Abigail, Huldah, and Esther). The Bible tells us her husband's name was Lapidot, and Judges 4:4 says she led Israel. Judges 4:5 tells us that Deborah sat under a palm tree, and "...the children of Israel came up to her for judgment."

In addition to being a prophetess and judge, she commanded the armies of Israel to fight against their Canaanite enemies. She was so revered as a prophetess that the warrior Barak said he would wage war only if Deborah accompanied them (*see* Judges 4:8). Eventually Deborah agreed to join them (*see* Judges 4:9), and Israel so overcame the enemy that not a single man among the enemy survived (*see* Judges 4:16). When the battle concluded, Deborah triumphantly sang a prophetic song that is called the Song of Deborah (*see* Judges 5:1-31).

Deborah's role was great in the Old Testament, and ancient sources refer to Deborah as a *prophetess* of God.

- ***Hannah*** was the wife of Elkanah (*see* 1 Samuel 1:1,2), from the hill country of Ephraim. She was the mother of the prophet Samuel. Hannah is recognized as one of the seven women whom ancient rabbis referred to as *prophetesses* (the others were Sarah, Miriam, Deborah, Abigail, Huldah, and Esther).

  First Samuel begins with the story of Elkanah and Hannah, the mother of the prophet Samuel. Before the Temple was built in Jerusalem, the center of worship activities was in Shiloh, where Eli was serving as high priest at that time. Three times a year, faithful Jews would travel there to bring sacrifices. Although Hannah was deeply loved by her husband, she was incapable of producing children (*see* 1 Samuel 1:6).

  Once when Hannah accompanied her husband to Shiloh to sacrifice, she poured her anguish out to God and vowed that if He would give her a son, she would dedicate him to the work of God (*see* 1 Samuel 1:10-12). Eli, the high priest at that time, responded and told Hannah that God would grant her petition (*see* 1 Samuel

1:17). As prophesied, Hannah gave birth to a son whom she named Samuel. As vowed, when he was weaned, she took the young Samuel to Shiloh to serve alongside Eli (*see* 1 Samuel 1:24-28).

In addition to being the mother of the prophet Samuel, ancient sources refer to Hannah as a *prophetess* of God.

- ***Eli*** (c. 2888-2790 BC) was high priest in the ancient city of Shiloh, according to First Samuel, and was second to the last Israelite judge before the institution of the kings of Israel and Judah.

  Eli's two sons, Hophni and Phineas, were noted for their wicked behavior associated with taking more for themselves as priests than was allotted by law and for having sex with women at the entrance to the holy place (*see* 1 Samuel 2:22). Even though Eli was aware of his sons' vile behavior, he did not or could not stop their evil activities. People felt so abused by them that they stopping coming to the house of God (*see* 1 Samuel 2:16,17). As a result, God told Eli that he and his family would be destroyed and all male descendants would die (*see* 1 Samuel 2:27-34).

  Later when the Philistines captured the Ark of the Covenant, Eli's two sons were killed in a single day (*see* 1 Samuel 2:34; 4:10,11). When Eli heard about it, he fell backward out of a chair and died from a broken neck (*see* 1 Samuel 4:18). When his daughter-in-law who was pregnant and near delivery heard the news that the Ark of God had been captured and that her father-in-law and husband were dead, she went into labor, gave birth, and died in the process. But as she lay dying, she named the newborn boy Ichabod, which meant, *The Glory has departed from Israel* (*see* 1 Samuel 4:19-22).

Although the story of Eli is a warning to erring spiritual leaders, it nevertheless remains a fact that ancient Jewish sources refer to Eli as a *prophet* of God in his time.

- ***Samuel*** was the fifteenth judge over Israel and started his ministry after Eli, appearing on the scene from approximately 1154-1085 BC. He became recognized as the national prophet of Israel after the death of Eli (*see* 1 Samuel 7:5,6), and it is impossible to overstate the importance of Samuel's prophetic role in the history of Israel and the Bible. Samuel's mother was Hannah (*see* 1 Samuel 1:20), who is noted as one of the seven prophetesses of Israel, and his father was Elkanah, whose genealogy is found in the pedigree of the Kohathites (*see* 1 Chronicles 6:3-15). Samuel played a key role in the transition of Israel from the period of biblical judges to kings. He installed the first king, Saul, and later transitioned the kingdom from Saul to King David.

  Samuel was renowned as a prophet and seer from a very young age (*see* 1 Samuel 3:1-21). Throughout his ministry, he traveled in a circuit to deliver the prophetic word of the Lord, to preach, to rebuke, and to call people to holy living. In addition to being a national prophet, he also stood as a biblical judge. When Israel demanded a king like neighboring nations, it was Samuel whom the Lord used to anoint Saul as the first king of Israel (*see* 1 Samuel 10:1).

  When Saul arrogantly rebelled and disobeyed the word of the Lord, Samuel prophesied that Saul's house would not sit upon the throne, and that the kingdom would be taken from him and given to another man (*see* 1 Samuel 15:28). A short time later, Samuel arrived at the house of Jesse the Bethlehemite to anoint a new king among his sons, and that new king would be David, whom Samuel secretly anointed (*see* 1 Samuel 16:13). As years passed, Samuel's relationship with Saul was never mended, and Samuel provided sanctuary for David on occasion when Saul attempted to kill David (*see* 1 Samuel 19:18).

Just before his retirement, Samuel gathered the people at Gilgal to deliver a farewell speech in which he emphasized how prophets and judges were more important than kings, that kings should be accountable to God, and that Israel should not fall into the practice of idol worship. Samuel promised that if the people disobeyed these injunctions, God would subject them to foreign invaders (*see* 1 Samuel 12:14,15).

Samuel's function was so significant that ancient rabbis wrote that his prophetic role was nearly equal to that of Moses.[6] Biblical narrative states that Samuel was buried in Raman (*see* 1 Samuel 25:1). According to Jewish tradition, Samuel's tomb is located in a village that is visited by many devoted Jews today.

Ancient sources refer to Samuel as one of the most significant *prophets* to ever live.

- ***Saul*** (c. 1050-1000 BC) was the son of Kish, a member of the tribe of Benjamin, which was one of the 12 tribes of Israel, and he came from Gibeah. Saul married Ahinoam, daughter of Ahimaaz, with whom he had at least seven sons named Jonathan, Abinadab, Malchishua, Ishvi, Armani, Mephibosheth, and Ish-bosheth, and two daughters named Merab and Michal. He also had a concubine named Rispah, a daughter of Aiah, who bore two of his sons. Saul's only male descendant to survive was a crippled son of Jonathan who was five years old at the time of Saul's and Jonathan's tragic deaths.

  According to First Samuel 10:1, Saul was anointed by the prophet Samuel to be the first king of Israel. Samuel foretold that the Spirit of God would come upon Saul and change him into a different man. As Saul was traveling, he encountered a group of prophets who were prophesying and playing the lyre, tambourine, and flutes, and as Saul encountered them, First Samuel 10:10 says the Spirit of God came upon him and he began to prophesy with them (*see* 1 Samuel 10:17-24). Those who stood nearby and saw it, said, "Is Saul also among the prophets?" (*see* 1 Samuel 10:11).

Later when Saul once again encountered a group of other prophets who were prophesying and playing music, the Spirit of God once again came upon Saul and he began prophesy. Eventually, Saul falls in with the prophets momentarily and prophesies among them (*see* 1 Samuel 19:24).

Saul's tumultuous reign as the first king of Israel lasted for more than 20 years. It began with a severe break in his relationship with the prophet Samuel when Saul arrogantly disobeyed the word of the Lord. Because Saul veered from God's leadership early in his reign, Samuel prophetically told him, "Thou hast done foolishly: thou hast not kept the commandment of the Lord thy God, which he commanded thee: for now would the Lord have established thy kingdom upon Israel for ever. But now thy kingdom shall not continue: the Lord hath sought him a man after his own heart, and the Lord hath commanded him to be captain over his people, because thou hast *not kept that which* the Lord commanded thee" (*see* 1 Samuel 13:13,14).

Soon Samuel filled his horn with oil and went to the house of Jesse the Bethlehemite where he secretly anointed David as the new king of Israel (1 Samuel 16:1,13), which instigated a love-hate relationship that Saul felt toward David for the rest of his life.

At the very end of Saul's life, the Philistines made war with Israel, and Saul chose to lead his army to confront them at Mount Gilboa. The battle tragically fell to the Philistines.

The defeated Israelites fled and Saul found himself abandoned, so he asked his armor bearer to kill him. The armor bearer refused, so as First Samuel 31:4 says, Saul took his sword and "fell upon it," committing suicide rather than be taken prisoner by the Philistines. Three of Saul's sons (Jonathan, Abinadab, and Malchishua) died with him at the battle at Mount Gilboa (*see* 1 Samuel 31:2; 1 Chronicles 10:2).

When Saul died at the battle at Mount Gilboa (*see* 1 Samuel 31:3-6; 1 Chronicles 10:3-6), he had reigned for more than 20 years. He was buried in the region of Benjamin (*see* 2 Samuel 21:14), and Ishbosheth became king of Israel for a short period of time. But at the age of 40, Ish-bosheth was killed by two of his own captains. David then stepped into position as the anointed king of Israel.

It is worth noting that with all of Saul's struggles to faithfully follow God, during his lifetime and reign, there was no idolatry in Israel. Even though Saul strayed from God, the Spirit of God came upon him and he prophesied with prophets and even joined himself to the prophets.

For this reason, ancient sources refer to Saul as a *prophet* of God.

- ***David*** (c. 1040-970 BC) was the eighth and youngest son of Jesse (*see* 1 Samuel 16:10), of the tribe of Judah (*see* 1 Samuel 16:1; 2 Samuel 2:4), a descendant of Ruth (*see* Ruth 4:17), and the gospels of Matthew and Luke write that Jesus was a descendant of King David (*see* Matthew 1:1-17; Luke 3:23-32).

The prophet David began his life as a shepherd, but when God rejected Saul as king, the prophet Samuel came to the house of Jesse to anoint a new king, and David was remarkably chosen and anointed in the presence of his father and brothers as God's choice (*see* 1 Samuel 16:13). When King Saul was tormented by evil spirits and searched for someone to sooth his soul with prophetic music, David was summoned to play for him (*see* 1 Samuel 16:16-23). And afterward, David remained in Saul's service as a prophetic musician.

After King Saul died in battle (*see* 1 Samuel 31:4), David succeeded him as king, and his first action was to capture what is now the city of Jerusalem (*see* 2 Samuel 5:6-9).

In the 40 years in which David led Israel, he united the people, led them in many battles, and prophesied, planned, and supplied resources for the construction of the Temple at Jerusalem that would eventually be constructed by his son Solomon. First and Second Samuel, First and Second Kings, and First Chronicles are the primary biblical sources for the narrative of King David.

In spite of many personal struggles with enemies, with his own family, and with his own self-inflicted wounds that included adultery with Bathsheba and arranging for the murder of her husband Uriah, the Bible nevertheless states that David was "a man after God's own heart" (*see* 1 Samuel 13:14; Acts 13:22). After serving Israel for 40 years, David died at the age of 70 and was buried in the city of David (*see* 1 Kings 2:10). God prophetically promised David that his son Solomon would follow him as king, and that is precisely what occurred.

David wrote portions of the books of Psalms and Proverbs, and he is noted in Acts 2:29-31 and Hebrews 11:32, as well as ancient sources, as a *prophet* of God.

- ***Ahijah the Shilonite*** lived in the Eleventh Century BC and is mentioned in First Kings 11:29, which states that he was a prophet from the city of Shiloh in the days of King Solomon.

  In First Kings 11:29, Ahijah prophesied that Jeroboam would become king, and it was Ahijah who prophesied in First Kings 11:31-39 the separation of the Northern ten tribes from Solomon's united kingdom of Israel.

  In First Kings 11:38, the prophet Ahijah told Jeroboam that if he followed the Lord and was faithful to the Law, he would have God's promise that He would build for him a dynasty as enduring as the one He'd built for David and that He would give Israel to him.

  However, because of Jeroboam's rebellious conspiracy against Solomon's throne, Solomon tried to kill him, so Jeroboam fled to Egypt and stayed there until Solomon died. First Kings 12:4 says that upon hearing of Solomon's death, Jeroboam returned to encourage Solomon's son Rehoboam to lighten the load of labor that his father Solomon had imposed upon the people of Israel. But First Kings 12:13 and 14 says Rehoboam rather *increased* the load. The people of Israel rose up against Rehoboam, and everything Ahijah had prophesied was fulfilled: The kingdom was split, with Jeroboam as king over the northern kingdom of Israel, and with David's descendants ruling over the tribe of Judah.

  First Kings 12:26-30 tells us that because Jeroboam did not want the people to return to Jerusalem to worship the Lord, he set up a golden calf in Bethel and another in Dan where people could participate in idolatrous worship. In his life, Jeroboam continuously promoted idol worship, and his rebellion against God became so offensive that it is recorded in First Kings 13:33 and 34 that God prophesied He would destroy Jeroboam's entire household. Soon Jeroboam's son Abijah fell ill, and in First Kings 14:1 and 2, we read that Jeroboam asked his wife to clandestinely disguise herself to visit the prophet Ahijah with a gift and to ask for his help. Although Ahijah was elderly, the Lord allowed him to discern it was Jeroboam's wife in disguise.

Ahijah told her, "Go, tell Jeroboam that this is what the Lord, the God of Israel, says: 'I raised you up from among the people and appointed you ruler over my people Israel. I tore the kingdom away from the house of David and gave it to you, but you have not been like my servant David.... *You have done more evil than all who lived before you.* You have made for yourself other gods, idols made of metal, and you have aroused my anger and turned your back on me. Because of this, I am going to bring disaster on the house of Jeroboam. I will cut off from Jeroboam every last male in Israel — slave or free. I will burn up the house of Jeroboam as one burns dung, until it is all gone. Dogs will eat those belonging to Jeroboam who die in the city, and the birds will feed on those who die in the country. The Lord has spoken'" (1 Kings 14:7-11 *NIV*).

Ahijah prophesied that Jeroboam's son would quickly die and that his kingdom would be uprooted because of sin. Little more is known about Ahijah. The last mention of his name is found in First Kings 15:29 in connection with the fulfillment of his prophesy about the complete destruction of Jeroboam's family.

We are told in Second Chronicles that Ahijah authored a book described as the "Prophecy of Ahijah the Shilonite" (*see* 2 Chronicles 9:29). That book contained information about Solomon's reign, but it has not survived and is one of the non-canonical books referred to in the Bible. Jewish tradition credits Ahijah with having lived a very long life, linking his life-span with that of patriarchs like Methuselah.

In First Kings 14:4, Ahijah is described as being already extremely aged in Jeroboam's time. Rabbinical tradition states he was one of the seven long-lived saints whose successive lives extend over the whole history of mankind, each having transmitted the truth and history from his predecessor to the one succeeding him. One tradition says Ahijah was a Levite, a disciple of Moses, one of those who went out of Egypt, a member of David's court, and, finally, was the teacher of Elijah.

Ancient sources refer to Ahijah as a *prophet* of God.[7]

- ***Gad*** (c. 1649-1564 BC) lived concurrently with the reign of King David. He was a prophet and seer who served in King David's court, and he is referred to both in the Scriptures and also in the writings of the Jewish historian Josephus.[8] According to Jewish tradition, some of Gad's writings are recorded in portions of the books of First and Second Samuel.

  Gad appears for the first time in Scripture when he urges David to return to the land of Judah from his time of hiding in the land of Moab (*see* 1 Samuel 22:5). The next references to Gad appear after King David confesses his sin of taking a census of the people of Israel and Judah (*see* 2 Samuel 24:11-13; 1 Chronicles 21:9-13). An angel appeared to Gad and gave him instruction to go to King David and to deal with him about the egregious nature of his sin.

  God dispatched Gad to call David to repentance and to offer him three forms of divine punishment (*see* 1 Chronicles 21:9), and David chose pestilence as punishment. Gad is mentioned a final time in Second Samuel 24:18, where he is noted for coming to David to tell him to build an altar "in the threshing floor of Aranuah the Jebusite" to offer a sacrifice to stop the pestilence David had chosen as a form of his punishment for taking a census of the people.

Due to his significant role in King David's life, ancient sources refer to Gad as a prominent *prophet* during the time of King David.

- ***Nathan*** lived approximately in the Eleventh Century BC and concurrently with the reigns of King David and King Solomon. God used the prophet Nathan to confront David about his adultery with Bathsheba and the subsequent murder of her husband Uriah.

  Like the prophet Gad, Nathan was a court prophet and was involved in the highest levels of both David's and Solomon's courts. It was Nathan who prophesied that David's dynasty would endure forever (*see* 2 Samuel 7:16), and it was Nathan who, with Zadok the priest, anointed Solomon to be king after King David's death (*see* 1 Kings 1:32-39).

  In addition to Bible verses that vividly describe Nathan's prophetic activities, he is specifically called a *prophet* of God in Second Samuel 7:2; 12:25; First Kings 1:8,10,22,23,32,34,38,44,45; First Chronicles 17:1; 29:29; and Second Chronicles 9:29; 29:25.

  First Chronicles 29:9 and Second Chronicles 9:29 record that Nathan wrote a narrative about the reigns of King David and King Solomon, and he also wrote what was called the book of Nathan the prophet.

  Ancient sources refer to Nathan as a significant *prophet* during the eras of David and Solomon.

- ***Abigail*** lived concurrently in the time frame of King David. Abigail is recognized as one of the seven women whom ancient rabbis referred to as *prophetesses* (the others were Sarah, Miriam, Deborah, Hannah, Huldah, and Esther). Ancient rabbis recorded that Abigail was one of the most remarkable women in Jewish history and one of Israel's four great beauties, the other three being Sarah, Rahab, and Esther. David was smitten not only by her beauty, but also by her moral strength, integrity, and dignity (*see* 1 Samuel 25:20-35).

Due to the fact that she foretold David's future kingship shortly after the death of the prophet Samuel, ancient sources refer to Abigail as a *prophetess.*

- ***Asaph*** also lived concurrently during the time of King David. He was the son of Berechiah, the grandson of Shimea, and was a Levite from part of the Gershomite clan. He was born into an ecclesiastical line, but he could not serve as a priest because he was not descended from Aaron. He later became a musician and a cymbal player (*see* 1 Chronicles 15:16,17,19).

  After David captured Jerusalem and wanted to give the Ark of the Covenant a permanent dwelling place, the Bible says that David erected a tent for it and gave the order for the Ark of the Covenant to be transported there (*see* 1 Chronicles 15:1-3). To welcome the Ark to its new resting place, David led a celebrative parade that included a musical procession that was led by the Levites (*see* 1 Chronicles 15:25,28). At David's request, the Levites appointed musicians to play various instruments, and Asaph was appointed at that time to play the cymbal alongside Heman and Ethan (*see* 1 Chronicles 15:16-18).

  David later appointed Asaph as Chief Musician responsible for the music ministry during his reign (*see* 1 Chronicles 16:4,5). Asaph prophesied through the many songs and psalms he wrote and also prophesied by playing the cymbals. First Chronicles 25:1 refers to

Asaph as a *prophet* and a *seer* who had ability to prophesy and to see into the spirit realm (*see also* 2 Chronicles 29:30).

Ancient sources also refer to Asaph as a *prophet* who served in the court of King David.

- ***Heman*** lived in the Eleventh Century BC, concurrently with the time of King David. He was the grandson of Samuel the prophet, a Kohathite. Second Chronicles 29:1,15 records that, at first, Heman and others gathered together at the king's command on the high places of Gibeon to sanctify themselves, and, together with Jeduthun, they worshiped and cleansed the house of the Lord.

  First Chronicles 6:33 refers to Heman as "the singer," and in First Chronicles 15:16-22, we read that Heman was appointed with Asaph and Ethan to lead vocal and instrumental worship for the temple during the reign of David.

  First Chronicles 25:5 identifies Heman as one of King David's *prophetic seers*, and other ancient sources refer to Heman as a *prophet* of God in the court of King David.

- ***Jeduthun*** lived in the Eleventh Century BC concurrently with the life of King David. First Chronicles 16:41,42; 25:1; and Psalm 39:1 inform us that Jeduthun was appointed to be one of David's chief musicians along with Asaph and Heman. The music for several Psalms is attributed to these musical leaders.

  First Chronicles 25:3 tells us that Jeduthun had sons who were named Dedaliah, Zeri, Jeshaiah, Shimei, Hashabiah, and Mattithiah, and they were also musicians who joined him in playing the harp, cymbals, and lyre.

Second Chronicles 35:15 tells us that in addition to being a chief musician, Jeduthun was the "king's *seer*," and this means he not only led music for David, but also *prophesied* to him and observed things in the spirit realm on David's behalf.

Ancient sources refer to Jeduthun as a *prophet* of God.

- ***Solomon*** lived approximately 990 to 931 BC. He was the son of King David and Bathsheba. He followed David as king, he was fabulously wise and wealthy, and he was the ruler of the united kingdom of Israel. Jewish tradition states that Solomon was a Jewish prophet.

  Solomon was born as the second-born child of David and Bathsheba, who was the widow of Uriah the Hittite. When Solomon became king, he used the vast wealth provided by his father, along with his own additional resources — plus resources supplied by his leaders — to carry out his father's plans to build the First Temple in Jerusalem and to dedicate the Temple (*see* 1 Chronicles 29:1-8). He is the subject of many other later references and legends, but the primary source of information about Solomon comes from Second Samuel, First Kings, and Second Chronicles.

  Solomon was instructed by his father to begin his rule with an extensive purge that included killing Joab, his father's former military general, and Solomon further consolidated his position by appointing friends throughout his administration. He expanded his military strength, especially the cavalry and chariot arms, and founded numerous colonies, some of which doubled as trading posts and military outposts. He continued his father's profitable business relationship with Hiram I, king of Tyre. Together they sent out expeditions to distant lands to engage in the trade of luxury products such as gold, silver, sandalwood, pearls, ivory, apes, and peacocks.

In First Kings 3:5-9 and Second Chronicles 1:7-10, God asked Solomon what He most wanted from Him, and Solomon answered that he sought wisdom. As a result, God granted wisdom to Solomon that has never been exceeded by any leader. Solomon's wisdom is recorded in biblical books, and he is traditionally considered the author of Proverbs, Ecclesiastes, and the Song of Solomon.

But in spite of God's goodness to Solomon, First Kings 11:4 tells us that Solomon's "wives turned away his heart after other gods." Though it is hard to comprehend, First Kings 11 tells us that the influence of Solomon's pagan wives led to his descent into idolatry. First Kings 11:9-12; 30-34 communicates that it was on account of these sins that the Lord punished Solomon by removing most of the tribes of Israel from rule by Solomon's house.

According to the Bible, Solomon was the last ruler of a united Israel, and after his reign of 40 years, he died of natural causes at about 60 years of age (*see* 1 Kings 11:42,43). When Solomon died, his son, Rehoboam, followed him as the next king, but because ten of the tribes refused to accept him, the kingdom was split, and Jeroboam ended up ruling over the larger, northern kingdom while Rehoboam ruled the smaller southern kingdom of Judah that consisted of the two tribes Judah and Benjamin.

Ancient sources refer to Solomon as a *prophet* of God.

- ***Iddo*** also lived in approximately the Eleventh Century and Tenth Century BC. He was a biblical prophet who lived during the reigns of kings Solomon, Rehoboam, and Abijah. Although much is not known of Iddo, we are told that the events of Solomon's and Abijah's reigns and many of Iddo's prophecies were recorded in ancient prophetic writings that are not known today. Iddo is also credited with providing the histories of King Rehoboam and his son King Abijah (*see* 2 Chronicles 13:22).

Other early Jewish writings have identified Iddo as the unnamed prophet of First Kings 13, as the Jewish historian Josephus also does. The unnamed prophet in First Kings 13 prophesied against Jeroboam. After being ill-advised by an older, lying prophet, the unnamed prophet was killed by a lion (*see* 1 Kings 13:11-25), and the older, lying prophet then buried the unnamed prophet in a tomb he had previously prepared for himself (*see* 1 Kings 13:30).

Second Kings 23:17,18 tells us that nearly 300 years later, during the rule of King Josiah, Josiah burned human bones to ritually defile Jeroboam's altar, but in the process of unearthing human remains at those burial sites, Josiah noted engravings on an ancient tomb for an unnamed prophet that had been buried there. When Josiah inquired about the identity of the unnamed prophet, he was told it was the tomb of the prophet who had accurately forecasted the destruction of Jeroboam's altar. Upon hearing this, Josiah gave the charge that the tomb remain untouched as a commemoration of his accurate prophecy.

In addition to Iddo possibly being the unnamed prophet of First Kings 13, some ancient writers also identify Iddo as Oded the prophet who courageously removed abominable idols from the land (*see* 2 Chronicles 15:8). Erza 5:1 additionally states that Zechariah was the son of the prophet Iddo.

Scripture and ancient sources refer to Iddo as a *prophet* of God.

- ***Shemaiah*** lived in approximately the Tenth Century BC. Shemaiah was a prophet during the time of King Rehoboam (*see* 1 Kings 12:22-24). According to First Kings and Second Chronicles, ten of the 12 tribes of Israel separated from Judah and Benjamin. To restore them, King Rehoboam assembled an army of 180,000 men to fight, but the intervention of the prophet Shemaiah prevented the war from occurring. He prophesied that God had declared "this thing is from me" (referring to the separation) and that Rehoboam was not to fight against the Northern tribes (*see* 1 Kings 12:24). In addition, Second Chronicles states that the prophet Shemaiah prophesied the eventual punishment of Rehoboam by the Egyptian Pharaoh, Shishak (*see* 2 Chronicles 12:5).

  Ancient sources refer to Shemaiah as a *prophet* of God.

- ***Azariah*** lived in approximately the Tenth Century and Ninth Century BC. We read of Azariah in Second Chronicles 15 where the Bible says the Spirit of God came upon him, and he was prophetically moved to go out and meet King Asa of Judah to exhort him to return Israel to God and to restore the influence of the priesthood and the law to the land (*see* 2 Chronicles 15:1-7).

  Because Asa received Azariah's exhortation, he carried out a number of great reforms that included the removal and destruction of false idols, repairs to the altar in the complex in Jerusalem, and Second Chronicles 15:19 says an extended period of peace followed Asa's obedience in carrying out these reforms.

  Although little more is known of the prophet Azariah, his prophetic role was substantial in calling the people back to their relationship with God.

  Ancient sources refer to Azariah as a *prophet* of God.

- ***Hanani*** lived in approximately the Ninth Century BC. It seems that in addition to being the father of the prophet Jehu, Hanani was the prophet that God also used to speak a corrective word to King Asa of Judah when he wrongly entered into a political, military, and business league with Ben-Hadad I, King of Syria (*see* 2 Chronicles 16:1-4). Asa did not receive the prophetic correction Hanani delivered — instead, he ordered the prophet to be arrested and imprisoned in stocks (*see* 2 Chronicles 16:7-10). In spite of the hardships he endured, Hanani remained faithful to God and to his prophetic responsibility.

  Ancient sources refer to Hanani as a *prophet* of God.

- ***Jehu*** was the son of the prophetic seer named Hanani who rebuked King Asa of Judah (*see* 2 Chronicles 16:7-10). Jehu served as a prophet during the time Baasha was king of Israel and Jehoshaphat was king of Judah. It was Jehu who foretold the destruction of the house of King Baasha (*see* 1 Kings 16:1-4), and he rebuked Jehoshaphat for joining King Ahab in the attack on Ramoth Gilead (*see* 2 Chronicles 19:2,3). The chronicler of First and Second Samuel attributes portions of those books to Jehu.

  Ancient sources refer to Jehu as a *prophet* of God.

- ***Micaiah*** lived in approximately the Eighth Century BC. He was the son of Imlah, a prophet who foretold the death of King Ahab (*see* 1 Kings 22:7-28). Micaiah as a rule did not acquiesce to say whatever the king wished to hear. This explains why King Ahab said, "I detest him, for he does not prophesy good concerning me, but evil" (*see* 1 Kings 22:8). Other prophets at that time falsely prophesied Ahab and his allies would have victory, but when Micaiah prophesied contrarily to the word of the false prophets, he was imprisoned for a time (*see* 1 Kings 22:26,27).

In spite of his ill-treatment by Ahab, Micaiah bore no animosity toward him and even attempted to prevent his death and the defeat of Israel. Micaiah is remembered for his uncompromising commitment to the word of the Lord, and his uncompromising stand was especially evidenced at one point when he stood alone against 400 false prophets that Ahab gathered together in his court, and Micaiah boldly called them false prophets (*see* 1 Kings 22:28).

Ancient sources refer to Micaiah as an uncompromising *prophet* of God.

- ***Obadiah*** lived in approximately the Ninth Century BC. According to ancient Jewish tradition, Obadiah was a convert to Judaism from Edom. He was a descendant of Eliphaz (the friend of Job) and was identified with the Obadiah who was the servant of Ahab. Obadiah was chosen to prophesy against Edom because he was himself an Edomite. Having lived with two godless persons such as Ahab and Jezebel, Obadiah loathed wickedness and was deemed to be the most suitable prophet to prophesy against Edom.

  Obadiah was said to be very rich, but all his wealth was expended in feeding other poorer prophets. Jewish tradition says that Obadiah's fear of God was great and that if the house of Ahab had been capable of being blessed, it would have been blessed for Obadiah's sake (*see* 1 Kings 18:3).

  Obadiah was supposed to have received the gift of prophecy for having hidden the "hundred prophets" from the persecution of Jezebel (*see* 1 Kings 18:4). According to the account, he hid the hundred prophets in two caves so that if those in one cave were discovered, those in the other could escape.

  Ancient sources refer to Obadiah as a *prophet* of God.

- ***Oded*** lived in approximately the Tenth Century BC. He is mentioned in Second Chronicles 15:1 as the father of Azariah the prophet, whom God used to initiate major national and spiritual reforms during the reign of King Asa in the kingdom of Judah.

  Ancient sources refer to Oded as a *prophet* of God.

- ***Jahaziel*** lived approximately in the Tenth Century and Ninth Century BC. There are multiple Jahaziels in the Old Testament, but one of them, a Levite, is recorded as one who delivered a prophetic message from God at a time when an attack was being waged on Judah by the nations of Moab, Ammon, and Edom in the days of King Jehoshaphat.

  After Jehoshaphat declared a fast and prayed for God's direction and protection, Second Chronicles 20:14,15 says, "Then in the midst of the congregation the spirit of the Lord came upon Jahaziel son of Zechariah son of Benaiah son of Joel son of Mattaniah the Levite, of the sons of Asaph, and he said, 'Give heed, all Judah and the inhabitants of Jerusalem and King Jehoshaphat; thus said the Lord to you, "Do not fear or be dismayed by this great multitude, for the battle is God's, not yours…."'"

  As a result of this prophetic message delivered by Jahaziel, the following morning, King Jehoshaphat called upon his people to trust in the Lord and supernaturally led them forth with praise and worship into battle. In this famous story, they saw their enemies turn in disarray against each other, and Jehoshaphat and his forces returned to Jerusalem in joyous celebration.

  Ancient sources refer to Jahaziel as a *prophet* of God.

- ***Eliezer*** lived in approximately the Ninth Century BC. He was the son of Dodavah or Mareshah, and he is recorded as delivering a divine rebuke to King Jehoshaphat when he formed a league with Ahaziah (the king of Israel) and together with him built ships that were intended to be used for trade with Tarshish.

  Eliezer prophesied to Jehoshaphat and told him, "Because thou hast joined thyself with Ahaziah, the Lord hath broken thy works" (*see* 2 Chronicles 20:37). The verse goes on to say, "And the ships were broken, that they were not able to go to Tarshish." The ships sank as a divine retribution upon Jehoshaphat for forming an alliance with an ungodly king.

  Ancient sources refer to Eliezer as a *prophet* of God.

  Hosea lived in approximately the Eighth Century BC. He is noted as the author of the book of Hosea, and he is the first of 12 minor prophets whose prophetic writings were compiled in the Second Temple period. It seems that Hosea conducted his prophetic ministry primarily in the northern kingdom of Israel, where he was a native.

  Scholars have often referred to Hosea as a prophet of doom, but beneath his message was a promise of restoration. Jewish tradition states he was the greatest prophet of his generation.

  Very little background information is known about Hosea, but the book of Hosea states that he married Gomer, a daughter of Diblaim, who proved to be unfaithful. Hosea knew she would be unfaithful, but the marriage was arranged by God as a prophetic symbol of Israel's unfaithfulness to God, and he and Gomer's marital union illustrated the breakdown between God and His people Israel. Hosea's prophetic ministry was quite long, extending approximately 60 years and covering the span from the reign of Jeroboam II to the reign of Hoshea, and it ended sometime before the fall of Samaria. Hosea was the only prophet of Israel of his time who left any written prophecy.

Ancient sources refer to Hosea as a *prophet* of God.

- ***Amos*** lived in approximately the Eighth Century BC. He was a prophet from the southern kingdom of Israel, a contemporary with Hosea and Isaiah, and was one of the 12 minor prophets of the Old Testament. He is regarded to be the author of the book of Amos. His prophetic ministry spanned the reigns of Israel's King Jeroboam II and Uzziah of Judah. It is believed that Amos was the first prophet to write the prophetic messages he received. No earlier instance of a literary prophet is known.

  Before he was called to be a prophet, Amos was a shepherd and farmer. In Amos 7:14, he wrote that he was not "a son of a prophet," and some scholars take this to mean he was not descended from prophets, nor was he trained in a school of prophets. His prophetic ministry occurred at a time of peace and prosperity, yet at a time of great neglect of God's Law, when there was also a vast disparity between the wealthy and the poor. As a result, Amos prophetically addressed many issues having to do with justice. Although he came from the Southern kingdom, Amos's prophetic messages were directed to the Northern kingdom.

  Although it cannot be determined with certainty, one Jewish tradition states that Amos was killed by the son of Amariah, a priest of Bethel, but that he made his way back to his homeland before he died, and he was subsequently buried there.

  Ancient sources refer to Amos as a *prophet* of God.

- ***Amoz*** is mentioned in Isaiah 1:1; 13:1 and in Second Kings 19:2,20; 20:1, and he was the father of the prophet Isaiah.

  One ancient tradition says that when the name of a prophet's father is given, the father was also a prophet, so this means Amoz would have been a prophet like his son. Ancient rabbis wrote that Amoz was also the brother of King Amaziah, who was King of Judah at that time. This being the case, it would mean that Isaiah himself was a member of the royal family.

  Some speculate that Amoz is the "the man of God" referred to in Second Chronicles 25:7-9 who warned King Amaziah to free the Israelite mercenaries he had hired.

  Ancient sources refer to Amoz as a *prophet* of God.

- ***Elijah*** lived approximately in the Ninth Century BC. According to the books of First and Second Kings, he was a miracle-working prophet who lived in the Northern kingdom of Israel during the reign of the wicked King Ahab.

  The kingdom of Israel was divided into the Northern kingdom of Israel and the Southern kingdom of Judah, with Jerusalem as the Southern kingdom's capital. Omri was the king of the Northern kingdom, and he enacted policies that were contrary to the Law, which were intended to lead the people away from Jerusalem (*see* 1 Kings 16:25,26).

  To secure peace with his neighbors, Omri arranged a political marriage between Jezebel and his son Ahab (*see* 1 Kings 16:31). This union brought peace and prosperity to Israel for a time, but Jezebel invited a large entourage of priests and prophets of Baal into the country. In First Kings 17:1, the prophet Elijah warns Ahab that catastrophic famine was coming to the land because Ahab had "done evil in the sight of the Lord" (*see* 1 Kings 16:30).

King Ahab despised Elijah and denounced him as being the "troubler of Israel" (*see* 1 Kings 18:17). Elijah, however, retorted that Ahab was the one who had troubled Israel by promoting the worship of false gods (*see* 1 Kings 18:18). To demonstrate whose power was greatest, Elijah suggested a confrontation between God's power and Baal's power at Mount Carmel (*see* 1 Kings 18:19). At Elijah's prodding, Ahab accepted the challenge and summoned 450 prophets of Baal and 400 prophets of Asherah to Mount Carmel for a confrontation of divine powers. At the conclusion of that event, fire fell from Heaven to consume the sacrifice and the earth and the water in the trench around the altar, and Elijah ordered the slaughter of the prophets of Baal (*see* 1 Kings 18:38-40).

Many pages are needed to cover the miracle-working ministry of the prophet Elijah. In the biblical narrative, we find that Elijah had both high and low moments, including everything from his victory over the false prophets at Mount Carmel — to his running from Jezebel and hiding from her — to his experience of God's mighty presence as he was hiding in a cave, after which God dispatched him again to anoint Hazael as King of Aram, Jehu as King of Israel, and Elisha as his own prophetic replacement.

Time and time again, Elijah encountered wicked King Ahab, and in First Kings 21, Elijah prophesied Ahab's bloody death (*see* 1 Kings 21:17-19), that Jezebel would be eaten by dogs in Jezreel (*see* 1 Kings 21:23), and that Ahab's entire family would be eliminated (*see* 1 Kings 21:21). As prophesied, Ahab died a bloody death (*see* 1 Kings 22:29-36), Jezebel's body was eaten by dogs (*see* 2 Kings 9:30-37), and Ahab's sons were all destroyed (*see* 2 Kings 10:1-17).

The story of Elijah goes on and on, but he is remembered for many miracles that included resurrections from the dead and, as noted, even calling fire down from Heaven. Finally, a chariot of fire appeared and Elijah was taken up into Heaven, supernaturally transported by a whirlwind of God's power (*see* 2 Kings 2:11). As Elijah was finally lifted up into Heaven, he dropped his prophetic mantle to the ground, and Elisha picked it up to continue his prophetic ministry (*see* 2 Kings 2:13).

The influence of Elijah goes well into the New Testament, where we are told that Elijah appeared to Jesus with Moses on the Mount of Transfiguration (*see* Luke 9:28-31). The ministry of John the Baptist was likened to Elijah (*see* John 1:19-21), and James referred to Elijah's passions, struggles, and powerful prayers (*see* James 5:17,18).

Ancient sources refer to Elijah as a notable *prophet* of God.

- ***Elisha*** lived approximately in the same time frame as the prophet Elijah. In the biblical narrative, we read that he became a disciple of Elijah the prophet. Elisha was the son of a wealthy farmer and landowner (*see* 1 Kings 19:19). When Elijah first met him, Elisha was "one of them that was plowing with twelve yokes of oxen" (*see* 1 Kings 19:19). Elijah threw his mantle over Elisha's shoulders and the prophetic mantle came upon Elisha at that moment. Surrendering everything he had to follow Elijah, Elisha killed the yoke of oxen and burned the wood of his plough (*see* 1 Kings 19:20,21). After he told his family and friends farewell, he "went after Elijah, and ministered unto him" (*see* 1 Kings 19:21).

  From that point onward, Elisha became Elijah's attendant and apprentice until Elijah was taken up into Heaven.

Eventually a moment came when "sons of the prophets" told Elisha that Elijah was going to depart (*see* 2 Kings 2:3-5). Knowing this was about to occur, Elisha requested a "double portion" of Elijah's anointing (*see* 2 Kings 2:9). When the chariot of fire appeared to transport Elijah into Heaven, Elijah threw his mantle to the ground and Elisha picked it up (*see* 2 Kings 2:13). When that mantle fell on Elisha, he was divinely empowered to continue Elijah's dramatic ministry. He had requested a "double portion" of Elijah's anointing and throughout the ministry of Elisha, he performed *exactly double* the number of the miracles that Elijah had done (*see* 2 Kings 2-11).

In a style similar to Elijah, Elisha became known as a mighty prophet that performed many miracles that included the miraculous birth of a son, the resurrection of the dead, turning poisonous food into healthy food, feeding 100 men with 20 loaves of new barley, healing Naaman of leprosy, and so on (*see* 2 Kings 4:32-35; 4:41-44 and 5:10).

Elisha prophesied Hazael would become king of Syria (*see* 2 Kings 8:7-15), he directed one of the sons of the prophets to anoint Jehu as king of Israel (*see* 2 Kings 9:6), and he gave the orders for Ahab's 70 sons to be executed (*see* 2 Kings 10:10). Elisha prophesied many events, including many battles that were carried out successfully as he had forecasted.

It seemed the "double portion" of miracles that Elisha requested fell short by a single miracle. But according to Second Kings 13:21, about one year after Elisha's burial, a person's dead body was tossed into Elisha's grave, and when that body touched Elisha's remains, the dead man "revived and stood up on his feet." That resurrection brought the number of miracles performed by Elisha's presence to exactly "double" the miracles that had been performed by Elijah.

As with Elijah's ministry, to fully cover Elisha's ministry would take many pages and even books. But suffice it to say that ancient sources refer to Elisha as a mighty *prophet* of God.

- ***Jonah*** lived approximately in the Eighth Century BC. He was the son of the prophet Amittai, a prophet from the Northern kingdom of Israel. Jonah is the focus of the book of Jonah, which chronicles his reluctance to deliver God's prophetic message to the kingdom of Nineveh and Jonah's subsequently being thrown from a ship and swallowed by a large fish. The creature that swallowed Jonah is usually depicted as a whale, but the Hebrew text uses a word that means it was a "giant fish." In the belly of the fish, Jonah repented for not obeying God, the fish vomited him out, and Jonah went on to fulfill God's prophetic mandate to call the people of Nineveh to repentance, which they received and responded to and thus avoided divine judgment.

  Jonah's prophetic role is so important that even Jesus refers to this prophet of God, and ancient sources also refer to Jonah as a *prophet* of God.

- ***Joel*** lived in approximately the Eighth Century BC. He was originally from Judah, and it is quite possible that he was a prophet associated with the period of the Second Temple. In addition to being a prophet in Israel, Joel was the second of the 12 minor prophets and is the author of the book of Joel. Joel's name is mentioned only once in the book of Joel (*see* Joel 1:1), but he is significantly referenced by Peter on the day of Pentecost when Peter speaks of a last-days outpouring of the Holy Spirit (*see* Acts 2:14-36).

  Ancient sources refer to Joel as a *prophet* of God.

- ***Micah*** lived in approximately the Eighth Century and Seventh Century BC. He was from southwest Judah and prophesied during the reigns of kings Jotham, Ahaz, and Hezekiah. Micah is one of the 12 minor prophets who penned books of the Old Testament, and his prophetic ministry occurred during the same time as the prophets Isaiah, Amos, and Hosea.

  God spoke many prophetic messages through Micah. Many of them were directed toward the future of Jerusalem. It was Micah who prophesied the destruction of Jerusalem (*see* Micah 3:12; Jeremiah 26:18) — and its future glorious restoration. Micah promised that its eventual restoration would be more glorious than before (*see* Micah 4:1-3), and he prophesied a day of universal peace, during which time a governor would rule from the city of Jerusalem (*see* Micah 5:1,2). He rebuked the people of Judah for their dishonesty and idolatry (*see* Micah 3:8-11), and he prophesied that Bethlehem would be the birthplace of the Messiah (*see* Micah 5:2).

  It was Micah who famously wrote, "He hath shewed thee, O man, what is good; and what doth the Lord require of thee, but to do justly, and to love mercy, and to walk humbly with thy God?" (*see* Micah 6:8).

  Ancient sources refer to Micah as a *prophet* of God.

- ***Isaiah*** lived in approximately the Eighth Century BC. He is the prophet after whom the book of Isaiah is named. In Isaiah 1:1, he refers to himself as a prophet. We additionally read in Isaiah 1:1 that Isaiah prophesied during the reigns of Uzziah, Jotham, Ahaz, and Hezekiah. Ancient rabbis wrote that the prophet Amoz, Isaiah's father, was the brother of King Amaziah, who was King of Judah at that time. This being the case, Isaiah himself was a member of the royal family. Some early sources state that Isaiah's wife was a prophetess as well. But Isaiah lived until the fourteenth year of the reign of Hezekiah, and he may have been a contemporary of Manasseh for some years. Thus, it seems Isaiah served prophetically for possibly 64 years.

Shalmaneser, king of the Assyrian kingdom, determined he would subdue the Northern kingdom of Israel and destroy Samaria. But as long as Ahaz reigned, the Southern kingdom of Judah was untouched by the Assyrian power. When King Hezekiah sat on the throne, he was encouraged to rebel against the king of Assyria, entering an alliance with the king of Egypt (*see* 2 Kings 18:19-21). On account of that, the Assyrian king threatened Hezekiah and eventually invaded the land. The powerful Assyrian king, Sennacherib, led a large army into Judah, at which time Hezekiah was humiliated and ended up submitting to the Assyrians (*see* 2 Kings 18:14).

After a brief interval, war broke out again and Sennacherib led another army into Judah. One detachment threatened Jerusalem, and the prophet Isaiah encouraged Hezekiah to resist the Assyrians. When Sennacherib heard of this decision to resist, he sent a threatening letter to Hezekiah (*see* 2 Kings 19:10).

In response, the prophet Isaiah prophesied to Hezekiah, saying, "Thus saith the Lord, the God of Israel: Whereas thou hast prayed to Me against Sennacherib king of Assyria, this is the word which the Lord hath spoken concerning him: The virgin daughter of Zion hath despised thee and laughed thee to scorn; the daughter of Jerusalem hath shaken her head at thee. Whom hast thou taunted and blasphemed? And against whom hast thou exalted thy voice? Yea, thou hast lifted up thine eyes on high, even against the Holy One of Israel" (*see* 2 Kings 19:20-22; Isaiah 37:21-23).

Second Kings 19 records that an angel sent by God attacked the Assyrian army, and 185,000 of the Assyrian men were killed in a single night (*see* 2 Kings 19:35). The divine attack was so devastating that Sennacherib never recovered from it, and he made no more military expeditions against Israel after that event. The balance of King Hezekiah's reign remained peaceful.

Isaiah carried out his prophetic ministry in a stately manner for approximately 64 years. The time and manner of his death are not specified in the Bible, but an early Jewish tradition is that the prophet Isaiah was sawn in half during the reign of the wicked King Mannaseh. Second Kings 21:16 (*NKJV*) says, "Moreover Manasseh shed very much innocent blood, till he had filled Jerusalem from one end to the another...."

It is believed that during this rampage of bloodshed that the prophet Isaiah was killed with a wooden saw. Death by sawing was one of the most savage, vicious forms of slaughter ever to be conceived. When this hideous form of execution began, a victim was first stripped naked and then fixed in a position with his feet extending upward and his head downward. This caused a strong flow of blood to the torso and brain, which kept the victim alive longer and thus caused him to experience the maximum amount of suffering possible.

In fact, the victim often lived sufficiently long enough to see, hear, and experience the horror of the executioners violently heaving the saw back and forth through his flesh. The gore connected with this type of execution *cannot* be exaggerated.

The early Christian apologists, Tertullian and Justin Martyr, along with Origen of Alexandria, all recorded that Isaiah was sawn in half.[9] Even Hebrews 11:37 speaks of Old Testament saints who "...were stoned, they *were sawn asunder,* were tempted, were slain with the sword: they wandered about in sheepskins and goatskins; being destitute, afflicted, tormented." Scholars generally agree the words "sawn asunder" is a specific reference to the gruesome death that was experienced by Isaiah during the reign of Mannaseh.

Ancient sources refer to Isaiah as a *prophet* of God. Because he was of royal descent and performed his prophetic ministry in such a stately manner, he is referred to as *a prince of prophets.*

- ***Nahum*** lived in approximately the Seventh Century BC. He is among the minor prophets of the Old Testament and is regarded to be the author of the book of Nahum. Very little is known about his personal history except that he was from the town of Elkosh and his name means "comforter." The Bible tells us he lived peacefully among the Elkoshites and was even referred to as "the Elkoshite" (*see* Nahum 1:1).

  One account suggests that Nahum's prophetic writings were written just before the downfall of Assyria, while another account suggests he wrote this passage as liturgy just *after* its downfall in 612 BC, but it indeed seems his prophecies were focused on the end of the Assyrian Empire. One writer has stated that none of the other minor prophets even come close to matching the beauty or boldness that characterizes the prophetic sayings and writings of Nahum.

  Ancient sources refer to Nahum as a *prophet* of God.

- ***Habakkuk*** lived in approximately the Seventh Century and Sixth Century BC. He was one of the 12 minor prophets in the Old

Testament and is regarded to be the author of the book of Habakkuk. The name Habakkuk appears only in Habakkuk 1:1, and the etymology of his name is not clear, as it has no equal in the Hebrew language.

Nearly no background information exists to tell us about Habakkuk. This is indeed unusual, for in the case of other prophets, more information is given, such as the name of the prophet's hometown, his occupation, or information concerning his parentage or tribe. But although Habakkuk's home is not identified in Scripture, scholars generally conclude that Habakkuk lived in Jerusalem at the time he wrote his prophecy.

The book of Habakkuk suggests that Habakkuk was a man of great literary talent, and his book consists of five prophecies about the Babylonians and a song of praise to God (*see* Habakkuk 3). Habakkuk is noted as being unusual among the prophets because he openly questions the workings of God. In the first part of the first chapter, Habakkuk sees injustice and asks God why He does not take action. In Habakkuk 1:2, he cried, "O Lord, how long shall I cry, and thou wilt not hear! even cry out unto thee of violence, and thou wilt not save."

Some suggest that because the final chapter of his book is a song, Habakkuk may have been a Levite and possibly served as a musician in Solomon's Temple. In spite of the lack of background information about him, Habakkuk is noted among the 12 minor prophets of the Old Testament, and ancient sources refer to Habakkuk as a *prophet* of God.

- ***Urijah*** is described as being the son of Shemaiah. He was from Kiriath-Jearim, and he is clearly described as a prophet of God (*see*

Jeremiah 26:20). He was faithful to deliver the prophetic message of God during the reign of Jehoiakim, the king of Judah. Out of concern for retribution against him for speaking the word of the Lord, he fled into Egypt to hide from the cruelty of the king, but was brought back to be beheaded and his body was cast "into the graves of common people" (*see* Jeremiah 26:23).

Scripture and ancient sources refer to Urijah as a *prophet* of God.

- ***Zephaniah*** lived in approximately the Seventh Century BC. He was the great-grandson of King Hezekiah, ninth in order of the 12 minor prophets, a prominent prophet of God during the days of Josiah, king of Judah, and he is regarded to be the author of the book of Zephaniah. He was a contemporary with the prophet Jeremiah, and the place of his prophetic activity was primarily in the city of Jerusalem.

  During the reigns of Amon of Judah and Manasseh of Judah, the worship of Baal and Astarte was growing, and these vile forms of worship brought depraved moral activities with them. Many holy places were wrongly converted into places of idolatrous worship, and Josiah wanted to put an end to the misuse of these sacred places (*see* 2 Kings 23:1-25). To do so, Zephaniah stepped forward as one of his most zealous supporters.

  Zephaniah boldly prophesied that Judah would be destroyed because of the evil being committed by its residents, and he courageously prophesied against the religious and moral corruption that had penetrated even the sanctuary. He warned that God would "destroy out of this place the remnant of Baal, and the names of the idolatrous priests" (*see* Zephaniah 1:4). He pleaded for the people to return to the faith and simplicity of their ancestors (*see* Zephaniah 1:8).

Zephaniah lived at a time when the lands were being overrun by Scythians in the last decades of the Seventh Century BC. Zephaniah warned of impending judgment (*see* Zephaniah 1:7). It was a difficult time that needed a strong prophetic voice, and Zephaniah was that voice.

Ancient sources refer to Zephaniah as a *prophet* of God.

- ***Jeremiah*** lived in approximately the Seventh Century and Sixth Century BC. He was active as a prophet from the thirteenth year of the reign of Josiah, king of Judah, until after the fall of Jerusalem and the destruction of Solomon's Temple. This lengthy period spanned the reigns of Josiah, Jehoahaz, Jehoiakim, Jehoiachin, and Zedekiah. The prophet Zephaniah was Jeremiah's mentor, and the prophetess Huldah was a member of his family. Jeremiah was a major prophet in the Old Testament and regarded to be the author of the book of Jeremiah and the book of Lamentations. It is believed he also penned First and Second Kings with the help of Barach Ben Neiah, who was his scribe and disciple (*see* Jeremiah 36:4).

  Jeremiah was the son of the Jewish priest Hilkian and was from the Benjamite village of Anathoth (*see* Jeremiah 1:1). He prophesied that invaders would destroy Jerusalem because they had forsaken God by tolerating and practicing the worship of Baal and offering their children as offerings to Baal (*see* Jeremiah 1:14-16). The nation had broken their covenant with God by veering so far from the Law that it resulted in God withdrawing His blessings from the nation. Jeremiah gave prophecy after prophecy that Judah would suffer famine, foreign conquest, and would be led captive to foreign nations (*see* Jeremiah 23; 30,31; 33). Because of the gloomy nature of his prophetic utterances in the books of Jeremiah and Lamentations, he is referred to as the "weeping prophet."

It seems that in his earlier years, Jeremiah primarily was a preaching prophet who condemned idolatry and rebuked the greed of priests and false prophets. But according to Jeremiah 1:2 and 3, God called Jeremiah to active prophetic ministry about five years before Josiah king of Judah led the nation in repentance from its idolatrous practices. According to the books of Kings and Jeremiah, Josiah's reforms were insufficient to save Judah and Jerusalem from destruction that came upon them because of the sins of Manasseh. Jeremiah was appointed by God to address the sins of the nation and the punishment that was to follow.

Jeremiah felt unfit for the task, but God promised to place His words in Jeremiah's mouth and charged him to prophetically deliver exactly the message he had been given. God told him not to be afraid, but to stand up, to speak exactly what he had been instructed to speak, to go exactly where he was instructed to go, and to fear not those he was called to address.

The Lord told Jeremiah, in no uncertain terms, that the God-called prophet was to "...gird up thy loins, and arise, and speak unto them all that I command thee..." (Jeremiah 1:17). Then the Lord added, "...Be not dismayed at their faces, lest I confound thee before them" (v. 17).

In other words, the Lord admonished Jeremiah not to hesitate to deliver those words from God because of a sense of embarrassment, *or God was going to give Jeremiah something to be embarrassed about!* This is important lest we think God has changed His mind about the magnitude of His words and the significance of His plans today. He took the prophets' obedience, or lack of obedience, very seriously, and He is no less serious in our present time.

True prophets *then and now* were not placed into ministry to be popular with their audiences or to "tickle the fancy" of everyone who heard their messages. These men and women were set in place to obediently deliver the word of the Lord, even those words that many deemed unpleasant. Prophets of old often suffered at the hands of disobedient men — those who mocked the message. Some prophets were ridiculed and scorned, while others were imprisoned — still others paid the ultimate sacrifice to deliver the word of the Lord. But it was the price they were required to pay, if need be, in order to speak as God's mouthpiece and make the will of God known in a certain situation or season or hour. This is no less true concerning the prophetic ministry today.

Prophets of old often suffered at the hands of disobedient men — those who mocked the message. Some prophets were ridiculed and scorned, while others were imprisoned — still others paid the ultimate sacrifice to deliver the word of the Lord. But it was the price they were required to pay, if need be, in order to speak as God's mouthpiece and make the will of God known in a certain situation or season or hour. This is no less true concerning the prophetic ministry today.

As a result of Jeremiah's prophetic rebukes to so many on many different levels of society, many plots were orchestrated against the prophet Jeremiah. There were some who feared their prestigious religious positions would be lost due to his public denunciations of them, so they conspired to kill him (*see* Jeremiah 11:18). But God revealed the conspiracy to Jeremiah, thus protecting his life, and God prophetically declared through Jeremiah that those who sought his life would be destroyed (*see* Jeremiah 11:19-23). But a barrage of attacks continued to try to stop the prophet.

One example was a priest named Pashur, a temple official in Jerusalem, who was fearful of the effect of Jeremiah's words and ordered that Jeremiah be beaten and put in the stocks at the Upper Gate of Benjamin. After that incident, Jeremiah lamented the trouble that speaking God's word has caused him, but he noted that even if he tried to shut God's word inside, it nonetheless burns like fire in his heart and he was unable to resist speaking it (*see* Jeremiah 20:9).

In addition to troubles with corrupt spiritual leaders in Jerusalem, Jeremiah boldly prophesied against false prophets who were forecasting a time of peace when Jeremiah knew that God's forewarned destruction was en route (*see* Jeremiah 6:13-14; 8:10-11).

When Jeremiah prophesied Jerusalem would be handed over to the Babylonian army, the king's officials — including Pashur, the temple official in Jerusalem — tried to convince King Zedekiah that Jeremiah should be put to death for delivering discouraging prophetic messages that proved disheartening to the soldiers and the people (*see* Jeremiah 38:1-4). Under the influence of these wicked counselors, Zedekiah allowed Jeremiah to be cast into a cistern with the intent to kill Jeremiah by starvation (*see* Jeremiah 38:5,6). A Cushite pulled him out of the cistern, but, regardless, Jeremiah remained imprisoned until Jerusalem fell to the Babylonian army (*see* Jeremiah 38:13,28) Amazingly, the Babylonians released Jeremiah, treated him kindly, and allowed him to choose the place of his residence (*see* Jeremiah 39:11-14).

Scripture and ancient sources refer to Jeremiah as a significant and faithful *prophet* of God.

- ***Ezekiel*** lived in approximately the Seventh Century and Sixth Century BC. In the book of Ezekiel, we read that this prophet was the son of Buzi and that he was born into the priestly Kohanite lineage (*see* Ezekiel 1:3). The Bible tells us that Ezekiel and his wife lived during the Babylonian captivity on the banks of the Chebar River with other exiles from Judah (*see* Ezekiel 1:1). Ancient tradition suggests that Ezekiel did not actually write the book that bears his name, but that scribes of that time collected his words, experiences, prophecies, and utterances, and compiled them into the book of Ezekiel.

  Ezekiel prophesied the destruction of Jerusalem and its Temple, and he actually witnessed the fulfillment of this prophecy with the Babylonian attack on the city of Jerusalem. However, Ezekiel not only prophesied the destruction of Jerusalem, but he also prophesied the restoration of God's people to their land.

  According to the writings of Josephus,[10] Nebuchadnezzar's armies attacked Jerusalem, deposed King Jehoiakim, and took 3,000 Jews into Babylonian captivity — and Ezekiel was among them. But even during the time of captivity, Ezekiel remained active in his prophetic ministry. It seems the last recorded prophecy of Ezekiel dates to approximately 16 years after the destruction of Jerusalem. Thus, his prophetic ministry covered the space of about 22 years.

  Scripture and ancient sources refer to Ezekiel as a substantial *prophet* of God.

- ***Huldah*** lived in the Seventh Century BC and was the wife of Shallum, who was the son of Tikvah, the "wardrobe keeper" of the king. Additionally, Huldah is recognized as one of the seven women whom ancient rabbis referred to as *prophetesses* (the others were

Sarah, Miriam, Deborah, Hannah, Abigail, and Esther). Huldah is the only woman prophet referred to in the books of the Kings (*see* 2 Kings 22:14-20).

After discovering the Book of the Law during renovations being carried out during restoration work at the Temple, King Josiah consulted with Huldah and asked her to seek God's direction on his behalf (*see* 2 Kings 22:14). After authenticating the Book of the Law was genuine, Huldah prophesied future destruction for failure to follow it, but in Second Kings 22:20, she reassured King Josiah that due to his heartfelt repentance, "...Thou shalt be gathered into thy grave in peace; and thine eyes shall not see all the evil which I will bring upon this place...."

The name Huldah appears in only nine verses in the Old Testament (*see* 2 Kings 22:13-20; 2 Chronicles 34:22-28). But Huldah was nonetheless regarded as a noteworthy prophetess whom God used to speak to high priests and royal officials, as well as to kings and nations, prophesying their fates.

It is astonishing that when the Book of the Law was presented to Huldah, she became the first person God used to authenticate genuine Scripture — a remarkable feat for a woman at that time (*see* 2 Kings 22:3-20). But even with all of these remarkable facts, the biblical narrative goes cold in regard to Huldah's background, which is unusual since the Bible typically provides background information for pivotal prophets. Huldah's prophecies are contained in the books of the Kings.

Ancient and contemporary rabbis refer to Huldah as a *prophetess* of God.

- ***Haggai*** lived in approximately the Sixth Century BC. Haggai is a prophet who prophesied during the building of the Second Temple in Jerusalem. He was one of the 12 minor prophets in the Old Testament, and he is regarded to be the author of the book of Haggai. He was one of three post-exile prophets from the Neo-Babylonian Exile of the House of Judah along with the prophets Zechariah and Malachi, who lived about 100 years later. All these prophets belonged to the period after the return from Babylonian captivity. The Bible reveals very little of Haggai's background. Some speculate he may have been one of the captives taken to Babylon by King Nebuchadnezzar. It appears he began to deliver God's prophetic messages about 16 years after the return of the Jews to Judah.

  Haggai was the prophet through whom God prophetically commanded the Jews to rebuild the Temple in Jerusalem (*see* Haggai 1:1-8). Due to the interference of the Samaritans, the work of rebuilding the Temple had been suspended for years (*see* Ezra 4:17-24), but the work was resumed through the prophetic leadership of the prophets Haggai and Zechariah, who prophetically roused the nation from lethargy and exhorted them to rise and build and take advantage of a change in the policy of the Persian King, Darius I (*see* Ezra 5:1,2).

  Because the Persian Empire had become weak, Haggai saw it as an opportunity to restore much of what had been lost. He prophetically warned that if the people would not seize the moment to rise and build, poverty, famine, and drought would come upon the nation (*see* Haggai 1:7-11).

  Ancient and contemporary rabbis referred to Haggai as a *prophet* of God.

- ***Zechariah*** lived in approximately the Sixth Century and Fifth Century BC. The book of Zechariah introduces him as the son of Berechiah, the son of Iddo (*see* Zechariah 1:1). The book of Ezra states he was the son of the prophet Iddo (*see* Ezra 5:1; 6:14), but this likely means Iddo was his grandfather. He was one of the 12 minor prophets of the Old Testament, and is regarded to be the author of the book of Zechariah. His prophetic ministry seems to have begun in the second year of Darius the Great, who was the king of the great Achaemenid Empire (c. 520 BC). Along with Haggai, another contemporary prophet at that time, Zachariah was concerned with the building of the Second Temple.

  Ancient and contemporary rabbis refer to Zechariah as a *prophet* of God.

- ***Daniel*** lived in approximately the Seventh Century and Sixth Century. Daniel was a noble youth from Jerusalem taken into captivity at the time Nebuchadnezzar's armies attacked Jerusalem. At that time, many young noblemen were taken captive and transported to Babylon, and the Book of Daniel begins by telling how Daniel and his companions came to be in Babylon.

  While in Babylon, their oppressors changed Daniel's and his companion's Hebrew names *Daniel, Hananiah, Mishael,* and *Azariah* to the Babylonian names *Belteshazzar, Shadrack, Meshach*, and *Abednego* in an attempt to infuse them into Babylonian culture (*see* Daniel 1:3-7). But in spite of multiple pressures to conform and modify their faith and behavior to accommodate pagan gods, Daniel and his friends refused. In subsequent years, God promoted Daniel to lofty positions, and against all odds, over a long span of time, he served as a high-ranking official to the Babylonian, Mede, and Persian kings Nechadnezzar, Belshazzar, Darius, and Cyrus.

In the early years of their captivity, there was a moment of confrontation when Daniel's friends were thrown into a fiery furnace for not bowing to pagan pressures. When the king looked into the furnace and saw they were miraculously unburned and unharmed — and that, furthermore, he saw a "Fourth Man" in the fire with them — he ordered them to be removed, and he decreed that anyone who spoke against Daniel's God would be "...cut into pieces, and their houses...made a dunghill" (*see* Daniel 3:19-29).

Later, when an edict was issued that compelled Daniel not to pray to God, he refused, and when his enemies reported his noncompliance, he was thrown into a lion's den where he was divinely protected and untouched by the lions as a result of his obedience to God. Daniel's enemies were destroyed, and he was promoted in the kingdom (*see* Daniel 6:24-28).

It is shocking that Daniel is *not* considered a prophet in Judaism, because it is generally regarded that prophetic ministry ended at the time of Haggai, Zechariah, and Malachi. This is the reason why the book of Daniel in the Hebrew Bible is not found in the section with the Prophets.

Yet Daniel prophetically foretold many future events that were to occur in the "latter days" (*see* Daniel 10:14). He accurately prophesied various world empires (*see* Daniel 2 and 7), the "70 Weeks" (*see* Daniel 9:24-27), the persecutions of the saints (*see* Daniel 10:21), the emergence of the Antichrist (*see* Daniel 7:8), the abomination of desolation (*see* Daniel 9:27; Matthew 24:15,16) that Jesus also referred to (*see* Matthew 24:14,15), the very end of time (*see* Daniel 11:40), a time of trouble in the last days (*see* Daniel 12:1) that Jesus called a time of "great tribulation" (*see* Matthew 24:21), and Daniel even prophesied the resurrection of the dead (*see* Daniel 12:1).

But in spite of the fact that Jewish tradition does not refer to Daniel as a prophet, Josephus wrote that Daniel was a prophet. And most important is that Jesus spoke of "the prophet Daniel" in Matthew 24:15 and Mark 13:14.

Jesus, who is the most authoritative voice of all, referred to Daniel as a *prophet* of God.

- ***Esther*** lived in approximately the Fifth Century BC. Her Jewish name was originally Hadassah, but it was later changed to Esther, named after the goddess Ashtar. She is recognized as one of the seven women referred to as *prophetesses* (the others were Sarah, Miriam, Deborah, Hannah, Abigail, and Huldah).

  The Israelites were exiled to Babylon in 586 BC, and that is why Esther grew up as a Persian Jew. Orphaned at a young age, she was cared for by her relative Mordecai (*see* Esther 2:7). Because of her beauty, she was chosen to be the new queen for King Ahasuerus (*see* Esther 2:15-17) after he disposed of his insolent wife, Queen Vashti (*see* Esther 1:10-22). As the new queen, Esther moved into the palace, and her relative Mordecai advised her not to reveal her Jewish identity, as it would possibly be used against her (*see* Esther 2:10,20).

  An evil advisor named Haman plotted the extermination of the Jewish people in Persia and brought a liquidation proposal to King Ahasuerus (*see* Esther 3:7-15). Ahasuerus signed the decree not realizing his own wife would be executed according to the decree. Through a series of complicated events, Mordecai told Esther that she had "come to the kingdom for such a time as this" (*see* Esther 4:14) and urged her to find a way to boldly intervene for the Jews to be spared.

At a specially arranged banquet, Esther and Haman sat together with King Ahasuerus, and, in shock, Haman listened as Esther revealed that she was a Jew. By the conclusion of the dinner, the King ordered Haman be hanged on the very gallows he had prepared to use to execute the Jews in the kingdom (*see* Esther 7:10). Today Esther's bravery is still celebrated annually during the holiday of Purim.

Because of her prophetic role in the nation of Israel, ancient sources refer to Esther as a *prophetess of God*.

- ***Malachi*** lived in approximately the Fifth Century BC. It is interesting that many Jews of that age ascribed the book of Malachi to Ezra, but scholars have noted that if Ezra had been the author of the book, his name would not have been dropped. Other scholars speculate the book of Malachi was authored by Zerubbabel and Nehemiah. But the fact is that Malachi was a prophet and a Levite, and he was buried in the city of Jerusalem in the tomb of the prophets.

  The name Malachi means "one charged with a message" or "one charged with a mission." And because his name does not appear anywhere else except in the book of Malachi, "Malachi" seems to be a title rather than a name. Many scholars agree that Malachi was not this prophet's actual name, but rather a title to describe his prophetic function. The Jewish Encyclopedia of 1906 implies that Malachi, whoever he was, prophesied after the time of Haggai and Zechariah and possibly at the time of about 420 BC after the second return of Nehemiah from Persia.[11]

  Regardless of the true identify of Malachi, ancient sources refer to Malachi as a *prophet* of God.

In Summary

There were many prophetic voices in the span of the Old Testament — far too many to cover in a single chapter in this book. This chapter was intended to provide a smattering of information about these prophetic voices to show you the great spectrum of prophets who operated in the Old Testament and were recognized by ancient sources.

In the next chapter, we will be studying what the New Testament tells us about the role of Christ-given fivefold prophets in the Church Age. You are about to dive into powerful information about the role of prophets now and their role that will exist in the Church until we reach the maturity that God intends to exist in the Body of Christ, God's glorious House.

Questions for Deeper Consideration

Chapter 8

1. This chapter provides a long list of people whom ancient rabbis and other ancient sources referred to as prophets and prophetesses. Who in this list was the biggest surprise to you that ancient sources referred to him or her as a prophet or prophetess?

2. Enoch was the first in the Old Testament to be called a prophet. His prophetic ministry was so renowned that one of his prophetic utterances about the Second Coming of Christ is recorded in the New Testament. Can you identify the book of the New Testament where Enoch's prophecy about the Second Coming is found?

3. In addition to male prophets in the Old Testament, there were at least seven women whom ancient rabbis and other ancient sources recognized as significant Old Testament prophetesses. Can you name these seven women who were traditionally recognized as prophetesses?

4. As you look at the list of those whom ancient rabbis and other ancient sources referred to as prophets, it is clear that at times, there were multiple prophets in one family line. Can you name one or more prophets whose descendants were also prophets?

5. Daniel was such an influential, powerful prophet that Jesus referred to him as the prophet Daniel in Matthew 24:15 and Mark13:14. Yet in the Jewish Old Testament, the prophetic book of Daniel is strangely not included with prophetic books, but it is found among the books of Literature, Wisdom, and Poetry. Can you explain why it is not listed with other prophetic books of the Old Testament?

6. The book of Malachi is attributed to an Old Testament prophet named Malachi, but it is important to note that there is not a single record anywhere in the Old Testament that tells of a prophet named Malachi. And because the name Malachi does not appear anywhere else except in the book of Malachi, many scholars believe the name Malachi is a title rather than a name. From what you have read in this chapter, *if* the name Malachi is a title and not a name, what would the name Malachi mean?

7. In the next chapter we will see what is the greatest difference between Old Testament and New Testament prophets. But before you get there, can you postulate the biggest difference between Old Testament prophets and New Testament prophets?

CHAPTER 9

THE ROLE OF NEW TESTAMENT AND LAST-DAYS PROPHETS

Now therefore ye are no more strangers and foreigners, but fellowcitizens with the saints, and of the household of God; and are built upon the foundation of the apostles and prophets, Jesus Christ himself being the chief corner stone; in whom all the building fitly framed together groweth unto an holy temple in the Lord: In whom ye also are builded together for an habitation of God through the Spirit.
— Ephesians 2:19-22

In the last two chapters, we have looked at the meanings of the Hebrew and Greek words for a prophet and have seen a limited list of people who were referred to as prophets by the Bible and by ancient rabbis. In this chapter, we will look at various prophetic individuals that we read about, from the Gospels to the end of the early New Testament era.

Toward the end of this chapter, we will also importantly consider the difference between a fivefold-ministry prophet and one who merely prophesies. In no way should we minimize any person who prophesies in the context of a gathering of saints, but there is a huge difference between a person who merely prophesies and one who stands in the Christ-given fivefold ministry of a prophet.

As one studies how Old and New Testaments prophets functioned, it becomes clear that they each essentially functioned in the same ways — *with one major difference.* In Chapter Seven, we briefly studied Second Peter 1:20,21, which states that Old Testament prophets were God-anointed individuals who were gifted by God to hoist their spiritual sails so they could catch the wind, or movement, of the Holy Spirit when God was ready to move upon them to speak. They lingered for long periods and waited for God's Spirit to come upon them *from without*, and when He did, they spoke as the Spirit moved them. But when the Spirit was finished speaking, He "lifted" from them and departed until God was ready to move upon them again to speak.

Herein we find *the major difference* between Old and New Testament prophets. New Testament prophets are born again, as is true of all New Testament believers, and they, therefore, have the Spirit of God permanently residing not just *upon* them, but also *within* them. Old Testament prophets lingered for a gust of the Spirit and never knew exactly when it would come. But New Testament prophets — and, as noted, every New Testament believer — holds a higher status because the Holy Spirit dwells *within* them and does not simply come *upon* them from time to time.

But like Old Testament prophets, New Testament prophets are gifted to hoist their spiritual sails to catch the movement of the Holy Spirit and to speak when the Spirit moves upon them. But because they are born again and carry the Spirit within them at all times, a New Testament prophet (as is true of all believers):

- is permanently sealed with the Holy Spirit (*see* Ephesians 1:13).
- has the inward witness of the Spirit at all times (*see* Romans 8:16).
- can expect to be led by the Holy Spirit (*see* Romans 8:14).
- anticipates the gifts of the Holy Spirit to be at his or her disposal at all times as the Spirit wills (*see* First Corinthians 12:7,11).

In Chapter Seven, I referred to one author who noted that all prophets — whether Old or New Testament prophets — have a navigational dimension to his or her ministry. Because that statement is so well written, I wish to refer again to that author's words. He aptly stated that a prophet will have four primary dimensions to his or her ministry. I have modified his text as follows:

1. Prophetic Insight

Like Old Testament prophets, New Testament prophets will also at times have the supernatural ability to understand the root issues in situations — the circumstances and people's motivations, agendas, and plans. Prophets have a God-given ability to peer into a matter, evaluate the problem, and see in-depth. New Testament prophetic individuals (prophets) have extraordinary insight to counsel, provide wisdom, and bring divinely inspired solutions. They have divine insight to puzzle together critical, hard, or obscure cases — not mentally or intellectually, but by God's Spirit.

2. Prophetic Foresight

Like Old Testament prophets, New Testament prophets will also at times have the supernatural ability to see into the future — to see things ahead of time, before they happen. They have the visual acuity to predict events, happenings, and future things that are pending, or are yet to take place.

3. Prophetic Oversight

Like Old Testament prophets, New Testament prophets will also at times have the supernatural ability to understand prophetic context, ecosystems, service roles, functions, and perspectives — for example, how people relate within their callings to the season they find themselves in, "for such a time as this" (*see* Esther 4:14).

4. Prophetic Hindsight

Like Old Testament prophets, New Testament prophets will also at times have the supernatural ability to also see things in the past and understand their relevance to current or future events. Indeed, they frequently have the ability to comprehend things that have occurred in someone's past or events that consequently affect the present and could potentially alter the future. These prophetic individuals often have eyes to read the writing on the walls of a person's history and a powerful ability to see someone's spiritual background."[1]

In previous chapters, we have seen that the apostle Paul enumerated a list of the fivefold ministry gifts in Ephesians 4:11 and 12. In those verses, he wrote, "And he [Christ] gave some, apostles; and some, prophets; and some, evangelists; and some, pastors and teachers; for the perfecting of the saints, for the work of the ministry, for the edifying of the body of Christ…."

In each instance where the word "some" is used, it is a Greek word that should be taken as *an emphatic*, *exclamatory*, or *a categorical* remark. It could be translated: "And he [Christ] gave *indeed*, apostles; and *indeed*, prophets; and *indeed*, evangelists; and *indeed*, pastors and [it is understood to mean *indeed*] teachers…." Or it could be translated, "And he [Christ] gave *categorically*, apostles; and *categorically*, prophets; and *categorically*, evangelists; and *categorically,* pastors and [it is understood to mean *categorically*] teachers...." Or it could be translated, "And he [Christ] gave *emphatically*, apostles; and *emphatically*, prophets; and *emphatically*, evangelists; and *emphatically,* pastors and [it is understood to mean *emphatically*] teachers...."

But notice the word "prophets" follows the word "apostles" in this verse. This specific ordering of *apostles* and *prophets* occurs again in First Corinthians 12:28, where Paul wrote, "And God hath set some in the church, first *apostles*, secondarily *prophets*...."

This close relationship between *apostles* and *prophets* is referred to again in Ephesians 2:20, where Paul wrote that the church is "...built upon the foundation of *apostles* and *prophets*...." Each of these verses demonstrates the foundational ministry of the apostle, but also the prophet, who has a critical role to help ensure the foundations in the Church, including local churches, are laid properly.

Before we study New Testament prophets, you need to understand that ancient and contemporary Jewish rabbis generally believe Old Testament prophetic ministry ended with the book of Malachi in the Old Testament. According to their thinking, the book of Malachi was God's last prophetic words to be spoken in the Old Testament prophetic era. Jewish thinking furthermore generally states that the intertestamental years between the Old and New Testaments were prophetically silent.

But *were* they?

Intertestamental Prophets

God has never been silent and has always been speaking for anyone "who has ears to hear what the Spirit" desires to communicate (*see* Matthew 11:15; 13:9,43; Mark 4:9; Luke 8:8; 14:35; Revelation 2:7,11,17,29; 3:6,13,22).

And upon closely examining the alleged prophetically silent intertestamental years, it is very obvious that God was indeed still speaking from time to time through prophetic individuals even in that period. It is true that they were not major prophets, as those who existed before that era — but prophetic voices were nevertheless speaking. History shows that God has *always* been speaking through prophetic voices to those who have an ear to hear what He is saying.

The prophetic voices of the intertestamental years were different from their predecessors in that they did not write Scripture as was the case with many Old Testament prophets. However, in the intertestamental years, God's people still longed to hear His voice, and there was a great fascination with the future. Many scholars and voices of those intertestamental years were alert to the warnings the Holy Spirit was giving them even about end-time happenings — and they accurately prophesied many events we are witnessing today. But what most readers do not understand is that even the gospels began in the intertestamental years before the death and resurrection of Jesus, which officially gave birth to the New Testament period. For example, John the Baptist was an intertestamental prophet — a *notable* one (*see* Matthew 11:11; Luke 7:28) — which we will see in this chapter.

In the earliest accounts in the New Testament, we see that the spirit of prophecy was not silent and was in fact very active. In particular, we read that there were two individuals in the city of Jerusalem at the time of Jesus' birth who were noted for their ability to operate in a spirit of prophecy, and they were viewed to be contemporary prophets of that time. One was a religious leader named *Simeon* and the other was an intercessor and prophetess by the name of *Anna*. We read about them in the book of Luke (*see* Luke 2:25-38).

Some mistakenly refer to Simeon and Anna as New Testament prophets because their stories are recorded in the gospels. But because Simeon and Anna lived *before* the death, burial, and resurrection of Jesus, they were technically *intertestamental prophets* and lived between the eras of the Old and

New Testaments. The examples of *Simeon* and *Anna* clearly demonstrate that prophetic ministry was active and vibrant even beyond the book of Malachi.

Who Was Simeon the Prophet Who Prophesied Over Jesus?

When Joseph and Mary came to the Temple to present Jesus to the Lord as required by Old Testament Law, Luke 2:25,26 tells us, "And, behold, there was a man in Jerusalem, whose name was Simeon; and the same man was just and devout, waiting for the consolation of Israel: and the Holy Ghost was upon him. And it was revealed unto him by the Holy Ghost, that he should not see death, before he had seen the Lord's Christ."

Those who are well-versed in Jewish history have importantly pointed out that in Jerusalem exactly at that time, there was indeed a religious leader named Simeon who was revered for his spiritual and theological acuity. He was furthermore viewed to be an individual who operated in the spirit of prophecy. This respected, historical figure named Simeon was reputedly the son of Hillel, the prominent founder of a major Jewish theological circle. Eventually Simeon became so revered that he replaced his legendary father Hillel as the eminent leader of the Hillel theological group. And because he was honored above all others as the greatest scholar and theologian of his time, Simeon was regarded by some as the most respected leader in the Jewish Sanhedrin during that period.

Although Jerusalem was the largest city in Israel at that time, scholars generally believe its resident population was about 100,000. By today's standards, 100,000 sounds small, but in the ancient world, that was a large city. Some have alleged Jerusalem's population to be between 600,000 and 1,000,000, but historical records do not bear this out. However, Jerusalem *could* swell temporarily to more than 1,000,000 people when Jewish pilgrims came to Jerusalem three times a year for holy days, as required by the Law of God.[2]

The reason I mention Jerusalem's size is, many famous personalities we read about in the Bible were familiar with each other due to the smaller size of the city. This *Simeon* is an example of one who held a celebrity-type status and was well-known around the time Jesus was presented in the Temple.

I told you in Chapter Five that at a young age, the apostle Paul (still named Saul) relocated to Jerusalem to study theology under the renowned Pharisee named Gamaliel who is referred to in Acts 22:3. Gamaliel was the son of Simeon ben Hillel — who is said by many to be this very same Simeon we read about in Luke 2:25-28, who came into the Temple and prophesied over Jesus at the time his parents brought him to be dedicated.

In Acts 22:3, we read that as a young man, Paul studied "at the feet of Gamaliel." The words "at the feet" indicate he was submitted to Gamaliel and followed in his footsteps — in his doctrine and his strict manner of life. I find it remarkable that Paul's teacher Gamaliel was reputedly the son of this Simeon who prophesied over Jesus in the Temple — and this fact may explain why Gamaliel seemed tolerant of the Christian faith (*see* Acts 5:33-39). It is within the realm of possibility that his father Simeon had told him of the birth of Jesus, and that could thusly explain why Gamaliel was more lenient than others on early Gospel preachers.

But regardless, the Jewish leadership in Jerusalem about the time of Jesus' birth generally accepted that this Simeon — this powerful, celebrity-like theologian in Jerusalem — was endued with a supernatural spirit of prophecy and had the unique God-given gift to prophetically discern the times. In Luke 2:25, we are specifically told that Simeon was actively waiting for the consolation of Israel — that is, for the coming of the Messiah. Because the nation of Israel had been harassed and oppressed by Rome for many years, the coming of the Messiah would finally be a consolation — *it would bring great comfort* — to the Jews. And the spiritual leadership in Jerusalem was aware that Simeon had prophetically noised it abroad that God promised he would see the Messiah's appearance with his own eyes before he died.

When writing about Simeon, Luke said, "And, *behold*, there was a man in Jerusalem...whose name was Simeon..." (Luke 2:25).

The word "behold" in this verse is a translation of the Greek word *idou*, and it describes *bewilderment, shock, amazement, and wonder*. The use of this word tells us that even as Luke was recalling this event and writing about it, he was *still* astonished about what he was about to describe. It was as if he said, "*Wow*...can you imagine it?" Then with a sense of total amazement at what he was about to describe, he proceeded to tell the shocking events that occurred when this renowned Simeon came into the Temple in Jerusalem on the day Jesus was dedicated. In one moment in time, prophetic events concerning the promised Savior were rapidly unfolding, and Simeon's own word from God was coming to pass right before his eyes. I'm sure it was a surreal moment in the mind of the prophet.

As we have seen, the narrative states Simeon was "waiting" for the consolation of Israel. The word "waiting" in Luke 2:25 is translated from a form of the Greek word *prosdechomai*, and it pictures *a hope* or *an expectation*. It pictures one who is ready *to embrace, to gladly welcome*, or *to fully and completely take something without reservation or hesitation*. Because this word is used, it lets us know that Simeon was earnestly looking for and anticipating the "consolation of Israel." The word "consolation" is a form of the Greek word *paraklesis*, and in this verse it describes *comfort, encouragement, support*, or *solace*.

Simeon was filled with a prophetic expectation and anticipation that at any moment, the long-awaited Messiah would appear to free the nation of Israel from its Roman oppressors. Because the word "waiting" is used, it emphatically means Simeon's faith was engaged. He was on the edge prophetically — his faith was on the line — and he staked his reputation on what he believed God had prophetically communicated to him.

Luke 2:25 additionally tells us that "...the Holy Ghost was upon him." This is an unusual statement made to depict Simeon as having a unique anointing of the Spirit "upon" his life. The word "upon" is a translation of the Greek word *epi*, which literally means *on* or *upon*. And as already noted, the top Jewish leadership in Jerusalem regarded Simeon to be a man who operated with a spirit of prophecy "upon" him, and they held him in high esteem regarding his prophetic inklings. Simeon was reputed to be a reliable prophetic voice, and here Luke confirmed what was believed about Simeon — that the gift of prophecy, by the power of the Holy Spirit, operated "upon" him.

Luke 2:26 goes on to tell us, "And it was *revealed* unto him [Simeon] *by* the Holy Ghost, that he should not see death, before he had seen the Lord's Christ."

The words "revealed" and "by" in this verse are very important. The word "revealed" is a translation of the unusual Greek word *chrematidzo*, a term that was used to depict *a business transaction between two people*. The use of this word demonstrates the divine interactions that occurred between Simeon and God. It lets us know that his interactions with the Spirit were so close and frequent that he and the Holy Spirit were regularly interacting and conducting prophetic transactions with each other.

But the Greek word translated "revealed" also carries the idea that the recipient was charged by God to become a mouthpiece to speak revelation to others. This means God *expected* Simeon to communicate with others what the Holy Spirit had divinely communicated with Him — specifically, that he *and they* would see the Messiah in their own lifetime. Because God entrusted this revelation to Simeon, He expected Simeon to become a divine mouthpiece in Jerusalem to prophetically declare that the coming of the Messiah was upon them. Whether others fully believed him or not, because of Simeon's renowned status, what *he* believed about this event was well-known in Jerusalem.

Luke 2:26 says, "And it was revealed unto him [Simeon] *by* the Holy Ghost...." The word "by" is a translation of the Greek word *hupo*, which means *by, under, under the direction of, under the guidance of, or under the influence of* — and in this context, *"under the guidance, direction, and influence of"* the Holy Spirit. Because Simeon was a man in submission to the Holy Spirit, the Spirit was able to prophetically reveal information to him. He was a spiritually sensitive individual who was in submission to and in touch with the Holy Spirit — and was known for his spiritual sensitivity.

Luke 2:27 further gives us a picture of Simeon's prophetic sensitivity when it says, "And he came *by* the Spirit into the temple...." In this verse, the word "by" is not the same word for "by" used in verse 26. It has changed from the Greek word *hupo* in verse 26 to the Greek word *en* in verse 27. In context, the word *en* unquestionably means Simeon came *in the Spirit* or *in the control of the Spirit*, and it reinforces the understanding that Simeon was divinely operating *in* the control of the Holy Spirit. He was being supernaturally led and directed by the Spirit to come into the Temple at that precise moment that day.

Then Luke 2:27-29 tells us, "...And when the parents brought in the child Jesus, to do for him after the custom of the law, then took he [Simeon] him up in his arms, and blessed God, and said, Lord, now lettest thou thy servant depart in peace, according to thy word."

Some causal readers assume Simeon was an older man because he said, "Lord, now lettest thou thy servant depart in peace, according to thy word" (Luke 2:29). But nothing in this verse ever states that he was elderly. In fact, history shows that he was *not* elderly at this time of this event. But his words meant that now, even if he died at this point in his life, he would be satisfied because with his own eyes he had seen what God promised he would see — that is, the Messiah. In that reverent moment, Simeon exclaimed, "For mine eyes have seen thy salvation, which thou hast prepared before the face of all people; a light to lighten the Gentiles, and the glory of thy people Israel" (*see* Luke 2:30-32).

Luke 2:33 then tells us, "And Joseph and his mother *marvelled* at those things which were spoken of him."

The word "marveled" is important because it is a form of the Greek word *thaumadzo*, a word that means *to be so amazed that it leaves one at a loss of words*. It indicates *shock*, *amazement*, and *bewilderment*. Mary and Joseph were stunned that this renowned prophetic man was speaking such remarkable words over their newborn son. That these words were coming from the mouth of this recognized prophet must have been shocking. As we have seen, Simeon was perhaps the most highly respected theological leader in the Great Sanhedrin, and he was known for the spirit of prophecy that operated upon him. Now Joseph and Mary marveled in a speechless state as this legendary Simeon prophesied over their Child.

Who Was Anna the Prophetess Who Also Prophesied Over Jesus?

When Simeon finished speaking his prophetic words over Jesus, *Anna* suddenly entered the scene. We read about it in Luke 2:36, where the Bible says, "And there was one Anna, *a prophetess*, the daughter of Phanuel, of the tribe of Aser: she was of a great age, and had lived with an husband seven years from her virginity."

Luke identifies this Anna as a *prophetess*. Even though all these events occurred in what some have called the silent prophetic intertestamental years, it is clear that God was still moving by His Spirit. And in addition to the spirit of prophecy that operated upon Simeon, Anna was yet another prophetic individual *through and upon whom* the spirit of prophecy was operating in the city of Jerusalem.

Luke 2:37 says, "She [Anna] was a widow of about fourscore and four years...." A score is 20 years, so "fourscore and four" years would mean she was 84 years of age. But the Greek text is completely unclear as to whether she was 84 years old or if *she had been a widow* for 84 years. If the latter is true, it would mean Anna was about 100 years old at the time of this event. But whatever the case, she was an older woman — very old for that time period — and she was recognized as being an indisputable prophetess of God in Jerusalem.

Luke 2:37 goes on to say that Anna "...departed not from the temple, but served God with fastings and prayers night and day." This implies that Anna actually had living quarters somewhere on the Temple premises. The words "she prayed night and day" depict her total devotion to God's presence and a life of prayer and intercession. As a prophetess who knew the voice of the Holy Spirit, she kept her spiritual sails hoisted to catch the wind of the Spirit when He wanted to move upon her to speak. And for years, she had prophetically heard and proclaimed that the coming of the Messiah was near. Similar to Simeon, Anna had prophetically forecasted the Messiah would soon come to bring redemption.

But the words "departed not" in verse 37 are important because they demonstrated Anna's total devotion to be near where the Messiah would one day be manifested. It is a translation of a Greek phrase that means *to not step away from*. It indicates Anna was so expectant to see the Messiah with her own eyes that she didn't take one step away from the Temple because she did not want to miss that long-awaited moment. Out of her deep devotion, she'd stayed on-site at all times for decades with "fastings and prayers day and night."

But Luke 2:38 goes on to say, "And she coming in that instant gave thanks likewise unto the Lord, and spake of him to all them that looked for redemption in Jerusalem." In Greek, the words "in that instant" means *in that very hour* — and it is intended to show that she and Simeon were nearly synchronized in their being led by the Spirit *at that very moment* into the Temple area where Jesus was, with his parents. Luke 2:38 says that arising from her prophetic spirit, she "...spake of him to all them that looked for redemption in Jerusalem."

The word "looked" is the Greek word *prosdechomai*, the same word used in Luke 2:25 to depict Simeon's "waiting" for the consolation of Israel. Just as Simeon engaged his faith, was on the edge prophetically, and staked his reputation on what he believed God had prophetically communicated to him, the prophetess Anna was *filled with expectation* because she, too, had embraced the divine revelation God gave her about the coming Messiah. And when the prophetess Anna saw Jesus, she immediately perceived He was the Messiah. With Joseph, Mary, the Child, and Simeon at hand, she prophetically *welcomed Him without hesitation or reservation.*

So it is clear that even though some allege that God was silent during the intertestamental years, God was clearly speaking and moving prophetically in those so-called silent years for those who had ears to hear. Although most readers ascribe Simeon and Anna to be prophets of the New Testament, they in fact lived before Christ's death, burial, and resurrection, the events that commenced the New Covenant, or New Testament — and, thus, Simeon and Anna functioned as intertestamental prophets.

John the Baptist

After the prophets Simeon and Anna, the next prophet we read about in the Gospels is John the Baptist — another intertestamental prophet because he functioned before the death, burial, and resurrection of Jesus. Although John the Baptist introduced Jesus as the Lamb of God that takes away the sin of the world, his ministry predated the actual period belonging to the New

Testament, which commenced only after the resurrection. Hence, John the Baptist was also an intertestamental prophet.

Many pages could be devoted to the life and ministry of John the Baptist, but here, it is sufficient to say that he was a relative of Jesus and was also born as a result of a prophetic word. That divinely inspired word was delivered to his father Zacharias by an angel when Zacharias was performing his priestly duties inside the Temple (Luke 1:8-17). Elizabeth, Zacharias' wife, was barren, but God supernaturally healed her and she and Zacharias were enabled to give birth to John exactly as the angel that appeared to Zacharias had foretold (Luke 1:5-24). From a young age, it had been ingrained in John by his parents that God had explicitly given him the purpose of prophetically announcing the arrival of Jesus.

In Matthew and Mark, we read of John that at nearly 30 years of age, he was already located near the Jordan River, where he began his public prophetic ministry. The powerful nature of his prophetic ministry caused biblical writers to compare John's ministry to the ministry of the prophet Elijah. The Gospels of Matthew and Mark specifically describe his garments of camel's hair and the leather belt around his waist as similar to the attire of the prophet Elijah (*see* Second Kings 1:8).

Jesus Himself called John the Baptist the "Elijah who was to come" (*see* Matthew 11:14, 17:11-13), and many take this to mean that John came in a power and anointing that was similar to the anointing that operated in the prophet Elijah. When the angel spoke to Zacharias and foretold John's birth and ministry, he said that John would turn many of the sons of Israel to the Lord their God and "...go before him in the spirit and power of Elias [Elijah]..." (Luke 1:16,17).

Isaiah 40:3 prophetically foretold "the voice of him that crieth in the wilderness, Prepare ye the way of the Lord, make straight in the desert a highway for our God." New Testament writers took this prophecy as a description of John the Baptist, and in the gospel of Mark, the narrative states that John the Baptist's ministry was a fulfillment of multiple prophesies from the books of Isaiah, Malachi, and Exodus. In those texts, John the Baptist is pictured as the prophet who would cry in the wilderness to prepare the way of the Lord.

And at about the age of 30, John went into the wilderness to take his place at the Jordan River and to prepare the way of the Jesus. His preaching was so fiery that renowned religious leaders, publicans, sinners, and politicians trekked into the wilderness to hear his preaching, where he boldly commanded them to repent and to prepare for the coming Messiah.

In the gospel of John, the apostle refers to John the Baptist in its opening chapters, where it speaks of him as "a man sent from God" who "...came for a witness, to bear witness of the Light, that all men through him might believe" (*see* John 1:6,7). Later when people asked John exactly who he was, he plainly answered that he was "...the voice of one crying in the wilderness..." (*see* John 1:23). As one who was sent to make the way clear for the Messiah, John the Baptist was the prophet who first publicly introduced Jesus as "the Lamb of God that takes away the sin of the world" (*see* John 1:29).

In Luke 3:7-9, we read of John's bold preaching. It says, "Then said he [John] to the multitude that came forth to be baptized of him, O generation of vipers, who hath warned you to flee from the wrath to come? Bring forth therefore fruits worthy of repentance, and begin not to say within yourselves, We have Abraham to *our* father: for I say unto you, That God is able of these stones to raise up children unto Abraham. And now also the axe is laid unto the root of the trees: every tree therefore which bringeth not forth good fruit is hewn down, and cast into the fire."

Luke 3:12 tells us that publicans (and people of all types) came to the wilderness to witness John's sizzling prophetic ministry. Verse 15 tells us that many wondered if he himself was the Messiah, but in Luke 3:16-18 we read, "John answered, saying unto them all, I indeed baptize you with water; but one mightier than I cometh, the latchet of whose shoes I am not worthy to unloose: he shall baptize you with the Holy Ghost and with fire: whose fan is in his hand, and he will thoroughly purge his floor, and will gather the wheat into his garner; but the chaff he will burn with fire unquenchable. And many other things in his exhortation preached he unto the people."

But later when asked about John's ministry, Jesus described his prophetic ministry as a "burning and shining lamp" (*see* John 5:35) that was sent to penetrate darkness and to prepare the way of the Lord. On one occasion, Jesus began to speak to the multitudes about His great respect for the prophetic ministry of John. Matthew 11:7-9 says, "And as they departed, Jesus began to say unto the multitudes concerning John, What went ye out into the wilderness to see? A reed shaken with the wind? But what went ye out for to see? A man clothed in soft raiment? behold, they which are gorgeously appareled, and live delicately, are in kings' houses. But what went ye out for to see? A prophet? yea, I say unto you, and *much more than a prophet."*

In Matthew 11:9-15, Jesus plainly stated that John the Baptist was greater than any other prophet due to his monumental role in introducing Jesus' ministry. In those verses, Jesus said, "For this is he, of whom it is written, Behold, I send my messenger before thy face, which shall prepare thy way before thee. Verily I say unto you, Among them that are born of women there hath not risen a greater than John the Baptist: notwithstanding he that is least in the kingdom of heaven is greater than he. And from the days of John the Baptist until now the kingdom of heaven suffereth violence, and the violent take it by force. For *all the prophets* and the law prophesied until John. And if ye will receive it, *this is Elias* [Elijah], which was for to come. He that hath ears to hear, let him hear" (Matthew 16:10-15).

Mark 6:19 tells us that John the Baptist on one occasion rebuked Herod Antipas for his sinful marriage to the ex-wife of his brother Philip. Herodias — his new wife — insisted that Herod Antipas execute him for rebuking them for their marriage. The narrative tells us that rather than execute John, Herod Antipas had him arrested and put in prison (*see* Mark 6:17; Luke 3:19,20). Even though John the Baptist had publicly rebuked Herod Antipas, the ruler held John in great respect "as a holy and righteous man" (*see* Mark 6:20) and refused to capitulate to his wife's murderous demands.

But later when Herod asked his wife's daughter to perform a dance for him and his guests at his birthday party, he ridiculously offered to give her *anything* — including up to half his kingdom in exchange for her performance (*see* Mark 6:21-23). Hearing this audacious offer, the unnamed daughter danced for him, and at her mother's suggestion and behest, she then asked for the decapitated head of John the Baptist (*see* Mark 6:24,25). Herod was sorry and did not want to do it, but because his guests heard him make the promise, he delivered on his promise to "give her anything" and reluctantly ordered the beheading of John the Baptist, commanding that his head be bought on a silver platter (*see* Mark 6:27,28).

John the Baptist's role was so prominent that he is even mentioned by the Jewish historian Flavius Josephus in his renowned historical book *Antiquities of the Jews*. But because John prophetically ministered before the death, burial, and resurrection of Jesus Christ — between the eras of the Old and New Testaments — John the Baptist was technically an intertestamental prophet.

When God's Spirit moved upon him, John the Baptist's spiritual sails caught the movement of the Spirit and he was enabled to prophetically function. In every respect, he functioned like all the Old Testament prophets. But those who are born again today have the Spirit continually residing *within* them and possess a blessed state that even John the Baptist never experienced in his lifetime. This explains why Jesus said, "...He that is least in the kingdom of God is greater than he [John the Baptist]" (*see* Luke 7:28).

JESUS CHRIST HIMSELF AS AN INTERTESTAMENTAL PROPHET

As we've seen, a study of the life and ministry of Jesus clearly demonstrates that He stood in all five of the fivefold ministry gifts. He was the *Perfect Apostle,* the *Perfect Prophet,* the *Perfect Evangelist,* the *Perfect Pastor,* and the *Perfect Teacher.*

But because the events of the four gospels occurred in the period between the Old and New Testaments, Jesus technically began His ministry in the intertestamental era — until His death, burial, resurrection, and ascension, which started the period of the New Testament. In both Acts 2:33 and Ephesians 4:10 and 11, we read that when Christ ascended on high, one of His first actions was to pour the gift of the Holy Spirit on the Church and to give supernatural gifts to men. Those spiritual gifts are multifaceted, but they include the apostle, prophet, evangelist, pastor, and teacher, and as noted, this chapter is dedicated to New Testament *prophets.*

As early as the book of Deuteronomy, God was foretelling that Christ would stand in the office of a prophet. Deuteronomy 18:15 says, "The Lord thy God will raise up unto thee a *Prophet* from the midst of thee, of thy brethren, like unto me; unto him ye shall hearken." And in verse 18, Moses said again, "I will raise them up a *Prophet* from among their brethren, like unto thee, and will put my words in his mouth; and he shall speak unto them all that I shall command him."

Then in Peter's message on the Day of Pentecost, Peter quoted Moses in Acts 3:22 and affirmed that Jesus is a *Prophet* when he said, "For Moses truly said unto the fathers, A *prophet* shall the Lord your God raise up unto you of your brethren, like unto me; him shall ye hear in all things whatsoever he shall say unto you."

And as Stephen was preaching just before he suffered martyrdom (the first martyr in the Early Church), he also quoted Moses' words about Christ being a Prophet, when Stephen said, "This is that Moses, which said unto the children of Israel, A *prophet* shall the Lord your God raise up unto you of your brethren, like unto me; him shall ye hear" (Acts 7:37).

But as we journey through the life of Christ in the four gospels, we find there are a host of verses that refer to and affirm that Jesus is a *Prophet.* For example:

- Matthew 21:11 says, "And the multitude said, This is Jesus the *prophet* of Nazareth of Galilee."
- Matthew 21:46 says, "But when they sought to lay hands on him, they [the religious leaders] feared the multitude, because they took him for a *prophet.*"
- Mark 6:4 says, "But Jesus said unto them, A *prophet* [referring to Himself] is not without honour, but in his own country, and among his own kin, and in his own house."
- Mark 6:15 says, "Others said, That it is Elias. And others said, That it is a *prophet,* or as one of the *prophets,*" speaking of the fact that Jesus was a prophet.
- Mark 8:28 says, "And they answered, John the Baptist: but some say, Elias; and others, One of the *prophets,*" referring to that moment when Jesus asked who did the people say He was.
- Luke 4:24 says, "And he said, Verily I say unto you, No *prophet* is accepted in his own country." This is Luke's account of what was also recorded in Mark 6:4.
- Luke 7:16 says "And there came a fear on all [after seeing numerous miracles]: and they glorified God, saying, That a great *prophet* is risen up among us; and, That God hath visited his people."

- Luke 9:8 says, "And of some, that Elias had appeared; and of others, that one of the old *prophets* was risen again." This is Luke's account of what was written in Mark 6:15 that affirms it was widely believed even by many in Herod's circles that Jesus was a prophet.

- Luke 9:19 says, "They answering said, John the Baptist; but some *say*, Elias; and others *say*, that one of the old *prophets* is risen again."

- Luke 24:19 says, "And he said unto them, What things? And they said unto him, Concerning Jesus of Nazareth, which was a prophet mighty in deed and word before God and all the people." This is a record of what two apostles said to Christ about Himself as they spoke with Him on the road to Emmaus.

- John 4:19 says, "The woman [the woman at the well] saith unto him, Sir, I perceive that thou art a *prophet*."

- John 6:14 says, "Then those men, when they had seen the miracle that Jesus did, said, This is of a truth that *prophet* that should come into the world," speaking of the apostles response to Jesus multiplying the loaves and fishes to feed a multitude.

- John 7:40 says, "Many of the people therefore, when they heard this saying, said, Of a truth this is *the Prophet*." This is the recorded response of many who heard Him speak in the city of Jerusalem at the time of the Great Feast.

- John 9:17 says, "They say unto the blind man again, What sayest thou of him, that he hath opened thine eyes? He said, He is a *prophet*." This is the recorded response of the blind man whose sight was restored by Jesus.

Jesus Christ is indeed a Prophet. And Hebrews 13:8 says, "Jesus Christ is the same yesterday, and to day, and forever." This means that since He *was* a prophet, He is *still* a prophet, and He will *always be* ministering prophetically in the Church. To help those who question Jesus' current-day prophetic ministry in the Church, let's look closer at the words in Hebrews 13:8 to see what it means.

In Hebrews 13:8, the Greek word translated "same" emphatically means that Jesus Christ is *unchangeable.* Jesus is the one Person we can depend on to be the same, regardless of the time or the spirit of the age. That means we don't need to refigure who Jesus is, what He thinks, or what His message is, because He is the *same* — and everything He represents is the *same* — yesterday, today, and forever.

Jesus is the one Person we can depend on to be the same, regardless of the time or the spirit of the age. That means we don't need to refigure who Jesus is, what He thinks, or what His message is, because He is the same — and everything He represents is the same — yesterday, today, and forever.

The word "yesterday" is a translation of the Greek word *exthes*, and it depicts *all time that ever was up until this present moment.* In other words, it describes *the past.* The word "today" is a translation of the Greek word *semeron*, and it means *today*, *this very moment*, or *this current age.* It depicts *the present.* But when the words "yesterday and today" are used in one phrase, as they're used here, it portrays *continuity.* In fact, the words "yesterday and today" are an Old Testament expression that denotes *continuity* (*see* Exodus 5:14; 2 Samuel 15:20).

So based on Hebrews 13:8, we find that Jesus wasn't one way in the past and another way in the present. Whoever He was in the *past* is exactly who He is in the *present*. There is *continuity* in Jesus Christ! So if you discover who Jesus was in the *past*, you have also discovered who Jesus is in the *present* — and you have also discovered who Jesus will be in the *future* — because *He is continuously the same*. And the word "forever" in Greek means *into all the ages of the future*, which depicts *all future time to come*, including all ages that will ever be known.

Hebrews 13:8 presents this exact thought, *"Jesus Christ is exactly the same in the past, in the present, and in the future."* So whoever He *was* in the past is who He *is* in the present and who He *will be forever*. And in regard to His prophetic ministry, it means this Eternal One *was* a prophet, He is a prophet, and He will *forever be* a prophet.

And through the operation of the Christ-given fivefold gift of the prophet in the Church today, Jesus is still ministering as a Prophet. Seeing how intrinsically Jesus operated as a Prophet and seeing the prophetic anointing upon Him past-day, present-day, and forever, it lets us know that to reject the prophetic ministry would be the equivalent of rejecting an entire facet of Jesus Christ's ministry in the Church today.

Seeing how intrinsically Jesus operated as a Prophet and seeing the prophetic anointing upon Him past-day, present-day, and forever, it lets us know that to reject the prophetic ministry would be the equivalent of rejecting an entire facet of Jesus Christ's ministry in the Church today.

Other Prophets in the Time of the New Testament

On the Day of Pentecost, Peter quoted the prophet Joel (*see* Joel 2:28,29) when he said in Acts 2:16-18, "But this is that which was spoken by the prophet Joel; and it shall come to pass in the last days, saith God, I will pour out of my Spirit upon all flesh: and your sons and your daughters shall prophesy, and your young men shall see visions, and your old men shall dream dreams: and on my servants and on my handmaidens I will pour out in those days of my Spirit; and they shall prophesy."

Joel and Peter prophesied that when the Holy Spirit was poured out on the Church, it would initiate a new period when all believers would, to some extent, begin to speak prophetically on behalf of God. With the outpouring of the Holy Spirit on the Day of Pentecost, a door was thrown open for God to prophetically speak through all of His sons and daughters, and it was foretold that young men would see visions, old men would dream dreams, and servants and handmaidens would *prophesy*.

In the Old Testament, such happenings primarily occurred only with prophets who moved supernaturally from time to time when the Spirit suddenly would come upon them. But today we live in the New Testament period, and the Holy Spirit now miraculously indwells every believer. In this sense, just as all believers are a member of a spiritual priesthood, they are also members of a Church-wide "prophethood," because the Spirit is present inside every born-again believer all the time, and each Christian — at least in some measure — can speak for God as His representative. In the Church Age, it should be expected that prophetic activity will increase and *continue* to increase as we come closer to the end of age. We are told in Revelation 19:10 that "...the testimony of Jesus is the spirit of prophecy." Thus, any person who personally knows Jesus Christ is enabled in some measure to function prophetically.

But besides the common spirit of prophecy that can work through any believer, there additionally is the Christ-given gift of a *prophet* that is enumerated in Paul's fivefold listing in Ephesians 4:11. The gift of a prophet is a distinct fivefold gift, which is separate from the simple gift of prophecy. The fivefold gift of the prophet was given expressly for the upbuilding of the *naos* Temple of God, called the Church.

And as is the case with the other fivefold gifts of apostle, evangelist, pastor, and teacher, the gift of the prophet is given: "For the perfecting of the saints, for the work of the ministry, for the edifying of the body of Christ: till we all come in the unity of the faith, and of the knowledge of the Son of God, unto a perfect man, unto the measure of the stature of the fulness of Christ" (*see* Ephesians 4:12,13). Thus, until the Church has reached this long-awaited status, the gift of the prophet will be needed along with all the other fivefold gifts.

The Word 'Prophet' Wrongly Used

But as we saw in the case of the apostle, the word "prophet" is being used in the modern Church very sincerely, albeit wrongly, over and over again. I am convinced that if the apostle Paul were alive today and saw the growing list of people who are called "prophets" in magazine articles, on television, and in other media, he would be *appalled*. At the time the New Testament was being written and the Church was being established, the word "prophet" was a respected term that was only applied to those who were bona fide Christ-given fivefold prophets.

But in our day, just as the term "apostle" is being too freely used, the word "prophet" is also being used so freely that, in a certain sense, the weight of what it means to be a prophet has been diminished. Indeed, many have a *drawing* to prophetic things — or have experienced supernatural things that often accompany this ministry gift — and have heard marvelous things from the Holy Spirit. This should be expected in the Church Age as a fulfillment of Joel's prophecy that Peter quoted on the day of Pentecost. But these inklings and experiences and tendencies *do not* mean everyone who has had them is a Christ-given fivefold prophet.

Many love reaching the lost, but that does not mean they are a Christ-given fivefold evangelist. Furthermore, many deeply care for the well-being of people's souls, but that doesn't mean they are a Christ-given fivefold pastor. Many love teaching and sharing insights from the Word of God, but that does *not* mean they stand in the office of a Christ-given fivefold teacher. My prayer is that this book will help people be more careful about who they call an apostle or a prophet and that it will assist in bringing clarity to you about who is a real fivefold apostle or prophet according to the New Testament.

Prophets are *real* and *powerful* as a fivefold ministry gift, but only a *handful* of those who claim to be prophets today are real prophets — that is, compared to an ever-growing list of those who claim to be prophets or who are incorrectly called prophets by others. By the way the word "prophet" is being used today, I am convinced that people who use this word wrongly are simply uninformed about *what* and *who* a prophet is. Anyone who really grasps what and who a prophet is and what a prophet does would not freely apply that title so casually to so many people.

I kindly address those who incorrectly call themselves prophets or who incorrectly call others prophets — as I believe the misuse of this term is largely because of *unclear teaching* on the subject of what is and is not a prophet. Words and terms are very important, and when a very specific term — like the word "prophet" — is used too freely or loosely, it gives the false impression that there are a *plethora* of prophets in the Body of Christ, and there simply are not. However, most who incorrectly use the term "prophet" do it sincerely and out of ignorance because there is so little clarity on the subject. One purpose of these chapters is to help you gain a biblical grasp on the gift of the prophet.

'Built Upon the Foundation of the Apostles and Prophets'

The ministries of apostles and prophets are so closely connected that in Ephesians 2:20, Paul wrote that the Church, including every single member, is "...built upon the foundation of the apostles and prophets, Jesus Christ himself being the chief corner stone." In Chapter Two of this book, we saw construction terminology used to explain the various roles of the fivefold ministry, and I particularly noted that the team of "apostle and prophet" operate in the following ways:

- **Apostles** and their teams select the construction site where the Church has never been established before. When they enter a new location, they are anointed by God's Spirit to clear spiritual rubbish out of the way and to lay a foundation for the Church. And as team leader, the apostle works side by side with his God-called team to lay a rock-solid foundation on which others can come along to do their parts in building a magnificent structure.
- **Prophets** are like building inspectors who also play a key role to make sure the construction is being carried out properly and up to code. After the foundation has been laid, the Christ-given fivefold *prophet* enters the "apostolic" picture to do his or her part in building the House of God. Often prophets operate like anointed building inspectors because they are divinely enabled to see what others may not see, including what is done correctly or incorrectly. With Christ-given insight, Christ-given prophets impart courage to build correctly and at times, they address issues that need to be fixed in the building process so that the structure can stand for a long time.

In the Old Testament, we find a marvelous type and shadow of apostolic builders working hand in hand with prophets at a critical moment in history.

The story begins in Ezra 1:1-3, where we read:

> **Now in the first year of Cyrus king of Persia, that the word of the Lord by the mouth of Jeremiah might be fulfilled, the Lord stirred up the spirit of Cyrus king of Persia, that he made a proclamation throughout all his kingdom, and put it also in writing, saying, Thus saith Cyrus king of Persia, The Lord God of heaven hath given me all the kingdoms of the earth; and he hath charged me to build him an house at Jerusalem, which is in Judah. Who is there among you of all his people? his God be with him, and let him go up to Jerusalem, which is in Judah, and build the house of the Lord God of Israel, (he is the God,) which is in Jerusalem.**

A time miraculously came when God touched the heart of King Cyrus, and as a result, Cyrus gave the order for the Temple in Jerusalem to be rebuilt. He even miraculously ordered that all the resources be supplied that were needed to rebuild it. Soon exiles joyfully returned to Jerusalem to begin the building process, but as work commenced, the builders encountered severe opposition from surrounding enemies who made nonstop attempts to stop its construction. Ezra 4:4 and 5 records the story of this resistance when it says, "Then the people of the land weakened the hands of the people of Judah, and troubled them in building, and hired counsellers against them, to frustrate their purpose, all the days of Cyrus king of Persia, even until the reign of Darius king of Persia."

The resistance of enemies continued unabated until the exhausted builders succumbed to pressure and discouragement. They stopped building until "the second year of the reign of Darius king of Persia (*see* Ezra 4:24). But then the prophets Haggai and Zechariah began to prophetically stir the hearts of the people to cast off discouragement and to rise once again to build.

In Haggai 1:3, we read that the prophet Haggai confronted the people for not continuing their work to rebuild the house of God. Haggai 1:3,4 says,

"Then came the word of the Lord by Haggai the prophet, saying, Is it time for you, O ye, to dwell in your cieled houses, and this house lie waste?" And in Haggai 1:7,8, we read that the prophet Haggai continued to prophesy, "Thus saith the Lord of hosts; Consider your ways. Go up to the mountain, and bring wood, and build the house; and I will take pleasure in it, and I will be glorified, saith the Lord."

Together, the prophets Haggai and Zechariah began to prophetically stir the hearts of the people by prophesying to them about their need to resume building the Temple in Jerusalem. In Ezra 5:2, we read, "Then rose up Zerubbabel the son of Shealtiel, and Jeshua the son of Jozadak, and began to build the house of God which *is* at Jerusalem: *and with them were the prophets of God helping them.*"

When Nehemiah did his part to lead the project of rebuilding the walls around Jerusalem, once again enemies attempted to thwart the progress being made. The assaults made against the builders were so intense that the workers were required to build with a tool in one hand and a weapon in the other hand. In Nehemiah 4:15-18, Nehemiah reports:

> **And it came to pass, when our enemies heard that it was known unto us, and God had brought their counsel to nought, that we returned all of us to the wall, every one unto his work. And it came to pass from that time forth, that the half of my servants wrought in the work, and the other half of them held both the spears, the shields, and the bows, and the habergeons; and the rulers were behind all the house of Judah. They which builded on the wall, and they that bare burdens, with those that laded, every one with one of his hands wrought in the work, and with the other hand held a weapon. For the builders, every one had his sword girded by his side, and so builded....**

In both cases with the prophets Haggai, Zechariah, and Nehemiah, as the Temple and walls were being built and the builders busily worked at the site, those prophets stayed near to prophetically encourage and stir them to keep building. In many respects this is an Old Testament type and shadow of how prophets today work alongside apostles and other God-called builders to advance the Gospel and to build the *naos* Temple of God. First Corinthians 10:11 and Colossians 2:17 clearly state that many Old Testament events were foreshadows of realities now found in Christ, and certainly this rebuilding of the wall in Jerusalem was a prophetic foreshadowing that depicted the complimentary roles of apostles and prophets working together in the Church Age.

But in Ephesians 2:20, Paul says the ministries of apostles and prophets are so closely connected that the Church is "...built upon the foundation of the apostles and prophets, Jesus Christ himself being the chief corner stone."

Some scholars say this verse is Paul's illustration of the manner in which the writings of Old Testament prophets and New Testament apostles are joined together in the Person of Jesus Christ. While it is absolutely true that Christ is the One on whom the Old Testament and New Testament lean and is the One who gloriously brings it all together, in Ephesians 2:20, it is nevertheless clear that Paul is uniquely referring to the New Testament ministries of Christ-given fivefold apostles and prophets. He was not giving a theological dissertation on how the two Testaments come together in Christ, albeit it is indeed the case that the Old and New Testaments "hinge" on the Person of Jesus Christ.

In this chapter, where we are looking at various early New Testament prophets, please know that what you are about to read is certainly not an all-inclusive list. The book of Acts tells us that there were whole groups of traveling prophets, and we do not know all their names. After reading the following pages that list early New Testament prophets from the Bible, it may at first seem that this list is small compared to the lengthy list in the previous chapter that covered Old Testament prophets. But considering the New

Testament covers a much shorter span of time than the Old Testament, this listing is actually quite significant.

A thorough reading of the New Testament shows there were many active prophets in the time of the early New Testament. They were closely related to the work of apostles, a fact that we will cover in greater detail in the next and last chapter of this book. You will see that there were local prophets, traveling prophets, some apostles who were also prophets, female prophets, and you'll also see that there was a problem with *false* prophets, which has always been the case throughout history.

As we proceed, let's begin by looking in the book of Acts at the first group of prophets that are referred to in the emerging Church.

A Hub of Prophetic Activity in Antioch

The city of Antioch was located approximately 490 miles north of Jerusalem in what is today modern-day Turkey. It was the third largest city in the Roman Empire during early New Testament times with only Rome and Alexandria exceeding it in size. Because it was situated on a crossroads between East and West, Antioch became a thriving commercial center and a true melting pot of cultures and peoples. The multiplicity of cultures found within the thriving urban environment of Antioch naturally resulted in a colorful and diverse Christian community and experience for those who were privileged to be a part.[3]

The Gospel was first brought to Antioch in the wake of Stephen's martyrdom, and tradition states that it was brought there by Peter who started the church in Antioch in about 34 AD. Because Peter was an apostle to the Jews, he focused on the Jewish community when he first preached in Antioch, but eventually other preachers arrived, and Acts 11:20 and 21 tells us, "...When they were come to Antioch, spake unto the Grecians, preaching the Lord Jesus. And the hand of the Lord was with them: and a great number believed, and turned unto the Lord."

Notice that verse 21 says "a great number" of Grecians responded to the Gospel message. The word "Grecians" refers to Greek-speaking pagans. But the words "a great number" is a translation of the words *polus te arithmos*. The word *polus* means *much*; the word *te* means *then* or *at that time*; and the word *arithmos* means *a fixed and known number* — it is the root for the word *arithmetic*. Together, these words picture *a massive amount of people who came together at one precise time*.

Verse 21 says many Greek-speaking pagans "...turned unto the Lord." The word "turned" is a form of the Greek word *epistrepho*, and it means *to turn around* or *to physically turn*. It is not a metaphorical change; it is *a real change that can be witnessed by outside observers*. This word describes an outward change that accompanies genuine repentance and tells us that when a person genuinely repents, there is an undeniable change that can be observed by others.

In verse 21, it specifically says they turned "unto" the Lord. The word "unto" is a translation of the Greek word *epi*, which means *upon*, *leaning fully upon*, or *resting one's entire weight upon*. These individuals experienced a genuine saving faith as they placed their faith "upon" (*epi*) the Lord.

The word "Lord" is the Greek word *kurios*, which means *lord* or *supreme master*. We find that although Peter first went to Antioch to preach to the Jewish community, other preachers later arrived whose message was warmly received as pagans left their old lives behind and accepted Jesus into their hearts. Before long, a thriving church was established as believers in Antioch began to actively evangelize their city and the surrounding region (*see* Acts 11:19-26). Finally, the church of Antioch had grown so rapidly that it was second in size only to the church of Jerusalem.

However, despite the distinction of these two churches being the two largest congregations in the mid-First Century, the two churches were very different for various reasons. As noted, many new believers in Antioch were Gentiles who came from pagan backgrounds, whereas believers in Jerusalem were nearly all of Jewish ancestry, and as we will see, this disparity resulted in two completely different approaches to the kind of church that emerged in both settings.

Pliability in the Hands of the Holy Spirit

In the earliest years of the Church, the Holy Spirit's primary activity was focused in the city of Jerusalem, where the Holy Spirit was first poured out on the Day of Pentecost. That is where Peter preached his famous first sermon in which he referred to Joel 2:28 and 29, where thousands of unsaved people came to Christ, and where the apostles worked powerful miracles throughout the city.

Indeed, the long-awaited new wine of the Holy Spirit had been poured out in Jerusalem — but as the years passed, a significant problem arose. The church of Jerusalem became in many respects *an old, inflexible wineskin*. In Mark 2:22 (*NKJV*), Jesus said, "And no one puts new wine into old wineskins; or else the new wine bursts the wineskins, the wine is spilled, and the wine-skins are ruined. But new wine must be put into new wineskins." This analogy actually appears in three of the four gospels (*see* Matthew 9:17; Mark 2:22; and Luke 5:37-39), and it teaches the importance of being ever receptive and pliable to the working of the Spirit.

To help you understand the point of new and old wineskins, let me tell you a little about wineskins so you will see the point Jesus is making in these verses.

During the time of the early New Testament, wineskins were watertight containers, usually crafted from pliable goatskin, that were used to hold wine as it aged. When new wine was put in a wineskin, it would continue to ferment.

This fermentation would produce gas as a byproduct, which would cause the wineskin to expand and stretch. However, if new wine was poured into an old wineskin that had been already been stretched on multiple occasions until it was no longer flexible, the subsequent expansion of the gas could cause the material to burst, spilling the wine and destroying the bag.

It seems that just like an "old wineskin," the church of Jerusalem had grown inflexible very quickly. The believers there were preoccupied with tradition and rules because Jerusalem had been the center of Judaism for many centuries. Consequently, the city epitomized the rituals, ceremonies, rules, and regulations of the Jewish religion. Because the congregation in Jerusalem was primarily comprised of people who had been devout Jews before their conversion, many carried these Jewish customs over into their Christian walk. The religious traditions of these believers' past eventually became entrenched in the new church, and as a result, the congregation wasn't flexible enough to move with God as He sought to advance His Church.

When the new wine of the Spirit was poured out in their midst, the church of Jerusalem attempted to contain it within the context of Judaism. For example, even from its infancy, the congregation in Jerusalem squabbled over the issue of circumcision (*see* Acts 15). Fierce arguments ensued as various factions within the church debated how much of the Law should be kept. This argument and others like it caused schisms to form within the church and hindered the Holy Spirit from continuing to move as mightily as He had in the beginning.

Another reason the church in Jerusalem quickly became an old wineskin was that the believers there initially believed that the Gospel was for the Jews only and that Gentiles could not receive salvation. This very narrow mindset severely limited their point of view on many vital doctrinal questions during the early years of the church's existence — and as a result, the work of the Holy Spirit among them became significantly restricted.

The exclusion of Gentiles from the church at Jerusalem also had the negative consequence of eliminating diversity from their congregation. Only one nationality was represented within the church in Jerusalem — former Jews who were still very Judaic in their views. This was not a true picture of the new man God was creating. It was not — *and will never be* — His will for the makeup of any congregation to be restricted as the Church at large is intended to be a mixture of people from all nations. If we attempt to restrict the Church to a single race or nationality, we will derail our mission. This means when we receive salvation, all considerations of ethnicity and nationality disappear because such distinctions do not exist in the mind of Christ.

As I told you in Chapter Two, the Church of the Lord Jesus Christ isn't bond or free, Jew or Gentile, circumcised or uncircumcised, barbarian or Scythian, male or female — but it is one unified family that has all been made to drink of one Spirit. We are all one in Christ (*see* Galatians 3:28; Colossians 3:11). However, the church at Jerusalem was primarily a Jewish church filled with Jewish people and Jewish thinking, and thus they became very limited in their thinking. When it became apparent that this would not change, God's Spirit began to move mightily 490 miles to the north in the church of Antioch, where a diverse congregation allowed every believer to be a participant and all were equal partners in the church as the Body of Christ in that locality.

When we receive salvation, all considerations of color and nationality disappear because such distinctions do not exist in the mind of Christ.

But to understand just how unique the environment at Antioch actually was, we must look at the mixture of cultures among the spiritual leadership in

Antioch. Acts 13:1 says, "Now there were in the church that was at Antioch certain prophets and teachers; as Barnabas, and Simeon that was called Niger, and Lucius of Cyrene, and Manaen, which had been brought up with Herod the tetrarch, and Saul."

Notice Acts 13:1 begins with the word "now." The word "now" is a translation of the Greek word *de*, which serves as an exclamation mark to make a powerful and dramatic statement. It is as if the Holy Spirit in this verse is lifting the tone of the narrative to alert us to something significant happening in Antioch that was not occurring in other locations. It means, "Now *amazingly...*" Then the verse goes on to tell us that what was happening there was indeed remarkable.

We find that in Antioch, there was an unusual emergence of fivefold ministry. Acts 13:1 mentions five specific individuals — Barnabas, Simeon, Lucius, Manaen, and Saul. Although the information provided about these men in Acts 13:1 may at first seem limited, there is some knowledge about their lives that can be gleaned, and it is important for us to understand. For example:

- ***Barnabas*** was a Levite from the Gentile country of Cyprus, which was a region in Greece (*see* Acts 4:36). He was a Jew descended from the tribe of Levi, but because he was raised so far from Jerusalem, it is likely that he didn't grow up around the strict religious environment that was so characteristic of that city.

- ***Simeon*** is referred to in Scripture as "Niger," which is the Latin word meaning *black*. Scholars speculate that this particular Simeon was probably a black man from Africa and may have even been the slave of a Roman family. Regardless of his social status at that time, he nonetheless served alongside other leaders in a position of authority in the church of Antioch.

- ***Lucius of Cyrene*** was from the region of Cyrene which is located in northern Africa. Some have speculated that this may actually have been Luke, but it is unlikely since Luke is the author of Acts and does not identify himself here. Others have argued that Lucius was most likely a man of North African heritage. The name "Lucius" actually means *light* or *bright* and hence some scholars imply he was a black North African, but with lighter skin. If this is the case, it is likely that he, too, was first brought to Antioch as a slave. Regardless of his cultural identity, he had come to Antioch from Northern Africa.

- ***Manaen*** is recorded to have been brought up with Herod the tetrarch and was, in fact, probably a relative of the family of Herod. Because Manaen was Roman and likely descended from the royal family, he had received a Roman education. This is especially significant because educated Romans were raised to look down on foreigners as being uncouth barbarians who were classed as *"less"* than Romans. And in Antioch, Manaen's position alongside other ethnicities, skin colors, and social classes lets us know that he had broken free from the prejudices of his upbringing to work alongside two Africans and two Jews, whom he had been raised as a Roman to despise.

- **Saul** is the last-mentioned leader in the group. He eventually came to be called the apostle Paul. He was born into a very well-connected, tremendously wealthy Jewish family in Tarsus, who were rich enough to purchase Roman citizenship, a sum that in today's currency would exceed $250,000. Being raised in a wealthy home, he was afforded the best education that money as a rabbi and a Pharisee could buy. As a result, he was very well educated. After his prior education at the university of Tarsus, still at a young age, Saul had relocated to Jerusalem to be theologically trained at the feet of

> Gamaliel. Because of his former station and position, Saul was the most religiously instructed and possessed the greatest breadth of scriptural knowledge of any of his peers in the leadership in Antioch.

To assemble this particular group — with all of these ethnicities, skin colors, and social classes — into a single group broke all norms of society in the First Century and was truly a supernatural occurrence that only God could have arranged as the people remained hungry for and pliable to the working of the Spirit. In Antioch, blacks, whites, Jews, Gentiles, bond, and free all mingled together in leadership and worship. This was something that had never existed before. Remarkably, God used a plethora of nationalities and cultures that represented a broad perspective of the Gospel and its mission to paint a powerful picture of what the Church should look like — a colorful tapestry of people from all walks of life.

Through the death, burial, and resurrection of Jesus Christ, God was demonstrating His desire for one new man — the Body of Christ — and the wall separating ethnicities, skin colors, and social classes had been broken down and destroyed. In Antioch, it became remarkably visible that salvation was equally available to all mankind, and the new status was "one new man" (*see* Ephesians 2:15).

In Antioch, it became remarkably visible that salvation was equally available to all mankind, and the new status was "one new man."

In this rich spiritual environment, an interesting blend of prophets and teachers emerged. Acts 13:1 says, in effect, "Now *amazingly*…there were in the church that was at Antioch certain *prophets* and *teachers*…."

The word "prophets" is the plural form of the Greek word *prophetes*, which we studied in-depth in Chapter Seven. We saw there that it is a compound of *pro* and *phemi*. The preposition *pro* carries a wide range of meaning, and the second part of the word, *phemi*, means *to say, to speak*, or *to communicate*. The use of the word *phemi* immediately lets us know that a prophet is a *speaking* or *saying gift* or one who is intended *to communicate the heart and mind of God*. It is sometimes used in the New Testament to simply denote religious teachers — instructors sent from God — without particular reference to future events, for to teach the people in the doctrines of faith was a part of the prophetic office.

If you did not read Chapter Seven, I encourage you to return there now to read the section called, "The Use of the Word 'Prophet' By Greek Writers in Antiquity." It will give you a fuller understanding of the Greek word *prophetes*, the word used in the Septuagint Greek version of the Old Testament and in the New Testament to depict a *prophet*.

But Acts 13:1 tells us that in Antioch, there were also "teachers." In the original text, the word "teachers" is the plural form of the Greek word *didaskalos*, which is primarily translated as "teacher" throughout the New Testament. The word *didaskalos* is used 47 times in the gospels and the verb form of *didaskalos* is used more than 200 times in the Greek Septuagint version of the Old Testament and in the Greek New Testament. Any word used with such frequency is well-established with a clearly defined meaning. As we saw previously, the word "teacher" — translated from the Greek word *didaskalos* — describes *a fabulous and masterful, gifted teacher*.

But *didaskalos* is also importantly the Greek equivalent for the Hebrew word "rabbi." The word "rabbi" depicts *a teacher-scholar who is respected for his accumulation of facts and knowledge*. If translated literally from the Hebrew, the word "rabbi" means *great in number*, but if used as a title, it pictures the great number of facts and knowledge possessed by a well-versed rabbi.

So the word "teacher" — translated from the Greek word *didaskalos* — can be used interchangeably with the words *teacher*, *master*, and *rabbi* in the New Testament. All of these describe an *outstanding, masterful, great teacher.* In Ephesians 4:11, where Paul listed the various Christ-given fivefold ministry gifts and he included "teacher," it is translated from *didaskalos* and it describes any person who operates in the fivefold ministry gift of *teacher.*

'Who's Who' in Antioch?

The question often arises, "Which of the leaders in Acts 13:1 were *prophets* and which ones were *teachers* — or is it possible that these various leaders were a combination of both?"

Acts 13:1 does not expressly say who was a prophet or teacher in the group, but the Greek text uses certain parts of speech that seem to separate *the first three as the prophets* and *the last two as teachers.* If this is the case, it would mean *Barnabas*, *Simeon that was called Niger*, and *Lucius of Cyrene* functioned primarily as *prophets* — while *Manaen* and *Saul* functioned in Antioch primarily as *teachers.* Roles were expanded later on, but at least when Acts 13:1 begins, it seems these were the gifts that these various leaders operated in at that time.

Indeed, we also cannot overlook the fact that it is possible for two gifts to be united in a single person. Paul, as an apostle, had the capacity *if needed* to function in all of the fivefold ministry gifts. However, Paul specifically later said of his own calling, "Whereunto I am appointed a *preacher*, an *apostle*, and a *teacher* of the Gentiles (2 Timothy 1:11). In this verse, Paul acknowledges that he was a preacher, an apostle, *and* a teacher. Some scholars suggest that the word "preacher" refers to Paul also standing in the office of a *prophet.* Due to the numerous revelations and divine utterances that he expressed repeatedly throughout the course of his ministry, it is certain that Paul had the traits of a *prophet*.

But if one ponders the resumés of the various leaders listed in Acts 13:1, it becomes clear that the first three individuals — *Barnabas*, *Simeon*, and *Lucius* — were very different in their life experience and educational backgrounds compared to the life experience and educational backgrounds of *Manaen* and *Saul*.

If the first three men in our list in Acts 13:1 primarily functioned as prophets — as it seems is the case as implied by the Greek text — we must note the differences among these first three compared to Manaen and Saul. The first three — *Barnabas, Simeon that was called Niger*, and *Lucius of Cyrene* — were less educated in terms of the Scripture simply due to the fact that they were either non-religious Jews, possibly pagan in their heritages, perhaps even from different continents.

To function prophetically, these three individuals were gifted by Christ to supernaturally hoist their prophetic sails to catch the movement of the Spirit when God longed to speak. But due to their various backgrounds, it is probably the case that they did not have within them the reservoir of knowledge and facts that would be necessary for a teacher who is called upon to share a breadth of biblical information, albeit under the unction of the Holy Spirit. Having a strong biblical foundation and a grasp on Scriptures indeed helps any prophet be more accurate — and all prophetic individuals should seek to form a solid doctrinal foundation to undergird their prophetic ministries.

But the fact that these first three men were either unreligious, pagan in background, or possibly even from a different continent strongly suggests that due to their various backgrounds, they did not have biblical knowledge to exegete verse by verse from the Scriptures, which requires more than a gust of prophetic inspiration. To be a masterful teacher, one must possess a wealth of biblical and scriptural information.

The perfect example is Saul, whose many years of study provided him with a wealth of knowledge and enabled him to provide the believers in Antioch with unprecedented access to Jewish culture and the teachings of the Old Testament.

Whether the subject was the story of creation, the Old Testament covenants, praise and worship, Jesus' lineage, Messianic prophecies, the Shekinah glory of God, or simply Jewish history — all of it was comfortable territory for Saul because he was trained as a rabbi and theologian. When it came to drawing on a reservoir of this biblical information, he was like a fish in water. Saul's fellow team members in Antioch must have treasured his knowledge, and in a sense, he probably served as their "walking Hebrew concordance and Bible commentary." And because he was well-versed in the Word of God, he was able to discern what was doctrinally sound and what was contrary to the teaching of Scripture.

But wait...in addition to Barnabas, Simeon, Lucius, and Saul, there is one more person on the list in Acts 13:1 that we have not commented about yet, and that is Manaen. Manaen had been brought up with Herod the tetrarch. As noted earlier, the Greek participles in Acts 13:1 indicate that Manaen would have been in the second category in this group of leaders who were the *teachers.*

Manaen, a noble Roman, was highly educated and possessed a wealth of knowledge. Hence, it is not surprising that Christ tapped that reservoir of knowledge inside Manaen and called him to be a *teacher* in the church at Antioch. This emphatically does *not* mean having a high level of education is necessary to be a fivefold teacher, but by the same token, it does not hurt either.

All these factors — the diversity and backgrounds of these various men — may have had an impact on the way Christ gifted them.

APOLLOS, A TEACHER IN EPHESUS AND CORINTH

Let me provide another example of a fivefold ministry teacher — and that is *Apollos*, who for a time served alongside Aquila and Priscilla in the city of Ephesus.

As an Alexandrian Jew, Apollos had been educated in the best schools of theology in the city of Alexandria. Alexandrian scholars were noted for their intelligence and sophistication. Few excelled more in intellectual brilliance or education regarding matters of theology, history, geography, philosophy, and finance than the Jewish scholars of this great city. This was the environment where Apollos received his education and where his views of theology were developed as a younger man.

It is also important to note that Alexandrian Jewish scholars were famous for their careful interpretation of Old Testament Scriptures. Therefore, it is likely that Apollos' views had been shaped by the pervading theological beliefs held by the Jews of this city, where he had spent most of his life. His high level of education and his personal dedication to the careful interpretation of Old Testament Scripture is also made clear in Acts 18:24, where it states that he was "...an eloquent man, and mighty in the scriptures...."

The Greek word for "eloquent" in the Greek text reveals Apollos' advanced level of education. It is a translation of the word *logios*, which explicitly describes a person who is *highly learned* or who has *an advanced education*. This word denotes *one who has become eminently distinguished by his study and commitment to education*. The use of *logios* to describe Apollos indicates that this man's educational pedigree was impressive.

Because the word *logios* could also describe *one who has mastered the art of public speech,* it is worth noting that early documents written by historians of the Church affirm that Apollos was a gifted orator and an eloquent, persuasive public speaker. Because he was so educated and his vocabulary was so large, he was highly skilled in speaking persuasively. When people heard him speak and sensed his spiritual passion, they knew they were in the presence of a brilliant man who was passionately committed to studying and proclaiming the truths of God's Word accurately.

Additionally, Acts 18:24 states Apollos was "mighty in the Scriptures." The word "mighty" is the Greek word *dunatos*, which means *powerful*. But as used here, it carries the idea of one who has a *masterful grip* on something, and it refers to Apollos' *masterful grip* on Scripture. Only a person who was serious about theological study and reflection would possess such an extensive command of the Scriptures.

Acts 18:25 also adds, "This man was instructed in the way of the Lord; and being fervent in the spirit, he spake and taught diligently the things of the Lord...." The word "instructed" indicates Apollos possessed expert knowledge about this subject that had been passed on to him in the synagogue by rabbis or in the classrooms of Alexandrian schools of theology. Furthermore, the Greek tense for the word "instructed" in this verse is continuous, and it means Apollos wasn't a student who simply wanted to graduate and receive a diploma. Rather, he was thoroughly committed to the Word of God and had proven it by giving himself to continuous study and instruction over the years.

The effect of God's Word on Apollos' life is made plain in Acts 18:25, which states Apollos was "fervent" in the spirit. The word "fervent" means *to be full of enthusiasm*. Thus, Apollos was a man who *enthusiastically bubbled over* with love for the Word of God — and when people heard him speak, they were struck by this man's deep passion for the Word of God.

Eventually Apollos left Ephesus and relocated to Corinth to help the church there. The reason why he relocated is not specifically stated in the New Testament, but an addition in the Codex Bezae (an ancient Greek-Latin translation of the text) suggests Corinthian believers heard Apollos preach in Ephesus and asked him to come teach and make a significant contribution to the churches throughout Achaia.[4] Acts 18:27 indeed tells us that when Apollos arrived in Achaia, he "...helped them much which had believed through grace."

Before Apollos converted to Christ, his mind was already a treasure-trove of scriptural knowledge due to his Jewish theological training in Alexandria. It is no surprise that Christ called him to stand in the office of a fivefold teacher after he converted. Everything in his past prepared him to eventually teach New Testament truths in the emerging Early Church.

Next I want you to see that at the same time this particular group of five prophets and teachers were ministering in Antioch, there was another group of traveling prophets from Jerusalem who arrived in Antioch to bring them a prophetic word.

Agabus: Another Example of a New Testament Prophet

Acts 11:28 tells us that a prophet named Agabus arrived in Antioch from Jerusalem with a group of unnamed prophets who traveled with him. This entire group of prophets seemed to have been endowed with remarkable prophetic insight concerning future events and with the power of explaining divine mysteries. As the story unfolds, it is clear that Agabus had the God-given ability to foretell certain future events.

In Acts 11:27 and 28, we read, "And in these days came prophets from Jerusalem unto Antioch. And there stood up one of them named Agabus, and signified by the Spirit that there should be a great dearth throughout all the world: which came to pass in the days of Claudius Caesar."

Verse 28 states that Agabus "signified" by the Spirit that a famine was coming to the Roman world. The word "signified" is a form of the Greek word *semaino*, which means *to signify*, *to give a sign*, or *to give an alert.* It pictures a dramatic foretelling of a coming event, and in this case, it was a dramatic warning that "a dearth [or famine] throughout all the world" was coming.

Notice that verse 28 says Agabus gave his prophetic alert "by" the Spirit, which is a translation of the Greek word *dia*. It means *through* the Spirit, *by* the Spirit, *through the instrumentality* of the Spirit, or *by the agency* of the Spirit. Here we find Agabus was divinely informed and empowered to speak *by the agency* or *instrumentality* of the Holy Spirit. Because his spiritual sails were hoisted and he was prepared, Agabus caught the wind of the Spirit in his prophetic sails and was thusly "propelled" to supernaturally foretell this coming event.

And just as Agabus foretold it in Acts 11:28, a famine occurred that took place during the fourth and sixth year of Claudius' reign. Worst of all, it affected the regions near Judea and Jerusalem, and it was so severe that the historian Josephus even referred to it in his historical work called *Antiquities of the Jews*. In that record, Josephus described the event as a "very great famine, in which many died for want of food."[5]

Because the church in Antioch had been forewarned by Agabus — through the *agency* and *instrumentality* of the Holy Spirit working through him — and they believed what he prophesied, they were prepared in advance for the impending famine. The believers in Antioch were so convinced this was a true prophetic message that verse 29 says they were "determined" to take action. The word "determined" is translated from a form of the word *horidzo*, which, interestingly, means *to be bound* or *to be obligated*. The use of this word lets us know the saints in Antioch were bound with a sense of covenant obligation to fellow believers in other places, so they *determined to act* on what had been signified to them by the Spirit though the mouth of the prophet Agabus.

So working together as a team, the believers in Antioch gathered a relief offering so money would be available to be distributed to believers when the famine hit the hardest. Acts 11:29 says, "Then the disciples, every man according to his ability, determined to send relief unto the brethren which dwelt in Judaea." The action of those believers *before* a time of crisis made them God's agents of provision and deliverance for others when the crisis actually occurred.

We will return to Agabus again soon, but first we must see what the Bible tells us about Philip the evangelist's four daughters who were prophetesses and who were widely known as such in the Early Church.

Philip's Four Daughters Who Prophesied

In Acts 21:8-10, we read, "And the next day we that were of Paul's company departed, and came unto Caesarea: and we entered into the house of Philip the evangelist, which was one of the seven; and abode with him. And the same man had four daughters, virgins, which did prophesy. And as we tarried there many days, there came down from Judaea a certain prophet, named Agabus."

The Philip here was one of the original seven deacons (*see* Acts 6:5-7). However, at some point in his early ministry, Christ called him to be a fivefold evangelist. It was Philip who first preached the Gospel to the Samaritans with powerful signs and wonders (*see* Acts 8:5-8), and over time Philip took the Gospel to many villages of the Samaritans (*see* Acts 8:25). He preached the Gospel to the Ethiopian eunuch and baptized him (*see* Acts 8:26-39) before he was supernaturally translated by the Holy Spirit to Azotus (*see* Acts 8:40). After preaching in all the cities and villages of the coast, Philip came to the seaside city of Caesarea (*see* Acts 8:40) where he remained for 20 years. From there, Philip regularly took his ministry as an evangelist up and down the coasts of Israel and Phoenicia.

In Acts 21:8, we read that as Paul and his companion headed toward Jerusalem, they stopped at "the house of Philip the evangelist, which was one of the seven," and they spent "many days" with him. Notice that although Philip was a noted evangelist by that time, the text refers to him as "one of the seven" — a title that could only be applied to the legendary first seven men who served as deacons at the outset of the church in Jerusalem. Imagine how thrilling it must have been for Paul and his companions to stay in the home of one of the legendary "seven" and to have an opportunity to ask Philip questions about the earliest days of the book of Acts and the earliest events in the church at Jerusalem.

In Acts 21, we have the final narrative recorded about Philip in the book of Acts. Acts 21:9 says, "And the same man had four daughters, virgins, which did prophesy."

Notice the verse begins with the word "and." This is a translation of the Greek word *de*, which is a conjunction intended to be an exclamation mark to make a significant point. It carries the idea, "And *emphatically, categorically, remarkably*, this man had four daughters, virgins, who did prophesy." The word *de* draws attention to these daughters and lets us know that the fact they were known to prophesy is significant.

We've seen in Joel 2:28 and 29 and Acts 2:17 and 18 that God stated He would pour His Spirit out on men *and women*. And in the last chapter, we saw there were women in the Old Testament who were called into prophetic ministry. Now we see that there were women prophetesses in the household of Philip the evangelist. And the use of the Greek word *de* indicates these daughters were *emphatically recognized* and possibly *well-known* for their prophetic giftings as Christ-given fivefold prophetesses.

This text should challenge anyone who suggests Paul's writings were opposed to women being in the ministry. Nothing in this passage suggests that Paul or his companion had any issue with these women being fivefold prophetesses. As the author of the book of Acts, Luke was traveling as one of Paul's companions at the time of this writing, along with other travelers in Paul's group, and Luke was so impressed with these women as prophetesses that he began the verse with the Greek word *de* to emphasize this powerful fact. These four daughters were just as recognized as bona fide Christ-given *prophetesses* as their father was recognized as a Christ-given fivefold *evangelist.*

Agabus at the House of Philip the Evangelist

But look who else showed up at Philip the evangelist's house while Paul and his companions tarried in Caesarea. In Acts 21:10, Luke tells us, "And as we tarried there many days, there came down from Judaea a certain prophet, named Agabus."

Like metal that is attracted to a magnet, the prophet Agabus felt a spiritual connection to Philip's household, where there were four resident prophetesses. Reading the Old and New Testaments, we discover that prophets in both Testaments tended to be drawn to one another. They moved in prophetic groups, and they were frequently aware where other prophets lived and functioned. And now, in a similar fashion, we see that Agabus was likely drawn *like metal to a magnet* to the house of Philip, where there lived four prophetesses.

There is no indication in the text to give the impression that Agabus came there *only* to deliver a prophetic message to the apostle Paul. We do not even know if he was aware Paul was there when he arrived to visit Philip and his prophetic daughters. It's possible that visiting Philip and his four prophetic daughters may have been a regular activity for Agabus to exchange prophetic insights with them. Then when Agabus showed up this time, it's possible that only then did he discover that Paul and his companions were there.

When Agabus came into the house, the Spirit of God moved upon him to prophesy. Acts 21:10,11 says, "And as we tarried there many days, there came down from Judaea a certain prophet, named Agabus. And when he was come unto us, he took Paul's girdle, and bound his own hands and feet, and said, Thus saith the Holy Ghost, So shall the Jews at Jerusalem bind the man that owneth this girdle, and shall deliver him into the hands of the Gentiles."

When Agabus saw Paul, he was suddenly moved by the Spirit to deliver a prophetic word about what awaited Paul in Jerusalem. As a prophet, Agabus had his spiritual sails hoisted, so he caught what God wanted to say and then began to prophetically foretell future events to Paul and to forewarn him about what awaited him in Jerusalem. Agabus accurately foretold that Paul would be bound, arrested, and handed over to Roman authorities, and all of it came to pass exactly as prophesied by Agabus. Note that Agabus never told Paul not to go, but seemed to simply warn him of what awaited him there. It was Paul's companions, who took the word of Agabus so seriously and "besought him [Paul] not to go" to Jerusalem (*see* v. 12).

But notice Paul and his companions had been there "many days" before Agabus arrived. There is no indication that in the "many days" he had been with those four recognized prophetesses that the prophetesses ever gave any prophetic indication that trouble awaited Paul in Jerusalem. It seems what was prophetically revealed to Agabus had *not* been revealed to them, and that this revelation to Agabus likely only occurred upon his arrival when he saw Paul there. So how is it possible that four recognized and well-known prophetesses did not pick up on what was revealed to Agabus so suddenly? I will answer that question in the following sections.

Paul's Instruction to Prophets in First Corinthians 14:29-32

In First Corinthians 14:29-32, we read that Paul addressed multiple fivefold prophets who resided in the church at Corinth. Referring to their prophetic operation in the church, he told them, "Let the prophets speak two or three, and let the other judge. If any thing be revealed to another that sitteth by, let the first hold his peace. For ye may all prophesy one by one, that all may learn, and all may be comforted. And the spirits of the prophets are subject to the prophets."

Notice the word "prophets" is plural, which affirms there were multiple prophets in the church at Corinth. But notice that Paul also said, "...Let the prophets speak...." This means if prophets are present, and they have something to say, Paul said they should be allowed to speak.

As noted earlier, the Greek word for a prophet is *prophetes.* One component of this word is derived from the Greek word *phemi,* which means *to say, to speak,* or *to communicate.* The use of *phemi* emphatically tells us a prophet is a *speaking* or *saying gift* or *one who verbally communicates the heart and mind of God.* So in accordance with that gift, Paul said that if a prophet (or multiple prophets) has a word to express, time should be allocated for him to "speak" what God has given him. Indeed, prophets are primarily *speaking gifts* and, hence, need space allocated so they can speak *if* they are so moved.

Discerning — 'Judging' — a Prophetic Message or Revelation

In First Corinthians 14:29, Paul adds that while one prophet is publicly speaking what he or she has to say, the other present prophets should "judge" the message. Certainly, if a prophetic message — or *any* message given in *any* form, for that matter — is contradictory to the Word of God, those who are in spiritual leadership have a God-given responsibility to correct it. But the word "judge" used here is a translation of the Greek word *diakrino,* which in this context means *to carefully discern.* The other present prophets are called to carefully listen to and discern every facet and nuance of what is being prophetically communicated.

Paul also implied that as the other prophets carefully listen and discern what is being said, it should not be surprising if another prophet that is present suddenly senses that something else needs to be said or added to the message being communicated. That is why in verse 30, he said, "…If any thing be revealed to another that sitteth by, let the first hold his peace."

Paul importantly added that from among the other present prophets who are carefully discerning what is being said, it is possible that additional revelation may be "revealed" that also needs to be spoken and added in order to give the message more fullness or completeness. This is no different than a teacher who triggers additional insights in other fivefold teachers who are listening to a teaching in a meeting. In that Spirit-saturated environment, the Holy Spirit opens the floodgates of revelation and new insights are divinely added to the mix of others who are listening. Paul said, likewise, it is not unusual if additional insights are suddenly "revealed" to other prophets in the room who are listening to the one who is speaking.

The word "revealed" in Greek is a form of *apokalupto,* which is a compound of the words *apo* and *kalupto*. The word *apo* means *away*, and the verb *kalupsto* is the Greek word for *a veil, a curtain*, or some type of *covering*. When compounded into the word *apokalupto*, it means *to remove the veil* or *to remove the curtain* so you can see what is on the other side. It refers to *something that was veiled or hidden, but suddenly the covering is removed so that what is on the other side becomes clear and visible to the mind or eye.*

It is like pulling the curtains out of the way so you can see the scene outside your window. Even though the view was always there for you to enjoy, the curtains blocked your ability to see it. But once the curtains were drawn apart, you suddenly were able to see what was previously hidden from your view. In such a moment when you can see "beyond the veil" to observe what wasn't previously visible to you, that is what the Bible calls a *revelation* — translated from the Greek word *apokalupto*.

Thus, the word "revealed" that Paul used in First Corinthians 14:30 speaks of a prophet who suddenly sees something that had been previously veiled or hidden, but which has become clear and visible to the mind or eye. In the flash of a moment, the obstructing veil is removed and something previously not understood miraculously comes into clear view. In Spirit-saturated atmospheres, such obstructing veils are frequently pulled out of the way, thus enabling one to suddenly *see* or *hear* what he has personally never seen or heard before.

I can testify to moments when I have been in such anointed meetings, and, suddenly, the Holy Spirit began to supernaturally open my mind to see and to hear what I never saw or heard before. As I listened to what a speaker was saying, suddenly my spirit was opened up to see other things in addition to what was being spoken. In that atmosphere of revelation where hearts are open and where the Holy Spirit is working, many new things can be "revealed" to people in the anointed atmosphere of that meeting.

What the Prophet Can and Cannot Control — *'The Spirits of the Prophets Are Subject to the Prophets'*

Knowing this and having likely experienced it himself, Paul wrote that if one prophet is speaking — and another prophet suddenly sees, hears, or discerns something that needs to be publicly shared — the first prophet must "hold his peace" and allow space for that other prophet to share what he or she has received from the Spirit of God. Perhaps something the first prophet said triggered an insight or revelation in another prophet. In that case, Paul says that, eventually, the prophet who is speaking and holding the congregation's attention must "hold his peace" to allow the other to give his insight as well.

The words "hold his peace" are a translation of the Greek word *sigao.* It means *to be silent*, but it pictures one who needs to calm himself down, quiet himself, or to "hold his peace" as the *King James Version* translates it. It is often the case that when a prophet speaks, he or she is absorbed spiritually and emotionally in the message that is being communicated as the speaker endeavors to focus intensely to impart both the message and the heart of God accurately.

The Greek word *sigao* — translated as "hold his peace" — implies that when a prophet imparts a message, he or she may be so engrossed in the declaration that the prophet may need to "calm" himself or herself to make room for another to speak. Prophets are to be controlled by the Spirit, not by emotion — therefore, Paul said that person can calm, quiet himself, and "hold his peace" if it is evident that someone else has something to add that he or she has received from the Holy Spirit.

If someone replies, "But when the Spirit is speaking through me, I can't control myself," it is not altogether true. Such a claimant is inexperienced and immature in his or her gift, or that person is simply in error and deceived. Paul clearly added in First Corinthians 14:31 and 32, "For ye may all prophesy one by one, that all may learn, and all may be comforted. And the spirits of the prophets are subject to the prophets."

In verse 31 when Paul says, "…Ye may all prophesy one by one…," it depicts the presence of multiple prophets in a single congregational setting. Paul was teaching that they may each prophesy one by one, if needed. In other words, taking turns one after the other in a polite and orderly fashion, they each can "hold their peace" and allow other prophets to speak.

When I was younger, I attended the meetings of one of the nation's most established and well-known prophets, and I often observed that he would stop at times and call on other prophets in the room to ask if they had anything to add. He clearly understood something — that he did not have all the revelation himself and needed to graciously make room for the Spirit of God to speak through others.

Prophecy *Instructs* and *Inspires*

Paul added in verse 31 the reasoning for God's order in such a meeting — "...that all may learn, and all may be comforted..." by prophetic ministry. The word "learn" is a form of *manthano,* a Greek word that pictures students who gain intellectual and applicable knowledge from what is being communicated. The use of *manthano* lets us know that genuine prophetic ministry is more than a burst of emotion that affects us momentarily. It carries with it an instructional element as well. A real prophetic word may stir the emotions of listeners, but it also provides practical instruction. It is intended to *instruct* as well as to *inspire.*

The word "comforted" in verse 31 is a form of the word *parakaleo*, a compound of the words *para* and *kaleo. Para* means *alongside* and *kaleo* means *to call, to beckon, or to speak to someone.* When these two words are compounded, it depicts *someone who is right alongside a person, urging him, beseeching him, begging him to make some kind of correct decision.*

A real prophetic word may stir the emotions of listeners, but it also provides practical instruction. It is intended to *instruct* as well as to *inspire.*

In the ancient Greek world, this word was often used by military leaders before they sent their troops into battle. Rather than hide from the soldiers the painful reality of war, the leaders would summon their troops and speak straightforwardly with them about the potential dangers of the battlefield. The leaders would inspire their troops by telling them about the glories of winning a major victory.

Instead of ignoring the clear-cut dangers of battle, these officers came right alongside their troops and urged, exhorted, beseeched, begged, and pleaded with them *to stand tall, throw their shoulders back, look the enemy straight on — eyeball to eyeball — and face their battles bravely.* Thus, we discover that when prophetic ministry occurs, God's Spirit comes right alongside us to give a call to action and may even warn listeners of ensuing battles and their need to stand tall and to act bravely in the face of aggression. Nearly every prophetic word will give *a call to action or ask the listeners to respond in some way.*

For example, if a prophetic word says there is "sin in the camp," it will follow with a call to repentance. If a prophetic word forewarns of hard times, it will follow with a call to face the enemy in the power of the Spirit and to endure until victory is achieved. Thus, we learn from Paul's words in First Corinthians 14:31 that prophetic ministry is never simply foreboding. It is also filled with practical instruction and a call to action — a way to respond to what God is saying — that will equip those who have an ear to hear with the power to overcome.

But then in First Corinthians 14:32, Paul importantly added, "And the spirits of the prophets are subject to the prophets."

The word "subject" in this verse is translated from a form of *hupotasso*, a Greek word that was used militarily to picture soldiers who recognized the authority of their superior officers and who were in submission to their authority. The word *hupotasso* inherently implies that one knows his place, rank, or assignment in the army or in any type of organization. It pictures one who is submitted to authority and who knows that he or she must act according to rules that are established by that specific authority. Interestingly and significantly, this word *hupotasso* — translated "subject" in verse 32 — can also mean *to hide behind someone's back*, and it is intended to give the impression that *there is protection in submission.*

There is protection in submission.

In verse 32, Paul is corporately speaking to multiple prophets in the church at Corinth. He reminds them that each prophet is to know his or her file and rank among the other prophets, to respect one another, and to have an attitude of submission as someone publicly operates prophetically in their midst. Because the word *hupotasso* strongly implies *protection in submission*, it also tells us when a prophet has a submitted attitude, if he honestly makes a prophetic mistake, he can be corrected by the other listening prophets. That loving correction provides protection for him, and because of his submission to other prophets who sit nearby to judge what he is saying, it likewise provides protection for the church from prophetic error.

The entire passage in First Corinthians 14:29-32 demonstrates that no prophet has all the revelation and knowledge needed by himself. God speaks through many, and it takes every participant doing his or her part for the whole counsel of God to be imparted to a local church and to the Church in general. Paul clearly gives the encouragement that, if needed, other prophets must be afforded the time to speak so additional insights that are revealed to those prophets can also be heard.

As we continue, we will return to the subject of Philip's four prophetic daughters and Agabus the prophet. But for now, let's see what else Paul wrote about our limited knowledge and limited prophetic capabilities.

'We Know in Part, and We Prophesy in Part'

In reference to what we do and do not know, Paul said in First Corinthians 13:9, "For we know in part, and we prophesy in part." And then in verse 12, he added, "For now we see through a glass, darkly...."

First, I want you to notice Paul says that at this present time we both "know in part" and "prophesy in part." The words "in part" are used twice in this verse, and both times are translated from the Greek words *ek merous*, which literally means *from pieces*. It pictures something like the pieces of a jigsaw puzzle. While each piece of a jigsaw puzzle holds vital information and is valuable and important, each piece *alone* is insufficient to give a full picture. For the whole picture to be seen and understood, each piece must be added to the puzzle.

So Paul used the words *ek merous* — "from pieces" — to depict our fragmentary knowledge and prophetic abilities. Even if one person holds one piece of the puzzle and knows it very well, there are nevertheless other pieces of the puzzle that must be supplied. We must master what we know as best as possible, but if we think we've mastered a subject, we should reconsider our position, as there are always more pieces of the puzzle that we probably have not seen yet.

This is why in First Corinthians 8:2 (*NKJV*), Paul wrote, "And if anyone thinks that he knows anything, he knows nothing yet as he ought to know." Likewise, I have found that as a serious student of God's Word and early Christian history, I am fairly confident in what I know — yet as the years pass, I am always delighted to find a piece of a story or a part of history that I have never read or heard before that makes the full picture become even more complete for me. Those are euphoric moments when new rays of revelation come beaming into my spirit and soul. It reminds me of Psalm 119:18 where the Psalmist writes, "Open thou mine eyes, that I may behold wondrous things out of thy law." As much as the Psalmist already knew, he was aware there were more wondrous things that he had not yet seen.

Similarly, in regard to prophetic ministry, one could think he has a full and clear prophetic word for the hour — while, in reality, he or she holds only a *piece* of the picture, even if at times, it is a very *vivid* one. But he or she does not likely see the whole picture yet. Just as each piece of a jigsaw puzzle holds vital information — and each piece alone is insufficient to give the full picture — there is no prophet so gifted that he or she can see the whole picture by himself, or independently of others. He or she may clearly see a piece that is vital, but it is only a *piece*. That is why it is critical that each prophet learn to hold his peace and "keep silent" to see "if any thing be revealed to another that sitteth by" (1 Corinthians 14:30).

'We See Through a Glass, Darkly'

In First Corinthians 13:12, Paul wrote that "for now we see through a glass, darkly...." The word "now" is a translation of the Greek word *arti*, which means *presently* or *in this very moment in time*. Then Paul adds that in this present moment, *"we see."* The words "we see" are the plural form of the Greek word *blepo*, which means *to discern*, *to perceive*, *to observe*, or *to see.*

This, first of all, is Paul's acknowledgement that there really are certain things "we see" in this present moment. For example, we see many biblical truths clearly, we see many biblical doctrines clearly, and there are many prophecies about the future we confidently understand. But Paul goes on to also say we see "through a glass, darkly" — and that implies that as much as we confidently know, we must realize there is more God wants to reveal to us more clearly.

The word "glass" is a translation of the word *esoptron*, a Greek word that commonly depicted either Roman glass or a hand mirror from the time when Paul was writing. To understand the impact of both of these examples, it is imperative for you to know something about Roman glass and hand mirrors from that period.

Roman glass was a great technological breakthrough at that time, but it was crude, rough, blob-like, full of inclusions, blurry, and usually had a tint of blue or green. Although it was technologically considered to be highly advanced, all these factors nevertheless made it very difficult to look "through" Roman glass. If the dense glass with all of its inclusions was held to the sunlight, someone could indeed see bursts of light behind it, and those bursts of light cast gorgeous hues for that person to see. But because of the blurry condition of the glass, that individual could only see blurry images generated by bursts of light. The light was beautiful, but because the glass was blurry, the person viewing the glass could not see clearly through it.

However, the Greek word translated "glass" in First Corinthians 13:12 was also the word that was used to depict hand mirrors. These ancient hand mirrors were held in a person's hand, and because of their small size, the mirror could only "reveal" one small area at a time. Once one area had been exposed by the mirror, the person holding the mirror would have to move it to another angle to view what needed to be seen next. Thus, such mirrors were inadequate to give a full image at any one specific moment. Additionally, these mirrors were not made of silver-plated glass like mirrors today, but were fashioned from highly polished metal. Even if the metal was highly, highly polished, even the most highly polished mirrors provided only images that were hazy and indistinct.

This explains why Paul adds in this verse that we see through a glass "darkly." The word "darkly" is a translation of the word *ainigma,* a Greek word that depicts *something that is obscure* or *a riddle*. It is where we derive the English word "enigma," which depicts that which is hard to understand, that which is mysterious, that which is a paradox, or something we see or hear that challenges our understanding.

Thus, First Corinthians 13:9 and 12 are intended to remind us that we only hold smaller pieces of a bigger puzzle. And while we are thankful for what we do know and see, at best, the image before us is incomplete. To see everything God wants to reveal, we need the other pieces in order to see the full picture God wants to unveil. And just as Roman glass allowed the viewer to see bursts of wonderful light, as wonderful as that was, the knowledge and prophetic insights we hold are likely blurry on certain points. And just like an ancient hand mirror — even if we have highly polished knowledge and our prophetic insight is advanced — we, left just to ourselves, cannot with perfect clarity see the whole picture God wants us to see. We need the pieces of the puzzle that are held by others if we want to see and to hear clearly and correctly.

Agabus the Prophet and the Four Prophetess Daughters of Philip

This leads us back to the story of Agabus and the four prophetic daughters of Philip the evangelist.

The story in Acts 21 about Agabus and the four prophetesses perfectly illustrates what Paul wrote in First Corinthians 14:29-32: "Let the prophets speak two or three, and let the other judge. If any thing be revealed to another that sitteth by, let the first hold his peace. For ye may all prophesy one by one, that all may learn, and all may be comforted. For the spirits of the prophets are subject to the prophets."

These four daughters were bona fide prophetesses and likely had shared many prophetic revelations and insights with Paul and his companions in the "many days" Paul had already been there in their father's house (*see* Acts 21:10). But when Agabus arrived, they held their peace to make room for *his* prophetic gift to function. Although the four women were genuine prophetesses, something was revealed to Agabus that had not been revealed to them. But as a result of holding their peace and making place for Agabus' gift to operate, when Agabus arrived, he was given space to minister and God's Spirit provided direction and guidance for the apostle Paul.

I am sure that as well-regarded prophetesses, these prophetic daughters had shared their own prophetic observations with Paul in the days before Agabus arrived. They may have been thrilled with the "pieces" of prophetic revelation they held in their hands, but when Agabus arrived, they respected his authority and yielded so Agabus could add his prophetic piece of the puzzle and get it into place so the complete picture of what God wanted Paul to know could be conveyed.

THE PROPHETS SILAS AND JUDAS

At an important leadership convocation in Jerusalem, questions were being raised about pagans who were coming to Christ and what should be required of them. In Acts 15:22,30, and 32, we read, "Then pleased it the apostles and elders, with the whole church, to send chosen men of their own company to Antioch with Paul and Barnabas; namely, Judas surnamed Barsabas, and Silas, chief men among the brethren.... So when they were dismissed, they came to Antioch...Judas and Silas, being *prophets* also themselves, exhorted the brethren with many words, and confirmed them."

This narrative states that the spiritual leadership in Jerusalem had decided to dispatch two reputable brothers with Paul and Barnabas to Antioch with the final resolutions of that convocation of leaders. The two men they dispatched with Paul and Barnabas were Judas and Silas. And in addition to being reputable spiritual leaders, verse 32 states that these two men were *prophets.*

As prophets, Judas and Silas were filled with the Spirit of God and were divinely enabled to foretell events and to also scripturally teach the doctrines of faith as a part of their prophetic ministry. But remember, prophetic ministry is intended to *instruct* as well as to *inspire*, so within their prophetic ministry there was an instructional element. But the Greek word *prophetes* — where we derive the word "prophet" — depicts a *speaking gift* or a *saying gift*, and this explains why Acts 15:32 says Judas and Silas "…being prophets also themselves, exhorted the brethren with many words, and confirmed them."

The ancient Syriac version of the book of Acts says Judas and Silas exhorted the believers "with a rich word," indicating that in addition to supernatural prophetic ministry, they additionally brought the believers in Antioch a rich treasury of the instructional ministry of the Word of God. Thus, in Judas and Silas, we see clear examples of prophetic ministry that is marvelously mingled — divine utterance with sound biblical instruction.

Prophets in the Church at Thessalonica

We observed that in Paul's instructions to the Corinthians, he acknowledged that there were multiple prophets functioning in the church at Corinth. So many prophets were active there that Paul found it necessary to give instructions about when they were to speak, when they were to be silent, and how they should make room for other prophets to speak.

By reading the books of First and Second Thessalonians, we know that there were also prophets (plural) who were active in the church at Thessalonica. But because they were apparently not in submission to other established prophetic voices and were making prophetic errors, they had destabilized the faith of many in the church by a "prophetic mess" they had thusly created there. It is likely that if they had been in submission to other recognized prophets, as Paul instructed in First Corinthians 14:32, these erring prophets would have been corrected and the mess they created could have been avoided.

We saw in Chapter Seven that there were individuals in Thessalonica who purported themselves to be prophets, however, they were wrongly using the prophetic gift and were making grave prophetic errors. So when Paul wrote First and Second Thessalonians, he addressed this issue, and from what he wrote, we know that some visible leader — and possibly more than one leader — had wrongly prophesied that Jesus had secretly returned, and the Thessalonian believers had missed His return. If a system of "judging" had been in place in Thessalonica, as Paul wrote about in First Corinthians 14:29, this error could have been quickly corrected, but it seems such a system was not in place.

But because of the error the apostle Paul sought to correct, by the inspiration of the Spirit of God, we have Paul's teaching on the return of Jesus Christ, the apostate Church, the revealing of the Antichrist, and so much more (*see* 1 Thessalonians 4:15-18 and 2 Thessalonians 2:1-17). In this case, we see how Paul's gift was engaged by God to bring correction to others who had made serious prophetic errors, and this is an illustration of how every gift is needed to ensure that balance and doctrinal integrity is maintained in the Body of Christ.

We are not sure who the so-called prophetic individuals were who were upsetting the believers in Thessalonica, but whoever they were, they must have been influential because many in the church took their prophetic words seriously. They really feared that Jesus had come and that they had missed His return. The so-called prophetic utterances that so deeply disturbed them must have closely resembled a real prophetic message — thus the reason the congregation received it so seriously. Someone there had wrongly declared, "Thus saith the Lord" and took the church into a state of panic.

Finally, when the church woke up and understood that Jesus hadn't come yet, they were so upset by the *inaccurate prophecies* they had heard that they were tempted to turn a deaf ear to *all* prophetic utterances. However, closing their hearts to prophetic utterances because of a bad experience would have been a wrong response. Even though they felt that they had been exploited by bogus prophecy, it had not changed the value of genuine prophecy, which was a real gift from God that they needed. If they had shut their hearts to it because of a bad experience, it would have robbed them of fresh words from the Holy Spirit that God wanted to give them.

In a similar fashion, many people have been negatively affected by inaccurate prophecy at one time or another in our own day, but that doesn't mean all prophecy is untrustworthy. Lots of things are used inaccurately in life. For example, a car can be driven in such a reckless manner that it results in a collision — but that doesn't stop us from getting in *our* cars. Those mistakes might make us freshly aware of our need to drive more carefully and responsibly. But if we decided to never drive a car again because someone was once wounded in a car accident, it would be an irrational response.

Likewise, when Paul wrote to the Thessalonians, he didn't put a "ban" on all prophecies because of a negative prophetic experience. He simply told them to check their hearts regarding what they heard and to test prophetic utterances *before* they embraced them. In fact, Paul told them, "Quench not the Spirit" (*see* First Thessalonians 5:19). The word "quench" is a translation of the Greek word *sbennumi*, which means *to extinguish*, *smother*, *suppress*, *douse*, *put out*, *snuff out*, or *quell*. It most often pictures *a fire being doused with water*, and in other places, it is translated *to evaporate* or *to dry up*.

By urging them not to quench the Spirit after having a bad experience with prophets and prophetic ministry, Paul let us know that the church in Thessalonica was so put off by those who had misled them that they were tempted to put a lid on all prophetic ministry and to stop it from operating altogether. But "throwing the baby out with the bathwater" is never the correct response, so quenching the prophetic work of the Spirit was not the right response either. That is why Paul went on to tell them to "prove all things; hold fast that which is good" (*see* First Thessalonians 5:21).

Paul clearly taught our God-given responsibility to "prove" the prophetic words spoken over our lives. God doesn't expect us to blindly accept every prophecy as from the Lord. And prophetic ministry is so important for us that once we have determined a prophetic word is legitimate, Paul said we are to "hold fast" to it. In fact, Paul was so certain of the importance of authentic prophetic utterances that he later urged Timothy to "war a good warfare" by the prophecies that had been spoken over his life (*see* First Timothy 1:18).

But because people have a tendency to throw out the prophetic work of the Spirit when they become disappointed, Paul, in essence, told them (and thereby was telling us as well), "With the firmest grip, hold tight to authentic prophets and genuine prophetic ministry, because it is something noble and desirable that is needed in your midst."

Prophets Who Prophesied Over Timothy

In the New Testament, we also read about prophets and prophetic ministry who were active in Timothy's life and ministry. In First Timothy 1:18, Paul said, "This charge I commit unto thee, son Timothy, according to the prophecies which went before on thee, that thou by them mightest war a good warfare."

Most scholars agree this verse is a reference to the moment when Timothy was installed as the presiding leader of the Ephesian congregation. Apparently, at his installation, hands were laid upon him and prophetic utterances were spoken over him, but the verse does not explicitly say who spoke these prophecies. Whether it was Paul or someone else who uttered these prophetic words is not stated, and neither does the verse tell us if this was the simple gift of prophecy in operation or if it was delivered from the mouth of a recognized fivefold prophet. However, considering the stature of the church in Ephesus where this ordination event took place, it would be odd if other fivefold gifts were *not* present at Timothy's ordination, and, hence, it is likely that prophets were present along with other of the fivefold gifts.

We do know the prophetic words spoken over Timothy were *directional* and *navigational* — exactly the type of prophetic utterance one would expect to be spoken by a fivefold prophet. The words "went before on thee" are a form of Greek word *proago*, which means *to lead onward* or *to lead forward*, and it indeed tells us there was a *directional* or *navigational* dimension to these prophetic words that provided *direction* and *navigation* to Timothy about how to proceed in his ministry from that moment onward. The words "war" and "warfare" are both a form of *strateuo*, which means *to fight* or *to wage war*, but also importantly means *to strategize*. This means the prophetic words were intended to help provide Timothy with a *strategy* about how to move forward to accomplish his God-given ministry.

Then in First Timothy 4:14, Paul again referred to Timothy's ordination when he said, "Neglect not the gift that is in thee, which was given thee by prophecy, with the laying on of the hands of the presbytery."

In this verse, Paul acknowledged that this event occurred in the presence of the "presbytery." The word "presbytery" is translated from *presbuterion*, a Greek word that depicts *all the fivefold gifts who were present along with others who were recognized as elders of the church*. He states that certain divine enablements were imparted to Timothy with the accompaniment of a prophetic utterance or utterances. So we once again see that prophetic ministry played a respected key role at Timothy's installation as leader of the church in Ephesus.

Two End-Time Prophets in the Book of Revelation

Finally, we come to Revelation chapter 11, where we read of two end-time prophetic witnesses whom God will speak through during the Great Tribulation. These prophets will be endued with such supernatural powers that the Bible says no one will be able to stand against them until a time comes when "the beast" (*see* Revelation 11:7) will kill them, after which their bodies will lay in the streets visible to the entire viewing world. On the third day, they will be raised from the dead (*see* Revelation 11:11), and they will ascend into Heaven (*see* Revelation 11:12).

The Bible never tells us explicitly who these two end-time prophets are, but scholars have alleged this to be Moses and Elijah or Enoch and Elijah — or that God will raise up two previously unknown end-time believers to be His prophetic voices during the time of the Great Tribulation. Again, some speculate these witnesses to be Moses and Elijah because of the nature of miracles they will perform, which are so similar to the miracles that accompanied their prophetic ministries in the Old Testament.

Others speculate this will be Enoch and Elijah because neither of them ever tasted of death, as they were miraculously taken into Heaven, and that perhaps God will dispatch them to the earth to continue their work during the time of the Great Tribulation. And once again, some suggest it will be two previously unknown believers that God will raise up to speak and act on His behalf during the period of the Great Tribulation.

Although the book of Revelation does not identify who these two prophetic witnesses will be, Revelation 11:4 says, "These are the two olive trees, and the two candlesticks standing before the God of the earth." This is a reference to Zechariah, where the Scripture speaks of God's supernatural power in operation. So while we cannot know with certainty from the book of Revelation the identities of these two end-time prophetic witnesses, we do know the world will stand in awe of them as God mightily uses them in great power during the time of the Great Tribulation.

What About False Prophets?

In a previous chapter, I wrote about those who intentionally abuse the Church. If you did not read that section or have forgotten it, please read or reread it, as it is so important for you to understand and remember.

You must know that if there is a real prophetic gift, it is certain the devil will manufacture a counterfeit prophetic gift as well. Hence, just as there are real prophets, there are also *false* prophets. But *any* ministry gift can be counterfeited. Indeed, there can be *false apostles, false teachers, false evangelists, false pastors* (whom Jesus called "hirelings" in John 10:12), and likewise there can be, and there *are, false prophets.* In both the Old and New Testaments, there was an issue with false prophets from time to time, but if one has been burned by a bad experience or allows the dread of being misled affect him, it will cause him to miss what God has to say to him through legitimate prophetic ministry.

Remember that people counterfeit all kinds of things. For example, fake currency is regularly being produced and circulated from place to place. But just because there are counterfeit bills in circulation, does it mean you refuse to use money? Of course not, because you need money to live. Hence, rejecting money simply because of a few counterfeit bills would be a wrong response. In the same way, to reject all prophets and all prophetic ministry simply because you've had a bad experience with them is a wrong response. Since God gives nothing needlessly — or to no purpose — and He has given prophets to the church, we *need* them. Therefore, you need to learn how to recognize the legitimate ones, as well as the telltale signs of those who are illegitimate prophets. My sincere prayer is that this book will help you learn to discern the difference.

In the New Testament, we read that there are various kinds of false people, including false ministers. For example, there can be:

- ***"False brothers"*** (*pseudeoadelphos*, 2 Corinthians 11:26; Galatians 2:4)

  This is the word *pseudo* — meaning *false, deceptive,* or *untruthful* — compounded with *adelphos*, which is the Greek word for *a brother*. While this person may in reality be a *real* brother in Christ, something has changed so radically in his behavior and actions that he has become *false, deceptive*, and *untruthful.* Hence the relationship ceases to be honest. It has become corrupted, and he has become *a false brother* who is pretending to be what he is not.

- ***"False apostles"*** (*psuedoapostolos,* 2 Corinthians 11:13)

  This is the word *pseudo* — meaning *false, deceptive,* or *untruthful* — compounded with the word *apostolos*, which is the Greek word for an *apostle*. The fact that these individuals were in the leadership of the church tells us they were not outsiders who somehow invaded the church. They were resident members of the church, known by others, and perhaps long-term leaders. But somewhere along the way, they assumed a title that was never given to them by Christ. Although they claimed to be apostles, they were not, and therefore they were *false*, *deceived*, *deceptive*, or *untruthful*. They may have even believed that they were apostles — nevertheless, they were not; therefore, they were a corruption of the real apostolic gift.

- ***"False teachers"*** (*psuedodidaskalos*, 2 Peter 2:1)

  This is the word *pseudo* — meaning *false*, *deceptive*, or *untruthful* — compounded with the word *didaskalos*, which is the Greek word for *a teacher*. The fact that these individuals had public positions as teachers tells us they were not newcomers or unknown individuals in the church. But like the word "false apostles" previously discussed, this word indicates that somewhere along the way, their gift had become corrupted and they no longer represented the "teaching" gift that Christ intended for them to be to the Church.

- ***"False prophets"*** (*pseudoprophetes*, Matthew 7:15; 24:11; Revelation 16:13; 19:20)

  This is the word *pseudo* — meaning *false, deceptive,* or *untruthful* — compounded with the word *prophetes*, which is the Greek word for

> *a prophet*. It is primarily used in the four gospels to refer to outright false prophets, and in the book of Revelation, it was used to depict "the false prophet" who will work side by side with the Antichrist at the end of the age. However, as in the other instances noted, the word *pseudoprophetes* may also describe a genuine prophet who has become corrupted and therefore, a false representation of the God-given prophetic gift.

Jesus Himself specifically warned in Matthew 7:15, "Beware of *false prophets*, who come to you in sheep's clothing but inwardly are ravenous wolves." Pay careful attention to the fact that in this verse, Jesus depicted a particular category of "false prophets" that would come in "sheep's clothing." The words "sheep's clothing" clearly shows intent and tells us that this category knowingly operates in disguise and projects themselves to be sincere when they are not.

But Jesus adds that this particular category of false prophets are also "inwardly ravenous wolves." The word "inwardly" is translated from the Greek word *esothen*, a word that pictures something *concealed* or *hidden* and thus pictures a covert, clandestine, hush-hush, malevolent, underhanded, and surreptitious operation.

The word "ravenous" in Matthew 7:15 is translated from the Greek word *harpax*, a very specific word usually translated as *extortioner* in other places in the New Testament. It can also be translated *to rob* and pictures one who *brazenly* and yet *sneakily and stealthily* steals from another. And the use of *esothen* ("inwardly") and *harpax* ("ravenous") together in this single verse emphatically means the false prophets Jesus is describing are those who have their eyes on other people's money and who are working clandestinely to worm their way into the midst of God's people so they can coax money out of the pockets of others into their own pockets.

Jesus furthermore adds that this category of false prophets will operate like "wolves." This immediately brings to mind the image of a wolf, but there is much more to this word "wolves" than first meets the eye. The word "wolves" is the plural version of the Greek word *lukos,* which is a word that indeed pictures *a wolf or jackal,* and it was used to depict wolfish individuals who come to attack, victimize, and take advantage of others.

Very importantly, the word "wolves" — the plural version of the Greek word *lukos* — was the exact slang word widely used in the ancient world to depict *prostitutes* who wandered up and down streets at night to lure men into their dens of immorality, where they seduced them — and in that opportune moment often robbed them. These sexual predators, who were called "wolves," were famous for wandering the streets at night. They "howled" like *she-wolves* to make their presence known, and for this reason they were called "wolves." Because this slang term was so well-known in Jesus' time, when He spoke of false prophets as ravenous wolves in this verse, it is important to take it into consideration as being applicable to Jesus' description of and warning about false prophets as "wolves."

This means that just as prostitutes prowled the streets at night in order to sell themselves and their sexual services for money, Jesus tells us that false prophets will prowl through the church as they look for people to take advantage of with their errant ministries. Like "she-wolfs," they will "howl" or advertise themselves to make their presence known — and they are so seared in their consciences that they gladly "sell" or "prostitute" themselves and their services as they give a so-called prophetic utterance for financial profit. By using this word "wolves" that depicts prostitutes, Jesus clearly states that false prophets are those who spiritually prostitute themselves for some type of advantage or financial gain.

Unfortunately, there were those who were false from the start, but there were others who started out pure, but who through the lure or advantage of profit veered off course and prostituted themselves. Rather than being pure vessels who spoke on behalf of God by the Holy Spirit, they began using their spiritual giftings for self-gain or self-promotion to work money out of sincere people's pockets into their own pockets. Thus, due to their hidden agendas and ulterior motives, nearly everything in their so-called prophetic operation had become "false."

The words "false prophets" are a translation of the Greek word *pseudoprophetes*, a compound of *pseudo* and *prophetes*. The word *pseudo* carries the idea of *any type of falsehood*, and it pictures *one who projects an image of himself that's false*, *one who walks in a pretense*, or *one who intentionally misrepresents facts or truths*. The word *prophetes* is the Greek word for *a prophet*. But when these words *pseudo* and *prophetes* are compounded, the new word *pseudoprophetes* depicts outright false prophets or those who began as authentic prophets, but veered off course. Indeed some began as genuine, but have swerved and have thus become bogus in their prophetic operations.

False Christs or a Misuse of the Name of Christ?

But then in Matthew 24:5, Jesus added that in the time frame just before He returned at the end of the age, "...many shall come in my name, saying, I am Christ; and shall deceive many."

I once assumed that those Jesus referred to in Matthew 24:5 who declared themselves to be "Christ" would be "guru" types who appeared on the scene claiming to have a messianic calling. Certainly there have been many over the past 2,000 years who have claimed to be *a* messiah or even *the* Messiah. The Greek does use a definite article in front of the word Christ, which would seem to point to a concrete individual who will eventually claim to be the Messiah.

But if one considers the entirety of Matthew 24:5 in the Greek language, the text seems to imply that Jesus was also referring to a time when notable spiritual leaders would go astray in the very last hours of time. In this verse, Jesus said many would come "in My name." The words "in My name" can actually mean *on the strength and reputation of My name*. It appears that Jesus was prophesying about revelators who would wander onto a path of deception at the end of the age, but who would nevertheless use Him and His name as a cloak for their activities.

The apostle Paul also prophesied this would occur when he wrote about a "departure" from the faith that will take place at the conclusion of the Church Age. In First Timothy 4:1, he wrote, "Now the Spirit speaketh expressly, that in the latter times some shall depart from the faith, giving heed to seducing spirits, and doctrines of devils."

I have written entire books about the erring Church at the end of the Age (*Signs You'll See Just Before Jesus Comes*, *How To Keep Your Head on Straight in a World Gone Crazy*, and *Last-Days Survival Guide*) that detail what you need to do to ensure you are never a part of the erring Church. I recommend you obtain and read these books, as in them, you will see that the Holy Spirit indisputably says *some* notable people will depart from a right spiritual path as we come closer to the conclusion of the last days.

False Apostles and False Ministers Who Deliberately Deceive for Gain

In Chapter Four, we looked at Second Corinthians 11:13 and 14, where the apostle Paul described the growing problem of false apostles that existed in the First Century. In those verses, Paul described them when he wrote, "For such are false apostles, deceitful workers, transforming themselves into the apostles of Christ. And no marvel; for Satan himself is transformed into an angel of light."

Though we covered these verses in respect to false apostles, what Paul said in these verses could be applied to *anyone* who intentionally walks in falsehood — including *false prophets.*

Notice that Paul wrote about "deceitful workers." The word "deceitful" is translated from the Greek word *dolios*, a word derived from a root word that describes *bait that is put on a hook to catch fish*. It conveys the idea of *craftiness, cheating, cunning, dishonesty, fraud, guile*, and *trickery intended to entrap someone in an act of deception*. This word pictures something akin to a fisherman who carefully camouflages a hook with bait. Counterfeit prophets dangle what looks real to the eyes of the untried and lures sincere people closer and closer until they finally "bite the bait." Once the hook is in their victims' mouths, counterfeit prophets "jerk the hook" to catch people in order to exploit them for advantage of some kind.

Paul said they are deceitful "workers." The word "workers" is translated from the Greek word *ergates*, and it denotes *someone who actively works at what he is doing*. Because of this word, it is clear Paul was emphatically saying that there is nothing accidental about these blatant acts of deception. Those who intentionally operate in falsehood put forth great effort to impersonate real prophetic ministry. But remember, if there is a *false* prophetic ministry, it means there is also an *authentic* prophetic ministry, which counterfeits are attempting to copy or impersonate. The words Paul used in these verses very clearly make the distinction between these two categories.

Furthermore, Paul wrote that such individuals are so deceptive, they are able to "transform" themselves to look like they are something that they are not. The word translated "transform" is the Greek word *metaschimatidzo*, which means *to disguise oneself, to deliberately change one's outward appearance,* or *to masquerade in clothing that depicts a person as different than he really is.* Paul here is referring to individuals who intentionally attempt to pass themselves off as being legitimate, but are not — hence, Paul is picturing blatant acts of deception.

God Commands Us To 'Try' the Spirits

Just as Christ commended the church at Ephesus in Revelation 2:2,3 for developing criteria to determine who *was* and *wasn't* a real apostle, First John 4:1 urges us to do the same with those who claim to be prophets. That verse says, "Beloved, believe not every spirit, but try the spirits whether they are of God: because many false prophets are gone out into the world."

In First John 4:1, the apostle John, who is the author, acknowledged that at that particular time there was already an emerging "false-prophet" problem in the Early Church. In fact, such a large number of people were professing to be prophets who were not that John urged his readers (and us) to develop a criteria — *a paradigm* or *model* — to determine who *was* and who *wasn't* an authentic fivefold prophet.

But please notice the word "try" in First John 4:1. It is a translation of the word *dokimadzo*, a Greek word that was used to picture any *intense test that was intended to prove the quality and trustworthiness of a product.*

For instance, the word *dokimadzo* often denoted an *intense examination* of individuals who were running for public office to determine if their character was fit for the job. Because those who hold a public position were so influential, before they could be selected for office, they were *intensely examined* to determine if their character was sufficient for a powerful public position. Only after passing such a character test could they be permitted to run for office or be chosen for office. The process of examination was fiery, and if a person had flaws in his character, the test was designed to expose it.

But the Greek word *dokimadzo* is also the very word that portrayed the intense process of purifying and refining metal before it was used in construction. In the ancient world, to assure metal was free of defect and safe to use, it was put through multiple degrees of fire and intense heat to expose any hidden impurities that were invisible to the naked eye. Such flaws could significantly weaken a piece of metal and endanger lives if the structure collapsed. So before the metal was approved to be used, it was first placed into a fire that burned at a certain degree of heat; then it was placed into a second fire burning at an even higher degree; and finally, it was placed into a third blazing fire that burned at the highest degree of all. Three such tests were needed in order to remove all the unseen impurities from the metal that were hidden from the naked eye. Once its purity and trustworthiness was proven, it could be used freely, but this test was deemed very important to protect people from potential disaster.

But there is more. The word *dokimadzo* was also used in Greek literature to depict an intense test used to determine what was real or counterfeit coinage. A huge debasement of currency occurred after Nero's great fire of Rome in 64 AD. Prior to that, coins circulating in the Roman Empire were minted with a high percentage of precious metals so they would have a tangible value. But after the great fire when Nero needed massive sums of money to rebuild Rome, he devised a clever scheme to accumulate money for his construction projects. He ordered the silver content of the Roman denarii to be reduced and replaced with cheaper, more accessible metals; then he appropriated the unused silver for his own purposes. To the common eye, the new coins looked identical to the old ones, but the purity of the coins was radically reduced. The new coins appeared to have been struck from silver, but in reality, they were composed of cheap metal centers that were dipped in silver, leading people to think their money was worth more than it actually was.[6]

This practice of falsifying coins continued through subsequent emperors, and eventually a process was implemented to prove whether or not a denarius was legitimate or falsified. Attempting to determine the trustworthiness of a coin simply by judging its weight or giving it a quick visual inspection was usually insufficient to uncover the deception. Therefore, coins were thoroughly analyzed, examined, inspected, and scrutinized with a series of tests — including fiery tests — to determine if it was real or bogus. After a scrutinizing test was performed, the bona fide coinage stood up to the test, and the counterfeit coinage failed the test. But once a batch of denarii was proven to be genuine, it was then "bagged and tagged" with a piece of clay that declared it had passed official inspections and was genuine.[7]

But just as the counterfeit coins of the First Century contained a measure of silver so they wouldn't be easily detected and rejected, some false prophets possessed some qualities that appeared correct, but overall, they were defective. Hence, John encouraged his readers (and us) to make a deeper analysis of what we see or hear before we endorse it. Like people running for public office in the ancient world needed to have impeccable character, we need to be sure that those who prophesy to us have proven character.

And like metal that needed to be tested before it was used in construction, we need to know there are no hidden flaws in those who claim to be prophets that might spiritually endanger the lives of those who listen to them.

And like the coins that were tested to see if they were legitimate or bogus, we need to know that those who stand before us are legitimate. If we use our minds to analyze and allow the Holy Spirit to help us discern what we are hearing or seeing, and it passes the test, we can joyfully "bag and tag" the prophecies we are hearing as being legitimately from the Lord.

I personally have great respect and trust in those whom I trust to be authentic prophets. Nevertheless, God expects me to use my mind. So if I hear something that pings my spirit in a wrong way, I pay attention to it. Simply having great respect in those whom I believe to be authentic prophets does not exempt me from using my mind and listening carefully to discern what I hear from them.

Just as I would use my mind about anything I hear a teacher teach from the Word of God, First John 4:1 gives us a clear scriptural mandate to think about what we hear from the mouth of anyone, and that includes *prophets.* Remember that anyone can make a mistake, even those who are very sincere and who are called of God. So while we enjoy and need prophetic ministry, it is also imperative that we employ the use of our minds to be sure what we are consuming is good for us. The instruction in First John 4:1 confirms we are to "try" what we hear.

While you never want to allow a spirit of suspicion to affect you, the mere fact that you are called to "try the spirits" means some spirits need to be tried. God *commends* you for your genuine desire for truth, and if a prophet and his or her prophetic words are really from God, they will easily pass a biblical test, and you can joyfully "bag and tag" them as legitimate words from Heaven that you need.

What Does It Mean To Be 'Bewitched'?

It seems some believers in Galatians had been led astray, so Paul asked them in Galatians 3:1, "O foolish Galatians, who hath *bewitched* you...."

The word "foolish" is a translation of the Greek word *anoetos,* and it is a word that depicts *a person who isn't using his mind.* The problem wasn't that they didn't *have* minds; they just weren't *using* their minds. I see this as a warning for those of us living in the current age when digital devices provide information so quickly that *thinking* is no longer needed. People's minds are inundated with stimulating visual images and constantly updated information — and a great number of people online claiming to be a prophetic voice and to have a word about this, that, or the other thing.

A great number of untested individuals who have no spiritual accountability are sharing these so-called revelations. And because they are "online," many take them as being legitimate even when they are not. While there really are some good, legitimate voices worth paying attention to, the Internet is also flooded with wacky so-called prophetic voices that should not be taken seriously. So we each have to exercise our God-given responsibility to keep our minds engaged and our heads on straight.

If the believers in Galatia whom Paul was addressing had been *using their brains* and *thinking* about what was being put on their spiritual plates before consuming it, they wouldn't have ended up being bewitched. But they were so led astray that Paul asked them, "Who hath *bewitched* you...?"

The word "bewitched" is a translation of the Greek word *baskaino,* a word that means *to cast a spell on someone.* Paul's language tells us that their thinking was *clouded*, as if they were under a spell that affected their ability to correctly reason. They were mesmerized by something they were hearing, but as exciting as it sounded, it was wrong and was leading them off track spiritually.

Paul's readers in Galatia were feasting on the spiritual fare that was being put on their plates without deeply thinking about the quality of what they were consuming. And in the same way, people today who don't use their minds to think things through before they consume them, are the easiest to lead astray. So again, we see the scriptural mandate to use our minds and to "try" the spirits that claim to speak prophetically to us.

THE IMPORTANT DIFFERENCE BETWEEN *WRONG* PROPHETIC MINISTRY AND *FALSE* PROPHETIC MINISTRY

I feel the need to say here that there is a vast difference between *wrong prophetic ministry* and *false prophetic ministry* — and the difference between these two is very important for you to understand.

As noted earlier in this chapter, we all currently "see through a glass darkly" (1 Corinthians 13:12), and this means anyone can make an honest mistake. I cannot think of a single minister of the Gospel who has not preached or taught something that he or she later regretted and possibly even publicly retracted.

As I have grown in my own ministry over many years, there are things I have come to see more clearly than when I was younger, and I have had to correct some things from my own earlier teaching. At that earlier moment, I was doing my best, but as time passed and I grew in knowledge and understanding, I've had moments when I found myself to be sincerely wrong on some earlier points. Hence, I apologized and retaught correctly what I had sincerely, albeit *incorrectly*, taught in order to ensure a correction was brought to what I'd taught earlier.

I know of no other minister who hasn't had occasion to do similarly over the course of his or her ministry. It is simply a fact that our understanding grows over time and that we see through a glass *"darkly,"* or incompletely. In other words, the further we go in life as we study to "rightly divide the Word of truth," the brighter the light of revelation shines (*see* 2 Timothy 2:15; Proverbs 4:18 *AMPC*).

Likewise, there will be moments when even a bona fide prophet will make a sincere, but wrong prophetic statement — perhaps because he spoke out of his own soul or because he added his own commentary that God never asked to be added. Or perhaps a prophetic statement was incorrect because the person spoke by emotion and not by the Spirit of God.

All humans are imperfect and make mistakes. As long as we are in these imperfect vessels, even sincere mistakes can be made by each of us, but that does not mean everyone who has made a mistake is false. We have seen that there certainly are false prophets, and God's Word warns us about them. But many authentic Christ-given fivefold prophets have made prophetic mistakes, were embarrassed and sincerely regretful about it, and brought correction to themselves or to what they said.

But much of this potential error is very avoidable if a fivefold prophet is in relationship with other fivefold gifts who have authority to speak into his or her life. I can think of times as a younger man when those who were older in the ministry loved me enough to challenge me to rethink certain points in my teaching. I was never offended by their challenge and was thankful because it helped me think more deeply about what I publicly taught, and it actually served to sharpen my teaching gift.

The man who mentored me in ministry regularly met with me to show me when my scriptural analysis was defective and when it was right. He taught me how to judge what I wanted to teach *before* I brought a message to the public. Proverbs 24:6 says there is safety in having wise counselors, so I advise those in fivefold ministry to ensure they have voices with authority who can speak into their lives to bring correction and encouragement when needed. I have this in my life to this day (and always will), and I am so thankful for each voice who loves me enough to challenge or encourage me as needed.

But a real danger exists if any fivefold ministry gift becomes a "free floater" with no relationships who have authority to speak into his or her life. This kind of "free floating," places both that person and those who follow him or her in jeopardy.

'Stars' Versus *'Wandering Stars'*

In Revelation 1:16,20 and Revelation 2:1, Christ symbolically refers to His spokesmen as being similar to "stars." In my book *A Light in Darkness, Volume One*, I extensively cover this comparison. As I state in those pages, it is a scientific fact that every natural star in the heavens above has a predetermined orbit from which it veers very little, even over a time span of thousands of years.

And just as natural stars have an appointed orbit, God also has a predetermined course — an "orbit" if you will — for each of His God-appointed messengers to follow in the course of his or her life and ministry. This would include the details that make his or her call to minister the Gospel distinct and unique, such as where he is called to serve, what culture he is called to touch, and which people he is called to minister to. Moreover, in the same way that stars cross the paths of other stars in the heavens above, each minster's course will cross the paths of others that God intends for him or her to fellowship with, interact with, and be influenced by.

Like natural stars have a predetermined orbit from which they do not veer, it is vital for any spiritual leader to know those he is called to orbit with in his or her life and ministry. He or she must determine not to get out of sync with that God-appointed orbit and to not veer from those God-appointed relationships.

In Jude 13, we find a remarkable verse in which Jude addresses the topic of *wandering stars*. He refers to unaccountable, "free-floating" ministers who may have started out authentically, but somewhere along the way, their course was disrupted, they strayed off track, and they got out of sync in their accountability to other fivefold ministry gifts that God had appointed them to orbit with in life.

The words "wandering stars" are translated from the Greek words *asteres planetai*. They depict real stars whose course has somehow been disrupted, and as a result, they have swerved off track and strayed from their God-appointed orbit. Jude used this illustration to depict fivefold gifts who have broken rank, strayed off course, and moved out of their God-appointed relationships. Note that Jude never argued whether or not they were real stars. But even though they started as God's spokesmen and messengers and may still be emanating a measure of authentic light, Jude writes they began to "wander" off track, and thus they have veered into a dangerous spiritual place.

Just as natural stars have an appointed orbit, God also has a predetermined course — an "orbit," if you will — for each of His God-appointed messengers to follow in the course of his or her life and ministry. In the same way that stars cross the paths of other stars in the heavens above, each minster's course will cross the paths of others that God intends for him or her to fellowship with, interact with, and be influenced by.

Furthermore, the word "wandering" in Jude 13 is translated from a form of the Greek word *planao,* a word that describes *a deception*, *a wandering*, and it can depict *a person who has veered from a solid path and is now adrift*. But this word *planao* can also be translated as the word *delusion*. It tells us that such "wandering" individuals may have been duped themselves into believing what they are doing or saying is right when it is not. And in this wandering state, they are causing others to veer off track as well.

But if this particular category of ministers had stayed in the orbit of accountable relationships that God intended for them to possess and retain, there would have been reasonable voices to help recognize if they began to get off balance and needed help retaining their trajectory or getting back on course. But because they veered from those God-appointed relationships that provided protection — or because they outright rejected those relationships — Jude 13 says some of those authentic ministers became "wandering stars," that is, free-floaters with no accountability.

This is especially dangerous in regard to prophetic ministry, for when a prophet gets out of sync with other prophetic voices with no one to hold him or her in-check, the wandering prophet can veer further and further off track until he or she begins to *regularly* make incorrect prophetic declarations and statements. Again, everyone makes sincere mistakes, but having a measure of accountability helps one to correct his or her mistakes. But if there are no authoritative voices in one's life to bring mistakes to his or her awareness, the possibility for that person to float further and further off track with grave consequences for himself or herself grows more probable and more dangerous. And it is not only dangerous for the one who is adrift, but also for those who listen to and who follow his or her ministry.

Let me remind you again that First Corinthians 14:32 says, "And the spirits of the prophets are subject to the prophets." As we saw earlier, the word "subject" is a military term used to describe *soldiers who were under the command or authority of superior officers*, and it implies *knowing one's place, rank, or assignment in any type of organization*. It pictures *one submitted to authority* and *one who is expected to act according to the rules established by that specific authority*. Again, the word "subject" importantly means *to hide behind someone's back*, and it shows that *there is protection in submission*.

When fivefold ministry gifts are in submission to others and remain in the orbit that God appointed for them, it reveals and ensures several things:

- They are submitted to authority and therefore better enabled to stand humbly and soberly in an authoritative role.
- They are not free-floaters without accountability, but are rather established in a community of fellow ministers who can speak into

their lives and ensure that what those ministers are giving out has been tested and can stand up under scrutiny.

- Their submission provides continued protection both for them and those who follow them. It first protects the prophet because he knows that if he does anything wrong, those with authority will bring it to his attention. Simply knowing that correction is possible is a strong incentive to stay on track and to weigh one's words before saying, "Thus saith the Lord."

Knowing that a certain prophet is in submission to others also means the church can be at peace knowing that the prophet who is speaking to them is under authority with sound, seasoned voices speaking into his or her own life. But Jude lets us know that the one who functions without this accountability has placed himself or herself in a vulnerable position to possibly become a "wandering star" as described in Jude 13.

False Prophets Who Intentionally Mislead and Even Forge Prophecies for Their Own Benefit

In my book *How To Keep Your Head on Straight in a World Gone Crazy*, I cover in-depth Peter's words about the problem of false ministry that will emerge in the Church at the end of the age. If you have not read that book, I encourage you to obtain and read it entirely. But because I cannot improve on what I wrote in that book about falsehood in the Church at the end of the age, I include the follow modification of that passage for you here:

> Even in the First Century, errant spiritual leaders were emerging in the Early Church, who were beloved and well-known brothers within the Christian community who had veered off track. Because they were beloved, it made it difficult for believers at that time to know how to deal with them in love when they veered off course. Despite these leaders' high-ranking visible positions in

their local churches and the esteem of their fellow believers, something had caused them to succumb to false ministry.

When Peter wrote his second epistle, he referred to this attack that was taking place *inside* the Church. In Second Peter 2:1, he wrote, "But there were false prophets among the people, even as there shall be false teachers among you, who privily shall bring in damnable heresies, even denying the Lord that bought them, and bring upon themselves swift destruction."

Notice Peter stated there were "false prophets" among the people in the Old Testament. The words "false prophets" are a translation of the Greek word *pseudoprophetes*, a compound of *pseudo* and *prophetes*. The word *pseudo* carries the idea of *any type of falsehood*. It pictures *one who projects an image of himself that's false*, *one who walks in a pretense*, or *one who intentionally misrepresents facts or truths*. The word *prophetes* is the Greek word for *a prophet*.

When these words are compounded, it forms the word *pseudoprophetes,* which depicts prophets who may have begun as authentically God-called prophets, but over a period of time, they somehow progressively veered off course. Peter continued in Second Peter 2:1 to add, "But there were false prophets among the people, even as there shall be false teachers among you, who *privily shall bring in* damnable heresies, even denying the Lord that bought them, and bring upon themselves swift destruction."

The phrase "privily shall bring in" is a translation of the word *pareisago*, a compound of three Greek words: *para*, which means *alongside*; *eis*, which means *into*; and *ago*, which means *I lead*. The word *para* in this context indicates that the false revelators Peter referenced would walk *alongside* other believers. The word *eis* means they would bring their false revelation right *into* the church. But finally, the word *ago* suggests that these individuals would hold visible positions of *leadership*. These false revelators would not be outsiders trying to get inside — *they would be trusted insiders working within the Church*. Furthermore, when the Greek words *para*, *eis*, and *ago* are compounded, as they are in Second Peter 2:1, the new word *pareisago* often denotes *a smuggler attempting to covertly transport illegal contraband across a border while using a disguise, or stealth, to conceal his activities.*

Deliberately smuggling contraband is not accidental, so Peter's use of this word reveals that the particular false revelators he was describing would be neither ignorant, nor innocent concerning their activities. Peter was therefore speaking of leaders who act seductively to take advantage of God's people.

But in these verses, Peter also speaks futuristically to let us know that errant leaders will arise at the end of the age to smuggle some type of false ministry into the Church. He uses the word *pareisago* to inform us that their activities will be carried out so covertly that his or her deeds may be difficult to detect. The Greek word that Peter uses depicts a conscious effort — at least on the part of the seducing spirits behind the deception — to clandestinely smuggle hidden agendas and ulterior motives in a veiled way that prevents it from being easily detected.

Especially in the last days, it is essential for Church leadership to take their responsibility seriously to guard the flock over which the Holy Ghost has made them overseers (*see* Acts 20:28). As spiritual leaders had to do in the First Century, spiritual leaders today must be diligent to watch over the flock Heaven has placed in their charge so that error is not able to take up residency among God's people.

Saying No to the Lord

Peter states that this particular category of end-time errant leaders will *deny* the Lord who bought them. The word "denying" in the text is a translation of the Greek word *arneomai*, which means *to knowingly deny*, *to knowingly disown*, *to knowingly reject*, *to knowingly refuse*, or *to knowingly renounce.* It refers to *a person who knowingly disavows, forsakes, walks away from, or washes one's hands of another person or group of people.* It depicts something that is done with one's full consent and understanding of what he or she is doing.

The word *arneomai* is used in this verse to depict someone who hears what Christ has to say as the One who holds the position of CEO in his or her life, but then rejects His counsel. Those Peter described apparently did not like the instruction or correction the Lord had given. So rather than accept the Lord's counsel and obey Him, they rejected the counsel of the Lord. The choice before these individuals may have been to disobey the Lord or to obey Him and face the prospect of losing a following. Regardless, they chose to go their own way and to ignore the warning of the Holy Spirit.

We have all been guilty of ignoring the promptings of the Holy Spirit at some point in our Christian experience. However, if we are in error — and if we knowingly persist in it — we are opting for an outcome we will ultimately regret. That is why Peter added in Second Peter 2:1, "But there were false prophets among the people, even as there shall be false teachers among you, who privily shall bring in damnable heresies, even denying the Lord that bought them, *and bring upon themselves swift destruction.*"

The words "bring upon" are a translation of the Greek word *epago*, a word that was used in contemporary writings of New Testament times *to denote the letting loose of wild dogs to tear victims apart, limb from limb.* By using this very graphic word, Peter forewarns that when a spiritual leader denies the Lord's corrective voice — or the voice of other people who have or had authority to speak into his life — and chooses to go his own way, his actions may *let loose* his destruction. This verse does *not* say God brings destruction upon this person, but that they "bring upon *themselves* swift destruction." This is judgment that they self-release upon themselves by becoming a free-floating, wandering star with no accountability to anyone else.

Peter referred to these consequences with the words "swift destruction." The word "swift" is a translation of the Greek word *tachinos*, which describes something that takes place *suddenly* or *quickly*. The word "destruction" is a translation of the Greek word *apoleia*, and it describes *destruction, decay, rottenness*, or *ruin*. This depicts exactly what happened to the prophet Eli and his sons. Judgment came to this threesome in a "swift" manner because they persisted in their prolonged errant behavior and because they refused correction. (*See* 1 Samuel 3:11-14; 4:1-22.)

'With Feigned Words Make Merchandise of You'

Peter continued his warnings about error emerging at the end of the age in Second Peter 2:3 by adding that "...through covetousness shall they with *feigned* words make merchandise of you..."

The word "feigned" is from the Greek word *plastos,* which is a word that denotes *molding* something into a specific form, and it is where we get the word "plastic." Peter used this word to regretfully tell us that the errant revelators will *mold their words* at will to fit their own purposes. The word *plastos* was also the very word used in the First Century when Peter was writing to describe *forgery* — like one who *forges* a piece of artwork, a type of currency, or someone's signature. Since it is impossible to forge artwork, currency, or a signature by accident, this describes a *deliberate deception.* Peter said that just as a potter molds clay into any shape that pleases him, errant revelators will mold their words to benefit themselves.

The ulterior motive described by Peter's words is that they "...shall with feigned words make *merchandise* of you." The word "merchandise" is a translation of the Greek word *emporeomai.* This is where we get the word "emporium," which is the English word for a commercial center where assorted goods are sold.

In the times of the early New Testament, *emporeomai* portrayed the activities of *marketers* who set up tents in marketplaces to sell all kinds of goods. After the marketers analyzed each new market and determined what would best appeal to each audience, they proceeded to rave with enthusiasm about whatever product they deemed would sell best in each respective community. These ancient marketers were notorious for peddling flawed products that

> they claimed were fabulous. Their ability to work words to their advantage made them well known in the ancient world. These individuals were masterful manipulators who knew how to fashion their speech in the most effective way to get money out of their listeners' pockets and into theirs.
>
> These are the words the Holy Spirit chose to use to warn about a group of deceptive spiritual revelators who would emerge at the end of the age and enter the modern "Church market." Like the notorious marketers who worked in the natural markets of the ancient world, these end-time errant revelators will seek to reshape, redesign, and "mold" their words, *almost like plastic*, to meet their own purposes. All of this is included in the phrase "with feigned words make merchandise of you."
>
> By using the Greek words *plastos* and *emporeomai*, Peter forewarned of a type of errant spiritual revelator that will emerge at the wrap-up of the age who will say anything to establish himself or herself as a popular voice in the Christian market.[8]

But in spite of those who have prostituted themselves or veered off course, there are reputable, solid prophets in the Church today. And as stated previously, we need the ministry of authentic Christ-given prophets. They are *real* and *powerful*, and they are *needed* in the Church in this last hour of the Church Age.

Just as a real fivefold apostle is an extension of *Christ the Apostle* to the Church, just as the real fivefold evangelist is an extension of *Christ the Evangelist* to the Church, just as a fivefold pastor is an extension of *Christ the Pastor* to the Church, and just as the fivefold gift of teacher is an extension of *Christ the Teacher* to the Church, so also authentic Christ-given fivefold prophets are supernatural extensions of the prophetic ministry of *Christ the Prophet* to the Church.

Without the powerful and supernatural ministries of fivefold prophets, the Church lacks a crucial element of Christ. Ephesians 4:12 clearly states that fivefold prophets are given by Christ to the Church and that they will be operative with the other fivefold gifts until the conclusion of the Church Age.

The Difference Between the Ministry of a Prophet and One Who Simply Gives a Prophetic Message

Although this is not the focus of this book, it is important to understand the difference between a Christ-given fivefold prophet and the simple gift of prophecy. I am hesitant to call any gift of the Spirit "simple," as each of them are such marvelous gifts. I use the phrase "the simple gift of prophecy" to distinguish between the weighty ministry of a fivefold prophet and a prophetic word that can be given by any Christian as the Spirit prompts him or her to do so.

Paul listed the simple gift of prophecy in First Corinthians 12 and 14 as one of the nine gifts of the Holy Spirit. The word "prophecy" in First Corinthians 12:10 means *to speak on behalf of God, to speak in advance of a situation, to foretell an event*, or *to assert the mind of God to others*. The one who operates in the simple gift of prophecy is not necessarily called into the full-time ministry of a prophet. In First Corinthians 14:1, Paul encouraged *everyone* to seek to operate in the simple gift of prophecy and affirmed in verse 31 that it is possible for *everyone* to operate in it.

But First Corinthians 14:3 states that the primary objective of the simple gift of prophecy is to provide *edification, exhortation*, and *comfort* to the listeners. And when a person moves in the simple gift of prophecy, the operation of this spiritual gift results in an individual or congregation receiving new understanding about a truth, insight, or directive from the heart of God that helps strengthen, encourage, and instruct the listeners so they can walk with Him more accurately.

The word "edification" in First Corinthians 14:3 is a translation of the Greek word *oikodome*, which is an architectural term that pictures either *strengthening an existing structure* or *enlarging it* to accommodate a greater space. Hence, it means when the simple gift of prophecy is in operation in the Church, it causes God's people to be spiritually strengthened and it expands their spiritual capacity.

The word "exhortation" in First Corinthians 14:3 is translated from a form of *parakaleo*, a Greek compound of the preposition *para* and *kaleo*. The preposition *para* means *alongside*, and the word *kaleo* means *to call* or *to beckon*. When these two are compounded into a single word as in First Corinthians 14:3, it means *to come alongside someone else to passionately call out to them* or *to beckon them to some kind of action*. The word *parakaleo* is so strong that it can be translated *to beg or to plead for an individual to do something*. It pictures *someone who comes right alongside a person to urge, beseech, or plead with him to take some kind of action*.

When Paul was writing these verses, the word *parakaleo* was used by military leaders to depict a moment before they sent their troops into battle. They would gather them and rouse them to fight. Rather than hide them from the reality of war, the commanding officer would summon his troops together and speak straightforwardly to them about the potential dangers of the battlefield. In that moment, the military officer came right alongside the troops to urge, exhort, beseech, beg, and plead with them *to stand tall, to throw their shoulders back, to look the enemy straight on, eyeball to eyeball, and to face their battles bravely*. Rather than ignore danger or pretend it didn't exist, a good commander knew it was his moment to prepare and stir the troops for war. Hence, he would urge, exhort, encourage, and beseech his troops to face their battle with steadfast courage.

Because this is the word translated "exhortation" in First Corinthians 14:3, it tells us that when the simple gift of prophecy is in operation, it is God's way of coming alongside His people to passionately beckon them to take some kind of action. As the Commander of the saints, God used the simple gift of prophecy to prophetically urge, exhort, beseech, beg, and plead with His people to stand tall, to throw their shoulders back, to look the enemy straight on, eyeball to eyeball and, yes, to face whatever battle they are in with steadfast courage. It is a prophetic exhortation that stirs listeners to cast off any temptation to surrender to defeat, and to press onward until ultimate victory has been achieved.

But in First Corinthians 14:3 Paul says the simple gift of prophecy will also bring "comfort." The word "comfort" is translated from a form of the word *paramuthia*, which is a compound of the preposition *para* and *mutheomai*. The preposition *para* means *alongside* and the word *mutheomai* means *to speak*. When compounded into a single word as in First Corinthians 14:3, it gives the image of one who draws as near as possible to speak *consolation* or *encouragement* to *cheer up* a person or group. Thus, when the simple gift of prophecy is in operation, it is God's special way of drawing near to His people to prophetically console them in hard times, to encourage them to stay on track, and to keep fighting until victory is achieved. It is His way of cheering up the troops in the midst of their circumstances.

The impact of the simple gift of prophecy is so mighty that Paul writes in First Corinthians 14:4 that the one who prophesies "edifies" the church. The word "edifies" is a translation of the Greek word *oikodomeo*, which is a compound of *oikos* and *demoo*. The word *oikos* is the Greek word for *a house*, and *demoo* is a word that depicts *construction*. When compounded, it forms *oikodomeo* and it describes the *enlarging of a house*. By using this word, Paul reminds us again that when the simple gift of prophecy is in operation, God uses this gift to spiritually enlarge the capacity of the Church.

If you fully appreciate how powerful the simple gift of prophecy is, you'll see why I hesitate to call it "the simple gift of prophecy." This is a powerful gift that can also bring correction to sin if needed. In First Corinthians 14:24,25, Paul elucidates that when this simple gift of prophecy is in operation in a congregational setting, its operation can even bring conviction of sin to any unbeliever who is in the meeting. Paul said, "But if all prophesy, and there come in one that believeth not, or one unlearned, he is convinced of all, he is judged of all: and thus are the secrets of his heart made manifest; and so falling down on his face he will worship God, and report that God is in you of a truth."

At the first of verse 24, in Greek, Paul used the conjunction *de* as an exclamation mark and to make the point that when the simple gift of prophecy is in operation it can "convince" any unbeliever who has wandered into the meeting. The word "convince" is a form of a Greek word that means *to expose, convict, or cross-examine for the purpose of conviction*, as in convicting a lawbreaker in a court of law. It is the image of the Holy Spirit working like a divine lawyer to bring forth evidence that is indisputable and undeniable, so that the accused person's actions are irrefutably brought to light and the outcome is, the sinner is exposed and convicted.

As a result of the simple gift of prophecy, Paul declared that an unbeliever who is present can suddenly become aware of his or her personal sin as God's divine searchlight is turned onto his own "heart" to convict him or her.

The word "heart" is a translation of the word *kardias*, the Greek word that pictures *the heart* or *the inner secret life* of an individual that no one else knows about. But Paul wrote that when the simple gift of prophecy is in operation, all of a sudden, a sinner who is present can feel as if the secrets of his whole inner life, which were before known only to him, are supernaturally brought to the surface so strikingly that he feels as if the secrets of his heart have been laid bare. *This is a work of God that can only be performed by the Holy Spirit.*

The simple gift of prophecy was operative throughout the time of the early New Testament along with all nine gifts of the Holy Spirit, and its operation is a significant fulfillment of what was prophesied by the prophet Joel and quoted by the apostle Peter on the day of Pentecost — in effect: "I will pour out my Spirit on all people. Your sons and daughters will prophesy, your old men will dream dreams, and your young men will see visions. Even on my servants, both men and women, I will pour out my Spirit in those days" (*see* Joel 2:28,29; Acts 2:17,18).

In Summary

Certainly an entire book could be written on the subject of prophetic ministry in New Testament times. Many wonderful books have been written about prophets. But my prayer is that this chapter about prophetic ministry will provide a scriptural foundation to help you move deeper in your study and your experience of prophetic ministry.

Just as cessationists argue that apostles passed away with the end of the Apostolic Age, they also argue that prophets ceased to exist at the same time. But in Ephesians 4:12 and 13, Paul clearly states that Christ-given fivefold gifts are given to the Church, "For the perfecting of the saints, for the work of the ministry, for the edifying of the body of Christ: till we all come in the unity of the faith, and of the knowledge of the Son of God, unto a perfect man, unto the measure of the stature of the fulness of Christ."

The word "till" is a translation of the Greek word *mechri,* a word that would be better rendered "until," and it points to the end of the age when the Body of Christ will finally reach the full maturity God is waiting it to reach. The use of *mechri* expresses that apostles, prophets, evangelists, pastors, and teachers will continue "until" the Church has "…come in the unity of the faith, and of the knowledge of the Son of God, unto a perfect man, unto the measure of the stature of the fulness of Christ."

In the same way we need to understand and embrace the genuine gift of apostleship, it is important that we understand and embrace the gift of the fivefold prophet because it is an important extension of Christ's ministry to the Church. Remember, Jesus is the same yesterday, today, and forever (*see* Hebrews 13:8). As *the Perfect Prophet*, Jesus is still ministering prophetically through the gift of the fivefold prophet that He has given to the Church. Especially as we come to the close of the last days, we must embrace the full expression of fivefold ministry in the Church. It is imperative that we understand the *real* versus the *counterfeit* so we can know the difference and experience the marvelous gifts that Christ has bestowed upon us for a spiritual-equipping, especially for the last days.

Especially as we come to the close of the last days, we must embrace the full expression of fivefold ministry in the Church.

In addition to the apostle and prophet, there are also the Christ-given fivefold gifts of *evangelist*, *pastor*, and *teacher*, which I may cover more fully in a future book. But because of some confusion that has been widespread in recent years in regard to apostles and prophets, this book has been written to help guide you as you walk out your own journey in the latter-day ministry of the end-time Church.

QUESTIONS FOR DEEPER CONSIDERATION

Chapter 9

1. In this chapter, it has been demonstrated that Christ-given fivefold ministry prophets are often equipped with: 1) prophetic insight; 2) prophetic foresight; 3) prophetic oversight; and 4) prophetic hindsight. What do these four points about prophetic ministry mean to you?

2. Between the Old and New Testaments was the intertestamental period that lay between the two Testaments. According to what you have read in this chapter, name some of the individuals in the gospels who functioned as intertestamental prophets?

3. In Matthew 11:11, Jesus stated that John the Baptist was greater than any other prophet due to his monumental role in introducing Jesus' ministry. And yet in Luke 7:28, Jesus said, "...He that is least in the kingdom of God is greater than he [John the Baptist]." Since John the Baptist was the greatest prophet to live up to that moment, how is he that is least in the Kingdom of Heaven greater than John? Can you explain this seemingly contradictory statement?

4. We saw that in Malachi 4:5, God said, "Behold, I will send you Elijah the prophet before the coming of the great and dreadful day of the Lord." In the same way that John the Baptist prophetically prepared the way for Jesus at His first coming, this verse declares that there will be a supernatural rising

up of Elijah-type, Christ-given prophets at the end of the age to prepare the way of the Lord again. As we come closer to the end of this age, we can anticipate that God will be speaking even more widely through prophetic voices. Can you list someone you believe is one of those prophetic voices that God is using to prophetically speak in these current days?

5. On the Day of Pentecost, Peter quoted the prophet Joel (*see* Joel 2:28,29), saying, "But this is that which was spoken by the prophet Joel; and it shall come to pass in the last days, saith God, I will pour out of my Spirit upon all flesh: and your sons and your daughters shall prophesy, and your young men shall see visions, and your old men shall dream dreams: and on my servants and on my handmaidens I will pour out in those days of my Spirit; and they shall prophesy" (*see* Acts 2:16-18).

   All believers have the Holy Spirit indwelling them in the Church Age and are thusly enabled to speak as the Spirit moves them to do so. In this sense, all believers have become members of a Church-wide priesthood of prophetic voices, and at least to some measure, every believer can speak as a representative of God. So in the Church Age, it should be anticipated that prophetic activity will increase as we come closer to the end of the age. Where do you see prophetic activity increasing in our own time? How have you experienced it?

6. Paul wrote in First Corinthians 13:9 that at this present moment, "…we know in part, and we prophesy in part." Then in verse 12, he added, "For now we see through a glass, darkly…." After reading this chapter, what does it mean to you that we know in part, prophesy in part," and now "see through a glass darkly"? How do these verses have application to prophetic ministry in our times?

7. Jesus warned in Matthew 7:15 that false prophets are like "ravenous wolves." Why did He use this verbiage to describe false prophets? What message is concealed in the words "ravenous wolves" that we need to understand?

CHAPTER 10

'NO MORE CHILDREN, TOSSED TO AND FRO'

*And he gave some, apostles; and some, prophets;
and some, evangelists; and some, pastors and teachers;
for the perfecting of the saints, for the work of the ministry,
for the edifying of the body of Christ: till we all come in the unity
of the faith, and of the knowledge of the Son of God, unto
a perfect man, unto the measure of the stature of the fulness
of Christ: that we henceforth be no more children, tossed to and fro,
and carried about with every wind of doctrine, by the sleight
of men, and cunning craftiness, whereby they lie
in wait to deceive.*

— Ephesians 4:11-14

We began the first chapter of this book by looking at key verses in Ephesians chapters 2 and 4 that deal with God's vision for the Church and the specific roles of the Christ-given fivefold ministry in that divine building process. In this final chapter, we will return to Ephesians 4 to cover additional verses that clearly define the long-term vision and effects — God's desired outcome — of healthy fivefold ministry in the Church and why fivefold ministry is needed until the end of the Church Age.

But first, we will return to Ephesians 2, and we'll begin in verse 20, where Paul stated that the Church is "...built upon the foundation of the apostles and prophets, Jesus Christ himself being the chief corner stone."

As we saw before, the words "built upon" are a translation of the Greek word *epoikodomeo,* which depicts *a predesigned, well-planned, thought-out plan to build upward on a strong and solid foundation.* The word "foundation" is a translation of the Greek word *themelios,* which pictures *a foundation that is set in stone and that cannot be easily moved.* It pictures *a foundation so solid that it will endure the test of time* — or *an unmovable, unshakable, solidly fixed foundation.*

Ephesians 2:20 could be rendered that the Church "...has been built, and continues to be built, upward based on a predesigned, well thought-out plan — and upon a foundation put in place by apostles and prophets that is *unmovable, unshakable,* and *solidly fixed.*"

But then Paul added "...Jesus Christ himself being the chief corner stone." The words "chief corner stone" are translated from the single Greek word *akrogoniaois,* which is borrowed from the world of masonry. It pictures *the central stone in the middle of an arch* on which both sides of the arch come together. It is also *the central stone* on which the two sides lean, with the central piece holding the two sides together. That central stone is so vital that if it didn't exist, the arch would collapse, as both sides of the arch depend entirely on that central stone. That central stone is so critical to the structure that its absence would mean the total collapse of the entire structure.

As a linguist, Paul well understood the meaning of this word *akrogoniaois*, and he used it in this verse to emphasize the centrality of Jesus Christ in the Church and how everything is to come together and lean entirely upon His lordship. The work of apostles and prophets and other Christ-given fivefold ministry gifts is to focus on and come together in Christ. Indeed, if it does not come together in Christ, it will come to naught — for Christ is the *only* safe, steady, and sure focus in the *naos* Temple of God. He is the *Chief Cornerstone* and the *Supreme Head of the Church*, which is a very important point we will return to as we come to the conclusion of this chapter.

Paul added in Ephesians 2:21, "In whom all the building fitly framed together growth unto an holy temple in the Lord."

The word "building" in this verse is from the Greek word *oikodome*, and it pictures *an architectural plan to enlarge, increase, or amplify a structure*. It can be translated *to edify*, *to enhance*, *to improve*, *to intentionally increase*, or *to bring to a state of being larger and stronger*. The use of this word *oikodome* tells us that God never intended His *naos* Temple to be small, irrelevant, or nearly not noticeable. His plan for the Church is *grand*. He longs for it to grow, grow, and grow until it is an amplified, massive House that is composed of a multitude of living stones (souls) that are redeemed to God by Christ's blood from every kindred, tongue, people, and nation (*see* Revelation 7:9) that has been incorporated into the building of His House.

But Paul also added the words "fitly framed together." These words are a translation of the Greek word *sunarmologe*, which is an unusual triple compound of the Greek preposition *sun* and *harmos* and *lego*. The word *sun* means *together with*; the word *harmos* depicts *a physical joint*, like a joint between two structural beams in a building; and the word *lego* means *I say*, but can also mean *to put together*.

The use of this word *oikodome* tells us that God never intended His *naos* Temple to be small, irrelevant, or nearly not noticeable. His plan for the Church is *grand.* He longs for it to grow, grow, and grow until it is an amplified, massive House that is composed of a multitude of living stones (souls) that are redeemed to God by Christ's blood from every kindred, tongue, people, and nation

This *sunarmologe* word is so rare that it is only used twice in the New Testament — here and also in Ephesians 4:16. In both places, it is correctly used to depict a *joint* in a building that interconnects vital parts of a structure that must be linked together. Such joints are intended to bring vital elements together, but also allow its independent components to move as needed with respect to each other.

When the Greek components *sun*, *harmos*, and *lego* are compounded into a single word, thus becoming *sunarmalogeo,* it gives the image of Christ — the Master Builder — *speaking* direction (*lego*) and providing oversight to other fivefold ministry builders as they put *together* (*sun*) all the various materials to *join* and *connect them* in the Temple that God is building, called *the Church.* Like joints, every person must be fit together into his or her correct place in the Structure that is being built. Thus, Paul uses *sunarmalogeo* to picture Christ as the Chief Apostle of the Church and as One who is speaking words of direction to fivefold ministry gifts and to other believers in order to frame each of them into their proper places so they can be rightly connected in God's House.

Especially in the Western Church, such a consumeristic mentality exists that *wants what it wants*, and this could explain a lot in terms of people being wrongly connected, not recognizing or esteeming right connections, or being completely isolated and disconnected altogether. People who argue against the traditional "construct," or model of the local church, including the *assembling together* thereof (*see* Hebrews 10:25), could not maintain their argument in the light of this revelation. The truth is, rather, that they must divinely *"fit into"* something larger than themselves if they are to be aligned with the thinking — the heart, mind, will, design, plan, and purpose — of the Chief Architect, the Head of the Church.

In Ephesians 2:21, Paul also added, "In whom all the building fitly framed together groweth...." The words "in whom" would be better translated "in Him," and they refer to Christ. But notice the word "groweth" in this verse. It is crucially used at this juncture to tell us that when the Church is being built correctly, it always grows. That growth includes spiritual and numerical growth. On the other hand, if there is a lack of growth, it should be taken as a divine indicator that adjustments need to be made or that it is not being constructed correctly. When the Church is being assembled by the Chief Builder on a solid foundation that is laid by apostles and prophets and with the assistance of other Christ-given fivefold gifts, it grows miraculously.

I must add that there are seasons, especially in seasons of numerical growth, in which a pause in growth for a time is needed. No farmer lives in continuous harvest. When one season of harvest concludes, it is time for rest and then sowing seed again, watering it for the next period of growth, and harvesting once again. This is true of each and every church and ministry.

It must also be taken into account that a church may reach the pinnacle of the building thereof according to the blueprints of Heaven — that is, that particular church experiences growth that would be considered sufficient. From there, the church may be led to launch into church *planting* — which is also growth, although on a different scale. Spreading to various campuses, building an online church, etc. — all of this could be considered blueprint-perfect growth.

In Colossians 1:6, Paul wrote that the correct preaching of the Gospel naturally produces fruit. As a Christian leader, I find this truth to be so vital. If my own ministry has come to a point of stagnancy, it always causes me to seek God and to reassess what we are doing, for a lack of growth is a "neon sign" that something has gone awry. According to Paul in Colossians 1:6, the Gospel is always accompanied with growth. Certainly there can be different stages of growth, but if there is a continual lack of growth, it should be taken as a divine indicator that it is time to seek wisdom from above about what needs to change. The Gospel is so powerful that when it is properly declared, one can expect all types of growth to be forthcoming.

But particularly notice the word "groweth" in Ephesians 2:21: "In whom all the building fitly framed together growth unto an holy temple in the Lord." It is a translation of the amazing Greek word *auxano.* It denotes something that is being *amplified*, *augmented*, *enlarged*, or *enhanced.* It has to do with quantity and quality. Many fear that the larger a church gets, the more quality it will lose. But in this verse, we find that God longs for the Church to *escalate* and *multiply* in size *and* to increase in terms of quality. By using this word, Paul was explicitly telling us God's ultimate objective for the Church, His end-time Temple, is that it become a massive and quality constructed House for His presence in the earth. God is not interested in sacrificing quality for quantity — He desires *both* for the Church.

As we have seen before, the word "temple" in this verse is translated from the Greek word *naos*, and it pictures *a magnificent, splendid, stunning, highly decorated temple.* It pictures a sanctuary with vaulted ceilings, marble, granite, gold, silver, and highly decorated ornamentations. The word *naos* is the exact word used in the Greek Septuagint version of the Old Testament to describe *the Holy of Holies* in the Temple in Jerusalem — exactly where the Shekinah presence of God dwelled in the earth at that time.

But today God's Spirit is no longer satisfied to dwell in physical buildings made by human hands (*see* Acts 7:47; 17:24). Instead, He dwells in the hearts of His people. That is why in Ephesians 2:22, Paul added, "In whom ye also are builded together for an *habitation* of God through the Spirit."

The word "habitation" is translated from a form of the Greek word *katoikeo*, which is a compound of the preposition *kata* and the word *oikeo*. The preposition *kata* means *down*, and the word *oikeo* is from *oiko*, which is the Greek word for *a house*. But when *oikos* becomes the verb *oikeo*, it means *to live in a house*. When the words *kata* and *oikeo* are compounded into one, as in this verse, it means *to permanently settle down and to permanently live in a fixed location*. It pictures a person who feels so completely *at home* that he has chosen *to settle down and live there* forever. And because the verb tense indicates *continuous action*, it means the one who has settled down plans *to continually dwell* in that location forever. Thus, it has become his *habitual place of residency*. That is why the *King James Version* translates it as "habitation."

This categorically means God has established His physical residence *in the Church*, and He is so *at home there* that He has moved His permanent earthly residence into the Church. Hence in the earthly realm, the Church itself has become *God's dwelling place* and *His place of permanent residence*. That means the Holy Spirit is a perpetual, never-to-move-out Occupant of the universal Church, the Body of Christ. Therefore, He is the Occupant of *individual believers* who *collectively comprise* the Church — God's Temple, or House.

The Ultimate Purpose of Fivefold Ministry

In Ephesians 4:12-14, Paul wrote that Christ has given all the fivefold gifts of the apostle, prophet, evangelist, pastor, and teacher as *builders* to assist in the building of the Church. He stated these gifts are given: "For the perfecting of the saints, for the work of the ministry, for the edifying of the body of Christ: till we all come in the unity of the faith, and of the knowledge of the Son of God, unto a perfect man, unto the measure of the stature of the fulness of Christ: that we henceforth be no more children, tossed to and fro, and carried about with every wind of doctrine, by the sleight of men, and cunning craftiness, whereby they lie in wait to deceive."

These verses are where we will conclude this book. But this passage is so important that we will glean everything we can from it first.

The word "that" in Ephesians 4:14 is a translation of the Greek word *hina*, and it means *in order that* or *explicitly for* and it points to the long-term purpose for Christ-given fivefold ministry in the Body of Christ and in the *naos* — Temple of God.

According to this verse, fivefold ministry gifts are given explicitly "that we henceforth be no more children...." The word "henceforth" means to be *no more*, *no longer*, *not even a little*, or *not even in the smallest way* and in this context, Paul was saying we should *no longer*, *in the slightest way* be like immature children. This phrase implies that because so many were spiritually childish, a transition from spiritual childhood to spiritual adulthood needed to occur. At the time Paul was writing, the Church was in its infancy, and that was a reason for widespread immaturity.

But it is now some 2,000 years later, and the Church still has widely not reached a state of spiritual adulthood. One would think that after 2,000 years, this state of maturity would have already been reached. But because the Christ-given fivefold gifts over two millennia have not been fully recognized or embraced, the maturing process God intended for those gifts to help bring to the Church has been thwarted. As a result, the Church in many respects remains childish. But Paul stated that if fivefold gifts are fully released to do their work, God will use them to divinely assist the Church in leaving a childish and immature status and in growing up spiritually.

Ephesians 4:14 goes on to explicitly communicate that these ministry gifts are given for the purpose "that henceforth we be no more children...." There are many words in Greek for "children," but this is a translation of the word *nepios*, the word for "children" used here.

- The Greek word *nepios* gives the image of an *infant* still being nurtured at his mother's breast. It is precious to see such a tender moment when a child nurses at his mother's breast, but adult behavior could never be expected from such a newborn.
- The Greek word *nepios* also pictures *a toddler* who stumbles and falls as he or she is learning to walk. It is memorable to watch a child learn to crawl, pull himself or herself up, and then to take his or her first steps. As a toddler stumbles and falls in the process of learning to walk, it is obvious that toddlers are simply too immature to walk about in an adult manner.
- The Greek word *nepios*, likewise, projects the image of a child that is only beginning to learn how to speak. As that child utters his or her first words, he or she makes a lot of childlike mistakes that may seem cute or funny for a child, but talking in this childish way would be inappropriate for an adult.
- The Greek word *nepios* also pictures *an uneducated child* or a child who either skipped or has been deprived of education and training. Even though the child has physically grown, he or she is *unprepared* for life — for adult responsibilities — because he or she has either skipped education or has never been properly instructed. This last picture is one of *deprivation* or *deficit* — in this case, a deprivation and deficit of *education*.

As it is true with any young child that is nursing, a toddler that is just learning to walk, *or* a little child who speaks with a very limited and childlike vocabulary — either because of his age or because he has been deprived of teaching and training — Paul likewise uses the Greek word *nepios* to illustrate that the Church at large is, in many respects, similar to a child that is not ready for life or adult responsibilities. This was true in the First Century, and it is still true today. Although the Church has 2,000 years of history behind it, it still grapples with maturity issues. The Church should have reached adulthood by now, but it is still largely being "...tossed to and fro...."

What Does It Mean To Be 'Tossed To and Fro'?

The words "tossed to and fro" in Ephesians 4:14 are translated from the word *kludonidzomai* — a very specific word that means *to be tossed by waves.* It fully pictures *waves that are being blown back and forth by the wind*; *the rising and falling of waves*; *the surging upward and downward of waves*; or *the blowing back and forth of waves.* When used in regard to people, it means *to fluctuate up and down, to be tossed back and forth*, or it refers to those who are *unstable.* Figuratively in the New Testament, it pictures people who are spiritually tossed up and down, to and fro, and who are habitually vacillating back and forth or are indecisive — again, referring to those who are spiritually unstable.

In James 1:6, we find this same word was used by James when he wrote, "...He that wavereth is like a wave of the sea driven with the wind and tossed." The word "wavereth" in this verse is translated from the same root as the words "tossed to and fro" in Ephesians 4:14. In James 1:6, it pictures *one wave after another wave* or *a succession of rising and falling waves.*

If you've ever been to the ocean, you've probably watched the waves. Looking out over the water, you can see them as they build and grow bigger and bigger until, finally, they peak and then fall and tumble backward into the sea from which they came. As you continue to watch, waves continue to form — gathering height, volume, and speed. Once more, they rise and grow bigger and bigger until they finally peak and crash, tumbling back into the sea from which they came.

Over and over, this never-ending process continues, giving us a vivid analogy of a person who is *unstable.* In one moment, he seems to believe or think one thing, but soon changes his mind. When he changes his mind, like a wave of the sea, he falls back into a maze of confusion, where he rethinks everything again until he rises up to another new idea or conclusion. Finally, it seems like he is really moving forward, but then, abruptly, he is affected by the blowing winds around him, and once again, he changes his mind and returns to the maze of confusion.

James 1:6 says this type of "up and down" person is continually "tossed" back and forth by waves. The word "tossed" in this verse is a translation of the Greek word *rhipidzo*, a verb that pictures *a dangerous undercurrent.* Some scholars suggest the Greek word *rhipidzo* is the source for the word "riptide." A riptide is a dangerous undercurrent caused by atmospheric disturbances that has the potential to drag people into an inescapable undertow where they drown after being carried far away from safety.

These words in James 1:6 emphatically tell us that spiritually immature individuals are easily moved by what they hear and habitually vacillate back and forth in what they say or believe. As a result, they are dragged into a state of spiritual bedlam that seems to "drown" them. Their condition is so serious that James warned: "A doubled-minded man is unstable in all his ways" (*see* James 1:8).

The Results of Being Double-Minded

The word "doubleminded" in James 1:8 is translated from the Greek word *dipsuchos*, an unusual word that means a *two-souled man*. No one has two souls or two minds, but here James figuratively is portraying *a person with two heads.*

Think of what a monstrosity it would be to see a person with two heads. One head directs the man to do or say one thing, while the other head directs him to do or to say the opposite. This indeed would be monstrous on more than one level. But James used this word *dipsuchos* ("doubleminded") to alert us to the fact that people who are tossed to and fro spiritually are often like a man with two heads. Because they are not established in the Word of God, they are tossed here and there, and they are spiritually "unstable" — or constantly going "back and forth" like that man with two heads.

In James 1:8, the word "unstable" is a translation of the Greek word *akatastatos*. It means *restless, unstable, unsteady, and up and down*. It is importantly the same Greek root from which we derive the word *anarchy*. Thus, when a person is unstable, he is spiritually restless, spiritually unstable, spiritually unsteady, and spiritually up and down in his or her spiritual life. If he or she doesn't eventually level out, this state of anarchy — from the Greek word *akatastatos* — will throw that person into a state of confusion in every sphere of life.

This is precisely why James added that a double-minded man is unstable in "all his ways." The word "all" is the Greek word *pas*, and it pictures the totality of one's life. The word "ways" is translated from the word *hodos*, the Greek word for *a road* or *a path*. By using these words, James warned that if the habitual instability this kind of person lives in does not stop, it will eventually begin to seep into and affect *every road* or *path of life* on which he or she walks. Again, if such a person remains in this state of spiritual instability, it will begin to show up in every area of his or her life. This teaching from James may seem a diversion, but keep it in mind as you look at Paul's words about the need for the Church to leave a state of childishness and spiritual immaturity.

Do Not Be Carried About by Every Wind of Doctrine

Paul continued in Ephesians 4:14, "That we henceforth be no more children, tossed to and fro, and *carried about....*"

The words "carried about" are translated from the Greek word *periphero*, which is a compound of the preposition *peri* and the word *phero*. The word *peri* means *around*, like something that is *circular*, and the word *phero* means *to be carried*. When compounded into the word *periphero,* it pictures something that is *being carried around*.

The word *periphero* can also depict something similar to a leaf that has been *picked up and is being carried by the wind*. It is like a leaf that is blown here or there, whichever way the wind may be blowing at the moment. In one moment, it is blown in one direction, but when the wind begins to blow in a different direction, the leaf will be headed somewhere else because it is tossed and turned and carried *wherever* the wind is blowing at any given moment.

Paul used this word *periphero* to picture how spiritually immature people are easily moved and carried all over the place spiritually. They are spiritually unstable, spiritually unsteady, and spiritually unpredictable.

Paul furthermore said they are "carried about with every wind...." The word "wind" is translated from the Greek word *anemos,* a word that depicts *fierce winds* or *atmospheric turbulence* that has the potential to wreak havoc and destruction. The word *anemos* could illustrate the damaging effects of a tornado or hurricane or *winds that agitate peaceful water* and that cause *ripples* on a body of water that otherwise would be calm and serene. The Greek word *anemos* is the very word used in Mark 4:39 to depict the violent storm that Jesus and His disciples confronted as they journeyed by boat to the country of the Gadarenes.

Paul used this word "wind" — from the Greek word *anemos* — to depict the upsetting effects that strange "winds of doctrine" bring upon people who are immature in the Body of Christ. Because spiritually immature people are not grounded in the Word of God, they often tend to gravitate toward spiritual silliness. All of this tells us that "winds of doctrine" can produce devastating consequences in people's lives. Such "winds of doctrine" *agitate peaceful waters* in the Body of Christ and cause *ripples* that have a negative effect.

"Winds of doctrine" can produce devastating consequences in people's lives. Such "winds of doctrine" *agitate peaceful waters* in the Body of Christ and cause *ripples* that have a negative effect.

Obsessions With Unprofitable Spiritual Nonsense

Hebrews 13:9 says, "Be not carried about with divers and strange doctrines. For it is a good thing that the heart be established with grace; not with meats, which have not profited them that have been occupied therein."

This is a scriptural prohibition that we are not to be "carried about" with "divers and strange doctrines." This prohibition is especially important in our times when the Internet is filled with a plethora of "divers and strange doctrines." While a lot of wonderful ministry can be found on the Internet, a lot of information can also be found that is sensational or non-scriptural personal revelation. Those who are spiritually immature often buy into this kind of spiritual nonsense because they are not rooted and grounded in truth.

This lack of grounding in the Bible makes them susceptible to error that sounds good and looks appealing. As a result, they are thrown off course by whatever doctrine is blowing their direction at a given moment. Again, in our age especially, there are plenty of tantalizing teachings that are scripturally off-base — and personal revelations that also have no basis in the Word — thus, we need to heed the Bible's injunction that we are not to "be carried about with divers and strange doctrines."

The words "carried about" are a form of the Greek word *paraphero,* a compound of the preposition *para* and the word *phero.* The word *para* means *alongside*, like something taken closely to one's heart or *closely to one's side.* The word *phero* means *to carry.* But when these two words are compounded into the word *paraphero,* it portrays one who is being *led astray* or *misled* by something he has taken closely to his or her heart as genuine and sincere. If you've ever known a person who sincerely embraced a wrong teaching and you observed how "carried about" they became with it, then you understand exactly the meaning of Hebrews 13:9.

Hebrews 13:9 also refers to these erroneous teaching and revelations as "divers and strange doctrines." The word "divers" is the plural form of the Greek word *poilikos,* and it means *manifold, variegated,* or *various.* It is the same word used in the Greek Septuagint version of the Old Testament in Genesis 37:3 to describe the coat of *many colors* that Jacob gave to Joseph.

The word "strange" is a qualifier to inform us about the nature of these various teachings. It is translated from the Greek word *xenos*, a word that depicts anything that is *novel* or *foreign.* Although the idea is interesting to hear, upon close examination in the light of Scripture, it is clear that it is *off-color* and *a distraction.* But for the spiritually immature, these strange doctrines often sound like a doctrine worthy of their consideration. I recommend you read my book *How To Keep Your Head on Straight in a World Gone Crazy.* In that book, you will read how to judge what you are hearing and how to measure it in the light of Scripture.

When I speak of spiritually "novel" or foreign ideas, they often have to do with visitations of angels, frequent visits to Heaven, material objects (like gold and oil) appearing in meetings, or an obsession with demons and the occult that captivates the listener to the point of controlling them instead of their living victoriously over these spiritual entities in Jesus Christ. Certainly divine visitations, visits to Heaven, and unexplainable supernatural occurrences are real. But when these become infatuations that people obsess over, it is unhealthy and unproductive. Even authentic experiences of this nature are not central truths on which a person can build his or her life, and they must be kept in perspective. Unfortunately, many today build their ministries on such things, and people who are unstable become obsessed by these personal revelations that have little impact on how they can live effectually for Christ.

Again, Hebrews 13:9 says, "Be not carried about with divers and strange doctrines. For it is a good thing that the heart be established with grace; not with meats, which have not profited them that have been occupied therein."

This verse clearly states that "divers and strange doctrines" do "not profit them that have been occupied with them." The word "profited" is a form of the Greek word *ophelos*, a word that depicts an *advantage*, *benefit*, or *gain*. Thus, Hebrews 13:9 says that although some people have been tantalized by sensational teaching that is indeed entertaining, it has *added* nothing substantially life-transforming to their lives. Many of these "revelations" are distractions that divert them from teaching they need in order to establish their hearts solidly in the Bible and help them become a better Christian.

Particularly notice that this verse says people who follow these types of teachings become "occupied" with them. The word "occupied" is the continuous form of the Greek word *peripateo*. The word *peripateo* is a compound of the preposition *peri* and the verb *pateo*. The preposition *peri* means *around*, as in *something that is circular*, and the verb *pateo* means *to walk*. But when the word *peri* and *pateo* are compounded into a single word, it depicts *a person who walks around and around in one general vicinity*. It is used in this verse to convey the message that a person can become so *obsessed* with a particular "strange doctrine" that it becomes an obsession he cannot break free from. As a result, his thoughts habitually revolve around this off-track doctrine as he or she becomes more and more obsessed with it.

Can you think of anyone you know who became so obsessed with a new teaching that it diverted them and led them off track?

My Personal Concern

As I wrote in my book *Build Your Foundation*, I expressed that we have a good reason today to be very concerned about the state of the modern Church. What bothers me the most as I travel and visit churches, especially across the Western world, is that I often see an absence of good Bible teaching. And where there is an absence of the Bible, other voices quickly flood into its rightful space in a believer's heart and mind.

In my personal travels, I have heard a lot of good motivational and inspirational preaching and have encountered amazing praise and worship music. In fact, it's possible that the Church has never produced better music. However, I see a real void in the area of solid, foundational Bible teaching. This is a very serious state of affairs within the Church at large. When there is an absence of the teaching of Scripture, an unstable situation is created for the people of God that will ultimately prove catastrophic because they are unable to face victoriously the challenges and trials of life. They lose their ability to discern what is *right* and what is *wrong* or to make decisions, based on godly wisdom, about what they should and shouldn't do in their lives.

The Bible is the immovable plumb line, and where the Bible is the immovable plumb line in people's lives, it causes them to become firmly established on the immovable and unshakable foundation of God's Word. For this reason, I am doing my part to pray and work for a revival of the Bible in the Church at large — and I'd ask you to please join your faith and your prayers with mine to that end.

In Hebrews 5:12, the writer well described our current dilemma when he said, "For when for the time ye ought to be teachers, ye have need that one teach you again which be the first principles of the oracles of God; and are become such as have need of milk, and not of strong meat."

The Bible is the immovable plumb line, and where the Bible is the immovable plumb line in people's lives, it causes them to become firmly established on the immovable and unshakable foundation of God's Word. For this reason, I am doing my part to pray and work for a revival of the Bible in the Church at large — and I'd ask you to please join your faith and your prayers with mine to that end.

The believers that were being addressed in Hebrews 5:12 were spiritually immature at a time when they should have already been very advanced. Unfortunately, they were like children who had skipped the ABCs of their Christian faith. Although they were physically older Christians, they were so ungrounded in the teaching of the Bible that they needed to be established in those ABCs — basic, foundational doctrine — again.

Let me share an illustration to bring my point home. Let's say that you're walking down a school hallway and you look into a classroom of first-graders, where you see a room full of children sitting at their little desks, studying along with their teacher. But then you notice that right in the middle of all those first-graders is a 60-year-old man sitting in his little chair at a tiny desk. There he sits, oversized and squeezed into his tiny chair, studying the ABCs and other elementary principles, along with all the other first-graders.

If this man had never had the opportunity for an education, it might seem admirable that he would humble himself to attend a first-grade class and learn. But what if that man had been sitting at that tiny desk for *years and years and years* and was required to repeat the first grade over and over again because he didn't apply himself? Was he too lazy, or did he not make the time to study and grow? Suppose his failure to be promoted to the next grade was a result of his lack of commitment to learn — and that was why he was still sitting in the same chair at the same desk more than 50 years later. What if *that* is the reason all his former classmates grew up and went on to have families and careers while this man remained stuck right where he began.

To behold such a scenario would be bizarre indeed, especially if that 60-year-old man was mentally sound. This illustration may sound very strange, but it is actually happening in the Church all the time. People come to Christ, and in a certain sense, they go to first grade spiritually. They are new Christians, and it's time for them to learn *"the ABCs"* of the Christian faith — the fundamentals of the Word of God. But often, because these believers didn't apply themselves or were never correctly taught — or they gravitated toward "divers and strange doctrines" and never really embraced foundational principles of the Bible and applied them to their lives — they spiritually never graduated to more mature levels. They remained stuck in "first grade."

We read that the writer of Hebrews was concerned his readers were not where they were supposed to be spiritually by this time in their lives. That is why the verse says, "For when for the time ye ought to be teachers, ye have need that one teach you again which be the first principles of the oracles of God; and are become such as have need of milk, and not of strong meat" (Hebrews 5:12).

The word "ought" in this verse is a translation of the Greek word that describes *an obligation, a necessity, something that should be achieved or accomplished, something that is owed*, or *a moral duty*. In this particular case, this word refers to Christians who have heard and seen a great deal of God's truth and are now *morally obligated* to be able to correctly communicate it, apply it, and even teach that truth to others. They've been in class so long that they should know the subject inside and out.

That is why the verse continues to say, "You ought to be *teachers*." The word "teachers" is the plural form of the Greek word *didaskalos*. This word *didaskalos* is a very important term here, describing *a masterful teacher* or *someone who is superior in his field of expertise*. It was the very word used in the First Century to describe *rabbis*. So the writer of Hebrews was basically saying to his readers, *"After all the church meetings you've attended and after everything you have heard with your ears and seen with your eyes, you are actually morally obligated by this time to be masterful at your subject."*

The message being conveyed by the writer of Hebrews is clear: *"You need to be superior in this field of expertise — in foundational biblical truths. In fact, with all you've seen and heard, you ought to be like a spiritual rabbi by now — qualified to teach someone else because of everything you've heard and everything you've seen."*

But the writer of Hebrews went on to say, "...[But] ye have *need* that one teach you again which be the first principles of the oracles of God...." The word "need" is a translation of the Greek word *chreia*, which describes *a lack*, *a need*, or *a deficit that needs to be met*. So when the verse says, "Ye have need," it means, "You have *a deficit*; you have *a lack* — and now you need someone to teach you the *first principles* of the oracles of God."

The word "principles" is a translation of the Greek word *stoicheion*, a word that describes *basic elements, fundamentals, or rudimentary knowledge*. The word "first" is the Greek word *arches*, which describes *the first*, *the beginning*, or *something elementary*. Early philosophers used this word *stoicheion* to describe the *arche* (first) elements — in other words, the elements without which nothing else could find existence. These are the elements that form the "building blocks" comprising all of constructed creation. Thus, these doctrinal principles are the basic truths upon which rests the entire house of New Testament truth.

In Hebrews 5:12, the word *stoicheion* refers to *foundational* knowledge, or as the verse states it, "first principles." By saying "first principles" the writer is describing *the fundamental knowledge that every believer is required to obtain before he can advance to a higher level of spiritual education.*

These are the elements that form the "building blocks" comprising all of constructed creation. Thus, these doctrinal principles are the basic truths upon which rests the entire house of New Testament truth.

But just as the believers in the First Century needed to be taught, much of the Church today needs to be instructed in the elementary principles of the Word of God. When that foundation is laid under one's life, it gives him or her the ability to discern what is *right* or *wrong.* But an untaught Church remains vulnerable to being blown "here and there" by winds of doctrine because they are not being rooted and grounded in truth.

Scoundrels With Ulterior Motives

In Ephesians 4:14, Paul said, "That we henceforth be no more children, tossed to and fro, and carried about with every wind of doctrine, by the sleight of men...."

The word "sleight" is an old English translation of the word *kubos,* a Greek word that pictures low-level people who throw dice in a game of trickery to intentionally take advantage of other people. These were professional *dice-players* in the ancient world who won a game of dice by the "sleight of hand." Paul used the word *kubos* to picture *unscrupulous people in ministry who toss dice with doctrine* and who lure saints into a game that those unscrupulous ministers play with their souls for some type of personal gain.

But Ephesians 4:14 goes on to say, "That we henceforth be no more children, tossed to and fro, and carried about with every wind of doctrine, by the sleight of men, and cunning craftiness...."

The words "cunning craftiness" are translated from the Greek word *panourgia*, which is a word to emphatically portray *an unscrupulous person* who is willing to do or say anything to achieve his or her goal or to get some positional, authoritarian, or financial advantage over others. Although this word sounds harsh, the word *panourgia* depicts *a scoundrel.* Paul, a linguist who knew the meaning of this word, used it to alert us to the fact that there is indeed an unscrupulous category of people who "play dice" with doctrine. *Doctrinal correctness* is not their goal, but instead, they are more focused on what will create *a sensational stir* to attract attention. They toss dice with doctrine in a spiritual game to get the attention of unstable souls so they can take advantage of them.

Paul additionally stated that these "...lie in wait to deceive." The words "lie in wait" are translated from the word *pros*, which implies *a specific plan and a specific purpose*. The word *pros* is quickly followed by the word *methodeia*, the Greek word from which we get the word "methods." It depicts *a well-devised plan to strategically accomplish a goal.* The use of *methodeia* at this juncture means there is nothing accidental in what these people are doing. Indeed, they are actively and strategically devising methods to garner the attention of spiritually immature people who do not have enough spiritual sense to recognize the silliness that is being advocated to them. Because those who are spiritually immature tend to be gullible, they fall for this faster, thus making them easier prey for people who have wrong motives.

Paul furthermore stated this particular group of revelators are lying in wait "to deceive." That word "deceive" is a form of the Greek word *planao*, a word that depicts someone who has intentionally caused *one to wander from a well-known, well-established, well-worn, trusted path.* It is the very word used to picture sheep that have strayed so far from the flock that they cannot find their way back home without the assistance of shepherds who come looking for them to bring them home.

An End-Time Challenge for the Church

When Paul wrote First Timothy 4:1 about a departure from the faith at the end of the age, he used the word *planao* to describe the activity of "seducing" spirits that will operate even in the Church as the Church Age comes to a close. In that verse, he wrote, "Now the Spirit speaketh expressly, that in the latter times some shall depart from the faith, giving heed to seducing spirits, and doctrines of devils...."

The Holy Spirit inspired Paul to use the word *planao* in that verse to prophetically foretell a time when a *wandering* from the solid and trusted teaching of the faith will occur at the end of the age. The Holy Spirit forecasted that spirits of delusion will be unleashed by the devil at the end of the age to stealthily, methodically, and seductively entice people away from long-held established truths and into doctrines that are advanced by demon spirits.

Upon hearing this, I pray you see how vital it is that we have reputable Christ-given fivefold ministry gifts operating in the Church at the end of the age. When authentic Christ-given ministries fulfill their assignments in the Church as Christ commands, it causes the Church to grow and mature and learn how to discern right and wrong. This thus protects the Church and sets it on a sure foundation.

In First Timothy 4:1, Paul prophetically pointed to the end of the age — *to our very time* — to alert us that "deception" will be activated in the end of the age. Certainly this deception is mainstream in society today, but we must understand that the Holy Spirit forewarns it will also attempt to penetrate some segments of the Church.

We are living in the age when the Bible prophesied these things will occur. Already a spirit of delusion is working full force in the secular world today. But we must heed the warning of the Holy Spirit and stand guard against loose delusional teachings that will emerge in the last days to blow unstable souls here and there by "winds" filled with many "divers and strange doctrines."

The Need 'To Know Them Which Labour Among You'

Because of advances made in technology, the Christian world today is exposed to all kinds of Christian celebrities and personalities and a wide array of teaching. Through the avenues of Christian publishing houses, television and Internet programs, radio shows, and even entire Christian television networks, this generation has had the marvelous opportunity to access more information about the Gospel of Jesus Christ than any previous generation before us.

But this unprecedented access to information also heightens the possibility of error creeping into our personal spaces. The continual influx of information requires us to use great disernment regarding whom we allow to speak into our lives.

I am thankful for the vast array of Christian television programs that are available today. After all, I am also a TV broadcaster who seeks to extend my voice through these various media outlets. However, I must tell you that I cautiously guard my home and am careful even about which Christian TV programs are allowed into our personal space. I agree with the old saying that "everything that glitters is not gold." It is our individual responsibility to determine to use our sound minds, hold fast to the Scriptures, and refuse to budge from God's truth. In other words, *let's keep our heads on straight.*

We must pay heed to Paul's exhortation in First Thessalonians 5:12 where he wrote, "And we beseech you, brethren, to know them which labour among you, and are over you in the Lord, and admonish you."

If that verse was ever needed, it is needed today when so many are gaining notable, influential positions whom we know nearly nothing about. Hence, it is reasonable to ask:

- Who are they?
- Where were they trained?
- What ministerial circles do they run in?
- Who are their comrades in the faith?
- With whom are they in spiritual relationship?
- To whom are they spiritually accountable?

These are not periphery questions. They are important questions you need to ask before you open your heart and mind to anyone who has the ability to affect your spiritual life and thinking. Paul emphatically stated that we are to "know" them that labor among us. Since that was true 2,000 years ago, it is true for us today.

The Greek word translated "know" in First Thessalonians 5:12 is a form of *oida*, a word that depicts knowledge one gains *by personal experience* or *by personal observation.* Hence, before you throw open your heart in a trusting manner for someone you don't really know to exercise spiritual influence in your life, you are commanded in God's Word to *know* something about them. Nothing is more serious than your spiritual life. What happens at your core affects every area of your life. This is why Proverbs 4:23 tells us, "Keep thy heart with all diligence; for out of it are the issues of life." We are commanded by Paul to be confident in those who have spiritual authority in our lives and who feed us spiritually.

I especially urge you to make certain those you are following in media are in solid spiritual relationship with someone who has authority to speak into his or her life and to bring correction if needed. I urge you to avoid following a disconnected "wandering star" that roams freely with no accountability. Who feeds your spirit and soul is so very important that you need to carefully consider who you are listening to, who you are following, and who you are supporting with your finances. It is imperative that you are confident in your heart that you are following someone who has a life and teaching you can trust.

As you take the whole of Paul's message in Ephesians 4:12-15, notice he stated that when Christ-given fivefold ministry is active in the Church, a major part of its function is to assist the Church to grow to a point of spiritual maturity so that it is "no longer tossed to and fro and carried about by every wind of doctrine." If reputable fivefold ministry is embraced and fully released to do its job, it will help the people of God grow in their knowledge to a point that they will not be easily led astray by the "sleight" and "cunning craftiness" of those who toss doctrinal dice for the sake of attracting attention or to leverage others for their own advantage.

It's Time To Grow Up Spiritually

Finally, in Ephesians 4:15, Paul said, "But speaking the truth in love, [the Church] may grow up into him in all things, which is the head, even Christ."

Paul said, "But...." In Greek, this is the conjunction *de*, which is a exclamatory marker intended to make a significant point. It is the essence of saying, "*Instead of all this immature behavior*, the Church will at long last rise to a level of maturity, where it will speak the truth in love and '...*grow up* into him in all things....'"

The words "grow up" are translated from the word *auxano*, the same word we saw in Ephesians 2:21 that denotes something that is being *amplified*, *augmented*, *enlarged*, or *enhanced*. It carries the idea of something that *escalates* and *multiplies*. And as noted earlier, it denotes both increase in terms of *quantity* and *quality*. So Paul makes it unequivocally clear that it is God's intention for the Church to grow spiritually and numerically — in quality and quantity — until it becomes the mighty Temple and habitation that God longs for it to have in this earthly sphere.

In Ephesians 4:15, Paul then added that the Church is to "...grow up into him in all things, which is the head, even Christ." As I told you in Chapter One, the Greek word for "head" is *kephale*, which is the word that describes *a physical head* or *chief cornerstone* or *capstone* that connects two sides of an arch in the center. We saw in Ephesians 2:20 that Christ is the *Head* of the Body of Christ and the *Chief Cornerstone* or *Capstone* on which everything in the Church leans and relies. In keeping with Paul's apostolic vision of building a *naos* Temple of God, he once again used the word *kephale,* the word in this text for a Head, Chief Cornerstone, or Capstone, to depict the utter centrality of Christ in His Church.

Because this word *kephale* was used by many famous ancient Greek writers, and their use of this word gives us powerful additional insights into what it means for Christ to be the Head of the Church, let's review how they used it. As noted earlier:

- Plato used *kephale* to picture what is *main*, *basic*, or *core* and also used it to picture *investing a substantial sum of money* into a project. Thus, *kephale* became known as *the central point of investment.*[1]

- Aristotle used *kephale* identically to picture whatever is *main*, *basic*, or *core* and to portray *investing a substantial sum of money* into a project — thus, it was also used in his writings as *the central point of investment.*[2]

- Plutarch used the word *kephale* to depict a person who was considered to be *the chief* or *the head* of something.[3]

When all of these historical nuances are carried into Ephesians 4:15, where Paul described Christ as the "Head" of the Body of Christ, the Church, it emphatically means Christ is the *Chief* and *Head* of the Church, and He is so *central* that He is the very *core* of it. In Ephesians 4:15, Paul clearly stated that God's ultimate, long-term objective is that we grow up into Him, who is the *Head* and the *Apex* of the Church — that is, *Jesus Christ.*

A Final Word

In Ecclesiastes 3:1, we read, "To everything there is a season, and a time to every purpose under the heaven."

According to this verse, God has made everyone and everything for a special season and with a special purpose. In the same way, we can be confident that each of the Christ-given fivefold ministry gifts — including the *apostle* and *prophet* (which has been the focus of this book) — has been designed by God for the season of the entire Church Age and for a specific purpose to be fulfilled in the Church. And according to Ecclesiastes 3:1, if they exist under the heavens — and they *do* — it means they have God-designed purpose in the Church that the Great Designer planned Himself.

In conclusion, I remind you this book was *never* meant to be a manual about how to be an apostle or prophet, but rather, it is a biblical examination of the roles God has assigned to apostles and prophets in the Body of Christ and in the *naos* Temple of God.

We conclude based on the witness of Scripture that apostles and prophets indeed held vital roles in the past, they indeed hold vital roles in the present — and, contrary to what cessationists have alleged, Paul stated unquestionably in Ephesians 4:11-16 that these gifts will *continue* to hold a vital role in the Church until the consummation of the Church Age.

My prayer is that this book has shed clarity on this subject for those who have seeking hearts — and that you will take this knowledge of the ministries of *apostles* and *prophets* with you in your own experience.

**And he gave some, apostles; and some, prophets;
and some, evangelists; and some, pastors and teachers;
for the perfecting of the saints, for the work of the ministry,
for the edifying of the body of Christ: till we all come in the unity
of the faith, and of the knowledge of the Son of God, unto a perfect
man, unto the measure of the stature of the fulness of Christ: that
we henceforth be no more children, tossed to and fro, and carried about
with every wind of doctrine, by the sleight of men, and cunning
craftiness, whereby they lie in wait to deceive; but speaking the truth
in love, may grow up into him in all things, which is the head, even
Christ: from whom the whole body fitly joined together and
compacted by that which every joint supplieth, according
to the effectual working in the measure of every part,
maketh increase of the body unto
the edifying of itself in love.**

— Ephesians 4:11-16

Questions for Deeper Consideration

Chapter 10

1. Paul stated in Ephesians 2:20 that the Church is built upon the foundation of apostles and prophets, with Jesus Christ Himself being the Chief Cornerstone. As you have learned in this book, the chief apostolic vision for the Church is that of a mighty Temple that is being constructed of living stones to become a habitation for God's Spirit in the earth. Can you express what the words "Chief Cornerstone" mean in regard to Jesus' central role in the Church?

2. According to Colossians 1:6, when the Gospel is proclaimed in power, it always produces supernatural growth. God is interested in spiritual growth and numerical growth. But from what you have read in this chapter, what indicator is manifested if either form of growth stops and the Church stagnates? What does it mean and what action should be initiated to see growth begin again?

3. In Ephesians 4:11-15, Paul stated the ultimate purpose for the fivefold ministries of apostles, prophets, evangelists, pastors, and teachers. How would you very simply describe God's purpose for giving these ministry gifts to the Church?

4. Paul wrote that when fivefold ministry gifts are embraced and allowed to fully function, they assist the Church in leaving a childish state and to

enter spiritual maturity. Paul stated in Ephesians 4:14 that a sign of spiritual immaturity is when God's people are "tossed to and fro" by various winds of doctrine. After reading this chapter, what does "tossed to and fro" now mean to you — and how have you witnessed this kind of spiritual instability in yourself or others?

5. Hebrews 13:9 warns about God's people being recklessly "carried about with divers and strange doctrines." That verse states that although such doctrines are unprofitable, immature Christians often get caught up in them to the point of obsession. Can you think of novel doctrines that have caused ripples in the Body of Christ or among people you know personally?

6. In Ephesians 4:14, Paul wrote that by the "sleight of men," unscrupulous people take advantage of immature, sincere, naive believers. Paul used the Greek word *kubos* — translated "sleight of men" — to describe spiritual scoundrels who play dice with doctrine and use their positions to take advantage of people. Can you think of an instance in which you saw someone "play dice" with doctrine — who played a game of trickery with the saints?

7. In First Thessalonians 5:12, Paul admonished us to know those whom we permit to speak into our lives and to know something about those whom we permit to exercise spiritual authority in our lives. What steps do you take to ensure those speaking into your life are reputable, submitted to authority, and are bringing you sound doctrine and trusted teaching?

8. Paul stated that if all the elements in the Church — including every fivefold ministry gift — are functioning as God intended, it will cause the Church to grow up in Christ as the Head (*see* Ephesians 4:15). After reading this book, what do you believe needs to happen for the Church to arrive at this level of spiritual maturity? Do you see all the fivefold gifts in operation? What do you believe needs to transpire so they can each be received, embraced, and released to bring their various portions of Christ to the Church at the end of the age?

ENDNOTES

Chapter 1

[1] *Ancient Greek-Russian Dictionary, Volumes I and II.* Compiled by Joseph Dvoretsky (Moscow: State Publishing House of Foreign and National Dictionaries, 1958). Pindar.
[2] Ibid., Herodotus.
[3] Ibid., Plato.
[4] Ibid., Aristotle.
[5] Ibid., Plutarch.
[6] Rick Renner, *A Light in Darkness: Volume One, Seven Messages to the Seven Churches* (Tulsa, Oklahoma: Harrison House Publishers in partnership with Rick Renner Ministries, 2010), pp. 264-279.
[7] Aristotle, *Politics*, I.5.
[8] Herodotus, *The Histories*, IV.1-15,99-117.
[9] *Ancient Greek-Russian Dictionary, Volumes I and II.* Compiled by Joseph Dvoretsky (Moscow: State Publishing House of Foreign and National Dictionaries, 1958). Herodotus.
[10] Ibid., Euripides, Thucydides.
[11] Ibid., Plato.
[12] Ibid., Aristotle.
[13] Ibid., Lysias, Demosthenes, Lucian, Plutarch.
[14] Ibid., Polybius.
[15] Ibid., Herodotus, Plato.
[16] Ibid., Euripides, Aristotle.
[17] Ibid., Sextus Empiricus.
[18] Ibid., *euangelistes.*
[19] Ibid., Xenophon.
[20] Ibid., Demosthenes, Plutarch, Lucian.
[21] Ibid., Plutarch.
[22] Ibid., *evangelist.*
[23] Ibid., *euangelistes.*
[24] Ibid., Homer.
[25] Ibid., Aeschylus.
[26] Ibid., Euripides.
[27] Ibid., Plato.
[28] Ibid., Theocritus.
[29] Ibid., Lucian.
[30] Ibid., Aeschylus.
[31] Ibid., Herodotus.
[32] Ibid., Aristophanes.

[33] *The New International Dictionary of New Testament Theology & Exegesis,* Abridged, s.v. "didaskalos," (Grand Rapids, MI: Zondervan, 2014).
[34] Rick Renner, *No Room For Compromise: Christ's Message to Today's Church, Volume Two* (Tulsa, Oklahoma: Harrison House Publishers in partnership with Rick Renner Ministries, 2010), pp. 152-153.
[35] *Ancient Greek-Russian Dictionary, Volumes I and II.* Compiled by Joseph Dvoretsky (Moscow: State Publishing House of Foreign and National Dictionaries, 1958). Herodotus.
[36] Ibid., Plutarch.
[37] Ibid., Polybius.
[38] Ibid., Diodorus.
[39] Ibid., Galen.
[40] Ibid., Herodotus.
[41] Ibid., Plato.
[42] Ibid., Aristotle.
[43] Ibid., Plato, Aristotle.
[44] Ibid., Plato.
[45] Ibid., Demosthenes.
[46] Ibid., Polybius.
[47] Ibid., Plutarch.
[48] Ibid., Sextus Empiricus.
[49] Ibid., Plato, Aeschylus, Xenophon, Polybius.
[50] Ibid., Herodotus.

Chapter 2

[1] *Ancient Greek-Russian Dictionary, Volumes I and II.* Compiled by Joseph Dvoretsky (Moscow: State Publishing House of Foreign and National Dictionaries, 1958). Pindar.
[2] Ibid., Herodotus.
[3] Joshua J. Mark, "The Seven Wonders," World History Encyclopedia, September 2, 2009, https://www.worldhistory.org/The_Seven_Wonders/
[4] Mark Cartwright, "Statue of Zeus at Olympia," World History Encyclopedia, July 24, 2018, https://www.worldhistory.org/Statue_of_Zeus_at_Olympia/
[5] History.com Editors, "Parthenon," History, April 27, 2021, https://www.history.com/topics/ancient-greece/parthenon
[6] ArcheoRoma editorial staff, "Pantheon," ArcheoRoma, https://www.archeoroma.org/sites/pantheon/
[7] Rick Renner, *No Room For Compromise: Christ's Message to Today's Church, Volume Two* (Tulsa, Oklahoma: Harrison House Publishers in partnership with Rick Renner Ministries, 2010), p. 21.
[8] Alexander Meddings, "The Sack of this Ancient Temple Funded the Building of the Colosseum," History Collection, August 14, 2017, https://historycollection.com/sack-ancient-temple-funded-building-colosseum/
[9] "Western Stone," Megalithic Builders, 2021, https://www.megalithicbuilders.com/asia/israel/jerusalem-western-stone

[10] *Ancient Greek-Russian Dictionary, Volumes I and II.* Compiled by Joseph Dvoretsky (Moscow: State Publishing House of Foreign and National Dictionaries, 1958). Aeschylus.
[11] Ibid., Herodotus.
[12] Ibid., Euripides.
[13] Ibid., Aristotle.
[14] Christopher Siwicki, "Finding Wonderful Things," History Today, Vol. 70, Issue 4, April 2020, https://www.historytoday.com/archive/behind-times/finding-wonderful-things
[15] *Ancient Greek-Russian Dictionary, Volumes I and II.* Compiled by Joseph Dvoretsky (Moscow: State Publishing House of Foreign and National Dictionaries, 1958). Lucian of Samosata.
[16] Ibid., Aristotle.
[17] Ibid., Herodotus.
[18] Ibid., Sophocles.
[19] Ibid., Plato, Aristotle.
[20] Ibid., Xenophon, Demosthenes.
[21] Ibid., Herodotus, Plutarch.
[22] Ibid., Herodotus, Homer, Pindar.
[23] Ibid., Homer, Plato.
[24] Ibid., Xenophon.
[25] Ibid., Aristotle.
[26] Ibid., Herodotus.
[27] Ibid., Lucian of Samosata.
[28] Rick Renner, *No Room For Compromise: Christ's Message to Today's Church, Volume Two* (Tulsa, Oklahoma: Harrison House Publishers in partnership with Rick Renner Ministries, 2010), pp. 8-13.
[29] *Ancient Greek-Russian Dictionary, Volumes I and II.* Compiled by Joseph Dvoretsky (Moscow: State Publishing House of Foreign and National Dictionaries, 1958). Plutarch.
[30] Ibid., Herodotus.
[31] Ibid., Euripides.
[32] Herodotus, *The Histories*, I.
[33] Britannica, T. Editors of Encyclopaedia. "Claros." *Encyclopedia Britannica*, February 15, 2016. https://www.britannica.com/place/Claros

Chapter 3

[1] *Ancient Greek-Russian Dictionary, Volumes I and II.* Compiled by Joseph Dvoretsky (Moscow: State Publishing House of Foreign and National Dictionaries, 1958). Euripides, Thucydides.
[2] Ibid., Aristotle.
[3] Ibid., Herodotus.
[4] Ibid., Plutarch.
[5] Ibid., Plato, Polybius.
[6] Ibid., Lucian, Lysias, Demosthenes, Plutarch.
[7] Mark Cartwright, "Greek Colonization," World History Encyclopedia, May 7, 2018, https://www.worldhistory.org/Greek_Colonization/

[8] *Ancient Greek-Russian Dictionary, Volumes I and II.* Compiled by Joseph Dvoretsky (Moscow: State Publishing House of Foreign and National Dictionaries, 1958). *Apostolos.*
[9] Rick Renner, *A Light in Darkness: Volume One, Seven Messages to the Seven Churches* (Tulsa, Oklahoma: Harrison House Publishers in partnership with Rick Renner Ministries, 2010), p. 419.
[10] Eusebius, *Church History*, III.i.1.
[11] Gregory of Nazianzus, *Oration* 33.XI.
[12] Jerome, *Ep. ad Marcell.*, XXII.
[13] Theodoret, *On the Psalms*, CXVI.
[14] Nicephorus, *Short History*, II.39.
[15] Eusebius, *Church History*, V.x.3.
[16] Eusebius, *Church History*, III.24.6.
[17] Nicephorus, *Ecclesiastical History*, II.40.
[18] Eusebius, *Church History*, II.xv.1-2.
[19] Irenaeus, *Against Heresies*, III.i.1.
[20] Clement of Rome, *Letter to the Corinthians*, V.
[21] Ignatius, *Letter to the Romans*, IV.3.
[22] Eusebius, *Church History*, II.xxv.8.
[23] Tertullian, *Scorpiace.*
[24] Eusebius, *Church History*, II.25.7.
[25] Eusebius, *Church History*, II.xxv.5.
[26] Arthur Stapylton Barnes, *St. Peter in Rome and His Tomb on the Vatican Hill* (London: Swan Sonnenschein and Co., 1900), p. 26.
[27] Moses of Chorene, *History of Armenia*, IX.
[28] *Ancient Greek-Russian Dictionary, Volumes I and II.* Compiled by Joseph Dvoretsky (Moscow: State Publishing House of Foreign and National Dictionaries, 1958). Plutarch.
[29] Ibid., Thucydides.
[30] Ibid., Herodotus.
[31] Ibid., Aristotle.
[32] Ibid., Herodotus.
[33] Ibid., *ambassadors.*
[34] Ibid., *ambassadors.*
[35] Ibid., Thucydides.
[36] Ibid., *kerux.*
[37] Ibid., *dokimasia.*

Chapter 4

[1] Rick Renner, *Sparkling Gems From the Greek I* (Shippensburg, PA: Harrison House Publishers, 2003), p. 809.

Chapter 5

[1] New World Encyclopedia contributors, "Gamaliel," *New World Encyclopedia*, https://www.newworldencyclopedia.org/entry/Gamaliel.

[2] *Ancient Greek-Russian Dictionary, Volumes I and II.* Compiled by Joseph Dvoretsky (Moscow: State Publishing House of Foreign and National Dictionaries, 1958).
[3] Ibid., Herodotus, Plutarch.
[4] Ibid., Plato.
[5] Ibid., Plato, Euripides.
[6] Ibid., Demosthenes.
[7] Ibid., Chesiphron, Metagenes – Temple of Artemis.
[8] Ibid., Phyromachos – Alter of Zeus.
[9] Ibid., Ictinus, Callicrates – Parthenon.
[10] Ibid., Apollodorus – Pantheon.
[11] Ibid., *architects.*
[12] Charles Haddon Spurgeon, *Spurgeon on the Blood of Christ*, Compiled and Edited by Beverlee J. Chadwick (Newberry, FL: Bridge-Logos, Inc., 2015), p.28.
[13] Mark Cartwright, "Corinth," *World History Encyclopedia*, September 2, 2009, https://www.worldhistory.org/corinth/
[14] *Ancient Greek-Russian Dictionary, Volumes I and II.* Compiled by Joseph Dvoretsky (Moscow: State Publishing House of Foreign and National Dictionaries, 1958). Homer.
[15] Ibid., Pindar.
[16] Ibid., Plato.
[17] Ibid., Xenophon, Demosthenes.
[18] Ibid., Aristotle.
[19] Ibid., Polybius.
[20] Mark Cartwright, "Slavery in the Roman World," *World History Encyclopedia*, November 1, 2013, https://www.worldhistory.org/article/629/slavery-in-the-roman-world/
[21] *Ancient Greek-Russian Dictionary, Volumes I and II.* Compiled by Joseph Dvoretsky (Moscow: State Publishing House of Foreign and National Dictionaries, 1958). Homer, Euripides, Herodotus, Aristophanes, Xenophon.
[22] Ibid., Hesiod, Herodotus.
[23] Ibid., Euripides.
[24] Ibid., Plato.
[25] Ibid., Thucydides, Xenophon, Lysias, Herodotus, Aeschines, Plato, Plutarch.

Chapter 6

[1] Dennis E. Smith, ed., *Chalice Introduction to the New Testament* (Atlanta: Chalice Press, 2004), p. 108.

Chapter 7

[1] Rick Renner, *No Room for Compromise: Christ's Message to Today's Church, Volume Two* (Tulsa, Oklahoma: Institute Books, 2014), pp. 231-242.
[2] Pliny the Elder, *Natural History*, XXX,II,11.
[3] Eusebius, *Preparation for the Gospel*, IX.8.
[4] Origen, *Contra Celsum*, IV.51.

[5] David Noel Freedman, ed., *The Anchor Bible Dictionary, Vol. 3* (New York: Doubleday, 1992), p. 638.
[6] This information originated from the studies of the word "prophet" from Pastor Keith Trump. https://gettinggreek.org
[7] Naim Collins, *Realms of the Prophetic*, (Destiny Image, Inc., 2019).
[8] *Ancient Greek-Russian Dictionary, Volumes I and II.* Compiled by Joseph Dvoretsky, (Moscow: State Publishing House of Foreign and National Dictionaries, 1958). Herodotus, Plato.
[9] Ibid., Euripides, Aristotle.
[10] Ibid., Sextus Empiricus.
[11] John Gill, "Ezekiel 3 Commentary - *Gill's Exposition of the Whole Bible*," Bible Study Tools, 2021, https://www.biblestudytools.com/commentaries/gills-exposition-of-the-bible/ezekiel-3-3.html
[12] Robert Jamieson, A. R. Fausset, David Brown, "Ezekiel 3 Commentary - *Jamieson-Fausset-Brown Bible Commentary*," Bible Hub, 2021, https://biblehub.com/commentaries/jfb/ezekiel/3.htm
[13] John Gill, "Ezekiel 3 Commentary - *Gill's Exposition of the Whole Bible*," Bible Study Tools, 2021, https://www.biblestudytools.com/commentaries/gills-exposition-of-the-bible/ezekiel-3-3.html
[14] Rick Renner, *How To Keep Your Head on Straight in a World Gone Crazy: Developing Discernment in These Last Days* (Shippensburg, PA: Harrison House, 2019), pp. 181-183.
[15] *Ancient Greek-Russian Dictionary, Volumes I and II.* Compiled by Joseph Dvoretsky, (Moscow: State Publishing House of Foreign and National Dictionaries, 1958). Anacreon.
[16] Ibid., Euripides, Pindar.
[17] Ibid., Plato.
[18] Ibid., Sextus Empiricus.

Chapter 8

[1] "Abraham," Jewish Virtual Library, https://www.jewishvirtuallibrary.org/abraham
[2] Jeffrey, David Lyle. 1992. *A Dictionary of Biblical Tradition in English Literature* (Grand Rapids, Michigan: W.B. Eerdmans).
[3] "Moses," Jewish Virtual Library, https://www.jewishvirtuallibrary.org/moses
[4] Philo, *On the Life of Moses,* II.12,17-24.
[5] Flavius Josephus, "*The Words of Flavius Josephus: Translated by William Whiston; Antiquities of the Jews,*" II.9.
[6] New World Encyclopedia writers, "Samuel," New World Encyclopedia, https://www.newworldencyclopedia.org/entry/Samuel
[7] H. L. Ellison, *The Prophets of Israel from Ahijah to Hosea*, (Grand Rapids: W.B. Eerdmans Pub. Co, 1969).
[8] Flavius Josephus, "*The Words of Flavius Josephus: Translated by William Whiston; Antiquities of the Jews,*" VII.7.5.
[9] Richard A. Bauman, *Crime and Punishment in Ancient Rome* (New York: Routledge, 1996), p. 67.
[10] Flavius Josephus, *The Antiquities of the Jews*, X.6.3.
[11] Singer, Isidore. *The Jewish Encyclopedia: 1906 Edition*, (New York: Funk and Wagnalls Company, 1901-1906).

Chapter 9

[1] Naim Collins, *Realms of the Prophetic* (Shippensburg, PA: Destiny Image, Inc., 2019).
[2] Ralph Martin Novak, *Christianity and the Roman Empire: Background Texts* (Harrisburg, PA: Trinity Press, 2001).
[3] Dennis E. Smith, ed., *Chalice Introduction to the New Testament* (Atlanta: Chalice Press, 2004), p.108.
[4] Regarding the statement in Acts 18:27 that says, "Then he [Apollos] was disposed to pass into Achaia…," Bible scholar Adam Clarke writes this: "There is a very long and important addition here in the Codex Bezae, of which the following is a translation: 'But certain Corinthians, who sojourned at Ephesus, and heard him, entreated him to pass over with them to their own country. Then, when he had given his consent, the Ephesians wrote to the disciples at Corinth, that they should receive this man. Who, when he was come, etc.' The same addition is found in the later Syriac, and in the Itala version in the Codex Bezae." *Adam Clarke's Commentary*, Electronic Database, Biblesoft, 1996.
[5] Flavius Josephus, "*The Words of Flavius Josephus: Translated by William Whiston; Antiquities of the Jews*," XX.2.5.
[6] Kenneth W. Harl, *Coinage in the Roman Economy: 300 B.C. to A.D. 700* (Baltimore, MD: The Johns Hopkins University Press, 1996), p. 91.
[7] Alison E. Cooley, *The Cambridge Manual of Latin Epigraphy* (Cambridge: Cambridge University Press, 2012), p. 197.
[8] Rick Renner, *How To Keep Your Head on Straight in a World Gone Crazy* (Shippensburg, PA: Harrison House, 2019), pp. 261-277.

Chapter 10

[1] *Ancient Greek-Russian Dictionary, Volumes I and II.* Compiled by Joseph Dvoretsky (Moscow: State Publishing House of Foreign and National Dictionaries, 1958). Plato.
[2] Ibid., Aristotle.
[3] Ibid., Plutarch.

ILLUSTRATION AND PHOTO CREDIT ACKNOWLEDGMENTS

RENNER Ministries would like to thank the following picture libraries as well as individual copyright owners for permission to reproduce their images. Copyright inquiries should be directed to Rick Renner Ministries, social@renner.org.

All images are presented in the order in which they appear and are reproduced by permission. All images are © Balage Balogh, *Archaeology Illustrated* — https://archaeologyillustrated.com/ unless otherwise credited.

COVER:

Jewish man in a tallith prayer shawl against dramatic sky © John Theodor / Stock.Adobe.com; *Rock abstract brown wall background* © elen31 / Stock.Adobe.com

ILLUSTRATION PAGES:

1. *Builders of the Temple of Solomon Resting After Work* — Archaeology Illustrated

2. *Paul the Apostle Teaching* — Archaeology Illustrated

3. *Fisherman on the Sea of Galilee* — Archaeology Illustrated

4. *Jerusalem, Temple of Herod the Great, Second Temple, Court of Women, in Morning Light, 1st Century AD* — Archaeology Illustrated

5. *The Roman Forum, Basilica Julia and Basilica Aemilia, 1st Century AD* — Archaeology Illustrated

6. *Ephesus, The Temple of Artemis. One of the Seven Wonders of the Ancient World. Hellenistic and Roman Periods* — Archaeology Illustrated

7. *The Pergamon Altar, The Altar of Zeus on the Acropolis of Pergamon, Festival Scene, 2nd Century BC-4th Century AD* — Archaeology Illustrated (Alternate Title: *Altar of Zeus*)

8. *Athens, Acropolis, The Interior of the Parthenon with the Cult Image of Athena, 5th Century BC* — Archaeology Illustrated

9. *Rome, The Pantheon, 2nd Century AD* — Archaeology Illustrated

10. *Pompeii, House of the Vettii Family, The Reception Hall and Rainwater Pool, 1st Century AD* — Archaeology Illustrated

11. *Jerusalem, Temple of Solomon, 10th-7th Centuries BC* — Archaeology Illustrated

12. *Jerusalem, The Interior of the Temple of Solomon, According to Biblical Descriptions, 10th-8th Centuries BC* — Archaeology Illustrated

13. *Rome, Stone Relief on the Arch of Titus Depicting the Sacred Objects of the Destroyed Temple of Jerusalem being Paraded in Rome* — Archaeology Illustrated

14. *Jerusalem, The Temple of Herod the Great, The Second Temple, The Beth-haMikdash in Morning Light, 1st Century AD* — Archaeology Illustrated

15. *Early Christians Discussing Scripture* — Archaeology Illustrated (Alternate Title: *House Church: Early Christians Discussing Scripture*)

16. *Karnak, The Hypostyle Hall of Ramesses II, 13th Century BC* — Archaeology Illustrated

17. *Father and Son and a Jug of Wine in Ancient Greece* — Archaeology Illustrated

18. *Builders in the Greek and Roman World* — Archaeology Illustrated

19. *The Stone Mason* — Archaeology Illustrated

20. *Ezra and Nehemiah Reading the Scroll of the Law to the Israelites Assembled in the Temple Court in Jerusalem, 455 BC* — Archaeology Illustrated

21. *Jerusalem, Temple of Herod, The Second Temple, in the Court of the Israelites, Morning Light* — Archaeology Illustrated

22. *Jewish Pilgrims in Jerusalem* — Archaeology Illustrated

23. *Priestly Benediction* — Archaeology Illustrated

24. *"Sing Psalms in the Lord's honor with the lyre" (Psalm 98)* — Archaeology Illustrated (Alternate Title: *Psalm 98*)

25. *Paul the Apostle in a House Church* — Archaeology Illustrated

26. *Jesus and His Disciples at the Last Supper, a Passover Meal* — Archaeology Illustrated

27. *Paul the Apostle at Sea* — Archaeology Illustrated

28. *Phoenician Shipwrights at Work* — Archaeology Illustrated

29. *Greeks at Sea* — Archaeology Illustrated

30. *Phoebe Reading Paul's Letter to the Roman Christian Community* — Archaeology Illustrated

31. *Ur, Sumer, Southern Mesopotamia, The Great Harbor and Ziggurat* — Archaeology Illustrated

32. *Scribe of Qumran* — Archaeology Illustrated

33. *Roman Warships* — Archaeology Illustrated

34. *Jesus Teaching in the Temple of Herod* — Archaeology Illustrated

35. *Jesus and His Disciples in the Kidron Valley, Jerusalem* — Archaeology Illustrated

36. *Ephesus, Western Turkey, The Curetes Street, 2nd Century AD* — Archaeology Illustrated (Alternate Title: *Ephesus, Curetes Street, Looking towards Downtown and the Harbor, 1st-6th Centuries AD*)

37. *Ephesus, The Harbor Gate and City Center, 2nd Century AD* — Archaeology Illustrated

38. *Ephesus, Upper (Roman) Agora with the Temple of Domitian, Bouleterion (or Odeon) and Temple of Julius Caesar and Rome* — Archaeology Illustrated

39. *Ephesus in the Roman Period, Looking West, Late Afternoon* — Archaeology Illustrated

40. *The Forum of Corinth: the Bema, Triumphal Arches, Temple of Apollo and the Peirene Fountain, View from the Stoa towards the Gulf, 2nd Century AD* — Archaeology Illustrated

41. *Corinth, Southern Greece, The Forum, 2nd Century AD* — Archaeology Illustrated

42. *Corinth, The Bema on the Forum, The Political and Judiciary Center of the City where Paul the Apostle was Taken to be Tried, 1st Century AD* — Archaeology Illustrated

43. *Philippi, Northern Greece, 1st Century AD* — Archaeology Illustrated

44. *Corinth, Roman Period, The Lechaion Road (Harbor Road) Terminating at the Forum, the Civic and Religious Center, 2nd Century AD* — Archaeology Illustrated

45. *Corinth, House Church, 1st Century AD* — Archaeology Illustrated

46. *Corinth, The Peirene Fountain and Spring in the 1st Century BC-AD* — Archaeology Illustrated

47. *Capernaum, a Jewish Settlement by the Sea of Galilee, Looking towards Magdala, 1st-3rd Centuries AD* — Archaeology Illustrated

48. *Thessalonike, Northern Greece, The Royal Palace Area, Looking Towards Mount Olympus, Byzantine Period* — Archaeology Illustrated

49. *Greek Builders at the Temple of Artemis, Ephesus* — Archaeology Illustrated

50. *Abraham Receives Three Angels at his Tent in the Oak Grove of Mamre Near Hebron (Genesis 18)* — Archaeology Illustrated

51. *Moses on Mount Sinai on a Memorable Occasion. View Based on Actual Early Morning Photo Taken at the Summit* — Archaeology Illustrated

52. *The Prophet Samuel Anoints David, a Teenager, Among His Family in Bethlehem to Be King Over Israel* — Archaeology Illustrated

53. *The Prophetess Deborah and Commander Barak Discussing Strategy* — Archaeology Illustrated

54. *Jesus Baptized in the Jordan River by John the Baptist* — Archaeology Illustrated

55. *Jesus and the Money Changers and the Silver Half Shekels in Herod's Temple* — Archaeology Illustrated (Alternate Title: *Jesus and the Money Changers*)

56. *Nehemiah Directing the Rebuilding of Jerusalem's Walls after Returning from the Babylonian Exile, 440 BC* — Archaeology Illustrated (Alternate Title: *Nehemiah*)

57. *Prophets of Antioch: Barnabas, Simeon, Lucius of Cyrene, Manaen and Saul (Paul)* — Archaeology Illustrated

58. *Agabus Prophesying in the House of Philip and his Four Daughters in Caesarea about Paul the Apostle Being Arrested in Jerusalem* — Archaeology Illustrated

NOTABLE 'ANCIENTS'

Philosophers, Early Church Theologians, and Historians

Aeschines (c. 389-c. 314 BC) – a Greek statesman and one of ten famous Athenian orators who advocated for peace with Macedonia. He was a bitter opponent of Demosthenes. p.399

Aeschylus (c. 525-455 BC) – one of the great writers of Greek tragedy and the principal creator of Greek drama. Often recognized as the father of tragedy. pp.55,62,91,132

Ambrose (c. 340-397 AD) – also known as Saint Ambrose and Ambrose of Milan: a theologian and very influential ecclesiastical figure of the Fourth Century. He was unexpectedly exalted as bishop by popular acclamation while he was serving as a governor. p.227,542

Anacreon (c. 582-c. 485 BC) – a notable Greek lyrical poet whose poems were composed to be sung or recited with musical accompaniment. p.510

Antipater of Sidon (c. 200-c. 100 BC) – an ancient Greek poet and writer best known for his list and observations of the Seven Wonders of the World. p.109,111

Aristophanes (c. 450-386 BC) – an acclaimed comic playwright from ancient Athens who is sometimes referred to as the father of comedy. pp.63,397

Aristotle (384-322 BC) – the noted Greek philosopher, scientist, and founder of the Lyceum. He was taught by Plato and tutored Alexander the Great (356-322 BC). pp.18,31,42,44,83,87,133,135,138, 156,206,237,379,485,729

Caius, also known as Gaius – Presbyter of Rome and a Christian author in the early Third Century whose writings helped establish the canon of the New Testament. p.226

Callimachus of Cyrene (c. 305-c. 240 BC) – a Greek poet and scholar. Known as the most influential poet of the Hellenistic age. p.109,111

Clement of Alexandria (c. 150-c. 215 AD) – also known as Titus Flavius Clemens: a philosopher who was converted to Christianity by Pantaenus. As a Christian theologian and philosopher, he taught at the Catechetical School of Alexandria and was also a missionary theologian to the Hellenistic world. Among his students were Origen and Alexander of Jerusalem. pp.224,226

Clement of Rome (c. 35-99 AD) – also known as Pope Clement I and Saint Clement of Rome: thought to be the fourth bishop of Rome and considered to be the first Apostolic Father of the Church. p.226

Demosthenes (c. 384-322 BC) – an Athenian statesman and powerful orator. He is recognized as one of the greatest patriots from ancient Greece. pp.24,42,47,89,138,206,207,210,350,379

Diodorus Siculus (c. 90-c. 30 BC) – also known as Diodorus of Sicily: an ancient Greek historian who is known for his monumental work *Bibliotheca historica.* p.76

Dionysius (c. late-First or early- to mid-Second Century-171 AD) – also known as Bishop Dionysius of Corinth: known for his letters closely adhering to "the rule of faith" and warning against heretics. p.226

Ephrem (c. 306-373 AD) – also known as Ephrem the Syrian, Saint Ephraem Syrus, and Aprem of Nisibis, and bynames Deacon of Edessa and Harp of the Holy Spirit: a prominent Christian theologian and writer. He is revered to be the most notable hymnographer of Eastern Christianity. p.227

Euripides (c. 484-406 BC) – a tragic playwright of Classical Athens. pp.41,44,55,133,183, 206,213,350,397,485,510

Eusebius (of Caesarea) (c. 260-339 AD) – also known as Eusebius Pamphili: a theologian and Greek historian of Christianity. Served as a bishop of Caesarea Maritima and was a scholar of the biblical canon. His account of First Century Christianity, *Ecclesiastical History* (or *Church History*), is a landmark in Christian historiography. pp.222,223,224,226,477

Galen (129-c. 216 AD) – a Greek physician, surgeon, writer, and philosopher in the Roman Empire whose works influenced medical theory and practice through the mid-Seventeenth Century. p.79

Gregory of Nazianzus (c. 330-c. 389 AD) – also known as Gregory the Theologian and Gregory Nazianzen: a Fourth-Century Archbishop of Constantinople and theologian who defended the doctrine of the Trinity. p.222

Gregory of Tours (c. 538-c. 594 AD) – also known as Georgius Florentius, Bishop of Tours, and Saint Gregory of Tours: a bishop and Gallo-Roman historian whose most notable works include *Ten Books of Histories*. p.227

Herodotus (c. 484-425 BC) – a Greek writer and geographer and credited with being the first historian. Most known for having written *The Histories*, he was also the first writer to do systematic investigation and analysis of historical events. He is referred to as the "Father of History." pp.11,33,41, 44, 62,75,83,92,100,109,111,115,132,138,153,155,156,183,206,231,237,349,397,485

Hesiod (flourished c. 700 BC) – also known as Hesiodos: one of the earliest Greek Epic poets and is often called the "father of Greek didactic poetry." One of his writings, *Works and Days*, expounds upon peasant life. p.397

Homer (flourished Ninth or Eighth Century BC) – considered to be the greatest of all epic poets and Greek writers. Presumed author of the *Iliad* and *Odyssey*. pp.55,155,156,371,397

Ignatius (birth date unknown-c. 110 AD) – also known as Bishop Ignatius of Antioch and Ignatius Theophoros (Greek: "God Bearer") – Ignatius' letters and correspondence are a central part of a collection of works known to be authored by the Apostolic Fathers. His letters also serve as an example of Early Christian theology. p.226

Irenaeus (c. 130-c. 203 AD) – also known as Saint Irenaeus: a bishop of Lugdunum (Lyon), apologist, and leading Christian theologian of the Second Century. He is noted for his influence in expanding Christian communities in the southern regions of present-day France. pp.224,226

Jerome (c. 342-420 AD) – also known as Jerome of Stridon and Saint Jerome: a Christian priest, confessor, theologian, and historian. He is known for his teachings on Christian moral life and how a woman devoted to Jesus should live her life. pp.222,226,227

Josephus (c. 37-c. 100 AD) – or Flavius Josephus (born Joseph Ben Matthias): a First Century Jewish priest, scholar, and historian of Jewish history. His works include *The Jewish War* and *The Antiquities of the Jews*. pp.472,549,550,565,571,593,598,620,648

Justin Martyr (c. 100-c. 165 AD) – an early Christian apologist and Greek philosopher. His most well-known work passionately defends the morality of the Christian life and provided philosophical arguments to the Roman emperor to abandon the persecution of the Church. p.586

Lucian (of Samosata) (c. 125-180 AD) – the Hellenized Syrian satirist and rhetorician known for his superlative use of Greek. pp.42,47,56,135,156,206,207,210

Lysias (c. 445-380 BC) – a speech writer in Ancient Greece whose works were known for being unpretentious and simplistic. His works became the model for a plain style of classical Greek. pp.42,206,207,210

Moses of Chorene (c. 410-c. 490 AD) – also known as Moses of Khoren or Movses Khorenatsi: an Armenian historian, poet, hymn writer, and grammarian. He is the author of the *History of Armenia* and considered to be the father of Armenian history and sometimes referred to as the "Armenian Herodotus." p.228

Nicephorus (c. 758-829 BC) – also known as Saint Nicephoros or Nikephoros I of Constantinople: a Greek Orthodox theologian, historian, and patriarch of Constantinople whose chronicles of Byzantine history provide information otherwise unavailable on Early Christian thought and practice. pp.223,225

Origen (of Alexandria) (c. 185-c. 254 AD) – also known as Origen Adamantius: a Christian scholar, theologian, and ascetic, and was one of the most influential and controversial figures in Early Christian theology and apologetics. Once described as "the greatest genius the Early Church ever produced." pp.222,223,477,586

Pantaneus (c. Second Century-c. 200) – also known as Saint Pantaenus the Philosopher: a former Stoic philosopher who converted to the Christian faith. He was a key figure in the Catechetical School of Alexandria where he influenced Christian theology and the interpretation of the Bible. For a time he was a missionary, traveling as far as India, where he found communities using the gospel of Matthew written in Hebrew letters. He was also Origen's spiritual mentor. p.223

Papias (c. 70-c. 130 AD) – also known as Bishop Papias of Hierapolis: one of the Greek Apostolic Fathers and author of the five books the *Exposition of the Sayings of the Lord*. p.226

Paulinus (of Nola) (354-431 AD) – also known as Saint Paulinus of Nola, and byname Pontius Meropius Anicius Paulinus: a Roman senator who walked away from his political career to become a poet, writer, and a bishop of Nola. Regarded as one of the most important Christian Latin poets of his time. p.227

Philo of Alexandria (c. 20 BC-c. 50 AD) – also known as Philo Judaeus: an ancient Greek theologian and writer. One of the first historians to attempt to reconcile the doctrines of the Greek philosophers with the revelation of God as contained in the Hebrew scriptures. pp.471,472,549

Philo of Byzantium (c. 280-c. 220 BC) – also known as Philo Mechanicus: a Greek engineer, physicist, and writer on mechanics. His writings include the first literary account of the Seven Wonders of the World. pp.109,111

Pindar (c. 518-c. 438 BC) – considered to be the greatest lyric poet of ancient Greece. His choral odes were often used to celebrate the victors of the ancient games. pp.10,100,155,371,510

Plato (c. 428-c. 347 BC) – the famed Athenian philosopher and founder of the Platonist school of thought and the Academy (the first institution of higher learning in the Western world). He was a student of Socrates and teacher of Aristotle. pp.18,24,42,44,56,83,87,89,90,91,138,156,206,207,210,349,350,379,397,400,485,510,729

Polybius (c.200-c. 118 BC) – a Greek statesman and historian of the Hellenistic period who was noted for his work on *The Histories* that covered the period 264-146 BC in which Ancient Rome become a dominant world power. pp.42,75,90,91,206,207,210,379

Plutarch (c. 46-c. 119 AD) – a Greek Platonist philosopher, historian, biographer, and essayist whose historical writings influenced the evolution of the essay and the biography. pp.18,42,47,75,90,153, 174,206,207,210,231,349,400,730
Sextus Empiricus (c. 160-210 AD) – a noted Greek philosopher-historian, physician, and Pyrrhonian Skeptic whose writings provide the most comprehensive account of Greek Skepticism. pp.44,90,485,510
Sophocles (c. 496-406 BC) – one of classical Athens' three great tragic playwrights (with Aeschylus and Euripides). He is thought to have written over 100 plays but only 7 fully survive today. p.138
Tertullian (c. 160-c. 220 AD) – often called "the father of Latin Christianity" and "the founder of Western Theology." He was a prolific Early Christian author who was the first to produce an extensive compilation of Latin Christian literature and is recognized for being the first writer in Latin known to use the term translated "trinity." pp.226,586
Theocritus (c. 300-c. 260 BC) – a Greek poet from Sicily and the reputed creator of pastoral poetry. p.56
Theodoret (c. 393-c. 458 AD) – also known as Theodoret of Cyrus or Cyrrhus: an influential theologian of the School of Antioch, biblical commentator, and Christian bishop of Cyrrhus. His writings contributed to the development of the Christian theological vocabulary. p.223
Thucydides (c. 460-c. 400 BC) – an Athenian general and historian who chronicled nearly 30 years of war and unrest between Athens and Sparta. He has been called the "father of scientific history" and the "father of the school of political realism." pp.41,206,213,231,239,399
Xenophon (c. 430-c. 354 BC) – an Athenian-born military leader, philosopher, and historian noted for his works depicting late Classical Greece. pp.47,53,91,138,156,379,397,399

ABOUT THE AUTHOR

Rick Renner (renner.org) holds an earned ThD (Doctor of Theology) from a prominent Russian university and is a respected Bible teacher and leader in the international Christian community. He is the author of an extensive list of books, including bestsellers *Sparkling Gems From the Greek 1* and *2*, and his accumulated titles have sold millions of copies worldwide. Rick's understanding of the Greek language and biblical history opens up the Scriptures in a unique way that enables his audience to gain wisdom and insight while learning something brand new from the Word of God.

Today Rick is the overseer of the Good News Association of Churches, founder of the Moscow Good News Church, pastor of the Internet Good News Church, founder of Media Mir, and president of the Good News Channel — the largest Russian-speaking Christian satellite network in the world, which broadcasts the Gospel 24/7 to countless viewers in more than 83 nations. He is also founder of TBV, a national channel that broadcasts to all of Russia.

Rick is the founder of RENNER Ministries in Broken Arrow, Oklahoma, and host to his TV program, also seen around the world in multiple languages via television, Internet, and satellite. He leads this amazing work with Denise — his wife and life-long ministry partner — along with their sons and committed leadership team.

CONTACT RENNER MINISTRIES

For further information about RENNER Ministries or to reach out for prayer, please contact the office nearest you or visit the ministry website at:
www.renner.org

ALL USA CORRESPONDENCE:
RENNER Ministries
1814 W. Tacoma St.
Broken Arrow, OK 74012
(918) 496-3213
Or 1-800-RICK-593
Email: renner@renner.org
Website: www.renner.org

CANADA OFFICE:
P. O. Box 275
Abbotsford, BC V2T 6Z6
Phone: 877-498-3427
Email: information@rickrenner.ca

MOSCOW OFFICE:
RENNER Ministries
P. O. Box 789
101000, Moscow, Russia
+7 (495) 727-1467
Email: blagayavestonline@ignc.org
Website: www.ignc.org

OXFORD OFFICE:
RENNER Ministries
Box 7, 266 Banbury Road
Oxford OX2 7DL, United Kingdom
+44 1865 521024
Email: europe@renner.org

RIGA OFFICE:
RENNER Ministries
Unijas 99
Riga LV-1084, Latvia
+371 67802150
Email: church@goodnews.lv
Website: www.goodnews.lv

facebook.com/rickrenner • facebook.com/rennerdenise

youtube.com/rennerministries • youtube.com/deniserenner

instagram.com/rickrrenner • instagram.com/rennerministries_
instagram.com/rennerdenise

BOOKS BY RICK RENNER

Apostles and Prophets
Build Your Foundation*
Chosen by God*
Christmas — The Rest of the Story
Dream Thieves*
Dressed To Kill*
Easter — The Rest of the Story
Fallen Angels, Giants, Monsters, and the World Before the Flood
The Holy Spirit and You*
How To Keep Your Head on Straight in a World Gone Crazy*
How To Receive Answers From Heaven!*
Igniting a Powerful Prayer Life
Insights on Successful Leadership*
Last-Days Survival Guide*
A Life Ablaze*
Life in the Combat Zone*
A Light in Darkness, Volume One,
Seven Messages to the Seven Churches series
The Love Test*
My Peace-Filled Day
My Spirit-Empowered Day
My Victory-Filled Day
No Room for Compromise, Volume Two,
Seven Messages to the Seven Churches series
Paid in Full*
The Point of No Return*
The Rapture, the Antichrist, and the Tribulation
Renner A to Z
Comments and Quotes by Rick Renner on 400 Bible Topics A to Z!
Renner Interpretive Version of James and Jude (RIV)
Repentance*
Signs You'll See Just Before Jesus Comes*
Sparkling Gems From the Greek Daily Devotional 1*
Sparkling Gems From the Greek Daily Devotional 2*
Spiritual Weapons To Defeat the Enemy*
Ten Guidelines To Help You Achieve Your Long-Awaited Promotion!*
Testing the Supernatural
365 Days of Increase
365 Days of Power
Turn Your God-Given Dreams Into Reality*
Unlikely — Our Faith-Filled Journey to the Ends of the Earth*
Why We Need the Gifts of the Holy Spirit*
The Will of God — The Key to Your Success*
You Can Get Over It*

*Digital version available for Kindle, Nook, and iBook.
Note: Books by Rick Renner are available for purchase at:
www.renner.org

DRESSED TO KILL

A Biblical Approach to Spiritual Warfare and Armor

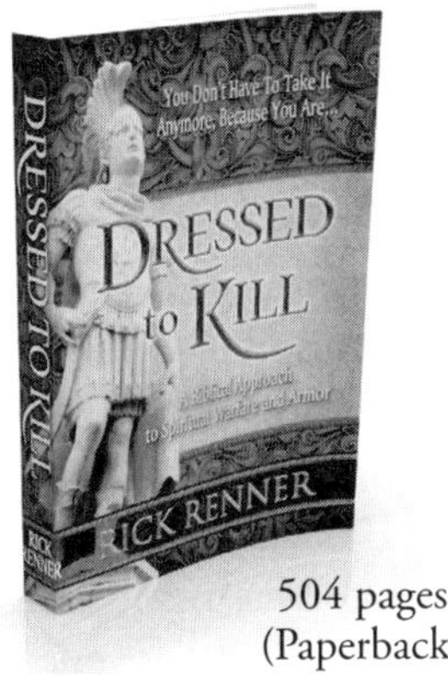

504 pages
(Paperback)

Rick Renner's book *Dressed To Kill* is considered by many to be a true classic on the subject of spiritual warfare. The original version, which sold more than 400,000 copies, is a curriculum staple in Bible schools worldwide. In this beautiful volume, you will find:

- 504 pages of reedited text in paperback
- 16 pages of full-color illustrations
- Questions at the end of each chapter to guide you into deeper study

In *Dressed To Kill*, Rick explains with exacting detail the purpose and function of each piece of Roman armor. In the process, he describes the significance of our *spiritual* armor not only to withstand the onslaughts of the enemy, but also to overturn the tendencies of the carnal mind. Furthermore, Rick delivers a clear, scriptural presentation on the biblical definition of spiritual warfare — what it is and what it is not.

When you walk with God in deliberate, continual fellowship, He will enrobe you with Himself. Armed with the knowledge of who you are in Him, you will be dressed and dangerous to the works of darkness, unflinching in the face of conflict, and fully equipped to take the offensive and gain mastery over any opposition from your spiritual foe. You don't have to accept defeat anymore once you are *dressed to kill*!

To order, visit us online at: **www.renner.org**

Book Resellers: Contact Harrison House at 800-722-6774
or visit **www.HarrisonHouse.com** for quantity discounts.

THE RENNER INTERPRETIVE VERSION (RIV) OF JAMES AND JUDE

A Parallel Study Bible for People of Faith

288 pages
(Hardback)

Do you long for deeper insight into your personal study of the Word of God? If so, the *RIV* is for you!

Equipped with footnotes and commentary, the *RIV* will open up the world of the New Testament in a whole new way. While it is not a word-for-word translation — the *RIV* is a conceptual interpretation that draws upon concepts in the Greek language and expresses them in a way that supplies a broader comprehension of Scripture. By bringing out imagery presented in the Greek language and conveying it to readers using contemporary speech, Rick helps draw lovers of the Bible into a deeper study of God's message to people for all time.

This first installment of the *RIV* is taken from the books written by James and Jude. James and Jude were Jesus' half-brothers, younger sons of Joseph and Mary, and in this representation, their Spirit-inspired words will thrill your heart, challenge your thinking, and open the eyes of your spirit in greater ways to see the unchanging nature of God — His wisdom, goodness, power, and love.

To order, visit us online at: **www.renner.org**

Book resellers: Contact Harrison House at 800-722-6774
or visit **www.HarrisonHouse.com** for quantity discounts.

TESTING THE SUPERNATURAL

How To Biblically Test Dreams, Visions, Revelations, and Spiritual Manifestations.

Have you ever struggled with whether a supernatural occurrence you heard about — or even experienced yourself — was really from God?

To help answer this question and more, Rick Renner wrote the book *Testing the Supernatural — How To Biblically Test Dreams, Visions, Revelations, and Spiritual Manifestations.*

96 pages
(Paperback)

Topics include:

- Testing False Apostles
- Four Questions You *Must* Ask
- Forbidden Ways To Receive Revelations
- How God Speaks
- The Basis of Deception
- When Error Is Mixed With Truth
- *And more!*

In this book, Rick scripturally examines how to know what *is* and what *isn't* the voice of God or a manifestation from Heaven. With the "litmus tests" Rick provides, learn to perk up your spiritual ears and fortify yourself in the truth so that you won't fall prey to spiritual deception!

To order, visit us online at: **www.renner.org**

Book Resellers: Contact Harrison House at 800-722-6774 or visit **www.HarrisonHouse.com** for quantity discounts.

UNLIKELY

Our Faith-Filled Journey to the Ends of the Earth

1,116 pages
(Hardback)

Rick Renner shares his life story in detail in his autobiography *Unlikely — Our Faith-Filled Journey to the Ends of the Earth.* In this book, you'll see how our smallest decisions can lead to something *big* if we'll determine to stay the course and follow God's plan for our lives wholeheartedly.

Rick and Denise Renner's lives are "proof positive" that this is true. From their humble upbringings in small Oklahoma towns, a lack of understanding from their peers growing up, and evil assaults from the enemy that threatened to undermine God's plan, the Lord drew Rick and Denise together and sent them, with their three young sons, to live in the former Soviet Union. Rick and Denise live and minister powerfully in the former USSR to this day — and not one of their hurtful, *harrowing* experiences was wasted!

You'll enjoy reading about Rick's adventures of flying in unsafe planes across 11 time zones in the former USSR, of circumventing criminal opportunists, and of dealing with deficits of food, fuel, and heat during harsh winters just after the fall of the Iron Curtain. Rick and his family were gloriously, and, at times, *hilariously* delivered so they could deliver the message of restoration and hope God sent them to give.

You have an unlikely story too. Life is not a game of chance. It can be a thrilling adventure when you give God your *yes* and "buckle up" to receive Heaven's directive for your life. This book can show you how!

To order, visit us online at: **www.renner.org**

Book Resellers: Contact Harrison House at 800-722-6774
or visit **www.HarrisonHouse.com** for quantity discounts.

FALLEN ANGELS, GIANTS, MONSTERS, AND THE WORLD BEFORE THE FLOOD

How the Events of Noah's Ark and the Flood Are Relevant to the End of the Age

512 pages
(Paperback)

In his book *Fallen Angels, Giants, Monsters, and the World Before the Flood — How the Events of Noah's Ark and the Flood Are Relevant to the End of the Age* — which includes more than 300 photos and illustrations — Rick Renner answers long-held questions about the fascinating story of Noah's Ark.

Presenting Scripture as well as the recordings of early writers, such as Irenaeus, Josephus, Origen, Tertullian, and many others, Rick explains such details as the population explosion on the earth just before the Flood; the likely reason the writings of Enoch survived the Flood; who "the sons of God" and "the daughters of men" in Genesis were; why God ultimately saved only Noah and his family of eight; what happened when they finally exited the Ark; Jesus' own prophecy that certain elements of Noah's day would happen again; *and much, much more!*

Using findings from his own expedition of the remains of Noah's Ark in the Ararat mountains — along with other empirical evidence of the Ark's present location — Rick fascinates readers in this book and helps the Bible *come alive* concerning this favorite childhood story from the Bible!

God has had a plan from the beginning concerning Jesus as "the Seed born of a woman" who would destroy the works Satan wrought in the Fall of man. And just as God has faithfully executed that plan in the past, He will continue to carry it out until Christ's rapture of His Church *and beyond.*

To order, visit us online at: **www.renner.org**

Book resellers: Contact Harrison House at 800-722-6774
or visit **www.HarrisonHouse.com** for quantity discounts.

Equipping Believers to Walk in the Abundant Life

John 10:10b

Connect with us for fresh content and news about forthcoming books from your favorite authors...

Facebook @ **HarrisonHousePublishers**

Instagram @ **HarrisonHousePublishing**

www.harrisonhouse.com